JOB THROKMORTON'S KINDRED

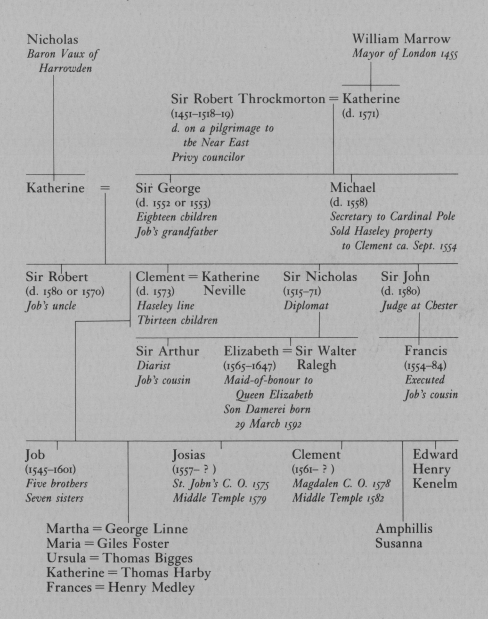

Nicholas
Baron Vaux of
Harrowden

William Marrow
Mayor of London 1455

Sir Robert Throckmorton = Katherine
(1451–1518–19)   (d. 1571)
d. on a pilgrimage to
the Near East
Privy councilor

Katherine = Sir George
                   (d. 1552 or 1553)
                   Eighteen children
                   Job's grandfather

Michael
(d. 1558)
Secretary to Cardinal Pole
Sold Haseley property
to Clement ca. Sept. 1554

Sir Robert
(d. 1580 or 1570)
Job's uncle

Clement = Katherine
(d. 1573)   Neville
Haseley line
Thirteen children

Sir Nicholas
(1515–71)
Diplomat

Sir John
(d. 1580)
Judge at Chester

Sir Arthur
Diarist
Job's cousin

Elizabeth = Sir Walter
(1565–1647)   Ralegh
Maid-of-honour to
Queen Elizabeth
Son Damerei born
29 March 1592

Francis
(1554–84)
Executed
Job's cousin

Job
(1545–1601)
Five brothers
Seven sisters

Josias
(1557– ?)
St. John's C. O. 1575
Middle Temple 1579

Clement
(1561– ?)
Magdalen C. O. 1578
Middle Temple 1582

Edward
Henry
Kenelm

Martha = George Linne
Maria = Giles Foster
Ursula = Thomas Bigges
Katherine = Thomas Harby
Frances = Henry Medley

Amphillis
Susanna

Martin Marprelate, Gentleman

A Dialogue vvherein is plainely laid o-
pen the tyrannicall dealing of Lord Bb.
against Gods children.

The speakers are these, { Puritane.
Papist.
Iacke of both sides.
Idoll minister.

Puritane.

Ou are well ouertaken sir, doe you
trauell far this way I pray you?
Iacke Towards London sir.
Puritane I shall willingly beare
you companie if it please you?
Iacke With all my heart, I shall
be very glad of yours.
Puritane From whence came you this way?
Iacke I come out of France.
Puritane Out of what part of France came you I
pray you? I came from *Rochell* my selfe, which is a part
of France.
Iacke It is so, but I came not neere that place.
Puritan Out of what parte of Fraunce came you
then?
Iacke I came from *Orleans*.
Puritan I pray you what newes from thence, is
there any likelyhoode of peace there?
Iacke Yes surely, there is some hope of peace, for
where the Kings powers come, they doe commonly
yeelde presently.
Puritan It is a good hearing.
Iacke What is he that comes after vs so fast?
Puritan He seemes to be some preacher or dumb
minister, it may be he goes our way, if he doe I hope
we shall haue his company whereby wee may passe a-
way

The beginning (folio A2 *recto*) of *A Dialogue*, an anonymous
treatise now proven to be the work of Job Throkmorton,
completed in April 1589.

Martin Marprelate, Gentleman

MASTER JOB THROKMORTON

LAID OPEN

IN HIS COLORS

———————————

BY LELAND H. CARLSON

HUNTINGTON LIBRARY · SAN MARINO

Copyright 1981
The Henry E. Huntington Library
San Marino, California 91108
All rights reserved
Printed in the United States of America
Library of Congress Catalog Card Number: 80–26442
ISBN: 0–87328–112–8
Printed by Kingsport Press
Designed by Ward Ritchie

Dedicated
to
my family
LAVERNE, TIMOTHY, and KAY,
my sisters
JEANNETTE, VERNA, and VIVIAN,
and my kindred
JEANNA, BERNICE, and WILLIAM,
FRED, RUSSELL, JOHN, NORMAN

CONTENTS

PREFACE   xi

ACKNOWLEDGMENTS   xiv

A CHRONOLOGICAL OUTLINE   xvii

INTRODUCTION   I

    The Church of England in the Sixteenth
      Century

    Causes Provoking the Marprelate Campaign

    A Synopsis of the Martin Marprelate Books

    Dramatis Personae

    Surmises on the Identity of Martin Marprelate

PART I

I.   THE GATHERING OF EVIDENCE   31

II.   THE ANTI-MARTINIST ATTACK   53

III.   THE PROSECUTION OF MARTINIST PARTICIPANTS   75

PART II

IV.   JOB THROKMORTON'S LIFE AND WRITINGS   95

V.   THROKMORTON'S AUTHORSHIP OF *Master Some
Laid Open in His Coulers*   132

    The Occasion for Writing the Book

    The Date of the Book

    Seven General Arguments

    The Argument from Parallels

    Scholarly Judgment on the Authorship of
      Master Some Laid Open in His Coulers

Contents

VI.   THROKMORTON'S AUTHORSHIP OF RELATED WORKS   158
      *A Dialogue. Wherin Is Plainly Laide Open the
         Tyrannical Dealing of Lord Bishopps against Gods
         Children*
      More Worke for Cooper
      "Martins Interim, or a Briefe Pistle to the
         Cursed Prelates and Clergie"
      The Crops and Flowers of Bridges Garden

VII. STYLISTIC PECULIARITIES AND PARALLELS IN
      THROKMORTON'S AND MARTIN'S WORKS   178

VIII. THROKMORTON'S AUTHORSHIP: THE MARPRELATE
      BOOKS   210
      An Epistle
      *The Just Censure and Reproofe of Martin Junior
         (Martin Senior)*
      *Certaine Minerall, and Metaphisicall Schoolpoints
         (Mineralls)*
      Theses Martinianae (Martin Junior)
      The Protestatyon of Martin Marprelat
      An Epitome
      Hay Any Worke for Cooper

IX.   THROKMORTON'S AUTHORSHIP: BASIC ISSUES   237
      Throkmorton's Status and Character
      Throkmorton's Indictment and Denial
      Throkmorton's Clandestine Practices
      Throkmorton's Anonymous and Pseudonymous
         Writings
      Throkmorton's Stylistic Characteristics and
         Techniques
      Throkmorton's Irony, Sarcasm, and Lampoons
      Throkmorton's and Martin's Special Interests
         and Topics
      Other Summary Arguments for Throkmorton's
         Authorship

PART III

X.   JOHN PENRY AND MARTIN MARPRELATE:
     COMPARISONS AND A CRITIQUE   271

XI. CONCLUSION   308

APPENDIXES
     "An Answer to Certen Peeces of a Sermon"   314
     An Exhortation to the Byshops   319
     Certaine Articles   322
     A Second Admonition to the Parliament   324
     "A Friendly Caveat to Bishop Sands"   328
     The State of the Church of Englande   332
     Anonymous Relevant Works in the
        Short-Title Catalogue   338
     Job Throkmorton's Petition to
        Lord Treasurer Burghley   341

NOTES   344

A SELECT BIBLIOGRAPHY   408

INDEX   419

ILLUSTRATIONS
     A Dialogue (April 1589)   ii
     An Epitome (November 1588)   236
     Hay Any Worke for Cooper (March 1589)   237
     A Treatise (January 1589/90)   272
     Petition to Lord Treasurer Burghley (April
        1587)   343

PREFACE

THE PROBLEM of establishing the authorship of anonymous and pseudonymous books is complicated, and the road to successful attribution is paved with many good intentions. For more than 210 years scholars have discussed the authorship of the letters of Junius. In 1978 appeared the most recent edition, *The Letters of Junius*, edited by John Cannon, who provided a list of 61 candidates who have been identified as Junius. For more than 390 years scholars have debated the identity of Martin Marprelate. Fortunately, only 22 candidates have been proposed, in addition to the suggestions of composite authorship by Jesuit conspirators and by a cabal of Puritans. In the twentieth century four serious contenders for Martin's role remained: Henry Barrow, Sir Roger Williams, John Penry, and Job Throkmorton. In the last two decades the publication of complete editions of the works of Barrow and Sir Roger enables us to remove their names from further consideration as serious candidates. Much research has been expended on Penry by John Waddington, William Pierce, Albert Peel, Donald J. McGinn, and David Williams, but very little work has been done on Throkmorton.

When I was planning an edition of Penry's writings, I had to decide whether to include or exclude the works of Martin Marprelate. At first I desired a quick categorical answer: yes or no, but as I assumed the role of an amateur detective, I became intrigued with the problem. I took a course on computers and literary analysis, and corresponded with a computer analyst who was experimenting with Martin's material. Initially, I was uncertain as to what problems could be solved by the computer, and subsequently, after spending a year compiling data, I was convinced that the computer could not think, that it could not isolate colorful writing, foreign expressions, proverbs, legal expressions, and other stylistic characteristics. The computer is a superb tool for providing data for glossaries, dictionaries, concordances, and word counts, but the problems of evaluating data, selecting salient features, and establishing criteria must still be resolved by the researcher. In the beginning I did not know which questions to propound to the computer, and I decided to become my own computer.

I collected about 7,000 items from Penry's nine books, from seven Marprelate items, and from twenty-three writings of Throkmorton. The wilderness gradually began to appear as a cleared forest. The tedious and laborious method enables one to distinguish between irony, humor, and sarcasm, between ordinary words and unusual expressions; it facilitates the task of attribution; it suggests new questions; and it enables the student to judge his data and to capture enroute obiter dicta. After compiling my data, I prepared three or four drafts of this book, including four chapters in refutation of the thesis of Penry's authorship, and six chapters on Throkmorton. In effect, I had two books in the making. To achieve a sharper focus, to keep my book within decent limitations, and to concentrate on Throkmorton, I eliminated the Penry chapters, but I relegated a summary of this material to chapter ten.

In this work I have not altered the spellings of quotations, but I have occasionally added capitalization and punctuation, extended abbreviations, and regularized the use of "i" and "j," "u" and "v." I have followed the sixteenth-century dating, Old Style, but all dates between 1 January and 24 March inclusive are given in both Old Style and New Style for the year. Therefore, the Convocation of January 1562, Old Style, is given as January 1562/63, and Archbishop Whitgift's death, which occurred on 29 February 1603, Old Style, is dated as 29 February 1603/04.

I have kept in mind three main objectives: to eliminate John Penry as a viable candidate; to present Job Throkmorton as the real Martin Marprelate; and to establish a canon of his writings, many of which are unknown because of their anonymity and pseudonymity. I have also tried to paint

Throkmorton in his true colors, "nothing extenuate," with all his "roughness, pimples, warts," as an idealist and reformer, sincerely committed to his cause, sometimes transgressing the boundaries of decorum, frequently using dubious means to achieve a desirable end. He deserves to be better known, and his works need to be more widely available to students of literature and history. He is a forerunner of Jonathan Swift, who improved the art of sarcasm, and he is a precursor of Voltaire, who enhanced the art of irony. Throkmorton, the English *episcopomastix* par excellence, would have admired Voltaire's crusading spirit and would have approved his militant exhortation: *écrasons l'infâme.*

ACKNOWLEDGMENTS

I WISH TO EXPRESS my sincere appreciation to many friends who have aided me in the preparation of this book. Six professors of English history and literature have carefully read the entire typescript and have contributed invaluable suggestions and constructive criticisms: Patrick Collinson, University of Kent; Daniel J. Donno, Queens College, Flushing, New York; Joel Hurstfield, University of London; Alice Scoufos, California State University at Fullerton; Paul S. Seaver, Stanford University, and one anonymous reader. Other friends have read portions of the book, or have aided me with counsel and information, especially B. W. Beckingsale, University of Newcastle-upon-Tyne; Horton Davies, Princeton University; Elizabeth Story Donno, Columbia University; Hallett Smith, William A. Ringler, Jr., Winifred Freese, Virginia J. Renner, and Mary K. Wright of the Henry E. Huntington Library; Craig R. Thompson, University of Pennsylvania; Jerald C. Brauer and John M. Wallace of the University of Chicago. To Professor S. T. Bindoff and the late Sir John Neale of the University of London I acknowledge a special debt for their seminars in Tudor history and for the opportunity of presenting papers for critical discussion on Robert Browne, Henry Barrow, John Penry, Job Throkmorton, and Martin Marprelate. I wish to thank E. G. W. Bill, E. S. De Beer, Norah Fuidge, James G. McManaway, Peter Milward, Ralph B. Pugh, David Quinn, and Conrad Russell for suggesting or supplying documents. I owe special thanks to Leo F. Solt, dean of the Graduate School, Indiana University, for a final reading of my typescript, and to my esteemed colleague, Martin Ridge.

Many scholars have provided inspiration and guidance by their writings or discussions. In addition to those already mentioned, the following authors deserve special gratitude: Hardin Craig, Richard W. Davis, Christopher Hill, Louis

Lecocq, Leonard W. Levy, Geoffrey F. Nuttall, Leonard J. Trinterud, David Williams, and Glanmor Williams. Previous scholars with whose writings I have had almost daily communion and rapport are Dean Matthew Sutcliffe, the Reverend John Strype, Professor Edward Arber, Bishop Walter H. Frere, the Reverend William Pierce, Dr. Albert Peel, Professor William Haller, Dr. Marshall M. Knappen, and Regius Professor John Dover Wilson.

It has been my delightful privilege to utilize the rare books and manuscripts in many rich repositories. To the directors, librarians, and staff of the following institutions I wish to record my appreciation for efficient and courteous help: the British Library, the Public Record Office, the University of London Library, the Institute of Historical Research, Inner Temple Library, Sion College Library, Dr. Williams's Library, Lambeth Palace Library, the Bodleian Library, the University of Cambridge Library, the collegiate libraries of Corpus Christi, Emmanuel, Gonville and Caius, and Peterhouse, the Pierpont Morgan Library, the Sterling Memorial Library, the Houghton Library, the Library of Congress, the Folger Shakespeare Library, where I enjoyed a fellowship in 1973–74, the Newberry Library, the Honnold Library of Claremont University Center, the University of Southern California Library, and the Henry E. Huntington Library and Art Gallery, where I have worked for many years. To the National Library of Wales I am indebted for a reproduction of a unique item—Penry's *Exhortation*, second edition, *S.T.C.* 19605.5. To the Northamptonshire Record Office and P. I. King I am indebted for information on the mayors of Northampton in 1588 and 1589. And to Dr. Marjorie Blatcher (Mrs. S. T. Bindoff) I express my gratitude for assistance in searching for elusive membranes in the King's Bench materials in the Public Record Office.

Mrs. Orin Tramz and Mrs. Faye Willams have provided expert typing, and Michael E. Moody has aided me in proofreading. Mrs. Betty Leigh Merrell, Mrs. Jane Evans, and Holly Bridges have skillfully guided this typescript from its submission and have put their editorial expertise and imprimatur on this and other volumes for the Huntington Library Publications program of scholarly books.

Leland H. Carlson

Henry E. Huntington Library
11 August 1980

A CHRONOLOGICAL OUTLINE

1545–1604

1545–1582
Throkmorton born in 1545. Oxford University 1562–66. "An Answer to Certen Peeces," *An Exhortation to the Byshops, An Exhortation to the Bishops, A Second Admonition to the Parliament, Certaine Articles*, all written by Throkmorton, 1572. "A Friendly Caveat to Bishop Sands," 1573

1583
6	July	Archbishop Edmund Grindal dies
23	September	John Whitgift confirmed as archbishop of Canterbury

1584
13	January	Throkmorton's letter to Ralph Warcuppe
23	March	Thomas Cooper confirmed as bishop of Winchester
	April	*A Dialogue concerning the Strife of Our Church*

1586
23	June	Star Chamber decree on printing
4	November	Throkmorton's Speech on Mary Queen of Scots
		Throkmorton an M.P. in Elizabeth's sixth Parliament, 29 October 1586 to 23 March 1587

1587
23	February	Throkmorton's Speech on "The Low Countries"
27	February	Throkmorton's Speech on "The Bill and Book"
	February	Penry's first book published—*A Treatise Containing the Aequity of an Humble Supplication*. Presented to the House of Commons 28 February by Edward Dunn Lee
	March	Penry imprisoned in the Gatehouse for a month by the Court of High Commission
23	March	Elizabeth's sixth Parliament adjourned. Throkmorton absent throughout March, since he was in hiding
3	April	Throkmorton's petition to Lord Burghley
16	April	Easter
?	June	Dean John Bridges' *A Defence of the Government Established* published
?	November	Dudley Fenner's *A Defence of the Godlie Ministers* published. This is a reply to Dr. Bridges' *A Defence*

1588
	March	John Field, Puritan co-ordinator, dies. Buried 26 March
	March	Penry's *Exhortation* published, or possibly in February
7	April	Easter
16	April	Throkmorton's book, *The State of the Church of Englande* (also known as *Diotrephes*), confiscated in Waldegrave's shop

16	April	Waldegrave's printing office raided
13	May	The Stationers' Company orders the destruction of Waldegrave's press, type, and equipment
	May	Penry's *Exhortation*, second edition, published
	May	Dr. Robert Some's first *A Godly Treatise* published
	June	John Udall removed as vicar of Kingston and silenced
	August	Penry's *A Defence of That Which Hath Bin Written* printed by Waldegrave
4	September	Robert Dudley, earl of Leicester, dies
5	September	Penry marries Eleanor Godley at Northampton
	September	Dr. Robert Some's second *A Godly Treatise* published
15–20	October	First Marprelate book, the *Epistle*, published at East Molesey
	October	John Udall's *Demonstration* published
10	November	Dr. Robert Some's sermon at Bartholomew Church in the Exchange. Throkmorton in attendance
14	November	The Queen commands Archbishop Whitgift and the Court of High Commission, with the aid of privy councilors, to apprehend the author, printers, and dispersers of Marprelate's *Epistle*
14	November	Depositions made by Cutbert Cook, John Good, Nicholas Kydwell, and William Staughton
15–20	November	Deposition of Stephen Chatfield
29	November	Examination of Walter Rogers
25–29	November	Marprelate's *Epitome* published at Fawsley
6	December	Giles Wigginton examined before the Court of High Commission

1589

1	January	Wednesday. Henry Barrow interrogated in the Fleet on his reply to Dr. Some
10 ca.	January	Thomas Cooper, bishop of Winchester, publishes his *An Admonition to the People of England*. First reply to Marprelate
26–28	January	Marprelate's *Mineralls* published at Coventry (not 20 February)
29	January	Penry's study in Henry Godley's home raided by the pursuivant, Richard Walton. Udall's *Demonstration* and Penry's manuscript reply to Dr. Some seized
4	February	Elizabeth's seventh Parliament assembles on Tuesday
8	February	Penry's *A Viewe (Supplication)* published at Coventry
9	February	Richard Bancroft's sermon at Paul's Cross. Denounces Martinists. Sermon expanded and published in March
13	February	Royal proclamation against Marprelate's books and broadside issued
15	February	Nicholas Tomkins examined by Richard Cosin, Master in Chancery
	February	Attempt to arrest Henry Sharpe at Northampton
2	March	Penry begins his residence as a guest of Throkmorton at Haseley, Warwickshire. Sought by pursuivants
20–27	March	*Hay Any Worke*, the fourth Marprelate work, published
30	March	Easter. Henry Sharpe consults with Sir Richard Knightley about confessing his own complicity in binding and selling Marprelate's books
4–5	April	Waldegrave departs from Coventry and Wolston
26	April	Andrew Perne dies at Lambeth
	May	Dr. Robert Some's third *A Godly Treatise* published
	May	Mar-Martine published

	June	Leonard Wright's *A Summons for Sleepers*, and *A Whip for an Ape: Or, Martin Displaied* published
13–14	July	John Hodgskin confers with Job Throkmorton and John Penry at Haseley Manor
14	July	Part of manuscript of *Martin Junior* found along the path
18	July	Job Throkmorton visits printers on Friday at home of Roger Wigston in Wolston
22	July	*Theses Martinianae*, or *Martin Junior*, printed. Printers leave Wolston for Warrington 29 July
29	July	*Martin Senior* published
	July	*Antimartinus*, a Latin treatise, published
1	August	Printers reach Warrington—probably Hodgskin's home
4	August	Cart and press arrive at Warrington. Type spilled on the ground. Probable cause for capture of printers
7	August	Printers move to Manchester. Press set up in a house
14	August	On Thursday, Hodgskin, Symmes, and Thomlin captured at Manchester while printing *More Worke for Cooper*
23	August	Saturday. Captive printers arrive in London
24	August	Hodgskin, Symmes, and Thomlin examined before the Privy Council
	August	"Martins Interim" completed. Not printed
	September	Henry Sharpe arrested—about 7–10 September
11–12	September	Hodgskin sent to the Tower for racking
10–15	September	Sharpe's preliminary examination
21	September	Summary Report on Marprelate and Penry and printers sent to Lord Burghley. Endorsed 21.7.1589 (Old Style)
20–30	September	Penry's *Appellation* published. Probably printed in July at La Rochelle. Delivered by Waldegrave to Throkmorton
20–30	September	Throkmorton's *Master Some Laid Open* published. Probably printed in July at La Rochelle. Delivered by Waldegrave
20–30	September	Throkmorton's *A Dialogue. Wherin Is Plainly Laide Open* published. Probably printed at La Rochelle in August. Delivered by Waldegrave to Throkmorton
20–30	September	Last Marprelate work, the *Protestatyon*, published
30 ca.	September	Second raid on Henry Godley's house in Northampton
2	October	Penry leaves Haseley and flees to Scotland
10	October	Symmes and Thomlin examined
15	October	Henry Sharpe examined by the commandment of Sir Christopher Hatton, lord chancellor
20	October	Sir Richard Knightley's first examination
20	October	*The Returne of the Renowned Cavaliero Pasquill of England* published. Possibly by Thomas Nashe
20	November	Sir Richard Knightley's second examination
25	November	John Hodgskin examined
27	November	John Hodgskin examined
29	November	Second examination of Nicholas Tomkins, by Dr. William Aubrey and Dr. William Lewin
10	December	Symmes and Thomlin examined before the lords commissioners
11	December	R. Jeffes' examination
11–12	December	Lawrence Jackson examined
	December	Hodgskin examined by the lords commissioners

1590

| | January | Penry's *A Treatise (Reformation No Enemie)* printed at Edinburgh by Waldegrave |

9	January	John Udall arrives in London, in response to a subpoena from the Privy Council. He left Newcastle-upon-Tyne on 29 December
13	January	John Udall examined at Lord Cobham's house in Blackfriars, by Lord Cobham; Lord Buckhurst; Lord Chief Justice Edmund Anderson of the Court of Common Pleas; John Young, bishop of Rochester; John Fortescue, chancellor of the Exchequer; Thomas Egerton, solicitor-general; Dr. William Aubrey; and Dr. William Lewin
19	January	Leonard Wright's *A Friendly Admonition* entered in the Stationers' Register
	February	The Puckering Brief compiled
13	February	Sir Richard Knightley, John Hales, Roger Wigston, and Mrs. Roger Wigston tried and sentenced in the Court of Star Chamber
	February	*An Almond for a Parrat*, probably by Thomas Nashe, was published in February or March
12	March	Richard Holmes examined
6	April	Sir Francis Walsingham, principal secretary, dies
ca.	June	Penry's *A Briefe Discovery* printed at Edinburgh by Waldegrave
3	June	Mr. Grimston examined
9	July	Humphrey Newman examined
24–25	July	John Udall arraigned before the judges of Assize at Croydon
1–5	October	Job Throkmorton indicted by a grand jury at Warwick
10–15	October	Throkmorton's letters of submission to Archbishop Whitgift and to the judges of Assize
14	October	Throkmorton's letter of submission to Sir Christopher Hatton, lord chancellor
6	November	Jenkin Jones, a kinsman of Penry, examined

1591

18–20	February	John Udall at the Assizes in Southwark. Sentenced to death on 20 February, but reprieved
	April	Throkmorton's court appearance—Easter and Trinity terms
	July	Penry in London because of the Hacket–Coppinger–Arthington scheme
28	July	William Hacket executed. Edmund Coppinger died the next day in prison
28	July	Penry flees from London to Scotland
18	August	Penry arrives in Scotland
26	August	Penry's third daughter, Safety, born
3	October	Henry Kildale, or Kyndall, examined. Waldegrave's assistant
20	November	Lord Chancellor Christopher Hatton dies
		Richard Cosin's *An Apologie: of, and for Sundrie Proceedings by Jurisdiction Ecclesiasticall*

1592

	June	Throkmorton's *A Petition Directed* printed by Schilders at Middelburg
	October	Penry arrives in London. Joins the Separatists
	December	Matthew Sutcliffe's *An Answere to a Certaine Libel Supplicatorie* published. Reply to *A Petition Directed*

1593

	March	Richard Hooker's *Of the Lawes of Ecclesiasticall Politie*
22	March	Penry captured in Ratcliffe, in Stepney

6	April	Henry Barrow and John Greenwood hanged at Tyburn. Friday
15	April	Easter
21	May	Penry arraigned before the Court of Queen's Bench. First indictment. Monday
25	May	Penry arraigned before the Court of Queen's Bench. Second indictment. Convicted and sentenced to death. Friday
29	May	John Penry hanged at Thomas à Watering, Southwark, Tuesday afternoon
		Bancroft's *A Survay*, his *Daungerous Positions*, and the Puritans' *A Parte of a Register* published

1594

	April	*The Defence of Job Throkmorton* published at Middelburg by Richard Schilders. Only book with Throkmorton's name
29	April	Thomas Cooper, bishop of Winchester, dies
3	June	John Aylmer, bishop of London, dies

1595

| ca. | June | Matthew Sutcliffe's *An Answere unto a Certaine Calumnious Letter* published |

1596

A Brief Apologie of Thomas Cartwright. The preface is by Throkmorton. Printed by Richard Schilders at Middelburg

1597

| 8 | May | Richard Bancroft consecrated as bishop of London |

1601

| 23 | February | Job Throkmorton dies |

1603

| 24 | March | Queen Elizabeth dies. James VI of Scotland succeeds as James I. Waldegrave returns to England about April–May |
| 27 | December | Thomas Cartwright dies |

1604

| 29 | February | Archbishop Whitgift dies. Funeral solemnities 27 March |
| 10 | December | Richard Bancroft confirmed as archbishop of Canterbury |

INTRODUCTION

FOR ALMOST four hundred years the identity of Martin Marprelate has remained a mystery. Who was the facile writer and irrepressible satirist that published the seven Marprelate works? Why did he conceal himself behind such pseudonyms as Martin Marprelate, Martin Junior, and Martin Senior? What is the explanation for the launching of his bitter attack on the ecclesiastical hierarchy shortly after the Spanish Armada had been driven from the English Channel? And what was the provocative power of Martin's books, which produced an immediate response from the queen, the privy councilors, leaders of the Church of England, high commissioners, contemporary writers and playwrights? These questions have intrigued scholars, and the solutions have varied widely.

It is the thesis of this book that the idealistic reformer who wrote the Marprelate works was Job Throkmorton, a country gentleman from Haseley, Warwickshire, who had written against the prelates ever since the outbreak of the Admonition Controversy in June 1572. As a member of Parliament in 1586/87, he had played a prominent role in seeking reform. Not willing to divulge his identity, and not yearning to suffer imprisonment as a martyr, since he did not enjoy "the ayre of the Clinke or Gatehouse" during the cold winter months, he wrote under at least eleven pseudonyms.[1]

For a clear understanding of the Marprelate controversy, a brief statement on the condition of the *Anglicana Ecclesia* in the sixteenth century will be presented. The causes arising from the situation in the church and provoking the outbreak of the controversy in October 1588 will be delineated. The course of the polemic will be illustrated by a brief discussion of the seven Marprelate books and a presentation of the *dramatis personae*. And on the vexed question of authorship a résumé will be given of the numerous surmises on Martin Marprelate's identity.

The Church of England in the Sixteenth Century

During the seventy-one years from the consecration of Archbishop Thomas Cranmer on 30 March 1533 to the death of Archbishop Whitgift on 29 February 1603/04, the English church experienced changes unparalleled in its rich history of twelve centuries. In 1534, by Act of Parliament, Henry VIII was designated "the onely supreme heed [head] in erthe of the Churche of England callyd *Anglicana Ecclesia*."[2] During the next six years the dissolution of the monasteries drastically altered the status and functions of the regular clergy, even more than the position of the secular clergy had been changed by the enactments of 1532–34. Under Edward VI the first Book of Common Prayer of 1549 introduced significant changes, and the second Book of Common Prayer of 1552 brought startling alterations. The Mass became the Eucharist or the Lord's Supper, as differing interpretations of the sacrament emerged, and communion in both kinds was celebrated. Services were conducted in the vernacular by clergymen, who were permitted to marry. Reversal and upheaval followed upon the accession of Mary Tudor. Apprehension spread as the half-Spanish queen married King Philip II of Spain on 25 July 1554. On 30 November the papal legate, Cardinal Reginald Pole, absolved the schismatic nation and, on 6 December, the Convocation clergy. There followed a restoration of the ancient rites and ceremonies, the arrest and imprisonment of nonconformists, the flight to the Continent of the Marian exiles, and the burning of the Protestant martyrs, including such prominent leaders as bishops Nicholas Ridley, Hugh Latimer, John Hooper, and Archbishop Thomas Cranmer.

On 17 November 1558, at the age of twenty-five, Elizabeth became queen. The cataclysmic changes of the previous quarter of a century coincided with her life from her birth in 1533 to her coronation on 15 January 1558/59. Therefore it is understandable that the queen and her advisors hoped to establish a regime of ecclesiastical stability, steady progress, and rational compromise. The first Parliament of 1559 enacted the Act of Supremacy by which "all foreign spiritual jurisdiction" was abolished and the monarch was designated the "supreme Governour" of the church, "aswell in all Spirituall or Ecclesiasticall Thinges or Causes as Temporall."[3] The Parliament also passed the Act of Uniformity, which restored an Anglican form of worship, as prescribed in the Elizabethan Book of Common Prayer of 1559—essentially the same service book as that of 1552 with a few changes. Despite the government's hope for agreement, all Catholic bishops except Anthony Kitchin, bishop of Llandaff, refused to take the oath supporting the royal supremacy in the church. The deprivation of the Catholic prelates ended their power in the House of Lords and weakened the church temporal. In August 1559 Matthew Parker was elected by the Canterbury chapter as the first Elizabethan archbishop and was confirmed and consecrated in December. Within the next three months eleven bishops, loyal to the Elizabethan regime, were consecrated. During the next three decades the Anglican hierarchy was confronted by problems posed by the rise of the Presbyterians under the leadership of Thomas Cartwright, Walter Travers, and John Field; by the emergence of the Separatists under the guidance of Robert Browne, Robert Harrison, John Greenwood, and Henry Barrow; and by the revival of the Catholic party under the direction of Cardinal William Allen, Robert Persons, and Edmund Campion.

Causes Provoking the Marprelate Campaign

The background causes for the Marprelate attack were inseparable from the history of the Elizabethan period. The Act of Uniformity of 1559 was a compromise measure which satisfied neither conservative Anglicans nor liberal reformers. Although the latter considered the Act as a point of departure toward more radical reform, the queen regarded further change as undesirable. In the Convocation of 1562/63 the attempt to promote reform failed.[4] Three years later the vestment struggle came to a crisis with the insistence of the queen and Archbishop Parker that dignity and uniformity of priestly apparel be observed. Rather than wear the hated "popish rags" and "badges of Antichrist," some of the more militant clergy accepted suspension or deprivation. In 1570 the area of disagreement widened from the *de bene esse* to the *esse* of the church when Thomas Cartwright, Lady Margaret professor at Cambridge, delivered his popular lectures on The Acts of the Apostles. He advocated a revolutionary presbyterian polity which would replace archbishops, bishops, deans, chancellors, commissaries, and archdeacons, and their ecclesiastical courts, with a tetrarchy of pastors, doctors, elders, and deacons, and with a system of discipline at the congregational, classis, and synodical level. Consequently, Cartwright was deprived of his professorship in December 1570, and of his Trinity College fellowship in September 1572. Nevertheless, from 1570 to 1590 he remained the acknowledged leader of the presbyterian classis movement.[5]

In June 1572 the provocative *An Admonition to the Parliament* appeared, written by two zealous reformers, John Field and Thomas Wilcox. This Presbyterian manifesto attracted immediate attention, and was followed in October or November by Throkmorton's *Second Admonition to the Parliament.*[6] Both books were attacks upon the Book of Common Prayer, vestments, prelates, and unlearned non-preaching clergy of the Church of England. John Whitgift, then master of Trinity College, Cambridge, published his *An Answere to a Certen Libel Intituled, An Admonition to the Parliament,* against which Cartwright in 1573 wrote *A Replye to an Answere Made of M. Doctor Whitgifte. Agaynste the Admonition to the Parliament.* The master then published a rejoinder, *The Defense of the Aunswere to the Admonition against the Replie of T. C.,* in 1574, to which Cartwright replied in 1575 and 1577. Since Whitgift decided not to answer these last two works of Cartwright, he was later accused by Martin of running away from the battle.[7] Evidently the queen disagreed, since she elevated him to the episcopal bench as bishop of Worcester in 1577. When Arch-

bishop Edmund Grindal died 6 July 1583, Whitgift was translated in September to the archbishopric of Canterbury.

Within two months of his confirmation, the new archbishop had prepared a list of articles to be subscribed by
the clergy.[8] Supported by the queen, Whitgift sponsored a
rigorous policy designed to achieve the medieval ideal of
unity and uniformity. To carry out this program, the archbishop utilized the Court of High Commission, which was
unencumbered by a jury. He effectively supported the famous
Star Chamber edict of 23 June 1586, which mandated a stricter
censorship of the press and more careful supervision of printers—especially of those who printed presbyterian or Catholic
books. Nonconformists were suspended, deprived, or imprisoned if they refused the self-incriminating oath ex officio.[9]
At the same time, despite strong opposition which would
have frightened a weaker man, the tireless metropolitan en-
listed the aid of friends in Parliament and supporters in the
Privy Council, such as Lord Chancellor Christopher Hatton,
William Brooke, Lord Cobham, and Thomas Sackville, Lord
Buckhurst. In the parliaments of 1584/85 and 1586/87 the Court
party opposed efforts to promote reform. Presbyterian bills
were shunted aside by governmental spokesmen in the House
of Commons, effectively blocked by the spiritual peers in
the House of Lords, or quashed by the firm order of the
queen, who was kept *au courant* by her faithful "little black
husband," Archbishop Whitgift. It is understandable that
the reformers became exasperated and bitter. Their own deep
sense of frustration was reflected in the writings of one of
their parliamentary members—Job Throkmorton, who assumed the pseudonym of Martin Marprelate.

The immediate cause of the Marprelate controversy was
the publication in 1587 of a large tome of 1,401 pages by John
Bridges, dean of Salisbury, entitled, *A Defence of the Government Established in the Church of Englande for Ecclesiasticall
Matters.*[10] This book was a reply to an influential presbyterian
manifesto, *A Briefe and Plaine Declaration*, sometimes referred
to as *A Learned Discourse* from its running title.[11] Probably
written in 1572 by William Fulke, an ardent Presbyterian,

5

it remained in manuscript until 1584, when it was published anonymously without the permission of the author. In the meantime Fulke had reconciled himself to the Church of England and become master of Pembroke College, Cambridge (1578–89).

In his book Dr. Bridges refuted some of the standard presbyterian teachings as set forth in Fulke's book and in Théodore de Bèze's work, *The Judgement of a Most Reverend and Learned Man from Beyond the Seas, concerning a Threefolde Order of Bishops*.[12] Since Bridges' volume was verbose and diffuse, replete with biblical and patristic learning and copiously documented from Continental theologians, it was an inviting target for critics. In 1587 Dudley Fenner, a brilliant young Presbyterian serving a partly reformed church at Middelburg in the Netherlands, replied with his *A Defence of the Godlie Ministers, against the Slaunders of D. Bridges*. In 1588 Walter Travers, a former lecturer at the Temple Church and later provost of Trinity College, Dublin, also answered Bridges with *A Defence of the Ecclesiastical Discipline*.[13]

One other immediate cause for the launching of the Marprelate attack was a fortuitous concurrence of events affecting Throkmorton, John Penry, Robert Waldegrave, and John Udall. On 23 February 1586/87 Throkmorton delivered in the House of Commons his "Speech on the Low Countries," which was critical of England's foreign policy and of such monarchs as Henry III, Philip II, and James VI. Alarmed by Throkmorton's aspersions against the Scottish king, Lord Treasurer Burghley wrote a mollifying letter on 2 March to the Scottish ambassador, Archibald Douglas, concerning "the lewd and blasphemous speechis usid in the Commons house by one Job Throgmorton ageynst the honor of the Kyng of Scottis, for which cause he shall be committed to morrow to the Towar as a close prisoner, and shall therby, for the rashnes of his tong, fele smart in his whole body. His fault is not excusable, and therfor the sharplier to be punished." Throkmorton escaped the Tower by fleeing to Hillingdon, but his parliamentary career came to an abrupt end. Unable henceforth to promote his reforms in Parliament, the frustrated Puritan resorted to writing anonymous diatribes.

Five days after Throkmorton's speech, Penry presented a petition to Parliament, with a copy of his first book, *A Treatise Containing the Aequity of an Humble Supplication Which Is to Be Exhibited unto Hir Gracious Majesty and This High Court of Parliament in the Behalfe of the Countrey of Wales, That Some Order May Be Taken for the Preaching of the Gospell among Those People*, one of the earliest books printed by Joseph Barnes at Oxford. This book was so upsetting to the hierarchy that almost the entire edition of 500 copies was confiscated by the wardens of the Stationers' Company. Penry was brought before the Court of High Commission and then committed to the Gatehouse for a month. Penry expressed his frustration in a letter of protestation of 8 March 1586/87, to John Field:

> Concerninge the men with whom I have to deale . . . I protes[t] and professe by Gods assistaunce never to have peace with them, etc., as longe as that league of theyrs, wherein they are linked with Sathan in a chayne that threatneth fatall over-throw unto all sinceritye, doth continew.

On 16 April 1588, the printing shop of Waldegrave "at the sign of The Crane in St. Paul's Churchyard" was raided, and copies of Throkmorton's book, *The State of the Church of Englande, Laide Open in a Conference betweene Diotrephes a Byshop, Tertullus a Papist, Demetrius an Usurer, Pandocheus an Inne-keeper, and Paule a Preacher of the Worde of God*, were seized. Waldegrave escaped with type hidden under his cloak, but on 13 May by order of the Stationers' Company, his "printing presse and Letters were taken away: his presse being timber, was sawen and hewed in pieces, the yron work battered and made unserviceable, his Letters melted, with cases and other tooles defaced (by John Woolfe, alias Machivill, Beadle of the Stacioners, and most tormenting executioner of Walde-graves goods)." As one who had been previously arrested for printing unlicensed books, as a man with "a wife and six small children," the foremost Puritan printer faced the gloomy prospect of imprisonment and unemployment (see

Appendix F, which presents reasons for attributing *The State of the Church* to Throkmorton).

Although not directly implicated in the Martinist series, John Udall was also embittered because he had lost his position as the curate of the church at Kingston-upon-Thames. Fulfilling his threat to write against the bishops, he penned *A Demonstration of the Trueth of That Discipline Which Christ Hath Prescribed in His Worde for the Government of His Church, in All Times and Places, untill the End of the World,* which Waldegrave printed secretly at East Molesey concurrently with Martin's *Epistle* in October 1588. Two months later, with the assistance of Henry Hastings, third earl of Huntingdon, he obtained an appointment as pastor in St. Nicholas Church at Newcastle-upon-Tyne, where he remained for a year.[14]

Thus, the Marprelate books were partly a result of the indignation and frustration of the author—Throkmorton—of the sympathetic collaboration of the co-ordinator of the project—Penry—and of the resentment of the printer—Waldegrave. The secret publication of Martin's works was also a consequence of and a challenge to the Star Chamber decree of 23 June 1586, which sought to curb unlicensed books, and of Throkmorton's deep hostility to the policies of Convocation, Whitgift, and the Court of High Commission.

A Synopsis of the Martin Marprelate Books

The Martinist series comprised six books and a broadside. *More Worke for Cooper* was intended as the eighth treatise, but the manuscript was confiscated in the course of printing and was never published. Ostensibly a reply to Dean Bridges' *Defence*, the first Marprelate book, the *Epistle*,[15] included a sustained attack on the Church of England, a series of threats and taunts against the supporters of the English church, and a defense of well-known Presbyterians. Since only one-fifth of the *Epistle* was directed against the *Defence*, Martin failed to grapple with many of Dr. Bridges' arguments. Instead, he presented a caricature of the *Defence* and a lampoon of the dean of Sarum, whose writings allegedly were senseless, whose style was obscure, and whose logic was fallacious.

The *Epistle* presented a severe indictment of the episcopal hierarchy. Martin libeled the archbishop and the bishops as "that swinishe rable," as "pettie Antichrists, pettie popes, proud prelates, intolerable withstanders of reformation, enemies of the gospel, and most covetous wretched priests."[16] Since he regarded "lord bishops" as unscriptural and unchristian, he accused them of usurping their authority by keeping ordinary pastors under episcopal jurisdiction. He also challenged them to show how they, by urging subscription to archiepiscopal articles, could avoid the accusation of violating the statute of praemunire[17] and the "Act to Refourme Certayne Dysorders touching Ministers of the Churche."[18] In a vehement tirade Martin denounced Thomas Cooper, bishop of Winchester, as "a flattering hypocrit" for asserting in a court sermon that not since the apostolic age had there been such a thriving institution as the Church of England, and in several pages of vivid prose he accused John Aylmer, bishop of London, of blasphemy and insolent behavior.

Martin deplored the lack of qualified clergymen. He criticized the Church of England because it tolerated nonresidency and pluralism, and he intimated that bribes and simony were factors in clerical promotion. He was especially critical of the leaders who failed to encourage the general preaching of the Word, and was scornful of official spokesmen whose sermons he regarded as insipid, flimsy, and unorthodox. Martin described the Court of High Commission as "turned cleane contrarye to the ende wherefore it was ordayned," and as guilty of excommunicating persons for trivial reasons. Dr. Edward Stanhope, chancellor of the diocese of London and a high commissioner, was satirized as "Tarquinius Superbus D. Stanop."

The *Epistle* defended such Presbyterians as Giles Wigginton, pastor at Sedbergh, Yorkshire, who had been deprived for nonconformity; it gave an ex parte account of Penry's appearance before the Court of High Commission; and it pleaded the cause of Udall, who had been silenced by Dr. John Hone, archidiaconal judge and Official to Dr. James Cottington, archdeacon of Surrey.[19] The *Epistle* also included four gibes: against Dr. Richard Cosin, vicar-general of the province of Canterbury and dean of the Arches, for his lack of learning and failure to reply to Dudley Fenner's *A Counter-poyson, Modestly Written for the Time;* against Dr. John Copcot, master of Corpus Christi College, Cambridge, for not refuting the confutation of his Paul's Cross sermon; against Dr. Bridges for not replying to Fenner's *A Defence of the Godlie Ministers, against the Slaunders of D. Bridges;* and against Archbishop Whitgift for not answering Cartwright's *The Second Replie agaynst Maister Whitgiftes Second Answer* and his *The Rest of the Second Replie agaynst Master Whitgifts Second Answer.*[20]

Unlike the systematic replies of Fenner's *A Defence of the Godlie Ministers* and Travers' *A Defence of the Ecclesiastical Discipline,* Martin's answer to Bridges was a motley array of stories and gossip, an assorted collection of accusations and denunciations, a humorous list of books he intended to write such as "Martins Dreame," or "Of the Lives and Doings of English Popes," a compilation of illogical and invalid syllogisms exposing Bridges' stupidity, and some impossible "Conditions of Peace to Be Inviolablie Kept for Ever" with the lord bishops. Since Martin indulged in banter, caricature, sarcasm, and derision, as well as jocularity, humor, imaginary conversations, and posturing, the *Epistle* provided fascinating reading and captured the attention of friend and foe. At a time when anti-Catholic feeling ran high, just three months after the attempted invasion by the Spanish Armada, Martin's accusation that "your Canterburinesse and the rest of the lord bishops favor papists and recusants, rather than puritans," and that the archbishop dealt more leniently with Catholic printers than with the Puritan printers such as Waldegrave, touched a sensitive nerve. Perhaps no other book in the Elizabethan period combined such unrestrained iconoclasm with irrepressible mirth and unflagging readability.

The *Epitome* was a continuation of the *Epistle,* but it comprised fewer topics and expressed less criticism of the

bishops.[21] In his introduction Martin revealed his elation at
the success of the *Epistle*, and his pleasure that his book had
been received in court. He claimed that he was "favored of
all estates (the puritans onely excepted)" and that he was
the subject of avid conversation and that many had tried
to obtain his book. When four alarmed bishops—Whitgift,
John Aylmer of London, Cooper, and William Wickham,
bishop of Lincoln—attempted to discover his whereabouts,
Martin feigned surprise that they thought he was lost. And
he expressed disappointment that the Puritan preachers were
angry with him. He justified his frankness and jocosity by
insisting that he "must needs call a spade a spade, a pope a
pope."

Most of the *Epitome* was a straightforward refutation of a
few of Dr. Bridges' arguments, with tangential derisive comments on the dean and ridicule of Aylmer's book, *An Harborowe for Faithfull and Trewe Subiectes.*[22] Martin maintained that
true church government consisted of pastor, doctor, elder,
and deacon, as prescribed in the New Testament by Christ
himself and the apostles. This government was established
in perpetuity and could not be altered by royal decree or
episcopal decision. Bridges had contended that Christ gov-
erned "the inward and spirituall government of the heart"
but did not prescribe an external government for the church.
Therefore ecclesiastical polity was not of the essence of religion, was not necessary for salvation, and was not immutable.
Thus, pragmatically, civil and ecclesiastical government
could be established on reason and experience. Martin insisted that justifying faith was the only absolute requisite
for salvation but that church polity and preaching of the
Word were prescribed in the Scripture and therefore not
to be altered "at the pleasure of man."

Throughout the *Epitome* Martin combined levity with ear-
nestness. Regarding Bridges as ignorant and "leadenheaded,"
he ironically referred to him as "thrise learned brother
Bridges," and asked him sarcastically if he could "decline
what is Latine for a goose." He grossly insulted the dean
when he wrote: "Thou knowest not how I love thee for thy

wit and learning sake, brother John (as for thy godlines, I might cary it in mine eye, and see never a whit the worse)." And twice he alluded to Dr. Bridges as one who "plaide my Lord of Winchesters foole in his sermon at Sir Maries Church in Cambridge." More serious were Martin's accusations that Bridges proffered "popish reasons," relied on the Jesuitical teachings of Robert Bellarmine, deferred to Whitgift, and lacked sincerity.

In the *Epitome* Martin devoted about ten pages to Bishop John Aylmer and his book, *An Harborowe for Faithfull and Trewe Subiectes.* This volume reflected Aylmer's ideas in the 1550s when he was a Marian exile in Strassburg and Zurich. It is not surprising that Martin praised the bishop's earlier views that Parliament had acted wisely in resisting Henry VIII's efforts to give proclamations statutory status, that ecclesiastical and civil offices should not be "jumbled together," that "Paules commission is to teache obedience; therefore hee hath nothing to doe to call for a redresse of matters in civil pollicie." Aylmer had also advocated that the bishops should give up their excessive wealth: "Let the queen have the rest of your temporallities and other landes . . . that every parrishe church may have his preacher, everie citie his superintendent, to live honestly and not pompously." Yet, since he had accepted a bishopric, Martin charged, Aylmer had become "a paterne of hypocrisie" and "a continuall oppressor of the Churche of God."[23]

The Marprelate attack might have ended in November 1588 with the publication of the *Epitome,* had it not been for the appearance two months later of *An Admonition to the People of England,* written by T.C. It was quickly discovered that "T.C." was not Thomas Cartwright but Thomas Cooper, bishop of Winchester, who refuted the stories and assertions in Martin's *Epistle.*[24] In effect, Cooper provided a new inviting target, and Martin immediately attacked the bishop in an interim broadside, *Certaine Minerall, and Metaphisicall Schoolpoints,* consisting of thirty-seven theses, somewhat distorted or exaggerated, to be defended in academic fashion by the bishops and deans.[25] Cooper was named a defendant in sixteen points, Bridges in five, Whitgift in four, Aylmer in three, the entire episcopal bench in three, Dr. Robert Some in two, and Convocation in one. With six other bishops and deans, there were thirteen defendants.[26]

The *Mineralls* comprised a list of beliefs and practices allegedly advocated by the Anglicans. Intended to embarrass or ridicule the hierarchy, the schoolpoints misrepresented some of the Anglican positions on doctrines and ceremonies. Among points at issue were the authority of creeds and the Apocrypha, the role of preaching, New Testament polity, and baptism administered by women. Other differences pertained to the wearing of the surplice, the use of the cross in baptism, church organs, public fasts, pluralism, and lay appropriations. Some of the schoolpoints were startling:

2. That a Lord Bishop may safely have two wives *in esse* at once; the defendant in this point, is father Marmaduke [Middleton], Bishop of S. Davids, who hath two now living: the one, Elizabeth Gigge, the other Ales Pryme. Prooved against him before the High Commission.[27]

15. That our Lord Bishops in England, are the bishops of the divell: the defendant in this point (I thank him) is father John O Sarum, pages 339, 340.[28]

Essentially, the *Mineralls* was a *divertissement*, compiled hurriedly within a week, to provide a brief reply to Cooper's *Admonition* until Martin could complete his *Hay Any Worke for Cooper*.[29]

This latter book[30] was a reply to Bishop Cooper's *Admonition* (252 pages). Since Cooper devoted only about one-fourth of his book—68 pages—to Martin's *Epistle*, and perforce omitted some of the Martinist accusations, Martin made the dubious assumption that whatever the bishop had not refuted could be accepted as true, and that the prelate had "confyrmed rather than confuted" Martin's assertions. Martin also gloated that since two passages in the first edition had been patched over, he had "made the bishops to pull in their hornes."[31]

Hay Any Worke, with fewer digressions, was more systematic than the other Marprelate books. It concentrated on three main topics: the essence of true church government, the supposed difficulties and dangers that would ensue by adopting Presbyterianism, and the faults of church governors. Martin alleged that true church government was a divine institution. Even as Moses left a perfect government, so Christ established an exact and immutable polity which consisted of pastor, doctor or teacher, elder, and deacon. To omit any of these offices was to maim the church; to establish any new office was to deform it. Since the Church of England, according to Martin, had maimed and deformed the body of Christ, it supported an ecclesiastical government which was "not allowed in the sight of God." Thus, Martin maintained the position that a true church governor was not subject to the jurisdiction of the magistrate but to the Lord alone. The Anglican bishops, however, believed that polity, unlike doctrine, sacraments, and faith, was a historical development, subject to the dictates of time and circumstance.

Cooper had enumerated some of the dangers that would be encountered if a Presbyterian platform were to be introduced. He feared that such a platform would "bring the Governement of the Church to a Democracie or Aristocracie," and that the danger would spread "to the governement of the common weale." Martin retorted that Presbyterian government was "monarchicall in regarde of our head Christ, aristocraticall in the eldership and democraticall in the people." The civil government would be "monarchicall in Her Majesties person; aristocraticall in the higher house of Parliament, or rather at the Councell table; democraticall in the bodie of the Commons of the lower house of Parliament." Cooper warned that a Presbyterian polity would bring in the "judiciall lawe of the Jewes." To this Martin replied that "the most of that law is abrogated," and that only the moral aspects of the Mosaic judicial code would be applicable. Again, Cooper indicated that "the canon law must [would certainly] be utterly taken away," that "the use and studie of the civill law will be utterly overthrowne," and that civilians would suffer. Martin contended that it was "treson by statute, for any subject in this land, to proceed doctor of the canon law," and that civilians could practice in Admiralty, Arches, and other prerogative courts, and that they could deal with tithes, wills, and matrimonial causes.[32]

Cooper defended the bishops not only against the extreme accusations of Martin but also against the general criticism that the prelates were covetous, that they did not contribute to the poor, and that they opposed reformation. Even though bishops made mistakes, they should be treated with kindness and understanding. Martin's riposte was a sarcastic exhortation in which he appealed with mock kindness:

> Good John of Canterbury, leave thy popedome; good father John of London, be no more a bishop of the divell; be no more a traytor to God and his Worde. And good sweet boyes, all of you, become honest men; maime and deform the church no longer. Sweet fathers now, make not a trade of persecuting.

As a special example of persecution, Martin reported several instances of the imprisonment of Waldegrave during the 1580s.[33]

After Martin had published his *Hay Any Worke*, he pressed on with his plan to complete *More Worke for Cooper*. His schedule, however, was upset when Waldegrave withdrew in April 1589 and not until 13 July did the newly hired printer, John Hodgskin, arrive at Throkmorton's home, with the expectation of receiving the manuscript of *More Worke*. Since it was not ready, Hodgskin was informed that he should remain briefly at Wolston to print an interim publication, *Theses Martinianae*, usually called *Martin Junior*.[34] It consisted of a title page and three pages of introduction, together with a compilation of 110 theses or "unanswerable conclusions," which represented Martin's beliefs and criticisms. This first portion was placed along a path by a bush, then picked up by Hodgskin on 14 July and brought to Wolston. The remaining portion—"Martin Juniors Epilogue"—was composed between 14–17 July, delivered secretly by Throkmorton to the printing room of Valentine Symmes, Hodgskin's compositor, on 18 July, and printed by 22 July. *Martin Junior*, written in great haste, was poorly organized; Martin himself acknowledged that it was an imperfect first draft and that there were "tautologies" in the "unanswerable conclusions."

The theses approximated thirty or forty words each. They set forth the novel idea that the true doctrine of the Church of England was that taught by such martyrs as John Frith, William Tyndale, John Lambert, and Robert Barnes in the reign of Henry VIII, and by bishops John Hooper, Nicholas Ridley, and Thomas Cranmer in the reign of Mary.[35] These teachings, according to the questionable reasoning of Martin, were essentially Presbyterian, were supported by the statute of 13 Elizabeth, c. 12, pertaining to the faith and sacraments,[36] by John Foxe's *Acts and Monuments,* published *cum privilegio,*[37] and by the royal prerogative. Approximately twenty-five theses pertained to "true" or reformed teachings on church polity; thirty-five denounced "lord bishops" as unscriptural; sixteen pointed to the error of uniting civil and ecclesiastical offices and to the danger for the commonwealth in permitting bishops to serve in the House of Lords and in allowing Whitgift to function as archbishop and president of the Privy Council. Other theses criticized enforced subscription to the Articles of Religion, episcopal licensing of preachers, citations, censures, excommunication by church courts, and the use of the ex officio oath, together with self-incriminating evidence, in the Court of High Commission.

The most fascinating section of *Martin Junior* was the "Epilogue" in which an imaginary stripling of "the reverend Martin Marprelate the Great"—actually Martin himself—praised his father "as a defender of the doctrine of our Churche." Martin Junior lampooned the bishops and especially Whitgift as adversaries of Christ and the apostles, as enemies "unto the doctrine of the Church of England sowed heere by the holy martires, and sealed with their blood." Martin Junior also poured scorn upon Mar-Martin, an anti-Martinist writer, who allegedly was employed to carry "Long Meg of Westminsters handbasket," and later was promoted to serve "some laundresse in a bishoppes house," where he was engaged in publishing "bawdery and filthinesse." Martin Junior had a fling at those authors who had published "haggling and profane pamphlets" against him. He was particulary incensed with the stage players, "poore seelie hunger-starved wretches," who had succeeded in attracting "many thousande eie witnesses, of their witelesse and pitifull conceites."[38]

The Just Censure and Reproofe of Martin Junior, usually referred to as *Martin Senior*, purported to be a rebuke by the older brother of his younger brother for writing *Martin Junior*.[39] Martin Senior reprimanded his brother for undutifulness, inconsideracy, and rashness in publishing his father's imperfect writings. By his despicable scrabbling, Martin Junior had infringed the privileges of his older brother who had inherited the right of "pistling the bishops." Furthermore, Martin Junior had provoked Whitgift to maniacal zeal in searching out Martin the Great. To illustrate the extreme measures the metropolitan would adopt, Martin Senior concocted a clever speech wherein the archbishop goaded his pursuivants into pursuit of Martin the Great, with a threat to dismiss them if they failed. Whitgift incited his henchmen to search out "Waldegrave the printer, Newman the cobler, Sharpe the booke binder of Northampton, and that seditious Welchman Penry, who you shall see will proove the author of all these libelles." The pursuivants were ordered to watch the Court area, Paul's churchyard, Richard Boyle's bookshop in Blackfriars, and Lincoln's Inn; they were spurred on to spy upon the houses of Puritan preachers, to check on the common inns, and to inspect packs. Unless the pursuivants captured the libeler, the archbishop warned, he would "grow starke madde" with them.[40]

Martin Senior revealed to his brother a plan to unite "lordes, knights, gentlemen, ministers, and people, to become joint suiters in one supplication unto Her Majestie and the lords of her honorable Privie Counsell." Such a petition would seek the redress of grievances and would command the support of one hundred thousand of "Her Majesties most loyall and trustie loving subjects." Also, it would request a quiet disputation on issues dividing the Anglicans and Puritans. Should the conference be refused, the petitioners would then insist on having remedy at the Court of King's Bench.

Martin Senior included a delightful discussion of the bishops' English—an amusing presentation of episcopal doubletalk. He was unable to understand why a petition to redress "the miseries of the church" should be translated in the prelates' language "to seeke the overthrowe of the State," or why a "dutifull supplication" should be rendered "to rebell against Her Majestie," or why "humbly and dutifullie to intreate" should signify "by unbrideled force undutifullie to compel." To understand the bishops' English, Martin Junior was advised to study his father's books, such as his *Grammar*, his *Lexicon*, and his *Capita Concordantiarum*. One month's study would enable the young man to penetrate the prelatical obfuscations and "to overturne anie catercap of them all."[41]

The Just Censure and Reproofe was professedly directed against Martin Junior but actually against Martin's favorite adversaries. Solemnly Martin propounded and proclaimed his denunciations against the archbishop and humorously suggested that Whitgift's household should consist of Dean Bridges as his court jester; Dr. John Underhill, rector of Lincoln College, as his almoner; Dr. Richard Bancroft, chaplain to Lord Hatton, and "drunken [William] Gravate," vicar of St. Sepulchre, as "yeomen of his cellar"; Mar-Martin and John Frégeville, a French writer, as "groomes of his stoole"; with Leonard Wright, an anti-Martinist writer, in attendance carrying the fool's sceptre; and Tobias Bland, a clergyman, holding a mirror to enable the jester to be certain that "his catercap doth every way reach over his eares." In two concluding derisive pot shots, Martin Senior, putting words into the mouth of Bishop Aylmer, "that Beelzebub of London," fired a "madmonition" against the pursuivants and aimed two pages of coarse doggerel against Mar-Martin.[42]

The *Protestatyon* was a helter-skelter work, written from memory, abominably printed and replete with misspellings and overturned letters in signature A.[43] As a protest against the capture of the Martinist printers, together with press, type, and the manuscript of *More Worke for Cooper*, it manifested a bravado spirit, coupled with indignation and frustration. Martin urged his readers not to be discouraged, not to reason from the government's success to the rightness of its cause—a *non sequitur*—and not to forget that Martinism would continue and that the reformation would triumph.

Martin provided some valuable biographical details on his motivation and status. He described himself as one desiring "onely the glory of God, by delivering of his churche from the great tyrannie and bondage, wherewith these tyranntes doe oppresse the same." He claimed that he prized a clear conscience, and disclaimed any desire for monetary rewards or "ambicious preheminence." Replying to those who said he had endangered his wife and children by his writings, he averred that he was a bachelor, although he might soon marry. If so, he would be cheered "to see a dozen of good and honest lord bishops daunce" at his wedding. He revealed himself as a man of substance when he wrote: "I have, I thanke God, of mine own, wherwith I am better content, than they [the bishops] are, with all their spoyle and robberie."[44]

Familiar themes recurred throughout the *Protestatyon*. Martin criticized the Court of High Commission for its browbeating tactics, its secrecy, and its use of the ex officio oath to compel men to accuse themselves. He pleaded for a public disputation, and taunted the prelates for not confuting the books of Cartwright, Fenner, Penry, Travers, and Udall. He particularly denounced bishops Aylmer and Cooper as "beasts," and reviled Whitgift as "that antichrist of Lambeth." Especially vehement was his general berating the bishops for resorting to "slanders, ribaldry, scurrillity, reviling, imprisonment, and torture." Their use of such weapons as the "halter, axe, bonds [fetters], scourging, and racking" was characterized as "whorish impudencie." To expose the prelates, Martin threatened to set up public notices of his victory throughout the land, and also to "make forraine nations ring of their villanies and ungoldlines."[45]

One of the valuable features of the *Protestatyon* was the summary of the confiscated manuscript, *More Worke for Cooper*. Martin affirmed that it contained a true characterization of a Martinist, as one who was not a "Browniste, Cooper-ist, Lambethist, schismatic, papist, atheist, traytor," or "lord bishop"; a true Martinist opposed all the enemies of God and the queen, and belonged to the "best affected subjects Her Majestie hath." Included in the summary were scornful comments against those who had written against Martin, such as Mar-Martin—described as "John a Cant. his hobbie-horse," and as one who had been ejected from a Morris-dance and discharged forever from "shaking his shins about a May-pole." Dr. Robert Some, a Cambridge don, who had "crazed his braine at Lambeth, and his conscience at Gyrton," was ridiculed for his egotism, and especially for his three repeti-tious books.[46] In *More Worke for Cooper* it is highly probable that Martin had confuted at length Some's book, *A Godly Treatise*,[47] and it is certain that he included "a large confuta-tion of Friar Fréguevil,[48] and of wringlefaced Wrighte."[49] Martin boasted that he had "slived [cleaved] Dick Bancroft over the shulder" probably by contemning his sermon of 9 February 1588/89. He also made demeaning remarks against Dr. John Underhill, shortly to be consecrated bishop of Ox-ford, and Dr. William Wood, a censor of books.

Unable to resist his penchant for burlesque, Martin said he had written a funeral oration upon the death of "olde Andrew Turne-coate" [Andrew Perne, master of Peter-house], preached by the "quick-witted Bridges." There was also a preamble, "to be song antiphonically in his Graces chappell, on Wednesdays and Frydayes, to the lamentable tune of Orawhynemeg." Martin had spoken of his Tolbooth, in which was a "great ashen chaire, wherin John a Bridges was placed by patent during his life." Around the prison was a "ranke of catercaps, conferring and disputing hotly, about the thirde declension, the churching of women, or such like matters of life and death. On the first fourm, sate in ranke, John, John, and William; on the seconde, Richard, Richard, and Thomas; on a third, John, William, and Marma-duke, etc."[50]

In the *Protestatyon* Martin stated that in *More Worke for Cooper* he had presented proof of some of the 110 theses which had been listed in *Martin Junior*. He may have been provoked by the anonymous Pasquill, author of *A Countercuffe Given to Martin Junior*, whose book was published about three weeks after *Martin Junior* had been issued. It is likely that Martin was late in procuring a copy, since he promised to talk elsewhere with "that blinde asse Pasquill."[51] Furthermore, Martin stated that in *More Worke for Cooper* he had included a discussion with the Puritans, whom he wished to mollify despite their criticisms. Martin promised that if any Puritans had justly reproved him, he would mend his faults. And in the list of errata Martin ridiculed Dr. George Bullen, or Boleyn, dean of Lichfield, for his heretical teaching on the subject of grace and for his antics in the pulpit. Previously Martin had depicted Bullen as a defender of pluralism.[52]

Dramatis Personae

There were at least twenty-three persons involved in the production and distribution of the Marprelate books. We shall conclude that Throkmorton was the writer (in Part II). Waldegrave printed the *Epistle*, the *Epitome*, the *Mineralls*, and *Hay Any Worke for Cooper*, assisted by his apprentice, Henry Kildale. When Waldegrave abandoned his task, he was replaced by John Hodgskin, with two assistants, Valentine Symmes and Arthur Thomlin, who printed *Martin Junior*, *Martin Senior*, and a small part of *More Worke for Cooper*. The first signature of the *Protestatyon* was printed by amateurs, probably Throkmorton and Penry, but the last three signatures were printed by Waldegrave. Proofreading for the first four items was probably done by Waldegrave, Kildale, or Throkmorton; Symmes confessed that he was the proofreader for *Martin Junior* and *Martin Senior*; it is likely that Penry and Throkmorton or Waldegrave read the proof for the *Protestatyon*. Kildale and Waldegrave did most of the binding, but Henry Sharpe, a Northampton bookbinder, assisted with *Martin Junior* and *Martin Senior*. Penry served as business manager.

Two presses were involved in the printing of the Martinist

series, one in the custody of Penry and the other in Hodgskin's control.[53] The harborers of Penry's press were Mrs. Elizabeth Crane, a London Puritan[54] who permitted the printing of the *Epistle* in her East Molesey house, and Sir Richard Knightley, a Puritan magnate who provided a building on his estate at Fawsley, Northamptonshire, for the printing of the *Epitome*. John Hales, a kinsman of Knightley, made available a house called "White Friars" in Coventry for the printing of the *Mineralls* and *Hay Any Worke for Cooper*, and also of Penry's *A Viewe*. In Wolston, Warwickshire, Roger Wigston, a country squire, and his wife granted quarters to Hodgskin and his assistants for the printing of *Martin Junior* and *Martin Senior*. Hodgskin's press was delivered to his home at Warrington, Lancashire, and then carried to a rented house near Manchester, where a few pages of *More Worke for Cooper* were printed. The last Marprelate book, the *Protestatyon*, was printed at Wolston on the Wigston premises.[55]

The persons mainly responsible for the distribution of the books were Humphrey Newman, a cobbler, and Penry, but Mrs. Waldegrave and Sharpe rendered assistance, and John Bowman and Augustine Maicocke, agents of Throkmorton, aided by distributing or selling books; Richard Holmes and a Mr. Grimston, both of Northampton, transported paper, ink, type, and equipment, to Wolston after Hodgskin's press had been seized at Manchester. One Garnet, also of Northampton, brought warning of the pursuivants' second raid on the home of Penry's father-in-law, Henry Godley, and aided in transporting 1,600 books to Banbury for concealment in widow Adams' house. As compensation for providing ink and other services, James Meddowes, another agent of Throkmorton, was promised a part of the expected profits from the printing of Throkmorton's *The Crops and Flowers of Bridges Garden*. In addition, five servants rendered assistance.

Surmises on the Identity of Martin Marprelate

The fact that at least twenty-two candidates have been suggested for Martin's role illustrates the complexity of the problem of authorship of the Marprelate books. One of the first suspects to be questioned by the high commissioners was Giles Wigginton, an eccentric clergyman from Sedbergh, Yorkshire, whose troubles with Archbishop Whitgift had been described in the *Epistle*. He was arraigned on 6 December 1588, but his examination elicited no information leading to Martin's identity.[56] Since the *Epistle* also contained material derived from a report of John Udall's troubles with clerical officials, he was suspected as a possible author. Stephen Chatfield, vicar of Kingston-upon-Thames, deposed that after being silenced, Udall had said that it was best for the bishops "not to stopp his mouth; ffor yf they did, he would then sett himself to writing, and geve the Bishoppes suche a blowe as they never had the lyke in their lyves."[57] A third suspect was John Field, the organizing secretary of the Puritan clergy. Since he had collected a large corpus of correspondence, complaints, and reports, there was a suspicion that his material was the source of some of Martin's biographical references. Also, according to Sharpe's testimony, Penry had intimated that the *Epistle* was at least partly dependent on notes found in Field's study after his death.[58] A fourth candidate was Dudley Fenner, who had served as minister in Cartwright's former church in Middelburg, Zeeland, and had published anonymously a reply to Dean Bridges—*A Defence of the Godlie Ministers.*[59]

Nicholas Tomkins, a servant of Mrs. Elizabeth Crane, had heard that Francis Marbury (or Merbury), father of the more famous Anne Hutchinson who migrated to Massachusetts, was regarded as a possible author of the *Epistle* and the *Epitome*, but this was mere rumor. Martin himself reported that "lame" Eusebius Pagit, a suspended Puritan preacher from Old, or Wold, Northamptonshire, and Kilkhampton, Cornwall, was wrongly considered to be Marprelate. Even Martin's close friend Cartwright was accused of being Martin or at least of knowing his identity.[60] William Maskell, an Anglican clergyman and liturgist, suggested that Walter Travers was perhaps responsible for the Marprelate books.[61]

All eight of the previously named suspects were Puritan clergymen. The death of Fenner late in 1587 and of Field in March 1587/88 ruled out any possibility of their candidacy, and the absence of Udall in Newcastle-upon-Tyne during the entire year 1589 precluded his role as Martin. The lack of any evidence against Wigginton, Marbury, Pagit, Cartwright, and Travers eliminates these clerics from serious consideration as likely candidates for the authorship of the Marprelate books.

Among non-clerical candidates, four prominent political figures have been proposed as the real Martin. An unlikely candidate was Michael Hickes, one of Lord Burghley's secretaries, who had a reputation for culture, wit, and financial expertise.[62] Another political personage who has been suggested was Laurence Tomson, an agent of Sir Francis Walsingham, whose writings indicated a Puritan stance. Even more unlikely was the conjecture that Robert Cecil, Lord Burghley's younger son, was masquerading under Martin's mantle. Despite wild rumors that Robert Devereux, second earl of Essex, was Martin, there are no clues which would incriminate the vain and mercurial earl.[63]

It is surprising that Gabriel Harvey, a cantankerous Cambridge poet and Fellow of Trinity Hall, was suspected of meddling in the Marprelate controversy. John Lyly, the probable author of *Pappe with an Hatchet* (1589), intimated spitefully or irresponsibly that Harvey was "a notable coach companion for Martin," but Harvey actually was anti-Martinist in his writings.[64] Another candidate who deserves mention is George Carleton, from Overstone, Northamptonshire. An active Puritan, member of Parliament, stepfather to Sir Anthony Cope (who sponsored the drastic "Bill and Book" legislation in Parliament in February 1586/87), Carleton was the kind of person who would be suspected of Martinist leanings. Furthermore, he was the second husband of Elizabeth Crane, at whose country house both Udall's *Demonstration of Discipline* and Martin's *Epistle* were printed. After *Hay Any Worke* was published, Carleton was summoned to appear before the Privy Council in April 1589 and was ordered to give daily attendance until permitted to depart.[65] The proponent of Carleton as a possible Martin is Miss Katherine M. Longley, whose unpublished paper, "A New Approach to the Marprelate Tracts," has provided fresh information on Carleton. Her suggestion that Martin's reference to the comedian, Richard Tarleton, was a misspelling and actually referred to Carleton cannot be maintained. Nevertheless, in Miss Longley's favor, it should be added that Dr. Patrick Collinson gave Carleton a high priority when he wrote that Martin "may conceivably prove to have been a gentleman from this part of the country [the Midlands]. If not Throckmorton, why not George Carleton, Mistress Crane's husband of 1589, perhaps abetted by that shadowy 'chief director' of Puritan strategy in Northamptonshire, William Fludd?"[66] It is possible to consider Fludd a tentative candidate, since he was a kind of nonconformist district superintendent, but I have found no evidence pointing toward his role as Martin. Perhaps further research may reveal collaboration by either Fludd or Carleton.

Having excluded fifteen candidates on whom very little Martinist research has been expended, we turn to four suspects who have been subjects of research and for whom we have scholarly articles and books: Henry Barrow, Sir Roger Williams, John Penry, and Job Throkmorton.

The leading advocate for Barrow's candidacy was Henry M. Dexter, a prominent American clergyman and editor, and a competent student of Puritanism, Separatism, and Congregationalism. Dexter regarded Martin as a bachelor, a lawyer, a trenchant writer, and a fearless opponent of the hierarchy. Barrow was a bachelor, a lawyer, a trenchant writer, and a fearless opponent of the hierarchy. Ergo, Barrow was Martin. It was an intriguing hypothesis, and one could almost wish it were true. It conjures up a picture of all the agents of the government—Privy Council, Court of High Commission, pursuivants, sheriffs, justices of the peace—searching high and low for the impudent satirist who dared to ridicule the church and hierarchy. While the pursuivants were scurrying around the country, Barrow was safely ensconced in the Fleet prison, chuckling at the futile efforts to find him. Somehow, the anomalous situation tickles our fancy and appeals to our sympathy. But we must conclude that Dexter's wish was the father to his thought. Martin praised Cartwright inordinately whereas Barrow criticized him; Martin was a humorist and a satirist and a Presbyterian; Barrow was a somber Separatist with no interest in humor or satire. It is a kind of tragedy to see the demolition of a beautiful big hypothesis by some ugly small facts.[67]

In 1912 John Dover Wilson published two articles entitled: "Martin Marprelate and Shakespeare's Fluellen. A New Theory of the Authorship of the Marprelate Tracts," in which he speculated that Sir Roger Williams, a famous Welsh officer and author of two books on war and military strategy, was a likely candidate for Martin's writings. Concluding that the Marprelate books were a product of composite authorship, he ascribed the *Epistle*, the *Epitome, Hay Any Worke*, and the text of *More Worke for Cooper* to Williams, as well as the 110 theses of *Martin Junior*. To Throkmorton he assigned *Martin Senior*, the opening section of *More Worke*, entitled "The Epistle to More Worke," and pages 15–32 of *The Protestatyon of Martin Marprelat*. To Penry he attributed pages 1–14 of this latter work and also the "Prologue" and "Epilogue" of *Martin Junior*.[68]

Wilson acknowledged that his "argument has been based upon a number of remarkable coincidences." Upon close scrutiny, one finds that Wilson's time chart of coincidences proves nothing of significance. There is no correlation between the battle of Gravelines on 29 July 1588 and the setting up of the Marprelate press on 29 September; the synchronization of "Williams goes to Netherlands with Norris" about 9 October 1588 and the publication of the *Epistle* about 15 October leads to no valid conclusion on authorship. Wilson's next synchronization indicates that Williams returned to England on 10 November, and that the *Epitome* was published about 29 November. The implication that Williams wrote the *Epitome* incurs the danger of being a *post hoc, ergo propter hoc* fallacy. The linking of Williams at Dieppe in September 1589 and Waldegrave's arrival at Haseley in the same month lends itself to an imaginative exegesis.

Wilson admitted that the styles of Martin and Williams

were different. He further weakened his case by stating that Throkmorton wrote *Master Some Laid Open in His Coulers.* Once this is admitted, it follows that the same author wrote the Marprelate books, since they all cohere beautifully.[69] Although Wilson's theory is clever, ingenious, and delightfully innovative, his pursuit of striking coincidences was a seeking for a will-of-the-wisp.[70] His hypothesis has not stood the test of time. John X. Evans, the recent editor of Williams' writings, concluded: "Indeed seldom has a thesis that is so demonstrably wrong been so lavishly praised."[71] Most of the lavish praise came from the pen of Ronald B. McKerrow, distinguished editor of Thomas Nashe's works, who reviewed Wilson's two articles. In effect, McKerrow rejected Wilson's theory but mitigated his criticism by unmitigated praise. He lauded Wilson's two articles as "among the most important contributions to the history of the great controversy that have appeared," and predicted that "further investigation may easily turn what is at present an ingenious and fascinating theory into established history." More correct though less polite was William Pierce, who rejected Wilson's thesis outright. Wilson summarized Pierce's intransigent views on his hypothesis by saying: "Indeed, he will not touch it with the end of the proverbial barge pole."[72] To Wilson's credit it should be noted that three of his articles added new information and his essay on "The Marprelate Controversy" remains the best succinct presentation of the subject. Perhaps the explanation for his own conflicting views on Martin is that Wilson had a predilection for the adventurous, the conjectural, and the unusual.[73]

Both Wilson and Pierce came very close to identifying Martin as Throkmorton, but Wilson flirted with the Williams hypothesis; and Pierce, after emphatically rejecting Penry's candidacy, held out the possibility that a "dark horse," a "Great Unknown," a distinguished member of Parliament such as Robert Beale, Sir Francis Knollys, or James Morice, was Martin Marprelate. J. B. Marsden wrote that "it has been conjectured, not unreasonably, that the Mar-prelate papers were also written by the Jesuits, and were a part of the great popish conspiracy against the protestant faith and the throne of Elizabeth."[74] Numerous suggestions have been made by William Camden, Sir George Paule, Peter Heylyn, Jeremy Collier, John Strype, and other historians that Marprelate's works were written by a junto, a club, a "pack." Combinations vary, but the names of Fenner, Field, Barrow, Udall, Penry, and Throkmorton recur most frequently. Since the evidence indicates that throughout the writings of Martin and Throkmorton the same stylistic features, the alliteration, the parallels, and the colorful writing are prevalent, we may safely reject the composite theory of authorship. Champlin Burrage, a nonconformist scholar, asserted that "it appears hardly probable that at this late date [1912] the true Martin will ever be discovered," and Albert Peel, a Penry specialist, concluded that "it hardly seems likely that the secret will be revealed at this time of day [1944]. But one or two facts furnished by the notebook [of Penry] may stimulate further research."[75] Since all the evidence, in my judgment, points strongly toward Throkmorton as author and Penry as manager and business agent, Part II will examine the life and writings of Throkmorton, and chapter ten will examine the role of Penry in the Marprelate drama by comparing his ideas with those of Martin.[76]

Part I

THE GATHERING
OF EVIDENCE

"And if any person have had knowledge of the Authors, Writers, Printers, or dispersers thereof, that shall within one moneth after the publication hereof, discover the same to the Ordinarie of the place where he had such knowledge, or to any of her Majesties Privie Counsell: the same person shall not for his former concealement be hereafter molested or troubled." (Proclamation of 13 February 1588/89. See Edward Arber, *Introductory Sketch*, pp. 109–11)

WITH THE PUBLICATION in mid-October 1588 of the *Epistle* at East Molesey, Surrey, ripples of laughter immediately spread, but criticisms of the work and author also escalated. The book became the subject of lively conversation not only among tradesmen and artisans but also among the intelligentsia and officialdom. The queen, hierarchy, and Privy Council were predictably incensed. They regarded the book as a "daungerous example to encourage privat men in this covert manner to subvert all other kyndes of government under Hir Majesties charg, both in ye church and commen weale." Therefore on 14 November the queen commanded Lord Chancellor Christopher Hatton and William Cecil, Lord Burghley, to urge Archbishop Whitgift to set in motion secretly the machinery of the Court of High Commission to "serch [fetch] out the authors hereof and the[i]r complices, and the pryntors and the secret dispersers of the same; and to cause them to be apprehended and committed." For assistance the archbishop was to confer with the bishops and utilize the services of Lord Cobham, Lord Buckhurst, and John Wolley, the Latin secretary—all privy councilors. Once captured, the offenders would be dealt with by the Privy Council.[1]

The ferreting out of information was aided by rampant rumors. On 14 November Nicolas Kydwell, William Staughton, Cutbert Cook, and John Good, all of Kingston-upon-Thames, Surrey, made depositions.[2] The government learned that copies of the *Epistle* were to be sold at the homes of Markes Collyns and Robert Doddeson in the Surrey parish. It also discovered that the former curate of Kingston-upon-Thames, John Udall, who had both preached and written against the polity of the Church of England, reputedly had employed an amanuensis for three weeks during September or October in Richmond, Surrey. On 29 November the minister of Richmond, Walter Rogers, deposed before Dr. William Aubrey, a master of Requests and master in Chancery, that he had heard of a certain person who was busy writing a book for Udall at the home of a zealous Puritan—Thomas Horton of Richmond. More damaging testimony against Udall was given about the same time by Stephen Chatfield, Udall's successor as vicar of Kingston-upon-Thames. He asserted that in 1586 he had held a private conference in his study with Udall, who had showed him written papers and manuscript books which Chatfield had read in part but refused to finish. Some of the titles, he said, suggested material similar to that in the *Epistle*. Chatfield also deposed that after Udall's silencing in June 1588, they had conversed in a small field about 15 September, and that Udall, bitter because of his silencing by Dr. Hone and because of the policies of the bishops, had spoken harshly against the bishops.[3]

One of the earliest examinations of Martinist suspects was that of the former vicar of Sedbergh, Yorkshire—Giles Wigginton—who had been a cantankerous Cambridge scholar, Fellow, and reformer. He was disliked by Whitgift, who was master of Trinity College when Wigginton was a scholar there, and later had been deprived, degraded, and imprisoned. Wigginton was apprehended on 6 December 1588 by Anthony Munday, a pursuivant, on the basis of a general warrant of the Court of High Commission to "search and apprehend all connected in any way with the boke entitled *Martin Marprelate.*" On the way to Lambeth Palace, Wigginton lectured the pursuivant for serving the prelates in that capacity and also told him the tale of the goose which he had read in Martin's second book, the *Epitome.*[4] At the archiepiscopal residence Wigginton appeared before six ecclesiastical commissioners—John Whitgift, Thomas Cooper, and William Aubrey, as well as Richard Cosin, dean of the Arches, Gabriel Goodman, dean of Westminster Abbey, and Justice Richard Young, a special commissioner. Munday and Abraham Hartwell, the archbishop's notary, also were present.[5]

The proceedings began when Whitgift, "with a glowringe countenaunce," charged that "there is a booke called *Martin Marprelate,* a vile, seditious, foolish, and intollerable booke: you are suspected to bee a dealer in it, and therefore you are to sweare what you know." Wigginton refused to swear, demanded the names of his accusers, and asserted that he would not accuse his neighbors nor "thrust a knife" into his own thigh. The archbishop could have remanded him immediately to prison for refusing the ex officio oath, but, needing information, condescended to allow the suspect to answer a list of questions. Not unexpectedly, Wigginton, according to the questions, was evasive, obdurate, saucy, insinuating, or silent. And not surprisingly, Whitgift charged that Wigginton in his replies had been obstinate and "worse than a papist."

The metropolitan asked Wigginton if he had composed or printed any part of the *Epistle* or if he had seen any portion of the manuscript before publication. Receiving a categorical denial, the archbishop inquired "whether have yow not bene a meane to publish it, or do you not know who hath published it, or had or read the same; did you not deliver some copies of it in the countrey, one to Mr. [John] More [minister of

St. Andrews and 'apostle of Norwich'], another to Mr. Cartwright?" To this six-pronged question, Wigginton impertinently replied that he had heard that "many lords and ladies, and other great and wealthy personages of all estates" had read the book. He slyly suggested that the archbishop should examine impartially not only poor people, as he usually did, but rich ones as well. The prelate continued his multiple interrogatories: "Whome do you believe, suppose, thinke, or gather any presumption, suspicion, likelihood, or conjecture, to be the author, writer, or printer, of it, or of any part of it, or helper any wayes towards it? Whether yow made any othe or promise to others, or vow in your selfe to conceale the same booke, being asked? What printing presse, print, or furniture for printinge have you knowne any where unauthorised within these two yeres last past?" When Wigginton responded negatively and reminded Whitgift that he was wasting his time, the archbishop replied: "Yea, but yow are vehemently suspected for it, and *publica fama* is against you in it." In the *Epistle* Martin had told a story about Wigginton and a parishioner named Atkinson, who, first prosecuting his pastor, had recanted and pleaded for his reinstatement. According to Martin, many of the good parishioners of Sedbergh had been "infected" by Wigginton "with the true knowledge of the gospell, by the Worde preached (which is an heresie, that His Grace doth mortally abhorre and persecute)." Others appealed to Whitgift to deprive Wigginton. Martin reported that the "pastor defied the archbishop to his face, and would give him no better title than John Whitgift, such buggs [threatening] words, being in these daies accounted no less than high treason against a Paltripolitan."[6] One can readily imagine the archbishop's feelings about this ex parte version. Suspecting Wigginton, Whitgift asked how the story happened to appear in the *Epistle*. The former vicar evasively answered that Atkinson had "told the story to many" people. Accused of reading the *Epistle* and the *Epitome*, Wigginton replied that "witnesses were produced in all good courts, and answers on oath were popish." When the questioning shifted to John Penry's role, the ex-vicar was asked if he thought that the Welshman had written *A Demonstration of the Trueth of That Discipline, Which Christe Hath Prescribed,* or Martin's *Epistle*. Wigginton did not believe that Penry had written either book and stated that the commissioners were as mistaken in thinking Penry was the author as they were in suspecting Wigginton himself.

It is apparent that Wigginton was a defiant, impertinent, and exasperating witness. He frankly asserted that we "follow the instructions of learned counsellers in these matters, who we trust will stand by us when neede shall require," and bluntly warned, "be you ready, when you shall be called to an accompt, to answer on the contrary touching the course of your dealings, you know whence your examination *ex officio* came (meaning even the Pope's cannons)." It is no wonder that Whitgift committed Wigginton to the Gatehouse prison. Ostensibly he had refused the oath ex officio but the real reason was that he had divulged nothing of importance and had showed himself—according to the archbishop— "contemptuous of the authority of the High Commission." Then the archbishop issued a veiled threat: "you shall obey and yeld unto the high commissioners ere I have don with yow."[7]

Lord Chancellor Hatton and Lord Burghley had promised aid to Whitgift in his task of finding the author, printer, and publisher of the Marprelate books. Assistance was given by the Privy Council, which sent commissioner Richard Young, Edward Tirrell, the warden of the Fleet prison, and Dr. Robert Some, a Fellow of Queens' College and later master of Peterhouse, to interview Henry Barrow, a leading Separatist and close prisoner in the Fleet. The interrogators, informed that two manuscript replies to Dr. Some's first *A Godly Treatise Containing and Deciding Certaine Questions* had been seized in Barrow's cell, regarded him as a possible Martinist. Desiring more information, they questioned him in his prison chamber on 1 January 1588/89. Unfortunately, only a one-folio fragment of his examination is extant, but from it one may conclude that the committee obtained very little information about Martin. It did confirm, however, that Barrow had written against Dr. Some, disliked the ecclesiastical hierarchy of the Church of England, and in emphasizing the headship of Christ seemed to minimize the queen's role as the supreme governor of the English church.[8]

By February 1588/89 the high commissioners had discovered that a book had been printed in Mrs. Elizabeth Crane's country home at East Molesey. The information came from a comment by David Howell, a friend of Penry, and the book was *A Demonstration of Discipline*. The commissioners had also learned that Mrs. Crane's servant, Nicholas Tomkins, owned a copy of the *Epistle*. On 15 February Tomkins was examined at Lambeth Palace by Richard Cosin, Whitgift's vicar-general and a master in Chancery. Interrogated about Udall's writings, Tomkins said nothing about authorship but confessed that *A Demonstration of Discipline* had been printed in Mrs. Crane's house. He did conjecture, however, that *Diotrephes* [*The State of the Church*] (*S.T.C.* 24505), which had been published in April 1588, had been written not by John Davidson, a Scottish preacher, but rather by Udall. Tomkins admitted that he possessed a copy of the *Epistle*, confessed at first that he had received it from Wigginton but later "upon better remembrance" thought he had received it from Waldegrave. He acknowledged he had said that, although the book cost nine pence, he could have purchased as many copies as he wished at six pence, and by selling them could have made a profit of twenty marks (£13 6s. 8d.). Questioned about the author, printer, and publisher of the *Epistle* and the *Epitome*, Tomkins denied any knowledge but mentioned rumors that Field, Wigginton, Penry, or Francis Marbury, a Puritan clergyman from Alford, Lincolnshire, had written the Martinist books. Queried about the place of printing, he implied—probably with the hope of shielding Mrs. Crane—that both books had been printed in Northamptonshire. Tomkins also disclosed that Waldegrave had brought a case of type to Mrs. Crane's London house about May, and that Waldegrave and Penry had been in Mrs. Crane's East Molesey house during late June-early July and at the end of September but not after 1 November 1588.[9]

In March 1589 the fourth and longest Martinist production—*Hay Any Worke for Cooper*—was published.[10] The book was witty, sarcastic, and patronizing, but also infuriating to the government, which intensified its search for the authors and printers. The officials established surveillance at Paul's churchyard and bookstores.[11] They learned that a servant of Sir Richard Knightley had delivered a letter and packet of books to Edward Seymour (1539?–1621), the earl of Hertford, in London. After perusing one of the books, the earl requested the servant to inform Knightley, his brother-in-law, that he "liked not that course" and to warn him that "as they shoote at bishoppes now, so will they doe at the nobilitie, if they be suffered." Shortly afterward, the servant indulged in too much wine, told a friend of the incident, and divulged additional information about a West Smithfield spurrier who had supplied the Martinists with paper and other printing materials.[12]

During April, May, and June Martin published nothing because his printer, Waldegrave, had relinquished his difficult task before 5 April.[13] He had complained about the dangers, the secrecy involved, the long hours, lack of warm food, and the Puritans' dislike of Martinist jesting. His assistant's illness had complicated matters, and the added work in composing, presswork, and binding had become formidable. Moreover, he had disagreed with Penry, most likely on the printing schedule of his *Appellation*, which Penry wished to present to Parliament while it was still in session. Waldegrave must have learned from Penry that Sharpe, in the hope of saving his own skin, was considering in March the possibility of co-operating with the authorities and turning state's evidence. Furthermore, Waldegrave wished to go to Devonshire and there begin the long-desired and congenial task of printing Cartwright's refutation of the Rhemish New Testament.[14] Perhaps, however, the principal reason for his withdrawal was fear of arrest by the pursuivants who were searching for Penry and Sharpe as well.

The Martinists unsuccessfully tried to obtain the services of Sharpe, the bookbinder, but he refused to set type. In

May Throkmorton, Penry, and Newman employed another printer, John Hodgskin, who hired two assistants, Valentine Symmes and Arthur Thomlin. Planning on secret printing in the North, Hodgskin sent his own press to his home in Warrington, Lancashire, but he and his men completed the printing on Penry's press of *Martin Junior* by 21 July and *Martin Senior* by 29 July. On the same day Hodgskin and his assistants, afraid of arrest, decided to leave. Dismantling Penry's press, they left it in the custody of Roger Wigston and his wife at Wolston. They also loaded a cart with "three payre of cases," three kinds of type, twelve reams of paper, and ink. By Friday, 1 August, the printers reached Hodgskin's home; on the following Monday the cart arrived. During the unpacking some of the type spilled on the ground. When curious bystanders, never having seen printing type, inquired about the small objects, they were informed that the pieces were metallic pellets or "shot." On 7 August the printers moved to a rented house in Newton Lane near Manchester; by 11 August they had transported Hodgskin's press and equipment from Warrington. Finally, on Thursday, 14 August, they began to print *More Worke for Cooper,* but after working for three hours and completing six quires on one side, they were arrested by the agents of Henry Stanley, the fourth earl of Derby. Press, type, printed sheets, and manuscript copy—all were seized. Within two days the nobleman, after interrogating the printers, ordered them sent to London.[15]

When the prisoners arrived in London on 23 August, Archbishop Whitgift was informed immediately at Canterbury. On the following day he sent a reply to Lord Burghley, assuring the Lord Treasurer that, although he had not been disturbed unduly by the Martinists' "lewde libles," he respected his episcopal position and was concerned about the impact of gossip and scandal on the credulous. Whitgift reminded Burghley that "if wee weare [were] such men as they wold make us, we weare [would be] not worthy to lyve, much lesse to injoy owre places, and yet [ought] not to be used in that manner and sort." Twice in his letter he urged that the prisoners be dealt with "according to the[i]r desertes." The archbishop expressed his preference for a trial by the privy councilors rather than by the bishops or high commissioners, so that the "world may know that wee are men not cast off on all sydes, as abjects of the world, but that justice shal as well take place in owre causes, as yt doth in all other mens."[16]

On the same day—Sunday, 24 August—the Privy Council held an emergency meeting at Oatlands, by Walton-on-Thames. Five councilors—Hatton, Burghley, and Wolley as well as Charles Howard, the lord high admiral, and Henry Carey, Lord Hunsdon—hastily assembled, examined the three printers, but were unable to obtain any useful information. Lamenting that the captives "will confess nothing," the councilors ordered them imprisoned separately in the Bridewell prison. They also appointed a special committee to interrogate the prisoners, consisting of John Fortescue, a privy councilor, Dr. Ralph Rokeby, a master of Requests, William Fleetwood, recorder of the City of London, and, in case of Fortescue's absence, Richard Young, a zealous investigator.[17]

The instructional letter from the Privy Council to the special committee explained that Hodgskin already had been questioned in Lancashire by the earl of Derby, that Symmes was a typesetter and Thomlin a press worker, and that all three had been interrogated unsuccessfully by the Council. The committee, therefore, with the aid of the printed quires of *More Worke for Cooper,* was requested to formulate questions for use at the Bridewell. If confessions could not be obtained, the prisoners were to be tortured and if necessary sent to the Tower for racking until they disclosed the truth. The questions asked at the Bridewell are not known, but when confessions were not extracted, Hodgskin was taken to the Tower for racking about 11 September. The committee found him to be a difficult and stubborn prisoner; an account of his protestation at a later arraignment indicated that his confession was "forced . . . by rackinge and great torments."[18]

The second phase in the gathering of evidence began late

in August 1589 after the arrest of the printers, and in the next six months the government was successful in unraveling the knotty Martinist skein. In September, with the help of the local bailiff, Henry Sharpe the bookbinder was apprehended. Since the bailiff was a tenant of Roger Wigston at Wolston, and since the squire realized that he himself might be implicated for harboring the press, he threatened the bailiff with reprisals. Sharpe had been in hiding since February, but he had been daringly and ironically designated by name in the pages of *Martin Senior* as one who ought to be apprehended. His preliminary examination in September is not extant, but extracts of his confession are available in summaries of the testimony of various implicated individuals. Sharpe confessed that an unnamed person [probably Edward Sharpe, minister of the Fawsley church], visited an acquaintance [possibly Henry Sharpe himself] in Northampton; the visitor was taken to Sir Richard Knightley's house in Fawsley where he received copies of Martinist books from Waldegrave. Sharpe also admitted that Edward Baker, the Northampton official principal, had discussed with him rumors concerning the secret printing at Fawsley. More important were Sharpe's accounts of his conversations with Penry and Hodgskin. According to Sharpe, Penry had put Hodgskin to work, had admitted that Hodgskin printed *Martin Junior* and *Martin Senior*, and had urged Sharpe himself to help Hodgskin with the printing. Sharpe also revealed that Newman and Penry distributed Martin's books, and that Hodgskin had declared, without divulging its location, that he had a printing press.[19]

After Sharpe's preliminary confession, a "Summary of the Information," endorsed 21 September, was prepared for Lord Burghley and possibly for other privy councilors and examiners.[20] This brief report included extracts from Sharpe's preliminary testimony and from Tomkins' examination of 15 February 1588/89 concerning the type brought by Waldegrave to Mrs. Crane's house. The compiler concluded that the type was known as "Waldegraves letters," that it had been used in the printing of the *Demonstration of Discipline*,

Martin Junior, and *Martin Senior,* and that it was identical with that captured with Hodgskin near Manchester. The report conjectured that because Dr. Some "hath somethinge sharply confuted Penries fansies," because *More Worke for Cooper* was "very longe and most bitter and virulent" against Dr. Some, that Penry had written this diatribe. But at this time the compiler did not know that Throkmorton had written *Master Some Laid Open,* which did not begin to circulate until the next month, and which was "very longe and most bitter and virulent" against Dr. Some. Nor did the compiler know anything of Throkmorton's role or style, or of his books and handwriting. The "Summary of the Information," representing the first serious attempt to identify Martin Marprelate, was inchoate and speculative. It did not incorporate the later testimony of Symmes and Hodgskin, or of Knightley, Wigston, and Newman. Although the lines of incomplete evidence seemed to converge on Penry, the government, in September 1589, needed fuller information and more reliable witnesses.[21]

In the meantime, torture of the printers was producing fragments of truth, used in turn to elicit further information. From the evidence of Hodgskin's later complaint, it is likely that the first confessions of Symmes and Thomlin had been "violent[ly] extorted from them." The two workers, when they were examined on 10 October, revealed that Hodgskin had imposed upon them an oath of secrecy and a promise never to reveal the name of Roger Wigston. This was the real reason they previously had admitted only the obvious, but now they confessed that *Martin Junior* and *Martin Senior* had been printed at Wigston's home at Wolston.[22]

Five days later, on 15 October, Henry Sharpe was "sworn and examined by the appointment" of Lord Chancellor Hatton.[23] As early as February the pursuivants had sought him at Northampton, and thereafter he had discreetly gone into hiding. In March he had discussed with Knightley his plight and his intention to surrender to the lord chancellor, who was also lord lieutenant of Northamptonshire. Knightley had dissuaded him from any precipitate action, warning him that feeling had reached such intensity that the authorities would probably hang him and advising him to remain in hiding until the officials were "better pacifyed." Sharpe followed the advice for two months, but then sent his wife to London to ask Hatton for a remission, presumably in return for his confession of guilt. When the pardon was denied, Mrs. Sharpe returned to Northampton about 20 June. In July Sharpe again left Northampton to live with his mother-in-law at Wolston, and there he discovered that the printers were in Wigston's house. He did aid in binding and packing the Martinist books, despite his real apprehensiveness.

At his main examination, Sharpe decided in self-interest to tell all he knew, or believed, or conjectured. Referring first to the *Epistle*, he wrongly stated that it had been printed at Kingston-upon-Thames and speculated that it had been proofread by Udall. He deposed that R. Jeffs of Upton, a tenant of Knightley's son Valentine, had brought the press by cart to the Fawsley house; he also asserted that although he never had seen the press there he had known of its presence from credible witnesses. He related an account of his conversation with Knightley, which suggests a lack of inhibition about incriminating his friends. He said that he had asked Knightley if he feared trouble and danger by allowing the *Epitome* to be printed on his premises. Did he worry that his house might be searched? According to Sharpe, Knightley replied: "Let me alone. The knaves durst not search my house. Yf they had, I wolde have courst [chased] them, they know well inough; but now yt ys gone, and that danger is past." The bookbinder then related that Stephen Gyfford, a servant, had brought the press by cart to the house of John Hales, a Coventry squire and Knightley's nephew by his first marriage, where Waldegrave printed the *Mineralls*, Penry's *A Viewe*, and *Hay Any Worke*. He admitted that he had bound the latter two, which Newman transported to London. He confessed that he went to Wolston to escape capture, and that he found Hodgskin there at work in Wigston's house. He provided gratuitous information when he stated that Mrs. Wigston had obtained permission from her husband to have work done in their home but had not informed him of its nature. Wigston, Sharpe testified, when later learning of the printing in his house of *Martin Junior* and *Martin Senior*, was "very angry with his wyfe," but permitted the work to continue. Sharpe also related his conversations with Penry, whose business activities he described, and frankly conjectured that Penry was the author of the Martinist books.[24]

Sharpe's testimony provided new information on the Wigstons, Hales, one Pigot, Gyfford, and Jeffs. It also included additional data on Waldegrave, Newman, and Hodgskin. The examiners acquired from Sharpe new and erroneous details about the printing of the second, third, and fourth Marprelate books, conjectures about proofreaders, and information on the binding and transporting of books. More important was the information which the examiners obtained regarding printing sites—Fawsley, Coventry, and Wolston—and regarding the complicity of such prominent people as Knightley, Hales, and Wigston; but on the question of authorship the interrogators acquired only speculations.

Sharpe's examination not only produced a farrago of information, misinformation, and conjecture, but also confirmed various reports previously received by the investigators. As early as December 1588 rumors had circulated in Fawsley about the existence of a press on Knightley's premises, and in March a servant had confessed that he had brought printed books from Fawsley to London. After Sharpe's colorful testimony, the investigators considered it imperative to interrogate Sir Richard Knightley. One of the foremost citizens of Northamptonshire and a landowner whose holdings reputedly yielded an annual income of £13,000, he had served as deputy lieutenant, high sheriff, and member of Parliament. His second wife, Elizabeth Seymour, was both the daughter of Lord Protector Edward Seymour, duke of Somerset, and the cousin of King Edward VI. Despite his wealth and influence, Knightley was arrested and informally questioned about 20 October. At almost the same time, as a result of Sharpe's testimony, John Hales and the Wigstons, both Roger and his wife, were apprehended.[25]

On 16 November the Privy Council appointed a special commission consisting of John Young, bishop of Rochester, eight privy councilors, Sir Edmund Anderson, lord chief justice of the Court of Common Pleas, William Aubrey, a master in Chancery, and William Lewin, judge of the Prerogative Court of Canterbury. From these twelve, a select committee of any two privy councilors and one other committee member, with William Bedill serving as registrar, was designated to interrogate Knightley, Hales, and the Wigstons. Bishop Young was ordered to come to London immediately; he and the other commissioners were informed that "yt is discovered that Sir Richard Knightly, Roger Wigston, and John Hales have bene acquainted with the printing and publishing of the said bookes, and have bene favorers and abettours of the said Martin Mar Prelate in his disordered proceedinges." These men, the letter intimated, probably knew the author's identity.[26]

When Knightley was examined by the select committee on 20 November, he confessed that Penry had spoken with him in September 1588 and had requested a room in one of his houses where he could reprint a book similar to one previously published but confiscated [*Aequity*], on the "unlerned ministri of Wales." Knightley also acknowledged that the *Epitome* had been printed in his house by Waldegrave and admitted that he had aided Newman by allowing him to wear the livery of his staff. Knightley revealed as well that he had ordered Stephen Gyfford to transport the press and type to John Hales's home in Coventry. Regarding the author of the *Epitome*, he disclaimed knowledge but conjectured "unless yt were Penry."[27]

The select committee next questioned six of Knightley's employees or residents. Jeffs testified that he brought the press from East Molesey to Fawsley and delivered it to Lawrence Jackson, keeper of Knightley's house. Jackson informed the examiners that he had received Knightley's gimmal ring from Penry as a token, along with a message to receive a shipment. Gyfford related the story that in November 1588 a visitor named Sheme, or Shamuel, came to Fawsley, ostensibly to inspect Knightley's legal papers, leases, mortgages, and contracts. Sheme's real name, according to Gyfford and Jackson, was Waldegrave. Gyfford also confessed that with horses and a cart provided by Knightley he had brought the press from Fawsley to Norton and then to Coventry. Two other servants, John Wright and Peter Greye, spoke of the presence at Fawsley of Newman, the distributor of the books. And Edward Sharpe, the Fawsley clergyman, stated that he had visited Waldegrave's indisposed servant— probably Henry Kildale—and that he had seen the press as well as either printed sheets or bound copies of the *Epitome*, and that he had taken one copy to Knightley to ascertain whether the squire knew of the printing in his house.[28]

John Hales testified that in January 1588/89 Waldegrave had delivered to him a letter written by Knightley earlier in the month. Since the letter requested him to provide a room for the printer, he had made available his house, "White Friars," and had given the keys to Waldegrave. He also said Penry had brought him to the site of the press and about 8 February had given him a copy of his *Viewe*, printed in his own house.[29]

Roger Wigston admitted that he had seen *Martin Junior* and *Martin Senior*, read their titles, even heard one of the books read to him, but claimed he had disliked it. His wife then disclosed that she had urged the printing of books, that the work continued for two weeks, and that the press had remained in her custody for many weeks. She acknowledged that when the printers were planning to transfer their work from Wolston to Warrington, she had "wished the printers to stay to print some better books"—that is, she had urged them to print *More Worke for Cooper* in her house. Mrs. Wigston readily admitted that she had furnished provisions for the printers and when they left had given each worker half a crown.[30]

Although John Hodgskin's examinations are not extant,

it is possible to reconstruct his confessions from related sources. He had been interrogated three times before he was sent to the Tower, and after his racking in September he was examined on 25 and 27 November, and probably once in December by the lords commissioners. He stated that he had negotiated in London with Newman, Throkmorton's agent, agreed to print books for the squire, hired Symmes and Thomlin, and informed them of his intention to print Latin grammars or "accidences." He disclosed that at Throkmorton's house he had arranged to print *Martin Junior* and *Martin Senior*, had received £5 for printing these works, and had printed a part of *More Worke for Cooper*. Despite previous equivocations, he admitted he had brought a letter written by Throkmorton to Mrs. Wigston, requesting permission to print books in her house. He also revealed that Throkmorton had arranged for the manuscript of *Martin Junior* to be left beside a bush "about one birdebowe shot from the said Master Throckmortons house," and finally confessed that on 18 July Throkmorton had promised him *"More Worke for Cooper* should come to his handes shortly." Hodgskin's earlier statements tended to exonerate Throkmorton and inculpate Penry. Therefore the student must heed the warning of one of the compilers of testimony: "It is to be noted, that the said Hodgkins in diverse of his examinations, went about to conceale his being at Master Throckmortons for delivering or freeing of him from suspicion of any such matter."[31]

Valentine Symmes's examination of 10 December 1589 is very important, since the printer divulged for the first time the leading role played by Throkmorton. As the typesetter hired by Hodgskin and as the compositor who set type from the original manuscripts, Symmes had consulted with Throkmorton and Penry regarding unclear passages in the manuscript copy and had proofread the printed sheets. Therefore he was an excellent witness for details of manuscript copy, handwriting, interlineations, and proofreading. Furthermore, Symmes's examination was valuable because it provided an effective check on Hodgskin's testimony and not only complemented but corrected the cautious and misleading information from his employer. Unlike Hodgskin, Symmes was honest and straightforward; he had no obligation to protect Throkmorton.

Symmes described his trip from London to Wolston. The printers stopped first at Adderbury, Oxfordshire, where Symmes's father, Richard, lived. Then Hodgskin went alone to Haseley on 13 July; Thomlin traveled to Coventry, and Symmes continued to Warwick where he met Hodgskin on 14 July 1589. The two men then proceeded to Wolston and during the trip Hodgskin showed him the incomplete manuscript of *Martin Junior*, consisting of only one or two sheets, as well as the letter to Mrs. Wigston, which Symmes thought was "written from Mr. Throckmorton." Symmes reported that printing began on Thursday, 17 July; then he presented the surprising developments of the following day:

> The Friday after as they do think a gentleman came unto them as they were printinge whom since they understand to be Job Throkmorton and badd God speed them. Immediately after his cominge he read that which was in printinge, and found fault in some places with the orthography. Then he looked upon the written copy and bicause it was in diverse places interlined, he asked Simmes yf he could read the sayd places so interlyned, poynting him unto them. Among the which places ther were two, wherin Simmes doubted. And Mr. Throckmorton did presently read them distinctly and readily unto him. Furthermore at the sayd time he asked Hodgkins softly in his eare, whether these examinants were good workmen and able to serve the turn: and Hodgkins answered yea.

Symmes deposed that at first he had only one or two sheets of *Martin Junior*, and he implied that Throkmorton had secretly delivered the second part and mysteriously joined it with the first part. Symmes also admitted he had discussed with Throkmorton the reading of specific interlined passages in the manuscript and the misspellings and misreadings in the printed sheet. On the same day, 18 July, Symmes learned that the copy of *Martin Senior* had been delivered to Hodgskin. During the next week he began setting type, and consulted

47

Hodgskin about difficult readings in the manuscript of *Martin Senior*. Since Throkmorton was not present, Hodgskin referred the questions to Penry, who deleted material and inserted corrections. Thus Symmes was able to compare the handwritings on the same folio of Penry and Throkmorton. Both Symmes and Hodgskin deposed that on 18 July Throkmorton promised Hodgskin he would receive the copy of *More Worke for Cooper* shortly. About a week later the manuscript was secretly dropped by Penry or Newman from an upper chamber into a low parlor where Hodgskin worked. Symmes concluded that *More Worke for Cooper* "was likewise of Mr. Throckmortons penninge: for that it was the same hand" as seen in *Martin Junior* and *Martin Senior*. The question of handwriting was of significance later at Hodgskin's arraignment, when he was found guilty of printing *Martin Junior* and Throkmorton was adjudged the author on the basis of Symmes's testimony. Thus, Symmes helped to establish Throkmorton's authorship of the letter to Mrs. Wigston and of three Martinist books.[32]

Symmes had clearly presented Throkmorton as a Martinist author, but the authorities were still suspicious of Udall's role. As early as November 1588 several deponents had said Udall employed an amanuensis in Richmond, and Stephen Chatfield, the vicar at Kingston-upon-Thames, had found some similarities in Udall's papers and Martin's *Epistle*. Davy Howell, Penry's friend, had said that the *Demonstration of Discipline* was printed at East Molesey and that Udall had visited there. Tomkins had conjectured in February 1588/89 that Udall wrote *Diotrephes*, and Sharpe had incriminated Udall in his October deposition. Examined a second time on 29 November 1589, Tomkins stated positively that Udall wrote the *Demonstration of Discipline* and conjectured once more that he wrote *Diotrephes*.[33] Therefore the authorities decided to interrogate Udall himself. Henry Carey, Lord Hunsdon, on behalf of the Privy Council, sent in mid-December a letter mandatory to the mayor of Newcastle-upon-Tyne, William Selby, ordering him to send Udall to London. Traveling with his escort, Christopher Applebie, Udall left town on 29 December; after a tiring trip he arrived in London on 9 January 1589/90. Four days later, on Tuesday, 13 January, he appeared before eight commissioners at William Brooke, Lord Cobham's home in Blackfriars.[34]

Udall's examination was conducted primarily by Sir Edmund Anderson, chief justice of the Common Pleas, and Thomas Sackville, Lord Buckhurst. Udall was willing to answer questions on Martinist books, since he was no longer suspected of being Martin Marprelate, but when Anderson asked Udall if he wrote the *Demonstration of Discipline* or the *Dialogue* [*Diotrephes*], Udall refused to answer. Anderson asked him why he was willing to exonerate himself from the charge of writing Martin's books but not those purportedly from his own pen. Udall responded that he agreed with the content but not with the style and manner of presentation of the Marprelate books. As to the *Demonstration* and the *Dialogue*, he expressed approval of the content, style, and presentation but would not elaborate.

Lord Buckhurst, querying Udall if he knew Penry and receiving an affirmative answer, asked him directly: "And doe you not know him to be Martin?" Udall answered: "No surely, neither doe I thinke him to be Martin." Asked for his reason, Udall replied that "when first it [the *Epistle*] came out, he [Penry] understanding that some gave out that he was thought to bee the author, wrote a letter to a friend in London, wherein he did deny it, with such tearmes as declare him to bee ignorant and cleere in it." To Buckhurst's final question regarding the reason for Udall's frequent association with Penry, Udall stated that Penry "being a scholler and student in Divinity, and one whom I alwaies thought to be an honest man, your Lordships may easily conceive the cause." Then the interrogation ceased, and Udall was committed to the Gatehouse prison to await trial.[35]

After Udall's imprisonment, since the authorities had considerable substantive but also conflicting and concordant evidence and rumor about Udall, Penry, Waldegrave, and Throkmorton, they decided to summarize their information both for the use of the investigators and for the anticipated arraignments of Knightley, Hales, and the Wigstons. The result was the Puckering Brief, completed about the end of January, and extending to eighteen printed pages, fourteen pages longer than the "Summary of the Information" of September 1589. It summarized data incriminating thirteen persons for Martinist activity: Udall, Mrs. Crane, Waldegrave, Penry, Knightley, Newman, Hales, Wigston and his wife, Throkmorton, Hodgskin, Symmes, and Thomlin. The accusations were based on the depositions or confessions of nineteen witnesses, especially those of Sharpe, Tomkins, Hodgskin, Symmes, Knightley, Hales, and the Wigstons. The document was a valuable compilation, representing a significant increase of information from the time of the printers' arrest in August 1589 to Udall's examination in January 1589/90.[36] It should be noted, however, that although nine of the thirteen incriminated persons were in custody, three—Hodgskin, Symmes, and Thomlin—were printers, five—Mrs. Crane, Knightley, Hales, and the Wigstons—were harborers of the press, and only one—Udall—was a suspected author. The four most important Martinist participants—Throkmorton, Penry, Waldegrave, and Newman—were still at large; until their arrest, uncertainty would remain about the authorship of the Marprelate books.

About five weeks after the compilation of the Puckering Brief, the government arrested a Northampton citizen, Richard Holmes, and examined him on 12 March 1589/90. Another Northampton resident, a Mr. Grimston, was apprehended in May and examined on 3 June.[37] Since both men in August and September 1589 had transported printing materials from London to Wolston, the investigators learned for the first time how the Martinists had managed to print the *Protestatyon* on Penry's press even though Hodgskin's press and equipment had been confiscated.

About the end of June the main distributor of Martin's books was arrested, and on 9 July this peripatetic cobbler, Humphrey Newman, was examined. Although his examination is not extant, there are twenty-nine citations from his testimony in two reliable sources. These provide important information on Penry and Throkmorton, as well as precise data on times and places of printing, transportation of books, and the number of volumes printed. From Newman we learn that after the raid on Penry's study on 29 January 1588/89, Penry resided with Throkmorton at Haseley from 2 March to 2 October 1589, and that he collaborated with Throkmorton in the completing and proofreading of *Hay Any Worke for Cooper*. Newman revealed Penry's role as a manager, and mentioned he was directed by Penry to deliver 200 copies of Martin's *Epitome* to Waldegrave's wife. After these had been carried to London on Penry's mare, Newman returned to Northampton and made an accounting with Penry. Newman's association of his trips with St. Luke's tide, Christmas, and Shrovetide makes it possible to correct Sharpe's defective chronology. Throkmorton's *Epistle* was published about 18 October 1588; his *Epitome* appeared about 25–30 November; the *Mineralls* was printed about 26–28 January; and Penry's *A Viewe* was dispatched from Coventry about 8 February 1588/89.[38]

Newman confessed "he was dealt withall at Job Throkmortons house, to provide a printer to supply Walde-graves place," and that he sent Hodgskin to Haseley. Newman is our only source for the story that Throkmorton wrote *The Crops and Flowers of Bridges Garden*, that he conveniently dropped the manuscript when Newman was following, and that he promised Newman a share of the profits from the printing of the book. We are indebted to Newman for his report that Waldegrave delivered to Throkmorton at Haseley in September 1589, three consignments of printed books: 600 copies of [Throkmorton's] *Master Some Laid Open in His Coulers*, an unspecified number of his *Dialogue. Wherin Is Plainly Laide Open the Tyrannicall Dealing of Lord Bishopps against Gods Children*, and 500 copies of Penry's *Appellation*. Newman reported that when these books were being scrutinized, a messenger brought the news that Penry's study in Northampton had been raided a second time; consequently most of the books were hurriedly packed and carried to a house in Banbury.[39] As a result of Newman's implication that Throkmorton was probably the author of two of these books, along with Symmes's attribution of three Martinist books to the Haseley squire, the authorities presented their information to a grand jury, which indicted Throkmorton before the Assize judges in Warwick, during the summer of 1590.

In the autumn of 1590 the government arrested Penry's kinsman and agent, Jenkin Jones, and examined him on 6 November. Jones deposed that Penry's book, *Reformation No Enemie*, with the author's name, had been printed in Edinburgh about Christmas 1589. Jones admitted that of 800 copies printed, he carried 300 to London and that he returned to Edinburgh to make a financial accounting with Penry. When 700 copies of Penry's anonymous book, *A Briefe Discovery*, were printed in the summer of 1590, once more Jones transported 300 of them to London. It is likely that during this trip or shortly thereafter he was captured.[40]

It is not possible to date exactly the two depositions, but about 1590 two agents of Throkmorton, John Bowman and Augustine Maicocke, were captured. Bowman deposed that in a letter Throkmorton addressed him as "Archer" and expressed his desire to see a copy of his own newly printed book, *The Crops and Flowers of Bridges Garden*. Maicocke deposed that Throkmorton addressed him as "May," that the squire raised money for Penry's expenses and debts, and that he warned Maicocke not to trust Bowman.[41]

In the autumn of 1591 officials seized Waldegrave's assistant, Henry Kildale, and questioned him on 3 October. Kildale deposed that in May 1590 Waldegrave had printed 1,000 copies of an anonymous book, *An Humble Motion;* Kildale did not regard Penry as the author of the book, but said it had been sent to Edinburgh for printing. Kildale did testify, however, that Penry wrote *A Briefe Discovery*.[42] With Kildale, examinations ended, but later events in the lives of Martinist participants will be recounted in the third and fourth chapters.

 # THE ANTI-
MARTINIST
ATTACK

[Archbishop Whitgift recommends Richard Bancroft for the bishopric of London, and praises him for his anti-Martinist strategy]
"He was a special man that gave the instructions to her Majesty's learned Council, when Martin's agents were brought into the Star-chamber. By his advice that course was taken, which did principally stop Martin's and his fellows' mouths; viz. to have them answered after their own vain writings." (John Strype, *The Life and Acts of John Whitgift*, 2:387, from Inner Temple, Petyt MSS. 538[38], item 68, fols. 155–56)

WE MAY SAY that the campaign against the Martinists began on 14 November 1588, when Lord Chancellor Hatton and Lord Burghley wrote a letter to Whitgift. They informed the archbishop that it was Her Majesty's pleasure that he should utilize the Court of High Commission to arrest those responsible for the writing, printing, and distributing of Martin's *Epistle*. He was requested to seek the advice of other bishops and to consult with Lord Cobham, Lord Buckhurst, and Latin Secretary John Wolley, all privy councilors, who had been directed by royal command to give assistance. It is evident that the high commissioners acted quickly, since they obtained six depositions in November and dispatched a letter on 16 December, commanding the ecclesiastical commissioners at Canterbury Cathedral to search for Martin's books.[1]

The first anti-Martinist book, *An Admonition to the People of England,*[2] reminiscent of an earlier *Admonition* issued in 1572 by John Field and Thomas Wilcox, was published about 10 January 1588/89. The author's initials, "T.C.," were suggestive of Thomas Cartwright, but the new *Admonition* was as Anglican as the first had been Presbyterian, and readers soon learned that "T.C." were the initials of Thomas Cooper, bishop of Winchester. The work professedly was written for the moderate and godly, as seen in the author's comment that "the malicious back-biter and railer will never be satisfied; but the more he is answered, the worse he will be." The book, however, was defensive and ineffective in coping with Martin's satire and ridicule. Sweet reasonableness proved to be not a palliative but an irritant.

A distinguishing feature of the *Admonition* was its frankness. Cooper wrote that "the dartes, I confesse, of deceitfull and slaunderous tongues, are very sharpe, and the burning of the woundes made by them, will as hardly in the hearts of many bee quenched, as the coales of Juniper."[3] Such an admission could have been understood by all men of good will and sympathy. But the injured bishop continued: "when I call to my remembrance, the loathsome contempt, hatred, and disdaine, that the most part of men in these dayes beare, and in the face of the worlde declare, towarde the ministers of the Church of God, aswell bishops as other among us here in Englande, my heart can not but greatly feare and tremble at the consideration thereof."[4] From his own observation and experience the prelate deplored the sorry state of affairs:

> For who seeth not in these dayes, that hee who can most bitterly inveigh against bishops and preachers, that can most boldly blaze their discredites, that can most uncharitably sclaunder their lives and doings, thinketh of himselfe, and is esteemed of other, as the most zealous and earnest furtherer

of the gospel? Yea, they thinke it almost the best way, and most ready, to bring themselves in credite and estimation with many. A lamentable state of time it is, wherin such untemperat boldenes is permitted without any bridle at all. What man therefore that feareth God, that loveth his church, that hath care of his Prince and countrey, can remember this thing, and not dread in his heart, the sequele thereof?[5]

Fortunately the apprehensive and learned bishop could not foresee the consequences of his book nor could he envisage the literary immortality that would accrue to him in Martin's malapert replies, *Hay Any Worke for Cooper* and *More Worke for Cooper*.

Cooper's avowals were not only general but personal as well. The bishop, of course, was incensed by the offensive libels which were so "fraught with untruethes, slaunders, reproches, raylinges, revilings, scoffings, and other untemperate speeches, as I think the like was never committed to presse or paper, no, not against the vilest sort of men, that have lived upon the earth." He charged that a similar prejudice to the "honor of this State and government" had never been "offered in any age." Furthermore, the prelate criticized the author, declaring that he "calleth himselfe by a fained name, Martin Marprelate, a very fit name undoubtedly," and warning that "if this outragious spirit of boldenesse be not stopped speedily, I feare he will prove himselfe to bee, not onely *Mar-prelate* but *Mar-prince, Mar-state, Mar-lawe, Mar-magistrate*, and all together, until he bring it to an Anabapticall equalitie and communitie."[6] The bishop was old enough to remember the shocking events of Münster in 1534–35, and was not averse to invoking the specter of Jan of Leyden and Bernt Knipperdollinck.

Cooper particularly regretted that Martin's books had "spread abroad almost into all countreyes [regions] of this realme." A staunch patriot, the prelate could not understand, after the Lord's crowning mercies in delivering England from the Spanish Armada, why such widespread ingratitude should prevail. He was pained that "even now (I say) at this present time, wee should see in mens hands and bosomes, commonly slaunderous pamphlets fresh from the presse, against the best of the Church of England, and that we should heare at every table, and in sermons and lectures, at private conventicles, the voyces of many not giving prayse to God, but scoffing, mocking, rayling, and depraving the lives and doings of bishoppes, and other of the ministerie, and contemptuously defacing the state of government of this church" (pages 33–34).

The bishop of Winchester was irritated especially by the effectiveness of Martin's books. England had not been treated previously to such telling satire. The rollicking style, homely stories, clever alliteration, spicy gossip, and direct informal approach were calculated to catch and hold the readers' attention. Here was no euphuism smacking of John Lyly, no pompous poetry, no stilted elegance, no ponderous theological tome; here was delightful humor—sometimes crude but not vulgar—closely bound to a message, since the author was intensely earnest. Here were no vague generalities but instead specific incidents, no plaster-of-Paris saints but flesh-and-blood sinners. Cooper inadvertently revealed Marprelate's potency and success when he complained that Martin was not "contented to lay downe great crimes generally, as some other have done, but with very undecent tearmes, charge some particular bishops with particular faultes, with what trueth you shall now understand" (pages 36–37).

In his straightforward apologia for the Church of England as established by the queen and Parliament, Cooper valiantly defended himself, Whitgift, Bishop Aylmer of London, Bishop John Young of Rochester, and Bishop William Wickham of Lincoln. He justified the harsh treatment, graphically described by Martin, of Waldegrave, Penry, Wigginton, [Hugh?] Evans, and Barnaby Benison; he affirmed the superiority of bishops over presbyters, and cited the imperfections of foreign churches. He also challenged his readers to prove from Scripture that one necessary unchangeable form of church government had been prescribed for all ages and all countries. And in accordance with the title of his book, he warned Englishmen of the possible consequences if Presbyterianism should supplant Anglicanism—the necessary alteration of the laws, the ensuing innovations and inconveniences, and the subsequent confusion and chaos.[7]

During January 1588/89 rumors were rife in Northampton and Fawsley regarding books printed secretly in late November on the premises of Sir Richard Knightley. A maid talked freely of books recently printed; another servant mentioned the delivery of a printing press. Edward Baker, the official principal and a prebendary of Peterborough Cathedral, spoke openly about the printing; and Edward Sharpe, the vicar of Fawsley, visited Waldegrave's assistant, Henry Kildale, who was ill. The clergyman saw a printing press, printed sheets, and copies of the *Epitome*, one of which he brought to Sir Richard, "advertiseing him, what was done in his Howse." Moreover, Henry Sharpe, the Northampton bookbinder, had purchased copies of the *Epitome* to sell at a profit. And Penry's visits to Knightley's Fawsley house had not escaped notice of the servants.[8]

The high commissioners had good reasons to suspect Penry and Sharpe. In February 1586/87 Penry had published his first work, *A Treatise Containing the Aequity of an Humble Supplication*. The book, along with a written petition, had been presented on 28 February to the House of Commons by Edward Dunn Lee, a Puritan member of Parliament for Carmarthen. During February or March 1587/88 Penry's *An Exhortation unto the Governors, and People of Her Maiesties Countrie of Wales* had appeared and was followed in May by a second edition containing seventy pages of new material addressed to the Privy Council.[9] In July or August he had published *A Defence of That Which Hath Bin Written in the Questions of the Ignorant Ministrie, and the Communicating with Them*, in which he responded to Dr. Robert Some's first *A Godly Treatise Containing and Deciding Certaine Questions*, issued in May 1588. When Dr. Some's rejoinder, his second *A Godly Treatise . . . Whereunto One Proposition More Is Added*, was published in September, Penry prepared a second reply, which he hoped Waldegrave would publish immediately. Instead, Waldegrave printed Martin's *Epistle*, which appeared in October. It was not without reason that the authorities suspected Penry as the writer of the *Epistle* and that Wigginton had been questioned about him. The rumors from Fawsley, Northampton, and London also implicated Penry. Therefore, he wrote a letter to a friend in London, explicitly denying his authorship of Marprelate's work.[10] The high commissioners never saw Penry's letter, but, acting on the rumors, dispatched their pursuivant, Richard Walton, to Northampton where Penry was living with his father-in-law, Henry Godley. On 29 January 1588/89 Walton raided Godley's house and ransacked Penry's study. Among the seized writings were a printed copy of Udall's *Demonstration of Discipline* and Penry's manuscript reply to Dr. Some's second *A Godly Treatise . . . Whereunto One Proposition More Is Added.*[11]

The attempt to seize Penry indicated that the authorities were intensifying their efforts to silence Martin. During the preceding eleven weeks the High Commission had functioned swiftly and effectively. It had examined at least nine persons, and had acquired information on prime suspects such as Udall, Wigginton, Barrow, Waldegrave, Penry, and Sharpe. The commissioners had provided information to Bishop Cooper for his *Admonition*, had established a limited espionage system, alerted county and local officials, and sent agents to suspected areas. That these efforts would be strengthened was evidenced by four important developments in February: Lord Chancellor Hatton's speech to Parliament, a forceful sermon by Chaplain Richard Bancroft, the issuance of a royal proclamation against the Martinists, and an attempt to capture Henry Sharpe.

On Tuesday, 4 February 1588/89 Elizabeth's seventh Parliament assembled. In his opening address Hatton alluded to those zealots who "do greatly deprave the present estate and reformation of religion, so hardly attained to, and with such [intemperate Martinists] her danger continued and preserved; whereby her loving subjects are greatly disquieted, her enemies are encouraged, religion is slandered, piety is hindered, schisms are maintained, and the peace of the Church is altogether rent in sunder and violated." Hatton also emphasized that Elizabeth unequivocally believed in the Anglican form of ecclesiastical polity and opposed the Puritans. The lord chancellor said she was

> most fully and firmly settled in her conscience, by the Word of God, that the estate and government of this Church of England, as now it standeth in this reformation, may justly be compared to any church which hath been established in any Christian kingdom since the Apostles times; that both in form and doctrine it is agreeable with the Scriptures, with the most ancient general [seven ecumenical] Councils, with the practice of the primitive church, and with the judgments of all the old and learned fathers.[12]

On 9 February—the first Sunday of the parliamentary session—Dr. Bancroft preached his famous sermon at Paul's Cross. As Hatton's chaplain and Whitgift's agent, Bancroft was an aggressive member of the Court of High Commission; during the next five years he was the leader of the attack upon Presbyterians and Martinists. He co-ordinated the work of governmental agencies, sponsored a pamphlet campaign against Martin, and employed university wits to reply to the Martinists in a witty and sarcastic vein. By thorough and persistent methods of raiding Puritan homes, spying, and tampering with the mail service, he and his agents acquired important documentary evidence of conspiratorial leaders, meetings, and plans.[13]

The sermon, expanded to 106 pages when printed in March, was based on 1 John 4:1: "Deerly beloved, beleeve not every spirit, but trie the spirits whether they be of God. For manie false prophets are gone out into the world." Inveighing against Martinists, "false prophets," "libellers," and innovators, Bancroft condemned those who threatened to limit the queen's prerogative in ecclesiastical matters, overthrow the Church of England, and bring in by force a new polity. The future archbishop quoted the prediction of the author of *A Second Admonition to the Parliament* that "great troubles will come . . . if it [the new discipline] be not provided for,"[14] and cited Udall's warning that Presbyterianism "must prevaile; and if it come to passe . . . by that means which will make your harts to ake, blame your selves."[15] The chaplain also contended that "Martin, in his first booke threateneth Fists: and in his seconde, he wisheth that our Parleament, which is now assembled, would put downe Lord Bishops, and bring in the reformation which they looke for, whether Hir Majestie will or no." Certain that he understood Marprelate's intentions, Bancroft asserted that "whilest he talketh much of treason, I feare he wil be found a traitor himself."[16] The preacher further reiterated his concern in four rhetorical questions: how could Martin "conceive that such a thing should be brought to passe (if Hir Majesty do hir best to withstande it) without a rebellion at the least, that I may go no farther? Hath not Hir Highnes in making of lawes a negative voice? Is not *lex principis opus?* Hath not every law *vim cogentem* of the king?" Warning his audience that "these are desperate points to be stoode in," Bancroft asserted that unless "good order be taken, and that in time, these things will grow to some extremities."[17]

With Cooper and Whitgift, Bancroft probably was instrumental in procuring the queen's pronouncement against the Martinists and their books. Undoubtedly he had been influenced by the appearance of the *Mineralls* in late January, which may have been the catalyst precipitating the issuance on 13 February 1588/89 of a royal proclamation "against Certaine Seditious and Schismatical Bookes and Libels." Citing defamatory writings "in rayling sorte, and beyond the boundes of all good humanitie," it condemned the erroneous doctrines, "notoriously untrue" presumptions, and slanders against the State. Particularly singled out was the attack on the bishops and hierarchy as presaging a "monstrous and apparaunt daungerous innovation," a subversion of the queen's prerogative, and a dissolution of "one of the three auncient estates of this realm"—the lords spiritual. Somewhat unrealistically—and ultimately unsuccessfully—the proclamation commanded all who possessed seditious writings to deliver them to the Ordinary of the diocese; somewhat hopefully—and equally unsuccessfully—it urged all who had information about the authors, printers, or distributors to divulge their knowledge to the bishops.[18]

Toward the end of February the pursuivants attempted to arrest Henry Sharpe, suspected of binding and selling Marprelate's books. Although the binding had been done by Waldegrave and his assistant, Kildale, Sharpe had been involved in the precarious and easily detectable activity of distributing and selling the *Epitome*. The officials, however, were unable to capture him, since he had been apprised of the pursuit and had been "compelled with the hinderance of his family to absent himself from his calling." The high commissioners, therefore, issued mandatory letters to the mayor of Northampton, Thomas Crasswell, who was commanded to arrest Sharpe. If Crasswell failed to comply, he was ordered to appear personally before the Court of High Commission and neither leave without permission nor offer any excuse of official duties or distance.[19]

With the publication of Cooper's *Admonition* in January and Bancroft's *Sermon* in March, the government launched a campaign of pamphlet warfare against the Martinists. The literary onslaught continued in the spring with two books by Leonard Wright, an apologist for the Church of England. His first book, which may be dated about March 1588/89, was *A Summons for Sleepers*, in which he referred to "the sinfull crue of napping sleepers in generall," and also to the Martinists whose "pretence (as their Captaine saith) is to marre the Prelate, the auncient grave Pastors, reverend Fathers, and chiefe pillers of our Church." In his second book, entered in the Stationers' Register on 7 June, Wright discussed *The Hunting of Antichrist*. The main attack was directed against the Church of Rome, but pages 15–28 pertained to Puritans and Martinists.[20]

In early June 1589 *Mar-Martine*, an eight-page poem in rhyme, was published. This anonymous work apparently riled Martin, especially the last stanza:

> *If Martin dy by hangmans hands, as he deserves no lesse,*
> *This Epita[p]h must be engravde, his maners to expresse.*

Here hangs knave Martine a traitrous Libeler he was,
Enemie pretended but in hart a friend to the Papa,
Now made meat to the birdes that about his carkas are
   hagling.

Learne by his example yee route of Pruritan Asses,
Not to resist the doings of our most gratious Hester,
Martin is hangd, o the Master of al Hypocritical Hangbies.[21]

In June or July appeared *Marre Mar-Martin: or Marre-Martins Medling, in a Manner Misliked*, with three pages of doggerel, concluding:

> If all be true that Lawyers say,
> The second blowe doth make the fray:
> Mar-Martins fault can be no lesse,
> Than Martins was which brake the peace.
>   Martin, Marre-Martin, Barrow, Browne,
>   All helpe to pull Religion downe.[22]

Another edition, entitled *Mar-Martin*, without title page, followed shortly. Its first line reads: "I knowe not why a frutelesse lye in Print," whereas in the other edition the reading is: "I know not why a fruitles rime in print." *Mar-Martin* also lacks the seven lines of verse found on the title page of *Marre Mar-Martin*.[23] About the same time a similar work, and possibly by the same author, appeared, *A Whip for an Ape: or Martin Displaied*, reissued as *Rythmes against Martin Marre-Prelate*. It consisted of twenty-six stanzas of six lines each; the first stanza begins:

> Since reason (Martin) cannot stay thy pen,
> We'il see what rime will do: have at thee then.[24]

On 3 July a book by A.L. was entered in the Stationers' Register, entitled *Antimartinus*.[25] This volume, beautifully printed by George Bishop and Ralph Newbery, and displaying classical learning, was a warning to the students of Oxford and Cambridge to beware of the mendacity of Martin the libeler, who was linked with Machiavelli. A.L. defended the bishops against Martin's scoffs, and professed to have the best interests of the universities, the State, and the church in mind.

A manuscript book with a different emphasis, entitled "Asinus Onustus. The Asse Overladen," was delivered to the queen on 27 July. This manuscript book condemned Martin as one

> [who] blushed not to confesse himselfe to bee suborned, to be a marrer of prelates, that is, an overth[r]ower of the clergy, a captaine to caterpillers, a guide to church-robbers, and a ring-leader to the raskall sort, to bring the gospell of Christ, all religion, and the messengers thereof into utter contempt. But who seeth not, that not onely the breath, but the secret voice of a greater Martin was seene and heard in it, which gaped gredily for my confusion?

Essentially, the book was a plea for the parish clergy of England, who are "of all people most odious to courtiers." The preachers were likened to the donkey—despised, overburdened, and deprived of provender. The book was also a protest against the despoiling of the bishoprics by covetous officials, the impropriation and sale of benefices, and the imposition of heavy taxes by "horse-leeches" and "new-found politicians."[26]

Tobias Bland's book, which appeared in June or July, deserves a brief mention because he was the author of one of those "haggling and profane pamphlets" written against Martin. Bland was the chaplain to John Lord Saint John, baron of Bletsoe. His work, entitled, *A Baite for Momus, So Called upon Occasion of a Sermon at Bedford Injuriously Traduced by the Factious,* was a protest against "erronious spirites." He complained: "For now what uncircumcised hart and mouth dare not whet his style and sharpen his tongue to spit spight and venome, strife, and rebellion against the higher powers?" By "higher powers" Bland meant "our chiefe magistrates and high priestes," and by implication the Martinists were reproved.[27]

A Countercuffe, the first of the Pasquill publications, appeared in August. A brief, ineffectual treatise of eight pages, it denounced Martin as a "monster" and "an error of nature," and referred to "the maine buffets that are given him in every corner of this realme." Ostensibly a reply to *Martin Junior*, which was printed by 22 July, *A Countercuffe* scarcely dealt with his opponent at all. Pasquill ironically exhorted Martin Junior to play "the knave kindly as thou hast begun, and waxe as olde in iniquitie as thy father." He boasted: "Pasquill hath taken up your glove, and desires you to charge your weapon at him like a man. If you play with him, as your father and your selfe have doone with the bishops heretofore, if you barke like a curre and bite behind, he will have a tricke with his heele to strike out your teeth." Pasquill announced his intention to publish *The Owles Almanacke* and *The Lives of the Saints*, but his promise remained unfulfilled.[28]

During the summer of 1589 Francis Bacon, in the role of a peacemaker, wrote a book for private circulation, "An Advertisement Touching the Controversies of the Church of England." This treatise, which was not printed until 1641, was a carefully modulated and discreet essay.[29] Bacon's mother, Ann, one of the five famous daughters of Sir Anthony Cooke, was sympathetic with the nonconformists, and her son also exhibited a tolerance and wisdom unusual in the anti-Martinist literature. He deplored the current Martinist publications which sought to "turn religion into a comedy or satire," complained of those writers that combined "curious controversies and profane scoffing," and rebuked those who "intermix Scripture and scurrility." But he also reprimanded those anti-Martinists who added fuel to the fire and warned them that "the second blow maketh the fray." "*Qui replicat, multiplicat.*"

Bacon asserted that some Puritans were too contentious and extreme. In categorically denouncing the Roman Catholic Church, they disregarded its valuable features; in stressing the sermon, he said, they stirred up diversity of opinion; in seeking Scriptural sanction, they interjected private opinion; and in emphasizing polity, they failed to recognize that church government as practiced by Continental churches was not necessarily applicable to England. Councils and synods and consistories had their proper places, but "when voices shall be numbered and not weighed," truth does not always eventuate. But Bacon was even more critical of those bishops who regarded foreign churches with condescension and Presbyterian ordination with suspicion. He disliked subscription, oaths, and general warrants, and condemned the church courts for dispensing arbitrary justice on trivial matters by exaction of fees and fines. He rebuked the bishops for resisting reform and for their failure to promote parliamentary bills which would correct legitimate grievances. Bacon's treatise was eminently judicious, and deserves reading today for its common sense and its insights into human nature.[30]

Martins Months Minde probably appeared in October 1589.[31] One of the more imaginative and substantial of the anti-Marprelate books, it was written by Mar-phoreus, and purported to report Martin's death, funeral, and final will. Three causes allegedly produced his death: "foolerie," "ribaudrie," and "blasphemie." According to Mar-phoreus, Martin specified that he should not be buried in a churchyard, since that would be an act of profanation, but in a field or barn, and that his body should lie north and south. His epitaph should be placed on a post or tree, near to his grave, with the letters "M.M.M.," meaning *"Memoriae Martini Magni,"* but his critic interpreted the letters to signify *"Munstrum Mundi Martinus."* In his will Martin bequeathed to his sons his knavery and ribaldry, and his scolding and railing to the London gossip, Dame Margaret Lawson, whom he had defended in his Marprelate writings. Mar-phoreus alleged that when Martin's body was exhumed, his lungs were "huge and made to prate," his gall "overflowen with choller," his tongue "wonderfullie swolne in his mouth," and his head with "no crumme of braine within it." His epitaph was blazed in Latin:[32]

Hic iacet, ut pinus,
Nec Caesar, nec Ninus,
Nec magnus Godwinus,
Nec Petrus, nec Linus,
Nec plus, nec minus,
Quam clandestinus,
Miser ille Martinus,
    Videte singuli.

O vos Martinistae
Et vos Brounistae,
Et Famililouistae,
Et Anabaptistae,
Et omnes sectistae,
Et Machiuelistae,
Et Atheistae,
Quorum dux fuit iste,
    Lugete singuli.

At gens Anglorum,
Praesertim verorum,
Nec non, qui morum,
Estis bonorum,
Inimici horum,
Ut est decorum,
Per omne forum,
In saecula saeculorum,
    Gaudete singuli.

The second Pasquill book, published in October, was entitled, *The Returne of the Renowned Cavaliero Pasquill of England, from the Other Side the Seas, and His Meeting with Marforius at London upon the Royal Exchange.* It was a dialogue and a diatribe in which Pasquill denounced Martin as a Savonarola, a knave, and a thief. He accused Martin of distorting Scripture, introducing division into many households, slandering religion, and coveting gold, lands, and benefices. Nevertheless, Pasquill admitted that Martin had staunch supporters and "hath made some head, in some parts of Her Majesties dominions, not because his Worshippe is invincible" but because he had not encountered strong opponents. Pasquill also berated the Puritans whom he called "pruritans"—those suffering from a wanton itching. He chided Walter Travers for receiving a Presbyterian ordination at Antwerp and satirized William Dyke, of St. Albans, as a preacher "so bald, so bare, and yet so bold to flie into heaven with a fewe sicke feathers." Eusebius Pagit, sometimes referred to as "lame" Pagit because of a boyhood injury not to his foot but to his arm, was belittled as a man with two clubs, "one in his foote, another in his head." Other disparaging remarks were directed against Penry, Wigginton, Humphrey Fen, preacher at Coventry, and one [Christopher?] Rogers, a clergyman from Byfield, Northamptonshire.[33]

Pappe with an Hatchet, usually ascribed to John Lyly of *Euphues* fame, was published in October. The book is a long, tedious caricature of Martin and his two sons, who are called "Huffe, Ruffe, and Snuffe, the three tame ruffians of the church." Lyly had read *Martin Junior, Martin Senior,* and the *Protestatyon,* and had incorporated in his work some of Martin's expressions. He was contemptuous of Martin's coined words, and made an inventory of all his "uncivill and rakehell tearmes" in order to improve his own raillery and to reply to Martin with equally "lavish termes." Unfortunately, he was not an overwhelming success, although he boasted that if Martin should pistle him, "then have I a pestle so to stampe his pistles, that Ile beate all his wit to powder." In asking Martin Junior if his father had died at the Groyne [Corunna, Spain], Lyly said he knew Martin to be "sicke of a paine in the groyne." In addition to this sick humor, he invented a story of one of Martin's favorites who stupidly swore an oath not by his conscience but by his "concupiscence." Not content to call Martin merely a malcontent, who had "throwen fire, not into the church porch but into the chauncell," he described him as "some jester about the Court," well versed in obscenity and "squirrilitie," one who had undermined religion and castigated the bishops. Lyly added that William Elderton, the ballad writer, had written a rime for Martin, beginning:

> Come tit me, come tat me,
> Come throw a halter at me.

Lyly also reported that he himself once planned to write a ballad, entitled, "Martin and His Maukin" [country wench], "to no tune, because Martin was out of all tune."[34]

Shortly after Lyly's book was published, a work of a different character appeared, *Plaine Percevall the Peace-Maker of England,* usually ascribed to Richard Harvey, Fellow of

Pembroke College, Cambridge.[35] This was an exhortatory and didactic treatise, somewhat patronizing and repetitive, written by a neutral observer who hoped to quench the sparks before they became a conflagration. He had read some of Martin's books, and therefore was critical of "Counterfet Martin" and "Counter Martin," as he labeled him. Since he had also read Pasquill's *Countercuffe*, Mar-phoreus' *Martins Months Minde*, and Lyly's *Pappe with an Hatchet*, he professed to be weary of accusations, wranglings, and dissension, of pro and con, ergo, and verbal fisticuffs. He rebuked Martin for writing "Pistles" that were not Gospels, but he also objected to the "tuft mock-adoo mak-a-dooes; for *qui mocchat, moccabitur*, quoth the servingman of Abington." The conclusion of his exhortation was cogent: "Well then Martin, and you professed Mar-Martins, in presence of me, Percevall, shake hands and be friendes, meet halfe way."[36]

"An Advertisement for Pap-hatchet, and Martin Mar-prelate," dated 5 November 1589, was a learned work written by Gabriel Harvey, poet and Fellow of Trinity Hall, Cambridge. It remained in manuscript until 1593 when it was included in Harvey's *Pierces Supererogation, or a New Prayse of the Old Asse.*[37] Harvey wrote "An Advertisement" because Lyly, in his *Pappe with an Hatchet*, had called Harvey "a notable coach companion for Martin." Smarting under this indictment, Harvey vehemently denied he was Martin, and unmercifully derided Lyly. Harvey confessed that he began to think "basely" of Lyly "since thou began'st to disguise thy witt, and disgrace thy arte with ruffianly foolery." Having thrust in the dagger, Harvey twisted it: "The finest wittes preferre the loosest period in M. [Roger] Ascham, or Sir Philip Sidney, before the tricksiest page in *Euphues*, or *Paphatchet*." Then in a reference to the latter work, he sneered: "The whole worke, a bald toy, full of stale, and woodden jestes; and one of the most paltry thinges, that ever was published by graduate of either Universitie; good for nothing but to stop mustard pottes, or rub gridirons, or feather rattes neastes, or such like homely use."

Harvey's treatment of Martin was comparatively mild. He

disliked Marprelate's views on bishops, discipline, and Presbyterianism, and warned him that in promoting a reformation a deformation would ensue. Since "all men are not of
one mould," no progress would be achieved by innovation
or new forms of polity. Then he added: "Good Martin, be
good to the church, to the ministery, to the State, to thy
country, to thy patrons, to thy frends, to thy brethren, to
thiselfe: and as thou loovest thiselfe, take heede of old Puritanisme, new Anabaptisme, and finall Barbarisme."[38]

A Myrror for Martinists, published in late December or January 1589/90, written by T.T., has been ascribed to Thomas
Turswell; since Turswell died in 1584/85, a more likely attribution would be Thomas Timme or Tymme, translator and
author of at least eighteen works. T.T. was critical of the
"late Martine libellers" and the "repliers, who notwithstanding they have chosen the better part, yet handle it not so
charitably and modestly as it requireth." Drawing his examples from the Scripture and patristic writers, and warning
of the heresies of Origen, Sabellius, Arius, Apollinaris, and
Nestorius, the author exhorted his readers to follow peace,
sobriety, and prudence.[39]

In January 1589/90 Leonard Wright published his third
book against the Martinists: *A Friendly Admonition to Martine
Marprelate and His Mates*. In his "friendly and kindly way"
Wright desired that "the spirit of grace, wisedome and chari-
tie" would be given to Martin, who had disdainfully referred
to "wringlefaced Wrighte" in his *Protestatyon*. The writer
admonished Martin to stop his "grievous railing, disdainfull
mocking, and bitter contention." And in his defence of the
Church of England—its bishops, its sacraments, discipline,
and ceremonies—Wright adduced the authority of Dr. William Fulke, the recently deceased master of Pembroke College, Cambridge, and even of Thomas Cartwright, who had
written favorably of the English church in his letter to Robert
Harrison, the Separatist. But in a less friendly way Wright
concluded that Martin, like Edmund Campion, was sincerely
wrong, that he was too dogmatic and cocksure, and that the
Martinists were "so fierce, fell, and furious, so obstinat, wil-

full and malitious, so churlish, disdainful and presumptuous, so captious over other mens manners, so readie to spie a moate in other mens eies, so busy in laying open other mens infirmities," that they should reform themselves.[40]

An Almond for a Parrat, or Cutbert Curry-knaves Almes. Fit for the Knave Martin, and the Rest of Those Impudent Beggers, That Can Not Be Content to Stay Their Stomakes with a Benefice, but They Will Needes Breake Their Fastes with Our Bishops, published about February or March 1590, was probably written by Thomas Nashe.[41] The writer, who was acquainted with the Martinist books and quoted from the *Protestatyon,* referred to "sweete Martin sauce malapert," "good munckie face Machivell," and "Martin Makebate of Englande." In his *An Almond for a Parrat* the author produced a book rich in scandal and gossip. He dredged up from his teeming brain imaginative, scatological, and scathing details to concoct one of the most scurrilous and venemous accounts ever written. Penry, "his Welchnes," was called "as arrant a papist as ever came out of Wales"; he was labeled an Anabaptist, a Brownist, a Ramist, and Martin himself. He was "splay-footed," and endowed by "God and nature" with a "serpentine soule, like a counterfet diamond, more deepe in dong."

An Almond for a Parrat also included disparaging references to other Puritans besides Martin and Penry. The names of Cartwright, Travers, Udall, and Wigginton reappeared. Stephen Egerton, preacher at St. Anne's Blackfriars, was derided for his sermons, and Philip Stubbes, author of *The Anatomie of Abuses* (1583), was ridiculed. Pagit, previously mentioned as "lame" in his arm, was once more dragged into the narrative as "poltfoote Paget," a "schismatique" and a "whoremaster." Despite his supposed leg injury, he was allegedly seen running from Hounslow "for getting his maide with childe." No Martinist work ever reached the depths of scurrility exemplified in *An Almond for a Parrat.*[42]

The third Pasquill book, *The First Parte of Pasquils Apologie. Wherin He Renders a Reason to His Friendes of His Long Silence: and Gallops the Fielde with the Treatise of Reformation Lately Written by a Fugitive, John Penrie,*[43] published in July 1590, was primarily an attack on Penry and his book, *Reformation No Enemie*.[44] Pasquill depicted Penry as disloyal to the queen, privy councilors, judges, and other magistrates. Examining Penry's defense of Puritans, his views on nonresidency, preaching versus reading, and the equality of the clergy, he adjudged them erroneous. Pasquill once more likened Martin to Savonarola of Florence and accused him of stirring up factions at a time when the Spanish invasion was imminent. In three leading questions Pasquill implied that Penry was a Martinist agent:

> Who had the oversight of the libell at Fawslie? John of Wales.
> Who was corrector of the presse at Coventrie? John of Wales.
> Who wrote the last treatise of Reformation so full of slaunders, but John of Wales?

Pasquill also defended Archbishop Whitgift, "the byshop of my soule," prelates generally, and chaplain Bancroft. He praised the Church of England, which had been approved by such eminent scholars as Martin Bucer, Peter Martyr, and Bishop John Jewel. Although Pasquill contributed at least three treatises against Martin, and promised several more, he supposedly regretted dissensions when he wrote: "Contention is a coale, the more it is blowne by dysputation, the more it kindleth; I must spit in theyr faces to put it out."[45]

In July 1590 Anthony Marten, "gentleman sewer of the queens chamber" and royal librarian, published his *A Reconciliation of All the Pastors and Clergy of This Church of England*. Written in an irenical vein, the book was a plea for knowledge as well as zeal. There was no specific indictment of Marprelate, but the Martinists by implication were refuted. The author defended bishops and episcopal excommunication, and advocated degrees of ministers as set forth by Hadrian Saravia, author of the *De diversis ministrorum Evangelii gradibus*, published a month before Marten's book.[46] Although the early church "prescribed no certayne form of government for all times and places," as Whitgift and Cooper had affirmed, nevertheless Marten believed that the Church of England was closer to the apostolic model than the reformed churches were, despite their claims.

Thus, there were at least twenty-one books and pamphlets published by the anti-Martinists in the years 1589-90.[47] Some writers professed a dislike of the undignified controversy, but they continued their writing. Bacon informed his readers—and this may explain why he did not print his own treatise—that "bitter and earnest writing may not hastely be condemned; for men cannot contend coldly and without affection about things which they hold dear and precious." But he also warned that "it is more than time that there were an end and surseance made of this immodest and deformed manner of writing lately entertained, whereby matters of religion are handled in the style of the stage."[48]

Mar-Martine, as we have seen, was one of the earliest anti-Martinist writers, but he was also one of the first to deplore the appearance on the stage of the burgeoning spirit of Richard Tarleton the comic actor and Martin Marprelate the libeler:

> These tinkers termes, and barbers jestes,
>> first Tarleton on the stage,
> Then Martin in his bookes of lies,
>> hath put in every page.[49]

Both Mar-Martine and Bacon were vexed when the anti-Martinist writers joined forces with the stage players in producing burlesques and caricatures of Martin. One anonymous writer reported that during the early summer of 1589 "everie stage plaier made a jest of him, and put him cleane out of countenance." At Shoreditch outside the jurisdiction of the city magistrates, on the stages of the Curtain and the Theater, Martin was "drie beaten, and therby his bones broken, then whipt that made him winse, then wormd and launced, that he tooke verie grievouslie, to be made a Maygame upon the stage, and so bangd, both with prose and rime on everie side, as he knewe not which way to turne himselfe, and at length cleane marde."[50] The author of *A Whip for an Ape: or Martin Displaied* described an actor who mimicked Martin.

Hidden in a sack, the player suddenly emerged as an ape before the audience. Then the ape "delights with moppes and mowes [grimaces and mockings], with jesting and scoffing, with flouting and kicking."

> Such fleering, leering, jarring fooles bopeepe;
> Such hahaes, teehees, weehees, wild colts play;
> Such sohoes, whoopes, and hallowes, hold and keepe;
> Such rangings, ragings, revelings, roysters ray [dress].
>
> Then in he leapes with a wild Morrice daunce;
> Now strikes he up Dame Lawsens lustie lay;
> Then comes Sir Jeffries ale tub tapde by chaunce:
> Which makes me gesse (and I can shrewdly smell)
> He loves both t'one and t'other passing well.[51]

On one occasion Martin was appareled "with a cocks combe, an apes face, a wolfs belly, catts clawes, etc."; also:

> *Vetus Comoedia* beganne to pricke him at London in the right vaine, when shee brought foorth Divinitie wyth a scratcht face, holding her hart as if she were sicke, because Martin would have forced her, but myssing of his purpose, he left the print of his nayles uppon her cheekes, and poysoned her with a vomit which he administred unto her, to make her cast uppe her dignities and promotions.[52]

During the autumn of 1589 apprehension spread because of the indecency and bawdy character of the stage. Lord Burghley wrote to Richard Young, a special commissioner, urging him to consult with Mayor John Harte about the suspension of all plays within the London jurisdiction. On 5 November Harte summoned the players from the Lord Admiral's company and Lord Strange's group and ordered them "in Her Majesties name" to desist. The Admiral's men obeyed, but Lord Strange's servants "in very contemptuous manner" disregarded the order and played at Cross Keys the same afternoon. The Privy Council discussed the problem on 12 November, and then wrote letters to Whitgift, Mayor Harte, and Edmund Tilney, master of the Revels, enjoining the archbishop to appoint a person well versed in divinity,

73

and directing the mayor to select a representative for the city, who would serve as a committee with Tilney to inspect comedies and tragedies and eliminate material "unfytt and indecent to be handled in playes, both for divinitie and State." Thus, the attack against the Martinists was subverted, though John Lyly lamented: "Would those comedies might be allowed to be plaid that are pend [held back], and then I am sure he [Martin] would be decyphered, and so perhaps discouraged."[53]

THE PROSECUTION
OF MARTINIST
PARTICIPANTS

"Would it not bee a fine Tragedie, when Mardocheus shall play a Bishoppe in a Play, and Martin [shall play] Hamman, and that hee that seekes to pull downe those that are set in authoritie above him, should be hoysted up on a tree above all other?" (John Lyly, *Pappe with an Hatchet*, signature D2 v, D3)

WE HAVE ALREADY recounted the arrest and interrogation in the autumn of 1589 of Sir Richard Knightley, John Hales, Roger Wigston and his wife. On Friday, 13 February 1589/90 all four were arraigned before the Court of Star Chamber. The judges and prosecutors included Lord Chancellor Hatton, the vice-chamberlain, Thomas Heneage, the former lord deputy of Ireland, Sir John Perrot—all privy councilors—along with Attorney General John Popham, Solicitor General Thomas Egerton, and the queen's serjeant, John Puckering.[1] Popham spoke of the "prosperous and happy state of Her Majesty," but warned that "papists abroad" and the "seditious sectaries at home" had sought to disturb this prosperity and quietness. Both parties, he said, had been effectively repressed, but another group, the Puritans, had arisen, comprised of the "very vilest and basest sort," who contended for a new form of ecclesiastical discipline, and for a church government "in each province, in every diocese, yea, in every parish." Popham warned that if this new polity prevailed, "more mischief than any man by tongue can utter" would follow. He stated that dangerous books had been secretly printed and distributed in England, that the queen had ordained that printing be limited to London, Oxford, and Cambridge, that all publications "should be first seen and allowed," and that two proclamations had been issued in 1583 and 1588/89 against seditious books.

Reviewing Knightley's indictment, Popham asserted that the Marprelate book, the *Epitome*, as Sir Richard had confessed, had been printed on his Fawsley estate. Also, he stated that Knightley had "sent his man [Lawrence Jackson, the keeper] a ring for a token to receive the press into his house, who did so, and there they printed the *Epitome*." Furthermore, Popham asserted that Knightley had threatened to chase anyone who would dare to "search his house," and that when the press was at Fawsley, he had read the *Epitome*, kept secret the existence of the press, and had recommended Waldegrave to his kinsman John Hales, to whom he had sent a letter requesting a room for the press in one of his buildings in Coventry.

Knightley denied any malicious intent against the queen or State. Implying that he had no knowledge of any Marprelate book, he asserted that Penry had requested permission to reprint his *Treatise Containing the Aequity of an Humble Supplication*, a book allegedly unobjectionable to the government. Considering that the clergy were lacking in learning, that "for one good" minister there "were forty bad" ones, that for the most part they were "not worthy to sweep the church," Knightley admitted that in the summer of 1588 his "zeal for the furtherance of God's glory caused him to allow of this book." He minimized his role by stating the "press was never in his own home but in a house at the farther end of the town." He admitted he had requested Hales to provide a place for the press, but he did so because Waldegrave desired to print a book by Cartwright against the Jesuits [that is, a refutation of the Rheims version of the New Testament]. Moreover, he claimed these events had occurred before the issuance on 13 February 1588/89 of the proclamation against seditious Marprelate books. He concluded his testimony with a plea for the queen's forgiveness and a statement of remorse. Citing the example of King David, he said he had resolved that henceforth he would "not so much as to touch the hem of the Lord's Anointed." Despite his plea that the judges would be lenient and his assurance that he would heed the warning the lord chancellor had given, he was fined £2,000 and imprisoned at the queen's pleasure.[2]

John Hales, nephew of Knightley, confessed that out of respect for his uncle, he had acceded to his request for a house to be used for printing, but he disclaimed any knowledge of the printer, his purposes, and his books.[3] He admitted he had received a copy of Penry's *Supplication to the Parliament* [*A Viewe*], and stated he had learned of Penry's [Waldegrave's] intention to print Cartwright's book against The New Testament of Jesus Christ, printed in 1582 at Rheims under the Catholic auspices of the English College. Attempting to justify his actions, Hales asserted that he had received the *Supplication* before the proclamation of 13 February 1588/89 against Martin's books. Popham, however, reminded him there had been a proclamation in 1583 "against schismatical and seditious libels."[4] Hales then denied that Penry's book was a libel, and said that Penry had subscribed his name as author. Nevertheless, when Popham continued to characterize the book as a libel, Hales was discreetly silent. He also failed to mention that in addition to Penry's book, two Marprelate works, the *Mineralls* and *Hay Any Worke for Cooper*, had also been printed on his premises. Then the court fined him 1,000 marks [£666 13s. 4d.] and imprisonment at Her Majesty's pleasure.

Roger Wigston confessed that at his wife's request he had permitted the printers to carry on their work in his home at Wolston. Heneage criticized Wigston for his folly in allowing his wife to dominate him, and Perrot suggested that Wigston should be punished more severely "for giving such a foolish answer as that he did it at his wife's desire." But the court was lenient, and Wigston was fined 500 marks [£333 6s. 8d.], and imprisonment. Mrs. Wigston readily admitted that her zeal for the reformation in God's church caused her to invite the printers to work in her home. Attempting to shield her husband, she acknowledged that she had taken the initiative and that her husband, being neither over curious nor meddlesome, had complied with her wishes. She was fined £1,000—three times her husband's fine, and committed to prison.[5]

As early as February 1588/89, the investigators had learned from Nicholas Tomkins, servant of Mrs. Elizabeth Crane, that printing had occurred in her East Molesey house. When she was called before a commission of privy councilors and others, she refused to take an oath, said "she would not be her own Hangman," and declared that "she could not in her Conscience, be an Accuser of others."[6] The attorney general, Popham, prepared a Bill of Complaint, dated 11 February 1589/90, accusing Mrs. Crane of contempt toward the queen and her laws; the Bill requested that a writ of subpoena be issued, commanding her appearance forthwith before the Court of Star Chamber. Mrs. Crane, disdaining legal counsel, prepared an answer, which was considered "frivolous" and inadequate. In Trinity term 1590, she was brought before the court, fined 1,000 marks [£666 13s. 4d.] for contempt; she was also convicted for harboring the Martinist press, fined £500, and committed to the Fleet prison.[7]

After Humphrey Newman had been examined on 9 July 1590, he was remanded to prison, but in the spring of 1591 he was tried before the Court of Queen's Bench and found guilty of publishing and setting forth dangerous books against the queen and her officials, in violation of the statute of 23 Elizabeth, chapter 2, section 4, "An Acte against sedicious Wordes and Rumors uttered againste the Queenes moste excellent Majestie." On 16 May the Privy Council sent a letter to Archbishop Whitgift, informing him that Newman had been "condemned of felonie whose time of execution as yt is now appointed draweth verie neare." The privy councilors recommended that Whitgift appoint Alexander Nowell, dean of St. Paul's, and Dr. Lancelot Andrewes, vicar of St. Giles's, Cripplegate, and master of Pembroke College, Cambridge, to consult with Newman, and to persuade him to acknowledge his crime. If because of "obstinacie or wilful refusal" he did not submit, then "due execution of justice" was to follow according to his sentence, but if he agreed to sign a submission which Chief Justice Edmund Anderson of Common Pleas would prepare, then an application for mercy would be made to the queen.[8]

If we may infer from the results, Newman was persuaded by his interviewers. Since he had neither written nor printed any of the Marprelate books, since he was Throkmorton's employee and Penry's collaborator, and since he had "published" and "set forth" books only in the limited interpretation of making them public and putting them into circulation, his culpability was less than that of Hodgskin or Symmes. Furthermore, unlike Hodgskin, he had co-operated with his examiners by divulging significant information. Therefore the judges decided to accept his submission and urged his subscription to the following statement:

> Wheras I Humfraie Newman have heretofore bene a cheef dispercer and publisher of sondrie sortes of seditions [seditious?], infamies [infamous?], and slaunderous bookes and libells, not only against Her Majestie, her lawes, parlaments and godly government, but also against sundrie in authoritie, as well spirituall as temporall, under Her Majestie, tendinge to the erecting of [a] new forme of government contrarie to Her Majesties supremacie, crowen, regallitie, lawes, and statutes, for spreadinge wherof I am justly indicted and condict [convicted] as a fellone, sithence which tyme I have seene my great and foule offences, and doe nowe before God and all this presence, freely, voluntaryly, and humbly confes the lewdnes and greevousnes of my saide former practices, which I doe with all my hart and sole detest, . . . promisinge that if it shall please God, to move Her Majesties most royall hart, to have compassion of me, a moste sorrowfull condemned wreche, that I will forever hereafter forsake all suche undewtiefull and daungerous courses, and demeane my self dewtifully and peaceablye, as well to Her Majestie as to all authorities,

as well civill as ecclesyasticall, established under Her Highnes
in this realme, for I doe acckno[w]ledge them bothe to be lawe-
full and godly and to be obeyed by every faithfull subject.[9]

We may conclude that Newman signed this submission, since
he was granted a special pardon on 14 June 1592 by John
Puckering, keeper of the Great Seal. Thereafter Newman's
name disappeared from the records, and his date of death
remains unknown.[10]

It has been previously noted in chapter one that after his
capture in August 1589 Hodgskin had been examined at least
seven times. After spending ten months in the Tower—"a
great tyme and uppon Her Majesties chardg," as the privy
councilors observed—Hodgskin was transferred in July 1590
to the Marshalsea prison in Southwark. In late 1590 or more
likely in the spring of 1591, he was tried at the Court of
Queen's Bench on a charge of felony for having violated
the statute of 23 Elizabeth, chapter 2. Section 4 declared that
anyone who wrote, printed, or published a book which revealed "a maliciouse intente" against the queen, or contained
"any false, sedicious and slaunderous matter to the defama-
tion of the queenes majestie," or encouraged "stirring or
moving of any insurreccion or rebellion," was upon conviction guilty of felony. Although there were ten counts in
the indictment, the prosecutors pressed the charges of sedi-
tion, slander, and malice, and concentrated on the main accusation that Hodgskin, according to his own previous
confession before the lords commissioners, had printed Martin's *Theses Martinianae (Martin Junior)*, which "was devised
chiefly by the said Throckmorton, as also he is thought to
be the author of *Martin Senior* and *More Worke for the Cooper*."[11]

Hodgskin denied that the book contained any "matter of
sediccion and slaunder to Her Majestie and the State." When
this denial was refuted by specific citations, he disclaimed
any malicious intent against the queen or the government.
The court responded that "not the intent, which might be
secret, but the fact of the partie must shewe his minde."
Hodgskin then claimed the benefit of a legal exception, since

the statute under which he was charged provided that "the partie accused must be manifestly convinced by twoe witnesses produced *viva voce* and that within one moneth after the fact before one Justice of Peace or els must be indicted thereof within one yere next after the offence, where as nowe the[y] wanted wittnesses and also that one yere and more was since the first impression." The court then read the statute, section 8, which indicated that the proviso pertained to "speaking and reportinge, and printers and writers plainly exem[p]ted." Hodgskin then protested that "the confessions of the saide Symes and Tomlynes had bene violent[ly] extorted from them and by his one confession he was forced thereunto by rackinge and great torments." Francis Gawdy, justice of the Queen's Bench, responded that Hodgskin "did verie shamefully, himself being present at the examinacion which conteyned noe more in effect than he him self vollentarilie confessed, namely [that he was] the printer of the saide booke." Hodgskin continued to defend the contents of *Theses Martinianae* until he was adjudged guilty of felony. Thereupon, "in verie submise manner he renounced his former assercions and humblie praied the lords for his lif[e] and the furtherance to Her Majestie for her favor."[12] Sentence of death was pronounced against him, but in May 1591 Dean Nowell and Dr. Andrewes were appointed to interview him. Hodgskin must have submitted, since he received the queen's mercy and was released about 1593.[13]

The examination of Valentine Symmes on 10 December 1589 is extant, but thereafter no record exists for his activities until March 1594. As an employee of Hodgskin, and as one who had testified frankly and fully, he was less culpable than his employer, and therefore probably was not arraigned. By 1594 he had established himself in the printing business again, but his career for the next nineteen years involved difficulties with the Stationers' Company. There were minor infractions, such as "breaking order," "printinge a thing disorderly," and issuing at least two recusant books, one with a false imprint and the other without any imprint. More serious was his printing of *Grammar and Accidence*, which was a pirated edition of an old standard book by William Lily and John Colet, *A Shorte Introduction of Grammar* (1549). Symmes was ordered to bring his press to Stationers' Hall, perhaps only for a limited period, but his type was melted and some of his equipment was destroyed. In 1599 he printed *Nashes Lenten Stuffe*. This book, together with Sir John Davies' *Epigrammes*, John Marston's *The Scourge of Villanie; Three Books of Satyres*, and other risqué works, caused Archbishop Whitgift and Bishop Bancroft as licensers of the press to issue a sweeping list of commandments forbidding the printing of satires, epigrams, plays, and English histories unless allowed, requiring that the works of Thomas Nashe and Gabriel Harvey be seized wherever found, and stipulating that "none of theire bookes be ever printed hereafter." These decrees, published at Stationers' Hall on 4 June 1599, listed fourteen printers, including Symmes, who were regarded as potential offenders; they were designated as "unprivileged printers" and specially warned to observe the "commandments."

In 1601 Symmes printed *A Proclamacion* without allowance; in June 1603 he was fined for "printing disorderly a ballad," which was the property of Margaret, the mother, or Elizabeth, the wife, of Edward Allde, a printer who was in trouble with the Stationers' Company. In December he was ordered to bring to Stationers' Hall his broadsheets of *The Traitours Lately Array[g]ned at Winchester*, and also thirty copies of Thomas Powell's *A Welch Bayte to Spare Provender*, and in addition was fined 14s. 6d. Further difficulties developed in 1605 when Symmes printed an edition of Sir Edwin Sandys's book, *A Relation of the State of Religion;* since this work had been printed from a stolen manuscript without permission, it was burned by the order of the Court of High Commission at the request of Sandys. In 1607 Symmes was in deep trouble, and William Hall was "admitted to be a prynter in the place of Valentine Symmes." Consequently, Symmes printed no books in the years 1608–10 and only three books thereafter. In December 1622 he requested Archbishop George Abbot to restore him as a master printer, but his suit was rejected the following February. Nevertheless, he was given a pension of £6 annually for five years.[14] William A. Jackson has suggested that "Simmes had been a printer of recusant books and it may be that it was thought to be easier to pension him than to keep a watch on his work."[15]

During the years 1594–1612 Symmes printed at least 164 books and four broadsheets, of which some deserve special mention. He collaborated with Thomas Creede in reprinting Raoul Le Fèvre, *The Auncient Historie of the Destruction of Troy;* this was the first book which William Caxton had printed in English at Bruges in 1475. Symmes printed John Weever's *Epigrammes* (1599), which contained a sonnet (signature E6 *recto*) dedicated to William Shakespeare, and also issued the same author's *An Agnus Dei* (1601), one of the rarest miniature books of the period, with pages one inch wide and one and a quarter inches high. In 1603 he produced a folio edition of Michel de Montaigne, *The Essayes,* and in 1604 Joseph de Acosta's *The Naturall and Morall Historie of the East and West Indies.* In the same year Symmes—the Marprelate printer—issued *Sacro-sanctum Novum Testamentum Domini Servatoris nostri Iesu Christi, in Hexametros versus ad verbum et genuinum sensum fideliter in Latinam linguam translatum,* prepared by Bishop John Bridges, whose *Defence of the Government* in 1587 had provoked Marprelate's devastating attack. Prominent literary writers whose books Symmes printed were Samuel Daniel, Thomas Dekker, Michael Drayton, Stephen Gosson, Robert Greene, Benjamin Jonson, Christopher Marlowe, Thomas Nashe, Barnaby Rich, and Robert Southwell. Symmes also printed nine Shakespeare quartos, including one comedy, *Much Adoe about Nothing,* one tragedy, *Hamlet,* and seven history plays on Richard II, Richard III, and Henry IV.[16]

John Udall's interrogation by the lords commissioners and his committal to the Gatehouse prison on 13 January 1589/90 have already been noticed in chapter one. On the same day he had answered questions based on the testimony of Tomkins, Chatfield, and Sharpe. On 13 July Udall had verified the record of this examination and added three minor alterations. On 24–25 July 1590 he was tried at Croydon before the judges of Assize, Robert Clarke, baron of the Court of

Exchequer, and Puckering, queen's serjeant. The prosecutor, James Dalton, asserted that the substance of the indictment constituted felony, that Udall was the author of the *Demonstration of Discipline,* and that the book revealed a malicious intent against the queen and State. The proof, somewhat dubious, was based on Sharpe's testimony, which in turn was derived from Penry's remark that Udall was the author. It was also based on the deposition of Chatfield, who had been summoned to give evidence but to the annoyance of the judges had not appeared. According to bystanders, Chatfield had departed before the summons could be served. The third basis of Dalton's charges was the testimony of Tomkins, who had stated that Udall was the author. Tomkins had been sent overseas, ostensibly on business but more likely to remove him from the court's summons. Thus, not a single witness was present in the courtroom. Despite a warning from the Puritan lawyer, Nicholas Fuller, to the jury that it must prove malicious intent, Clarke instructed the jury merely to determine if Udall was the author. That being concluded, then the charge of felony was also true, since the judges had averred that the anonymous author of the *Demonstration* was guilty of felony. The jury decided that Udall was the author, and adjudged him guilty of felony on 24 July; on the following day discussions with the court continued on law, equity, and pardon.

Udall was not sentenced but was committed to the White Lion prison. He made a supplication to the queen, pleaded for a pardon, and denied any malicious intent or slander against Her Majesty. On 18–20 February 1590/91 he appeared at the assizes in Southwark, before judges Clarke, Puckering, and Edward Fenner. He maintained his belief in the cause of church reform, and asserted his innocence, but neither affirmed nor denied his authorship of the *Demonstration.* When he was asked if he would "acknowledge all the laws ecclesiastical and temporal of the land, to be agreeable to the Word of God," he replied that the judges knew what he held regarding ecclesiastical laws and that he could "yield no further than you have heard." Puckering responded:

"Then we must do our office, and pronounce sentence on you." When Udall replied, "God's will be done," the sentence of death was pronounced.

The execution of the sentence was deferred because Udall was reprieved by order of the queen, who sent her chaplain, Dr. Nicholas Bond, to confer with the prisoner on a form of submission. On 22 February Udall sent to Sir Walter Raleigh a letter in which he appealed for aid "to appease Her Majesty's indignation." Udall included a statement of his beliefs and a plea that if the queen would not pardon him, she would merely punish him by banishment. About the end of May Dr. Andrewes and Dean Nowell conferred with him about forms of submission. Even James VI wrote a letter on 12 June 1591 to the queen on Udall's behalf. In July the crackbrained conspiracy of Hacket-Arthington-Coppinger created such a strong anti-Presbyterian sentiment that Udall "thought it bootless to sue." In the spring of 1592 his petition to attend church services was denied, but he did obtain a copy of his indictment. On the basis of this document he formulated a new request for a pardon, petitioned the Privy Council for his liberty, wrote letters to the archbishop, and procured supporting letters from "honourable personages." But the unqualified acquiescence of the archbishop was not forthcoming. For a brief period, it seemed likely that some English merchants would be able to obtain permission to send Udall as a minister to serve their employees in Syria or Guinea. The archbishop required them to guarantee that Udall would go, which they were willing to do, and also requested the merchants to promise that Udall would not return until he had received Her Majesty's permission. Since neither the merchants nor Udall would accept this stipulation, and since the queen did not sign the pardon, he remained in prison, the trading ship sailed, and in 1593 he died, probably a victim of the plague or typhus.[17]

The last years in the life of Penry contrasted sharply with those of Udall and Throkmorton. Because of the danger from pursuivants, Penry fled from Throkmorton's Haseley residence on 2 October 1589 and arrived at Edinburgh in Novem-

ber. Still smarting because the Privy Council had issued a
warrant for his arrest, and had characterized him as "an enemie to the State," Penry completed the writing of his *Reformation No Enemie*, which Waldegrave printed about January 1589/
90 in Edinburgh. This book was an incisive defiance of the
rulers of England, who were stigmatized as a "multitude
of conspirators against God, against His truth, against the
building of His house." The hierarchy and clergy were reviled as a "troup of bloody soule murtherers, sacriligious
church robbers, and suche as have made them selves fatte
with the bloude of mens soules, and the utter ruine of the
church." Wicked lawyers and judges were denounced as men
who perverted justice and used the laws to "catch the peacea-
ble of the land." Even the Privy Council, which allegedly
delighted in the "violent oppression of Gods saincts," was
warned that God would afflict it "with an heavy plague."[18]
In the summer of 1590 Penry published a second book, *A
Briefe Discovery of the Untruthes and Slanders (against the True
Governement of the Church of Christ), Contained in a Sermon,
Preached the 8 of February 1588* [9 February 1588/89] *by D. Bancroft, and Since That Time, Set Forth in Print, with Additions
by the Said Authour. This Short Answer May Serve for the Clearing
of the Truth, untill a Larger Confutation of the Sermon Be
Published.*[19]

The English ambassador at Edinburgh, Robert Bowes,
prompted by Lord Burghley, kept a close watch on Penry.
On 24 April 1590 he informed the lord treasurer that the
Scottish ministers "have hitherto well entertained" Penry
and that he "no longer comes to public assemblies, but keeps
himself secret, with purpose to remove shortly." On 9 May
Bowes promised Burghley he would speak to James VI about
Penry's banishment, and a week later was able to report
that he had requested the king to banish Penry for publishing
a book advocating "the alteration of the government in England." On 23 July Bowes informed Burghley that despite
strong protests from Penry's friends, the king had decided
Penry should be publicly banished rather than extradited
to England. Bowes further related that some Scottish minis-

ters had urged their congregations to "pray for such as were persecuted in England for the Word of God, meaning such as Penry, seeking the alteration of the ecclesiastical order of the Church of England." On 14 August Bowes reported that on 6 August Penry had been banished by the "Act of the King in Council." Despite his apparent diplomatic success, Bowes complained in a conference with the king on 19 November that Penry was still in Scotland; the king and his chancellor replied that Penry had departed, but they also promised to make an inquiry. By 18 December Bowes informed Burghley the king had reported that though Penry had fled the realm, "his wife continues in Edinburgh, supported by his friends, some of whom say that he departed a good while past, and it is not known where he is." Penry, aided by friendly clergymen, probably lived incognito for a few months in the environs of Edinburgh.[20]

In 1591 Penry translated *Propositions and Principles of Divinitie*.[21] Since this Swiss theological treatise was a Presbyterian commonplace book, with no aspersions on the Church of England, it did not incur the hostility of the English ambassador. During the summer, having learned from correspondence with Henry Arthington, a gentleman from Wakefield, Yorkshire, and with Edmund Coppinger, a naive religious zealot in London, that a crisis was approaching, Penry made a secret trip to London. He had been disturbed by the collapse of the Puritan classis movement in 1590, by the arrest of such prominent Presbyterians as Cartwright and Edmund Snape of Northampton, and by their arraignment before the Court of High Commission and the Court of Star Chamber in 1590–91. Believing that "reformation must shortlie be enacted in England," Penry must have been disillusioned with the outbreak of a tumult in Cheapside on 16 July. Led by William Hacket, an illiterate and deluded charlatan, and abetted by Arthington and Coppinger, the conspiracy was pure farce. Arthington and Coppinger preached from a cart and proclaimed Hacket not only "King of Europe" but also of all Christendom; Hacket had defaced the queen's arms, and had urged that she should be deprived, since she "had forfeited her crowne." All three conspirators were quickly arrested. Hacket was tried at Newgate Sessions on 26 July and executed in Cheapside two days later; Coppinger starved himself for a week in the Bridewell prison and died on 29 July; Arthington confessed his guilt and was pardoned. On 28 July Penry hurriedly departed for Scotland, probably having witnessed the execution of Hacket, and rejoined his wife about 18 August; on 26 August she was delivered of a daughter whom the parents appropriately named Safety.[22]

For a year Penry remained in hiding, but about September 1592, he left Scotland for London. During the autumn he joined the recently organized Separatist church which had elected Francis Johnson as pastor and John Greenwood as teacher. For about five months he enjoyed membership in this congregation, which held its conventicles in the woods, in a schoolhouse, and in private homes, but he refused to accept any office in the pioneer church. In this period he was briefly united with his wife and children, who probably came from Scotland by ship, bringing a chest with his private papers. But on 4 March, while holding a worship service in Islington, the church members were captured. Although Penry escaped the same day, he was recaptured on 22 March, imprisoned in the Poultry Compter, and examined six times in the next two months. On 21 May he was arraigned at the Court of Queen's Bench; on 25 May a new indictment, based on 23 Elizabeth, chapter 2, charged him with having written seditious and slanderous passages in his book, *Reformation No Enemie*, even though it had been penned and published in Scotland. Found guilty of felony the same day, he was remanded to the King's Bench prison, and on 29 May was hanged at St. Thomas a Watering in Southwark.[23]

After Waldegrave had printed *Hay Any Worke for Cooper* late in March, he resigned his role as Martin's printer. Nevertheless, it is almost certain that he went to La Rochelle, worked at the shop of Les Haultin, printed Penry's *Appellation*, Throkmorton's *Master Some Laid Open*, and possibly his *A Dialogue. Wherin Is Plainly Laide Open*. Waldegrave left La Rochelle about the end of August 1589 and brought to Throkmorton's house at Haseley three or four consignments of books in September. He then departed for Edinburgh, where he arrived about November. On 13 March 1590 he received permission from "The Lordis of the Secreit Counsell" to print *The Confession of Faith Subscrived* [sic] *by the Kingis Majestie*, and on 9 October was appointed royal printer. During the year he printed thirteen books, including two books by Penry and one anonymous book, *An Humble Motion*. The last three books were without indication of place or printer and were offensive to the English ambassador. As early as April 1590 Ambassador Bowes had complained to Burghley that *Reformation No Enemie* had been printed "without the privity of the ministers," and on 20 November had informed the lord treasurer of his conference with James VI: "I shewed the king that it was marveiled in England . . . that Walgrave the printer might be permitted freelie to print seditiouse bookes against his native countrie of England, praieng . . . that Walgrave might be prohibited to exercise his science here, so appearantlie against the State of England." To this request the king and Sir John Maitland, chancellor and secretary of Scotland, replied that Waldegrave had admitted his mistake and that he had "entred into great bond with sufficient suretie in this towne, that he shall not hereafter imprint any thing without the allowance and warrant of the king first obtayned for the same." Furthermore, they added, Scotland needed a printer. It is possible that at this time Waldegrave gave a bond for his good behavior and also made a limited deposition of his faults, including his activities in La Rochelle, to which Dr. Matthew Sutcliffe, dean of Exeter, later alluded.

During the years 1592–94 the Scots made a concerted effort to obtain a pardon for Waldegrave. On 20 June 1592 James VI requested Lord Burghley to appeal to Queen Elizabeth:

The desire we have to releve Walgrave oure printer furth of his present conditioun moves ws to crave zoure favourable mediatioun for him to oure derrest suster the Quene zoure soverane . . . sa as he may have hir pardoun confirmed to him be write [by writing] . . . that he may the mair bouldly repair in his native cuntre as necesserly he sall have occasioun; and we undirtak and promiss for him that he sall wirk in his art na otherwyis then he salbe licensed be ws [by us], for quhilk he hes entered sufficient cautioun.

At the same time Alexander Hay, lord clerk register, also wrote to Burghley on Waldegrave's behalf, and in August Queen Anne made a further appeal to the lord treasurer and Elizabeth. No results followed these appeals. On 2 July 1593 Sir Robert Melville, former deputy chancellor of Scotland during James VI's trip to Denmark and Norway to meet his bride, petitioned Burghley "that His Majesty has given me command to crave pardon of Her Majesty for Waldegrave the printer." Unfortunately, in 1594, Waldegrave printed a book which displeased ambassador Bowes, who charged the king's printer "with his undutifulness in printing or publishing matter prejudicial to Her Majesty." Waldegrave readily admitted that he had printed a Latin book, *Principis Scoti-Britannorum Natalia*, which Andrew Melville, the rector of the University of St. Andrews, had penned, but he defended his action by insisting that he did so by royal command, that he did not understand Latin, and that he would not have printed the book had he realized that it would anger the queen.

Bowes informed Burghley that Waldegrave "seems very sorrowful for his fault," and "this error shall be a lesson to him in all times coming." Accepting Waldegrave's repentance, Bowes explained to James that Elizabeth and Burghley were offended because Melville had designated James as "King of all Britain in possession." The ambassador reminded the king that Elizabeth's "portion is the greatest part of Britain and his the less." James admitted that he had permitted Waldegrave to print Melville's work, but he confessed he had not read the book, and asserted that he did not "think that anything therein touched Her Majesty in any sort." He reminded Bowes that "being descended as he was, he could not but make claim to the crown of England after the decease of Her Majesty, who was well pleased to promise to him that upon his good behaviour towards her she would never hurt or impeach his title or right therein."

In December 1594 James once more urged Bowes to persuade Elizabeth to pardon Waldegrave. The English queen remained adamant, and Waldegrave remained in Scotland. During his thirteen years in Edinburgh, he printed about 120 books, more than the 88 books he printed in England from 1578 through 1589. In Scotland he reprinted books by William Perkins and Sir Philip Sidney, and had the satisfaction of printing Cartwright's long delayed book, *With God in Christ; The Answere to the Preface of the Rhemish Testament*, in 1602, shortly before Cartwright's death. Waldegrave also printed three of the best–known books of James VI: *Daemonologie, in Forme of a Dialogue* (1597); *The True Lawe of Free Monarchies* (1598); *Basilikon Doron* (1599, 1603). Upon the death of Queen Elizabeth on 24 March 1602/03 Waldegrave's exile of more than thirteen years came to an end. One of his last official acts was the printing of a proclamation announcing the accession of James VI to the throne of England. Waldegrave returned to London about May, but his new life in his own country continued for less than a year, since he died about January or February 1603/04.[24]

Part II

JOB THROKMORTON'S
LIFE AND
WRITINGS

"Who was Martin Marprelate? Not a trivial question, since the answer is the best English satirist before Dryden and Nashe's master in style." (John Carey's review, *Renaissance Quarterly* 20 [1967]: 375)

ONE EARLY CENTER of the Throckmorton family, which goes back at least to the thirteenth century, was in the parish of Fladbury, Worcestershire. In the sixteenth century an important branch of the Catholic Throckmortons was already established at Coughton, near Kenilworth, and a Protestant line was begun by Job's father, Clement, at Haseley, near Warwick. During the Tudor period the first prominent Throckmorton was Sir Robert, who died in 1519 on a pilgrimage to Jerusalem. His wife Katherine, daughter of William Marrowe, a lord mayor of London, lived on until 1571 when Job, her great grandson, was twenty-six years old.

Sir Robert's eldest son, Sir George, and his wife Katherine, daughter of Nicholas Vaux, lord of Harrowden, Northamptonshire, were the parents of nine sons and eight or nine daughters. Katherine was also the aunt of Katherine Parr, sixth wife of Henry VIII. Of the sons, the more prominent were Sir Robert, Sir Nicholas, an able diplomat, and Clement,

95

Job's father.[1] Sir Robert remained a Catholic, but Sir Nicholas became an ardent Anglican. He was an ambassador to the courts of France and Scotland, where he implemented the foreign policies of Elizabeth and Burghley. His son was Sir Arthur, Job's cousin, whose diary has been made available by A. L. Rowse in his *Ralegh and the Throckmortons* (1962), and his daughter was Elizabeth, who served as a lady-in-waiting to Queen Elizabeth and secretly married Sir Walter Raleigh about October 1591. Sir Nicholas had a younger brother John, who was a justice in Chester, a member of the Council of Wales, and an M.P. It was his son, Francis, also Job's cousin, who was executed in 1584 for his activities as a Catholic plotter in encouraging an invasion of England by Henry of Lorraine (1550–88), duke of Guise, and leader of the French Catholic forces in aiding his cousin, Mary Queen of Scots.[2]

Sir George's son, Clement, Job's father, was probably born in the 1520s. He participated in the capture of Boulogne in September 1544, became cupbearer to Queen Katherine Parr, his second cousin by half blood, and acquired considerable property during the 1540s and 1550s. When John Dudley, duke of Northumberland, was attainted and executed in 1553, his property reverted to the crown. Michael Throckmorton, Clement's uncle and secretary to Cardinal Reginald Pole, acquired the duke's property in Haseley, Warwickshire, and sold it to his nephew Clement about 1554. Clement became a member of the Merchant Adventurers Company of England in 1554/55, served as justice of the peace for Warwickshire, was employed in 1558/59 by the Privy Council to examine a complaint by the relatives of Bishop Nicholas Ridley against Edmund Bonner, bishop of London, and was appointed to the Court of High Commission in 1572. During the reign of Henry VIII Clement was a burgess in the parliaments of 1541/42 and 1545; in the reign of Edward VI he was in the parliaments of 1547 and 1553; in Mary's reign he was a member in 1553; and in the Elizabethan period he participated in the parliaments of 1559, 1562/63, 1571 (probably), and 1572: His absence from the later Marian parliaments reflected his protestant sympathies. Another indication of his Anglican views appeared in February 1554/55, when Thomas Hauckes was found guilty of nonconformity to the restoration of Catholicism in Mary's reign, and sentenced to death as a heretic. Clement promised Hauckes "to be a father and a wall of defence" for his son. After the burning of this protestant martyr at Coggeshall, Essex, on 10 June 1555, the son was delivered to Clement to be reared "in the fear of God and his laws."[3]

Clement's wife and Job's mother was Katherine Neville, the eldest daughter of Sir Edward, second surviving son of Sir George, who was second baron of Bergavenny. She was the great granddaughter of Sir Edward Neville, first baron of Bergavenny, who was the sixth and youngest son of Sir Ralph Neville, first earl of Westmorland.[4] Clement and Katherine were married probably about 1542, established a household with at least twenty servants, and reared a large family of seven sons and seven daughters, of whom Job was the eldest, born in 1545. Clement and Katherine were the founders of the protestant Haseley line of the Throkmortons, which continued in the male line to the great-great-grandsons in the period of Charles II. Job's six brothers were Josias, Jobe, Clement, Edward, Henry, and Kenelmus; his sisters were Frances, Martha, Katherin, Amphilis, Ursula, Suzann, and Martha (Mary?).[5]

Perhaps the strongest influence on Job's Puritanism came from his father, but the University of Oxford, which he entered in 1562, also strengthened his nonconformity. Although the University of Cambridge was reputed to be a stronger Puritan center in the 1560s, Oxford had Puritans in places of influence.[6] Laurence Humphrey, regius professor of divinity and president of Magdalen College, had been a Marian exile in Basel, Zurich, and Geneva, and was known to be a zealous anti-Romanist. Thomas Sampson, dean of Christ Church, and a militant reformer, had suffered exile at Strassburg and Geneva. At Oxford he refused to wear the required vestments and therefore was deprived of his deanship by the queen in 1565. Dr. William Cole, a Fellow and later president of Corpus Christi College, was a Marian exile who had come under the influence of Henry Bullinger and Rudolph Gualter, Reformed ministers at Zurich. John Field and Thomas Wilcox, authors of the provocative *Admonition to the Parliament* in 1572, whom Job later defended during their imprisonment, were Oxford students in the 1560s, and it is probable that their friendship began at the university. It is possible that Job first knew Eusebius Pagit as a chorister or scholar at Christ Church, who was twice deprived for nonconformity and was praised by Martin Marprelate. Ralph Warcuppe, with whom Throkmorton collaborated in 1583/ 84 in searching out and examining recusants, was a scholar at Christ Church from 1561 to 1565. Although unmentioned in Throkmorton's writings, Sir Thomas Bodley, founder of the Bodleian Library, may have crossed paths with Job, since Thomas received his B.A. from Magdalen in 1563 and his M.A. from Merton in 1566. As the son of John, a Marian exile, Thomas had listened to the lectures of Calvin and Théodore de Bèze in Geneva, and on his return had been instructed by the leading Calvinist professor of divinity, Dr. Humphrey.[7]

In addition to Humphrey, Sampson, and Cole, already mentioned as collegiate heads with nonconformist views, there were five other men of conformist outlook who were Job's contemporaries at Oxford, who later became collegiate administrators or vice-chancellors, and who were criticized in the writings of Martin and Throkmorton.[8] Nicholas Bond was a Fellow of Magdalen College from 1565 to 1575, president from 1589 to 1607, and vice-chancellor in 1589 and 1592.[9] Martin Colepepper or Culpepper, after receiving his B.A. in 1562 and his M.A. in 1566, was warden of New College from 1573 to 1599 and vice-chancellor in 1578. Thomas Cooper, Martin's bête noire, attended Magdalen College School and Magdalen College from 1531 to 1570, with some interruptions, as chorister, student, Fellow, and administrator. He received his B.D. and D.D. in 1567, acted as dean of Christ Church in 1567 and vice-chancellor in 1567–70. He became bishop of Lincoln in 1570/71 and bishop of Winchester in 1583/84. John Underhill secured his B.A. in 1564 at New College, became rector of Lincoln College, 1577–89, and bishop of Oxford, 1589–92. John Kennall, whom Martin satirized, was archdeacon of Oxford and vice-chancellor in the years 1564–67.[10] Martin's comments on these men reflect personal knowledge from his student days.

Among other prominent persons whom Throkmorton probably knew or heard of during his college years, and who were alluded to in his writings, mention may be made of five. Dr. John Day, Fellow and librarian of Magdalen College, and paramour of Mrs. Thomas Cooper, was a long-time resident of Oxford; he was a demy at Magdalen College School, 1544–51, Fellow at Magdalen College, 1551–86, proctor, 1559, D.C.L., 1579. In 1587 he became vicar-general to Thomas Godwin, bishop of Bath and Wells. Tobias Matthew, later accused by Martin of pluralism, received his B.A. degree in 1563/64 and his M.A. in 1566; then he served as president of his alma mater, St. John's College, 1572–77, vice-chancellor in 1579, and archbishop of York, 1606–28. Three well-known Roman Catholic students were contemporary with Throkmorton at Oxford. Edmund Campion, Catholic martyr, received his B.A. in 1561 and his M.A. in 1564/65. William Rainolds, of New College, brother of John, obtained his B.A. in 1563 and his M.A. in 1567. Gregory Martin, of St. John's College, principal translator of the first English version from the Vulgate, that is, the Rhemish New Testament of 1582, received his B.A. in 1560 and his M.A. in 1564.[11]

Job Throkmorton probably entered The Queen's College, Oxford, in 1562 at the age of seventeen.[12] During the two preceding decades the university had been adversely affected by the confiscation of the monasteries, the visitations of the colleges, and the vicissitudes involved in the religious changes during the reigns of Henry VIII, Edward VI, Mary, and Elizabeth. Enrollment had declined, resulting in a paucity of qualified Fellows and professors. During the first chancellorship of Sir John Mason, 1552–56, the departure of the Marian exiles and the persecution of the nonconformists had upset the fortunes of the university. Cardinal Reginald Pole, in whose favor Sir John resigned, acted as chancellor from 1556 to 1558, but was too busy with national affairs to give time to educational matters. Then Sir John was reelected in June 1559 and continued until 1564, when Robert Dudley, earl of Leicester, succeeded him. During his chancellorship until his death in 1588, significant changes occurred. In 1565 new university statutes prescribed that "a student in arts to qualify for a B.A. degree was to spend two terms (each of twelve weeks) over Grammar, four over Rhetoric, five over Dialectic, three over Arithmetic, two over Music. Some new books were recommended, but Aristotle's works remained imbedded in the foundations of Oxford studies."[13] Matriculation in the university from a college before the vice-chancellor became mandatory, and every student was required "to have a master or tutor in some college or hall."[14] Gradually the collegiate system in the sixteen colleges and eight halls was strengthened, individual instruction was encouraged, and "commoners," who paid fees according to their rank, were admitted in increasing number.

In 1564 approximately 1,200 students attended Oxford University, but The Queen's College was one of the smaller foundations with fifty-four residents, including a provost, ten Fellows, thirty "commoners," a chaplain, six "servientes" or "tabarders," and six "poor boys." During the period of transition from the Marian years through the first decade of Elizabeth's reign, major problems troubled the struggling college, such as religious differences, administrative inefficiency, and unethical practices. Hugh Hodgson, the first Elizabethan provost, 1559–61, either resigned or was deprived because of his religious scruples. Thomas Francis, 1561–63, lacking "statutable qualifications," was "by royal influence, intruded into the provostship," was opposed by some of the Fellows, and resigned. Lancelot Shaw, 1563–65, also withdrew because of accusations of "bad administration, waste of the College property, foul living, and resistance to the inculcation of good letters." Alan Scot, 1565–75, Senior Fellow in 1561, evidently inaugurated a stable period of tenure, continued by Bartholomew Bousfield, 1575–81, Henry Robinson, 1581–98, and Henry Airay, 1599–1616.[15]

After Throkmorton's graduation in February 1565/66, the records are silent on his activities for the next six years. It is likely that he spent his time at Haseley and London. Although his name does not appear in the admission records of the four Inns of Court, it is probable that he received some legal education, since his writings contain numerous legal allusions and phrases and indicate at least a general knowledge of the law befitting the son of a country gentleman and heir apparent to his father's estate. It is possible that he attended New Inn, an Inn of Chancery attached to Middle Temple, since his brother Josias attended New Inn about 1578 and transferred to Middle Temple in January 1579/80. Another brother, Clement, was admitted to Middle Temple in 1582, and Job's two sons were enrolled there, Clement in 1600 and Job in 1610.[16]

Throkmorton's writing career began in 1572 because of the publication in June of *An Admonition to the Parliament*, written by John Field and Thomas Wilcox.[17] When Cooper, bishop of Lincoln, preached a sermon against the *Admonition*, Throkmorton wrote a letter of protest, early in July, entitled, "An Answer to Certen Peeces of a Sermon Made at Paules Crosse on Sunday the xxvii[th] of June in Anno 1572." This was a sharp attack on the bishop as well as a denunciation of the liturgy, unscriptural clerical titles of dignity, and government of the Church of England.[18] In October Throkmorton's first printed work appeared, consisting of two treatises. The first, *An Exhortation to the Byshops to Deale Brotherly with Theyr Brethren*, was a plea for Christian treatment of Field and Wilcox, who had been imprisoned in "dreaded Newgate" as close prisoners. The second, *An Exhortation to the Bishops and Their Clergie*, was a request that the bishops publish an impartial and scholarly reply, based on scriptural arguments, to the *Admonition*. In October or November Throkmorton published *A Second Admonition to the Parliament*, commonly ascribed to Cartwright but actually written by the Haseley squire. It defended Field and Wilcox, denounced their imprisonment, and condemned the bishops. Since the first *Admonition* had emphasized the deficiencies of the church, the *Second Admonition* propounded specific suggestions for the reform of the Church of England. Appended to the *Second Admonition* was another treatise by Throkmorton, entitled: *Certaine Articles, Collected and Taken (as It Is Thought) by the Byshops out of a Litle Boke Entituled An Admonition to the Parliament, with An Answere to the Same. Containing a Confirmation of the Sayde Booke in Shorte Notes.* This book consisted of two parts: an Anglican treatise, entitled, "A Viewe of the Churche," which was a summary and criticism of the positions taken in *An Admonition.* The second part was Throkmorton's "A Reproufe of This Viewe," which answered seriatim the arguments in "A Viewe of the Churche."[19]

In June 1573 Throkmorton wrote an insulting letter, "A Friendly Caveat to Bishop Sands Then Bishop of London, and to the Rest of His Brethren the Bishops: Written by a Godly, Learned, and Zealous Gentleman, about 1567 [1573]."[20] By this time Field and Wilcox had already spent nine months in Newgate and three months in the custody of Archdeacon John Mullins. They had petitioned for complete liberty and had obtained a recommendation of favor from the Privy Council. Bishop Edwin Sandys complained to Lord Burghley that "the whole blame is layde on me for ther Imprisonment," and reported that Archdeacon Mullins desired to "be ridd of theym [because] ther is such resort unto theym." This situation was the occasion for Throkmorton's letter, which imperiously demanded the release of the prisoners and unmercifully berated Bishop Sandys.[21]

With the death of his father on 13 December 1573, Throkmorton became the lord of the manor at Haseley. For a decade he led the life of a country squire. Then on 13 January 1583/84 Throkmorton wrote a letter to Ralph Warcuppe, esquire and justice of the peace, who desired the collaboration of Throkmorton in executing an order from Robert Beale, secretary of the Privy Council, to apprehend William Skynner, search his house, and examine witnesses. Skynner was a staunch Catholic, who was suspected of harboring a Jesuit and defending the title of Mary Queen of Scots as the heir apparent to the English throne. Throkmorton's letter indicated his ardent anti-Catholic zeal and revealed his strong protestant inclinations. He reported that Skynner was "a perillous subjecte as any the Queen hathe of his coate, and hath ben a deadly enemye to the gospell and to the proceedinges thereof any tyme thease twenty yeare. The Lorde turne his harte or cutte him of[f] speedelye." Nine depositions of witnesses were enclosed with the letter. Throkmorton's frustration because of the reluctance of intimidated witnesses to testify was apparent from his report to Warcuppe:

> in the tryall whereof yow would not credyte what secrete laboring und[e]r hande and threatening of poore men there hath ben to keepe them from deposing their knowledge; men that promised mounteynes before hande have when yt camme to the pynche perfourmed but mole hills. O[u]r papistes heere are woondrous cunning, and frayle men without grace are easely corrupted. God be mercyfull unto us.[22]

In the autumn of 1586 Throkmorton decided to stand for election to Parliament as a burgess for Warwick. His decision perhaps was influenced by the example of his father, who had served in eight or nine parliaments from 1541/42 to 1572.[23] It is also likely he was incited by the Catholic conspiracy led by Anthony Babington during the summer of 1586 to assassinate Elizabeth and place Mary Queen of Scots on the English throne. Furthermore, John Field and other Puritans were making strenuous efforts to procure the election of "the best gentlemen of those places, by whose wisedome and zeale Gods causes may bee preferred."[24] The Parliament of 1584–86 had been prorogued until 14 November 1586, but it was suddenly dissolved on 14 September 1586, and a writ for a new election was issued on 15 September. The election campaign in October was turbulent and divisive. "Mr. Job Throkmorton made very great labor to many of the inhabitants of this borough for their voyces," though he was neither a burgess of the town nor a resident, as required by law.[25]

Supported by "the worst sort of the inhabitants," he was hastily sworn a burgess for Warwick, and despite the opposition of some of the principal burgesses and of John Fisher, the previous parliamentary incumbent in 1584–86, was elected to Parliament, which assembled on 29 October.[26]

This election was of sufficient importance to attract the interest of two leading modern historians. Sir John Neale discussed this Warwick election of 1586 wherein "religious zealots were putting forth their maximum efforts in a political campaign, the scope and organization of which seem astonishingly out of place in the sixteenth century."[27] Dr. J. H. Plumb, in an essay on "The Growth of the Electorate in England from 1600 to 1715," wrote:

> As we know, the Puritans had been exceedingly active in the elections for the Parliaments of the 1580s, and this is the decade when we get the first hints of appeal to a wider franchise in order to defeat the entrenched corporation oligarchies. In one case, Warwick, in 1586, a Puritan extremist, Job Throckmorton, forced his election by threatening to invoke the rights of the commonalty to vote.[28]

The three dominant issues debated by this sixth Elizabethan Parliament were the fate of Mary Queen of Scots, foreign policy, and religion, and Throkmorton delivered a speech on each subject.[29] Not one to hide his light under a bushel, this "freshman" legislator made an impassioned plea on 4 November, during his first week in Parliament, on the subject: "Againste the Scottishe Queene, That Shee Ought Not to Live: That Mercy in That Case is Both Dreadeful and Dawngerous." Some idea of the rhetorical and Marprelatian power of this turbulent Warwickshire squire may be seen in the following quotation:

> Yf I should tearme her the daughter of sedition, the mother of rebellion, the nurce of impietie, the handmaide of iniquitie, the sister of unshamefastenesse; or yf I should tell you that which you know allreaddye, that she is Scottishe of nation, French of education, papist of profession, a Guysian of bloude,

a Spaniarde in practize, a lybertyne in life: as all this were not to flatter her, so yet this were nothinge neere to dyscrybe her.

In the Parliament of 1572, as Throkmorton reminded the House of Commons, Elizabeth had granted mercy and clemency to Mary at the expense of instability and injustice. "It is now highe time for Her Majestie, I trow, to bee ware of lenitives and to fall to coresyves [corrosives] an other while and to launce an ynche deeper than ever shee did, yf shee meane to sitte quietly in her seate." Mary "ought in deed to dye the death," and Parliament must strengthen the hand of the queen.[30]

Throkmorton's second speech, "On the Low Countries," pertaining to foreign policy, was delivered on 23 February 1586/87. It was the longest of his three speeches, and was also the one to cause him the most trouble. He spoke sharply of Charles IX of France, "the same king that wept to the Admirall over night, and gave him up to the butcherye to bee cut in pieces in the morning." He castigated Catherine de Médicis and excoriated Philip II of Spain. This king "(howsoever hee holde there now by Stafforde law, as they say, that is, by the swoorde) hath in truth and equitie lost the right of his soveraignetye even by the judgment of the Catholykes themselves." He depicted Henry III of France as irresolute and uncertain, giddy and confused. He added: "Well, in whom ther is no religion, in him there is no trust: a Frenchman unreformed is as vile a man as lyves and no villeynye can make him blushe." Then he turned to James VI of Scotland:

Whether [whither] then shall wee cast our eye? Northewarde towardes the younge impe of Scotlande? Alas, it is a colde coast (ye knowe); and he that should sette up his rest uppon so younge and wavering a headde might happen finde colde comforte to[o], I tell yow. Yee knew his mother (I am sure), did ye not?

Elizabeth was in no mood to listen to criticisms of her fellow monarchs, and her government did not relish any upsetting of the delicate balance in foreign relations. As a result, Lord Chancellor Hatton rebuked Throkmorton, and Lord Burghley wrote an apologetic letter to the Scottish ambassador, Archibald Douglas, with the promise that Throkmorton would suffer imprisonment in the Tower for his irresponsible strictures.[31]

Throkmorton's third speech, "The Bill and Book," was delivered on 27 February 1586/87 after Sir Anthony Cope had introduced his revolutionary bill, together with a copy of the revised Genevan Prayer Book. This bill, which advocated the establishment of Presbyterianism in England, was a precursor of the "Root and Branch Bill" advocated in 1640–41. In effect, it proposed that Anglicanism be replaced by the reformed religion practiced in Scotland, La Rochelle, and Geneva; it also propounded that the Book of Common Prayer be supplanted by the Calvinist and Reformed *Booke of the Forme of Common Prayers*, and that the existing ecclesiastical courts and laws be nullified. Sir John Neale described the "Bill and Book" as "stark revolution. Its like was never seen before in English Parliament."[32] One of the staunch supporters of that revolution was Throkmorton, who was dead in earnest in his plea for Puritanism, and for freedom of speech in the House of Commons, and who was able to inject humor and irony into his speeches:

> This freedome of ours, as yt is now handeled heere amongst us, I can very well lyken to a certeine lycense graunted to a preachere to preache the gospell freely, provided allwayes that he medle neyther with the doctryne of the prophetes nor the apostles. Pardon mee (right Honorable), is not this, I praye you, the very image of our freedom in this House at this day? Ye shall speake in the Parleamente House freely, provided all wayes that ye medle neyther with the reformation of religion nor the establishment of succession, the verie pillers and grounde workes of all our blisse and happines, and without the which (let us solace our selves never soe much with songs of peace and all peace), dreadefull despayre will bee the end of our foolishe hope.[33]

Throkmorton made a strong plea for the elimination of the dumb (unpreaching) clergy and the establishment of a learned ministry. He also made a moving appeal for an understanding of Puritanism as an ethical label rather than an easy libel. With savage irony and deep frustration he declaimed:

> O mercifull God, into what lamentable dayes and times are we now fallen into? To bewayle the distresses of Gods children, it is Puritanisme. To finde faulte with corruptions of our church, it is Puritanisme. To reprove a man for swearing, it is Puritanisme. To banishe an adulterer out of the house, it is Puritanisme. To make humble sute to Her Majestie and the high courte of Parleament for a learned ministery, it is Puritanisme. Yea, and I feare me we shall come shortly to this, that to doe God and Her Majestie good service shalbe counpted Puritanisme.[34]

In the light of Throkmorton's denunciation of the bishops in 1588 and 1589, his criticism of the prelates in 1586–87 is illuminating. He asserted that since the clergy had failed to act on legitimate grievances, remedy should be sought not in Convocation but in Parliament. He warned that those who relegated religious issues to the "grave fathers" were remiss in their duty, and stated that "lamentable experience hath made us in a maner dispayre of any good successe from that coast; what wee may find of yt heereafter I know not, but hitherto wee may trewly say it hath been as a northern wynde that seldome bloweth good to the church of God."[35] By implication he indicted the queen, who quashed the radical proposals of the "Bill and Book" the very next day by demanding the delivery of this bill and Calvinist book to her at Greenwich.

During the next week Throkmorton fled Parliament to escape imprisonment in the Tower for his aspersions on monarchs. He went into hiding at his sister's home at Hillingdon, near Uxbridge, and kept out of range of the Privy Council.[36] On 3 April, after Parliament had adjourned, he sought to mitigate the queen's indignation toward himself by sending a petition to Lord Burghley. His letter was a model of brevity, suavity, and gentleness:

> May it please your Honor. To challenge any favor from your Lordship by deserte I can not: yet to dispayre of your favor

for all that I may not. The lesse deserte the more honor to yow. Neyther am I the first man, I know, by many a hundred, to whom yow have stoode an honorable frynde without cause.

After confessing his fault, Throkmorton minimized his guilt by characterizing his speech as rashness and "meere unadvys-ednesse." He then concluded: "for the which my humble sute is that your Lordship would vouchsafe me what favor yow may when yow see your tyme." Despite his efforts to obtain a pardon, Throkmorton did not receive Burghley's favor, and he never sat in the House of Commons again.[37]

Having failed to achieve his purposes in Parliament, Throkmorton began in earnest his literary campaign against the Church of England. During the years 1588–89 he wrote thirteen books, mostly against the archbishop, lordly prelates, deans, archdeacons, and the unlearned clergy. His first dialogue was published in April 1588, entitled, *The State of the Church of Englande, Laide Open*[38] *in a Conference betweene Diotrephes a Bishop, Tertullus a Papist, Demetrius an Usurer, Pandocheus an Inne-Keeper, and Paule a Preacher of the Worde of God.* Also known as a *Dialogue* or as *Diotrephes,* this book revealed irony and sarcasm, yet dealt *suaviter in modo, fortiter in re,* with some twenty-five favorite ideas and grievances of the author. Throkmorton depicted the Anglican Bishop Diotrephes as an insincere and scheming prelate whose hatred of the Precisians (Puritans) was emphasized. Tertullus the papist, who had become the confidant of Diotrephes, urged a relaxation of the laws against Catholics and recommended subtle tactics and devious procedures for curtailing Puritan influence. Diotrephes promised that incarcerated Catholics "shal have the best chambers in everye prison, and when anye Puritane falleth into our handes, you shal see him have the most stinck-ing place that can bee found" in the prison. This book at first enjoyed only a limited circulation, since many copies were confiscated in the printer's shop and burned, but it was reprinted in 1588 and 1593.[39] In the *Epistle* (page 13) Throk-morton was referring to his own book when he alluded to "the poore *Dialogue* that the bishops lately burned." This remark may indicate the natural indignation and frustration of an author whose book has been seized; it may also reveal one more incentive for launching the Marprelate attack.

In October 1588 Throkmorton's (or Martin's) first Marprelate book, the *Epistle*, was published at East Molesey; the *Epitome*, published at Fawsley, appeared in late November. About 26–28 January 1588/89 the third work, a broadside, known as the *Mineralls*, was printed at Coventry and the fourth Marprelate book, *Hay Any Worke for Cooper*, also printed at Coventry, was published in the latter part of March. Waldegrave printed all four works, but in April he departed for La Rochelle. With Penry and Newman as his agents, Throkmorton employed John Hodgskin and two assistants, Valentine Symmes and Arthur Thomlin. These men printed *Martin Junior* and *Martin Senior* in the latter half of July at the home of Roger Wigston in Wolston, Warwickshire. When the printers fled to Manchester on 29 July, they carried with them Throkmorton's lengthy manuscript of *More Worke for Cooper*. At Manchester on 14 August, after working for three hours, the printers were arrested by the earl of Derby's men, and their press, type, manuscript, and printed sheets were seized.[40]

Despite this disturbing development, which seemingly ended the Marprelate series, Throkmorton immediately began the writing of his *Protestatyon*, and in the period from 18 August to about 18 September completed the seventh Martinist book. The printing of the *Protestatyon* under adverse circumstances has long remained a mystery, but the work of John Dover Wilson and the discovery of new information in the Ellesmere Manuscripts clarify the problem. Throkmorton and Penry collaborated in obtaining necessary supplies. With the assistance of Grimston and Richard Holmes of Northampton, James Meddowes and Humphrey Newman, who brought from London to Wolston an iron frame, eight reams of paper, ink, and type, Throkmorton and Penry completed their preparation for the issuance of the *Protestatyon*.[41] They managed to print signature A, replete with mistakes such as overturned letters, wrong fonts, and misspellings, about 20 September. Then Waldegrave arrived with three consignments of books which had been printed during the summer at La Rochelle.[42] He probably was shocked or amused to see the bungling results in the first signature, but he assisted in the printing of the last three.[43] Essentially, the *Protestatyon* was a plea for the captured printers and a defiant challenge to the bishops, especially Whitgift, Aylmer, and Cooper. It also provided a brief summary of the contents of the captured manuscript, *More Worke for Cooper.*

This latter work had been written by Throkmorton in the period between March and July 1589, and was delivered to Hodgskin at Wolston on 25 July. After the seizure of this work at Manchester, as previously noted, the sheets and manuscript were brought to London where they were scrutinized by the committee of examiners appointed by the Privy Council, and later were carefully studied by Sutcliffe. According to Hodgskin, there was "an other copy of *More Worke for the Coop[er]*, which should serve them an other time; and that this was but the first p[ar]te of the sayd booke, the other p[ar]te being allmost as bigge agayne."[44] Unfortunately, neither the printed sheets nor the manuscript folios have ever been found.

One consignment of books which Waldegrave delivered to Throkmorton in September 1589, was *A Dialogue. Wherin Is Plainly Laide Open, the Tyrannicall Dealing of Lord Bishopps against Gods Children.* This was Throkmorton's second dialogue, written about April 1589, and printed in the summer by Waldegrave. Although not generally regarded as one of the Marprelate series, it should be, since it was written by the same author, and since its subject matter was mainly derived from the first four Marprelate works. The sources of this fascinating *Dialogue* and attribution of authorship are discussed in chapter six.

A second consignment of books which Waldegrave delivered to Throkmorton's home consisted of 600 copies of *Master Some Laid Open in His Coulers.*[45] This work was written in the winter of 1588–89 and was completed by the first week of April 1589. When Waldegrave departed from Haseley in

Easter week, 30 March–5 April, he possessed the manuscripts of Throkmorton's *Master Some Laid Open* and Penry's *Appellation*, which he hoped to print in the "West Countrye" and deliver to Haseley by Whitsuntide (18–20 May). Instead, he probably went to La Rochelle where he printed both books and delivered them in September to Throkmorton's home.[46] *Master Some Laid Open*, one of the most caustic books of the Elizabethan period, was a savage and satirical attack on Dr. Robert Some, and a refutation of Dr. Some's second *A Godly Treatise . . . After the Ende of This Booke You Shall Find a Defence of Such Points as Master Penry Hath Dealt against*, which had been published in September 1588. *Master Some Laid Open* was also a powerful and incisive defense of Penry and his teachings. Furthermore, as Throkmorton's longest work, 124 pages, it included unstinted praise for the doctrines of such Anglican Puritans as Laurence Chaderton, William Fulke, John Rainolds, Walter Travers, William Whitaker, and William Whittingham. Likewise, it included unrestrained criticism of the teachings of Dean Bridges, Dr. Cosin, Bishop Cooper, Dr. Perne, and Archbishop Whitgift—all favorite targets of the Haseley squire and Martin Marprelate. Reasons for attributing this book to Throkmorton are presented in chapter five.

Some time in the summer of 1589, Throkmorton completed another book, "Martins Interim, or a Briefe Pistle to the Cursed Prelates and Clergie." Since Humphrey Newman was unwilling to deliver the manuscript to the printers at Manchester in August, the work remained unprinted. Throkmorton later sent it to Penry and Waldegrave for printing in Edinburgh, but Waldegrave, who had printed in 1590 three books objectionable to the English ambassador, Robert Bowes, was unwilling or unable to print it because of its offensive character. When Penry's wife returned from Scotland by sea to England, it is probable that she brought her husband's papers in a chest. When the chest was seized in the London area about April 1593, the government acquired incriminatory papers that were used against Penry at his trial in May. It is probable that "Martins Interim" was in the chest, and it is certain that it was scrutinized by Dean Sutcliffe, who is our sole source for its contents.[47]

The last book which belongs to the Marprelate series, at least tangentially, is entitled *The Crops and Flowers of Bridges Garden*. It was written before Newman's testimony in July 1590, either in the autumn of 1589 or the winter-spring of 1589/90. According to Sutcliffe, the book was brought to Middelburg and printed there, presumably by Richard Schilders, the well-known Dutch printer of English nonconformist works. It is regrettable that the book is not extant, and one may only conjecture that it was seized by the customs authorities.[48] It is likely that the book was a continuation of Throkmorton's playful satire against the "dunce," the "patch," and the "quick-witted" Dean Bridges, as revealed in all the Marprelate books and especially in the *Epistle* and the *Epitome*. Thus came to an end the delightful and disturbing and dramatic series, beginning and ending with Dean Bridges, consisting of the familiar seven treatises, plus the second *Dialogue*, along with three non-extant works. If we include two other related books, the first dialogue—*The State of the Church of Englande*, and *Master Some Laid Open in His Coulers*—then we may say that Throkmorton produced thirteen books for his literary campaign against the hierarchy during 1588–89, but his three non-extant works never reached the public.

While Throkmorton was continuing his vendetta against the lord bishops, the net of evidence was closing in upon him. Since the testimony of Hodgskin, and especially that of Symmes and Newman in 1589–90, directly implicated the Haseley squire, he was indicted in the summer of 1590 by a grand jury at Warwick for "disgracing Her Majesties government, and making certaine scorneful and satyricall libells under the name of Martin." The jurors swore "that the bill of enditement was true" and the Assize judges "thought it worthy to be enquired of."[49] Therefore the cause was shifted to Westminster, and Throkmorton began to prepare for his arraignment. On 14 October 1590 he sought the aid of the highest legal official in the land, Lord Chancellor Hatton.

His petition, which revealed the same subtlety as found in his appeal to Lord Burghley in April 1587, acknowledged that he had already submitted himself to the archbishop of Canterbury and to the justices of Assize, Francis Gawdy and Edward Fenner, both judges of the Queen's Bench. He then submitted himself in all humility to Hatton "as the highest magistrate next under Her Majestie." Although Throkmorton pretended not to justify himself in all his actions, he tactfully suggested that he could sufficiently clear himself from the grand jury indictment. He gave no inkling that he had been indicted of felonious action which could have brought a death sentence, or that he had been accused of writing the Marprelate libels, of ridiculing the hierarchy, and of slandering the State. Furthermore, he downgraded his offenses by speaking of his "slipps and infirmityes," and craved vengeance on himself and his children if ever he entertained a felonious thought against the queen. The appeal was a clear illustration of Throkmorton's suave style, his clever approach, and his palliative equivocation.[50]

Since Throkmorton was in London intermittently from January to June 1591, his advice and collaboration were solicited by Edmund Coppinger, whose brother Ambrose had been an employee of Ambrose Dudley, the earl of Warwick. Edmund Coppinger was a naive Puritan visionary whom Throkmorton had first met at London in Hilary term 1590/91. Somewhat addicted to fasts, fervent prayers, extraordinary callings, and "phantasticall revelations," Coppinger was long on enthusiasm and short on common sense. He was also disturbed by the arrest of nine clergymen involved in the Puritan classis movement, distressed by their trial before the Court of High Commission and Star Chamber, and determined to promote innovations and ecclesiastical alterations. When Throkmorton visited Cartwright in the Fleet prison about March 1590/91, he related his encounter with Coppinger. Cartwright warned Throkmorton about Coppinger, whom he characterized as a man affected by "some crazing of the braine." In Easter term Coppinger visited Throkmorton, showed him various copies of letters he had written to

Lord Burghley, Ann Dudley, the countess of Warwick, and even to Queen Elizabeth, and warned him of "certaine horrible practices, treasons, and conspiracies intended against the Queene." Coppinger also prevailed upon Throkmorton to visit the lodgings of William Hacket, a self-proclaimed prophet, to partake in his prayers, and to meet Henry Arthington, another deluded reformer.[51] Throkmorton later described Hacket, "the very puffing and swellinge of his face, the staring and gogling of his eies, with his gahstlie [*sic*] countenance," and he likened his prayer to "the wildgoose chase, neither heade nor foote, rime nor reason."[52] When Coppinger solicited Throkmorton's collaboration in what would prove to be a fanatic and chimerical uprising, Throkmorton wrote a letter on 18 May 1591 to Coppinger:

> That course you speake of, intended by you, I was never, you know, in particular acquainted with, and therefore for me to like or dislike a matter I had no knowledge of, had bene, I take it, without ground or warrant. Onely I confesse I heard some buzzes abroad of a sole and singular course, that either you or some other, had plotted in his head, which was greatly feared, and condemned of the brethren. What that was, as I know not, so had I small reason to speake of it with prejudice. Onely I would wish you and all that beare good will to the holy cause, in this perillous age of ours, to take both your eies in your hands, as they say, and to be sure of your ground (and warrant) before you strive to put in execution.[53]

In the Easter term of 1591 (21 April–17 May) Throkmorton appeared in Westminster to answer the bill of indictment against him. He was accused of intermeddling in the Martinist books. He was charged with slandering the queen, the government, and the ancient orders of the kingdom, that is, the bishops in the House of Lords. He was also indicted for declaiming against the laws of the realm, for scoffing at matters of religion, and for libeling the clergy in a saucy and gibing manner. His case was deferred from Easter to Trinity term (4–23 June), and then the proceedings came to an end. We do not know all the reasons, but we have hints. His indictment was contested for lack of proper form, evidently a legal technicality. He had mollified the archbishop, the lord chancellor, and the judges of Assize by his letters of submission. By the importunity of friends he had obtained the special favor of Lord Hatton. Above all, the queen, who "had winked at so many lewd pranks of his," extended her clemency. It is likely that she remembered the kindness of Queen Katherine Parr, her stepmother, who was a friend and second cousin of Job's father Clement. It is possible that Elizabeth Throkmorton, Job's cousin, exerted influence, since she was one of the queen's ladies-in-waiting and still in favor at the court prior to her secret marriage to Sir Walter Raleigh.[54] Many friends regarded Martin Marprelate with amazement and amusement, as a gifted writer who knew how to tell humorous stories and keep the clergy in check. Peter Wentworth had suffered for discussing the liberties of the House of Commons and the succession problem, and John Stubbs had encroached on the queen's marriage diplomacy, but Throkmorton had provided mirth for the kingdom. Consequently, Throkmorton was neither arraigned nor pardoned after 1591 but was kept dangling on the hook. When pursuivants sought him at Haseley, he discreetly kept out of the way, thus avoiding taking his proffered oath that he was not Martin.

Despite his legal problems, Throkmorton regarded himself as innocent. Instead of reassessing his views and actions, he continued his opposition to the Church of England. Some indication of his defiant and flippant attitude is revealed in a letter he wrote to Penry at Edinburgh, as reported by Sutcliffe:

> O Sir (saieth he), hath not her Majestie raigned prosperously, and is it a time, thinke you, to alter all these, and so many blessings bestowed upon us: to raise turmoiles, and innovations, and to pull the crowne off her head? Well, your Worship (saieth he, meaning Penrie) will not meddle with any of these kind of seditious people. He doth also certifie him of Udals, Cartwrights and others imprisonment, and of the taking of the presse and copie of *More Worke* in Lancashire, by the noble earle of Darbie; for so he writeth in scorne of his lordship,

as the circumstance of the place declareth. He signifieth unto him further, that the Printers then taken had confessed, that Martin was made by Penrie and one of the Throkmortons. In the latter ende hee writeth, that her Majestie had lately bene in danger of poisoning, and that other shrewd plots had bene laied against her, and all by Penry[!].

Then Sutcliffe commented: "Great pitie it is, seeing the man is so busie, that he is not called to render a reason of these sayings."[55]

Throkmorton was unhappy with the course of events in 1590–92, as church and State sharpened their attacks against the Presbyterians. In 1590 the Puritan classis movement was effectively curbed, when nine presbyterian leaders, including Cartwright and Edmund Snape, a prominent clergyman from Northampton, were imprisoned. A year later the Hacket-Coppinger-Arthington uprising damaged the presbyterian cause. In 1590–91 an important anti-presbyterian book was published, first in Latin and then in English, *Of the Diverse Degrees of the Ministers of the Gospell*, written by a learned Reformed professor of Leyden who had migrated to England, Hadrian Saravia. Matthew Sutcliffe's book, *A Remonstrance*, a hard-hitting refutation of Udall's *Demonstration of Discipline*, appeared in 1591, and in the same year two editions of the same author's *A Treatise of Ecclesiasticall Discipline* were published. This book was an attack on the entire system of presbyterian polity and discipline. In 1591 Dr. Cosin published *An Apologie: of, and for Sundrie Proceedings by Jurisdiction Ecclesiasticall*, a learned defense of the jurisdiction, powers, and proceedings of spiritual courts and of the ex officio oath, against the views of Robert Beale, Humphrey Davenport, Francis Knollys, James Morice, Thomas Norton, and Throkmorton. Cosin also published in 1592 *Conspiracie, for Pretended Reformation: viz. Presbyteriall Discipline*, a detailed exposé of the Hacket-Coppinger-Arthington conspiracy, in which the author revealed some implicating letters between Coppinger and Throkmorton.[56] Also in 1592, as a complement to his attacks on presbyterian polity, Sutcliffe published his *M. Sutliuii de catholica, orthodoxa, et vera Christi ecclesia libri duo*, which was a defense of the Church of England.

In the summer of 1592 an anonymous book was printed by Richard Schilders in Middelburg, entitled, *A Petition Directed to Her Most Excellent Majestie, Wherein Is Delivered 1. A Meane Howe to Compound the Civill Dissention in the Church of England. 2. A Proofe That They Who Write for Reformation, Doe Not Offend against the Statute of 23 Elizabeth, c. [2] and Therefore till Matters Bee Compounded, Deserve More Favour.*[57] The author insisted that writers of presbyterian books were not defamers of the queen and were not guilty of fomenting rebellion. He presented the true beliefs of "Seekers of Reformation" and charged that the Church of England violated its own statutes, canons, injunctions, advertisements, and ordinals. He also added "Certaine Questions," consisting of forty-three ensnaring interrogatories needing resolution. The writer stated: "I doe not nowe write eyther to pull downe bishopprickes, or erect presbyteries. With whom the trueth is, I will not determine. For I knowe not. What seemeth most probable and true to me that I knowe."[58] This was a specious assertion to give the appearance of impartiality, since the entire book of eighty-three pages was a strong plea for a reformed church on the presbyterian model. The author adduced a wide array of patristic writers, Continental and English divines, to buttress his arguments. His suggestion of a "meane howe to compound the civill dissention in the Church of England" was embodied in his advocacy of a national or provincial synod to discuss reform, episcopal policy, and ecclesiastical polity, with the stipulation that the synodal discussion be published and that Her Majesty, the Parliament, and the Privy Council, not the Convocation, be judges. *A Petition* was essentially an apologia by Throkmorton, who defended himself against some of the counts in his indictment, such as slandering the queen, ridiculing the bishops, deriding the magistrates, and undermining the laws of the kingdom. The book was also a defense of John Udall, with implied criticism of his judges and the prosecutor, James Dalton.[59]

Throughout the treatise the style was partly modified to give the impression of equity and objectivity. The customary sharp language was blunted, the alliteration was reduced, the flippant aspects were eliminated, and the indignation was restrained in accordance with the literary fiction that the writer was petitioning Her Most Excellent Majesty. Nevertheless, there are clear indications of Throkmorton's and Martin's pen. He strikes at his familiar adversaries, such as Bancroft, Bridges, Cooper, Cosin, and Whitgift, in words reminiscent of his criticisms in his earlier writings. He refutes Dr. Sutcliffe, a civilian, who became dean of Exeter in 1588, and who as apologist for the Church of England began publishing his numerous and learned books in 1590/91.[60] Throkmorton misquotes Aylmer's *An Harborowe* in a passage which seems to be derived from the same misquotation in the *Epitome* (D4 v).[61] Sensitive to criticism for using such phrases as "twentie fistes about his eares," or "an hundred thousande handes to this supplication . . . would strike a great stroke," the author justifies these words as "tropologicall or metaphorical speach without intendement of anie harme"; God forbid that they "should come within the compasse of treason or rebellion." He discusses his own humorous views on the "Bishops English," or episcopal doubletalk, and how the bishops "pervert by sinister exposition the ordinarie proprietie of our English phrase." He pounces on a small error by Dr. Cosin, even as he had gloated over picayunish errors of Bridges and Cooper. Also, as in the last three Marprelate books, he scorns the anti-Martinist libels, especially *Martins Months Minde* and *An Almond for a Parrat*, which had been published after the Martinist series had been terminated.[62]

Other indications of Martin's and Throkmorton's pen recur in the author's listing of specific prisons (page 76), his familiar boast of the "uprightnesse of myne owne conscience" (page 59), his allusions to the writings of William Tyndale, Robert Barnes, John Hooper, and Hugh Latimer (pages 35, 76), and his frequent references to statutes.[63] His belief that the bishops should not be regarded as one of the three estates (page 17) is related to his assertion that "the lawes of Englande have bene made, when there was never a bishop in the Parliament, as in the first yere of Her Majestie." In his criticism of card playing as an "unlawfull game," though shooting was deemed an honest recreation (page 67), we find an echo of his denunciation of William Chaderton, bishop of Chester, for playing primero, an "unlawfull game" (related to modern poker), though shooting allegedly was permissible.[64] Throkmorton's interest in Robert Cawdrey's appearance before Bishop Aylmer and the Court of High Commission (page 24) is also indicated in the *Mineralls*, nos. 8, 22. His use of a dozen Latin expressions and his resort to alliteration, such as "professe and protest," or "manifolde miseries and molestations" (pages 14, 15, 57) reveal his old habit. His denunciation of the state of bishops replays an old refrain.[65]

There are some parallels in *A Petition* with expressions found in other Throkmorton writings and in Martin's books:

vos autem non sic (pp. 9, 45)
inter vos autem non sic (*Certaine Articles*, in Frere and Douglas, *Puritan Manifestoes*, p. 141)

a marprince, a marlawe, a marstate, and mar-all (p. 14)
Mar-prince, Mar-law and Mar-state (*Hay Any Worke*, p. 19)

whom can they flie unto (p. 14)
to flye unto your Lordship ("Petition to Lord Hatton"; P.R.O., 30/15/124; now in Lambeth Palace Library)

seekers of reformation (pp. 16, 18, 19)
seekers of reformation (*Epistle*, p. 2)

Christ knowinge the bondes of his calling, would not medle with externe pollicie, etc. (p. 8)
But Christ knowing the bounds of his office, would not meddle with externe pollicies (*Epitome*, D4)

Divines me thinkes by this example should not give them selves too much the bridle, and too large a scope to meddle too farre with matters of pollicie (p. 8)
Divines (me thinkes) should by this example, not give themselves too much the brydle, and too large a scope, to meddle with matters of pollicie (*Epitome*, D4)

[In these two last parallels, Throkmorton may be quoting from Aylmer's *An Harborowe* directly, or from his own *Epitome*, D4]

About December 1592 Sutcliffe published his refutation of *A Petition*, which he entitled, *An Answere to a Certaine Libel Supplicatorie, or Rather Diffamatory, and Also to Certaine Calumnious Articles, and Interrogatories.* Whereas *A Petition* contained eighty-three pages, Sutcliffe's book, with 230 pages, was more than twice as long. In addition to a refutation of the five sections of *A Petition*, it contained a list of fifty-seven "strange opinions" of the Presbyterian reformers, and concluded with a list of ninety-five captious questions, which offset Throkmorton's forty-three entrapping queries. Whereas Dr. Cosin had named Throkmorton as one involved in correspondence with Coppinger, Dean Sutcliffe queried "whether Job Throkmorton was not well acquainted with Hacket, Copinger, and Arthingtons intentes," and also "whether he be not an abettor, and concelour of their trecherous practises." To support his insinuation, Sutcliffe printed eighteen lines of Throkmorton's letter to Coppinger of 18 May 1591. He went a step further when he asked whether all of Throkmorton's "Libels, and scoffes published under the name of Martin, as namely his theses, protestations, dialogues, arguments, laying men out in their colours, and all his doings tending to the advauncement of the holy cause, as they call it, did not tend wholly to an insurrection."[66] In effect, he accused Throkmorton of writing three Marprelate books and three related works.

Sutcliffe's capable refutation of *A Petition* strengthened the Anglican position. In 1592/93 the Church of England received further support by the publication in March of the first four books of Richard Hooker's magisterial and judicious work, *Of the Lawes of Ecclesiasticall Politie*, which examined critically the main Presbyterian arguments, and which still retains a high place in literature and in cultural history, as well as in theology and church government.[67] In the same year Dr. Thomas Bilson, warden of Winchester College, a learned and deeply read divine who became bishop of Worcester in 1596 and of Winchester in 1597, produced *The Perpetual Governement of Christes Church*, with special attention to the Jewish, New Testament, and apostolic background, and to the patristic and early conciliar periods. He also contributed in 1593 *A Compendious Discourse Proving Episcopacy to Be of Divine Institution*. Bilson subordinated the role of lay elders to that of ordained clergy; unlike Jerome, he denied the parity of presbyters and bishops; like Saravia, he supported degrees or grades in the ministry; unlike Throkmorton, he justified the right of the patron on financial grounds to present clerics to livings and the power of Christian princes to nominate bishops. He also affirmed the offices of metropolitans and primates on the basis of historical development and practical necessity.

Less learned but more interesting and more damaging to the presbyterian cause were two books published anonymously in 1593, written by Dr. Bancroft. The first, *A Survay of the Pretended Holy Discipline*, was a denunciatory and historical treatise against the "English Genevaters" and their platform of government. Writing under the conviction that "to acquaint you with their discipline, is to overthrow it," Bancroft criticized Calvin and de Bèze, and derided their English followers such as Cartwright, Travers, Barrow, and Martin Marprelate for curtailing the role of the queen in ecclesiastical affairs, for misinterpreting the Scripture, and for misquoting the fathers of the early church. The second work, *Daungerous Positions and Proceedings*, published in the latter half of 1593, carried two running titles: "English Genevating for Reformation" and "English Scottizing for Discipline." Its purpose was to examine the diverse beliefs held by the reformers and to expose those zealots mainly responsible for introducing presbyterian discipline under the guise of reformation. Bancroft recounted presbyterian proceedings in Geneva, Scotland, and England. On the basis of Star Chamber records, he revealed for the first time the clandestine activities within the English classes or presbyteries. With the help of Dr. Cosin's *Conspiracie*, he documented the correspondence of Coppinger with English Puritans. Somehow, Bancroft had managed to obtain some of Field's correspondence from his study, and he referred at least sixty-one times to letters and reports sent to this Puritan leader and co–ordinator. He quoted from Throkmorton's *A Petition* three times, and he referred four times to *A Dialogue. Wherin Is Plainly Laide Open* "that came from Throgmorton." Also, he alluded fourteen times to Marprelate's writings.[68]

Partly to counterbalance the Anglican publications, a significant Puritan work appeared in 1593, *A Parte of a Register*, of 644 pages (iv-546–94), containing thirty-three items, with ten subdivisions. Many of the items were from manuscript sources, such as letters, questions, reports of examinations, petitions, complaints, and answers. These probably were quarried from Field's vast corpus of documents, although most of the material remained unpublished, as is apparent from the huge volumes A, B, C, which constitute the "Seconde Parte of a Register," preserved today in Dr. Williams's Library. There were twelve items from printed sources, approximating two-thirds of the book. Of these, two were reprints of Anthony Gilby's items, one of a letter by James Pilkington, bishop of Durham, two of Fenner's books incompletely, one of Udall's *Demonstration of Discipline*, and six anonymous items. Of the anonymous items, *The State of the Church of Englande* was written by Throkmorton, and *A Defence of the Reasons of the Counter-Poyson, for Maintenance of the Eldership*, usually wrongly attributed to Fenner, was probably by Throkmorton. In addition, one manuscript item, Throkmorton's "A Friendly Caveat to Bishop Sands Then Bishop of London," appeared in print for the first time. It has been conjectured with some plausibility that Lady Ann Bacon, mother of Francis and a fervent Puritan, aided financially in the publication of *A Parte of a Register*, and the inclusion of three items by Throkmorton suggests the possibility of his collaboration.[69]

Dr. Bancroft referred to this volume as follows:

> And now it seemeth, for feare that any of all their sayd Libels and rayling Pamphlets, (that have bin written in her highnesse time) should perish, (being many of them but triobolar chartals [worthless libels]:) they have taken upon them to make a *Register:* and to Print them altogether in Scotland, in two or three volumes: as it appeareth by a part of the sayde *Register*, all

ready come from thence, and finished: which containeth in
it three or foure and forty of the sayd Libels.[70]

The difficulty with this observation is that only one volume
appeared, and that it was not printed in Scotland by the
"old servant Waldgrave," as Bancroft implied, but was
printed in Middelburg by Richard Schilders.[71]

The attacks of Cosin, Sutcliffe, and Bancroft infuriated
Throkmorton, who issued a reply in the guise of a letter
written supposedly to a noblewoman, a lady of honor. This
response, entitled *The Defence of Job Throkmorton, against the
Slaunders of Maister Sutcliffe, Taken out of a Copye of His Owne
Hande as It Was Written to an Honorable Personage*, printed
by Richard Schilders at Middelburg in 1594 or 1594/95, was
the only one of his nineteen books that carried his name.
Throkmorton was irritated because Cosin and Bancroft had
revealed his correspondence with Coppinger, and he was
incensed because Sutcliffe had implied that he was guilty
of misprision of treason in not divulging his knowledge of
the Coppinger-Hacket-Arthington conspiracy. Sutcliffe had
also alleged that Throkmorton had "concurred in making
of Martin," and that he had written at least six libels, and
that his "manifolde lewde demeanours, and trecheries"
tended "wholy to an insurrection."[72]

Throkmorton's *Defence* was a stinging reply to Sutcliffe,
a kind of personal vendetta against the dean of Exeter. It
is remarkable that Throkmorton expended the entire treatise
in maligning Sutcliffe, belittling Coppinger, ridiculing
Hacket, and extenuating his own association with the conspirators. Inasmuch as he had not participated in this fanati-
cal enterprise, he was on safe ground in denying any role
therein and in projecting his inflated sense of righteous indignation. But what is especially significant is that he evaded
the substantive issue of writing the Marprelate books. In a
treatise of thirty-nine pages he devoted less than one page
to this topic. Somewhat recklessly, he asserted that Sutcliffe
might as well accuse him of writing all the Marprelate books
instead of one. By distorting Sutcliffe's accusation, he agreed

that he was merely a "candle-holder" to John Penry, John Udall, and John Field, "and no more in deede I am not, in regard of some of those Reverend men." He never mentioned that he was also a "pen-holder" and a "purse-holder," nor did he explain his role as a "candle-holder." Instead, he stigmatized Sutcliffe as an eagle-eyed "censurer of other mens labours," as an infamous slanderer in whose writings were revealed "the very sting and venime of the hart," and "the gall and vineger of his penne."[73] Enraged at Sutcliffe's strictures against Cartwright, Udall, and Stephen Egerton, the influential pastor at Blackfriars, Throkmorton wrote a devastating reply:

> Yet me thinkes it were much fairer play and an evener course, a great deale, to cleare them of treason first, and then to tender them the chalendge and disputation afterwardes, than thus to throw out the guantlet and chartell of defiance with one hande, and to shake the halter and shewe the hatchet with the other, or rather in plaine tearmes to doo what in him lieth to cut in sunder their windpipe first, and then to aske them why they whoppe not or lewre not afterward [lewre— cry, shout].[74]

Throkmorton also quoted the admonition of Richard Hooker to his "deere brethren": "To lay aside the gall of that bitternesse wherein their [your] mindes have hitherto over abounded, and with meekeness to seeke [search] the trueth, etc." Although Hooker's admonition was specifically directed to the Puritan advocates of the "Lords Discipline" and the "holy cause," Throkmorton implied that Hooker did "levell at his brother Sutcliffe above others," and promised Hooker, "or to anie man living of his complexion, that if among all those that have hitherto sued for reformation, he can picke me out but one that is comparable to Maister Sutcliffe, in that sea of bitternesse, and overflowing of the gall he speakes of, I wil forthwith yeeld him the bucklers, and passe him my recantation under seale."[75]

Throkmorton's offer to exonerate himself by an oath was hedged about with equivocation. He said he would willingly take an oath "whensoever it shall be thought so good by the State," by which he meant "before the Court of Parliament or the lordes of Her Majesties Privy Council." But he was not willing to swear that he had played no part in the writing of the Marprelate books, that he had nothing to do with financing, publishing, and distributing the books. Even the proffered oath was suspect: "I am not Martin [I am Job Throkmorton]. I knewe not Martin [he is a literary figment and not a person, even as his sons Martin Junior and Martin Senior were imaginary persons]. And concerning that I stande endighted of, I am as cleare as the childe unborne" [I never slandered the queen, but I did the State good service by exposing the bishops' wicked actions].[76]

On 19 April 1595 Sutcliffe received a copy of Throkmorton's *Defence*, and about four months later published his *An Answere unto a Certaine Calumnious Letter Published by M. Job Throkmorton*, dedicated to Sir Edmund Anderson, chief justice of the Court of Common Pleas. Whereas Throkmorton's *Defence* consisted of thirty-nine pages, Sutcliffe's *Answere*, which reprinted *in toto* the *Defence*, extended to 180 pages. Sutcliffe usually printed two or three paragraphs of Throkmorton's work and then replied in two or three pages of refutation. Also, he included a series of short marginal notes, sometimes ten to fifteen per page, totaling about 630 crisp, caustic, and curt retorts. His purpose was fourfold: to defend himself against Throkmorton's aspersions; to refute and deflate the Haseley squire; to indicate that Throkmorton was a consort of Coppinger and Hacket, an abettor of their treasonable practises, and a concealer of their treacherous plans; to prove that he was the writer and publisher of the Martinist libels.

Throkmorton had made the impudent assertion that "M. Sutcliffe himselfe (for anie thing he [Throkmorton?] knowes) was full as guiltie, and everie way as accessarie to those conspiracies, as he." To this preposterous charge, Sutcliffe replied that he never knew Hacket, never prayed with him, never received treasonable letters from Coppinger, and never had concealed himself when the uprising began.[77] He also retorted that Throkmorton's mistitled book should really be entitled: *A Defence of Throkmorton and Others, Together with a Bundle of Ridiculous and Slanderous Accusations against Matthew Sutcliffe.* Since Throkmorton had cavalierly accused Sutcliffe and Dr. Cosin of having printed his letter to Coppinger of 18 May 1591 "by patches and pieces with so many etcaeteraes," by dismembering, altering, mangling, "overstrayninge some wordes too," "renting one clause from another," Sutcliffe exposed Throkmorton's bluff by printing the complete letter.[78]

Resentful of Throkmorton's derision of his own labors, Sutcliffe answered that he was a busy servant of the queen, but that Throkmorton was "like a horse-leech living on the blood and sweate of others; and a man that taketh delight in writing of libels, and slaunderous and ribauld-like letters, and spreading of newes, and furthering of new devises, than in any service in the church or common wealth. But if he take to himselfe ease at home, and libertie to slugge [loaf] and loytre, like a swine in his cote, let him not calumniate others industry that travaile and serve Her Majestie abroad."[79] Sutcliffe stigmatized Throkmorton as an opinionative and dull makebate [troublemaker], ill equipped to engage in verbal combat, since he lacked intelligence and learning, and since his venomous tongue was biforked. Reminding him that he still remained under indictment for meddling in the Martinist books "and for slandering Her Majestie," the magistrates, and the clergy, Sutcliffe scorned Throkmorton's hypocrisy in justifying himself before an Honorable Lady; "he must appeare at the Bench, not declame from his alebench, and be acquited by twelve men, and not one woman."[80] His writings were merely a gallimaufry of kitchen rhetoric, ribaldry, scurrility, and malice. "Consider, I pray you, his satyricall epistles and treatises set foorth under divers counterfeit names, and marke his scurrilous scoffes and bitter invectives, his dog-rhetorike, and his fierie and vulcanical satyrs, his gunpowder libels printed by the gunpowder man" [John Hodgskin]. He then continued with a powerful and stinging indictment:

Forgetting the matter hee hath in hand, hee holoweth, shout-
eth, and whoopeth like a man of Bedlem, and crieth, so, ho,
ho. Forgetting himselfe, he falleth in scorning, with termes
unwoorthie to be spoken, or written. What should I speake
of his malicious railing against many honest men, that never
thought him hurt? He spareth none. Both the queene and the
lordes, and the judges, feele the smart of his stinging and malicious tongue.[81]

Retaliating for Throkmorton's invective, Sutcliffe inveighed
against Throkmorton as a snake, "a counterfeit Scoggin,"
whose "braine and wit had taken cold," whose mother had
"cursed him bitterly," one whom creditors would not "trust
on his bond." He charged that when Throkmorton was a
burgess in Parliament in 1586/87, he had escaped imprisonment for his intemperate speech by hiding at Hillingdon.
Although he said he was ready to take an oath that he was
not Martin, "yet Her Majesties messengers say, he is not
very ready, for as oft as he was sought for to that purpose,
he hid his head and lay like Saturne *in Latio*, lurking, and
would not come forth."[82]

Sutcliffe was specific in accusing Throkmorton of writing
the Martinist books. Whereas Throkmorton expended less
than one page on his Marprelate involvement, Sutcliffe concluded with twenty-four pages of significant evidence pertaining to this accusation. He adduced detailed proof of
Throkmorton's authorship of *Hay Any Worke, More Worke
for Cooper, Martin Junior, Martin Senior, Master Some Laid Open
in His Coulers, The Crops and Flowers of Bridges Garden*, and
"Martins Interim"; he also referred to Throkmorton's *Protestatyon*, his dialogues, epistles, and libels.[83] Therefore Sutcliffe's *Answere* constitutes one of the best sources for
Throkmorton's authorship of Martinist books, since he had
access to all pertinent documents, some of which have disappeared; since he based his conclusions on ten depositions
of important Martinist collaborators—cited thirty-eight
times; and since he alone had studied or discussed Throkmorton's non-extant works, *More Worke for Cooper*, "Martins In-

terim," and *The Crops and Flowers of Bridges Garden.* Whereas Throkmorton's *Defence* was clever, amusing, evasive, and digressive, Sutcliffe's *Answere* was substantial, learned, pertinent, and systematic.

One would expect that Throkmorton's *Defence* and Sutcliffe's *Answere* would conclude their four-year feud, but the controversy continued for one more year. In four previous books, Sutcliffe had attacked Throkmorton's friends, such as John Udall and especially Thomas Cartwright. Therefore, in 1596 Cartwright published *A Brief Apologie of Thomas Cartwright against All Such Slaunderous Accusations as It Pleaseth Mr. Sutcliffe in Severall Pamphlettes Most Injuriously to Loade Him with,*[84] in which he replied to nine of Sutcliffe's allegations, including the assertion that "Mr. Cartwright upon the comming forth of Martin is reported to have saied that it was no matter, if the Bishops were so handled, seeing they would take no warning."[85] What is pertinent is that the introductory epistle, "To the Reader," was written by Throkmorton, who defended Cartwright and requited old scores by deriding Sutcliffe as one who dealt in reproaches, slanders, and falsehoods.[86] Sutcliffe quickly retaliated with *The Examination of T. Cartwrights Late Apologie* (1596), in which he alluded to Throkmorton's preface and criticized Cartwright for utilizing such "a lewde and foule mouthed proctor to plead in commendation of his innocencie and patience." Thus ended Throkmorton's five-year conflict with the dean of Exeter and also his twenty-four-year battle with the bishops and the Church of England.

There are glimpses of Throkmorton during the last four years of his life. Among the manuscripts of W. Bromley-Davenport, esquire, M.P., formerly at Baginton Hall in Warwickshire, there is a document listed for 4 March 1597 [1597/ 98?] indicating that John Weale had "given, granted, and assigned to Job Throckmorton of Haseley, in the county of Warwick, esquire, and to his heirs for ever, all his right, etc., in a certain cottage or tenement, with the appurtenances in Haseley aforesaid, wherein one William Shakespeare now dwelleth."[87] Another impression of Throkmorton's last days, however, is an illusion. In his *D.N.B.* article on Throkmorton, Sir Sidney Lee reported that near the end of his life Throkmorton suffered from a consumption and a morbid anxiety concerning his soul. Desiring the spiritual ministrations of John Dod, "Decalogue Dod" and reputed author of the "Sermon on Malt," Throkmorton moved to Canons Ashby, Northamptonshire. Allegedly, "for thirty-seven years he sought in vain a comfortable assurance of his salvation, but secured it within an hour of his death." The implication that Throkmorton vainly sought salvific assurance from his university years to his death, 1564–1601, does not befit the self-assured and conceited country gentleman and belies his life and writings. John Dod did not go to Canons Ashby until about 1611, a decade after Throkmorton's death. Furthermore, the "Throgmorton" involved was "a pious and painfull Preacher of the Word," who died in 1628 or 1637.[88] A more realistic view of Throkmorton within three months of his death is given in "The Diary of an Elizabethan Gentlewoman," written by Margaret Hoby, wife of Sir Thomas Posthumous Hoby. She recorded that Throkmorton visited her on 4 and 6 December in London, probably at the home of her brother-in-law, Sir Edward Hoby, who was a colleague of Throkmorton in the Parliament of 1586/87.[89] About two and a half months later Throkmorton died and was buried in the Haseley churchyard on 23 February 1600/01.

Job married Dorothy, daughter of Thomas Vernon and Ellenor Shirley of Hownell or Houndhill, Staffordshire. She was the great-great-granddaughter of John Talbot, second earl of Shrewsbury.[90] Their oldest son was Clement, born about 1581. At the age of fifteen he enrolled as a pensioner at Emmanuel College, Cambridge, a newly established Puritan institution whose master was Laurence Chaderton, personally selected by the founder, Sir Walter Mildmay. In 1598 Clement migrated to The Queen's College, Oxford, where he was permitted to count eight terms from Emmanuel. He received his B.A. in 1599, and then entered Middle Temple in 1600.[91] In 1601, with the death of Job, he became the heir to the Haseley property and lord of the manor. Early in the reign of James I he was knighted. William Dugdale, distinguished antiquarian and historian, characterized him as "a Gentleman not a little eminent for his learning and eloquence, having served in sundry Parliaments as one of the Knights for this shire [Warwickshire], and undergone divers other publique imployments of note."[92] In 1610, when Francis Holyoke published *A Sermon of Obedience Especially unto Authoritie Ecclesiasticall*, preached at a visitation of Dr. William Hinton, archdeacon of Coventry, he dedicated the book "to the Right Worshipful and Thrice Worthy Gentleman Sr Clement Throckmerton Knight, his singular good Patron, all happines." Such a dedication and such a sermon topic, though a tribute to the dedicatee, would have been anathema to his father.[93] Sir Clement was elected to the last Jacobean Parliament of 1623/24 and to the first two Caroline Parliaments of 1625 and 1625/26. In 1634 he died.[94]

Clement (1604 or 1605–64), grandson of Job, received the dedication of Book III, "The Fourteenth Century," of Thomas Fuller's best known work, *The Church History of Britain*. Fuller wrote:

TO CLEMENT THROCKMORTON, THE ELDER, OF HASELEY IN WARWICK-SHIRE, ESQUIRE:

Let others boast of their French bloud, whilest your English family may vie Gentry with any of the Norman extraction.
1. For Antiquity, four Monosyllables being, by common pronuntiation, crouded into your name; THE, ROCK, MORE, TOWN.
2. For Numerosity, being branched into so many Counties.
3. For Ingenuity, charactered by Camden to be FRUITFUL OF FINE WITS, whereof several instances might be produced.

But a principal consideration, which doth, and ever shall command my respect unto your person, is, your faithful and cordial friendship, in matters of highest concernment, (whatever be the success thereof) to the best of my Relations, which I conceived my self obliged publickly to confes.[95]

Clement was knighted in 1660, and served in the Parliament of 1661–78/79. His three sons were Clement, Francis, and Robert. Of these three, only Robert had a son, Clement, who was the last male in the Haseley line. His daughter and heiress, Lucy, first married William Bromley, and then Richard Chester.

THROKMORTON'S AUTHORSHIP OF

MASTER SOME

LAID OPEN IN

HIS COULERS

"Now 'M. Some in his coulers,' the author of which is under no sort of restraint, is a riot of comic metaphor and humorous vision . . . I know no other piece of Elizabethan prose, not even in the works of Nashe, in which the comic imagination is more fertile in play, more varied in resource, than 'M. Some Laid Open.'" (John Dover Wilson, "Martin Marprelate and Shakespeare's Fluellen," *The Library* 3 [1912]: 250–51)

The Occasion for Writing the Book

IN THE SPRING of 1588 Waldegrave printed Penry's *An Exhortation unto the Governours and People of Her Majesties Countrie of Wales, to Labour Earnestly to Have the Preaching of the Gospell Planted among Them,* which pleaded that the preaching of the Word was necessary for salvation. Because the Welsh clergy merely read from the Book of Common Prayer and did not preach, the people were deprived of the interpretation of the gospel. Furthermore, Penry asserted that the Welsh clergy were not rightly called to their office, since a true vocation required that a man be called not merely by a lord bishop but by the Lord himself. This involved the possession of gifts of learning and sanctity of life, the approbation of the church, and the ordination by the eldership. Penry believed that the ministers in Wales, many of whom had not attended a university, did not fulfill these requirements completely, and therefore the sacraments which they administered, baptism and the Eucharist, were of doubtful validity. Since Penry considered the three distinguishing marks of a true church to be "the Word preached, the right administration of the sacraments, and the outward forme of governement," and since these were allegedly lacking in Wales, the Welsh church was in a perilous condition.

Dr. Some replied to these points in his first *A Godly Treatise Containing and Deciding Certaine Questions,* which was published in May 1588. Penry answered Dr. Some's arguments and defended his own theses in *A Defence of That Which Hath Bin Written in the Questions of the Ignorant Ministerie, and the Communicating with Them,* which appeared in July or August. Dr. Some rejoined with his second *A Godly Treatise . . . and a Confutation of Many Grosse Errours Broched in M. Penries Last Treatise,* published in September. The first portion of the book was a reprint of the first *Godly Treatise,* pages 1–36, with slight changes, but the latter portion, pages 41–200, was a vehement, arrogant, and patronizing reply to Penry. The contrasts between the courtesy, humility, and respectful tone of Penry's *Defence* and the rudeness, dogmatism, and disrespect of Dr. Some's second *Godly Treatise* are immediately apparent to any impartial reader. Dr. Some's superiority revealed a mind-set of one who assumed that his *ipse dixit* was the source of all dogmatic truth. It was this lofty stance that provoked Job Throkmorton to defend his friend Penry and also to deflate and humiliate Dr. Some. About November, Throkmorton began work on his answer and probably completed a first draft by the end of January 1588/89. Then he learned that on 29 January Richard Walton had raided Penry's study and carried away his unpublished manuscript reply to Dr. Some's second *Godly Treatise.* This event precipitated Throkmorton's decision to publish his own reply to Dr. Some, as we see in his own words: "having this [reply to Dr. Some] lying by me, without any purpose to publish it

133

as yet, I was advertized of the taking away of Master Penries book by the pursivant. Whereupon I resolved (though it should be some offence to my friende) not to closet it up any longer, lest the adversary shoulde too much triumph and insult."

After the raid, the question perplexing Penry was whether he should rewrite his answer to Dr. Some or continue his work on his *Appellation,* which was directed to the Parliament that would convene on 4 February. He decided the appeal to Parliament was more important but he continued to hope that he would be able to answer Dr. Some. Yet the overriding consideration in Penry's mind was that Throkmorton had decided to enter the lists. Throkmorton continued his work and completed his reply by the end of March. Then Waldegrave received the manuscript, and probably brought it to La Rochelle, where it was printed. The result was that *Master Some Laid Open in His Coulers* was published in September, when Waldegrave delivered the books to Throkmorton's home. This sardonic and clever diatribe against Dr. Some was one of the most incisive and devastating attacks that ever appeared during the Elizabethan period.[1] Add to this the humor, the irony, the learning, the sarcasm, and the brilliant style of writing, and the end-result was a work that ranks with Martin Marprelate's *Epistle* and his *Hay Any Worke for Cooper.*

The Date of the Book

There has been much confusion on the date of Walton's raid and seizure of Penry's manuscript reply to Dr. Some, and on the related questions of the dates of *Master Some Laid Open* and Penry's *Appellation.* The problem developed in 1879 when Arber interpreted the date in Penry's *Appellation,* 7 March 1589, to be Old Style.[2] Therefore the year date would be 1589/ 90, or 1590, New Style. Since *Master Some Laid Open* was printed at the same time as the *Appellation* by the same printer, F. J. Powicke dated both works as 1590 in his biography of Henry Barrow.[3] In 1907, however, in a special article,

John Dover Wilson concluded that 29 January 1588/89 was the correct date for the raid and 1589 for the publication of both books.[4] In full agreement with Wilson, Pierce accepted 1589 as the correct date and assigned *Master Some Laid Open* to the late autumn of that year.[5] In his edition of the writings of Thomas Nashe, R. B. McKerrow first dated the raid as 1589/90, but in his concluding volume he corrected himself, accepted the findings of Wilson, and opted for 1588/89.[6] In April 1944, Donald J. McGinn published his article, "A Perplexing Date in the Marprelate Controversy," in which he asserted that Wilson and McKerrow were in error; Dr. McGinn dated the raid as 29 January 1589/90, and asserted that the *Appellation* and *Master Some Laid Open* were published two months later in 1590. Once more, in his book published in 1966, McGinn reaffirmed his views and asserted that after Walton's seizure of "an answere unto Master D. Some in writing," Penry promised he would publish another "answere." "Shortly thereafter appeared the unsigned *M. Some laid open in his coulers*, which has every appearance of being this 'answere.'" Then McGinn compounded the confusion by stating that "Wilson continues with the assumption that the 'answere unto master D. Some in writing' seized in Penry's home was written by Throckmorton and printed along with the *Appellation* by Waldegrave at Rochelle in the summer of 1589. In this opinion Pierce concurs with Wilson."[7] Unfortunately, both in his article and in his book, McGinn is in error. The reason he has gone astray is that he has misinterpreted a passage in Penry's *Appellation*, which refers to the high commissioners:

> From this insolency of theirs it is, that of late they have in their mandatory letters, enjoined the Maior of Northampton, to surcease the execution of his office in the government of that towne under hir majestie, and either to become their pursivant, in apprehending one of his neighbours, or else personally to appeare before them at London, and not to departe their court without special leave, his affaires in her majesties service, and the distance of Place betweene Northampton and London, nothing considered. And yet required they of him that which

he coulde not bring to passe, because the party whome he
was to apprehend [a marginal note—M. Sharpe book binder
of Northampton], being wel known to be a dutiful subject,
and for the love he beareth unto Gods truth to have bene heeretofore
so cruelly dealt with at some of their hands, by long imprisonment,
and so evil dealt with, as his cause comming to be heard before the
Lords of her majesties privy counsel, their Honours judged the bishops
proceeding against him, to be against lawe and conscience, and so
were the meanes of his delivery, the party I say, nowe fearing
the like injustice, *that hee sometimes tasted of,* was compelled
with the hinderance of his family *to absent himself from his*
calling.[8] [McGinn's italics]

Dr. McGinn has interpreted this passage as a reference to
Sharpe's appearance before Lord Chancellor Hatton on 15
October 1589. Thus, he argues, Penry's *Appellation* must be
dated *after* 15 October; therefore it was printed in 1590 up
in Scotland. But if the reader will examine Penry's statement
carefully, he will perceive that *it has no relationship whatsoever*
to 15 October 1589. Penry was comparing Sharpe's predicament
in February 1588/89 and his previous difficulties with the bishops. The Court of High Commission and the bishops were
not involved in Sharpe's deposition before the lord chancellor, and the Privy Council was not trying a case that had
previously been a part of "the bishops proceeding against
him." Furthermore, Sharpe never suffered "long imprisonment" after 15 October 1589. In fact, he had given bond for
his appearance on that date, and there is no evidence that
thereafter he suffered imprisonment at all. Since Penry's
statement was written some time between 29 January and
7 March 1588/89 at least six months before Sharpe's deposition,
it could not refer to subsequent events. Since McGinn did
not use manuscript sources, he does not realize that Penry
was alluding to Sharpe's difficulties with the High Commission in 1579–81, some ten years earlier. The Privy Council's
letter of 9 July 1579 to John Aylmer, bishop of London, and
to the High Commission, ordered the commissioners not to
"vexe or molest the said Sharpe for unnecessary causes."
The Privy Council also decided to send Sharpe home because

of the illness of his wife, and ordered that his sureties and bond not be forfeited or jeopardized.[9]

Furthermore, there is new and indisputable evidence to resolve this long-standing problem. Newman, the Martinist distributor of books, deposed:

> Penry and Walgrave fell at some litle jarre. They parted in the latter ende of Easter week [30 March–5 April 1589]; Walgrave, having then in his hands *Some in His Colers* and Penryes *Appellation* to have printed immediatly after *Hay Any Worke for Cooper*, wold not redeliver them, but promised Penrye to print them in the West Contrye and to bringe them agayne unto him by Whitsontide.[10]

> Now abowt this time Walgrave returned to Penrye at Fawsley [Haseley]. In so much as Numan comming thither to Penrye, being sent for by him abowt three dayes before Michaelmas, 1589, fownd Walgrave there and fower other new printed bookes, viz., Penryes *Appelation, Some in His Coulers, a Dialogue,* and Martins *Protestatyon*.[11]

> Newman being at Hasely at Michaelmas, as is before mentioned, worde was brought thither by one Gardiner [Garnet] of Northampton that Godlyes howse was searched for Penrye [a second time] by certayne pursevaunts. Whereupon the sayd bookes at Haselye were packed up, viz., 500 of the *Protestations*, 500 of the *Appelations*, and of *Some in His Coulers* 600, and sent by the sayd Gardiner upon Penryes mare to widdow Adams howse in Banburye.[12]

Thus, it is conclusive that *Master Some Laid Open* and Penry's *Appellation* were in Waldegrave's possession early in April 1589 when he departed from Wolston, that he printed them in the summer, either in London or more likely at La Rochelle, and that he delivered them to Throkmorton's home in Haseley before 29 September 1589. It is also evident from this deposition that there was a second raid on Godley's home and Penry's study before Michaelmas, 29 September. We may conclude that contrary to McGinn's opinion Waldegrave did not sever himself from the Martinists in April 1589, since he printed most of the *Protestatyon* and delivered this consignment of books to Haseley. Inasmuch as Waldegrave possessed Penry's manuscript of the *Appellation* in April 1589, it is absolutely certain that Penry's date, 7 March, on page 2, must be 1588/89, and that the date of the first raid, to which he alludes, must be 29 January 1588/89.[13]

Seven General Arguments for Throkmorton's Authorship

The first argument for Throkmorton's authorship is based on the deposition of the book's printer, Waldegrave. Dean Sutcliffe, who had access to all the Martinist depositions and examinations impounded by the governmental authorities, and who was the leading investigator of Throkmorton's role, stated in 1595 that "the booke called *Some in His Colours* was likewise made by J. Throkmorton. That is proved first, by the deposition of Waldegrave that upon his oath testified so much, and at Rochel where he printed it, spoke it openly." In his *An Answere* of 1592 Sutcliffe had accused Throkmorton of being the author of *Master Some Laid Open*, and in his *An Answere* of 1595 had affirmed that Throkmorton did not "deny that treatise to be his, being charged with it." He had also concluded that "the saucinesse of the stile doeth declare who was the author," and had asserted that "it appeareth by the depositions of Newman and Holmes, that he dispersed divers hundreds of those bookes, and that he corrected the said bookes, and was earnest with Holmes that hee should not bewray him." An argument *a silentio* tends to be inconclusive, but the significant points are that Waldegrave spoke openly of Throkmorton's authorship and that Holmes testified to Throkmorton's fear of discovery.[14]

A second argument for Throkmorton's authorship is a statement on the title page: "Done by an Oxford man, to his friend in Cambridge." Since Throkmorton was an Oxford man and Penry a Cambridge graduate and friend, the natural explanation is simply that Throkmorton was defending Penry, who had been answered unfairly and outrageously by Dr. Some whose two *Godly Treatises* were so patently pa-

tronizing that when Dr. Some threw down the glove, Throkmorton was eager to accept his disdainful challenge. Moreover, there are three pertinent references in the text and
one in the preface which indicate that the writer was an
Oxford man. Addressing Dr. Some, a Cambridge man, the
author asked: "Doe you remember howe you were woont
to be girding at me for our Oxforde doctors, as Dr. [John]
Kennall, Dr. Barnard [Daniel Bernarde], etc.?" The "our"
comes in naturally. Also, Throkmorton's student days in the
1560s overlap the vice-chancellorship of Dr. Kennall at a time
when Penry was a baby in Wales. Again, the author wrote:
"If I shoulde name Oxforde men unto you, it may be you
woulde thinke me partial." And in scornfully deriding the
emptiness of Dr. Some's learning, acquired in Cambridge,
the writer ironically suggested that "there may be wine
enough in the seller [cellar], when there is non[e] in the
cuppe." He then added: "let your Doctor ruffle it never so
much in bigge words and countenances, yet I can tel you,
if he releeve us not better in his next supply than he hath
done hithertoe (be he as lerned as he wil), we Oxforde men
shal thinke that Master Penri hath a greate deale more cause
to feare the Archbishop his pursevant, than your Doctors
penne." It seems obvious that Throkmorton, an Oxford man,
was the writer of this last sentence, and also of a statement
in the preface, which referred to the author [himself] as an
Oxford friend, "who if he be thought in his pleasant veine
anye thing too snappish, the reader is to wey with what
kind of adversary [Dr. Some] he deales: namely, with the
snappishest gentleman, and most bitter mouthes, that ever
put pen to paper."[15] In his *Protestatyon* Throkmorton used
a similar phrase: "in a pleasant vain of writing." Perhaps a
contrasting statement by Penry will reveal his spirit; addressing Dr. Some in his *Defence*, written about six months earlier,
Penry wrote:

Not that I wold any way disgrace, you whom I reverence,
for that is no part of mine intent, the Lorde is my witnes.

139

Nay, I would be loth to let that syllable escape me, that might give you or any els the least occasion in the world, to thinke that I carrye any other heart towards you, than I ought to beare towards a reverend learned man fearing God.[16]

There is a biographical allusion which points toward Throkmorton; Dr. Some had written:

If you denie not that it is a sacrament, you affirm it.
For not to denie is to affirme.
Every childe can teach you that lesson.

This certainly was dubious logic, and the critic pounced upon the fallacy:

See then what a wit I have, that can at the first dash, upon the sight of one bare paterne, thwite you out an other straight, full as good as that:

Master Some denies not that I am a bastard,
Ergo, he affirmes it.
For not to denie is to affirme.
Every childe can teache him that.

Ye[a], howe nowe? What occasion did I give Master Some to call me bastard? Trust me, if he use me so, Ile have an action of the case against him. For I would he should knowe it, my mother is an honest gentlewoman, and nobly borne.[17]

This reference to his mother is revealing and telling. Penry's parents were of yeoman stock from Brecon in Wales. But Throkmorton, as we have noted previously, was a country squire. His father was a gentleman and a member of Parliament. His mother, Katharine, was born of nobility (see her genealogy). Therefore, one concludes that the reference points to Throkmorton as the writer rather than to Penry, whose mother was not nobly born.

On the last page of *Master Some Laid Open* the mysterious initials "I.G." appear. William Pierce thought these might refer to a particular individual or that they were meaningless symbols intended to mislead. Another student of nonconformity, Henry M. Dexter, conjectured that Henry Barrow's fellow prisoner, John Greenwood, was the author, and this unfortunate surmise was accepted by the editors of the *Short-Title Catalogue*. But Dexter himself sensed that the discrepancy of style was obvious, and therefore suggested that Barrow had collaborated with Greenwood. A. F. Scott Pearson, biographer of Cartwright, queried if "I.G." pertained to James Gibson, minister of Pencaitland, in Scotland. The letter "I" suggests James, John, Joseph, or Job, but the letter "G" could be any cognomen. Therefore, even careful guessing would be inconclusive. There is information, however, supplied by Dean Sutcliffe, which may solve the mystery. The dean of Exeter berated Throkmorton for writing anonymous books and accused him of acting as a Jesuit in changing his name or hiding his identity. Sutcliffe related that when Throkmorton wrote to Edmund Coppinger in May 1591, he did not sign his name, but when Coppinger and the letter were seized, the writer was revealed by the seal and by a copy of Coppinger's reply. Sutcliffe also stated that when Throkmorton wrote to Penry in Scotland he used a pseudonym. Among the aliases used by Throkmorton were Gravener, Grivel, Johnson, Juell, Robinson, Stone, Tomson, and Warner. Therefore, it is possible that "I.G." stands for Job Gravener or Job Grivel.[18]

There is a revealing passage in which the writer appealed to the views of Dr. William Fulke, master of Pembroke College, Cambridge, in order to discredit Dr. Some. The writer then denounced what he regarded as six somewhat weak, vapid arguments which Dr. Some had used rhetorically, and asserted that these with many more were "but the crops and flowers of his owne pretie garden." As previously mentioned, Dean Sutcliffe had related the story of how Throkmorton wrote a little book. The dean had also provided some specific details. In a room at the home of one Master Harvye, Throkmorton promised to give Humphrey Newman "a little booke" which would help defray the expenses Newman had incurred as Throkmorton's messenger and distributor of books. Throkmorton told him the title of the book: *The Crops*

and Flowers of Bridges Garden, and promised him that to pre-
serve anonymity he would drop the manuscript while taking
a walk so that Newman could pick it up. The conclusion
drawn from this story is that the similarity in the phrase
and the book's title is best explained by postulating one origi-
nator of both expressions, which are found in Throkmorton's
books and conversation.[19]

There is a sarcastic story which is relevant to the question
of authorship and to Throkmorton's contempt for Dr. Some:

> Beare witnesse, I pray you, that I speake heere of *sound preach-
> ing,* that is, of deviding the Worde aright which the Apostle
> calleth *orthotomein.* I speake not of *babling* or of handeling a
> text with a curricombe, in that I joine with Master Some with
> al my hart. And therefore I wish he had bene with me the
> 10 of November last, at a certaine church by the Exchange, I
> thinke they cal it Bartholomewe Church, where it may be
> his ears would have glowed, and (if he durst have bene so
> bolde), I doe not thinke but he would have condemned the
> preacher and that worthely for his babling. For there he might
> have heard him fetch many vagaries, and spend the most of
> his time in invectives against good men, telling the audience
> to this effect: "That for the papists, thanks be to God, we
> need not so greatly feare them, for they were through the
> vigilans and wisedome of the magistrate reasonably hampered.
> God be blessed for it. But now the magistrate was onely to
> cast his eye on the phantasticall crue, such as troubled the
> peace of the church, otherwise there might fall out many mis-
> chiefes. For so was it done to the Donatists in Saint Augustines
> time, and so to other heretikes in other times." And naming
> another doctor of the church, either Basill or Chrisostome, I
> take it, I knowe not well whether [which], he tolde them greatly
> to their comforts, that he would first tell them his wordes in
> Greeke, and afterward in English, and so he did, belike because
> they should know that he was a Grecian. What a sweet receipt
> was that, trow ye, to such of the people as were either sicke,
> or troubled in mind? I heare that Master Some useth to come
> to that church himselfe sometime. I pray you, when you see
> him, be in hande with him to shake up that snuffing preacher
> for his babling.[20]

Then follows a marginal gloss, so innocent, so impish, so cruel: "This preacher (as I understoode since) was Master Some himselfe."

What is pertinent to note about this anecdote, apart from the humorous technique of the writer, is the date, 10 November 1588, which was a Sunday. The writer was a part of the audience at Bartholomew Church in London. That writer, however, could not have been Penry, because about 1 November he had supervised the dismantling and removing of the printing press from Mrs. Crane's house in East Molesey. A servant, Jeffs of Upton, brought the press by cart to Sir Richard Knightley's estate at Fawsley, Northamptonshire, where he arrived about 12–15 November. Then Penry arranged with Lawrence Jackson, keeper of Knightley's house, for the reception of a load, and within an hour Jeffs appeared with his cart and press. From the testimony of Jeffs one may conclude that on 10 November Penry was either enroute to Fawsley or had arrived at his home in Northampton.[21] Therefore one may also infer that Throkmorton, not Penry, was the person attending service at Bartholomew Church. Since he had read Dr. Some's second *Godly Treatise* of September, he had already decided to refute it and was attending church to gather information on Dr. Some.

If one assumes that Penry wrote *Master Some Laid Open,* then one must accept the difficult thesis that Penry wrote about himself in the third person. In this treatise there are more than a hundred references to him. On the supposition that they were written by Penry, they are strained and inexplicable; on the supposition that they were written by Throkmorton, they are appropriate and readily understood. There are at least ten references, sympathetically ironical, to "proude Penrie," "the poore ignorant Welchman," and "the poore Welchmans head." McGinn asserted that "another indication of Penry's hand is the personal pique in the author's repetition of M. Some's 'poore ignorant Welchman.' " This is difficult to accept, since most authors would not relish the repetition of insulting phrases about themselves. Penry's pique disappears if one realizes that he was not the author of *Master Some Laid Open.* He was frank, direct, unsubtle, and open, and expressed his reverence for Dr. Some. All his writings were either signed or acknowledged. He stated: "I have delt al this while in the face of the sun, and nowe before the state of the land assembled together."[22] There would be more reason for concealing his name from his two printed supplications to Parliament in 1589 than from a reply to Dr. Some. Yet both his appeals to Parliament, and his *Defence* against Dr. Some, were signed.

The following statements are scattered throughout *Master Some Laid Open.* When ascribed to Penry they are *disjecta membra,* ill-fitting and illogical; when assigned to Throkmorton, they cohere with the ideas and style of his acknowledged writings.

1. Having this [manuscript of *Master Some Laid Open*] lying by me, . . . I resolved (though it should be some offence to my friende) not to closet it up any longer, lest the adversary shoulde too much triumph and insult. [A2]

   The clause, "though it should be some offence to my friende," is meaningless if Penry were the writer. The phrase, "triumph and insult," unused by Penry, is similar to Throkmorton's phrase, "triumphinge and insulting," in his "Speech on the Low Countries," folio 38.

2. It is sure, but the good luck that some men have over others, for if poore M. Penri had written thus, he should have bene chronicled, I warrant you, for a cobling Welchman while he had lived. [page 16]

   In *Martin Junior,* acknowledged in Court by the printers to be Throkmorton's, we read: "you deserve to be chronicled" [Civ]. "I warrant you" is a favorite phrase used by Throkmorton.

3. And therefore I dare say for M. Penri, that he will willingly with hart and hande subscribe to it. [page 17]

   The alliteration and the phrase "harte and hande" are typical of Throkmorton's writings. The phrase, "hartes and handes," occurs in Throkmorton's "Speech on the Scottish Queen," folio 7.

4. Only this much I thinke one may safely and truely say, that in all that ever M. Penri hath written (though M. Some have beprouded him I know not how many times), no man shal be able justly to finde any one dashe with a pen, savoring so palpably the corruption of the heart, thorow the good liking of himself, as in a hundred places of M. Somes book. Too long and loathsome it were to runne through all, and therefore I wil onely ad som few more to sute with the rest. [Then follow five quotations from Dr. Some.] How saye you, is not this a medicine to give a modest man a vomit? [page 47]

Penry could not have written this stinging indictment of Dr. Some. In his reply to Dr. Some, *A Defence*, there is not one caustic sentence in all his 63 pages. The word "beprouded" is typical of Throkmorton, who used fifty-two words beginning with "be," of which twelve were coined words, including "beprouded."

5. But what will you say, if the man that you reverence so [Dr. Some], be taken now and then with a tricke of a false finger? You would be sory for that, I am sure: you do not heare me say, that he can juggle or help a die, I would not have you to take me so. [page 79]

Penry said he reverenced Dr. Some, but Throkmorton used the word ironically. Penry regarded Dr. Some as an honest man, but Throkmorton accused him of logical legerdemain. Penry never referred to a die or dice, but Throkmorton frequently used gambling terms.

6. Furthermore in that point of the *magistracy* (which M. Penri is soe charged to have handled with very foule and bepitched hands), the very words which M. Doctor would seeme most to make vantage of, vz., *devise of man*, I cannot finde in al M. Penries booke, sure I am, they be not in the places quoted, betwixt the pages 47 and 51. And if they be not in the booke

at all (as I beleve they be not), then by your leave we charge him once more with a trick of a false finger, in that he hath thrust in more than was in the text. [page 80]

Penry would be certain of what was in his own work. "Be-pitched" points to Throkmorton, and also "by your leave," which is used in five of Throkmorton's works.

7. But I pray you, tell me, is it not a miserie, that such un-learned stuffe as this, should drop from the penne of anye man that beareth the face of learning? [page 95]

Penry wrote: "Master D. Somes booke was published this day. I have read it. The man I reverence from my heart as a godly and learned man." See John Penry, *Three Treatises concerning Wales*, ed. David Williams, page 98.

8. Therein I must hould with M. Some, that if M. Penri thinke so, he is much to blame. [page 27]

It is unlikely that Penry would incriminate himself.

9. Well, your Doctor hath yet an other wipe at the ignorant Welchman. [page 27]

Throkmorton liked the word "wipe," used it nine times, and Martin Marprelate employed it five times.

Throkmorton's Authorship: The Argument from Parallels

Master Some Laid Open in His Coulers is rich with parallels to Throkmorton's acknowledged works. In the following list of parallels there are 33 words, 46 examples of their use in Throkmorton's writings, and 39 examples of their occurrence in *Master Some Laid Open*, with 28 duplicates not counted. There are seven examples that are ordinary and unconvincing when they stand alone, but they have been retained because of their frequency, because they are not found in Penry's writings, or because they characterize Throkmorton's style. Such expressions as "I muse," "I warrant you," and the ironic "wee thanke him" smack of Throkmorton's pert style and rash confidence. There are eight ordinary phrases which have not been adduced as evidence, even though they do occur in many of Throkmorton's sentences: "for all that," "a greate deale," "in good earnest," "in a maner," "I am sure," "thinke you," "mee thinkes," and "I trowe."

To facilitate the task of footnoting, I have numbered the following twelve examples of Throkmorton's incontrovertible writings:

(1) "Letter to Mr. Warcuppe"
(2) "Speech on the Scottish Queen"
(3) "Speech on the Low Countries"
(4) "Speech on the Bill and Book"
(5) "Letter to Lord Burghley"
(6) *A Dialogue. Wherin Is Plainly Laide Open*
(7) *Master Some Laid Open in His Coulers*
(8) "Letter to Lord Chancellor Hatton"
(9) "Letter to Edmund Coppinger"
(10) *Defence of Job Throkmorton against . . . Sutcliffe*
(11) "Letter to the Bailiff and Principall Burgesses"
(12) Preface to Cartwright's *A Brief Apologie*

In the following list of parallels, all the arabic numbers refer to Throkmorton's writings, as numbered above. Thus, in the first entry, (3:42) refers to the "Speech on the Low Countries," folio 42; (7:32) refers to *Master Some Laid Open*, page 32; (10: Bi v) refers to *Defence of Job Throkmorton*, signature Bi *verso*. The above list includes only those writings which are indubitably by Throkmorton. There are eleven other works which I have attributed to Throkmorton, but some readers may regard one or two of these attributions as dubitable. Therefore, to avoid the impression of "loading" the argument from parallels, I have not utilized parallels from these eleven other works. My reasons for attributing these eleven works to Throkmorton are included in the text or in the appendixes, and the works themselves are listed in chapter seven as "other works attributed to Throkmorton."[23]

Parallels in *MASTER SOME LAID OPEN IN HIS COULERS* and in *Throkmorton's Writings*

ABJECT
  a very abject of the earth (7:32)
  the verie abjectes of the earth (10:Bi v)
  and we poore abjectes (3:42)

AFFLICTED
  succoured the afflicted (7:57)
  to succour the afflicted (3:48)

BLAST
  a blast of words (7:14)
  a blast of good wordes (4:15)

BLUNDER
  blunder you out an other proper figure (7:106)
  blunder out a trueth (12:A2 v)

BONES
  he made no bones (7:1)
  he made no bones (12:A3 v)

CHOKE
  choake him straight with a pill (7:105)
  choked me straight with his old common place (10:Dii)

COULERS
  laid open in his coulers (7:A1)
  featured out in his coulers (3:43)

CREW
  of the fantastical crewe (7:28, 48, 56, 62)
  of the fantasticall crue (6:A3 v)

CROPS
  the crops and flowers of his owne pretie garden (7:105)

The Crops and Flowers of Bridges Garden (Sutcliffe, *An Answere* [1595], 72 v)

EYE
  a man with halfe an eie may easily see (7:81)
  a man with haulfe an eye may easely beholde (3:36)

GLOWE
  his ears would have glowed (7:21)
  would make your eares to glowe (4:21)

GREVOUS
  guiltie of a grevous sin (7:108)
  so greate and greevous sinns (6:B2)
  without a grievous sinne (10:Aiv v)

HANDE
  with hart and hande (7:17)
  with hartes and handes lyfted up to heaven (2:7)
  lyfte up his handes to heaven (3:48)

HISSED
  is hissed out of the scholes (7:20)
  is hissed out of the schoole (4:21)

INSULT
  triumph and insult (7:A2)
  triumphinge and insulting (3:38)

LIGHT

should light on the name (7:95)
I can not light on his name
(4:22)

MARGINAL

woorth a marginal note (7:102)
by their marginall note
(10:Biii)
in the marginall note (10:Ci v)

MARKE

marke I pray you (7:8, 40, 53,
76, 110)
marke then (I pray you) well
(3:29)
marke yt I pray you well (3:32;
4:21)
it is worth marking (7:118)
it is worth marking (3:32)

MATTER

nothing to the matter (7:23, 23,
101)
nothing to the matter (6:B3 v)

MOODE

that good Christian moode
(7:9)
in his good moode (7:32)
in his angrye moode (7:35)
in his madde moode (6:D1)
in his better moode (10:Eii)

MOUTH

he closeth up the mouth of all
(7:123)
to cloze up the mouth of all
(3:30)

MUZE

I muse (7:17) (4:14) [marvel]
I muze (7:55, 105, 109, 117)
I muze (10:Bii, Biii, Biii v)

NECKE

Master Some coms in the
necke of this with his appeale (7:35)
in the necke of this should
have followed these words
(7:50)
huddleing one in the necke of
the other (2:7)
in the necke of this comes
Maister Sutcliffe with his
vie [bid] (10:Biii)

PATCHES

anye patches or peeces (7:110)
by patches and pieces (10:Bii)

PERSWADED

I am verely perswaded (7:15)
I am veryly perswaded (2:6)

SMAL

as I have smal reason (7:38)
we have small reason (7:39)
so had I small reason (9:18)

SPLEENE

as it were upon a spleene (7:15)
whether it be upon the
spleene (10:Bii v)

SWARVE

we shal but swarve from the
question (7:98)
wee shall not lightly swarve
much from the marke (9:18)

SWEETE

whose sweete sentences these
be (7:46) [ironical]
I remember this sweete sentence (10:Diii) [ironical]

THANKE

we thanke him (7:18, 70, 81)
we thanke him (3:36)
I thanke him (10:Biii, Div, Eii)
[all ironical]

WARRANT

I warrant you (7:16, 35, 56, 69, 92, 94, 122)
I warrant you (2:4; 3:31; 4:21, 21; 6:C3 v, C4 v, D2 v)
I warrant you (10:Aii v, Bii v)

UNMANGLED

to publishe it unmangled as he received it (7:A2 v)
publishe it altogither, as it was, unmangled (10:Bii)

WOUND

wound and disgrace his adversarie (7:11)
wounde and disgrace the persons (4:19)

Scholarly Judgment on the Authorship of
MASTER SOME LAID OPEN IN HIS COULERS

Without exception all scholars who have studied the Marprelate problem have agreed that the Martinist books and *Master Some Laid Open* were written by the same author. Dr. Henry M. Dexter noted a "decidedly Martinist flavor" in *Master Some Laid Open*, and added: "I am quite sure that all who are familiar with the Martinist tracts, will agree with me that these extracts [from *Master Some*] are so entirely in keeping with them, as to suggest a common authorship." Pierce concluded that the similarities in Martin's books and *Master Some* were "too great to be overlooked" and that "the easy idiomatic raciness of style is the same." Wilson commented that "style may be a doubtful touchstone for the test of authorship; but one cannot conceive that anyone familiar with the tracts of Martin could fail to see the same hand in *M. Some Laid Open*. In every way, it is similar, in that boisterous, rollicking, hustling manner of speech which has won them a place in the literature of the nation, and it deserves to share that place with them." And McGinn observed that *Master Some* and *A Dialogue. Wherin Is Plainly Laide Open* "in style and content closely resemble the Martinist tracts." Therefore the establishment of the authorship of *Master Some* is directly relevant to the authorship of the Martinist books.[24]

As a ninth argument, we may especially emphasize that

one of the weighty reasons for concluding that Throkmorton was the author of *Master Some* is the strong consensus of judgment reached by reliable witnesses and thorough students of the Marprelate problem. There are nine persons who have concluded that Throkmorton was the author: Robert Waldegrave, Matthew Sutcliffe, Edward Arber, Sidney Lee, Frederick J. Powicke, John Dover Wilson, William Pierce, Georges A. Bonnard, and Patrick Collinson. In addition, there are five scholars who have not specifically discussed the authorship of *Master Some* but are unanimous in asserting that Penry was not Martin: John Waddington, Albert Peel, Sir John Neale, Alexander J. Grieve, and David Williams. One writer, Dr. Dexter, conjectured that John Greenwood was the author, and three authors suggested that Penry was the writer of *Master Some:* William Maskell, Donald J. McGinn, and Charles Turney. By pausing to review the conclusions of these students, one will be in a stronger posture to attack the Penry thesis and to defend the position that Throkmorton was the author of *Master Some* and therefore of the Martinist books.

According to Dean Sutcliffe, as previously noted, the Marprelate printer, Waldegrave, spoke openly at La Rochelle of Throkmorton's authorship and also deposed upon his oath that Throkmorton wrote *Master Some.* It is probable that Waldegrave made his deposition at Edinburgh in 1590 when he was appointed the king's printer. It is difficult to reject Waldegrave's testimony, since he received the manuscript of *Master Some* at Haseley in March or April 1589, printed it in the summer of 1589, brought the consignment of 600 books to Haseley in September, and "came to Throgmorton, to know what he would have done with them."[25] He also printed five Marprelate books, seven Penry items, and three related Throkmorton writings. Sutcliffe, Waldegrave's contemporary, was one of the ablest apologists for the Church of England. In 1592 he asserted that Throkmorton was the author of *Master Some,* as well as of three specific Martinist writings: the *Mineralls, Martin Junior,* and the *Protestatyon;* and also of *A Dialogue. Wherin Is Plainly Laide Open.* Throkmorton replied to Sutcliffe in 1594 with his *Defence* but sidestepped the question of writing Martinist books. Sutcliffe rejoined in 1595, once more attributed *Master Some* to Throkmorton, and in addition to the above-mentioned five books, assigned to the Haseley squire five other works: *Hay Any Worke for Cooper, The Crops and Flowers of Bridges Garden, Martin Senior, More Worke for Cooper,* and "Martins Interim."[26]

Edward Arber was one of the first scholars in the nineteenth century to emphasize the role of Throkmorton and to place him alongside Penry as a Marprelate collaborator. In his *Introductory Sketch* he devoted four pages to a discussion of authorship, of which two pages were given to Throkmorton. By a process of elimination or exhaustion of the list of potential Martinist candidates, he arrived at the conclusion that Throkmorton wrote three works, including *Master Some Laid Open.*[27] Sir Sidney Lee, editor of the *Dictionary of National Biography,* biographer of Shakespeare, and a specialist in Elizabethan studies, was the author of eight articles in the *D.N.B.* on John Bridges, John Lyly, Thomas Nashe, John Penry, Andrew Perne, Job Throkmorton, Robert Waldegrave, and John Whitgift, all relevant to the Marprelate controversy. In his article on Penry (1895), he ascribed *Master Some* to John Greenwood, an erroneous attribution that derived from Dexter, but in his later article (1899) on Waldegrave, Lee ascribed *Some in His Collours* [sic] to Throkmorton, an attribution probably dependent on the judgment of Arber.

Frederick J. Powicke spent many years studying the origins of the Separatists. His articles in the *Transactions of the Congregational Historical Society,* his biography, *Henry Barrow Separatist,* his studies of Robert Browne, John Robinson, and Richard Baxter, and his acute criticisms of Arber's book, *The Story of the Pilgrim Fathers, 1606–1623 A.D.* (London, 1897), lend weight to his judgments. His discussion of the controversy involving Barrow, Dr. Some, and Penry is percipient and relevant. Noting that a friend intervened on the side of Penry, Powicke stated: "The friend, it appears, was Job Throckmorton, and his defence of Penry took the title, *Master Some Laid Open in His Colours, Wherein the Indifferent Reader*

May Easily See How Wretchedly and Loosely He Hath Handled the Cause against Mr. Penry." Thus, Powicke suggested that Throkmorton was the author of this work. But in Appendix I of his book he was more positive. He added: "Of course, since the writer of *Master Some Laid Open in His True Colours* was the 'clerk of Oxford' against whom Barrow girds so strongly, it is plain that Dr. Dexter cannot be right in (conjecturally) assigning the book to Greenwood. Since, moreover, the writer was Job Throckmorton, an extract or two may serve to show how extremely probable is the conjecture that he—Penry's friend—had a share in the writing of the [Marprelate] Tracts. If the following does not 'smack' of Marprelate it would surely be very hard to say what does." Thereupon he presented five quotations from *Master Some*, typical of Martin's style.[28]

John Dover Wilson was one of the keenest students of the Marprelate problem. His chapter on "The Marprelate Controversy" in the *Cambridge History of English Literature* is still the best succinct presentation of the story, and his scholarly articles on related subjects are helpful and scintillating. Wilson gave high praise to *Master Some*, concluded that it was "printed by Waldegrave at Rochelle in the summer of 1589," and was written "undoubtedly by Throkmorton."[29] In 1908 William Pierce noticed the similarity between Marprelate's three main works—the *Epistle*, the *Epitome*, and *Hay Any Worke*—and *Master Some*. He also sensed a relationship of this latter work with Throkmorton's *Defence*. Therefore he concluded that "the style and the circumstances in which the tract [*Master Some*] was produced point most strongly to Job Throkmorton as the Oxford man." In 1923 he referred to the writer of this book as one "who also may be Martin," and asserted that "it can scarcely be doubted that Job Throkmorton is the author." In these acute observations Pierce revealed his percipience as well as his scholarship and earned full credit for his accuracy.[30]

The Swiss scholar, Georges A. Bonnard, on the basis of Sutcliffe's and Newman's statements, set forth without disagreement the authorship of Throkmorton. He wrote:

L'attribution de ce traité à Throckmorton est le fait de Sutcliffe, *Answer*, 74 (Arber, *I.S.*, 180) sur la foi d'une déposition sous serment de Waldegrave. Throckmorton n'en a jamais nié être l'auteur. Newman, dans son interrogatoire, également cité par Sutcliffe, *loc. cit.*, affirma que Throckmorton s'occupa activement de la vente de *Some . . . in His Coulers*.[31]

Patrick Collinson, a master of Tudor sources and author of the excellent book, *The Elizabethan Puritan Movement* (1967), has concluded that Throkmorton wrote *Master Some*. He commented:

> Penry was almost his [Martin's] *alter ego*, but his [Penry's] voice and style were not Martin's. Job Throckmorton—whom Pierce came close to identifying with Martin and whose candidature is favoured by Sir John Neale—contributed to the secondary series of tracts, when Martin's "sons" had supposedly assumed their father's mantle, and with Penry he clearly managed the whole enterprise at this stage, probably as the senior partner. His sallies into what can best be called para-Martinist literature, especially in the tract called *M. Some laid open in his coulers*, printed by Waldegrave in La Rochelle later in 1589, expose a genius with a richly comic imagination. And now Neale's discovery of the parliamentary speeches of 1586–7, hitherto unknown, are a further revelation of his potentialities, and of a style close to that of Martin.[32]

Five prominent students of Penry and Throkmorton were John Waddington, Albert Peel, Sir John Neale, Alexander J. Grieve, and David Williams. Waddington published the first biography of Penry in 1854, and Peel edited his *Notebook* in 1944. There is no recorded judgment by these two scholars on the authorship of *Master Some*, but both men rejected Penry's candidacy as Martin. Since it seems an inescapable conclusion that the same person wrote both the Martinist books and *Master Some*, it may be inferentially possible to say that they would also reject the assertion that Penry wrote *Master Some*. In writing on the identity of Martin Marprelate, Neale wrote: "Both denied being Martin. That need weigh very little. Other arguments rule out Penry, and, as the evidence now stands, Throckmorton seems most likely."[33] Grieve, editor of Penry's *Aequity*, wrote that "of his authorship there is not a shred of evidence. Indeed the unlikeness, both in style and spirit, of the Marprelate tracts to Penry's known writings appears to be conclusive" (p. xv).[34] And Williams, the editor of three of Penry's treatises, concluded that "the consensus of scholarly opinion no longer holds Penry responsible. It is, indeed, unthinkable that he should have written the tracts, for they made their readers laugh at sin, whereas to Penry sin was odious." Williams is paraphrasing Samuel Clarke, who wrote: "When Martin Mar Prelate came first out, Master Greenham being to preach at St. Maries in Cambridge, spake freely against that Book, manifesting his dislike of the same: For (said he) the tendency of this Book is to make sin ridiculous, whereas it ought to be made odious."[35]

In 1879 and 1880 Dexter, a leading writer on Congregationalism and nonconformity, conjectured that Henry Barrow was Martin Marprelate and that John Greenwood was the author of *Master Some* because the final page (124) carried the initials "I.G." But Dexter qualified his own conclusion:

> So decidedly does it [*Master Some*] differ in style in parts, from other books bearing his [Greenwood's] name—I am persuaded Barrowe had a considerable hand. Incarcerated together, and paired in nearly all their experiences, even to the halter which at last pulled open heaven's gate for them, and avowedly joint authors of several volumes, I imagine both pens worked indiscriminately upon this.[36]

Dr. Dexter was wrong on two counts. Greenwood had no role in writing *Master Some*, and Barrow had no connection with the Marprelate tracts. But Dexter was right in detecting a similarity between these writings, and he was correct in concluding that they were so close "as to suggest a common authorship." There is a common author, but he is neither Greenwood nor Barrow, nor is he Penry.[37]

There are three writers who have assigned *Master Some* to Penry: William Maskell, Donald J. McGinn, and Charles Turney. In 1845 Maskell published *A History of the Martin Marprelate Controversy in the Reign of Queen Elizabeth*, the earliest book-length discussion (224 pages) of the subject. It was not so much a history as a running commentary on twenty-three books and items which were published by protagonists and adversaries. It was interesting as ecclesiastical history, with unblushing High-Anglican bias, with grave warnings against the Puritans, and with a patronizing digression about the misfortune that the recently reprinted Marprelate Tracts would be sent chiefly to America, "with no literature of their own, . . . where there is no attempt at discipline, and scarcely certainty even upon the most important doctrines." He alluded to Dr. Some's *A Godly Treatise Containing and Deciding Certaine Questions,* and in a marginal note suggested that *Master Some* was Penry's answer to Dr. Some, but gave no reasons for this erroneous attribution.[38]

McGinn argued that Penry wrote *Master Some,* that the book was printed at Edinburgh, and that it was published about March 1590. All three arguments are incorrect.[39] McGinn also contended that Penry's *Appellation* and *Master Some* are linked by date.[40] Although he misdated both books as 1590, it is correct that the two books were printed at the same time—during the summer of 1589 at La Rochelle, but the implication is false that dates of printing are substantive arguments for authorship. McGinn also argued that both books were printed from the same type. Again, the implication is wrong, since typographical likeness does not permit one to assert Penry's authorship of both books. Not all books printed from the same type are by a single author.[41] We may discount the arguments of linkage by date and type, but the absence of any linkage of authors by Newman arouses suspicions. Newman spoke of Penry's *Appellation* and the anonymous *Master Some.*[42] Why the omission of any author for the latter work? If Penry had written it, it is likely that Newman would have said so. When Newman testified in July 1590, Penry was ensconced in Scotland, but Throkmorton was on the verge of being indicted in Warwick. Therefore Newman may have remained discreetly silent. Furthermore, if Penry had written *Master Some,* it is highly probable that he would have included his own name. All of his works are signed or acknowledged, whereas all of Throkmorton's nineteen books, excepting his *Defence*, are either anonymous or pseudonymous. The reason Penry's name was not appended to *Master Some* is that he did not write it, would not have written such a caustic lampoon, and could not have penned such a rollicking and derisive reply to Dr. Some.[43]

There remains for consideration a doctoral dissertation which Charles Turney completed in 1965 at Rutgers University, with Professor McGinn as adviser. This is entitled: "A Critical Edition of the Puritan Pamphlet, *M. Some Laid Open in His Coulers* (1590)" [1589]. This is a useful edition, but Dr. Turney has bypassed the moot question of authorship. He admits that "it is of course possible that Throckmorton could have written *M. Some laid open,*" but then adds: "I accept McGinn's argument that Penry was Martin Marprelate and conjecture that Penry also wrote *M. Some laid open.*"[44]

As a concluding argument, we may state with assurance that *Master Some Laid Open* reflects the personality and style of Martin Marprelate. Ronald B. McKerrow, a specialist in Elizabethan literature, was impressed by the "dominant personality, the extraordinary figure of Martin himself." Likewise, Wilson was convinced of the uniqueness of the personality and style of Martin, of which he wrote: "Martin's freakish and audacious personality and his unusual vein of satire were something new and not easily forgotten. He was the great (most famous) prose satirist of the Elizabethan period and may rightly be considered as the (humble) forerunner of that much greater satirist whose *Tale of a Tub* was a brilliant attack upon all forms of religious controversy." Since he concluded that *Master Some*, "almost without doubt, is Throckmorton's," and since he believed that "Throckmorton was the principal, if not the sole, author of the Marprelate Tracts,"[45] we may infer that the satirical style of writing in *Master Some* and in the Marprelate writings emanated from the mind of one writer. And from the ten arguments in this chapter we conclude that McKerrow's "extraordinary figure" was Job Throkmorton.

THROKMORTON'S
AUTHORSHIP OF
RELATED WORKS

"In my edition of this tract I have reviewed the development of the literature of complaint in England from the sermons and Wycliffite tracts of the fourteenth century to the satirical complaints of the Puritan reformers in Renaissance England, where the complaint attained great popularity in the form of satirical dialogues. I have placed A DIALOGUE WHERIN IS PLAINLY LAIDE OPEN *in this tradition and have also discussed those qualities in which it represents a departure from the tradition."* [*This treatise is*] *"unique in its presentation of a character, Jacke of both sides, for whom there is no prototype in any of the other polemical religious dialogues."* (Joy Lee Belknap King, "A Critical Edition of *A Dialogue Wherin Is Plainly Laide Open, the Tyrannicall Dealing of L. Bishopps against Gods Children*," preface, p. [2] and p. xxxvii)

A Dialogue. Wherin Is Plainly Laide Open the Tyrannicall Dealing of Lord Bishopps against Gods Children

HENRY M. DEXTER alluded to *A Dialogue* as a collateral tract, A. F. Scott Pearson described it as an "interesting auxiliary pamphlet," and William Pierce referred to it as a "sprightly piece." In 1968 Joy Lee Belknap King completed a Ph.D. dissertation, a critical edition of this book, which linked *A*

Dialogue with the denunciatory and conversational satire extending from Gower, Langland, Wycliffe, and Chaucer in the fourteenth century to William Turner, Anthony Gilby, and George Gifford in the sixteenth century. This dissertation is helpful in associating *A Dialogue* with the Martinist works and with the printing activities of Waldegrave, but it misdates the tract as 1590 and it mistakenly supports the "supposition that Penry himself was the author of the work."[1]

The anonymous author probably began his composition of *A Dialogue* in March 1589, as soon as he had completed his *Hay Any Worke for Cooper.* This latter work was not quite ready by 16 March, but by Palm Sunday, 23 March, Newman had delivered to Sharpe at Northampton some 700 copies for binding. During the previous week Waldegrave had already bound more than 200 copies and dispatched them to London. Therefore, one may infer that during the latter half of March the author was preparing *A Dialogue.* This completion of the composition may be dated not *after* April, as Pierce suggested, but *in* April, since two internal clues help to date it after Easter (30 March) and before the death of Andrew Perne on 26 April 1589.[2] It is possible that Waldegrave had the manuscript in hand when he left Wolston about 5 April, and that he printed it at La Rochelle in the summer of 1589. On folio A2 *recto* there is a factotum—two naked cherubs—with no enveloping border, exactly like the factotum used by Waldegrave in *Master Some Laid Open,* also printed at La Rochelle in the summer of 1589, and in *An Humble Motion,* printed by Waldegrave in May 1590 at Edinburgh. The type used in Penry's *A Viewe,* in *Martin Junior,* and *Martin Senior* was probably cast by the house of Les Haultin in La Rochelle, and was closely similar to, if not identical with, the type used to print the three La Rochelle imprints—Penry's *Appellation,* and Throkmorton's *Master Some Laid Open,* as well as *A Dialogue.*[3]

This latter book is presented in a dialogue form, with Puritane, Papist, Jacke of Both Sides, and Idoll Minister as the four interlocutors. In the course of some thirty pages of discussion, questions, and accusations, Puritane accounts for

about one-half of the material, and the other three characters
are limited to the remaining half. One notes that Puritane
is proceeding from Protestant or Huguenot La Rochelle, and
that Jacke of Both Sides is coming from Catholic Orléans.

A Dialogue was mostly a recapitulation of material found
in the four previous Marprelate items—the *Epistle, Epitome,
Mineralls,* and *Hay Any Worke for Cooper.* Familiar accusations
against Archbishop Whitgift, bishops Aylmer, Cooper, and
Middleton, were repeated. The harsh treatment accorded
Waldegrave was again mentioned, and the superior learning
of Cartwright, compared with that of Whitgift, was once
more stressed. There were, however, three stories presented
in *A Dialogue* which were not found elsewhere. One related
the success of the women of Hampstead in resisting the cut-
ting down of trees in their town by the servants of Bishop
Aylmer. Another revealed the disappointment experienced
by Dean Bridges and one Thornby, master of the Savoy,
who met on the green at Richmond. Both men said they
had been promised a bishopric, but were shocked and disillusioned to learn that the appointment had been given to another candidate. The third story was an insinuation of
discourteous conduct by Dr. Martin Culpepper, archdeacon
of Berkshire, and of disgraceful deportment by Dr. Nicholas
Bond, chaplain-in-ordinary to the queen.[4]

There are substantial reasons for attributing *A Dialogue*
to Throkmorton. Waldegrave delivered the printed books
to him at Haseley in September 1589. Also, that master detective, Richard Bancroft, referred four times to *A Dialogue* "that
came from Throgmorton." Likewise, Bancroft's collaborator,
Dean Sutcliffe, in 1592 spoke of Throkmorton's "theses,
protestations, dialogues, arguments, laying men out in their
colours," and in 1595 he was more specific: "The most reverend father in God, my Lord of Canterbury, in a certaine
dialogue, that came from Job Throkmorton, that here plead-
eth not guiltie, is called *Belzebub of Canterbury the chiefe of
the divels.*" It is apparent that Bancroft and Sutcliffe, two of
the most knowledgeable investigators, were asserting the authorship of Throkmorton on the basis of their own study

of the examinations of 1589 and 1590, especially the deposition of Newman, and on the findings of the Warwick grand jury in 1590, when Throkmorton was indicted.[5]

Arguments from style may be somewhat subjective and debatable, but the differences in Throkmorton's and Penry's styles are so clear-cut that one can arrive at high probablility. Dr. McGinn rightly observed that *A Dialogue* resembles the work of Martin Marprelate "in style and content," but it should be added that the style and content of *A Dialogue* also resemble Throkmorton's non-Marprelate writings and that they do not cohere with the known writings of Penry. Therefore there is an immediate presumption in favor of Throkmorton as Martin. This presumption is strengthened when we notice Throkmorton's stylistic characteristics in *A Dialogue.* Of twelve criteria of his style presented in chapter seven, nine occur in *A Dialogue.* There are such expressions as "fel a beckoning, fel a swadling, were a dying." We find "and you wil" for "if you wil"; we see the use of a double negative: "have you no more but one benefice neither"; we observe the form "Ile"; and we especially note Throkmorton's pen in his omission of "to" or "for" with an indirect object: "he burst me out with a greate exclamation of him selfe." There is also the Throkmorton penchant for alliteration in thirteen examples, for legal terminology in eight cases, for colorful writing, and for resort to Latin words. We note also the Throkmorton irony in such lines as "he is so liberall, that he will not suffer the scraps to be bestowed uppon the poore," or "he was so good unto his men, as to hange them up three or foure in numbers." Such touches are nowhere found in Penry's acknowledged writings.[6]

Throughout *A Dialogue* there are twelve common phrases and clauses which individually have no evidential value but collectively occur at least 250 times in Throkmorton's Marprelate and non-Marprelate writings, and have some evidential value: "I assure you, in good earnest, with all my heart, it is no marvell, for mine owne part, I pray you, I thanke God, thinke you, trowe you, if it be true, I warrant you, by the way." There are similar topics, allusions, and persons mentioned in *A Dialogue* and the first four Marprelate items. We encounter the familiar references to Puritans and preaching, to persecution and pursuivants, and to prisons. When we read: "you will for all this lustines, kisse the Clinke or Gatehouse for this geare," we realize that this is pure Throkmorton, who constantly referred to specific jails and who repeatedly used "for this geare." Throkmorton harps on the same string in condemning simony and in reviling those who seek after promotion and "suche as gape after Bishoppricks."[7] He ridicules bishops Aylmer and his stinginess, Cooper and his Dictionary, Middleton and his two wives; he belittles Dr. Perne for his turncoat reputation, and Dr. Some for his nonresidency. When Throkmorton refers to Kennall, who was vice-chancellor of the University of Oxford, or to Dr. Bond, "Master of Magdalins in Oxford," or to "Doctor Culpepper of Oxforde," or to Bishop Cooper ("for I have heard of him in Oxford"), he is alluding to four men who were at the university during his undergraduate years, and with the exception of Dr. Bond were mentioned in the Marprelate books. When the author refers to Martin Marprelate, who "hath set downe a pretty thing in his *Epistle*," we remember his allusion to his own *More Worke for Cooper*—"it was so prettie, and so witty"—and we hear Throkmorton praising himself. Penry frequently indulged in self-depreciation, but Throkmorton was not averse to self-adulation.[8]

One of the strongest arguments for Throkmorton's authorship is derived from the numerous parallels found in *A Dialogue* and in both Throkmorton's writings and Marprelate's works. In the two following lists of parallels, the first line or entry is numbered (6:) indicating *A Dialogue*. Any arabic number from 1 to 12 indicates an indubitable Throkmorton writing, and a roman numeral indicates a Marprelate item.

Job Throkmorton's Writings

(1) "Letter to Mr. Warcuppe"
(2) "Speech on the Scottish Queen"

(3) "Speech on the Low Countries"
(4) "Speech on the Bill and Book"
(5) "Letter to Lord Burghley"
(6) *A Dialogue. Wherin Is Plainly Laide Open*
(7) *Master Some Laid Open in His Coulers*
(8) "Letter to Lord Chancellor Hatton"
(9) "Letter to Edmund Coppinger"
(10) *Defence of Job Throkmorton against . . . Sutcliffe*
(11) "Letter to the Bailiff and Principall Burgesses"
(12) Preface to Cartwright's *A Brief Apologie*

Martin Marprelate's Works

I *Epistle*
II *Epitome*
III *Minerall and Metaphisicall Schoolpoints* (*Mineralls*)
IV *Hay Any Worke for Cooper*
V *Theses Martinianae* (*Martin Junior*)
VI *The Just Censure and Reproofe* (*Martin Senior*)
VII *The Protestatyon*

Parallels Found in A Dialogue *and in Throkmorton's Works*

I can make quicke dispatche (6:A4 v)
we made the quycker dispatche (1:1)

our dumbe dogs (6:B2)
our dumbe doggs (7:117)

with a single eie (6:A3 v)
with a sengle [*sic*] eye (3:38)

it was never merry worlde (6:D2)
have a merrie worlde of it (7:104)

howe dare you presume to say (6:A4)
durst even presume to doe (3:34)

and [if] he will be ruled by me (6:D4 v)
if he woulde be ruled by me (7:121)

we wil give him the slip (6:D4 v)
lest in time he give us the slippe (7:26)
hath faier given it the slipp (7:92)

a knavishe tricke (6:B3)
a sluttish tricke (7:31, 51)
one prety tricke (7:36)
a Cambridg tricke (7:52)

Parallels Found in A Dialogue *and in* Marprelate's *Writings*

The following list of thirty ideas and expressions from *A Dialogue* and the first four Marprelate works indicates Throkmorton's propensity to repeat himself in similar language. The thirty items from *A Dialogue* (6:), longer than the previous eight parallels, correspond closely to eleven parallels in the *Epistle* (I:), six in the *Epitome* (II:), six in the *Mineralls* (III:), and ten in *Hay Any Worke for Cooper* (IV:), and also to a parallel in *An Exhortation to the Byshops* and two parallels in *Master Some*. These thirty-six parallels, which supplement the eight parallels previously listed, are especially fascinating and evidential, since they pertain to unusual topics and contain verbatim clauses or even whole sentences. With forty-four parallels in all, the inference is well-nigh inescapable that the author of *A Dialogue* was quoting from memory or more often copying extracts from the first four Marprelate items. Like a palindrome, the conclusion seems to run both ways: since Throkmorton wrote *A Dialogue*, he penned the first four Marprelate books; since he wrote the Marprelate items, he also wrote *A Dialogue*.

1. The Bishop of London [Alymer] hath published in print, and that in an Epistle or preface before Barnardeus de Loques booke of the Church, published in English, that the puritanes may as well deny the sonne to be consubstantiall with God the Father, as they may deny the superioritie of Archbishops and Lord Bishops, flat contrary to the saying of our Saviour Christ. Luke 22:[25, 26]. (6:B2 and B2 v)

> That the Puritans may aswell deny the sonne of God to be *Homouseos* [*Homoousios*], that is, consubstantiall with God the Father, as they may denie the superioritie of Archbishop and Bishops to be lawfull. The defendant in this point is father John [Aylmer] of Fulham, in his preface before Barnardeus de Loques booke of the Church, published in English. (III:thesis 1)[9]

2. Nay, what say you to a Bishop that hath two wives and both nowe living? . . . The Bishop of Saint Davids in Wales is the man . . . I referre you to the High Commissioners, where it is recorded, with his wives names, vz., Elizabeth Gigge and Ales Prime. (6:B2 v and B3)

> That a Lord Bishop may safely have two wives in *esse* at once. The defendant in this point, is father Marmaduke, Bishop of Saint Davids, who hath two now living; the one, Elizabeth Gigge, the other, Ales Pryme. Prooved against him before the High Commission. (III:thesis 2)[10]

3. And [if] he will be ruled by me. (6:D4 v)

> if they wad be ruled bai me. (II:F1)[11]
> if they will be ruled by me. (IV:35)

4. The Word preached is the onely ordinary meanes to salvation. (6:C2 v)

> The preaching of the Word (as being the onely ordinarie meanes to salvation). (II:F2)

5. The Bishope of London when he throwes his bowle (as he useth it commonly uppon the sabboth day), he runnes after it, and if it be toe harde, he cries, "rub, rub rub," and saith, "the Divel goe with thee." (6:C3 v)

> O well bowlde, when John of London throwes his bowle, he will runne after it, and crie, "rub, rub, rub," and say "the Divill go with thee." (I:43)[12]

6. What? Doctor Pearne? Why, he is the notablest turnecoate in al this land; there is none comparable to him . . . What say you to John of Glocester, Doctor Kennolde,

Doctor Bancroft, Doctor Goodman, the Abot that nowe is of Westminster? (6:D2 v)

> Some men would play the turncoats, with the Bishop of Glocester, Doctor Kenold, Doctor Perne (I wil let Dean Goodman, Abbot of Westminster, alone now.) (I:51)

7. Why, the Bishop of Winchester is most impudent in al his actions, for very blasphemously in his sermon, preached at Mary Overies at London, said that a man might as wel finde fault with the holy Scripture, as with our corrupt *Common Booke of Prayer.* (6:C1)

> But brother Winchester, you of al other men are most wretched, for you openly in the audience of many hundreds, at Sir Marie Overies Church the last Lent, 1587, pronounced that men might finde fault, if they were disposed to quarrell, as well with the Scripture, as with the *Booke of Common Praier.* Who coulde heare this comparison without trembling? (I:32–33)[13]

8. And the Bishop of Winchester in answering the same, saith thus, in page 62 of his booke, that our Saviour Christ usually sware by his faith in his sermons, for he saide, "Amen, Amen," which is as much to say (saith he) as "by my faith, by my faith." (6:B4 v)

> That our Saviour Christ in his sermons, usually sware by his fayth. For he said, "Amen, Amen," which is as much to say, as "by my faith." The defendant in this point, is father Thomas of Winchester, alias profane T.C., page 62. (III:thesis 4)

> Yea, and our Saviour Christ sware by his faith very often. "How so, good John? I never h[e]ard that before." Why, saith T.C., he sayd, "Amen, Amen," very often, and "Amen" is as much as "by my faith," page 62. (IV:45)[14]

9. Why would he not have answered M. Cartwrights workes, nowe a dozen yeares extant and more? (6:A3 v)

> Cartwrights bookes have bene now a dozen yeares almost unanswered. (I:3)

10. For I have heard that there was some good thinges in him before he was Bishop of London, for he wrote a book called the *Harborowe of Faithful Subiects*, against Bishops, wherein he saith: "Come downe yee Bishops with your thousands, and betake you to your hundreds; let your fare be Priestlike and not Princelike, etc." (6:B1 v)

> As John of London prophesied, saying: "Come downe you bishopps from your thousands, and content you with your hundreds; let your diet be pristlike and not princelik, etc.," quoth John Elmar in his *Harborow of Faithful Subiects*. (I:3)

> Come off you bishops, away with your superfluities, yeeld up your thousandes, be content with your hundreths . . . Let your portion be pristlike and not princelike. (II: D4 v)

> Come off you bishops, leave your thousandes, and content your selves with your hundreds, saith John of London. (IV:B1 v)[15]

11. [Dean Bridges] woulde have bribed some courtier to have dealt for him, as he did for his Deanry. (6:D1)

> I praye you, where may a man buie such another gelding, and borow such another hundred poundes as you bestowed upon your good patron Sir Edward Horsey for his good worde in helping you to your Deanry. (I:19)[16]

12. They have bin often challenged, and offerd by the Puritans, even to adventure their lives against their Bishopricks. (6:C4)

> you are challenged by the Puritans to adventure your Bishoppricks against their lives in disputation. (II:A2 v)[17]

13. The Bishop of Winchester [Cooper], who took upon him to confute it, hath confirmed it for the most part. (6:B3)

> For you [Cooper] have confyrmed, rather than confuted him. (IV:A2)

14. Cooper translated a peece of Robert Stephanus his *Thesaurus* and joined it to the same with a fewe phrases, and

so bereaved the famous Knight of his labor, and calls it by the name of Coopers Dictionary. (6:B3)

> He hath translated his Dictionarie, called Co[o]pers Dictionarie, verbatim out of Robert Stephanus his *Thesaurus*, and ilfavored to[o], they say. (I:46)[18]

15. [The thieves] at their deathes, confessed that to be the dyars cloth which the Bishop had, but the pore men were never the neere for their cloth, nor cannot get it or any parte of it to this day. (6:B3 v)

> And at their deathes confessed that to be the cloth which the bishop had, but the dyars coulde not get their cloth, nor cannot unto this day. (I:9)

16. That the Creed of the Apostles, Athanasius, etc., the Nicene, etc., containe in them many palpable lies. (6:C1)

> That the Creede of the Apostles and of Athanasius, the Nicen, etc., containe many palpable lyes in them. (III:thesis 34)

17. The holy Discipline is a platform devised he knowes not by whome. (6:C2)

> The platforme of government by Pastors, Doctors, Elders, and deacons, which you say was devised you knowe not by whom. (IV:11)

18. And uppon the words where he saith, *it is not denied*, there is pasted, at the commandement of the Bishop of Canterbury, *it is not yet prooved*. (6:C2)

> For there [page 135], having said, that they wil not denie the Discipline to have bene in the Apostles time, they have now pasted there upon that, *that is not yet proved*. (IV:38)[19]

19. [The] Bishop of Winchester saith, the Bishop of Canterbury *is a giddy head, and to be brideled*, because he authorised Doctor Whitaker his readings against Bellarmina, wherein the Apocripha is defaced. (6:C2)

That the Archbishop of Canterbury *is a giddie head and to be brideled,* because he alowed the defacing of the Apocrypha by Master Doctor Whitaker, in his readings against Bellarmina. The defendant is father Thomas of Winchester, profane T.C., page 49. (III:thesis 26)[20]

20. Dr. Some . . . calls the Archbishop of Canterbury *An absurde Heretike,* because he holds baptisme administred by weomen, to be the seale of Gods covenante, page 3 of his booke against Master Penri. (6:C2)

> That the Archbishop of Canterbury, etc., in holding baptisme administred by women to be the seale of Gods covenant, is *an absurd heretike.* The defendant in this point, is father Robert Some, in his table of Master Penries errors, page 3. (III:thesis 25)[21]

21. Yes Sir, I knowe there is such a booke named *Martin Marprelate,* a most vile and slaunderous libel, but I doe not thinke my Lorde of Winchester doth approove any thing that is set downe there in any of those books, for they have put forth three or foure books under that title. (6:B3 v)

> [The Bishop of Winchester]: There have bene within these fewe weekes three or four pamphlets published in print, against bishops. The author of them calleth him selfe Martin, etc. (IV:35)[22]

22. He speaks of the habilitie that shoulde be in every minister of the Worde, that he shoulde knowe his quarter strooks, to be able to convince the adversary, etc. (6:B1 v)

> When they come to handigripes, they must not onely flourishe, but they must know their quarter strokes, and the way howe to defende their head, etc. Such a precher, I say, as this, would quickly with his quarter strokes, overturne al religion. (II:D2)[23]

> But knewe their quarter stroke, (which knowledg you require in the minister, page 49). (II:E2)

23. Hee made the Porter of his gate, minister of Paddington, being blinde. (6:B1)

> Who made the porter of his gate a dumb minister? Dumbe John of London. (I:19)

> He was almost blinde, and at Paddington, being a small people, hee could not starve as many soules, as his Master doth, which hath a great charge. (IV:44)

24. And in the first session of Parliament, holden in the first yeare of Her Majesties raigne, there was never a Lord Bishop in the lande. (6:A4)

> The lawes of Englande have bene made, when there was never a bishop in the Parliament, as in the first yere of Her Majestie. (IV:26)[24]

25. If a man apply any newe writer his opinion of the re-formed churches, in defence of the Lordes trueth, as Master Calvine, Beza, or others, he will not also sticke to bragge and tel him, that he is able to teach Calvine and Beza, or any of them all. (6:C4 v)

> When the said Master [Thomas] Settle alleaged for him-selfe, that the doctrine taught by him, had not only the warrant of the holy Scriptures, but also the approbation and testimony of the best writers of our age, as, namely, of Master Calvin and others: "What tellest thou us of Cal-vin?" (quoth the Bishop in very disdainful sort), "I tel thee there are here that can teach Calvin." At which time, there satte in commission, the Archbishop him selfe, the Deane of Westminster, Doctor Pearne and Cousins, a proper band of musitians to teach Calvin. (7:35–36)[25]

26. He [Whitgift] wrote against the Discipline, for noe other end, but to get a Bishoppricke. (6:C4 v)

> For you wrote this foule heape against the holy Discipline of Christ (as Whitgift did the like) in hope to bee the next Pope of Lambeth. (I:17)[26]

27. They sticke not in the deade time of the nighte, to breake downe the maine wal[l]es of his house, and enter in with constables and pursivants. (6:B4)

who in November last [1588] violently rusht into his house [Waldegrave's], breaking through the maine wall thereof after midnight, taking away his goods, for some of the purcivants solde his books up and downe the streats. (IV:41)

28. At which time he had his presse and letters taken away from him, and destroyed for the same cause . . . the greate charge he hath of wife and six smale [small] children. (6:B4)

> Walde-graves printing presse and letters were taken away . . . having a wife and sixe small children. (I:23)[27]

29. For he [Bishop Cooper] may well be compared to a horse with a galde backe that hath bin so rubd, that he winces, frets, and chafes. (6:C1 v)

> wherein the bishops and prelates of this realme (much lyke to galled horsses, that cannot abide to be rubbed). ([Throkmorton], *An Exhortation to the Byshops to Deale Brotherly with Theyr Brethren*, preface, first signature, ii v). See Frere and Douglas, *Puritan Manifestoes*, pp. 60–61. *S.T.C.*, no. 10392.[28]

30. In *A Dialogue*, Throkmorton quotes Luke 22:25–26 and I Peter 5:2–3; he also cites Romans 12:[4–8], Ephesians 4:[11–16], and I Corinthians 12:[28–30]. (6:A4)

> The same biblical references occur in *Martin Junior*, theses 1, 19, 42, signatures Aiii, Aiv v, Bii.

More Worke for Cooper

When Martin Marprelate wrote *Hay Any Worke for Cooper*, he referred seven times to his contemplated sequel, *More Worke*, which he promised would be a further reply to Bishop Cooper.[29] One may assume therefore that the two works belong together and that they come from the same writer. From the summary report to Lord Burghley of 21 September 1589, it is clear that *More Worke* was very long, and from Hodgskin one learns there was supposedly a second part almost as long as the first part. The initial portion was written during April–

July 1589. When the book was being printed near Manchester, the printers completed six quires on one side after three hours of work. Then the printers were arrested, and the quires, together with the manuscript, were seized by the agents of Henry Stanley, the fourth earl of Derby, on 14 August 1589. Although this manuscript is not extant, there is a summary of it in the *Protestatyon*, and there are references to it by Sutcliffe. Since it was very "bitter and virulent" against Dr. Some,[30] this may indicate that it was at least partly a reply to Dr. Some's writings, and that it was a supplement to Throkmorton's *Master Some Laid Open* and also to *Hay Any Worke*.

There is a reasonable presumption, based on Throkmorton's authorship of these two latter works, that he was also the author of *More Worke*. This presumption is strengthened by the statement at Hodgskin's trial that Throkmorton was regarded as the author. There is the specific statement from Symmes, who set type from the manuscript, that *More Worke* "was likewise of Master Throkmortons penninge; for that it was the same hand" in which *Martin Junior* and *Martin Senior* were written.[31] There is also the important fact that Sutcliffe had compared the handwriting of *More Worke* with that of several letters which Throkmorton had written to Edmund Coppinger and John Penry, and he had carefully studied Throkmorton's style. Therefore his testimony carries weight. He asserted unequivocally that the handwriting, the diction, the stylistic features, and the interlineations and corrections proved that Throkmorton was the author. He noted that "one-half" or "most" of the manuscript was written by Throkmorton, but he said nothing of the other one-half or one-third, which presumably was copied by Penry or an amanuensis. Sutcliffe was cautious and conservative in asserting that Throkmorton wrote "most" of *More Worke*, but he also gave seven plausible reasons for concluding that Throkmorton was the real author:

> 1. First, that is proved by the testimony of J. Throkmortons owne hand writing, for the copy which every man may

see that doubteth hereof, is half of it written with Job Throkmortons owne hand.[32]

2. Besides this, the phrase and maner of writing, which is a
   certaine indice and signe of the authors affections, doth declare from whence the booke did come. So scurrilous,
   wicked, and railing stuffe could come from no other than
   Throkmorton.

3. Thirdly, he that made *Martin Senior* and *Martin Junior*, made
   also *More Worke*. Simmes and Tamlin do both depose, that
   both were written with one hand. And it is already proved
   that Throkmorton was author of *Martin Senior* and *Junior*.

4. Fourthly, the same booke is found in divers places corrected
   and enterlined with Job Throkmortons own hand. But no
   man useth or presumeth to adde, detract, or alter the origi-
   nall, beside the author.

5. Fiftly, at Penryes and Throkmortons intreaty, Newman was
   content to goe from Throkmortons house to London, to
   provide a printer for the printing of *More Worke for Cooper*.
   If he had not bene author, what needed he to have cared
   for the printing of it?

6. Sixtly, when Hodgskin was come to Throkmortons house,
   there the bargaine was made for the printing of the booke,
   as both Hodgskin and Newman doe testifie.

7. Lastly, it is deposed both by Hodgskin and Simmes, that
   Throkmorton while *Martin Senior* and *Martin Junior* were
   in printing, should say unto Hodgskin, that *More Worke for
   Cooper* should come to his handes shortly. And so it did,
   being dropped out of a chamber into a rome where then
   Hodgskin was. If he were not the author, or at least an
   actor in it, how could hee know how the booke should come
   to his handes? Could he prophesie that the booke would
   droppe out of the chamber, if he had not bene privie to
   the dropping of it?

Then Sutcliffe concluded with a powerful and direct paragraph:

If then Master Throkmorton made that booke which is called
More Worke, then is he doubtlesse Martin Marprelate. For the
author of that booke doeth in plaine termes confesse, that he
is Martin Marprelate. Let him disguise the name as he will,
and call himselfe now Martin, then Marprelate, or give to

Penry the name of Martin, and to himselfe the name of Marprelate, as if Martin Marprelate were a monster compounded of divers persons, and much wicked scurrilitie and ribaldry; yet this is certaine, that Job Throkmorton was author of *More Worke for Cooper*, and that the author of that booke was Martin Marprelate; and to go one streine further, that the same is a most infamous, wicked, prophane, and scurrilous libell, the author whereof deserveth not to live in any Christian common wealth.[33]

If the reader accepts the arguments for Throkmorton's authorship of the *Epistle*, as presented in chapter eight, then Throkmorton by his own admission was also the author of the *Epitome* and *Hay Any Worke*. If he wrote this latter book, he also penned *More Worke*, which was promised several times in *Hay Any Worke*. Further corroborating evidence was provided by the compilers of the "Summary of the Information" of 21 September 1589, whose report was completed about five weeks after the capture of *More Worke* on 14 August. The compilers reported that "the authoure of the written copie [of *More Worke*], that was taken by the Earl of Darbie, taketh upon him to be the same, that made the first three libells, and the stile doth not varie." In other words, the writer of *More Worke* admitted a second time that he had written the *Epistle*, the *Epitome*, and *Hay Any Worke*.[34]

Martins Interim, or a Briefe Pistle to the Cursed Prelates and Clergie

Sutcliffe is our sole authority for a manuscript book which is not extant. He stated that he had "seen a little pamphlet entitled 'Martins Interim.'" He said the title exemplified "the humor of the author," and then gave the full title: "Martins Interim, or a Briefe Pistle to the Cursed Prelates and Clergie." Among the epithets and "kitchen rhetoricke" directed against the ministers of the Church of England, Sutcliffe mentioned "a hellish rable," "godlesse men," "an ungodly swarme of caterpillers, dogges, and hirelings." This was Throkmorton's language, and Sutcliffe correctly assigned it to him because it was "full of rayling and ribaldery, of cursing, slaunder, and impietie." Sutcliffe also alleged seven reasons for Throkmorton's authorship: (1) the style; (2) his handwriting; (3) he was "reported to be the author of it"; (4) no one else was suspected to have written it; (5) the testimony of examinees and deponents; (6) the slanderous and unchristian name-calling; (7) Throkmorton sent the book with letters to Penry in Scotland.[35]

Although Throkmorton hoped that his book would be printed in Scotland, it was never set to type. It is understandable why Waldegrave did not print it, since he was under pressure from James VI to print nothing without license, lest he or the king give offense to Queen Elizabeth and her government. Furthermore, the English ambassador, Robert Bowes, kept a close watch on Waldegrave's activities. Therefore Penry kept the book and letters, but after he had dispatched his papers by sea to London, his chest of documents and letters was captured, together with "Martins Interim," probably in Stepney about April 1593.[36]

Since Sutcliffe had read the manuscript, his report is both informative and invaluable:

> In his booke called "Martins Interim," a booke knowen to be Throkmortons, he calleth the most reverend prelate in this land [Archbishop Whitgift], whom for his pietie and gravitie all men reverence, and for his justice, and humanitie, his enemies cannot chuse but honor, *the enemy of Christ*, and *Antichrist*, yea, and *contemptible varlet*; the bishops and clergie he calleth *miscreants, caterpillers, locusts, and divels incarnate*. And so he goeth on throughout his booke.

Sutcliffe concluded that "Martins Interim" was "a booke, by witnesses, and likenesse of stile, and divers other arguments, proved to be Job Throkmortons."[37]

The Crops and Flowers of Bridges Garden

Our knowledge of this book comes from the best of sources—the deposition of Newman. According to Sutcliffe's summary, Throkmorton promised that Newman would be rewarded by the sale of this work because of his "great pains" and small compensation. The manner of the delivery of the manuscript was characteristic of Throkmorton's caution and astute ingenuity. Even as he had arranged for the placing of the incomplete manuscript of *Martin Junior* under a bush, even as on 18 July 1589 he had furtively slipped the rest of this manuscript into Symmes's copy near the press, even as he had arranged to have Newman and Penry drop the manuscript of *More Worke for Cooper* from an upper chamber into an empty room at Roger Wigston's home in Wolston, just so he resorted to a typical device to cover his tracks in this instance. He informed Newman "that he would go forth to walk in the evening, and that if he [Newman] would follow him, he should find it [the manuscript]. Which fell out accordingly. He walked like a proper man, Newman followed, the book dropped down, Newman took it up, and Throkmorton dealt earnestly with him to print it."[38]

James Meddowes, who was also designated to benefit from this book's sales because of his assistance to Throkmorton's work, brought the manuscript to Middelburg, where Richard Schilders printed many secret books for English nonconformists. While the book was being printed, Throkmorton sent a letter to one of his agents, John Bowman, to obtain copies. According to Sutcliffe, who saw the letter or the deposition of Bowman, Throkmorton "had a great longing" to possess and peruse the finished product. "Even as foolish parents long to see their children, so he was desirous to see that worke which he without any paine and great meriment had brought forth into the world."[39]

This story is told with such intriguing detail that it rings true. It rests upon the main participant, Newman, and his deposition. It is supported by Throkmorton's letter to Bowman and by the latter's deposition. And it is further strengthened by an additional detail, which provides an excellent parallel. Newman testified that Throkmorton had told him the name of the book—*The Crops and Flowers of Bridges Garden*. This same phrase appears in Throkmorton's book, *Master*

Some Laid Open (page 105), where he speaks of "the crops and flowers of his owne pretie garden."[40]

Sutcliffe specifically said that the book was written and published. No copy seems to exist in the libraries of England, Wales, Scotland, the Netherlands, or the United States. There is still hope that a lone copy survives in some archive, in some collection of pamphlets, or in a record office. The likelihood is that the entire consignment was seized by censors. If a copy of the book does exist, it may be cataloged under "Crops" or "Martin Marprelate" or a pseudonym, or it may be listed as anonymous or mistakenly as by Dr. John Bridges. Despite persistent efforts in searching libraries and catalogs, I have been unable to find a copy.

STYLISTIC PECULIARITIES AND PARALLELS IN THROKMORTON'S AND MARTIN'S WORKS

VII

"Considerations of style are crucial to any discussion of Martin Marprelate's identity, for what is distinctive about his pamphlets is their own original and inimitable form of expression. And what almost everyone who has carefully read Martin's work and that known to have been written by Penry finds it impossible to accept, is that they could both be the products of the same pen. Penry's style is robust and vigorous enough, but not even his most ardent admirers could claim for him any qualities of sparkle or humour. His weapon was a rough-hewn bludgeon as compared with that deadly, polished, glittering Toledo blade of Martin Marprelate." (Glanmor Williams' review of Donald J. McGinn, *John Penry and the Marprelate Controversy*, in *The Welsh History Review*, 3 (1967): 312

No SCHOLAR has ever made a systematic comparative analysis and study of the writings of Penry, Throkmorton, and Marprelate. Some of the nine books of Penry are rare, such as the second edition of his *Exhortation*, which exists in a unique copy at the National Library of Wales. Two of his books, *A Treatise Containing the Aequity* and his *A Viewe*, have been reissued, and David Williams published his *Three Treatises concerning Wales* in 1960, but there is no edition of his collected works, and some of his manuscripts have remained unknown, even to his diligent biographers, John Waddington and William Pierce.

The study of Throkmorton's writings has been neglected because so many of his works are anonymous or pseudonymous. The British Museum *General Catalogue of Printed Books* and the *Short-Title Catalogue* list only one work by him—*The Defence of Job Throkmorton, against the Slaunders of Master Sutcliffe*. Since this book comprises only thirty-nine pages, the amount of material on which one could base a study of style has been inadequate. But fortunately there are five letters, three recently discovered parliamentary speeches, the preface to Cartwright's *A Brief Apologie, A Dialogue,* and *Master Some Laid Open,* all written by Throkmorton, so that there are twelve items on which we can certainly rely. In addition there are eighteen items which are anonymous and pseudonymous. Of these, seven are Marprelate books which I have endeavored to prove belong to Throkmorton. There are a few excerpts from three non-extant items described by Throkmorton, Sutcliffe, and Newman, which were probably written by Throkmorton. (See chapter six.) Also, we have six books and two manuscript items which I have assigned to Throkmorton, with evidence for their attribution to him. (See chapter nine and appendixes.) Consequently, we now have thirty probable items by Throkmorton, of which twelve constitute a firm foundation on which to build generalizations about the man, his ideas, and his style of writing. To be doubly cautious, I have been sparing in the use of the early works in 1572–73, since they were written fifteen or sixteen years before the Marprelate books, but I have frequently used *Master Some Laid Open,* with 124 pages, and *A Dialogue. Wherin Is Plainly Laide Open,* with thirty-one pages, in buttressing arguments relating to style, ideas, and persons, since I believe these two books are clearly and indubitably from Throkmorton's pen. The study of Martin's seven main tracts presents no problem, since we have all of them in print, although the third one—the *Mineralls*—exists in only two known copies, one at Lambeth Palace Library and one at the Bodleian Library. There is a facsimile edition from the Scolar Press and one modernized edition by William Pierce of Martin's works, besides the three reissues by John Petheram—the *Epistle*, the *Epitome*, and *Hay Any Worke.*

Twelve stylistic features, found in Throkmorton's and Marprelate's writings (and infrequently a few in other writers), *but not in Penry's*, are presented in this chapter. The first six are mainly grammatical, but some of the remaining six characteristics, being purely stylistic, reflect Throkmorton's temperament and playfulness. One does not find such an extensive use of alliteration in other writers, nor does one encounter the colorful writing and coined words which Throkmorton and Martin use. These special features reveal the writer's vivid and unique personality, his percipient eye, his sense of the humorous and the ridiculous, his participation in worldly pleasures, his legal interests, and his knowledge of Latin.

As before, in chapter six, I have assigned arabic numbers to Throkmorton's works and roman numerals to Martin's writings. Thus (3:22) indicates the third item, "Speech on the Low Countries," folio 22, and (I:4) indicates the source in the *Epistle*, page 4. The following list contains eleven items which I have attributed to Throkmorton. Since these anonymous works are newly assigned to Throkmorton, I have not built the stylistic argument on these items, but I have provided reasons in the text or appendixes for ascribing them to Throkmorton. They are included here to provide a complete list of all thirty of Throkmorton's writings, so far as this is possible. Future research may provide reasons for doubting an item or two in the list of eleven attributions, and it is hoped some future researcher may discover an additional rare book or an unknown manuscript, such as *The Crops and Flowers of Bridges Garden* or "Martins Interim," thus enlarging the canon of Throkmorton's writings.

Other Works Attributed to Throkmorton

(a) "An Answer to Certen Peeces of a Sermon Made at Paules Crosse on Sunday the xxvii[th] of June in *Anno* 1572 by Doctor Cowper, Bishop of Lincoln"

(b) *An Exhortation to the Byshops to Deale Brotherly with Theyr Brethren*
(c) *An Exhortation to the Bishops and Their Clergie*
(d) *Certaine Articles, Collected and Taken (as It Is Thought) by the Byshops out of a Litle Boke Entituled An Admonition to the Parliament, with an Answere to the Same*
(e) *A Second Admonition to the Parliament*
(f) "A Friendly Caveat to Bishop Sands Then Bishop of London, and to the Rest of His Brethren the Bishops"
(g) *The State of the Church of Englande (Diotrephes)*
(h) *More Worke for Cooper*
(i) "Martins Interim, or a Briefe Pistle to the Cursed Prelates and Clergie"
(j) *The Crops and Flowers of Bridges Garden*
(k) *A Petition Directed to Her Most Excellent Maiestie*

Use of Indirect Object and Reflexive Pronoun

One of Throkmorton's distinctive stylistic peculiarities is his use of the indirect object without the preposition "to" or "for." Another is his practice of using the personal pronoun as a reflexive. In my original compilation of eighty-one items, there were thirty-six examples from six of Throkmorton's works and forty-five examples from six of Marprelate's books. Usually these examples have been reduced to an average of two or three for each work.

Throkmorton's Works

he rappes mee out an othe (3:22)
shee hath brought us into this worlde suche a litter (3:33)
hee may sitte him downe in his chearyre (3:35)
I will never stande now to shape him an answere (4:16)
wee knowe not which way to turne us (4:23)
he burst me out with a greate exclamation (6:Ciii)
comes me in the same house very pleasauntly to them (6:Diii v)
to have drawne us his portraiture by (7:10)
carie his mother a stoole (7:30)

I referre me to the learned (7:77)
he casting me a cusshen (10:Aiii)
hee pulles me out of his bosome a bundle (10:Aiii v)
whispered me in the eare (10:Dii)

Marprelate's Works

say me that againe (I:4)
I crye him mercy (I:11)
worke your priesthood a woe (I:28)
answer me this point (II:D2 v)
very narrowly escape me a scouringe (II:D2 v)
what a pleasure you have done me (IV:A2)
and bring me him (IV:A4)
cary me this conclusion to John o Lambehith (IV:6)
whosoever can bring mee acquainted with my father (V:Ai)
they . . . have gotten them many thousande eie witnesses (V:Dii v)
I do by these my writinges, cast you downe the glove (V: Dii v)
have you diligently soght mee out Waldegrave (VI:Aii v)
hee hath chosen him such a methode (VI:Bii v)
I wil here set them down a waye (VII:10)
it would do me good at the heart (VII:16)
set me downe the particulars (VII:27)

Use of the Double Negative

There are thirty-two examples of the use of the double negative, of which twenty-one derive from six of Throkmorton's works, and eleven from five Marprelate items. Sixteen are listed here. The word "neither" occurs frequently in both sections.

Throkmorton

yet should yt not wante by theyr good willes an orator to smooth yt, an advocate to pleade for it, nor a champion to avowe yt (2:4)
hee is not exempted from the hand of God nether (3:34)
this is not spoken neyther to lull us (3:37)
and have you no more but one benefice neither (6:A4 v)

he knowes him not neither (7:12)
he will not spare him no more (7:19)
which is not so priviledged neither (7:123)
they should not bee verie well affected neither (10:C3 v)
and no more in deede I am not (10:Eii)

Marprelate

he hath no great skill in neyther (I:28)
and not these neyther without cure (I:38)
nor bapti[s]m neither (II:D1 v)
nay, nor twenty neither (II:E4)
nor it was not at that time (IV:42)
you have nothing neither your selves (VI:Aiii)
nor have nothing to doe with him (VII:30)

The Use of "A"

There are forty examples of the use of "a" before words. Eighteen are found in Throkmorton's works, and twenty-two occur in Marprelate's books. Twenty-four are presented here.

falles a praysing of him (3:44)
the weomen fel a swadling of them (6:C4)
then he fel a beckoning to the preacher (6:D3)
should fall a casting of the physitions water (7:104)
fall a setting Doctor Fulke to schoole (7:104)
wonderful treasons a brewing against the Queen (10:Di v)
say what you wil a Gods name (6:B4 v)
he comes a pace (6:B4 v)
that spied nowe a time (7:76)
his handes are a colde (7:116)

where he should be a printing books (I:42)
and went a heymaking (I:49)
cha bin [I have been] a seeking (IV:30)
children are like to go a begging (IV:48)
hee first fell a studying the arte of Pistle making (V:Ciii)
boyes will now be a Pistle-making (VI:Aii)
and fall a prooving of these thinges (VI:Bii v)
John a Bridges (III:11; IV:A2 v; V:Aiii; VI:Cii v; VII:30)

John a Cant. (VII:25)
put your corner cap a litle nere a toe side (I:48)
an a [if he] had bin my Worships printer (IV:39)
I could a told tis [this] (VI:Aii)
and set them a worke (VI:Aii v)
let a six or seven of you (VI:Aiii v)

Use of "and" or "an" for "if"

In all, there are twenty occurrences of "and" or "an" with the meaning of "if." It is employed in Throkmorton's *Dialogue* and nineteen times in six Marprelate items. Eleven examples are listed here.

and you will (6:C4)

and that be all you can say (I:4)
an thou takest that course (I:8)
an you doe (II:C1)
and they dare but raise up this slander (II:D3)
halfe a dozen and neede be (IV:11)
but and thou lovest me, never liken me to our bishops (IV:31)
and he doe (V:Ciii)
ant [if it] please your Worshippe (VI:Biii)
an I had beene (VI:Cii)
an thou be a goodfellow (VII:32)

Use of "his" for "its"

The masculine possessive pronominal adjective occurs eight times in Throkmorton's writings and three times in Marprelate's books.

and yet had it [tragedy] his patrons (2:4)
so have I given it his pasport (7:A2)
it is a limited power and hath his bounds (7:24)
belike it [sound preaching] had bin in some danger to have lost his credite (7:43)
till that same perillous pillorie . . . be shifted or remooved out of his place (7:56)

when this bugbeare is unvizarded once, . . . his visnomy appeares (7:59)
the sound of this bell by his clapper (7:104)
the Word of God is in his own nature an edifying woord
(7:117)

he hath given the cause sicken a wipe in his bricke (II:Bı)
lawful for the Church of Geneva to begin his sermon (II:Cı)
his chaplainship is never able to recover his credite (VII:26)

Use of "Any Thing," "Nothing," "Something," and "Somewhat"

There are nouns used adverbially; twenty-six are from
Throkmorton's works and six from Marprelate's books.
"Somewhat" is used both as an adverb and as a substantive.

in his pleasant veine anye thing too snappish (7:A2)
if my hands doe happen to smell any thing unsavorly (7:5)
may any thing satisfie youe (11:391)

if no comparison anye thing neere the fittest (V:Diii)

yet this were nothinge neere to dyscrybe her (2:5)
the cytye of Geneva . . . nothinge neare that thralldome (3:31)
ye that were nothing touched with the miseryes (3:45)
it is nothinge alltered but translated (4:19)
Master Some is nothing so bleare-eyed as Master Bridges (7:38)
his visnomy appeares nothing so terrible (7:59–60)
as if it were a thing nothing materiall (7:64)
did nothing answere those patheticall outcries (10:Aiii)
beeing nothing well before (10:Aiii)
though in words nothing so groslie (10:Biv v)

this word *unworthinesse*, is something too generall (7:23)
and thereby something too weake (7:23)
till the edge of these arguments be something overworne (7:42)
the poore schollers logicke was something too weak (7:54)
to talke something wildly (10:Aii v)
when I had something recovered (10:Aiii)
as men something amazed (10:Aiv v)
Sutcliffe would something recall him selfe (10:Civ v)
I was something amazed (10:Diii v)

one poynt which something troubled them (I:26)
the old man to be something discouraged (V:Ai v)
if he were not something touched with the coinquination of
    the flesh (VI:Cii v)
are they not then something too much overwayned (VII:15)

and somwhat to the purpose (6:A2 v)
they are somwhat neere (6:A4 v)
the preacher somewhat troubling him (6:D3)
he wil have somewhat els to doe (7:42)

howsoever it be, somewhat is not well (V:Ciii)

Use of "Ile," "Ise," "Ide," and "a"

There are forty-two examples of variants for the pronoun
"I," and two for the pronoun "he." Ten examples are derived
from Throkmorton's writings, and thirty-four from Marprelate's works.

ile tell you (6:C1, C3, D3)
ile (7:35, 54, 54, 72, 86, 86, 87)

ile (I:3, 4, 9, 15, 18, 18, 20, 29, 38, 46)
ile (II:A2, C1, C1, C4 v, F3, G1, G1 v)
ile (IV:A2 v, 36, 48, 48)
ile (V:Ai)
ile (VI:Aiv v, Dii)
ile (VII:22, 22, 30)
ise [I shall] (I:37; II:G1 v; IV:6, 37)
ide a [I would have] (IV:39)
I hope a [he] would (IV:2)
an a had bin [if he had been] my Worships printer (IV:39)

Alliteration

One of the stylistic peculiarities that is immediately apparent
to the reader of Marprelate's books is his use of alliteration,
which is deliberate, persistent, and effective. It is exciting
and amusing to note the same deliberate practice in all of
Throkmorton's writings. My original list of 267 items in-

cluded 140 examples from Throkmorton's works and 127 from Marprelate's books, but only a select list is presented here, consisting of 80 examples.

Throkmorton

    were well wrong [wrung] (1:1)

    the prayse and pryviledge (2:3)
    joyning of handes and joye of harte (2:6)
    in deed to dye the death (2:8)
    infinite frightes and feares (2:9)

    florishing in the feare and favour (3:31)
    a greate State to slyde, sometimes, to slyppe (3:34)
    shyver us and shatter us (3:37)
    serving us as a sheilde of securitie (3:37)

    warier than wee in watching (4:14)
    beaten his brayne to the botomme (4:15)
    seede men of sedition doe see (4:21)
    gyftes and graces of Godes spirit (4:23)

    a just judgment (5:148)

    greate and grevous (6:A3)
    sore pestered with sects and scismes (6:A3)
    I have heard how he (6:D3 v)
    let me loose my life (6:D4 v)

    canvasing of controversies in Cambridge (7:10)
    he will willingly with harte and hande (7:17)
    surcease your suites and supplications (7:18)
    by their leave, they lye, and they lye loudely too (7:57)
    crosse and controll in this case (7:63)
    cleave to the crosse of Christ (7:101)
    to smo[o]the it, or smother it (7:111)

    to reject or refuse (9:18)
    a sanctified cause, you know, would alwayes have a sanctified
      course (9:18)
    your love to loade mee with (9:18)

    neither in methode, matter, nor manner (10:Aiii)
    fastened some of his fooleries and phantasticall revelations
      (10:Aiii v)

printed and published by patches and pieces (10:Bii)
strayning and stretchinge (10:Biii)
so eger and sharpe sett to snappe (10:Biii)
shake the halter and shewe the hatchet (10:Civ)
falling flatte on his face (10:Di v)
groveling, groaning and foming (10:Di v)

I will willingly (11:391)

give the glory to God (12:A2 v)
to be troden and trampeled on (12:A3)
a fardle of fooleries (12:A3)
so slipper in the seare as Maister Sutcliffe is (12:A3 v)
thy condemners to be thy clearers (12:A4 v)
revell or revile (12:A4 v)

Marprelate

our cosen Cosins (I:2)
proud, popish, presumptuous, profane, paultrie, pestilent and
 pernicious prelates (I:6)
marke my masters (I:12)
being belike bankerout (I:34)
cannot nor could not chuse but committ (I:45)
made more manifest (I:53)

I will worke your woe (II:A2 v)
cannot keep them close (II:A2 v)
let John Cant. cast his cardes and consider (II:B1)
he hath behaved himselfe (II:B1 v)
true and tried trueth (II:B3 v)
brother Bridges (II:C2, E3)
predicables and predicaments (II:C2 v)
he hath in his hande (II:E3 v)

troubles and turmoiles (III:7)
crowne of Canterburie (III:37)

Thomas Tubtrimmer (IV:A2, 2, 31, 35)
confyrmed rather than confuted (IV:A2 v)
he had bin better to have hooped halfe the tubbes (IV:6)
you mar-prince, mar-law, mar-magestrate, mar-church, and
 mar-commonwelth (IV:23)

I doe disdaine to deale (IV:37)
Martin hath marred Richard Patriks market (IV:43)

mislike my manner (V:Aii)
fire and fagot, bands and blowes, railing and reviling (V:
    Aii v)
ministerie and the magistracie (V:Biii v)
suffering the sayde sermon (V:Cii)
Maister Martin Marprelate (V:Cii v)
praying your prelacie (V:Cii v)

Canturburie Caiphas (VI:Aii)
crakt the crowne of Canturbury (VI:Aii v)
die the death, that to the dog is due (VI:Diii)
himselfe or his hangIons [hanglons, hang-ons?] (VI:Ci)
discrying and displaying (VII:7)
an handsome halter to hang himselfe with (VII:20)
I then said, and so say I still (VII:28)
shaketh and quivereth, and shrinketh, as it were, in the sinowes
    (VII:9)
wringlefaced Wrighte (VII:31)

Colorful Writing

The writings of Throkmorton and Marprelate are studded
with sentences that are vivid, picturesque, and imaginative.
These qualities are not characteristic of Penry's writings,
since he lacked the gifted pen of Throkmorton.

Throkmorton

For ambition (you knowe) ys like a quicke eele in a mans
bowells that never giveth rest, and no julippe can queanch
the thirst of a kingdome, but only bloudde. (2:8)

But yet, as mighty as he is, it seemeth, by your leave, the
Lorde hath put a snaffle in his mouth for all that. (3:35)

This freedome of ours, as yt is now handeled heere amongst
us, I can very well lyken to a certeine lycense graunted to a
preachere to preache the gospell freely, provided allwayes that
he medle neyther with the doctryne of the prophets nor the
apostles. (4:13)

189

Well, I hope there bee no man heare of this minde, "that igno-rance is the mother of devotion." That wretched and ragged opynion is hissed oute of the schoole of our hartes long eare this, I hope. (4:20)

Tush, foe, he sites nowe uppon his cogging stoole, which may truly be called the chaier of pestilence; little may he doe if he cannot bragge, crake, and face it out. (6:C4 v)

Will you have it in English now? For Ile never dissemble you, I doe by my Latine, as that sweet babe of Sarum doth by his Greeke and Hebrue, begg and borrow here a patch, and there a patch, as the dictionaries that come in my way do yeeld me sustenance. (7:86)

Who woulde have thought that Master Some would ever have bestowed new varnishing of an olde rustie and cankred blade, which was so behackled before? (7:96)

In whose presence he so behaved himselfe, falling flatte on his face, groveling, groaning, and foming at the mouth (10:Di v)

And this was the first and the last time that ever I saw Hacket in my life. And to speake the trueth, this verie once was enough to distaste any man of never so meane judgement, I beleeve, unlesse he were bewitched, because the very puffing and swell-inge of his face, the staring and gogling of his eies, with his gahstlie [*sic*] countenance, did, me thought, sufficientlie deci-pher out unto me, what was in the man, at the first sight. (10:Dii v)

Yea, and of that which I beleeve the poorest scavenger in a towne would be loth to stoupe for, he with a little helpe and forbishing of Mr. *Surveiour of Discipline* [Dr. Bancroft], frameth for the most parte some irrefragable and tempestuous conclu-sion against these new plot-formers, and then forsooth to the presse it must in all post hast with some rhetoricall varnish of innovation, as if *quidlibet ex quolibet*, or as if the poorest and most patched record under the sunne (that blusheth, it may be, to see the light) were evidence strong enough against a Precisian. (12:A3)

Marprelate

At the hearing of this speeche, the waspe got my brother by the nose, which mad[e] him in his rage to affirme, that he woulde be Lord of Fulham as long as he lived, in despight of all England. Naye, softe there, quoth Master Madox, except Her Majestie I pray you. That is my meaning, ka dumb John. (I:21)

After that his Grace had eased his stomacke in calling him boy, knave, varlet, slanderer, libeller, lewde boy, lewd slaunderer, etc. (I:30)

Trust me truely, he hath given the cause sicken a wipe in his bricke, and so lambskinned the same, that the cause will be the warmer a good while for it. (II:B1)

Thou knowest not how I love thee for thy wit and learning sake, brother John (as for thy godlines, I might cary it in mine eye, and see never a whit the worse). (II:B4 v)

That the long prayers of the Puritanes, before and after their sermons, are nothing els, but beeble bable. (III:8)

Whau, whau, but where have I bin al this while? Ten to one among some of these Puritans. Why Martin? Why Martin, I say, hast tow forgotten thy selfe? Where hast ti bene? Why man, cha bin a seeking for a samons nest, and cha vound a whol crue, either of ecclesiasticall traitors, or of bishops of the Divel. (IV:30)

But did not I say truely of thee, that thou canst cog, face, and lye as fast as a dog can trot, and that thou hast a right seasoned wainscoate face of ti nowne, chwarnt tee, ti vorehead zaze hard as horne. (IV:39)

Published and set foorth as an after-birth of the noble gentleman himselfe, by a prety stripling of his, Martin Junior, and dedicated by him to his good neame and nuncka, Maister John Kankerbury. (V:Ai)

Let them be well assured it was not undertaken to be intermitted at everye blast of evill successe. Naye, let them knowe that by the grace of God the last yeare of Martinisme, that is, of the discrying and displaying of Lord Bishops, shall not be, till full two yea[r]s after the last year of Lambethisme. (VII:7)

Nexte to this (as I take it) followed a preamble to an Eblitaph [Epitaph] upon the death of olde Andrewe Turne-coate, to be song antiphonically in his Graces Chappell, on Wednes-dayes and Frydayes, to the lamentable tune of Orawhynemeg. (VII:26)

Allusions to Betting, Gambling, Cards, Drinking, Chance

Throkmorton was a worldly Puritan who believed in temperance but not in total abstinence. He knew by experience the life of a country gentleman, the selfish and shrewd ways of men, the relaxation of Court and club. Participation in normal pleasures he regarded as permissible in moderation, but he demanded a stricter code of conduct for clerical leaders whose indulgences he ridiculed. He did not disapprove of stage plays, but he denounced the excesses of the anti-Martinist productions. He did not frown on bowling, but he enjoyed catching Bishop Aylmer on the green during the sabbath. He approved of moderate imbibing, but roundly criticized parson William Gravat for drunkenness. Sins of the flesh did not greatly trouble him, but he was mightily concerned with influence-peddling, bribery, promotion-seeking, persecution, injustice, and tyranny.

Penry, however, was a rigorous Puritan, strict with himself, concerned about others, inclined to be censorious, and a hater of sin. He sought to be an exemplar of his beliefs, and did not hesitate to reprove wrongdoing by the rich and the powerful. He did not trifle with sin, nor did he give evidence of participation in secular pleasures. Since he believed strongly in predestination, and God's providence, he did not allude to luck, chance, or hap.

In all there are twenty references to cards, thirteen to chance, nine to betting, nine to gambling, and seven to quaffing. Of the total of fifty-eight allusions, twenty-five are from Throkmorton's writings and thirty-three from Marprelate's books. The following select list presents a total of twenty-six examples from six works by Throkmorton and six books by Marprelate.

    no julippe can queanch the thirst of a kingdome (2:8)
    he that should sette up his rest (3:43)
    twentye to one (4:20)
    the good luck that some men have (7:16)
    Master Penri goeth an ase [ace] further (7:24)
    and every hand whiles he bids them (7:31)
    he can juggle or help a die (7:79)
    I dare lay a good wager (7:116)
    in the necke of this comes Maister Sutcliffe with his vie [bid]
        (10:Biii)
    Mr. Sutcliffe was once taken with false dice (12:A2 v)

    one that will not sticke to play a game at cards (I:12)
    Sir Jeffry once in an alehouse (I:41)
    the gamesters his companions wan [won] all his monie at trey
        trip (I:42)
    by bowling and tabling (I:54)
    it would put a man to his trumps (II:B3 v)
    let John Canterbury cast his cardes (II:B1)
    his rare skill in juglinge (II:G1)
    two or three paire of trulling square dice (II:F3 v)
    play twenty nobles in a night (IV:A3 v)
    at Priemeero on the cards (IV:A3 v)
    a bishop such a cardplaier (IV:A3 v)
    as good a gift in pistle making as you have at Priemeero (IV:
        A3 v)
    tenne to one (V:Dii)
    with a draught of Darbie ale (VI:Div)
    I have long agone set up my rest (VII:14)
    as if the wager had bene (VII:19)

Legal Terminology

Throkmorton's and Marprelate's writings reveal a general interest in or a quasi-technical knowledge of legal matters, which is not found in Penry's books. In all there are 71 examples from Throkmorton's writings, and 91 from Marprelate's

works; of these 162 items, 62 are presented in the following
list.

Throkmorton

within the compasse of the statute (1:1)
enter into recognoissance (1:1)

perillous presidente [precedent] (2:8)
to cancell so greate a recognysaunce (2:8)

justitia et charitas validae sunt principis arces (3:46–47)

lyving witnesses agaynste all such unsavorye pleadinges (4:23)
we are at an outlarye [outlawry] (4:23)

a just judgment (5:148)

were not lord bishops established by Her Majestie and consent
    of the whole Parliament (6:A4)
if they wil not sweare, then to the Clinke (6:D1 v)
when sute is made unto him for their libertie (6:D1 v)
they will enter into bonds (6:D1 v)

surcease your suites and supplications (7:18)
might have bred a demur (7:19)
a judge may ride, may walk, may heare a sermon,may confer
    with the gentlemen and justices, may sit downe on the bench
    (7:20)
as the lawyers cal it, a *none est factum* (7:24)
I speak not here *de iure,* but *de posse* (7:24)
he hath his *supersedeas* and discharge (7:28)
with a *sursurare* to a higher court (7:35)

my submission aswell to my Lord of Canterbury as to our
    Justices of Assize (8:1)
cleare my self of the indightment (8:1)
yf ever I had so much as anie fellonious thought (8:1)

the next terme, you heare, I must appeare here again upon
    my bond (9:18)

my recantation under seale (10:Civ v)
a mans clearing and defence (10:Div v)
his band and recognoisance (10:Eii v)
the fellons and malefactours standing at the barre (10:Eiii v)

for the burgesship I may safely say (11:391)
by heresay and report (12:A2 v)
were evidence strong enough (12:A3)
while he was going to execution (12:A3 v)

Marprelate

to bee tryed in the Court of Requestes (I:20)
cleane contrary to the statute 13 Elizabeth (I:21)
popish doctors of the bawdie courts (I:22)
to the chauncellors courte (I:22)
did you get a decree in the High Court of Starchamber (I:24–25)
he will do little contrary to law for fear of a premunire (I:26)

Is there any law to force men to accuse themselves (II:A2 v)
urging an oth contrary to statute (II:A2 v)
which is a piece of the forraine power bannished by statute (II:A2 v)
get you the law to be against their lordly callings (II:E4)

prooved against him before the High Commission (III:no. 2)
may have a lawfull superior authoritie (III:no. 18)
it is not lawfull for Her Majestie (III:no. 35)

desireth the judge that the lawe may proceede against him (IV:B1)
to be tried with me in a judgement of life and death, at any barre in England (IV:13)
civillians live by the Court of Amraltie and other courts as well as by the Arches (IV:24)
the popes canon lawes, which are bannished by statute (IV:25)
the lawes of Englande have bene made when there was never a bishop in the Parliament, as in the first yere of Her Majestie (IV:26)
I hope he wil see both the *quare impedit* and the *premunire* (IV:43)

approved by the statutes of this kingdome, and Her Majesties royall prerogative (V:Bii)
this their doctrine is mainteined by statute (V:Bii v)
the citations, processes, excommunications (V:Biv)
the warrant of our laws and statutes (V:Ci)

contrarie unto her lawfull statutes and priviledges (VI:Biv v)
to have incurred the statute of *premunire facies* (VI:Biv v)
proceedings against law and equitie (VI:Biv v)
to have his remedie at the Kings Bench (VI:Ciii v)

when they be both sole judges, and sole witnesse[s] themselves
    (VII:21)
what remedie shoulde the partie that stands there alone have,
    by apeaching or complayning (VII:22)
ile have the *scandalum magnatum* against him (VII:22)
in a plaine statute of the 25 of Henry VIII (VII:23)

The Use of Latin

Throkmorton is fond of Latin words, phrases, and sentences,
which occur frequently in his works. In fact, in Throkmorton's books there are 129 examples, and in Marprelate's works,
69, totaling 198. In Penry's writings, however, there are a
few Welsh phrases, an occasional Greek or Latin word, and
one quotation of two lines from Horace's *De Arte Poetica* (lines
21–22). Following is a select list of 85 items, 44 from Throkmorton and 41 from Martin.

Throkmorton

mitissimum, clementissimum, pietatissimum, venerandae pie-
    tatis (2:4)
serpens oculata, ambitiosa mulier, fedifraga horribili vigilantia,
    celeritate in conficiendis malificiis (2:5)
cum applausu (2:6) sunt quaedam beneficia quae odimus (2:8)
    in cephalica (2:8) quid non (2:9)

quo cautius et secretius sacrum hoc foedus sanciretur (3:29)
umbras timet qui deum non timet (3:33)
rerum humanarum vicissitudo (3:39) filii dilecti (3:42)
omnis natura querit conservationem sui (3:45)
parcere subiectis et debellare superbos (3:48)
horrendum est incidere in manus Dei viventis (3:50)

peccavimus cum patribus nostris (4:14) omnia bene (4:14)
potius quam aliquid detrahatur de gloria Christi. Ruat non
    modo pax, sed et caelum et terra (4:15)

quicquid est causa causae est causa causati (4:21)
Impius Quintus [Pius V] (4:21) noli me tangere (4:22)
parum aut libris, aut legibus profici, quousque firmum et ido-
neum ministerium in ecclesiis constitutum fuerit (4:24)

Thesaurus (6:B3) Bellarmina (6:C2) rexe [rex] (6:C3 v)

index animi sermo (7:2) iudicium non preiudicium (7:2)
humile peccatum, quam superbam innocentiam (7:8)
Barnardus non videt omnia (7:10) Hercules furens (7:12)
Platonis (7:29) veritatis calculus (7:29) a latare (7:33)
ignorantia excusat non a toto sed a tanto (7:60)
demones credunt et contremiscunt (7:114)

laesum principium (10:Aiii v) inversio (10:Biv v)
hic quidem certum est hoc nomine declarari speciosum regiae
magnificentiae splendorem in spectantium oculos incurren-
tum (10:Ci v) per hyperbolen (10:Ei v)
licentia poetica (10:Ei v) in capite (10:Eiii)

si quam maledicendo voluptatem coepisti, eam male audiendo
amittes (12:A2) mihi vindicta (12:A2)
aequa lance (12:A3) quidlibet ex quolibet (12:A3)
hic murus ahenus esto, nil conscire sibi, nulla pallescere culpa
(12:A4)

Marprelate

decorum personae (I:1) ad practicandum (I:2)
Cato de moribus (I:5) Tarquinius Superbus (I:10)
in coram (I:24) in primis (I:38) bendicite (I:44)
anno pontificatus vestri quinto, (and I hope) ultimo (I:54)

sic foeliciter incipit (II:B1) de inveniendis mediis (II:C2 v)
indecorum person[a]e (II:D3) de ecclesia (II:D4 v)
epistomastix (II:D4 v) celarent (II:E4 v)
secundum usum Sarum (II:F2) pro and contra (II:F2 v)

in esse (III:2) cum privilegio (III:28)

non plus (IV:A2 v) in iudicium capitis (IV:24)
qui pergit quod vult dicere quae non vult audiet (IV:37)
dolus fraus insidiae (IV:47)
nemo confidat nimium secundis (IV:48)

nemo desperet meliora lapsus (IV:48)
Anglia Martinis disce favere tuis (IV:48)

Tygurium (V:Aiv) cum privilegio (V:Bii v)
cygneam cantionem (V:Civ) vi et armis (V:Diii)

quem honoris causa nomino, quoties nomino, nomino autem
   saepissime (VI:Bii)
patrizat sat bene certe (VI:Biii)
premunire facies (VI:Biv v) quatenus probabile (VI:Ci)
semper excipio Platonem (VI:Civ v)
capita concordantiarum (VI:Di) e verbo ad verbum (VI:Di v)
vernacula (VI:Di v) ave Marie (VI:Div)
Pater noster (VI:Div) magnificat (VI:Div)

scandalum magnatum (VII:22)

The Diction of Martin and Throkmorton

As a supplement to the presentation of the stylistic peculiarities found in Throkmorton's and Marprelate's works, a consideration of the use of words may be apposite. A comparative
study of the diction of Martin, Throkmorton, and Penry
reveals that the language of Martin and Throkmorton is similar, and that their rich vocabulary differs remarkably from
that of Penry. In compiling a list of unusual or out-of-the-
ordinary words, selected from an approximately equal number of writings of Martin, Throkmorton, and Penry, I obtained the following results: Martin's list comprised of 529
words; Throkmorton's, 375; Penry's, 150. Throkmorton's list
was more than double Penry's, and Martin's list was more
than treble. Martin and Throkmorton use strong, aggressive,
and threatening verbs such as "bangest, bepistle, besoop,
buckle, bumfeg, choaked, clapperclawed, cogge, girding, lev-
eling, lewre, mangle, stashed, thumped, thwacked." They
also utilize sexual words such as "bastardly, bawdie, brothel,
ribaudrie, stewes, strumpet, trull, virgine, whorehunters."
The most distinguishing features of their diction are their
employment of verbs with the prefix "be" and the use of

coined, playful, and colorful words. Consequently, with the diction of Throkmorton and Martin, (but not with that of Penry), one resorts to the specialized dictionaries and glossaries.

The following three lists indicate that Throkmorton and Martin are fond of words with the prefix "be." There are twelve coined words, printed in italics, by Throkmorton and Martin, but none by Penry:

MARTIN	*THROKMORTON*	*PENRY*
beblesse (VI:Diii)	beblesse (10:Ciii v)	beget
beceytfull (IV:A1)	befoole (7:64)	beloved
bedeaconed (IV:47)	*beglazed* (7:32)	bequeathed
befie (IV:48)	begrease (7:51)	bereaved
beminstrelled (IV:47)	*behackled* (7:96)	beseech
bepatched (VI:Diii)	bepitched (7:80)	besotted
bepistle (IV:36)	*beprouded* (7:47)	besought
beshrewe (VI:Dii)	*beseared* (7:32)	betide
besire (I:41)	besprinkled (10:Ciii)	betray
besoop (IV:36)	bestirre (2:1)	bewrapped
bethought (IV:14)	betake (6:B1)	(no coined
bethout (II:B4 v)	be thanke (7:118)	words)
(without)	bethinke (7:91)	

The following lists give the coined, playful, or colorful words and a few sentences in Martin's books:

EPISTLE

Sir Asse (Asaph)	fyckers	paltripolitans
catekissing	ile	paultripolitanship
Confocation	ise (I shall be)	(metropolitanship)
Conspiration	ilsample	raffodie
dissolve (resolve)	Lambathismes	seevillaines
Divillitie	Latenie (litany)	(civilians)
epistomastix	neverbegood	wan (won)
His Canterburinesse	(Wood)	
My Lords Grease	is us have I (yes we have, aye)	
is us do (yes we do)	by your sleeve (leave)	
O is (O yes)	tse tse tse	

Martin Marprelate, Gentleman

EPITOME

beetleheaded	fathermillerly	Perncanter-
bethout	fickers	burikenolde
bricke	fie fie	sicken
bommination	green heads	siginnes (seggones)
breakepulpits	leadenheaded	sourfaced
currats	neverlasting	steane
dissimblation	perceede	umbertie
Your Father-	your master-	yaw (you)
hoods	doms	Your Terribleness

They themselves say beath, and ai say brethren, that for the
stopping of your meathes and other causes, I wad counsell
them, if they wad be ruled bai me, to be nether nother (F1)

MINERALLS

beeble bable	ternal
catercorner	tubtrimmer

HAY ANY WORKE

argling	bommination	lalour
beceytfull	bumfeg	(labour)
bedeaconed	caperclawed	pistle
befie	(clapperclawed)	py hy hy hy
beministrelled	Capcase (Copcot)	squint gogled
bepistle	Culpable (Culpepper)	stealecounter
besoop	heez (he is)	trunchfiddle
bethought	hublication	

For ise so bumfeg the Cooper, as he had bin better to have
hooped halfe the tubbes in Winchester, than write against
my Worships pistles. (6)

Now you wretches (Archbishop and Lord Bishops I mean),
you Mar-state, Mar-law, Mar-prince, Mar-majestrat, Mar-
commonwealth, Mar-church, and Mar-religion. (18)

Whau, whau, but where have I bin al this while? Ten to one
among some of these puritans. (30)

Why Martin, I say, hast tow forgotten thy selfe? Where hast
ti bene? Why man, cha bin a seeking for a samons nest,
and cha vound a whole crue, either of ecclesiasticall traitors,
or of bishops of the divel. (30)

Thou hast a right seasoned wainscoate face of ti nowne,
   chwarnt tee, ti vorehead zaze hard as horne. (39)
An a [he] had bin my Worships printer, ide a [I would have]
   kept him from your clouches. (39)

MARTIN JUNIOR

catercaps	nethew (nephew)	tat (that)
ere heel (ere	nuncka (uncle)	vather (father)
he will)	nunckle (uncle)	Kankerbury
neame (eme)	popedome	(Canterbury)

MARTIN SENIOR

beblesse	heele (he will)	simoniarkes
bepatched	madmonition	starve-us booke
beshrew	pistling	thatle
hangIons	proper-sition	weele
(hanglons)		

PROTESTATYON

Alsolne College	ficker	Martinist
chaue (I have)	Lambethetical	orawhynemeg
Cooperism	Lambethist	proculstant
Cooperist	Lockwood	trodled (trobled?)
eblitaph	Martinism	wringlefaced
(epitaph)		

The following four lists give the coined, playful, or colorful
words in the works of Throkmorton:

A DIALOGUE. WHERIN IS PLAINLY LAIDE OPEN

affinite	dog him	Pearnd
betake	fye	pied face
cogging	galde	trunst
crake	mallepert	tush

MASTER SOME LAID OPEN IN HIS COULERS

Father Admonitor	catechising	Lockewood
befoole	kisse Cate	packsadle
beglazed	clotheade	papershott
begrease	Collyweston	pidling
behackled	Dorbel of Sarum	pharoicall
bepitched	evenimed	quavemires
beprouded	(envenimed?)	shavelings
beseared	hangbies	spurblinde
be thanke	horsekacke	Thrasonicall
bethinke	hungerbit	

THE DEFENCE OF JOB THROKMORTON

beblesse	egle-eied	lewre
besprinkled	farre fette	overslip
bethink	hysteron proteron	overswift
buckle	infirmation	rusteling
chartall	inversio	straggering
curtaile	jogged	scurvey Jacke
egger on	leveling	tenter-stretched

MANUSCRIPT ITEMS

hurleburleyes	Impius quintus	snaffle
valet de chambre	(Pius V)	varlet de chambre

There are no coined or playful words in Penry's writings, but there are a few unusual words.

contumeliously	derogatorious	pensation
Cymbrûbrittons	efflagitateth	timorouslie
curtisanlike	fallation	tympany

Verbal and Ideological Parrallels: A Recapitulation

The argument for authorship from parallels can be a tricky business. Two authors may use standard or similar phrases, or may paraphrase the same source. Anyone advancing arguments for authorship from verbal parallels must consider such factors as subjectivity, probability, frequency of use, ordinary versus unusual expressions, and the number of words involved. Sometimes a parallel with two or three unusual words may seem more evidential than one with four or five ordinary words. Occasionally a commonplace expression may point to one author if it is used frequently and if it is not utilized by an alternative writer. I have omitted most ordinary expressions, though they appear frequently, such as "thinke you," "mee thinkes," "I warrant you," and "I pray you" (about 110 times, including 26 occurrences in one treatise). Since these expressions are almost totally absent from Penry's writings, this difference is worth noting.

In the following four sets of sixty-one parallels, the argument is a cumulative one. The first twenty-one unusual parallels are sufficient to establish a strong presumption of Throkmorton's authorship of the Marprelate books. Even the first two parallels alone constitute clues that cannot be easily minimized. When one adds the ten parallels which have three or four like words, the presumption becomes a probability. Perhaps the remaining thirty suggestive parallels are of enough significance to establish high probability. The main point is that Throkmorton's and Marprelate's habitual language and similar terms indicate that they originate in one mind.

Unusual Parallels

olde Lockwoode of Sarum (7:81)
olde Lockwood of Sarum (VII:26)
   A distinctive reference to Dean Bridges, whom Throkmorton ridiculed unmercifully.

howsoever hee holde there now by Stafforde law, as they say, that is, by the swoorde (3:46)
I threatned him with blowes, and to deale by Stafford law (IV:A3)
   The reference is not to a person but to the county. The phrase is listed in Murray, *New English Dictionary*, with the meaning of club law, force, coercion. The earliest citation is given from Martin's *Hay Any Worke*, 1589, but Throkmorton used it in his "Speech on the Low Countries" in 1586/87. The phrase also occurs in 1557 in an anonymous translation of Erasmus' "Conjugium," *A Mery Dialogue*. The Latin

of Erasmus reads: "uteretur suo iure, et verberibus eam emendaret; "take Stafforde lawe" refers to a wife who "woulde not be rewled by wordes." The anonymous translator may be Edmund Becke or Richard Taverner, who translated some of the works of Erasmus. See Henry de Vocht, ed., *The Earliest English Translations of Erasmus' Colloquia, 1536–1566* (Louvain, 1928), p. 72, and E. J. Devereux, "English Translations of Erasmus, 1522–1527," in R. J. Schoeck, ed., *Editing Sixteenth Century Texts* (Toronto, 1966), pp. 48, 57. Michael Harding used the phrase as early as 1530. See G. R. Elton, *Star Chamber Stories* (London, 1958) p. 191.

that patch [Bridges] of Saint Maries pulpit (7:31)
after his [Bridges'] patched manner (7:31)
why doth the patch [Bridges] doe this (7:31)
his brother Bridges is a patch (7:72)
Master Bridges was a verie patch (I:1)
the patche [Bridges] can doe the cause (I:1)
as very a patch as Deane John [Bridges] (IV:38)
if this patch Thomas Cooper had not used two patches to cover his patcherie (IV:38)

the Bishop of Canterbury is a giddy head (6:C2)
the Archbishop of Canterbury is a giddie head (III:26)

if one have a coate or cloake that is turned, they saye it is Pearnd (6:D2 v)
and doe you thinke the Bishop of Canterbury will be as good a turner as his Master Doctor Pearne is (6:D2 v)
he [Pearne] is the notablest turn-coat (6:D2 v)
his old Patrone and benefactor, D. Pearne, for whoe but he could teach Calvin to fetch a turne, and a retorne (7:36)
the turnecoat [Pearne] is canonized (I:10)
his Grace Doctor turnecoats (Perne I shoulde saye) scholler (I:16)
wee will beleeve the turncoate Doctor Perne (IV:44)
upon the death of olde Andrewe [Pearne] turne-coate (VII:26)

to lay pillowes under our elbowes (3:40)
you sow pillows under Harvies elbowes (I:35)
   The Geneva Bible translation of Ezekiel 13:18 is: "Wo unto the women that sowe pillowes under all arme holes." The

American Standard Version reads: "Woe to the women that sew pillows upon all elbows." The Hebrew for "elbows" is "joints of the hands."

he shutteth up the whole with this good loose (7:52)
a fine sweete loose at the latter ende (VI:Div)
>This expression refers to the discharge of an arrow, or to the close of a matter, its upshot or conclusion. Here it seems to mean sarcastically a final parting shot.

catechising of them (7:122)
kisse Cate no more in the pulpit (7:65)
spake of Catekissing (I:49)
>This is typical of Throkmorton's and Martin's punning.

he that should sette up his rest (3:43)
I have long agone set up my rest (VII:14)
>A card-game expression associated with primero.

his good and learned discoursing brethren (7:35)
that good and learned discoursing brother (V:Cii v)

hee that hath given Calvine and Beza suche a blowe, as they could never speake word of good Irish since (7:30)
it maie bee, that thou haddest never, I tell thee trueth, learned a worde of Irish in thy life (VI:Bi)

the crops and flowers of his owne pretie garden (7:105)
the crops and flowers of Bridges garden (title of Throkmorton's book; see Sutcliffe, *An Answere unto a Certaine Calumnious Letter*, p. 72 v)

is the winde in that dore (7:53, 106)
is the winde at that dore (II:B4)

blessings and crosses come in *alternis vicibus*, by course (3:38)
they *alterius* [*alternis*] *vicibus*, shall be the groomes (VI:Cii v)
>The printer probably misread "ni" as "iu" in the manuscript. It is doubtful that either printer, Hodgskin or Symmes, knew any Latin.

let me spurre a question unto you (6:Bi)
let me . . . spur a question unto you (II:B4 v)

I am a shrewde fellowe (7:97)
Martin is a shrewd fellow (I:4)
thou [Martin] art a shrewd fellowe (IV:48)

I have reade and indeede long agoe (5:148)
I have read in my dayes (10:Cii v)
I have red somthing in my dayes (I:7)
I have bin a great schooleman in my daies (II:E4 v)

saving your reverence, Madame, plaine scabbe and scurvey Jacke (10:Biv v)
sauf vostre grace, Monsieur, Saint Paule, we dare warrant, hath no such woordes (10:Ci v)
saving your reverence that are bishops, that he is as very a knave, and enemy (I:1)
saving your reverence, uncle Canturburie, you lie in your throate (VI:Aiv v)

Nam qui pergit, ea quae vult dicere, ea quae non vult, audiet (Throkmorton, "An Answer to Certen Peeces of a Sermon . . . by Doctor Cowper," Inner Temple, Petyt MSS. 538[47], fol. 461)
Qui pergit quod vult dicere quae non vult audiet (IV:37)

quidlibet ex quolibet (12:A3)
quidlibet ex quolibet (Throkmorton, *Certaine Articles*, in Frere and Douglas, *Puritan Manifestoes*, p. 141)

thithacticoi (7:24)
didaktikos (Throkmorton, "An Answer to Certen Peeces of a Sermon . . . by Doctor Cowper," Inner Temple, Petyt MSS. 538 [47], fol. 460)
"Thithacticoi" is a misprint for "didacticoi." The printer probably read the delta as a theta. Thus we have "didacticoi" and "didaktikos," the plural and singular nominative of the same word, which means "one apt to teach." See 1 Timothy 3:2 and 2 Timothy 2:24.

Parallels with Three or Four Main Words

eyther of time, place, person, or circumstance (10:Aiv)
the circumstances of times, places, and persons (II:B2 v)
the circumstances of time, place, and persons (IV:14)

not to say black was his eie (7:34)
not once say blacke to your eies (IV:36)

nothing to the matter in question (7:23)
nothing to the matter in question (II:C1 v)

any certaine prescript rules (7:75)
the certaine prescript rule (II:B4 v)

limpeth and shrinketh in the sinowes (7:79)
quivereth and shrinketh as it were in the sinowes (VII:9)

have I not acquited my selfe worthily (7:54)
have not I quited my selfe like a man (I:7)

they goe more roundly to worke (7:109)
I may go roundly to worke (IV:6)

his book is *seene and allowed* (7:55)
finde *seene and allowed* in the title of the booke (I:2)

scarce make a good syllogisme (7:39)
never able to make good syllogisme since (IV:36)

men have runne themselves windlesse (7:25)
a man that had coursed him selfe windlesse (VII:8)

Verbatim Parallels with Two Main Words

an absurd hereticke (7:80, III:25)
ambitious wretch (6:C4 v, I:32)
and [if] you will (6:C4, I:24)
banished the land (4:25, II:C4)
bishops of the Divel (6:twelve times, III:15, IV:fourteen times)
blasphemous wretch (6:B2 v, I:33)
sufficiently confuted (6:C4 v, II:G1)
at the first dash (7:72, II:B2)
a hundreth of these (7:115, I:42)
letters of orders (7:25, II:F3 v)
palpable error (7:107, II:E2)
nay soft (7:25, 51, 67, I:21, II:B3 v)
to the view of al men (7:104, III:title)
to the view of the worlde (3:47, 4:19, V:Aii)
wrack and misery (7:29, IV:45)

Close Parallels with Two Main Words

The evidential value of parallels, whether verbatim or close, is debatable. It should be noted, however, that these parallels occur in the works of Martin and Throkmorton but not in the books of Penry. Moreover, it should be observed that when there are three or four parallels, they do not carry much weight, but when there are fifteen verbatim parallels of two terms and when there are seventy-five close parallels, the total of ninety such parallels poses a question of what is significant evidence. The probability that chance would explain the occurrence of these parallels is low, but the probability that they emanate from one mind increases as the number of parallels grows. Therefore the verbatim and close parallels with two main words tilt the scales a little when considered as supplementary to the thirty-one better parallels in the first two sections. The following list presents fifteen parallels—20 percent of the complete compilation of seventy-five examples.

to appeach or accuse (10:Eiii)
by appeaching and accusing (III:9)

manifestly bewraiing very grosse and palpable ignorance (7:68)
do notably bewray their vile ignorance (IV:9)

some crazing of the braine (10:Aiii v)
hath crazed his braine (VII:28)

if he can dissolve you of this doubt (7:96)
dissolve this one question (I:3)

have an eye to afterclappes (3:39)
have an eye to this geare (3:46)
have an eie to Boyles shop (VI:Aiii v)

bragge, crake, and face it out (6:C4 v)
he will cog, and face it out (I:33)
if we can face it out with a bragg (II:F2 v)

one of the porest haglers (7:18)
alas poore haglers (V:Dii)

jellous to suspect (7:84)
jealousie and suspition (7:91)
jelious suspicion (IV:47)

some such stale jeasts (7:93)
he is good at a stale jest (II:B2)

in good sadnesse (7:87)
in good sadnes (II:F1 v)

reviled and railed upon (10:Eiii)
railing and reviling (V:Aii v)

neither sappe nor edg (7:62)
without sappe or edge (VII:28)

hath faier given it the slipp (7:92)
have given the holye religion of God the slipp (VII:6)

by tyrany and bloudde (3:46)
but tyrannie and blood (VII:10)
their tyrannie and blood thirstie proceedinges (VII:21)

to publishe it unmangled (7:A2 v)
publishe it altogither, as it was, unmangled (10:Bii)

THROKMORTON'S

AUTHORSHIP:
THE MARPRELATE
BOOKS

"The honour of this battle of the books belongs, so far as literature is concerned, to Martin. The Marprelate tracts are part of English literature, the answers to them little more than materials for literary history." (John Dover Wilson, in *The Cambridge History of English Literature* [1930], page 397)

An Epistle

IN THE LAST three chapters an attempt has been made to establish specific criteria by which the writings of Throkmorton and Penry may be distinguished. The main criteria are twelve stylistic peculiarities, parallels in Throkmorton's and Marprelate's writings, diction, coined words, common phrases, writing techniques, invention, use of anecdotes and proverbs, examples of humor, irony, satire, raillery, and derisive epithets, frequent and specific allusions to contemporary personalities, and certain favorite topics and recurrent themes. In chapters five, six, and seven these criteria have been directed mainly to the writings of Throkmorton,[1] and in the present chapter the criteria are applied to the seven Marprelate books, especially to the *Epistle* as the most distinctive and exciting of the first four works of Martin, and to

Martin Senior as the best exemplar of the last three books, which were hastily written under great pressure during the summer of 1589. It will be sufficient to analyze and comment more briefly on the remaining five Marprelate items.[2]

The first argument for Throkmorton's authorship is a general one. If the reader will peruse the *Epistle*, then read Throkmorton's parliamentary speeches, his *Defence*, and his *Master Some Laid Open*, he will sense a coherence in these works. They all clearly reveal a vigorous, gifted, humorous, and satirical writer, who is utilizing mirth as a deliberate technique to influence his readers. Secondly, if the reader will examine any of Penry's books, he will find no coherence and will conclude that he is dealing with a different writer. He will notice that whereas Martin is racy, amusing, and pungent, Penry is serious, religious, and prosaic. In the second edition of his *Exhortation*, Penry discussed Dr. Bridges' book by presenting four reasons or syllogisms in a straightforward manner,[3] but Martin played with Dean Bridges, ridiculed his style, laughed at his foibles, exposed his fallacies, and resorted to name-calling and railing. In Martin's *Epistle* (page 29), there is a story of Penry's appearance before the Court of High Commission in March 1586/87. The writer stated specifically that he was using Penry's notes, and his style was so like that of Martin's other works and Throkmorton's writings, and so unlike that of Penry, who related the same story in an utterly different manner in his *Appellation* (pages 39–40), that one may be certain that Penry was not the writer of this account in the *Epistle*. Therefore, since Penry's works lack coherence with the *Epistle*, Penry is an unlikely candidate for Martin's role.

A third argument for Throkmorton's authorship of the *Epistle* derives from stylistic features. Chapter seven presents 12 stylistic peculiarities found in Marprelate's and Throkmorton's works but not in Penry's books, of which 11 are found in the *Epistle*.[4] There are 5 examples of the use of the indirect object without a "to" or "for," such as, "say me that againe," and 5 examples of the double negative, such as, "withstand not the knowen trueth no longer." We see the use of "a" in such expressions as, "he should be a printing books," or "went a heymaking." There are 10 examples of the use of "ile" for "I will," and 8 examples of the use of "an" or "and" for "if." In one sentence, the clause, "which something troubled them," illustrates Martin's and Throkmorton's practice of using a noun in an adverbial sense. In the *Epistle* there are 7 examples of the use of expressions referring to card-playing, drinking, bowling, and gambling. There are 20 examples of alliteration, 16 of the use of Latin, numerous and colorful expressions, and 20 of the utilization of legal phrases. In all, the *Epistle* has about 100 examples of the stylistic peculiarities found in Martin's and Throkmorton's works. Since these peculiarities are not in Penry's works, they point to Throkmorton, even though some of them are found in the writings of other authors.

A fourth argument stems from the use of coined or playful words. In the *Epistle* thirty examples of such words occur. For civilians we find "seevillaines," and for metropolitans we encounter "paltripolitans." Dean Bridges, doctor of Divinity, emerges as "Doctor of Divillitie." William Hughes, bishop of St. Asaph, is dubbed the "Bishop of Sir Asse." The clergy are referred to as "fyckers," "currats," and "cater-caps," and prelates are addressed as "uncle Canterburie," or "My Lord's Grease." Convocation becomes the "Confocation House" or the "Conspiration House." Playful and humorous expressions are "Latenie" for litany, "besire" for desire, "Catekissing" for catechising, "O is" for O yes, and "is us have I" for yes we have, aye. Since no coined, playful, or punning words occur in Penry's books, and since Throkmorton enjoys derisive name-calling, words with the prefix "be," and paronomasia, one may conclude that the thirty examples in the *Epistle* point toward Throkmorton as the author.[5]

A fifth argument for assigning the *Epistle* to Throkmorton is the presence of ten parallels in the writings of Throkmorton and the *Epistle*. These parallels suggest Throkmorton's pen, and the absence of convincing parallels in Penry's writings indicates that he was not the writer of the *Epistle*.

Parallels in Marprelate's Epistle *and Throkmorton's Works*

Master Bridges was a verie patch (I:1)[6]
his brother Bridges is a patch (7:72)

full learnedly handled after this manner (I:47)
after this manner, and full as learnedly as this doth he handle
   himselfe (7:75)

I con thee thank (I:16) [con—avow or acknowledge]
I con him thank (7:74)

hath he not bestowed his liberallitie (I:37) [ironic]
he hath so liberally bestowed (7:33) [ironic]

I have two strings to my bow (I:19)
having on[e] string more to our bowe (7:27)

do so much hurt (I:41)
did never so much hurt (6:D4)

unto Hir Majesties eare (I:13)
in Her Majesties eares (7:56)

till he come to the pinch (I:33)
when yt came to the pynche (1:1)

procure that the Puritans may one day have a free disputation
   (I:3)
procure a free disputation (6:C4)

wipe his mouth cleanly, and looke another way, as though it
   had not bene he (I:18)
he may wipe his mouth, and washe his hands, and wonder
   to whome they speake (7:28)

A sixth reason for assigning the *Epistle* to Throkmorton
is the presence of proverbs and common phrases which typify
his style. There are ten proverbs in the *Epistle*, and many
others occur repeatedly in Martin's and Throkmorton's
works.[7] One rarely finds a proverb in Penry's books, and if
it is found, it is likely to be a quotation from the Book of
Proverbs in the Old Testament. Martin repeats certain common phrases, such as "I warrant you," and "by your leave,"
and provides one punning example, "by your sleeve."

A seventh reason for associating Throkmorton with the *Epistle* is the wealth of anecdotal material in the treatise. Throkmorton is a superb storyteller who holds the interest of readers by his interspersing of humorous and scandalous stories. By contrast, one may read several of Penry's books without encountering a single anecdote to interrupt the even tenor of his style. In the *Epistle* there are fourteen anecdotes, which are fascinating to read. Eight of these are highly critical of the bishops, two are directed against the lower clergy, two are condemnatory of the Stationers' Company, one is a denunciation of the licensers of books, and one is an ex parte account of the proceedings of the Court of High Commission. Five of the stories are highly amusing, such as the simplistic, infantile sermon by John Bullingham, bishop of Gloucester; Bishop John Young's presentation of a benefice to himself; "Sir" Jefferie Jones's efforts to cope with an ale-wife and alehouse; the argument between Bishop Aylmer and John Madox; and the account of Dr. William Turner's dog which absconded with the episcopal corner cap. Some of the stories are informative, such as Giles Wigginton's problems with his own parishioners in Sedbergh, Yorkshire, and with Archbishop Whitgift. Also, Penry's appearance before the high commissioners, which is graphically described, and Waldegrave's difficulties with the Stationers' Company, which destroyed his press, type, and equipment, add to our information. The two most censorious stories pertain to Bishop Cooper's apologetic and polemical sermon and to Bishop Aylmer's alleged disgraceful avarice in his treatment of two merchant creditors.

The eighth reason for concluding that Throkmorton wrote the *Epistle* is that there is considerable name-calling in this work. Throkmorton is adept at raillery, invective, scoffing, and derisive epithets, as we see consistently in his books. But Penry is above derision and invective, since he regards terms of opprobrium as sinful, as expressions for which he must give ultimate account to his Maker in the Day of Judgment.[8] Therefore, the presence of derisive names is a prima facie indication that Penry was not the writer of the

Epistle. In it Archbishop Whitgift is belittled as "Dr. Pernes boy," and is referred to contemptuously as "My Lord of Cant.," as a "Canterbury Pope," and as "His Gracelessness of Cant." Bishop Cooper is called a "monstrous hypocrite," a "dunce," and a "liar"—one who "wil lie as fast as a dog can trot." Bishop Aylmer is accused of swearing "like a lewd swag." Stephen Chatfield, the vicar who replaced John Udall in Kingston-upon-Thames, is insulted directly: "go to you asse." Dr. John Hone, the archdeacon's Official, is called a "bawdy doctor," a "coxcomb," and a "popish dolt," and Dean Bridges is characterized as a "patch," a "knave," and a "hedge priest." His books, Martin smirks, seem to proceed from the "braynes of a woodcocke."

The *Epistle* was a treatise which startled, delighted, or shocked the people of England when it suddenly appeared on the national stage in October 1588, just three months after the Spanish Armada had been repelled. Although dedicated to the cause of reform, the *Epistle* was vestured in the trappings of a royal jester and adorned with colorful particularities. In this book almost every tone or color in the spectrum of humor and satire is revealed. There is simple mirth and gaiety, badinage and persiflage, raillery and invective, subtle and heavy irony. The satire may be good-natured, or it may descend to the level of lampoon and caricature, to diatribe and impudence, as it does in ridiculing Aylmer and Cooper. Inasmuch as Throkmorton had a reputation as a learned, mature man with a facetious and biting tongue, and inasmuch as Penry was utterly incapable as a young immature evangelist, age twenty-five, of writing brilliant satire, and in temperament disinclined to use humor or scurrility, one may conclude as a ninth argument that Throkmorton wrote the *Epistle.*

A tenth argument for Throkmorton's authorship is found in the similarity of topics and themes in his writings and in the *Epistle.* Certain salient features appear; certain interests, complaints, and projects dominate his thinking. He is especially interested in printers and Puritans and writers; he constantly alludes to prisons, praemunire, and treason;

he accuses his opponents of simony, bribery, sycophancy, and seeking for promotions; and he delights in playing with arguments and exposing errors. Like motifs in a musical refrain, prominent themes recur in his writings. In the *Epistle* there are references to six stationers and printers—Thomas Thomas, Robert Waldegrave, Thomas Chard, "knave" Thackwell, John Charlewood, and Thomas Orwin. One finds about twenty-five references to Puritans; there are allusions to such writers as Whitgift, Cartwright, Bridges, Aylmer, and Benedict Aretius, a Swiss theologian. We find at least nine references to prisons, such as the Bridewell, the Clink, and the Counter; allusions to pursuivants, and threats of praemunire. The crime of treason, charged especially against Dean Bridges, is alleged four times, with hints of disloyalty and insincerity. Also, there are a half a dozen references to syllogisms, especially fallacious ones. Since these topics do not occur in Penry's books, and since they are favorite themes in Throkmorton's books, these recurring features reveal the pen of the facile writer and gentleman of Haseley in Warwickshire.

An eleventh reason for attributing the *Epistle* to Throkmorton is the indication that the writer was an Oxford student and a resident of the Midlands. The clues in the *Epistle* are perhaps insufficient in themselves to prove the point conclusively, but they are suggestive, and if they are supplemented by the other clues in the remaining six Marprelate items and especially in Throkmorton's *Master Some Laid Open*, then they become evidence worthy of consideration. In the *Epistle* the writer refers to Father Thomas Bricot, a philosopher at the University of Oxford, whose book, *Cursus optimarum questionum super philosophiam Aristotelis cum interpretatione textus secundum viam modernorum*, Throkmorton may have read in folio at Oxford. There is also a cryptic reference to Doctor Terence of Oxford, who remains unidentified. The writer speaks of Thomas Cooper's revision of Sir Thomas Eliot's *Dictionary*, and of the *Thesaurus* by Robert Stephanus, which Cooper expanded and published in 1565, when Throkmorton was a student and Cooper was a schoolmaster at Oxford.

The story of "Sir" Jefferie Jones, the bibulous priest, pertains to a clergyman from Corley, in Warwickshire, a few miles distant from Throkmorton's home in Haseley. The references to Thomas Cartwright of Warwick and Ambrose Dudley, the earl of Warwick, two of Throkmorton's friends, and the brief allusions to Oxfordshire, Worcester, and Warwickshire, point to a man in the Midlands. Also, the unexpected reference to "D. Kenold" or John Kennall, archdeacon of Oxford and commissary or vice-chancellor of the university from 1564 to 1567, seems to imply a personal knowledge by Throkmorton from his university residence in 1562–66. Since Penry was born in 1563, in Brecknockshire, Wales, it is most unlikely that he would make allusions to the University of Oxford in the 1560s.[9]

A twelfth argument for Throkmorton's authorship is found in the unrelenting attack against the hierarchy of the Church of England and other officials. Throkmorton's writings from 1572 to 1594, especially his "An Answer" of 1572 to Bishop Cooper, his "A Friendly Caveat" to Bishop Sandys in 1573, his *Dialogue* and *Master Some Laid Open in His Coulers* of 1589, and his *Defence* of 1594, reveal a virulent anti-episcopal animus, which extends to deans, archdeacons, legal officials in the ecclesiastical courts, heads of colleges, and other clergy. Likewise, Marprelate's *Epistle* is par excellence a showpiece for anti-prelatical and anti-clerical attitudes. In this treatise two archbishops and thirteen bishops are denounced or ridiculed.[10] In addition, four deans are singled out for attack, John Bridges of Salisbury, Richard Cosin of the Court of the Arches, Gabriel Goodman of Westminster, and Andrew Perne of Ely. Two archdeacons are criticized, Dr. John Kennall of Oxford and Dr. James Cottington of Surrey. Also, two ecclesiastical judges, Dr. Edward Stanhope, chancellor of the diocese of London, and Dr. John Hone, Official to the archdeacon of Surrey, are roundly belabored. Even three heads of colleges are derided, Dr. John Bell, master of Jesus College, Cambridge, Dr. William Cole, president of Corpus Christi, Oxford, and Dr. John Copcot, master of Corpus Christi, Cambridge. Thus, we see that twenty-six ecclesiastical and legal officials are satirized or depreciated in this one book alone.

By contrast, in all nine of his books Penry refuted only five officials, Whitgift, Cooper, Bridges, Some, and Bancroft, and he did not ridicule them, though he dissented strongly from their views. The reason he selected these five was not personal animus but the fact that they all wrote influential books attacking Puritan ideas. Thus, of twenty-six officials whom Martin attacked in the *Epistle*, twenty-one were not discussed by Penry, who shunned flippant and derisory language, and who believed in the preaching of the Word, establishing a learned ministry, and eliminating the evils of nonresidency and pluralism. He disclaimed any desire to gall the bishops, but Marprelate was eager to mar a prelate and claimed the right of "pistling" the bishops. Also, Throkmorton in his own writings was just as eager to ridicule the hierarchy.

A thirteenth argument for Throkmorton's authorship of the *Epistle* is found in Penry's letter to Lord Burghley, which was never published until 1944 when Peel's edition of Penry's *Notebook* appeared. In this letter Penry disassociated himself from some of Throkmorton's ideas and expressed his dislike of Martin's style of writing:

> These things I speak not for any favour which at this present I have unto the gentlemans person [Throkmorton]. *For it is well knowen that hee being of the same judgment with the preachers of the land, differeth from mee at this present, even as farr in a maner as ever Marten and the prelates disagreed.* [Penry's italics]

> First when thes bookes first came out [the *Epistle* and *Epitome*] I ame well knowen to have dislyked them and disclaymed them so as I wished to have been but privy unto many thinges their sett downe, which in my conscience I saw not only unjustifiable but some thing yrksome for mee whoe altogether dislyked the whole brood of the Romane prelates to read.

> But to my self agayn I dislyked many things in Marten for his manner, and for his matter of writing.

> But this one thing for his maner I greatly dislyked, vz., that which hee sett downe touching him whome they call the Arch-

bishop of Canterbury. A long story or mome their is some
wher in his writinges sett down of him, as touching his cloc-
bagg [cloak-bag] carying, his servic done to D. Perne, etc. I
ame sory that I ame enforced to troble my self but especially
your Honour with such stuff; well, I dislyked it and I do dislyk
it and the rest of the thinges of that nature.[11]

Since this story of Whitgift and his carrying of Dr. Perne's
cloak-bag is found in the *Epistle* (page 32), we must conclude
either that Penry did not write the *Epistle* or that he is criticizing and contradicting himself. A natural inference is that
Penry was reproving Throkmorton for unfair dealing against
the archbishop and that Throkmorton wrote the *Epistle*.

A fourteenth reason for attributing the *Epistle* to Throkmorton is the utilization of stylistic techniques which are
also found in his non-Marprelatian writings. There is a kind
of posturing whereby the writer carries on a discussion with
an imaginary or real opponent; the writer puts himself into
the role of an adversary, either by inserting parenthetical
remarks or adding replies in marginal comments.[12] There
is constant resort to irony, to sarcasm and raillery. The use
of anecdotal material is a device to hold attention, especially
when the story contains a bit of gossip or scandal. Also,
there is the occurrence of an unexpected word or an unantici-
pated ending, which provides an element of surprise. A related technique is the clever formulation of imaginative devices
whereby the writer works out a mock or pseudo treaty of
peace with the bishops or provides two epitaphs for Dean
Bridges.[13] Above all, there is the presence of colorful writing
coupled with spicy humorous material. Throkmorton had
the ability to make his readers perceive an action, so that
they could picture the bishop raising his arms and flinging
them down again on the desk, or they could see the wasp
stinging the episcopal nose, or they could feel the blows as
John Madox hit the lord bishop over the thumbs. By dealing
in particularities, by avoiding abstruse writing, by resorting
to mirth and jesting, by making his paragraphs vivid and
graphic, Throkmorton succeeded in catching and holding
national attention and inculcating his message of reform.

A final argument comprises five small clues which militate

against Penry's role and support Throkmorton's authorship of the *Epistle*. When this treatise was published in October 1588, Penry, as reported by Sharpe, complained to the bookbinder "that Wal[de]grave had printed yt now agaynst his will, for that, sayth he, 'I wo[u]lde have had my Boke agaynst Doctor Some first printed.' " If Penry had written the *Epistle*, as well as his reply to Dr. Some's second *A Godly Treatise* of September 1588, he would have had no valid reason for complaint.[14] Also, as Udall testified, when Penry learned "that some gave out that he was thought to bee the author" of the *Epistle*, he "wrote a letter to a friend in London [Udall?], wherein he did deny it, with such tearmes as declare him to bee ignorant and cleere in it."[15] Thirdly, Penry's books reveal his interest in scriptural ideas, injustices, ecclesiastical shortcomings and church abuses; they do not indicate any special interest in persons who flourished in the Elizabethan period, since his writings average only nine personal references per volume. Whereas Penry's books, therefore, are impersonal, Throkmorton's and Martin's books are excessively personal, and reveal a wide aquaintance with Elizabethan writers, Puritans, officials, bishops, and clergymen. In the *Epistle* alone there are allusions to sixty-eight contemporary persons. Furthermore, as listed in chapter six, there are eight short parallels for *A Dialogue* and the writings of Throkmorton. In addition, there are listed thirty longer items in *A Dialogue*, topics and ideas which average three lines each, and thirty-six parallels, of which eleven are found in the *Epistle*. If the argument in chapter six for Throkmorton's authorship of *A Dialogue* is valid, then these eleven parallels, which are very close and difficult to explain away, are sufficient in themselves to indicate that Throkmorton wrote the *Epistle*. Moreover, also in chapter six, there are Sutcliffe's seven arguments indicating that Throkmorton wrote *More Worke for Cooper*. Since the writer of *More Worke* admitted that he also had written the *Epistle*, and since those who scrutinized *More Worke* after its seizure said that "the stile doth not varie," we have a fifth clue that Throkmorton wrote the *Epistle*.

The Just Censure and Reproofe of Martin Junior
(Martin Senior)

The previous section presented fifteen arguments indicating that Throkmorton wrote the *Epistle*. Therefore he also wrote the *Epitome* and *Hay Any Worke*, since the author of this latter book confessed he wrote the two former books. Also, the writer of *Hay Any Worke* referred frequently to his forthcoming *More Worke for Cooper*, which was summarized in the *Protestatyon*. Therefore the question of authorship remains unresolved mainly for *Martin Junior, Martin Senior*, and the *Protestatyon*. Of these, the former two belong together. Since *Martin Senior* is longer, more informative, and more deserving of careful analysis, it is presented here as the best example of what are sometimes referred to as the secondary or interim tracts, written by the sons of Martin. Sixteen reasons are presented to substantiate Throkmorton's authorship.

The Just Censure and Reproofe, familiarly known as *Martin Senior*, was written hastily in less than a week's time. It was based on memory and vivid imagination, repeated previous ideas, and revealed familiar topics, persons, and criticisms. Fortunately, the style is easily recognizable; verbal parallels exist, clues and literary devices abound, and thus the task of connecting *Martin Senior* with the other six Marprelate items is facilitated. When the twelve stylistic criteria utilized in examining the writings of Throkmorton and Marprelate (chapter seven) are applied to *Martin Senior*, eleven of these characteristics are exemplified by eighty-two items which illustrate Martin's and Throkmorton's style.[16] First, there are twenty-two occurrences of the indirect object without the preposition "to" or "for," as seen in the following expressions:

> bring me in Penry (Aii v)
> if you can finde us eyther young or olde Martin (Aiii)
> hee hath chosen him such a methode (Bii v)

The double negative is apparent in the statement: "you have nothing neither your selves" (Aiii). Nine times we observe the use of "a" in expressions such as "be a Pistle-making" and "goes a visiting." There are three examples of the use of "an" for "if," such as "an thou doest." The word "ile" for "I will" occurs twice, and "ise" for "I shall" is seen in the expression, "Ise abide by it." The word "something" for "somewhat" appears in the clause: "if he were not something touched with the coinquination [defilement] of the flesh" (Cii v). Alliteration, deliberately utilized by Throkmorton and Martin but not by Penry, occurs sixteen times:

> crakt the crowne of Canturbury (Aii v)
> die the death, that to the dog is due (Diii)

One example of colorful writing, which abounds on almost every page, will suffice. In addressing Martin Junior, the elder brother scolds him for treating Mar-Martin so leniently:

> Loe, youth, though I were loth to file my fingers with such a brothell beast as this Mar-Martin is, yet because thou diddest let him goe by thee (mee thought) halfe unbranded, I was the willinger, as thou seest, to give him a wipe or twoo, which I beleeve he wil never claw off with honestie while he lives (Diii v).

We note a little touch of betting and drinking, expressed in the phrases, "tenne to one" and "with a draught of Darbie ale." There are nine legal references, such as "the statute of *premunire facies*," and fifteen Latin expressions, such as:

> semper excipio Platonem (Civ v)
> patrizat sat bene certe (Biii)
> quem honoris causa nomino, quoties nomino, nomino autem
> saepissime (Bii)

The following list of nine parallels in *Martin Senior*, and in Marprelate's and Throkmorton's writings, reveals one originative mind. The signature reference in the first line is to *Martin Senior*; see chapter six for the numbered references to other items. The fifth and ninth parallels illustrate Throkmorton's tendency to repeat himself.

> have an eie also unto all the Puritanes houses (Aiv)
> have an eye to afterclappes (3:39)
> have an eye to this geare (3:46)

saving your reverence, uncle Canturburie, you lie in your
throate (Aiv v)
saving your reverence, Madame, plaine scabbe and scurvey
Jacke (10:Biv)

it maie bee, that thou haddest never, I tell thee trueth, learned
a worde of Irish in thy life (Bi)
hee that hath given Calvine and Beza suche a blowe, as they
could never speake word of good Irish since (7:30)

the synagogue of Sathan (Ci)
the very sinagog of Sathan (7:108)

the proofe of such points, as thou hast laid downe, will force
him to alter his purpose in, *More Worke for the Cooper* (Bii
v)
I must be brief now, but *More Warke* [*sic*] *for Cooper* shall examine your slaunders (IV:26; also Bi v, 30, 35, 37, 43)

to give him a wipe or twoo (Diii v)
an other wipe at the ignorant Welchman (7:27)
is it not a shrewd wipe (7:71)

a fine sweete loose at the latter ende (Div)
he shutteth up the whole with this good loose (7:52)

as for Mar-Martin, and John Fregneuile [Fréguevile], they *alter-*
ius [*alternis*] *vicibus* shall be groomes (Cii v)
blessings and crosses come in *alternis vicibus*, by course (3:38)[17]

if John Canturburie will needs have a fool in his house, wearing
a wooden dagger, and a cockes combe, that none is so fitte
for that place as his brother John a Bridges (Cii and Cii v)
John Bridges deserves to have his place that weares the wooden
dagger, the cockescombe (Ciii)
Some man in the land (say they) weareth a wooden dagger
and a coxcombe, as for example, his grace of Canterburies
foole, doctor Pernes cosen and yours: You presbyter John
Catercap [Bridges], are some man in the land: Therefore
by this reason, you weare a woodden dagger and a coxcombe
(I:48)

Martin Senior illustrates Throkmorton's use of words with
the prefix "be," such as "beblesse," "bepatched," and "be-
shrewe." It also reveals his delight in coined words, such

as "proper-sition," "madmonition," and "pistling," and it displays his colorful diction in such words as "coinquination," "dilling," "springall," "ka," and "thwacked." The style is further enriched by proverbial expressions, such as "a blacke tooth in their heads," "at blunt and sharpe," "with tooth and naile," "spunne a faire thread," "file my fingers," and "no biting to the old snake." *Martin Senior* also manifests Throkmorton's propensity to name-calling. Whitgift is called "uncle Caiphas" and "Esau," and Aylmer is stigmatized as "Beelzebub." Dean Bridges is "the poore old Drone o Sarum," and Dr. Perne is denigrated as a "Judas." These defamatory labels, absent in Penry's writings, are typical of Martin's and Throkmorton's numerous calumnies and libels throughout their books.

In the writings of Throkmorton and Martin there are special interests and themes which are repeated in *Martin Senior.* One finds allusions to printers and Puritans; one notes references to pursuivants, warrants, and prisons; the reader encounters the familiar accusations of praemunire and treason, as well as the complaints of persecution and oppression. Martin Senior discusses sermons and preaching; he criticizes the archbishop for his belief that the reading of the Book of Common Prayer is tantamount to preaching. There is a nice touch of irony as Martin indicates how careful the metropolitan is that the *"heresie of preaching maie not prevaile."*[18] A close parallel occurs in the *Epistle*, where Martin accuses the "paltripolitan" of willingness to act against law, God, and conscience in depriving a Puritan preacher rather than that *"heresie of preaching should prevail."* There is also the same delight in the "pistling of bishops," which "by right of inheritance" belongs to Martin Senior, the elder brother.

In *Martin Senior* one observes the same close attention to friends and adversaries as in Martin's other books. In Penry's works, as we have previously noted, one rarely encounters a reference to contemporary personalities, but with Martin Senior, as with Throkmorton and Marprelate, there is a special interest in persons. Martin Senior mentions thirty-six individuals, including his six main antagonists—Whitgift, Cooper, Aylmer, Bridges, Perne, and Some. Dr. John Prime, an elusive figure who was criticized in *Hay Any Worke*, reappears in *Martin Senior*. Dr. Bancroft, Dr. Underhill, and "drunken Gravate" are derided. Two new adversaries are introduced—Anthony Munday and Anthony Anderson; four writers previously alluded to in *Martin Junior*, who had recently written disparagingly of Martin, namely, Leonard Wright, Tom Blan o Bedford (Tobias Bland), Jean de Frégeville, and Mar-Martin, are again mentioned. At the same time, Martin Senior speaks approvingly of his friends, Waldegrave, Newman, Sharpe, and Penry, and sympathizes with eleven prominent Puritan clergymen who were marked for surveillance in the talks delivered by Whitgift and Aylmer to the pursuivants.

Throughout Martin's and Throkmorton's books the author constantly resorts to invention and special techniques. Likewise, in *Martin Senior* the writer employs several devices to spice up the narrative, to whet the interest of the reader, and to provoke a chuckle or a guffaw. One effective device is the archiepiscopal oration, a masterpiece of derision that exposes Whitgift's supposed exasperation. He becomes so incensed that he fears he will lose his mind unless the traitors are captured.[19] A similar invention is the imaginary "mad-monition" in which Bishop Aylmer harangues his pursuivants. He urges his spies to exercise special surveillance on Pagit in Hounslow, Travers in London, and Cartwright in Warwick, and also to keep watch on gentlemen, knights, and noblemen. Another device is a legal indictment in which Martin Senior propounds, affirms, and protests against the prelates.[20] Especially fascinating is the use of ironic humor. Since Martin Junior is troubled by the problem of double-talk, and confused by the semantic difficulties resulting from the distorting of plain meanings of words, Martin Senior recommends that his brother make a special study of episcopal semantics. He will quickly learn to detect the bishops' cunning treacheries. If then the prelates translate the Puritans' "sure upholding of the crown and dignitie of their dread soveraigne" into "the utter ruine and subversion of Ladie Elizabeth," Martin Junior will be able to refute the catercaps, and the queen will "welfavouredlie laugh at such a translation as this is."[21]

In *Martin Senior* the writer employs the technique of the unexpected humorous ending. He warns Martin Junior not to get in touch with his father, for if he does, he will be punished for his impertinence in such a way that he will never be a lord bishop. Martin used the same expression in the *Epistle*, where he requested a free disputation. He wrote: if the bishops "be not set at a flat *non plus*, and quite overthrowen, ile be a Lord Bishop my selfe." Another technique to which Martin Senior resorts is the use of doggerel, as found in two previous books. Two pages are given to a denunciation of Mar-Martin:

> From Sarum came a gooses egge, with specks and spots bepatched;
> A priest of Lambeth coucht thereon; thus was Mar-Martin hatched.[22]

Throughout *Martin Senior* we also note that the writer has recourse to nineteen marginal notes. This device, which is used in the *Epistle* and *Epitome*, exemplifies a kind of posturing by which the reader enjoys the repartee and feels he is participating in a tête-à-tête.

In conclusion we may list five other indications of Throkmorton's authorship of *Martin Senior*.

1. Martin Senior exonerated Penry and others from any role in writing Marprelate's books when he asserted that they "did never medle nor make at anie time, with the metropoliticall writings of our renowmed father."[23]
2. Throkmorton wrote a letter to Mrs. Wigston, requesting permission to print *Martin Junior* and *Martin Senior* at her house.[24]
3. Symmes testified that *Martin Senior* was written in the same handwriting as in *Martin Junior*, and he thought "that Mr. Throckmort[on] was the author of it."[25]
4. Sutcliffe stated that "both *Martin Senior*, [and] *Martin Junior* were written with that very same hand, that wrote most

of *More Worke for Cooper*, which is knowne to be M. Throkmortons."[26]

5. Upon his arraignment, Hodgskin was found guilty of printing *Martin Junior*. It was stated at the trial "that this booke was devised chiefly by the said Throck[morton]: as also he is thought to be the auther of *Martin Senior* and *More Worke for the Cooper.*"[27]

Certaine Minerall, and Metaphisicall Schoolpoints (Mineralls)

The *Mineralls*, printed as a broadside by Waldegrave at Coventry about 26–28 January 1588/89, was an interim publication, designed to maintain interest and keep the polemic going until *Hay Any Worke for Cooper* could be published. Bishop Cooper's attack on Martin, *An Admonition*, had been issued about 10 January, and within three weeks Martin had promulgated his preliminary challenge to the bishop of Winchester.[28] The first argument for Throkmorton's authorship is that Penry informed Sharpe the manuscript copy of the *Mineralls* "was sent him from London." If this statement is true—and there is no reason to doubt it—then Penry was not the author. It is certain that Penry was at Fawsley or Northampton and it is probable that Throkmorton was in London after the publication of the *Epitome*, and that Newman delivered the manuscript.[29]

Two of the schoolpoints (numbers 16 and 25) refer to Dr. Some, whom Throkmorton satirized in his *Master Some Laid Open*. The flippant manner of writing befits Throkmorton, but it is utterly unlike Penry's polite reply to Dr. Some in *A Defence of That Which Hath Bin Written*. At least six of the schoolpoints indicate an irritation with the ideas presented in the writings of Whitgift, Aylmer, Cooper, Bridges, Cosin, and Some. This same irritation is revealed in Throkmorton's books. Likewise, Martin's and Throkmorton's tendency to repeat familiar ideas in similar language is evidenced in the twelfth schoolpoint:

> that the magistrate may lawfully maime and deforme the bodie of Christ (III:12)

> no civil majestrat may lawfully either maime or deforme the
> body of Christ (IV:6)
> no magistrate may lawfully maime or deforme the body of
> Christ (V:Aiv, item 17)[30]

Another reason for assigning this broadside to the Haseley
squire is that it contains twenty names, including those of
six bishops and four deans. All of these names occur in Martin's and Throkmorton's writings, with a touch of derision
or sarcasm, but only six are alluded to, without contempt
or gibes, by Penry. With undisguised glee Throkmorton
charged Bishop Middleton with bigamy in marrying Ales
Pryme and Elizabeth Gigge, as he did in his *Epistle* and in
Hay Any Worke. He took a malicious delight in striking at
Bishop Cooper by referring to "Mistris Coopers husband"
in schoolpoint number 29. Mrs. Cooper's shrewish reputation
and her dalliance with Dr. John Day were common knowledge during Throkmorton's years at Oxford in the 1560s.
Penry, who was born in 1563, did not enjoy gossip, regarded
scandalous insinuations as sinful, and had no personal knowledge of Cooper's marital problem or Mrs. Cooper's reputation. Therefore, the six snide references to her in the
Mineralls, Hay Any Worke, and the *Protestatyon* are strong clues
pointing toward Throkmorton's pen.[31]

Although the *Mineralls* is only a single sheet, it contains
ten expressions which correspond to parallels in Throkmorton's writings. Of these, five are presented here:

> by appeaching and accusing (III:9)
> to appeach or accuse (10:Eiii)

> the Archbishop of Canterbury is a giddie head (III:26)
> the Bishop of Canterbury is a giddy head (6:C2)

> that reading is preaching: the defendant in this point, is father
> John a Bridges (III:11)
> Bridges saith that reading is preaching (6:C2 v)

> to the preventing of the cavels of these wrangling Puritans
> (III:title)
> to cut of[f] al cavels and wranglings (7:75)

Christe in soule descended into hell (III:3)
Christ in soule descended into hell (IV:39)

Four phrases are repeated verbatim: "an absurd heretike" (III:25; 7:80); "as before is set downe" (III:conclusion; 10:Di); "bishops of the Divell" (III:15; 6:A1 twelve times, and IV:26–34, fourteen times); "to the view of all men" (III:title; 7:104). Even more convincing are six parallels in Throkmorton's *A Dialogue. Wherin Is Plainly Laide Open* and in the *Mineralls*, set forth in chapter six, which presents thirty lengthy items with well-nigh irrefutable parallels.

Theses Martinianae (Martin Junior)

Martin Junior and *Martin Senior*, which complement each other, seem to emanate from one mind. Since it was indicated earlier in this chapter that Throkmorton wrote *Martin Senior*, there is a natural presumption that he also penned *Martin Junior*. Both treatises were published in July 1589, within a week of each other.

On the basis of depositions by Newman, Hodgskin, and Symmes, Dean Sutcliffe stated that Throkmorton contracted with Hodgskin to print *Martin Junior*, that he arranged for the pickup of the manuscript along a path, and that he requested permission by letter from Mrs. Wigston for printing the book at her house. Symmes testified that when Throkmorton visited the place of printing at Wolston on 18 July, he clarified the reading of the interlineations in the manuscript, corrected the spelling in the printed material, and inquired of Hodgskin "softly in his eare" whether the two assistants "were good workmen and able to serve the turn, and Hodgkins answered yea." Symmes also affirmed "that he receaved at first but on[e] or twoe sheets of *Theses Martinianae*: and he thinketh the rest was brought thither by the said Throckmorton." Both Symmes and Thomlin, as well as Sutcliffe, stated that the handwriting in *Martin Junior*, *Martin Senior*, and *More Worke for Cooper* was all the same, and they regarded Throkmorton as the author of *Martin Junior*. When Hodgskin was arraigned before Justice Gawdy of the Queen's Bench, upon the statute of 23 Elizabeth, chapter 2, section 4, pertaining to illegal printing, the court not only adjudged him guilty of felony for having printed *Martin Junior*, but also ascribed the authorship to Throkmorton.[32]

In four of the writings of Throkmorton we find six parallels to expressions in *Martin Junior:*

> unto the view of the world (V:Aii)
> to the view of the worlde (3:47)

> have you choaked him with a fat prebend (V:Ciii)
> he choked me straight with his old common place (10:Dii)

> you deserve to be chronicled (V:Civ)
> he should have bene chronicled (7:16)

> the planters of our churche (V:Di v)
> the first plantinge of a church (7:75)

> I beginne prettily well (V:Diii v)
> and began pretily well (6:C4)

> I shall take a pride in it (V:Div)
> I take a pride in it (7:86)

Martin Junior clearly illustrates Throkmorton's style of writing. Of twelve criteria of style established in chapter seven, ten examples or features are found in this treatise. There are familiar phrases such as "I tell you true," "I must needes say," "I pray you," "good leave have I," "to be of this minde," which are ordinary phrases but which in the aggregate differentiate Throkmorton's and Penry's writings. The constant resort to name-calling, not found in Penry's books, is seen in such epithets as "Kankerbury," "Pilate," and "Caiphas," and also in "Judases," "Diotrephes," and "Simon Maguses." Less specific are denunciations against "scullions," "kennel rakers," "disguised asses," "varlets," and "ribaulder." We find unusual words such as "nuncka," "nunckle," and "neame" for "uncle," and playful words such as "tat" for "that," "nethew" for "nephew," and "vather" for "father." Throkmorton's favorite themes of persecution, excommunication, treason, pluralism, nonresidency, printers, Puritans, syllogisms, and polity occur, and his special interest in prisons is seen in Martin Junior's ironical statement that his father would be satisfied with a less modest house than the Tower, Newgate, the Fleet, or the Gatehouse.[33] And Throkmorton's love of deliberate alliteration is seen in "maimed and mishapen members," "praying your prelacie," "preheminence and promotion," and one melodious example: "Fire, and fagot, bands, and blowes, railing, and reviling." He exhibits his intensive feeling by absolute adverbs: "cleane gone," "utterlye to reject," and "flatlie forbidden."

There are other small indications of Throkmorton's hand. One is his temptation to boast of himself, not flagrantly but subtly: "I have a prety smattering gift in this Pistle-making, and I feare in a while I shall take a pride in it." Covertly speaking of himself, he writes: "My father [Martin Marprelate] is of a kingly nature I perceive by him. Hee woulde doe good unto you, but he would not be recompenced for it againe." Referring to himself, he concludes: "And therefore I tell you true, I thinke it a great blessing of God that hath raised uppe this Martin." There is a touch of pride and self-justification in thesis 97: "That Maister Thomas Cartwright, together with all those learned men, and my selfe also that have written against the state of the Clargy, could do no lesse than we have done, except wee woulde betray the trueth of God, the lawes of this lande, and the doctrines of our church." Penry knew of Cartwright, but Throkmorton was his intimate friend, invited him to his home, traveled with him, and visited him when Cartwright was imprisoned in the Fleet. There is also a sense of mirth and cleverness as Martin refers to the manuscript of *Martin Junior:* "If you demaund of mee, where I founde this, the trueth is, it was taken up (together with certaine other papers) besides a bush, where it had dropped from some body passing by that way." Since Throkmorton himself had arranged the drop, he enjoyed his own action. He referred to his own treatise, *Hay Any Worke,* as "that woorthie Treatise," and alluded with pride to his forthcoming book, *More Worke.*[34]

The Protestatyon of Martin Marprelat

The *Protestatyon*, reflecting deep frustration and bold defiance, was the final Martinist publication, written in great haste after the capture of Hodgskin, his assistants, the press, type, printed sheets, and manuscript of *More Worke for Cooper* on 14 August 1589. Since Penry co-ordinated the work of printing the *Protestatyon*, and since the printed books were delivered to Throkmorton's home in Haseley, we may infer that one of these two collaborators was the author or that both men produced it.[35]

In writing to Lord Burghley, Penry stated that he "dislyked many thinges in Marten for his maner, and for his matter of writing." "Unseemely jestes, uncomly rayling I allow not." He also protested that there was no reason why he would controvert the bishops "under a visor," since he had acknowledged his own books, and added: "I sett my name unto all my writinges saving my first book." He assured Burghley that he had "disclaymed the prelates and their dealing . . . befor the face of the sun" and that he would "by the power of the Lord foyle them openly."[36] Penry also defended himself and indirectly implicated Throkmorton when he wrote in his *Notebook* (page 65):

> Lastly Marten him self hath evidently cleared mee in his writinges by affirming him self in one [of] the last bookes hee made to bee unmaryed, wheras it is openly knowen that I had both a wif and also a child or more, even long befor that tyme, nay I was maryed befor Marten or any Martinist as the[y] are called was knowen in England.[37]

We note the assertion "hee made" [he wrote], referring to the *Protestatyon*, which was the last Marprelate book. Therefore, presumably Penry did not write this book; he was not Martin; and the probable author was Throkmorton.

A second reason for assigning this treatise to Throkmorton is the summary of *More Worke* in the *Protestatyon* (pages 24–31). In chapter six the evidence for Throkmorton's authorship of *More Worke* is presented. If he was the author, as Sutcliffe and Symmes affirmed, then it is probable that he was also the summarizer of this book in the *Protestatyon*.

Thirdly, chapter five established Throkmorton's authorship of *Master Some Laid Open*. Inasmuch as Penry in his *Defence of That Which Hath Bin Written* replied courteously and
objectively to Dr. Some, without railing and rancor, and inasmuch as Throkmorton refuted Dr. Some with sardonic satire,
in a patronizing, censorious, and insulting manner, we have
available a sharp contrast in the *modus operandi* of these two
writers. When we compare the treatment of Dr. Some in
the *Protestatyon* (pages 28–29), the similarity to Throkmorton's
mode of refutation and the dissimilarity to Penry's method
and approach are startling and significant. The identical references in the *Protestatyon* and *Martin Junior* to Tyndale's
"Practize of Prelates, page 374," to "M. Tindall, M. Frith,
M. Barnes, M. Hooper," and the caustic allusion to "those
shamelesse speeches of that woorthye grayhead, Mistresse
Coopers husband," all point to Throkmorton. Penry never
could have written the humorous, autobiographical, derisive,
and jeering pages in the *Protestatyon*.[38]

A fourth argument revealing Throkmorton's pen is the
stylistic evidence. All twelve stylistic criteria in chapter seven
are exemplified in the *Protestatyon*. Throkmorton's favorite
themes are present: persecution, tyranny, scourging, bonds,
pursuivants, imprisonment, racking, Court of High Commission, ex officio oath, polity, Puritans, printers, open disputation, a good conscience, and syllogisms. Well-known phrases
appear: "as I said before," "tell them from me," "if you
marke," "give over my course," and expressions indicating
intensity: "clean foild," "flatt contrarye," "inviolablie kept,"
and "uterly extinguis[h]ed." Throkmorton's rich and vivid
diction is illustrated by such words as "appeache," "intermitted," "overwayned," "Proculstants," "rapping," "slived," and
"suborned." Coined words, never found in Penry's books,
are: "Cooperism," "Cooperist," "Lambethisme," "Lambethist," "Lambethetical," "eblitaph," and "orawhynemeg." Unable to resist contemptuous epithets, Throkmorton gives vent
to such invectives as "buchers," "horseleaches," "beasts,"
"whelpes," "dragons," "cormorants," and "Antichrist of
Lambeth." Throkmorton's predilection for mentioning particular names is evidenced by his specifying thirty individu-

als, including nine bishops, seven Puritan writers, four anti-Martinist authors, and his six main adversaries—Whitgift, Cooper, Aylmer, Dean Bridges, Dr. Perne, and Dr. Some.

Alliteration is an integral part of Martin's and Throkmorton's style and pervades all their works, but it is absent in Penry's writings. In the *Protestatyon* there are twenty-seven examples of alliteration, of which five are listed here:

> discrying and displaying (VII:7)
> an handsome halter to hang himselfe with (VII:20)
> I then said, and so say I still (VII:28)
> Friar Fréguevil (VII:31) wringlefaced Wrighte (VII:31)

Even though the *Protestatyon* is Martin's shortest book, it has parallels from Throkmorton's writings and also from earlier Martinist works. The following list presents fifteen examples:

> for I knowe them soe well (VII:4)
> I knowe him so well (7:69)
> They know you not yet so thorowly as I doe (IV:5)
>
> M. Tindall, M. Frith, M. Barnes, M. Hooper (VII:12)
> M. Tindall, M. Frith, M. Barnes, M. Hooper (V:Civ v)
> M. Tindall, M. D. Barnes, and M. Fryth (V:thesis 52)
>
> I have long agone set up my rest (VII:14)
> he that should sette up his rest (3:34)
>
> it would do me good at the heart (VII:16)
> that would do me good at the hart (IV:5)
>
> as M. Tindall hath verye well noted, Practize of Prelates, page 374. It is not possible naturally, there should be any good and honest lord bishopp (VII:16)
> it is not possible, that naturally there can be anie good lord bishop, Master Tindalls practice for prelates, page 374 (V:thesis 57)
>
> leake out of al cry (VII:20)
> leake out of all crye (IV:t.p.)
> this is out of all crie (IV:A2)
>
> to pull the crowne off her Majesties head (VII:21–22)
> to pull the crowne off of her head (VI:Civ v)

ile have the *scandalum magnatum* against him (VII:22)

lest a *Scandalum magnatum* should be had against me (I:23)

the doctrine of our church (VII:22, 31) (a slogan)

the doctrine of our church (V:82, 87, 95, 97, 98, 100, 104)

that before God, there was noe other waye of tryall [except
   by the High Commission], nor no state could stand and
   continue without it (VII:23)

that there is no other way of triall before the High Commission,
   but by appeaching and accusing a mans selfe, and that no
   State can stand, without such answering and swearing (III:
   no. 9)

the state of the cleargie (VII:24, 26, 31)

the state of the Clargy (V:thesis 97)

is to bee neither Browniste, Cooperist (VII:25)

nor yet a sottish Cooperist (IV:25)

olde Lockwood of Sarum [Bridges] (VII:26)

olde Lockwoode of Sarum [Bridges] (7:81)

without sappe or edge (VII:28)

without sappe nor edge (7:62)

Ficker of Hell (VII:25)

vickers of Hell (IV:31)

An Epitome

The *Epitome*, as a continuation of the *Epistle*, is a further
refutation of Dean Bridges, "cloyster master of Sarum,"
"whose writings and sermons tend to no other ende, than
to make men laugh."[39] On the basis of arguments presented
previously in this chapter, we may safely assign the *Epistle*
to Throkmorton. Therefore we may attribute the *Epitome*
to him, since he said therein he had "made some mention
to his [Bridges'] praise in the former *Epistle.*" Also, in the
Epistle he announced: "Mine *Epitome* is readie."[40] In this latter
treatise Throkmorton's familiar phrases, coined words, dia-
lectal expressions, irony, humor, and satire are plentifully
utilized. There are eighty-three parallels found in the *Epitome*
and Throkmorton's writings. Of Martin's and Throkmor-

ton's twelve stylistic characteristics, ten are revealed in the *Epitome*, with seventy-nine examples.[41] No man in Elizabethan England, certainly not Penry, could have duplicated Throkmorton's unique and inimitable manner of writing.

Hay Any Worke for Cooper

In chapter six the reasons for attributing *More Worke for Cooper* to Throkmorton are presented. Since this treatise was a continuation of *Hay Any Worke*, we may assume that Throkmorton wrote this latter book, wherein he alluded seven times to his forthcoming *More Worke for Cooper*.[42] Since this latter book was a virulent diatribe against Dr. Some, we may also associate it with Throkmorton's *Master Some Laid Open*.[43] Again, since the writer of *Hay Any Worke* admitted that he "published a Pistle and a Pitome, wherein also I graunt that I did reasonably Pistle them," we may assign *Hay Any Worke* to Throkmorton on the basis of his authorship of the *Epistle*.[44] Furthermore, of twelve stylistic criteria established, ten appear in *Hay Any Worke*, supported by thirty-four examples. Likewise, the occurrence of twenty parallels in *Hay Any Worke* and Throkmorton's writings are more than sufficient to indicate his pen.[45] In the *Epistle* there are sixty-eight personal allusions and in *Hay Any Worke* fifty-seven, of which thirty-six names occur in both treatises. The conclusion is clear that *Hay Any Worke* coheres with *More Worke*, *Master Some Laid Open*, and such Martinist books as the *Epistle*, the *Epitome*, and the *Protestatyon*.

Oh read ouer D. John Bridges, for it is worthy worke:

Or an epitome of the

fyrste Booke, of that right worshipfull vo=
lume, written against the Puritanes, in the defence of
the noble cleargie, by as worshipfull a priefte, John Bridges,
Prefbyter, Prieft or elder, doctor of Diuillitie, and Deane of
Sarum. Wherein the arguments of the puritans are
wifely preuented, that when they come to an=
fwere M. Doctor, they muft needes
fay fome thing that hath
bene fpoken.

Compiled for the behoofe and ouerthrow of
the vnpreaching Parfons, Fyckers, and Currats,
that haue lernt their Catechifmes, and are paft grace:
By the reuerend and worthie Martin Marprelat
gentleman, and dedicated by a fecond Epiftle
to the Terrible Priefts.

In this Epitome, the forefaide Fickers, &c. are very in=
fufficiently furnifhed, with notable inabilitie of moft vin=
cible reafons, to anfwere the cauill
of the puritanes.

And left M. Doctor fhould thinke that no man can write with=
out fence but his felfe, the fenceles titles of the feueral pages,
and the handling of the matter throughout the Epitome,
fhewe plainely, that beetleheaded ignoraunce, muft not liue
and die with him alone.

Printed on the other hand of fome of the Priefts.

Title page of the *Epitome*, the second Marprelate book, printed in November 1588 by Robert Waldegrave, at Fawsley, Northamptonshire. The first
eleven lines are identical with those of the first Marprelate book, the *Epistle*,
of October 1588.

Hay any worke for Cooper:

Or a briefe Pistle directed by waye of an
hublication to the reverende Byshopps/ counselling
them/if they will needs be barrelled vp/ for feare of smelling
in the nostrels of her Maiestie & the State/that they would
vse the aduise of reuerend Martin/for the prouiding of their
Cooper. Because the reuerend T. C.(by which misticall
letters/ is vnderstood/eyther the bouncing Parson of Eastmeane , or Tom Coakes his
Chaplaine) to bee an vnskil-
full and a deceptfull
tubtrimmer.

Wherein worthy Martin quits himselfe like a man
I warrant you/in the modest defence of his selfe and his
learned Pistles/and makes the Coopers hoopes
to flye off/and the Bishops Tubs to
leake out of all crye.

Penned and compiled by Martin the Metropolitane.

Printed in Europe/not farre from some
of the Bouncing Priestes.

Title page of *Hay Any Worke for Cooper*, the fourth Marprelate work, printed
in March 1589 by Robert Waldegrave, at Coventry, Warwickshire.

 # THROKMORTON'S AUTHORSHIP: BASIC ISSUES

"To the present writer at least there are in the whole range of English literature few characters more interesting, more curious, and, it may be said, more completely bewildering [than Martin]. (Ronald B. McKerrow, *The Works of Thomas Nashe* 5 [1910]: 35)

Throkmorton's Status and Character

JOB THROKMORTON, eldest son of a Warwickshire squire, completed his university education at Oxford in 1566, and probably continued with legal studies at London. With the death of his father, Clement, in 1573, he became the lord of the manor at Haseley, near Warwick. In the sixth Elizabethan Parliament of 1586/87, he served as a burgess for Warwick, delivered three significant speeches, and before Parliament adjourned he fled the House of Commons because of the threat to imprison him in the Tower for his aspersions on the queen's foreign policy. From 1572 to October 1588, when the first Marprelate book appeared, he had already written seven treatises, five of which had been printed, all revealing a remarkable power of humor, independent thought, and irresponsible wit and sarcasm.[1] Despite his carping spirit, he referred frequently to himself as a gentleman, emphasized

237

courtesy, good manners, and proper decorum toward one's betters. He was conscious of his status as a man of society, and enjoyed the friendship of his peers. As a person of strong likes and dislikes, he expressed his views with an extraordinary power of language, clarity, and satire, and impressed his contemporaries as a Puritan *politique*, subtle, elastic, and worldly.

Throkmorton was a zealous nonconformist. He belonged to the political circle of Sir Anthony Cope, Sir Richard Knightley, Robert Bainbridge, John Field, Robert Beale, James Morice, and Peter Wentworth. During the Admonition Controversy of 1572 he had befriended Field, the organizing head of the dissident Puritans, and had urged his release from Newgate prison. He was an admirer of Robert Dudley, the earl of Leicester, and of his older brother, Ambrose Dudley, earl of Warwick. It is evident from his speech on the "Bill and Book" that Throkmorton was a staunch believer in the Reformed Genevan tradition, a supporter of the presbyterian classis movement, and a zealous advocate of a learned ministry. He was a thoroughgoing Erastian who thought that Convocation had too much power in spiritual matters. With Peter Wentworth he believed in free speech for parliamentarians, even on sensitive subjects such as the succession problem or religious reform. Consequently, he resented the role of the bishops, and despised Archbishop Whitgift, who had enforced articles of subscription, curtailed the liberty of the press by the Star Chamber decree of 1586,[2] imprisoned nonconformists, bullied defendants, exacted ex officio oaths, intimidated adversaries, and displayed unwonted choler. Throkmorton criticized the Court of High Commission, which was dominated by Archbishop Whitgift, Bishop Aylmer, and Bishop Cooper, whose decisions he regarded as miscarriages of justice. It is no accident that these three ecclesiastical officials loomed large in the pages of Martin Marprelate's books.

The character of Throkmorton may be elucidated and evaluated with the help of contemporary judgment. In a letter to the Scottish ambassador, Archibald Douglas, Lord Burghley apologized for Throkmorton's rash tongue and his "lewd and blasphemous" language used in the House of Commons against monarchs, including James VI. Lord Burghley was incensed by the speech, and caused the queen to be informed of it. He mollified the ambassador by stating that Throkmorton's fault was "not excusable," and therefore was to be punished by close imprisonment in the Tower.[3] Dr. Bancroft regarded Throkmorton as an irascible man with a fierce disposition. William Camden, historian, headmaster of Westminster School, and Clarenceux king-of-arms, considered him to be a shrewd, experienced person, brilliantly satirical and sharp-tongued, a "royster," "a learned man, but a merry conceited fellow," and one who brought "the prelates in hatred with the people" by spitting out "slanderous venome" in his poisonous books.[4] Although Lord Chancellor Hatton regarded Throkmorton as indiscreet, irrepressible, and ill-mannered, the Haseley squire boasted that Hatton considered him to be an honest man. This boast must be taken *cum grano salis,* since Dean Sutcliffe refuted Throkmorton, ridiculed him for his attempt to hide behind Hatton's banner, and wrote scornfully of his braggadocio:

Is it likely that so grave and wise a counseller should give such a testimony to such a railer and libeller, or that he not onely in his owne house, but also in Her Majesties presence, and in open Parliament, should affirme Job Throkmorton to be an honest man? . . . I have bin certified by men of sound credit, and against Throkmorton certes no parties [certainly not biased], and that were neerer and farre better acquainted with the late Lord Chanceller, than ever was M. Throkmorton, *that his Lordship did accompt of him, as of a man of a lewd, and proude disposition, and of a dissembling, and factious spirit, and gave out very hard speaches against him.* They told me further, that what favour he shewed him in qualifying his manifold offences for which he was constrained to hide his head, and to keepe himselfe out of the reach of Her Majesties judges and commissioners, flying from place to place, the same was extorted from him by the importunitie of some friends, which are to [can] be named, and wonne by a counterfaite submission made unto him by Throkmorton, with an humble acknowledgement of his faults.[5]

Sutcliffe himself regarded Throkmorton as lacking in wisdom and sound judgment, as somewhat deficient in honesty and godliness, and as irresponsible and intemperate. In calling him a libeler, a slanderer, and a railer, who was unable to contain himself or his tongue, Sutcliffe also reported that Throkmorton's "owne friendes call him *gibing Job*."[6]

Throkmorton's estimate of his own qualities is revealing. He described himself as "a shrewd fellow." He was proud of his wide reading and deep learning, and he was enamored with his unique style of writing. He delighted in his ability to reason, to expose illogical syllogisms, and to ferret out erroneous statements. Above all, he was aware of his wit and humor. He described the "Epistle" to his *More Worke for Cooper* with a vainglorious statement: "To tel thee true, I sigh to remember the losse of it. It was so prettie, and so witty. And I know if thou hadst it, thou wouldest laye it up, among other thy honest recreations for thy delight."[7] He displayed an unchristian pride and self-confidence, which contrast sharply with the self-debasing and self-negating qualities disclosed in Penry's writings. Thus, from the status of Throkmorton as a country gentleman, a member of Parliament, and an ardent Puritan, and from the estimates of his contemporaries, we may conclude that he was the kind of person clearly delineated in the seven Marprelate books.

Throkmorton's Indictment and Denial

One of the telling arguments for Throkmorton's authorship of the Marprelate books was his indictment by a grand jury at Warwick in the summer of 1590. By this time the government possessed the final depositions and examinations of Symmes, Thomlin, Sharpe, and Newman.[8] In preparation for the summer Assizes, the local magistrates convened the jurors, who heard witnesses, pondered a bill of indictment, and swore that it was a true bill. The judges of Assize, Edward

Fenner and Francis Gawdy, averred that the charges of writing Martinist libels were deserving of further inquiry, and therefore Throkmorton was bound in a recognizance to answer before judges in Westminster. In 1591 proceedings were deferred and then suspended, probably because of a legal technicality in his indictment. Throkmorton was neither acquitted nor pardoned but kept on probation until he died a decade later.[9]

In 1592 Sutcliffe had accused Throkmorton of writing the Marprelate books, and on the basis of two or three letters which Throkmorton and Edmund Coppinger exchanged in May 1591, had also charged that Throkmorton had abetted the Hacket-Coppinger-Arthington conspiracy and that he had a foreknowledge of the plot. In 1594, in reply to these charges, Throkmorton published his *Defence*, in which he expended the entire treatise in extenuating his own association with the conspirators by criticizing Coppinger and ridiculing Hacket. Instead of honestly refuting Sutcliffe's accusations, Throkmorton injected irrelevant issues, made countercharges, and did his utmost to malign the dean of Exeter. What is obvious is that Throkmorton sidestepped the issue of authorship, since he expended less than one page on this accusation.

Throkmorton's Clandestine Practices

Throkmorton's furtive behavior points to his being the true Martin. Whereas Penry was an agent, the negotiator with Newman, Sharpe, and Hodgskin, and one who dealt openly "in the face of the sun," Throkmorton remained in the background, lurking in the shadows. He cautioned Richard Holmes not to expose his activities. He wrote to two of his agents, Maicocke and Bowman, under counterfeit names. He was proud of his clever plan to have somebody plant the manuscript of *Martin Junior* along the path by a bush. He arranged for the manuscript of *More Worke* to be dropped from an upper room into the printers' work area, and he instructed Newman to follow him and nonchalantly pick up the manuscript of *The Crops and Flowers of Bridges Garden.* In consulting with the printers, he "asked Hodgkins softly in his eare" if Symmes and Thomlin were capable workmen. When he brought the remaining portion of the manuscript of *Martin Junior,* he stealthily slipped it in with the earlier portion without informing Symmes.[10] These secret practices befit one who is seeking to conceal his identity and his actions, and they accord with the procedures of Martin but not of Penry.

Throkmorton's Anonymous and Pseudonymous Writings

Throkmorton's reputation for clandestine behavior is illustrated by his practice from 1572 to 1596 of writing anonymous works and utilizing pseudonyms. Of thirty items identified as his, only eight were acknowledged, and these were almost entirely his shorter items, which consist of four letters to Ralph Warcupp, to the Bailiff and Principal Burgesses, to Lord Burghley, and to Lord Chancellor Hatton; three parliamentary speeches; and one book—his *Defence.* There were six pseudonymous writings: The *Epistle,* the *Epitome, Hay Any Worke for Cooper,* and the *Protestatyon,* all by Martin Marprelate. *Theses Martinianae* allegedly was by Martin Marprelate and Martin Junior, and *The Just Censure and Reproofe* was by Martin Senior. The fourteen anonymous items were:

1. "An Answer to Certen Peeces of a Sermon." 1572. MS.
2. *An Exhortation to the Byshops.* 1572.
3. *An Exhortation to the Bishops and Their Clergie.* 1572.
4. *A Second Admonition to the Parliament.* 1572.
5. "A Friendly Caveat to Bishop Sands." 1573. MS.
6. *The State of the Church of Englande.* 1588.[11]
7. *Certaine Minerall, and Metaphisicall Schoolpoints.* 1588/89.
8. *A Dialogue. Wherin Is Plainly Laide Open.* 1589.
9. *More Worke for Cooper.* 1589. MS. Partly printed.
10. "Martins Interim." 1589. MS.
11. *The Crops and Flowers of Bridges Garden.* 1589 or 1590.
12. "Letter to Edmund Coppinger." 1591. MS.
13. *A Petition Directed to Her Most Excellent Majestie.* 1592.
14. Preface to Thomas Cartwright, *A Brief Apologie.* 1596.

Throkmorton's two books signed by initials were *Certaine Articles* (1572), which carried the letters J.T.J.S., indicating Job Throkmorton as author and John Strowd as printer and possibly as part author, and *Master Some Laid Open in His Coulers* (1589), which was signed I.G., probably indicating Job Grivel or Job Gravener, two of his pseudonyms. Throkmorton's penchant for anonymity is evident.

Throkmorton's Stylistic Characteristics and Techniques

All serious students of the Marprelate problem have recognized the radical differences in the stylistic characteristics found in Penry's and Throkmorton's writings. Whereas Penry is earnest and vehement, Throkmorton is sprightly and clever. Whereas Penry is heavy, Throkmorton is light and frivolous. Penry is importunate and pleading, given to apostrophe, but Throkmorton is playful, teasing, and jesting. Throkmorton is aware of good English and is conscious of style. He knows how to interest his reader, how to relieve didacticism, how to create suspense. He oscillates between the serious and the humorous, and designedly injects unexpected conclusions. He plays with his reader, assumes postures, and easily triumphs over his imaginary opponents. His style is fluent, clear, and fascinating. There is a graphic quality, a picturesque feature, even a droll character to his paragraphs, which provoke mirth, laughter, and hilarity. He enjoys the anecdotal and conversational approach. His allusions reveal wide reading, a rich vocabulary, maturity, worldly wisdom, knowledge of human nature, broad experience, legal and political knowledge. In his descriptions and accusations, he is specific, concrete, particular. As a practical cameraman, he provides not panoramas but close-ups. As a reporter, he uses vivid words, choice expressions, and vigorous sentences. He enjoys colorful language. Both Martin and Throkmorton freely use anecdotes and proverbs, but these are missing in Penry's books. Whereas Martin and Throkmorton are specific in presenting dates and places, Penry is more general or omits such data. Throkmorton and Martin habitually speak of the human body, either in a literal or figurative meaning. There are at least sixty references to the body, such as "crazing of the braine," "huddleing one in the necke of the other," "fel sicke of the splene," "with a wet finger," "to his Graces teeth," "twenty fistes about your eares," "a smooth tongue," "bleare the eyes," "noses can abide no jest," and "stashed his sweet face." There are also frequent references to blisters, bowels, bones, cheeks and jowls, loins, marrow, sores, veins, and windpipes. Such corporeal allusions are not found in Penry's writings.

Whereas Penry professes to write in a "free and plaine style" without embellishments, Throkmorton takes pride in his stylistic techniques, variety of learning, method, and pleasant style, and even suggests that "the like is not elsewhere to bee found." He delights in characterizing himself as "old excellent" and "old suersbie" [reliable]. He is eminently successful in establishing a sense of intimacy and rapport with his readers, by chuminess, conversation ploys, questions, and jesting. This is seen in his inviting Bishop Cooper to go out alone with him in the fields for discussion:

> Therefore (marke now, T.C., and cary me this conclusion to John O Lambehith for his breakefast), our church goverment by Archbishop and bishops, is an unlawful church goverment. You see, brother Cooper, that I am very courteous in my minor, for I desire therein no more offices to bee thrust out of the church at one time, but Archbishop and Bishops. As for Deanes, Archdeacons, and Chancellors, I hope they wilbe so kind unto my Lords Grace, as not to stay, if his Worship and the rest of the noble clergie Lords weare turned out to grasse.[12]

He adopts a posturing attitude which creates an atmosphere of discussion; he impersonates his opponents, and puts loaded answers into the mouths of his disputants: "Can you denie any part of your learned brother Martin his syllogisme?" "We denie your minor, M. Marprelat," the bishops reply.[13] Again, in disputing with Dean Bridges, Martin writes: "A most true and tried trueth, what then, brother Sarum? Do you assume from this, true goverment?"

Nay soft there, ka masse deane. I trow the Puritans will not drive me to make syllogismes in this booke. That is no part of mine intent, for if I had thought they would drive me to suche pinches, I would not have medled with them. Naye, by their leave, if the assumption or proposition bee eyther more than I can proove, or be against my selfe, I will omit them.[14]

When Bishop Cooper suggested that faults should be charitably and mildly dealt with, Martin replied with condescending mockery:

Gentle fathers, keep the people in ignoraunce no longer; good fathers now, maintain the dumbe ministerie no longer. Be the destruction of the Church no longer, good sweete babes nowe; leave your nonresidencie and your other sinnes, sweet Popes now, and suffer the trueth to have free passage. Lo, T.C., nowe I have mildely delt with the good fathers. I will nowe expecte a while to see whether they will amende by faire means; if not, let them not say but they have bin warned.[15]

In reprimanding Bishop Aylmer for his interpretation of Pauline teaching on civil policy, Martin wrote: "I see now it is no marvaile though Paul be put to silence within the diocesse of London, for I perceive there is an olde grudg betweene my Lord and him."[16]

Another technique used by Throkmorton and Martin was the inclusion of a qualification, a parenthetical phrase which catches the attention of the reader. In reference to the archbishop, Martin remarked: "I hope John of Canterburie whom I knowe (though I know no great good in him) . . . ." Replying to Bridges, he commented: "Ile never beleeve him though he saye so. Neyther will I saye that his Grace is an Infidell (nor yet sweare that he is much better)." Closely related to this stylistic device is the utilization of an unexpected conclusion. Martin Senior warns: "For an [if] thou doest, I can tell thee, heele give thee such a lesson for thy sawcinesse, as I thinke thou shalt never be Lord Bishop while thou livest." Again: "How sayst thou, hast thou anie skil in Musike? If thou have, then I am sure thou wilt confesse with mee, that this bastarde pentamenter [*sic*] verse hath a fine sweete loose at the latter ende, with a draught of Darbie ale."[17]

Martin and Throkmorton enjoy a play on words. "Civillians" are degraded to "seevillaines," and Dean Bridges, "Doctor of Divinity," is demoted to a "Doctor of Divillitie." The Service book (sarve us) is called the "starve us" book. Accusing Dr. Some, Throkmorton asserts: "he chargeth his adversarie to say flatlye, and yet it is but a *flat lye.*"[18] In alluding to the groom of Charles IX as a *valet de chambre du roy*, Throkmorton prefers to speak of him as a *varlet de chambre du roy.*[19] Dr. William Wood, a censor of books, is called "Neverbegood (Wood)," and Dr. Culpepper becomes Dr. "Culpable." When Bishop Aylmer, preaching at Paul's Cross, spoke of "Catekissing" (catechising), Throkmorton warned him that he "should *kisse* Cate no more in the pulpit."[20] In one of his sentences, Throkmorton contrasts the "leprosye of the body" with the "lethargye of the sowle," and in another, "litany" becomes "Latenie."[21] His use of balance is seen in one of his parliamentary speeches:

> The same God that can rayze up stones unto Abraham, for the defence of his church,
> can also rayne downe haylestones upon Pharao, for the overthrowe of the wicked.[22]

Martin used ridicule to further his purposes. When Mar-Martin wrote his verses against Martin Marprelate, he included a line:

O England now ful often must thou Pater Noster say.[23]

Martin urged his readers to scan it well, and added: "Where like a good Catholike hee counsels us (we thanke him) to say a rounde *Pater Noster* for Queen Elizabeth, I muze [marvel] thou saidst nothing to that regarde. And much more had shee beene, if hee had added an *Ave Marie* to it. Those both together, with a peece of St. Johns Gospell about ones loins, woulde have beene a principall receit [recipe] for the collicke." Then comes a query: "Whether likest thou better of these Nicholas Priestes that can so amble away with the *Pater*

Noster, or of that little priest of Surrey, who bade his maide in her extreamitie of sicknesse say, *Magnificat*, say *Magnificat*?"[24]

Martin Junior lampooned Mar-Martin unmercifully for his riming efforts. "Concerning Mar-Martin, if he be a Londoner, or an universitie man, tenne to one, but you shall see him, one of these odde days, carted out of the towne for his honestie of life. Why, that rime of his sheweth, that hee had no other bringing uppe, than in a brothel-house." Martin Junior suggested that Mar-Martin had been promoted "unto the service of some laundresse in a bishoppes house, where, in hope to bee preferred by his good lordes, he hath undertaken to mar-rimes, in publishing bawdery, and filthinesse, for the defence of these honest bishops."[25] In *Martin Senior* the writer chided Martin Junior for not producing a counter-riming attack on Mar-Martin. "But yet I would have born with all this, if thou haddest taken a little paines in ryming with Mar-Martin, that the cater-caps may knowe, howe the meanest of my fathers sonnes is able to answeare them, both at blunt and sharpe."[26] Then came two pages (fifty-five lines) of undignified burlesque verse-riming doggerel, which sets forth Mar-Martin's base origin and deserved epitaph. It is instructive to find that as early as 1572 Throkmorton had included on the title page of *Certaine Articles* eight lines of doggerel, entitled, "The Prynter to the Reader." Then followed two lines which were reminiscent of the imprints in Martin's *Epistle*, *Epitome*, and *Hay Any Worke for Cooper*:

> Imprinted we know where, and whan,
> Judge you the place and [if] you can.[27]

Martin also ridiculed Dean Bridges' writing style, and gave a mock example of the dean's poetical "rime doggrell":

> Is good inough for bishops I can tell,
>   And I doe much marvell,
> If I have not given them such a spell,
>   As answere it how they cannot tell.
> Doctor Bridges up and downe,
>   Writeth after this fashowne.[28]

Name-calling is a prominent characteristic and a deliberate device in Martin's and Throkmorton's writings but not in Penry's books. Some of the titles are humorous and ironical, such as "Your Holines," "Your Terribleness," "Fickers Generall," and "Worshipfull Paltripolitans." Other names are impertinent and degrading, such as allusions to Archbishop Whitgift as "Dr. Pernes boy," "Dr. turnecoats scholler," "His Gracelesnes of Cant.," and "Beelzebub of Canterburye," even as Bishop Aylmer is called "Beelzebub of London." The most imaginative and persistent name-calling is reserved for Dean Bridges, who is "Goffer Bridges" and "uncka Bridges." He is referred to as "Lockewoode of Sarum," "the Prince of all the Stumblers in the worlde," "olde Dorbel of Sarum," "that clotheade" [clod-pate], "that sweet babe of Sarum," "that packsadle," and "that sory chaplain of Sarum." Less imaginative descriptions are "duns," "patch," "pied faced foole," "drudge," "sot," and "symonical Deane." After Bishop Thomas Cooper had published his anti-Martinist *Admonition to the People of England*, he was termed "Father Admonitor."[29]

Pope Pius V is ridiculed as "Impius Quintus." Mary Queen of Scots is alluded to as a "wreatched Athalia," a "guysian impe," and a "Jezabel," and her son, James VI, is called "the younge impe of Scotlande." Dean Perne is called "Father Palinod," "Ambo," a "turncoat," a "turner," a "fox," and a "Judas." Doctor Hone, an archidiaconal judge, is designated as "the bawdie Doctor," "the veriest coxcombe that ever wore velvet cap," and "a popish dolt." Stephen Chatfield, vicar at Kingston-upon-Thames, is put down as a "bankerout and duns," whom Martin addressed directly: "Go to, you Asse." Scriptural characters such as Haman, Pilate, Caiaphas, Diotrephes, Simon Magus, and Antichrist are freely associated with Martin's adversaries, and the names of living creatures, such as caterpillers, serpents, dragons, beasts, dogs, and whelps are used pejoratively. Other terms of opprobrium are "hypocrites, bastardly governors, blockheads, sourfaced knave, ribaulder, massmonger, turnespit, scullions, varlets, sycophants, ignominious fooles," and a "journeyman in the shambles." Related to these epithets are about thirty references to the brain, which insinuate that an opponent is stupid, or that he is crazy, giddy headed, suffering from a swimming in the head or apoplexy.[30]

Even the title pages of Martin's and Throkmorton's books, which sometimes belie the author's purposes, represent devices and imaginative fictions designed to catch the readers' attention. The first Martinist book, the *Epistle*, is neither a letter "to the terrible Priests of the Confocation house" nor an epitome of Dr. Bridges' *Defence*. Its form suggests a list of indictments, complaints, or a legal suit, with sixteen phrases sprinkled throughout the book, such as "most pitifully complayning," and "may it please you." In essence, the *Epistle* is a series of anecdotes and denunciations of the hierarchy, warnings and threats, and ridicule of Dr. Bridges and the clergy. The literary devices are interest-catching artifices, which reveal an ingenious writer. There is an epitaph for Dean Bridges as a worthy presbyter. In case he should die as a bishop, as he actually did, a second epitaph is provided: "Here lies John Bridges late Bishop, friend to the Papa." In the *Epistle* Martin draws up "Conditions of Peace to Be Inviolablie Kept for Ever, betweene the Reverend and Worthy Master Martin Marprelate, gentleman, on the one partie, and the reverend fathers his brethren, the Lord Bishops of this lande." Martin lays down five conditions, and he promises "upon the performaunce of the premisses by you, never to make any more of your knavery knowne unto the worlde." Not unexpectedly, in his next book, the *Epitome*, Martin divests himself from any obligation to desist from "pistle-making," since the clergy masters have broken the conditions of peace.[31] *Hay Any Worke for Cooper*, with its catchy title, was a clever device; had Martin's book been entitled, *An Answer to Bishop Thomas Cooper*, it would have been less effective and more quickly forgotten. *Theses Martinianae*, or *Martin Junior*, which contains the fiction that the son found his material among his father's imperfect papers, seems a transparent device to camouflage the fact that the treatise was hurriedly prepared in a few days in order to supply copy for the printers, and the second fiction that the roll was found beside a bush seems a device to permit Hodgskin the printer to pick up the manuscript and still be able to deny any knowledge of the author. The suggestion that the manuscript was wet and weatherbeaten because of a sea journey probably indicates that the papers placed by the bush were affected by rain, with "never a drie threede in them."[32] Likewise, *Martin Senior* represents a fiction that the older brother is reprimanding his younger brother for his mistakes, but Martin the Great is really praising himself and denouncing the archbishop, Mar-Martin, and the stage players who had burlesqued him. Martin Senior appends a "proper-sition" for investing Dean Bridges into his rightful place as the official jester at Lambeth Palace. A similar device occurs in the *Protestatyon* where the author describes Martin's Tolbooth. Suggestive of a prison, a customs-shed, and a town hall, the Tolbooth contained "a great ashen chaire, wherin John a Bridges was placed by patent during his life."[33]

In the works by Throkmorton we notice the same practice of utilizing devices even in the titles. "A Friendly Caveat," written against Bishop Edwin Sandys in 1573, is more a fictitious title than a kind warning, since it presents Throkmorton's harsh denunciation of the bishop of London. *A Dialogue. Wherin Is Plainly Laide Open* ostensibly is a discussion carried on by four travelers, but actually is a presentation of Throkmorton's ideas and complaints found in his first four Marprelate publications, and is designed to expose the evil deeds of Whitgift, Cooper, Aylmer, and Bridges. Throkmorton's longest work, *Master Some Laid Open in His Coulers,* is a staunch defense of Penry against the attack of Dr. Some. The title itself promises an exposé. Another stratagem is the preface, "To the Reader," which pretends to be a statement by an anonymous publisher or editor as distinct from the author, "an Oxford friend." Both the preface and the text are obviously by Throkmorton himself. *A Petition Directed to Her Most Excellent Maiestie* is purportedly a plea to the queen, but clearly is a device by Throkmorton to attract attention and to attack his adversaries. Still smoldering from his indictment at Warwick, he sought to exonerate himself and the seekers after reformation from charges of defaming the monarch and inciting rebellion. *A Petition* was a direct promotion of presbyterian church government and an indirect and cautious criticism of protagonists of Anglican polity. It censured Whitgift, Aylmer, and Cooper, and repeated former accusations against Dean Cosin and Dr. Bridges. Its list of captious questions was a technique to entrap the ecclesiastical writers of the Church of England. Throkmorton's last book, *The Defence of Job Throkmorton, against the Slaunders of Maister Sutcliffe, Taken out of a Copye of His Owne Hande as It Was Written to an Honorable Personage*, carried a fiction in the title. The insinuation was that Throkmorton had written his *Defence* in the form of a letter to an honorable lady, perhaps his own mother or to such a distinguished person as Anne, countess of Warwick, widow of Ambrose Dudley, the earl of Warwick, and a close friend of the queen. Supposedly, this "Honorable Personage" had then published the letter without Throkmorton's knowledge or consent. This seems to be an obvious subterfuge, possibly used to disclaim any responsibility for printing the *Defence* in case the author was accused of circumventing the *censor librorum*.[34]

Throkmorton's Irony, Sarcasm, and Lampoons

In the writings of Throkmorton and Martin, but not in Penry's works, there are numerous examples of irony, sarcasm, and lampoon. Throkmorton exemplifies his irony by such words as "forsooth," "sweet," "smooth," and "worthy." When he describes the bitter and caustic writing of Dr. Some, he says: "And then he goeth on very sweetly thus." When he wishes to ridicule a foolish statement, he speaks of this "worthy" sentence. Occasionally, he throws in a parenthetical phrase, "we thank him," or "I thank him," when there is nothing to thank him for, or when an unkindness is involved.

Throkmorton's treatment of Dr. Some is a masterpiece of sarcasm and sharp repartee. He accuses him of making more than 400 bare and naked assertions which cloy the ears of his listeners. These peremptory pronouncements he likens to rigorous and thundering statutes which reveal the dogmatic character of the man. He asserts that Dr. Some's utterances are empty of content, trite, banal, without either "sappe or salt." When Dr. Some likens Penry to Demetrius, to Campion, to Judas, Throkmorton sarcastically refers to "that good Christian moode of his," wherein "it pleaseth him full sweetly" to make Penry "worse than a drudge and a turnespit." Although Throkmorton regards Dr. Some as an utterly unlearned man, and considers his treatise a blast of platitudes, yet in mock deference to an unrevealed potential knowledge he admits that there may be wine in the cellar "when there is non[e] in the cuppe."[35]

The sarcastic treatment of Dr. Bridges, both in the Marprelate books and in *Master Some Laid Open*, is in itself a strong indication that the frequent identical sentiments originate in one mind. We note the same kind of irony, jocularity, and sarcasm. The satire against Dr. Bridges is humorous and clever; the lampoons are abusive and malicious. Dr. Stumbler Bridges is described as a blear-eyed sot, who suffers from a "fiever Lourdaine" [feverlurden, the disease of laziness].

> I meane that proper scholler that could speake Englishe before I was borne; he that hath given Calvine and Beza suche a blowe, as they could never speake word of good Irish since . . . That pretie pigeon that wrote the sixteen great volumes in defence of the hierarchie of bishops, but as he hath handled it, it may serve as well for the foule cawsey betwixt Glocester and Bristow. I doe not meane Tarleton, man; tushe, no, I meane that musicall poet, that can so ingeniously translate rime into prose, and prose into rime againe. That patch of S. Maries pulpit, what should I call him? *Bridges, Bridges*, a shame on him, I shall hit on his name anon. This is he, I feare me, that taught M. Some this tricke, and yet when it is looked into, it wil be found but a sluttish tricke neither, I beleeve. This *Bridges* you must understand, is bound in a recognisance. The condition is this. *That if ever he hurt Puritane by any learning,*

reason, logicke, divinitie, or good grammaticall sense, then he forfaits
al that ever he hath to Her Majestie, and is utterly undone for ever.[36]

If the evidence in chapter five for Throkmorton's authorship
of *Master Some Laid Open*, which includes this passage, is credible, it is easy to believe that the same person wrote the following passage on Goffer Bridges in Marprelate's *Epitome:*

> Trust me truely, he hath given the cause sicken a wipe in
> his [its] bricke, and so lambskinned the same, that the cause
> will be the warmer a good while for it . . . What cannot a
> smooth tongue, and a schollerlike wit bring to passe? . . . His
> stile is as smooth as a crabtree cudgell. The reader cannot
> chuse but have as great delight therein, as a jacke an apes
> hath in a whip. He hath so thumped the cause with crosse
> blowes, that the Puritans are like to have a good and a sound
> cause of it as long as they live. In this one thing I dare preferre
> him before any that ever wrote: to wit, that there be not three
> whole periods for every page in the book, that is not graced
> with a verie faire and visible solacism. O most excellent and
> surpassing eloquence. He speaketh every thing so fitly to the
> purpose, that he never toucheth the matter in question. A
> rare gift in a learned writer.[37]

One never encounters this kind of writing in Penry's works,
since he, with Richard Greenham, believed that sin should
be made odious, not ridiculous. By nature and training Penry
was incapable of the jocosity and levity of the Marprelate
books, and he disliked the frivolity which seems second nature to Throkmorton.

Throkmorton's and Martin's Special Interests and Topics

In the writings of Throkmorton and Martin there are many
topics and themes which reveal something of their authors'
special interests. Since these topics are not discussed in Penry's writings, this negative evidence points toward Throkmorton's authorship of the Marprelate books. There are some
thirty references which display his unusual interest in printers and printing. His allusions to Waldegrave in his *A Dia-*
logue. Wherin Is Plainly Laide Open and in four Marprelate

books indicate that Throkmorton derived much of his information directly from the printer. There are contrasts between the harsh treatment of Waldegrave, who printed books pertaining to the bishops' mitres, and the favorable treatment accorded "popish" printers such as "knave Thackwell," Thomas Orwin, and John Charlewood. Since Waldegrave printed the first four Martinist items, and most of the *Protestatyon*, as well as Throkmorton's *Master Some Laid Open* and his *Dialogue*, and also his *The State of the Church of Englande*, which was confiscated in April 1588, and since he consulted with Throkmorton at Haseley, to whom he delivered his printed books in September 1589, it is understandable why Throkmorton's information on him is specific and informative.[38] Throkmorton referred to Richard Schilders, a printer at Middelburg, in the Netherlands, who printed Throkmorton's *The Crops and Flowers of Bridges Garden*, his *A Petition Directed to Her Most Excellent Maiestie*, and *A Parte of a Register*, which contained two sections by the Haseley squire. Schilders also printed *The Defence of Job Throkmorton* and Cartwright's *A Brief Apologie*, for which Throkmorton wrote the preface and served as editor.[39] Throkmorton alluded to the Puritan printer, Thomas Thomas, at the University of Cambridge, who had printed the *Harmony of the Confessions of Faith of the Christian and Reformed Churches*,[40] and had incurred the displeasure of the prelates. Throkmorton warned Thomas that he might receive the same treatment that Waldegrave had suffered for printing "my frend and deare brother Diotrephes his Dialogue" "that the bishops lately burned."[41] Throkmorton also stigmatized John Wolfe, beadle of the Stationers' Company, as a "Machiuill" [Machiavelli], and referred four times to Thomas Chard, publisher of Bridges' *A Defence*, a bulky volume of "an hundred three score and twelve sheets," expensive to print, which required a "protection" or subvention because of the high cost and low sales.[42] Throkmorton was also interested in the printers' product, since he spoke of books in folio, quarto, and octavo, of sheets, one-half sheets, leaves, and parchment. He noted that the first edition of Cooper's *An Admonition* had 252 pages, and he gloated that the book had been recalled for corrections. Throkmorton even made a cryptic reference to 1,401 and 812.[43] He also liked to remark, when it suited his humor, that a book had been printed *"cum privilegio"* and had been "seen and allowed."

Unlike Penry, Throkmorton and Martin refer to Puritans and Puritanism about 135 times. In his *Master Some Laid Open,* in his *A Dialogue,* and in his *Defence,* as well as in his parliamentary speech on "The Bill and Book," Throkmorton frequently alludes to Puritans. Likewise, in all seven Marprelate books, there are similar allusions to such prominent university Puritans as John Rainoldes of Corpus Christi College, Oxford, and Laurence Chaderton, master of Emmanuel College, Cambridge. Throkmorton is especially appreciative of William Whitaker, master of St. John's College, and William Fulke, master of Pembroke Hall, whom he regards as two of the most learned Cambridge men in the land. There are good words for Walter Travers, Stephen Egerton, the popular preacher at Blackfriars, and John Udall, and there is sympathy for those Puritans who had suffered for advocating reform, such as Dudley Fenner, Percival Wiburn, Eusebius Pagit, Robert Cawdrey, Giles Wigginton, Barnaby Benison, Thomas Settle, and William Charke. Other Puritans who were venerable or recently deceased such as John Foxe, Anthony Gilby, and Richard Greenham are mentioned. There are also brief references to John More, the "apostle of Norwich," John Knewstub of Cockfield, Suffolk, Robert Wright of Ipswich, Suffolk, and John Davidson, a presbyterian minister from Prestonpans, Scotland.

More than Penry and most other English writers in the Elizabethan period, Throkmorton and Martin reveal an interest in Continental authors. Among those mentioned are Benedictus Aretius, Théodore de Bèze, Martin Bucer, John Calvin, Lambert Daneau or Danaeus, Joachimus Camerarius, Franciscus Junius (Du Jon), Kemnitius (Martinus Chemnitius), Bertrand de Loque (François de Saillans), Immanuel Tremellius, and Petrus Loseler Villerius (Pierre Loyseleur de Villiers). Among Catholic writers there are allusions to

William Allen, Richard Bristow, Desiderius Erasmus, Thomas Harding, William Rainoldes, Sadel (Antoine La Roche Chandieu), Thomas Stapleton, and Franciscus Turrianus.

Throkmorton and Martin, but not Penry, charge treason against some of their opponents, especially Dean Bridges. Martin implies that the archbishop is guilty of misprision of treason in allowing flat treason to be published. He hints that "the foxe D. Perne" may have been the author of a treasonable passage on page 448 of Dr. Bridges' book. Treason is defined as affirming "Her Majestie to be an infidell," or asserting that a priest or archbishop "may have a lawfull superiour authoritie" over the queen. Dr. Bancroft is charged with being traitorous for implying that the queen was a "petty pope" who had usurped authority. Throkmorton, by straining a point, even asserts that Dean Bridges was proved guilty of treason "by the mouth of my Lord of Winchester himselfe, if it were he that fumbled us up that sodden *Admonition to the People of England.* For Martin (whom he cals the libeller) chargeth Doctor Bridges with flat treason, and I take it, he names both the place and the page." In this last sentence, Throkmorton is alluding to himself, and is boasting that he is specific, even as he did in the *Epitome*, signature C1 v. As a corollary to his charges, Throkmorton hopes that these traitors will be subject to the statute or writ of *praemunire facias.*[44]

Although highly critical of the prelates' policy of incarcerating opponents, Throkmorton seems to enjoy making constant allusions to specific prisons. He predicts that one of his literary characters will "kisse the Clinke or Gatehouse for this geare." Likewise, Martin mocks Bishop Cooper and his "loving and carefull brethren" for their thoughtfulness in pursuing him. He ironically explains that he has not revealed his whereabouts because he does not like the cool temperature of the prisons in the winter time. He warns the clerical authorities to restore Walter Travers to his preaching post at the Temple. Otherwise, another book such as Travers' *A Defence of the Ecclesiastical Discipline Ordayned of God* may "drop out of his budget." Then it would be "good for the bishops to lie a day and a night in Little Ease in the Counter." He issues a sarcastic plea that if anyone dares to "defend Christ Jesus and his prerogative," then the disputation will be quietly arranged, and the proceedings will continue within "the bare walles in the Gatehouse or some other prison." Martin protests against the archbishop's threat of sending Mrs. Thomas Lawson, a London shrew, to the Bridewell, and he reports that Bishop Aylmer sent Barnaby Benison, a London preacher, to the Clink. Martin modestly confesses that he doesn't need an expensive house such as the Tower, the Fleet, Newgate, or the Gatehouse, and he asserts that the bishops ought not to have prisons wherein to punish transgressors. In mockery Martin Junior asks if the bishops have secretly murdered Martin Marprelate in their prisons.[45]

In addition to the prison allusions, there are about thirty references to pursuivants, who are presented as the truckling agents of episcopal persecuters. Martin ironically speaks of the bishops' kindness in seeking for him, but he sarcastically refers to the pursuivants as "beasts." The pursuivants are reminded that their warrants from the Court of High Commission extend to gentlemen, knights, and even nobility. Both Martin and Throkmorton are disdainful toward the bishops and their agents, who reject any appeal for scholarly and modest writings, open disputations, and good and sound syllogisms. Having grown old and senile, the bishops are averse to arguments and controversy. "Alasse, they may leave that to [their pursuivants] Watson, or Walton, Haslop, or Munday, or some such sweete chapleine of theirs, whoe have excelent witts at whipcoard conclusions, to manicle these puritans with."[46] Instead of dealing with issues, ideas, polity, and reform, the bishops, "like furious and senceles brute beasts," "spare none, but with tooth and naile, cry out—'downe with that side that favoureth the gospel so. Fetch them up with purcivants, to the Gatehouse, to the Fleet, to the Marshalsea, to the Clinck, to Newgate, to the Counter with them.' "[47]

There are references to instruments of torture and execution. Martin speaks of "ravening purcivantes" who fly city and country to find their suspects, who in turn are threatened with the rack. Martin also refers to bishoprics which have been so depleted and despoiled that a bishop newly appointed to a diocese scarcely has enough to "purchase him a handsome halter to hang himself with." Likewise, Throkmorton accuses Dean Sutcliffe of desiring that John Udall be "honored with the gibbet."[48] In a blunt passage, which Penry never could have written, Throkmorton vents his rage against Sutcliffe, accusing him of shaking the halter with one hand and showing "the hatchet with the other."[49] When Dr. Some threatened Penry: "you dare not for your eares say," Throkmorton replied: "The onely way that I see is to couch under the board, and keepe close for the time, till that same perillous pillorie whiche so frighteth and threatneth men with their eares, be shifted or remooved out of his [its] place."[50] All these allegations on dishonorable utilization of prisons, pursuivants, racks, pillories, gibbets, and halters culminate in Martin's sweeping indictment of his enemies:

> Fire, and fagot, bands, and blowes, railing, and reviling, are, and have bene hitherto, their common weapons; as for slandering and lying, it is the greatest piece of their holy profession. And these with their bare assertions, and their wretched cleving to popish absurdities, are in a maner the onely proofes and tried maximes they offer unto the Church in this age.[51]

There are sixteen allusions to the theme of promotions in the clerical hierarchy, with specific references to Bridges, Whitgift, and Dr. Some. These allusions are about equally divided in the writings of Throkmorton and Martin, but they are not found in Penry's writings. Dean Bridges, "the pide faced foole," is depicted as a man who would do anything to obtain a bishopric. His mind is so set on his promotion that he is unable to finish a sentence properly. He wrote "this foule heape [*A Defence*] against the holy Discipline of Christ (as Whitgift did the like) in hope to bee the next Pope of Lambeth." Even though he had incurred "the ignomie, shame, and reproache" for writing *A Defence*, nevertheless he was double-crossed by the archbishop, who promised him and John Thornborough the same position and then awarded it to a third party.[52] Dr. Some is asked rhetorically whether a "sweet deanery" or a bishopric would not prevail more effectively with him than sound arguments in altering his views. Throkmorton concludes that "M. Some and some others should not be suffered to rove and range up and downe as they doe, neglecting theire charges, and breathinge after chaplainship, promotions, and I knowe not what." In a passage directed against both Dr. Some and Archbishop Whitgift, he writes:

> Wel, for all that, if he can make shift with all the skill he hath to fetch a jump from his benefice at Girton to some sweet Deanry or Bishopricke, it wil sure be one of the pretiest jumps that ever he made in his life. There be of his betters [Whitgift] that have made such Alemaine leapes in their dayes, and thereby may the better direct him the way, if neede be. How thinke you by these jumps? From Peter House to Penbrooke Hall, from thence to Trinitie Colledge, from thence to Lincolne, from Lincolne to Worcester, from Worcester you knowe whither.[53]

Martin then adds: "Beleeve me, he hath leapt lustily." "Is not this ambitious wretche at the highest, thinke you?"[54]

The striking contrast in the way that Penry and Throkmorton use the syllogism is a strong indication that Throkmorton is the author of and commentator on the syllogisms scattered throughout the Marprelate books. Whereas Penry in the second edition of his *Exhortation* utilizes the syllogism in a formal, academic, and humorless manner, Throkmorton and Martin play with this Aristotelian tool, expose the chinks in their opponents' logical armor, ridicule fallacious arguments, and scoff at invalid conclusions. There are about sixty-five allusions to syllogisms in the writings of Martin and Throkmorton, mostly flippant, humorous, or taunting, quite unlike the pedantic and serious references in Penry's works.[55] Often the syllogisms are characterized as "brave," "unmerciful," or "popish." Martin suggests that he and Cooper should "go out alone into the plaine fields, and there we wil try it out, even by plaine syllogismes, and that I know bishops cannot abide to heare of." For Martin, "one sound syllogism (w[h]ich, I tell you, is dainty ware in a bishopes breast), brought in for the p[r]oofe of their unlawfull callings, shall more dismay and sooner enduce me to give over my course than a thousand warants, a thousand pursevants, a thousand threts, and a thousand racks." In alluding to the polemic between Whitgift and Cartwright, Martin wrote: "I would not be so wel thwacked for the popedome of Canterbury, as he hath borne, poore man. He was never able to make good syllogisme since."[56]

Likewise, Dean Bridges is described as a man who "can scarce make a good syllogisme," without recourse to trickery, cunning, and sleights. Throkmorton asserted that Bridges' syllogisms "offended in form," and concluded in no mood. Nevertheless, in a sarcastic aside, Throkmorton said he would be willing to confirm his minor "by the sacred and inviolable authority of M. Bridges, *scilicet, si sanum haberet sinciput.*" In attacking Dr. Some's reasoning, Throkmorton discusses "the lame legge of both the consequents," and asserts that "his brave *ergo* limpeth and shrinketh in the sinowes unreasonably." His conclusion is tantamount to a "silogisme in Bocardo," and his "argument smells as if it were shaped at Salisbury." "And thereupon I reporte me to you, whether this conclusion have not a wry mouth." Throkmorton frequently accuses Dr. Some of begging the question, of presenting "a meere childish *fallax,*" and of perpetrating "a trick of a false finger." Although Martin professes to be unable to construct a hypothetical syllogism to shake or batter some foolish positions, even though he could gain a bishopric, he is really proud of his logical powers. He boasts that his "minor proposition is in it selfe sufficiently rampered against the strongest battery of the best lerned pen under heaven," and asserts that "his syllogismes, exioms [axioms], method and all are of his owne making."[57]

Both Throkmorton and Martin discuss the form of a syllogism, its mood and figure. Martin writes: "I finde the same syllogisme concluded in no mood." And Throkmorton declares: "And if you can tell me what figure it is in, Ile put you of doubt what moode it is in, so you and I betwixt us, shall, I hope, finde out the moode and figure, whence this stinging syllogisme is drawne." The problem arises because Dr. Some's arguments "are drawne from the passionat Mood and the threatning Figure."[58] Martin presents a formal valid syllogism, which is named after three of his ecclesiastical adversaries—Perncanterburikenolde. "The moode answereth unto Celarent, elder daughter to Barbara."[59]

PERNE	No civill magistrate can be an ordinarye preacher without sinne.	(Ce)
CANTERBURIE	Everie Lorde Bishoppe is a civill magistrate. Therefore,	(la)
KENOLDE	No Lord Bishop can be an ordinarie preacher without sinne.	(rent)

One of the persistent interests Martin and Throkmorton displayed was in the use of homely proverbs and practical apothegms which spice all their books. Here are some examples: "I hope to see you in for a bird"; "out of all scotche and notche"; "ye[a], but it is an old said saw, 'inough is as good as a feast' "; "blacke to your eies"; "threatened men (they saye) live long"; "blessing goeth by favour"; "they say it is an evill bargaine that no bodie thrives by"; "a lying tongue slaieth the soule." In addition to some sixty proverbs there are colorful expressions on almost every page, frequently enlivened by wit and humor.[60] Whereas Thomas Nashe and John Lyly reached a more sophisticated audience, Martin appealed to the rank and file reader by his directness, his earthiness, and his clarity. He was a clever stylist, who introduced his material with animation and "besprinkled" his pages with scintillating *obiter dicta* to make a point or check drooping attention or provoke a laugh.

Martin and Throkmorton stress the significant role of conscience, as evidenced by approximately forty-five allusions in their writings. In three of his books Throkmorton protests that he must satisfy and discharge his own conscience, that he is "bound in conscience," and that "in conscience, and in the reverence of God, we are forced to speake as we doe." Likewise, Martin boasts that "the possession and enjoying of a good conscience" is a prized virtue, and complains vigorously against the archbishop and bishops who "compel men against their consciences." In a special marginal note, Martin vows that "His Grace shall never get me to swear against my conscience." He denounces Bishop Aylmer as one who has "eyther a most seared, or a most guiltie conscience."[61] Closely related to Martin's sincere interest in moral sensitivity is his rationalizing effort to praise and defend and exculpate himself:

> Is Martin to be blamed for finding out and discovering traitors? Is he to be blamed for crying out against the Bishops of the Divel? If he be, then in deed have I offended in writing against bishops. If not, whether [which] is the better subject, Martin or our bishops? Whether I be favored or no, I wil not cease, in the love I owe to Her Majestie, to write against traitors, to write against the Divels bishops.[62]

Realizing that "there may be many that greatly dislike of my doinges," Martin asserts that his "purpose was and is to do good." Because he "sawe the cause of Christs government, and of the Bishops Antichristian dealing to be hidden," he decided that, since most people would not read serious books, he would resort to mirth and jesting. In self-justification he concluded: "The ende wherefore I have taken this worke in hand, was onely the glory of God, by delivering of his Churche, from the great tyrannie and bondage, wherewith these tyranntes doe oppresse the same." "And therefore I tell you true, I thinke it a great blessing of God that hath raised uppe this Martin, whome you can hardelie brooke, to holde tackling with the bishops."[63]

Unlike Penry, who was unable to flavor his books with anecdotes, Throkmorton possessed the ability and experience to favor his readers with fascinating stories. His anecdotes may be categorized as informative, humorous, and abusive.

His description of Penry before the Court of High Commission is more graphic and informative than Penry's own serious résumé of the same appearance before the commissioners. When Throkmorton tells the story of Giles Wigginton, the strait-laced Puritan preacher from Sedbergh in Yorkshire, whose parishioners had been "infected by him with the true knowledge of the gospell," he also includes one [Nicholas?] Atkinson, who had been infected and affected to such a degree that he wanted to deprive his vicar. The conference between Atkinson and Whitgift affords an insight into the problem of satisfying both sermon-lovers and ritualists. The account of an attempt by the earl of Warwick to place a Welshman, Master [Hugh?] Evans, in a Warwick benefice, and the refusal by the archbishop to do so unless Evans would subscribe to Whitgift's Three Articles, provides us with information on patronage and secular influence. Martin's narrative of Udall's difficulties in Kingston-upon-Thames, the influence of the usurer Harvey, and the role of Dr. John Hone and Archdeacon James Cottington in Surrey, are instructive. And the story of the success of some Hampstead women in blocking efforts to cut the elms, despite episcopal efforts, is informative.[64]

In all nine of Penry's books there is not a single account suggesting humor, mirth, or jollity, but in Martin's and Throkmorton's books we are richly supplied with jocular narratives. Among the humorous anecdotes we may include the plight of Sir Jefferie Jones, an incompetent clergyman in Corley, Warwickshire, who imbibed too much ale. Becoming angry at the alewife who demanded payment, "Sir" Jefferie made a rash vow never to go to the alehouse again. Unable to forgo his morning draught, and unwilling to break his vow, he hired a man to carry him on his back to the alehouse. There is also a story of old Dr. William Turner's dog, which ran away with a bishop's corner cap, and there is another account of a vicar in Halstead, Essex, one Glibberie, whose antics in the pulpit became public knowledge. When a boy in a red cap appeared in the audience, Good Glibberie's eyes became so transfixed that he was "cleane

dasht out of countenaunce." All he could say was: "take away
red cap there, take away red cappe there. It had bene better
that he had never bin borne. He hath marred suche a sermon
this day, as it is woonderfull to thinke." Martin thought it
regrettable that the queen and Privy Council could not have
heard this sermon. Equally humorous are Throkmorton's anecdotes about Dr. Some's sermon in London, Bishop Bullingham's sermon at Worcester, and Dr. Nicholas Bond's
appearance in a dancing house in Oxford.[65]

Throkmorton's stories pertaining to Bishop Aylmer and
his quarrels with two merchants and with John Madox are
both humorous and abusive. When two businessmen sought
to collect a grocery bill from the prelate, he "answered them
sweetly . . . in this maner":

> You are raskals, you are villaines, you are arraunt knaves. I
> owe you nought. I have a generall quittance to shew.
> "Sir" (sayd they), "shew us your discharge, and wee are satis-
> fied."
> No (quoth he), I will shew you none; go sue me, go sue me.
> Then sayd one of the merchants, "doe you thus use us for
> asking our due? Wee would you should know, we are no
> suche vile persons."
> Done [don] John of London (hearing their answere) cried out
> saying: Hence away. Citizens? Nay, you are raskcals, you
> are worse than wicked mammon (so lifting up both his hands,
> and flinging them downe againe, said): You are theeves, you
> are Coseners; take that for a bishops blessing, and so get
> you hence.[66]

When Bishop John Aylmer tried to interfere in a case pend-
ing at the Court of Requests, he became involved in a controversy with Master John Madox:

> Some rough words passed on both sides. Presbyter John sayde
> Master Madox was verye sawcie, especially seeing he knew
> before whom he spake, namely, the Lord of Fulham. Where-
> unto the gentleman answered, that he had bene a pore free-
> holder in Fulham before Don John came to be Lord there,
> hoping also to be so when he and all his brood (my Ladie
> his daughter and all) shoulde be gone. At the hearing of this

speeche, the waspe got my brother by the nose, which mad him in his rage to affirme that he woulde be Lord of Fulham as long as he lived, in despight of all England. "Naye softe there," quoth Master Madox, "except Her Majestie, I pray you." "That is my meaning," ka dumb John, "and I tell thee, Madox, that thou art but a Jacke to use me so." Master Madoxe replying, sayd that in deed his name was John, and if every John were a Jacke, he was content to bee a Jacke (there he hit my Lord over the thumbs). The Bishop growing in choller, sayd that Master Madox his name did shewe what he was, "for," sayth he, "thy name is mad Oxe, which declareth thee to be an unruly and mad beast." Master Madox answered againe, that the Bishops name, if it were descanted upon, did most significantly shew his qualities. "For," said he, "you are called Elmar, but you may be better called mar-elme, for you have marred all the elmes in Fulham, having cut them all downe."[67]

Other Summary Arguments for Throkmorton's Authorship

In addition to the seven main arguments presented thus far, we may conclude with fourteen brief reasons for ascribing the Martinist books to Job Throkmorton. One significant reason is that although uninformed public opinion associated Penry with the writing and publication of the Martinist books, informed private judgment implicated Throkmorton as the real author of the Marprelate books. Waldegrave asserted that Throkmorton wrote *Master Some Laid Open in His Coulers*. Newman associated him with the authorship of *The Crops and Flowers of Bridges Garden*. Bancroft referred four times to Throkmorton's authorship of *A Dialogue*. Once the authorship of these related books is established, Throkmorton's authorship of the Marprelate books is difficult to resist. Furthermore, Penry wrote in his private notebook that Throkmorton "made" the *Protestatyon*. Sutcliffe ascribed eleven books to the Haseley squire, including most of the Marprelate books. At the arraignment of Hodgskin, it was considered by the court that Throkmorton was the author not only of *Martin Junior*, but also of *Martin Senior* and *More*

Worke for Cooper, on the basis of the confessions of Symmes and Thomlin. These judgments by five friends of Throkmorton and two investigators are difficult to refute.[68]

Chapters five and six endeavor to prove that Throkmorton wrote *Master Some Laid Open* and *A Dialogue.* Of all the books attributed to him, these two deserve to be admitted to the Throkmorton canon with the least hesitation. When the authorship of these two works is accepted, then their coherence with Martin's books points to Throkmorton's authorship.

Chapter six presents Sutcliffe's closely reasoned arguments for assigning three non-extant works to the lord of the manor at Haseley—*More Worke for Cooper,* "Martins Interim," and *The Crops and Flowers of Bridges Garden.* Paradoxically, enough is known about these three non-extant books to provide evidence for Throkmorton's authorship of the *Protestatyon,* which summarizes *More Worke,* and of *Hay Any Worke,* which predicts its sequel.

Chapter seven presents evidence that twelve stylistic peculiarities differentiate Martin's and Throkmorton's books from Penry's works. The persistent use in Martin's and Throkmorton's books of alliteration, legal allusions, Latin expressions, colorful writing, rich vocabulary, and coined words indicates that Throkmorton and Martin write in a similar style. This chapter also sets forth sixty-one unusual, verbatim, and close parallels, which indicate that many of Martin's habitual expressions and ideas are the same as those of Throkmorton.

Chapter eight seeks to establish credible reasons for Throkmorton's authorship of the *Epistle,* which is the keystone of the Marprelate structure. Once these reasons are accepted, Throkmorton's authorship of the *Epitome* and *Hay Any Worke* ineluctably follows by his admission of writing these two works. Since *More Worke for Cooper* was promised and mentioned seven times in *Hay Any Worke,* since both Hodgskin and Symmes deposed that Throkmorton promised to deliver the manuscript of *More Worke* shortly, and since Sutcliffe affirmed Throkmorton's authorship, we need not doubt it.

Throkmorton's knowledge of and Martin's interest in Oxford are indicated by twelve references to persons who were at the university when Throkmorton was in attendance during the 1560s: Dr. Daniel Bernarde, Dr. Nicholas Bond, Dr. William Cole, Dr. Martin Colepepper, Bishop Thomas Cooper, Mrs. Cooper, Dr. John Day, Dr. Laurence Humphrey, Dr. John Kennall, Dr. John Rainolds, William Rainolds, and Dr. John Underhill. Throkmorton refers to "we Oxforde men," and "our Oxforde doctors." Since the Martinist books were written by an Oxford man, the evidence points toward Throkmorton.

All of Martin's and Throkmorton's books reveal a wide acquaintance with prominent people, who are inordinately praised, roundly criticized, or mockingly disparaged. Personal references to contemporaries by Martin average forty-one per volume, as compared with nine in each of Penry's books. There are sixty-eight in the *Epistle* and thirty-six in *Martin Senior*. In Throkmorton's *Master Some* there are forty-eight personal references and thirty in his *A Dialogue*.

Martin and Throkmorton but not Penry indicate a special interest in sermons. In 1572 and 1573 Throkmorton castigated Bishop Cooper's and Bishop Sandys's sermons; in 1588–89 Martin ridiculed the sermons of bishops Aylmer, Bullingham, Wickham, and Dean Bridges. He took issue with Dr. Copcot's sermon, satirized Dr. Some's sermon, and reproached Dean Perne for telling lies in the pulpit. Martin also taunts the archbishop for opposing the "heresy" of preaching.[69]

Martin and Throkmorton persistently mocked and satirized the prelates. Penry actually protested against the galling of bishops, but Throkmorton was the outstanding *episcopomastix* of the Elizabethan period.

Throkmorton financed Penry, provided a refuge for him in his own home, compensated Newman and Meddowes, and received at least four consignments of books in Haseley.

In 1587–93 Penry wrote nine books, of which seven carried his name and two were acknowledged. In 1588–94 Throkmorton wrote fifteen books, all of which were unacknowledged except his *Defence*.[70]

Throkmorton's books, delightfully written, are sprightly,

humorous, jocular, satirical, and derisive. Penry's books, plainly written, are earnest, didactic, and religious.

Martin refers to Penry by name in the *Epistle,* pages 29, 30; in the *Mineralls,* numbers 16, 25; in *Hay Any Worke,* pages 21, 36, 46; in *Martin Senior,* signatures Aii v, Aiii, Bii; and in the *Protestatyon,* page 12. Throkmorton refers to Penry repeatedly in *Master Some Laid Open,* and he also refers to Penry's book, in *A Dialogue. Wherin Is Plainly Laide Open,* signature C2. In this latter volume, on signatures B3, B3 v, and C3 v, Throkmorton refers favorably to Martin Marprelate's *Epistle,* and in his *Defence,* signature Ei v, Eii, Throkmorton denies that he was Martin Marprelate. Penry refers to Martin in *A Briefe Discovery,* page 42; in his *Notebook,* never intended for publication, he refers both to Throkmorton, pages 62, 63, 70, 76, and to Martin, pages 63, 64, 65, 66, 67, 70, 71, 75. These references indicate indubitably that Martin and Penry are two separate and distinct persons, and for a critical reader they rule out the possibility that Penry was Martin Marprelate.

In the summer of 1590 Throkmorton was indicted at Warwick for "disgracing Her Majesties government," and for writing scoffing and defamatory books under the pseudonym of Martin Marprelate. He made his submission to the archbishop of Canterbury, to Lord Chancellor Hatton, and to the judges of Assize. Penry was hanged in 1593 for writing in Scotland a "seditious" book against the English magistrates, but he was not accused of writing Martin's books. Penry's book, published in Edinburgh in 1590 by Waldegrave, was entitled: *A Treatise Wherein Is Manifestlie Proved, That Reformation and Those That Sincerely Favor the Same, Are Unjustly Charged to Be Enemies, unto Hir Maiestie, and the State* (also known as *Reformation No Enemie).* What seems to be the actual copy used by Attorney General Thomas Egerton, with underlining and marginal comments, is now in the Huntington Library.

Part III

JOHN PENRY AND

MARTIN MARPRELATE:
COMPARISONS AND
A CRITIQUE

"Now we have to turn to that highly subjective question of literary style. Doubtful a touchstone as it may be in the search for authorship, it has to be employed. On one score there is little scope for disagreement, however. There is an unmistakable difference, whatever may be the reason for it, between the style of the Marprelate Tracts and that of those writings which John Penry acknowledged as his own. The author of the former was one of the earliest masters of English prose satire: mocking, boisterous, flexible and nimble. John Penry, on the other hand, in his own name wrote in very different vein; earnest, impassioned, scriptural and slightly ponderous. Most earlier students have been convinced that the disparity between the two styles is so great that Penry cannot conceivably have been responsible for both. As far back as 1717, James Peirce declared, 'What I have read of Penry appears to me to be written with an entirely different style and temper from Martin Marprelate.' His opinion has been endorsed by many scholars of widely different endowment and background." (Glanmor Williams, "John Penry: Marprelate and Patriot?" *The Welsh History Review* 3 [1967]: 367)

ALTHOUGH PENRY WROTE nine serious books and Martin produced seven satirical works, their topical paths occasionally crossed. By comparing their treatment of common subjects,

A TREATISE
WHEREIN IS MA-
NIFESTLIE PROVED, THAT
REFORMATION AND THOSE
that sincerely fauor the same,
are vnjustly charged to be enemies,
vnto hir Maiestie, and
the state.

WRITTEN BOTH FOR THE
clearing of those that stande in that
cause: and the stopping of the sclaunderous mouthes of all the ene-
mies thereof.

(***)

ZEPHANIAH 3. 18.19.

After a certaine time wil I gather the afflicted, that were
of thee, and them that beare the reproch for it: behold
at that time will I bruise al that afflict thee, and I will
saue her that halteth, and gather hir that was cast out,
and I wil get them praise in al the land of their shame.
At that time wil I bring you again, and then wil I gather you, for I wil giue you a name, and a praise amõg
al the people of the earth, when I turn back your cap-
tivity before your eyes saith the Lord.

1590.

This *Treatise* by John Penry, usually referred to as *Reformation No Enemie*, was printed in late December 1589 or January 1590 by Robert Waldegrave at Edinburgh. Penry's indictment was based on this book. This title page is from the copy used by Attorney General Thomas Egerton for Penry's trial before the Court of Queen's Bench. It is at the Huntington Library.

we can determine if Penry and Martin are one and the same person or if we are dealing with two distinct personalities. We may begin with Penry's account in his *Appellation* of his appearance before the Court of High Commission in March 1586–87. He mentioned six commissioners—Whitgift, Aylmer, Cooper, Dr. William Lewin, Dr. Richard Cosin, and William Wickham, bishop of Lincoln. Since he had petitioned Parliament and not the High Commission, he protested that the court had no jurisdiction in his case and that the commissioners had compelled him to take the oath ex officio. Designating Whitgift as his accuser, he complained in a serious straightforward manner, without satire or sarcasm, that the archbishop had accused him wrongly of slander, treason, and blasphemy.[1]

Martin also described Penry's appearance before the commissioners, but with a significant difference in style and approach. Whereas Penry mentioned six judges, Martin referred only to Whitgift, Aylmer, and Cooper, and he ridiculed all three. He wrote:

> After that his Grace had eased his stomacke in calling him [Penry] boy, knave, varlet, slanderer, libeller, lewde boy, lewd slaunderer, etc. (this is true, for I have seene the notes of their conference), at the length a poynt of his booke began to be examined, where nonresidents are thought intollerable. Here the Lorde of good London asked M. Penrie, what he could say against that kinde of cattell [rubbish, nonsense].

When Penry emphasized the importance of the Word preached, his Worship of Winchester "rose up, and mildly after his maner, brast forth into these words: 'I assure you, my Lords, it is an execrable heresie.'" Then Martin added: "I will leave this storie for shame. I am weary to hear your Grace so absurd. What say you to this geare, my masters of the Confocation house? We shal have shortly a good religion in England among the bishops?[,] if Paule be sayd of them to write an heresie."[2] The writer stated specifically that he had seen Penry's notes of the court appearance, and there is no reason to doubt the assertion. The description of Whitgift's choler and Cooper's impetuosity, the expression "this geare" and "Confocation house," the flippant, sarcastic, and ironic features—all are lacking in Penry's narrative and all are characteristic of Throkmorton's style. The conclusion is clear that Penry did not write this Martinist account of his appearance, and therefore it is unlikely that he wrote Martin's *Epistle*. This conclusion is strengthened by the arguments in chapter eight for Throkmorton's authorship.

Penry's brief criticisms of Archbishop Whitgift are scattered mainly in three of his books.[3] He regarded the archbishop as an outward symbol of a system of church government that was unscriptural, and considered such archiepiscopal titles as "Metropolitan," "Primate," and "My Lords Grace" to be unfit for a true pastor, elder, and minister. He objected to Whitgift's role as president of the Privy Council, since this was properly a function of the civil magistrate. Therefore he criticized the archbishop as "a detected enemie unto the gospel," but he did not ridicule him. His ambivalent attitude may be summarized by a quotation from his *Notebook*, which was not published in his lifetime:

> I know that prelate to bee a great enemy of God, his sayntes, and truth, this day even [an] enemy unto Hir Majesties soule, the soules of hir people and his owne, yet I cary this mynd towardes hym, that yf at this very hour, his enemy assayled him in my presenc, I wold not only defend his lyf, but even his welfare, and that most willingly. Yea, and the Lord shewe favour unto him body and soul for evermore, which is all the disgrac I wish unto him.[4]

Martin was less concerned with the gospel and the salvation of souls, and more fascinated with labels and libels. The archbishop was designated as a "Worshipfull Paltripolitan," a "Canterburie Caiphas," "Pope of Lambehith," and "a plain Antichrist." Since Martin was determined to deflate the pride and pomposity of Whitgift, he dedicated his fifth book, *Martin Junior*, to "his good neame and nuncka, Maister John Kankerbury." He sneered at the archbishop as "doctor Pernes boy," as a poverty-stricken Cambridge scholar who "was so poor as he had not a napkin to wipe his mouth, but when he hadd gotten some fatte meat of[f] o[f] the Fellowes table, would go to the skrine, and first wipe his mouth on the on[e] side and then o[n] the other, because he wanted [lacked] a napkin. Judge you whether this bee not a meaner state, than to cary a cloakbag, which is not spoken to upbraide any mans poverty, but to pull the pride of Gods enemy an ase [ace] lower."[5] This was the proud prelate who went on his visitation with a train of 140 horses and a rabble of syco-phants wearing his livery. This was the popish persecutor who was a "beastly defendor" of a "bastardly church govern-ment." When the archbishop spoke of "traitors and enemies unto Her Majestie," Martin added a gloss: "Saving your rev-erence, uncle Cantur., you lie in your throate."[6]

The treatment of Whitgift by Penry and Marprelate indi-cates two writers, with different approaches. Penry's narra-tive, devoid of name-calling, was serious, brief, and prosaic; Martin's attacks, found in all seven of his books, were lengthy, jocular, satirical, and scurrilous. His personal caricatures and lampoons befit Throkmorton, who possessed a facetious and gibing tongue, and Martin's sly humor and sarcasm typify the satirical squire from Warwickshire. This was the critic who described the archbishop as one with a "giddie head" and a choleric temper, "a vile and a cursed tyrant," an abject person who lacked "any excellent naturall witte and learn-ing," and who was utterly unfit to serve as a privy councilor. "The Lorde hath passed by many thousands in this land farre meeter for the place than is poore John Whitgift."[7]

When Bishop Cooper defended the established hierarchy, Penry refuted his six arguments. It is possible to compare Penry and Marprelate in their replies to the bishop's fifth argument. In this fifth reason the bishop of Winchester had contended that foreign churches "professing the gospel have not this [Presbyterian] government." He wrote:

In *Denmarke* they have Bishops both in *Name* and *Office,* as it appeareth in certaine Epistles of *Hemingius* written to some of them. In which he saith: "they are greatly troubled with

275

continuall visitation of their Churches. In *Saxony* they have Archbishops and Bishops in *Office*, but not in *Name*."[8]

To this Penry replied:

Whereby the pretence that other churches professing the Gospel have not this government, is evidently shewed to be nothing else, but a profe that other churches have their imperfections and are not as yet so farr built, as the Lord requireth. Asa was a godly King, and reformed many things in the house of God: yet the Idolatrous high places remained al his daies.[9]

But Martin's reply was quite otherwise:

Thirdly, saith profane T.C., page 75: "All Churches have not the government of Pastors and Doctors; but Saxoni and Denma[r]ke have Lord bishops." You are a great State man, undoubtedly, T.C., that understand the state of other Churches so well. But herein the impudencie of a proude foole appeareth egregiously. As though the testimonie of a siely Schoolemaster [that is, Cooper, who had been master of Magdalen School, Oxford, 1549–67], being also as unlearned as a man of that trade and profession can be, with any honestie, would be believed against knowne experience. Yea, but Saxonie and Denmarke have Superintendents. What then? *Ergo*, Lord Archbishop and bishops? I deny it.[10]

Whereas Penry in one book devoted ten pages of impersonal arguments against Cooper's views, Martin attacked the bishop personally in six books and scattered his denunciations over eighty pages. Determined to "bumfeg [clobber, thrash] the Cooper," and to come at the "beceytfull tubtrimmer" with sharp "soopes," Martin was eminently successful.

As an Oxford don and dean, Cooper had gained the approval of the queen for his revision of Sir Thomas Elyot's *Dictionary* and especially for his improvement and augmentation of Robert Stephanus' *Thesaurus*, which at one stage of its preparation had been thrown into the fire by Cooper's unacademic and shrewish wife. But Martin depreciated the work of Cooper, and contrasted him with Walter Travers, an eminent Puritan, logician, and Latinist, to the detriment of the bishop. "And if my Lord of Winchester understood eyther Greeke or Hebrew, as they say he hath no great skill in neyther, I woulde praye your priestdomes to tell me which is the better scholler, Walter Travers, or Thomas Cooper." He added insult to injury by asserting ironically and erroneously that "his Lordship of Winchester is a great clarke, for he hath translated his Dictionarie, called Coopers Dictionarie, verbatim out of Robert Stephanus his *Thesaurus*, and ilfavored to[o], they say."[11]

Perhaps the cruelest and most caustic comments made by Martin related to Mrs. Cooper, a profligate woman who had cuckolded her husband in her dalliance with Dr. John Day. Cooper's friends offered to procure quietly a divorce for him, but the bishop refused. He believed in marriage and said he would not burden his conscience with such a scandal. With this background, one better understands Martin's snide remarks, couched in a playful statement:

> Now reverend T.C., I beseech you entreat Mistris Cooper, to write to Master Dr. Day, somtimes of Magdalins, that he may procure Dr. Cooper, to know of him that was the last Thomas of Lincolne [Cooper formerly was bishop of Lincoln], whether the now Bishop of Winchester [Cooper] be not perswaded, that reverend Martin hath suffi[ci]ently prooved it to be unlawful, for the civill magestrate, to abolishe any lawfull churche officer out of the church.[12]

> Concerning Mistresse Lawson, profane T.C., is it not lawfull for her to go to Lambeth by water, to accompanie a preachers wife, going also (as commonly godly matrons in London do) with her man? "No," saith T.C., "I doe not like this in women." Tushe, man, Thomas Lawson is not Thomas Cooper, he has no suche cause to doubt of Dame Lawsons going without her husbande, as the Bishop of Winchester hath had of dame Coopers gadding. But *More Worke for Cooper* will say more for Mistresse Lawson.[13]

Martin was especially infuriated with a sermon which Bishop Cooper had preached at the court during Lent 1587/88. The prelate had asserted "that there was not in the world at this day, nay, there had not bin since the Apostles time, such a flourishing estate of a church, as we have now in England." Martin replied to this boast with a stinging indictment of the church and the bishop:

> Is it any marvaile that we have so many swine, dumbe dogs, non-residents with their journeimen the hedge priests, so many lewd livers, as theeves, murtherers, adulterers, drunkards, cormorants, raschals, so many ignorant and atheistical dolts, so many covetous popish bishops in our ministery, and so many and so monstrous corruptions in our Church, and yet likely to have no redresse? Seeing our impudent, shamelesse, and wainscote faced bishops, like beasts, contrary to the knowledge of all men, and against their own consciences, dare in the eares of Her Majestie, affirme all to be well, where there is nothing but sores and blisters, yea, where the grief is even deadly at the heart. "Nay," saies my Lord of Winchester (like a monstrous hypocrite, for he is a very duns, not able to defende an argument, but till he come to the pinch, he will cog and face it out, for his face is made of seasoned wainscot, and wil lie as fast as a dog can trot), "I have said it, I doe say it, and I have said it."[14]

In none of Penry's books does this kind of fury and railing occur. He was temperamentally incapable of vindictive comments, and was averse to jesting and personal diatribes. Although he hated sin, he loved the sinner. He avoided innuendoes and insinuations and lampoons. He could not have written this assertion by Martin: "they [the queen and the State] know you [Cooper] not yet so thorowly as I doe."[15] But Throkmorton could have written this statement from personal experience. He was a student at Oxford in the 1560s when Cooper's *Thesaurus* was published, and when Mrs. Cooper, her husband, and Dr. John Day were all at Oxford. In June 1572, when Cooper, then bishop of Lincoln, delivered a sermon at St. Paul's, in which he denounced reformers, Puritans, and Field and Wilcox, the authors of the *Admonition to the Parliament*, Throkmorton was present. As a staunch supporter of his friends, the admonitioners, he reacted vigorously and immediately by writing a reply to Cooper.[16] When Cooper published his *Admonition to the People of England* in

January 1588/89, Martin (or Throkmorton) within three weeks replied with his broadside, the *Mineralls*, and within three months retorted with his *Hay Any Worke for Cooper*.

If Penry wrote the Marprelate books, one would be at a loss to explain the contrast between his brief, dignified and restrained manner, and the virulence of Martin's attacks. Why Penry should lampoon Bishop Cooper regarding events that occurred about the time Penry was born in Wales (1563) is inexplicable. But if Throkmorton as Marprelate was remembering from his university years Cooper's marital problems, and was continuing a vendetta that had begun in 1572, it is not only explicable but also obvious that the same person is involved. There is no evidence whatsoever that supports Penry's candidacy as the most virulent and vituperative enemy of the bishop of Winchester.

Penry's refutation of Dr. Bridges is a straightforward, serious, indignant, and sharp attack. It is restricted to eighteen pages in the second edition of his *Exhortation*, and was reprinted with a few modifications in *A Viewe*. Penry accused Bridges of overthrowing Her Majesty's title of supremacy, of alienating the hearts of her loyal subjects, and of defending the English prelacy in a manner that smacked of popery, since his arguments were similar to those found in the Catholic writings of Robert Bellarmine, Francis Turrian, Nicholas Sanders, and Thomas Harding. His reply consisted of four reasons or syllogisms pertaining to polity. According to Penry, the dean of Sarum advocated a form of church government which made Jesus "Christ inferior unto Moses"; he considered the ecclesiastical regimen to be merely a human constitution instead of a divine order; he followed procedures which went beyond what was included in Christ's commission; and he believed that church government was "a kingdome that cann be shaken, that is," could be altered "at the magistrates pleasure."[17]

Since Martin's treatment of Dr. Bridges is digressive, humorous, replete with name-calling, and fascinating, it is diametrically opposite to that of Penry. Whereas the Welshman described Bridges' *Defence* simply as a book having 160 sheets of paper, Martin characterized the volume as 172 sheets "of good demy paper," useful "to stop mustard pots," so heavy that a horse could scarcely carry it, and possessing "neyther wit nor learning." Martin repeatedly accused Dean Bridges of flat treason, but Penry regarded "the question concerning the popes supremacie (which is the point I urge, and not the treason)," as heinous and odious.[18] Whereas Penry limited himself to about eighteen pages in his discussion of Bridges, Martin expended seventeen pages in his *Epistle*, forty pages in his *Epitome*, and hounded the "poor old drone of Sarum" in all seven of his books. Likewise, Throkmorton pursued the dean relentlessly in *Master Some Laid Open*.[19]

The most striking contrasts between Penry's and Martin's discussion of Dr. Bridges are seen in Martin's and Throkmorton's use of pejorative terms, personal innuendoes, and humor, which are lacking in Penry's writings. Dean Bridges is a practitioner of simony, a "sot," a "knave," a "patch," a "dunce," and a "hedge priest." He has gained his deanship by simony and bribery. His mind is so set on his promotion to the episcopacy that he cannot write clear English. His obtuse sentences are so long and involved that "a man might almost run himselfe out of breath before he could come to a full point." And his book reveals deceptions:

> It would make a man laugh, to see how many trickes the Doctor hath to coosen the sielie Puritans in his book. He can now and then without any noyse, alleadge an author clean against himselfe, and I warrant you, wipe his mouth cleanly, and looke another way, as though it had not bene he. I have laught as though I had bene tickled, to see with what sleight he can throw in a popish reason, and who sawe him?[20]

The dissimilar treatment accorded Dr. Bridges indicates two different writers, one serious, one humorous; one impersonal and systematic, the other familiar, facetious, and clever. Penry never could have written Marprelate's *Epistle* or *Epitome* against the dean of Sarum, since he lacked the inclination, the temperament, and the ability necessary for Marprelate's rollicking jocular style. Unlike Robert Louis Stevenson's character, Dr. Jekyll and Mr. Hyde, Penry possessed no potion to transform his own nature.

There is no evidence that Penry was personally acquainted with Thomas Cartwright. In his first six books, published in the years 1586/87–89/90, Penry never discussed him at all. But in his seventh book, *A Briefe Discovery*, published in the summer of 1590 at Edinburgh, Penry referred to the Puritan leader in these words:

> As concerning M. Cartwright, whome you [Dr. Bancroft] (to keepe your tongue in ure [practice] with your naturall vaine), call our ringleader, wee blesse God, that ever he hath vouchsafed us such an instrument to stand in the defence of his holy government, and to give your hierarchie, and your High Prieste [Whitgift] the shamefull foile. But we follow him no further, than he attendeth upon the truth of his God.

There is only one other passage in which Penry wrote: "And yet M. Cartwright and others have long since proved these men to be unreconcilable adversaries unto the hierarchie."[21]

In Martin's books, Cartwright is referred to about thirty times. He is always mentioned with respect, as one who had been a professor of divinity at the universities in Cambridge and Geneva. In writing against T.C. [Thomas Cooper], Martin pretended that he was uncertain about the identity of the author. Therefore he designated Thomas Cooper as "profane T.C." to distinguish him from Thomas Cartwright. Of the latter he wrote: "And if I had thy learning, Thomas Cartwright, I would make them all to smoak." Martin also coupled himself with this learned Puritan leader when he wrote:

> That Maister Thomas Cartwright, together with all those learned men, and my selfe also that have written against the state of the Clargy, could do no lesse than we have done, except wee woulde betray the trueth of God, the lawes of this lande, and the doctrine of our church.[22]

A recurring theme in Martin's books is the famous literary duel between Whitgift and Cartwright, with the implication that the latter had obtained a signal victory and that the archbishop had been soundly "thwacked" and disgraced. This literary and religious conflict had begun in June 1572, when the *Admonition to the Parliament* was published as a shabby, poorly printed pamphlet of some fifty-two pages in a small black-letter or Gothic type. Whitgift replied to it in November with his *An Answere to a Certen Libel,* well printed in 300 pages. In 1573 Cartwright entered the lists with his *A Replye to an Answere Made of M. Doctor Whitgifte.* Then Whitgift rejoined with his *The Defense of the Aunswere*[23] in 1574, to which Cartwright replied with *The Second Replie of Thomas Cartwright* in 1575 and *The Rest of the Second Replie agaynst Master Whitgifts Second Answer* in 1577.[24] Since Whitgift never answered these last two replies, he was taunted by the Puritans for running away from the battle. Martin warned Dean Bridges and reviled Whitgift in a gloating remark:

> You shall not deale with My Worshipp [himself], as John with his Canterburinesse did with Thomas Cartwright, whiche John left the cause you defend in the plaine field, and for shame threw downe his weapons with a desperate purpose to runne away, and leave the cause, as he like a coward hath done. For this dozen yeares we never saw any thing of his in printe for the defence of his cause, and poore M. Cartwright doth content himselfe with the victorie, which the other will not (though in deed he hath by his silence) seeme to grant.[25]

The differences in Penry's neglect of Cartwright and Martin's intense interest in him personally and in his books is explained by the fact that Martin was Throkmorton, and that the latter was involved in the Admonition Controversy at a time when Penry was only nine years old. He was a close personal friend of Cartwright, who visited Throkmorton at Haseley in 1586, baptized his child, and preached a fiery forthright sermon in which he attacked the ecclesiastical establishment and advocated the Presbyterian discipline and polity. In the same year Cartwright and Throkmorton were entertained at the Swan in Stratford-on-Avon by the local magistrates. When Cartwright was imprisoned in the Fleet from 1590 to 1592, Throkmorton visited him there. In his *Defence* of 1594 Throkmorton defended Cartwright against Dean Sutcliffe's charges, and in 1596 Throkmorton served as editor for Cartwright's *A Brief Apologie* and wrote the preface, "To the Reader."[26]

In seeking to compare Penry's and Martin's treatment of Bishop Aylmer, one discovers that there is no basis for comparison. In one line Penry alluded to Aylmer as a member of the Court of High Commission, but Martin ridiculed the bishop of London unmercifully in every one of his books except *Martin Junior*. He characterized Aylmer's book, *An Harborowe for Faithfull and Trewe Subiectes*, as "a carnall and unlearned booke, smelling altogether of earth, without rime and without reason."[27] He exposed the cupidity, insolence, and hot temper of the bishop in his stories about thieves who had stolen cloth worth £30, about two merchants who tried to collect an episcopal debt, and about John Madox's quarrel with Aylmer. Martin struck a sharp blow at the bishop, who was depicted as wealthy and miserly, by quoting one of his famous statements, made when he was a Marian exile in 1558: "Come off, you bishops, away with your superfluities, yeeld up your thousandes, be content with your hundreths, as they be in other reformed churches, where be as great learned men as you are."[28] With this kind of reliable source material, Martin could not resist contrasting the earlier reforming archdeacon with the later conservative prelate whose life he regarded as a pattern of hypocrisy and avarice.

In searching for the views of Penry and Martin on Dr. Andrew Perne, one finds that Perne is never mentioned in any of Penry's published books. This fact alone is sufficient to refute McGinn's suggestion that Dr. Perne was Penry's foe and that the antagonism between Perne and Penry "had become legendary at Peterhouse." Since Penry was a student at Peterhouse during the mastership of Dean Perne, one would expect some reference to him, especially because of Thomas Nashe's assertion that Penry criticized Perne's role in formulating statutes for the University of Cambridge. Yet Penry's only reference to Dr. Perne occurred in his private notebook, a manuscript item seized by the pursuivants in April 1593. In this notebook there is a letter to Lord Burghley in which Penry actually defended the master of Peterhouse and the archbishop against Martin's gibing, and asserted: "I dislyked it and I do dislyk it and the rest of the thinges of that nature."[29]

A major theme of Martin's is the slippery reputation of Perne. Sir Sidney Lee has written that students at Cambridge punned on Perne's name in saying that the Latin verb *perno* meant, "I turn, I rat, I change often." Satirists suggested that the letters on the weathercock of St. Peter's Church—A.P.A.P.—denoted "either Andrew Perne, a Papist, or Andrew Perne a Protestant, or Andrew Perne a Puritan." In a sermon delivered on 23 April 1547, Perne asserted that the "pictures of Christ and the saints ought to be adored," but on 17 June he recanted this view as the doctrinal climate changed in the early months of the rule of Edward VI and the duke of Somerset. He vacillated in his belief about transubstantiation. In the reigns of Henry VIII, Edward VI, and Mary he adjusted his creed in keeping with prevailing political winds. In 1554 he accepted Roman Catholic articles of belief, but in the Elizabethan years he subscribed the Thirty-Nine Articles. In 1564 he defended the power of the church to excommunicate, but pulled in his horns when he was rebuked by the queen. Critics poured scorn on Perne's role as vice-chancellor in burning the bones of Paul Fagius and Martin Bucer in 1556 and acquiescing in the disinterment of these same bones in 1560. These events partly explain Perne's inclusion in John Foxe's *Book of Martyrs*, and also Martin's gibes. In five of his books, Martin referred twenty-five times to Perne, usually as a "turner" and a "turncoat," and even coined a new word—"Pearnd."[30]

In defense of Perne, one may note that as with many other individuals Perne was compliant, conforming, and cautious, but to Martin he was fickle, pusillanimous, and opportunistic. In derision Martin suggested: "let Andrew *Ambo* [both sides, double-dealer] judge betwene you; he is an indifferent man." Martin humorously designed a syllogism which he called

"Perncanterburikenolde," but maliciously labeled Perne an "apostate" and a "Judas." In reference to his projected books which he teasingly planned to write, Martin said: "I hope olde Father Palinod [recantation] Dr. Perne shall be in there by the weekes" [be fully discussed], and in distorting a portrait conceived by Bishop Cooper, Martin depicted himself as Innocency, drawn by the hair of his head by three characters—*Dolus, Fraus, Insidiae*—who are identified as Dr. Perne (trickery), Dr. Kennall (fraud or deception), and Dr. Cosin (snare or ambush).

Penry was incapable of such invention, and was motivated by religious scruples against derision, jocularity, and malice. But Martin and Throkmorton were displayed in their true colors by their writings, since they hated Dr. Perne, regarded him as a slippery eel, and resented his influence with Archbishop Whitgift, who had sought to promote Dr. Perne to a bishopric in 1584. When Dr. Perne died at Lambeth Palace on 26 April 1589, Martin reminded Whitgift:

> Dr. Perne, thou knowest, was thy joy, and thou his darling. Hee was the dragon from whose serpentine breasts, thou diddest first drawe this poyson, wherewith nowe thou infectest the church of God, and feedest thy selfe unto damnation. Hee lived a persecutour, an atheist, an hypocrite, and a dissembler, whome the worlde poynted at, and he died, thou knowest, the death due unto such a life as he ledde.[31]

When Penry published early in 1588 the first edition of his *Exhortation*, he lamented the lack of preaching clergymen in Wales. In May 1588 Dr. Robert Some published his first *A Godly Treatise*, in which he replied to three of Penry's arguments. He asserted that ministers, though unworthy, delivered a valid sacrament, that the communicant was not polluted who received from them the sacrament, and that the new Donatists had long ago been refuted by St. Augustine, who assigned an independent value and validity to the sacraments despite the unworthiness of priests or fellow communicants. It was this treatise which Penry answered in his *A Defence of That Which Hath Bin Written*, published in July or August 1588. This reply, unlike most sixteenth-century polemical treatises, was unusually courteous. Penry's attitude toward Dr. Some is reflected in the following statements:

> Not that I wold any way disgrace, you whom I reverence, for that is no part of mine intent, the Lorde is my witnes.

> I am sory that you whom I reverence, should be the instrument to opugne a truth. The Lord respect the cause of his owne glorie, and pardon our sinne.[32]

In September 1588 Dr. Some replied to Penry's *Defence* with a second *A Godly Treatise* (200 pages), about four times as long as Penry's book. Dr. Some's volume, according to Martin, was dogmatic, opinionated, and cocksure, and it reflected an egotistical writer and a patronizing antagonist. Penry wrote a reply to it that same autumn, but on 29 January 1588/89 his manuscript was seized in his study at Northampton by the pursuivant, Richard Walton. In February Penry's supplication to Parliament, *A Viewe*, was published; in "The Epistle to the Reader" Penry referred to Dr. Some in one paragraph, but there is neither rancor nor contempt.

In Martin's books there is no reverence for Dr. Some, no expression of being sorry, and no concern about possible words which would give offense to his adversary. Martin included two provocative theses in his *Mineralls* against Dr. Some, pertaining to baptism performed outside the church or administered by women. In *Martin Junior* he mimicked Dr. Some for his oft repeated phrase, "my reason is." In *Martin Senior* he described a mock ceremony for investing Dean Bridges as the "fool" of Lambeth. As an attendant of this jester, there should be "first and formost Doctor Robert Some for his confessor, who also, when his master John Sarum hath no use of his service, may be at my Lordes-Graces commandement, to read the *starve-us* booke [the service book] in his Chappell at Lambeth." And in his *Protestatyon* Martin summarized the contents of his captured *More Worke for Cooper*, including a parody of Dr. Some:

> The next prettie thing to this, was to my remembrance, Chaplain Some confuted with the balde sheath of his own dagger,

wherein al his short cuts, Latine apothegs, and childishe pen-an-inke-horne proverbs, were wholly inverted upon him-selfe . . . And this is he that hath crazed his braine at Lambeth, and his conscience at Gyrton; whose balde writings without sappe or edge, unworthye of a boye of twelve yeare olde, have (I am perswaded) made and will make (if it bee not looked unto) more Brownistes in our church, than al that ever they have hitherto published themselves.

This (if you know him not) is the verye same Doctor, that in publishing three prettie treatises, hath so handled the matter, by a geometricall dimension, that the last (if it be well scanned), is the same with the first, and the middlemost, all one with them both. The man in all likelihoode never goeth without a little saunce-bell in his pocket, and that doth nothing els but *Ting, Ting, Ting.* And what doth it *Ting?* If you give good eare, nothing els, I warrant you, but My sermons, My writings, My reasons, My arguments, and al is My, My, My, as if the depth of all learning, were included in the chanell of his braine. This is even he, that let him write as many books as he will (thogh he should never so much disguise himselfe, and conceale his name), yet we should be sure to knowe him by one of these rapping figures: eyther by hittinge the white, or by miss-inge the butt, or by resting on his reason, or by thirty-two dozen of full points, or by som such broken wooden dishe or other [that is, skirting the question, arguing the wrong point, or using short dogmatic sentences].[33]

Throkmorton's most brilliant book, and one of the most pungent and scintillating satires of the Elizabethan period, was his *Master Some Laid Open in His Coulers, Wherein the Indifferent Reader May Easily See, Howe Wretchedly and Loosely He Hath Handeled the Cause against M. Penri. Done by an Oxford Man, to His Friend in Cambridge.* Justifying his book, Throk-morton informs his readers that if they think he has been too impolite in his presentation, they must consider that he deals with an adversary who is the most uncivil gentleman, and one of the most bitter writers, "that ever put pen to paper." He is a nonresident from his benefice at Girton, one who slyly and closely did "glut downe a pretty prebend or two to help his disgestion." He is a man of inordinate ambition, who seeks a sweet deanery or a bishop's orphreyed miter. Here is a man in whom "the life blood of his owne conceit did tickle him a little too much." He has a special gift "of sounding forth the trumpet of his owne praises," so that one must conclude that among divines he is "the onely prince of conceyted writers in this age." Dr. Some is revealed as a Delphic oracle, the English Solon, the Anglican lawgiver, but when we listen to his arguments, we hear "a great noise and a rusteling, and we see before us as it were a swelling sea of big words," but no syllogistical proofs or sound demonstrations. "Then beholde, in liew of this, there appeares before us a man new come out of the cloudes (as it were) with his mace in his hand, and his sandalles on his feet (as it should seme), rather to make lawes than to handle controversies, pointing with his finger, at this and at that, telling us what he thinks, as if al the world were to gape upon him."[34]

Throkmorton charged that Dr. Some's scornful superiority and disdain did "but lay open the rottennesse and corruption of his harte, being very far from that spirit that teacheth: 'Let the greatest among you be as the least, etc.'" When Penry said he reverenced Dr. Some for his gifts, he was "cut short, and uncurteously rewarded for his paines." Dr. Some had the effrontery to say that "he liked better *humile peccatum, quam superbam innocentiam.*" "Had he not neede, thinke you, to be a litle clearer from that infection himselfe, than your doctor sheweth him selfe to be?" Where was Christian humility when Dr. Some "in a kinde of swelling and disdainfull contempt (which he hath notably layd open in above 200 places in his book) [had the temerity] to say that *He doth more esteeme of one Calvine, than of a thousand Penries*"? In a passage which Penry never could have written, Throkmorton says:

> In that good christian moode of his, it pleaseth him full sweetly, to call M. Penri an hereticall Catabaptist, and of his charitie to liken and compare him to Demetrius the silver smith, to Alexander the copper smith . . . to that honest man Judas that betrayed Christ. [Dr. Some's friends] would never have

suspected that any such raggs as these should have fallen from a man of that gravitie, so rich in guifts and graces as they take M. Some to bee.[35]

Whereas irony is absent from Penry's *Defence*, it is apparent on almost every page of Throkmorton's exposé. When Dr. Some expressed his liking and commendation of sound preaching prior to the administration of the sacrament, Throkmorton mockingly replied:

> Howe say you? Is not sound preaching much beholden to M. Some, that wil of his curtesie vouchsafe it both his likeing and commendation? Belike it had bin in some danger to have lost his [its] credite, if M. Some had not reached forth his hand to give it some alowance.

Throkmorton quoted some of Dr. Some's "sweet sentences" and pompous pronouncements, and then asked: "But howe say you, have I done him any wrong? The places you see I have quoted, be you your self the judge; here is neither swarving nor falting, but al sound, sure and direct. Therefore you may see what a treasure your universitie hath bred up to our church, such a sure card as we may be bold to trust unto, if there do chance to fall a dearth of learned men in this age."

Whereas Penry consistently praised Dr. Some as a learned man, Throkmorton repeatedly presented him as an ignoramus. "Is it not a miserie, that such unlearned stuffe as this, should drop from the penne of anye that beareth the face of learning?" Dr. Some may have learning, but he revealed none of it in his treatise, which Throkmorton regarded as a mere blast of words, a gallimaufry of bitter and spiteful speeches, a hodgepodge of naked assertions and *ipse dixits*, a farrago of platitudes and banalities. When Dr. Some boasted of his knowledge of divinity matters, Throkmorton sarcastically commented:

> The best is, if you marke it, he speaks heere only of divinitie matters, and nothing els, so that if a man should happen to deale with him in *Lawe*, *Phisicke*, or *Philosophie*, there is some

hope yet we should finde him more tractable. But in divinitie matters there is noe mercy with him; he hath tolde us what we shall trust unto, either arguments or nothing. Yet I woulde you would aske him in his eare, whether a Deanrye or a Bishopricke, would not prevaile as much with him in matter of Divinitie, as the best argument in Christendome.[36]

Master Some Laid Open is a most significant work in unraveling the mystery of Martin Marprelate's identity. Its treatment of Dr. Some is the same as that found in Martin's books, and is diametrically opposite to that of Penry's *Defence*. When we read in Throkmorton's book his denunciation of Dr. Some's egotism:

Indeede, if a man marke it, there is much a do through out his whole booke with *his writings, his words, his reasons, his answeres, his sermons,* etc., which it semeth he woulde faine fasten uppon posteritie for lawes and statutes, as if the ground of al good knowledge were graven in the very wrinkles of his forehead,

and when we compare Martin's denunciation, previously mentioned, of the same theme:

If you give good eare, nothing els, I warrant you, but My sermons, My writings, My reasons, My arguments; and al is My, My, My, as if the depth of all learning, were included in the chanell of his braine,

then we realize that one writer penned both statements and that Throkmorton is the real Martin Marprelate.[37]

Thus far we have compared Martin's account with Penry's narration of his appearance before the Court of High Commission. We have also contrasted the treatment which Martin and Penry accorded to seven prominent clerical leaders: Archbishop Whitgift, Bishop Cooper, Dean Bridges, Thomas Cartwright, Bishop Aylmer, Dean Perne, and Dr. Some. In concluding this section, we may note the attitudes of Penry and Martin toward bishops generally and specifically and also toward other clerical persons, college heads, and legal officials.

Penry alluded to Whitgift, Cooper, and Aylmer about 25 times in 7 books. These allusions average about 4 per book, as compared with 223 references in Martin's 7 books, with an average of 32 per book; furthermore, Martin's references are longer, more specific, more insolent, and more pejorative. Except for Whitgift, Cooper, and Aylmer, Penry did not write against any other English bishop either by name or title. He did refer, without names, to the Welsh incumbents of St. David's, St. Asaph, Bangor, and Llandaff, but he did not indulge in name-calling or invective or satire or even irony. What he objected to was that these men were lord bishops, that is, bishops exercising pontifical lordships and civil powers and utilizing lordly titles and pomp, which ought not to be associated with spiritual shepherds. For Penry a true bishop was not a lord bishop but the Lord's bishop, an *episcopos*, an overseer, a first among equals, a co-pastor, a fellow presbyter. In a remarkable passage Penry disavowed any intention of discrediting or vexing lord bishops *qua* bishops: "Let not their places withstand the salvation of my brethren, and the true service of God among them, and if ever I either write or speake more against them, any further than their places are like to be the ruine of Hir Majestie and the whole State, let it cost me my life."[38]

Martin Marprelate, however, is a critic who enjoys the discrediting and galling of bishops. He claims "by right of inheritance" that the "pistling of bishops" belongs to himself. He likes to pommel his episcopal enemies about the shoulders, and he is proud of his ability to "pistle" learnedly his "uncle Canterbury." He announces his plans to "place a young Martin in every diocese" and even in every parish, and hopes that all of them will be "as worthie Martins as their father is, every one of them able to mar a prelate." He intends to publish various books, such as his *Epistomastix*, and *Of the Lives and Doings of English Popes*, and he threatens to write an entire book on that "notable hypocrite," Edmund Scambler, bishop of Norwich, unless he stops his secret "dealing against the truth."[39]

Martin denounces all bishops as "petty popes" and "petty

Antichrists," as "ungodlie and slaunderous lyars" and as a
"swinish rabble." But he also specifically names bishops,
some of whom are ridiculed as cardplayers, unlearned "turn-
coats," and "massmongers." William Hughes of St. Asaph,
a double-dealer, is charged with trickery against one of his
parishioners in a divorce problem. Marmaduke Middleton,
bishop of St. David's, is accused of having two wives at the
same time, and of perfoming a marriage ceremony between
a dying woman and his own brother. Martin characterized
John Bullingham, bishop of Gloucester, as a "turncoat," a
"stealecounter masse priest," and ironically as "an excellent
pulpit man," whose sermon on St. John's Day (24 June), delivered at Worcester, he caricatured as follows:

> As he traversed his matter, and discoursed upon many points,
> he came at the length unto the very pithe of his whol sermon,
> contained in the distinction of the name of John, which he
> then shewing all his learning at once, full learnedly handled
> after this manner:
>> "John, John, the grace of God, the grace of God, the grace
>> of God; gracious John, not graceles John, but gracious John.
>> John, holy John, holy John, not John ful of holes, but holy
>> John."
> If he shewed not himselfe learned in this sermond, then hath
> he bene a duns all his life.[40]

William Chaderton, bishop of Chester, is charged with
cardplaying, gambling, spending twenty nobles (£6 13s. 4d.)
in an evening, and with making primero a business instead
of a recreation. John Young, bishop of Rochester, is accused
of cozenage, of presenting himself with a parsonage. "I John
of Rochester present John Young, 'quoth the bishop.' "
Among "proud prelates," "enemies of the gospell, and most
covetous wretched priests," Martin includes William Overton, bishop of Lichfield and Coventry, who presented the
chancellorship of his diocese both to Dr. John Becon and
his own son-in-law, Zachary Babington. Edmund Freke,
translated from Norwich to Worcester as the successor to
Bishop Whitgift, allegedly teaches that "papistrie is better
than the sincere profession of the gospell, which falsely men

call Puritanisme." Martin therefore hopes that the writ of praemunire will be "brought uppon the bones of Father Edmond of Worcester." William Wickham, bishop of Lincoln, is suspected of crypto-Catholicism. Martin asserts that at the cathedral of Peterborough on 2 August 1587 the bishop had prayed that "his soule and the souls of all the rest there present, might be with the soule of the unrepentant papist departed," even though the deceased, Martin alleges, had been "condemned by the lawe of God" and of the State for her conspiracies against the English queen and the nation, namely, Mary Queen of Scots. Martin treats comparatively leniently bishops John Woolton of Exeter and Thomas Bickley of Chichester, describing the latter as a man of little learning, the former as a "petty pope," but he adjudges Herbert Westfaling of Hereford as a "usurper" and a "pestilent and pernicious" prelate. He also labels Richard Howland, bishop of Peterborough, as a "petty Antichrist," whose church government should fall. Thus, although Martin's main targets are the archbishop of Canterbury, the bishops of Winchester and London, and the dean of Salisbury, he criticizes sixteen bishops.[41]

Of non-episcopal targets, Martin rebukes five deans and three archdeacons, seven college heads, and three other officials. Dean Bridges and Dean Perne have already been discussed. Dr. Cosin, dean of the Arches, is attacked because he had written his *An Answer to the Two First and Principall Treatises* (1584), in reply to *An Abstract, of Certain Acts of Parliament* (1583 or 1584), in which Throkmorton may have had a hand. Cosin was also challenged to reply to Dudley Fenner's *A Counter-Poyson* (London, 1584 or 1585). Martin deplores Cosin's lack of wit and learning, and describes him not only as a defender of the established church government but also as "that maidenly doctor who sits cheek by ioll" [jowl] with the archbishop.[42] Dean Gabriel Goodman, the "abbot" of Westminster, is a "dunce," who asserted in a sermon "that so much preaching as in some places we have is an unreasonable service of God." According to Martin, "popish Goodman" even claimed that "the crosse in baptisme, and organes in

Cathedral Churches, are as necessarie as a preaching ministery." To a sermon-hungry Martin, who despised ceremonies
as poor substitutes for the preaching of the Word, these sentiments were little short of scandalous.[43] Dean George Bullen
(or Boleyn) of Lichfield is roundly condemned for his pluralist view that a minister must have two benefices in order
to "furnishe himselfe of Bookes," for his un-puritan teaching
that "men might fal from grace," and for his pulpit antics.[44]

Dr. John Kennall, archdeacon of Oxford, is characterized
as a "Judas" and a "turncoat," who should be cast out of
his office. Martin had a special dislike of Dr. Kennall, who
is included in Martin's syllogism, which he humorously calls
"Perncanterburikenolde." The archdeacon is also identified
with *Fraus*, a character representing treachery.[45] Dr. James
Cottington, archdeacon of Surrey, is berated as a "bankerout," a sycophant seeking to borrow money from usurer
Master Harvey—who was a vehement enemy of Martin's
friend, John Udall. There is a passing slur against William
Redman, archdeacon of Canterbury, depicted as a person
proficient at cards and juggling. His position as prolocutor
of the lower house of Convocation in 1584 and 1586 may partly
explain Martin's animus.[46]

Heads of colleges are not exempt from Martin's denunciations. We have already listed John Kennall as an archdeacon;
though he was not the head of a college, he did serve as
commissary or vice-chancellor at Oxford from 1564 to 1567,
when Throkmorton was a student at the university. John
Bell, master of Jesus College, Cambridge, is characterized
as a man of no learning; his successor as master, Dr. John
Duport, is dismissed as merely one of Whitgift's chaplains.
Dr. William Cole, president of Corpus Christi, Oxford, is
also presented as a man devoid of learning and a "dunce."
Dr. Martin Culpepper, warden of New College, Oxford, is
described as a "hawker." Dr. John Underhill, rector of Lincoln College, Oxford, and consecrated as bishop of Oxford
in 1589, is mentioned as a chaplain for a "chaste Ficker of
Hell, called Sir James King," of Hertfordshire. And Dr. Nicholas Bond, twice vice-chancellor of the University of Oxford

and president of Magdalen College, is portrayed as a "dancer."[47] Noteworthy is Martin's special interest in John Copcot, vice-chancellor of the University of Cambridge and master of Corpus Christi College, who is called a "sot" and a "beast," a defender of the established church polity. In Martin's distortion of Bishop Cooper's anti-Martinist portrait, "the treader was cankered malice, his eyes were fierce, his face thinn and withered, pined away with melancholi, and this was D. Copcot" (*Hay Any Worke*, page 47; Cooper, *An Admonition*, pages 84–87).[48]

Martin despised the church courts which cited good men, enforced subscription and the oath ex officio, levied fines, and imprisoned nonconformists. A prime target was Dr. Edward Stanhope, chancellor of the London diocese and a high commissioner. Martin calls him "Tarquinius Superbus," and inquires: "And is it good dealing, that poore men should be so troubled to the chauncellors courte, that they are even wearie of their lives, for such horrible oppression as there raignes? I tell you D. Stannop (for all you are so proude), a premunire will take you by the backe one day, for oppressing and tyrannizing over Her Majesties subjects as you doe." Another legist was Dr. John Hone, a "journiman doctor," a "popish dolt," a "knave," "the veriest coxcombe that ever wore velvet cap." Martin was especially incensed against this "popish doctor," who served in the "bawdy" archidiaconal court in Surrey, as Official to Archdeacon Cottington, and administered injustice against his ancient foe, John Udall. Dr. Hone had charged Udall with being a "sectarie, a schismatike, yea, he affirmed plainly, that the gospell out of his mouth was blasphemie." "Popish Hone, do you say so? Do ye? You are a knave."[49] Martin's dislike of church courts extended to the censorship of Puritan books, rigorously enforced after the Star Chamber decree of 1586. He singled out one of the licensers of books, William Wood. When John Davidson presented his catechism for licensing to the archbishop, he referred it to Dr. Wood. According to Martin, Dr. "Neverbegood (Wood)" scrutinized it for six months. "The booke is a great one of two sheets of paper. In one place of the booke the meanes of salvation was attributed to the Worde preached. And what did he, thinke you? He blotted out the word (preached) and would not have that word printed, so ascribing the way to work mens salvation to the Worde read."[50]

The restrained, serious, and brief treatment accorded by Penry to three English bishops and Dean Bridges stands in sharp contrast to Martin's parody of sixteen bishops and eighteen other deans, university officials, and legists. Martin directs his attacks against thirty bishops and officials who are never mentioned by Penry. The conclusion seems inescapable that there were two writers with differing interests, methods, and values. This position is strengthened when we review the treatment of the seven prominent clerical leaders by Penry and Martin, previously discussed in this chapter. Therefore, Penry could not have written Martin's books, which are replete with criticism, satire, humor, badinage, invective, jesting, and scurrility. Penry was too conscious of the warning in Matt. 12:36: "But I say unto you, That every idle word that men shall speak, they shall give account thereof in the day of judgment."

The preceding comparison, derived from the foregoing ten contrasts, indicates that Penry and Martin Marprelate are two distinct persons. This view is substantiated by the sentiments of at least twenty-six competent scholars who concluded that Penry was not Martin. Matthew Sutcliffe (1595), John Cotton, relying on Arthur Hildersam's statement regarding his last conference with Penry (1647), and James Peirce (1710, 1717), reached this conclusion. In the nineteenth century such scholars as Benjamin Brook (1813), John Waddington (1854), Samuel Hopkins (1861), John Hunt (1870), Edward Arber (1879), Henry M. Dexter (1880), and F. J. Powicke (1900), decided that Penry did not write the Martinist books. In the twentieth century the research of sixteen scholars has produced a redoubtable consensus that Penry cannot be identified with Martin Marprelate. These writers are: T. G. Crippen (1901), W. H. Frere (1904), A. J. Grieve (1905), R. B. McKerrow (1908), William Pierce (1908), J. Dover Wilson

(1908), Thomas Gasquoine (1909), Champlin Burrage (1912), G. A. Bonnard (1916), Marshall M. Knappen (1939), Albert Peel (1944), David Williams (1945, 1960), Sir John Neale (1957), Glanmor Williams (1967), Patrick Collinson (1967), and Leland H. Carlson (1972).

Since Dr. McGinn is the leading proponent of Penry's identity with Marprelate, our final comparison will be McGinn's treatment of Penry and Throkmorton, and a critique of *John Penry and the Marprelate Controversy*. It is obvious that McGinn regards Penry as an anti-intellectual, as one who "pays lip service to scholarship," even though Penry insisted that an educated minister should know logic and rhetoric, Greek and Hebrew, history and philosophy, Scripture and classics. When Penry criticizes the bishops, it is "with mock piety he protests that he dislikes attacking them." And when Penry warns his Welsh countrymen, McGinn asserts that he "acidly reminds them." Penry is somewhat sneaky, since he "slyly slips in a reference to baptism," and he occasionally throws "in a reference to Wales" to disarm his reader, and he "evasively" remarks that he had received a manuscript from London. Penry's patriotism is suspect. "Whenever Penry's youthful enthusiasm overcomes his discretion, the mask of patriotism slips aside and reveals the Puritan countenance underneath." "We can almost see his lip curling with scorn as, knowing full well the attitude of the English bishops toward the Puritans, he sarcastically addresses himself to his Welsh readers on the subject of preaching as essential to salvation."[51]

Penry emerges as insincere, hypocritical, impudent, evasive, scornful, sly, sarcastic, sophistical, unpatriotic, and anti-intellectual. This portrayal of Penry contrasts strongly to that of Welsh dissenters who regard Penry as "the morning star of Protestant nonconformity in Wales." It also differs sharply from that of John Dover Wilson, who regarded Penry as "one of the finest spirits of an age exceptionally rich in spiritual and intellectual achievement." "His cause, as he tells us himself, was the cause of the oppressed, the weak, and the fatherless."[52] But McGinn's delineation, which conflates the figure of Martin with that of Penry, appears as a sheer caricature of a noble soul. Therefore his conclusion does not ring true that if Penry's admirers will accept his attribution to Penry of the Marprelate books, which "contain nothing that might sully the moral reputation of their martyred hero," then "Pierce's dream of a place for him in the great circle of Elizabethan writers will be realized. To Penry, then, will be awarded the title already given Martin, namely, that of 'the great prose satirist of the Elizabethan period.' "[53] But as the best biographer of Penry, and as the author of two books on Marprelate, Pierce devoted a lifetime in proving that Penry was not the clever satirist and jester of the Marprelate books but a dedicated religious reformer who sought to bring an improved intellectual and spiritual quality to his beloved Welsh nation.

Dr. McGinn fails to utilize available source material. He writes: "To this day the question of Martin's identity is one of the enigmas of the Elizabethan period as far as legal proof is concerned, for no new documents have come to light in the intervening centuries."[54] This startling statement explains why he has propounded an untenable thesis, which is merely a reaffirmation of his misleading article published in 1943, and which has confused Marprelate research during the past fourteen years since his book was published in 1966.[55] He has not utilized the thirty-four manuscripts in the Huntington Library, mostly in the Ellesmere collection, pertaining to Penry's examinations, his preparations for his arraignment, his correspondence, and his notebook. There are about forty manuscripts in the Public Record Office, including thirteen on Penry and his trial in the Court of King's Bench. The State Papers Domestic, and the State Papers Scotland, have some twenty-eight manuscripts, with useful material for Penry and Waldegrave. Lambeth Palace Library has four important manuscripts, and is the only library which possesses all seven Marprelate books, as well as relevant rare books. More than 135 documents have come to light on Martin and his associates since 1589. Consequently, as Dr. Paul S. Seaver justly observes in his review of McGinn's book: "He employs no manuscript material and offers no new evidence."[56]

Too many of McGinn's generalizations are sweeping and invalid. He asserts that "all the external evidence presented by the various suspects questioned by the Government points toward Penry as the author of the seven Martinist tracts."[57] But when we examine McGinn's list of twenty-four witnesses, we discover that fifteen do not mention Penry at all. Four point to Penry as the manager of the press, two point to Throkmorton, and only three point toward Penry as author. Of these three, Hodgskin at first shielded Throkmorton, as his examiners noted, but his last deposition as reported by Sutcliffe implicates the Haseley squire. When questioned about the author, Knightley replied: "he knoweth not, unless yt were Penry." And Sharpe's testimony, which is long on circumstantial detail, rumor, and conjecture, proves that Penry was a business agent but not the author. Therefore, McGinn's generalization that "all the external evidence . . . points toward Penry as the author" needs drastic revision.[58] Equally culpable is McGinn's argument that the internal evidence in Martin's books points to Penry as the author. The "content of the [Martinist] tracts also reflects the spiritual turmoil, either expressed or implied, on almost every page of his [Penry's] signed writings during this period."[59] This generalization is wide of the mark. Marprelate's books reflect the humor, irony, and satire of a very gifted writer, whereas Penry's writings reflect his fervent love of Wales and his passionate concern for the religious welfare of his people.

Dr. McGinn refers to his own "impressive body of evidence," but on close examination one discovers that it is neither impressive nor evidential. At best, it is a body of circumstantial detail, a collection of associations and linkings. One reviewer rightly pointed out that "the similarities which Professor McGinn detects between Penry's writings and that of Martin are nearly all of a superficial nature, characteristics which many Puritan works would share in common."[60] I shall cite two examples which McGinn regards as the strongest proof for Penry's authorship of two Martinist writings. McGinn writes somewhat triumphantly and perilously: "We submit the italicized passage in his [Martin's] apology as the most important evidence for Penry's authorship of this pamphlet [*Hay Any Worke*]—and since it is generally agreed that all the Martinist tracts were the product of the same pen, of the other six as well."[61] The stakes are high!

> *I bethought mee therefore, of a way whereby men might be drawne to do both, perceiving the humors of men in these times (especially of those that are in any place) to be given to mirth. I tooke that course. I might lawfully do it. I [aye], for jesting is lawful by circumstances, even in the greatest matters.* The circumstances of time, place and persons urged me thereunto. (*Hay Any Worke*, page 14).

Even in such a short passage there are four indications of Throkmorton's pen. He likes words beginning with "be," and uses "bethought him," "bethought themselves," and "bethinke himselfe." The reference to "those that are in any place" is more suited to Throkmorton, who was an M.P. and knew the Court, than to Penry. Furthermore, the course of mirth and jesting is one that Penry never pursued. He wrote: "Unseemely jestes, uncomly rayling I allow not, and judge them more beseeming the Prelates and theyr Parrasites than anie modest Christian" (*Notebook*, page 71). The last sentence points to two close parallels, one from Martin and one from Throkmorton:

> The circumstances of time, place and persons urged me thereunto (*Hay Any Worke*, page 14)
> The circumstances of times, places, and persons (*Epitome*, signature B2 v)
> Eyther of time, place, person, or circumstances (Throkmorton, *Defence*, signature Aiv)

Even apart from the arguments in chapter eight on Throkmorton's authorship of *Hay Any Worke* and the *Epitome*, we may conclude that this "most important evidence" does not point toward Penry.

The second example is McGinn's presentation of "the most

convincing evidence for Penry's authorship of *Martin Junior.*" This is "Martin's foreknowledge of how Penry was to convey the manuscript of this tract into the printer's hands."[62] According to Martin, the method was intriguing. "If you demaund of mee, where I founde this, the trueth is, it was taken up (together with certaine other papers) besides a bush, where it had dropped from some body passing by that way."[63] As background, we note that on 13 July 1589 Hodgskin had arrived at Throkmorton's house at Haseley to obtain the manuscript of *More Worke for Cooper.* Since it was not ready, Throkmorton hurriedly prepared the brief first part of *Theses Martinianae (Martin Junior),* which consisted of one or two pages of handwriting, as an incomplete interim publication. On Monday 14 July, Hodgskin and Penry set out for Warwick and Wolston. Near Throkmorton's house by a bush Hodgskin picked up a roll of paper, the initial portion of *Martin Junior.* On Thursday 17 July at Wolston, the printers prepared their forms and press, and began printing from the manuscript copy. This copy—depending on the size of the sheets and whether they were written on both sides, as they probably were—made possible the printing of signature A and probably signature B, each containing eight pages. By Friday 18 July they had made a trial "pull" of signature A at least. On the same day Throkmorton visited the newly hired printers at work in a low parlour at Mrs. Wigston's house, conferred with the printers, clarified some difficult words in the manuscript, and corrected what had already been printed. Symmes, who had received from Hodgskin only a portion of the copy, testified later that "he thinketh the rest was brought thither by the said Throkmorton,"[64] who secretly inserted it with the earlier copy.

Now, the significant point to be noticed is that Martin's account of how the manuscript was to be placed by a bush is not given in signature A or B, but is printed on signature C3 *verso,* as a part of "Martin Juniors Epilogue," which is the concluding section of *Martin Junior.* It is obvious that the copy for signatures C and D was that which was delivered on Friday 18 July, and had been written between 14 July and 17 July. Therefore Martin Junior is describing what actually happened on 14 July when the first part of the copy was picked up. Dr. McGinn's "foreknowledge" disappears and history replaces it. Furthermore, from the best authority, the deposition of Hodgskin, we know that the copy "came to Hodgskins hands by the appointment [prearrangement] of Throkmorton, being laide in the way betwixt his and Mistresse Wigstons house, ready for Hodgskin to take up."[65]

From 1589 to 1980 Throkmorton has been suspected of writing Martin's books. One would expect, therefore, a careful consideration of his role, but of twenty-three items written by him sixteen are not mentioned by McGinn, and nine other works are misattributed.[66] He does not weigh the evidence for Throkmorton's authorship of *Master Some Laid Open*, *The Crops and Flowers of Bridges Garden*, "Martins Interim," or *A Dialogue*, as asserted by Sutcliffe and Bancroft. He does not consider Throkmorton's indictment before a grand jury at Warwick in 1590, his submission to Archbishop Whitgift and Lord Chancellor Hatton, his submission to the justices of Assize, and his appearance before the court at Westminster in 1591. McGinn concludes that "in view of the glaring inconsistencies in the accusations of Sutcliffe, it seems unwise to substitute this latecomer [Throkmorton] into the Marprelate Controversy for Henry Sharpe, who was on hand almost from the start."[67] But there are no glaring inconsistencies in Sutcliffe's account; Throkmorton was no latecomer but an "earlycomer" who began his episcopal attacks in 1572; Sharpe was mistrusted by the Martinists, was not present at East Molesey, was kept waiting in a field at Fawsley, was refused access to Waldegrave at Coventry, and was not present at Manchester. Dr. McGinn further concludes that "from Sutcliffe's account, then, we are not convinced that Throkmorton wrote the *Epistle* or even the *Epitome*, but rather that he supervised the printing of *Martin Senior*, *Martin Junior*, and *Martin's Interim*."[68] But Sutcliffe bypasses the *Epistle* and the *Epitome* and begins his proof of Throkmorton's authorship with *Hay Any Worke for Cooper*. It was Penry, in Throkmorton's absence, who clarified the reading of *Martin Senior* and probably served as proofreader. On 18 July 1589 Throkmorton did supervise the incomplete printing of *Martin Junior*. Neither man supervised the printing of "Martins Interim," since it was never printed. Thus, for McGinn, Throkmorton's role is reduced to the supervision of the printing of one book. But my conclusion is that Throkmorton was on hand from the very beginning, though lurking in the shadows, that he wrote all the Marprelate books, the three parallel non-extant works, as well as *Master Some Laid Open* and *A Dialogue*. He was the mastermind behind the entire Marprelate project, provided living quarters for his agent Penry at Haseley from 2 March to 2 October 1589, and compensated Newman and Waldegrave for their work. He alone was responsible for the savage attack against the episcopacy and clergy, for the wit and satire, jesting and humor, which characterize his Marprelate and non-Marprelatian writings.

A Critique of John Penry and the Marprelate Controversy

Dr. McGinn's book is an outstanding example of special pleading; it is one long preconception in search of validating material. This preconception is alluded to by McGinn in his foreword where he has written: "I was spurred on, of course, by memories of the unfavorable reception given in certain quarters to an article that I wrote in 1944 [*PMLA*, March 1943] identifying John Penry as Martin. I undertook to retrace my steps and to examine all relevant controversial literature both attacking and defending the Church of England in the last quarter of the sixteenth century."[69] The result of this re-examination was the publication of his book in 1966, which repeats his preconception, transmutes it into an obsession, and increases his errors.

The basic reason why Dr. McGinn has gone astray is found in his own statement: "From the words of Henry Sharpe, who assisted Penry through the entire controversy, and John Hodgkins, who succeeded Waldegrave as printer, we can piece together the entire story."[70] This statement indicates that McGinn has improperly evaluated his sources. Henry Sharpe should not be puffed up as a witness because he supports McGinn's thesis; he should be deflated because his opinions on authorship are mere conjecture. He did not assist "through the entire controversy," since he did not participate in the beginning and the ending of the Marprelate program. He never saw the press at Fawsley and Coventry. His main contribution was his assistance in binding *Hay Any Worke*, *Martin Junior*, and packing *Martin Senior* for the carrier. He did purchase copies of the *Epitome* to sell at a profit, and this transaction was probably the main event that precipitated his arrest.

Hodgskin's testimony should be divided into two parts: his earlier testimony as given in the Puckering Brief and his later testimony as revealed in his final examination, in Sutcliffe's summaries, and in his arraignment before the Court of King's Bench.[71] McGinn relies on Hodgskin's earlier testimony, which is vitiated by his determination to shield Throkmorton, by his equivocations and insinuations, and by omission of pertinent information. To place credence on Hodgskin's earlier testimony without checking it against his later statements and balancing it with better evidence from Sutcliffe and Newman borders on credulity.[72]

The most reliable and informative sources are the summaries of Sutcliffe in his indispensable *An Answere unto a Certaine Calumnious Letter Published by M[aster] J. Throkmorton* (1595); the last examination of Symmes, and the statements of Newman. McGinn's treatment of Sutcliffe, especially in his 1943 article, is an horrendous array of defamatory and disparaging accusations against the dean of Exter, who was a learned man, author of some twenty-four books, and a powerful polemicist and apologist for the Church of England.[73] McGinn does his utmost to demolish the testimony of Symmes, who was honest and competent, and was the first witness to incriminate Throkmorton.[74] McGinn concludes: "And we may repeat that Symmes and Tomlyn in their extant depositions had nothing to say about authorship,"—although Symmes had testified that the manuscript of *Martin Senior* "was of the same hand writinge with the former [*Martin Junior*]. And Simmes thinketh that Mr Throckmort[on] was the author of it."[75] McGinn neglects the testimony of Newman, which is found in twelve extracts in Sutcliffe's *An Answere* (1595), and in Ellesmere MS. 2148, which contains eighteen excerpts from Newman, unused by McGinn.[76]

Not only has McGinn improperly evaluated his sources, but he has unjustly criticized his predecessors in the field of Martinist research. He reprehends the pioneer biographer of Penry, John Waddington, who "not only fails to appreciate Martin's contribution to English literature but also disregards a large part of the evidence relating to Penry's life."[77] Waddington's subject, however, was not Martin's literary contributions but a life of Penry, and he did not confuse or conflate the writings of Penry and Martin. Furthermore, he unearthed at least sixteen manuscripts relating to Penry, researched his subject at a time (1854) when calendars of State Papers were not readily available, produced a dozen volumes of research, all on a meager salary as a full-time clergyman. Professor David Williams, a leading Welsh historian and specialist on Penry, is criticized for not being "completely familiar with the address 'To the LL. of the Counsell,' " which is appended to the second edition of the *Exhortation*. But Williams reprinted the text of the second edition in his *Three Treatises concerning Wales*. He omitted the section, "To the LL. of the Counsel," because "it was superseded by a separate treatise," *A Viewe*, and because it did not pertain to Wales.[78]

McGinn's strictures against Pierce are unkind, undeserved, and unscholarly. He asserts that Pierce's "exaggerations have tended to confuse our understanding of the Marprelate Controversy." Again: "Today his picture of Penry or of any other Puritan as an apostle of freedom of thought seems almost ludicrous. Sometimes, indeed, Pierce writes almost as though he had never read the pamphlets that he is discussing."[79] But Pierce, who seems to have read everything pertaining to his work, produced three solid and significant books on the Marprelate problem: *An Historical Introduction to the Marprelate Tracts*, *The Marprelate Tracts, 1588, 1589*, which is the best edition of these writings, and the definitive biography, *John Penry, His Life, Times and Writings*, all of which have stood the test of time. Pierce is also censured because he frankly admitted his difficulty in locating the source of Martin's allusion to "M. Fenners, and M. Penries syllogismes, whereby Doctor Bridges his booke is confuted and the cause of reformation unanswerably prooved." McGinn comments with assurance: "If, however, he [Pierce] had examined the second edition of the *Exhortation* at the University of Wales and the third edition at the British Museum, he would have found in them Penry's fifty-three syllogisms against the 'dumb ministers,' to which Martin undoubtedly refers."[80] This unique copy of the second edition of the *Exhortation* was first announced in a letter sent in 1906 by Sir John Williams to Alexander J. Grieve, editor of the *Transactions of the Congregational Historical Society*. When John Dover Wilson informed the scholarly world in 1909 of this discovery, in his article, "A New Tract from the Marprelate Press," he acknowledged the help of Pierce, from whom he had learned of this unique item, and of Sir John, whose letter he had read.[81] This unique copy is not "at the University of Wales" but at the National Library of Wales, as Pierce correctly states.

When McGinn says that if Pierce had examined "the third edition at the British Museum, he would have found," I am troubled by the contrary-to-fact implication. If McGinn had examined carefully Pierce's book, *John Penry*, pages 190–93, and glanced at the illustrations facing pages 184 and 192, which reproduce the title page and the last page of the main tract of the third edition, he would have found Pierce's summary of the third edition, and the statement: "This is the edition in the British Museum and used in the preparations of these pages." The culmination of this bizarre censure of Pierce is that McGinn asserts that Martin undoubtedly refers to Penry's fifty-three syllogisms, but this is indubitably wrong.[82] Martin alludes to "M. Fenners, and M. Penries syllogismes, *whereby Doctor Bridges his booke is confuted*, and the cause of reformation unanswerably prooved" [my italics]. Penry's fifty-three syllogisms have no relationship whatsoever to Dr. Bridges' book. The four syllogisms to which Martin alludes are in the new portion of the second edition of the *Exhortation,* pages 73–81, are reprinted in *A Viewe,* pages 21–41, and in Williams' edition, *Three Treatises concerning Wales,* pages 124–38. McGinn's omission of the articles by Sir John Williams and Wilson in his bibliography, and his own four errors, indicate that his criticism of Pierce is unscholarly.

Arber is criticized for "obscuring the problem of Martin's identity for all succeeding investigators of the controversy," and for "his unwillingness to implicate Penry;" McGinn derides the idea of "lost documents" which "Arber imagines were seen by Sutcliffe," and he reports that "Arber, in presenting his own 'belief on this subject' [that Throkmorton is Martin] accepts Sutcliffe's belated emotional attack and thus implies distrust of the testimony of everyone immediately connected with the publication of the Martinist tracts."[83] Wilson is allegedly guilty of misdating the raid on Penry's study and the publication of Penry's *Appellation* as 1589, but Wilson is correct in both cases. Wilson is chided for unfortunately selecting "not Waldegrave's deposition as recorded in the state documents but Sutcliffe's unreliable account." But Wilson's selection is fortunate, Sutcliffe's account is reliable, and there is no need for debating this point.[84] McGinn even censures the "subjective approach of most students of the Controversy, who refer to the depositions given before the High Commissioners in 1588 and 1589 only when a sentence or two happens to fit in with their own hypotheses."[85] I think it is obvious that "most students of the Controversy" have slowly and steadily ascended the mountain of research toward the peak, and that McGinn has climbed the wrong mountain.[86] The thesis that Penry was Martin cannot be maintained today in the light of the evidence we now possess for both Penry and Throkmorton.[87]

 CONCLUSION

XI

"*The opportunity* [of attacking Dean John Bridges' *Defence*] *was seized on by a writer of genius, the most effective popular pamphleteer of the sixteenth century*" (G. R. Hibbard, *Thomas Nashe*, p. 22)

THE MARPRELATE BOOKS were not the product of an organized group. They cannot be linked with the Presbyterians or the Separatists. They cannot be associated with powerful political leaders such as the earl of Leicester or the earl of Essex. Although Throkmorton was a Puritan, the leaders repudiated his literary campaign. It was a great disappointment to Throkmorton that the Puritans were angry with him because he jested and treated sin too lightly. He admitted that the Puritans "like of the matter I have handled, but the forme they cannot brooke." He acknowledged that some Puritans had concluded that he had marred everything, but he dissented vigorously. To him the crux of the matter was the implementation of Christ's government as revealed in the New Testament, and the necessary curtailment of episcopal power. To these two principles of Christian polity and the limitation of prelatical policies, one may add Throkmorton's conviction that he was truly serving his queen and helping to avert God's vengeance against the nation. Throkmorton affirmed that the bishops were "the greatest enemies that now our State hath," that they blocked the free passage of the gospel and truth, and that they provoked God Almighty to punish the nation. To accomplish his purposes Throkmorton deliberately adopted the weapon of mirth and satire.

Not all of Throkmorton's motivations were idealistic. He coveted the plaudits of his hearers and readers. He liked the well-turned phrase, and was skillful in the use of a literary stiletto. He enjoyed scoring a success against his opponents, and he stooped to conquer. At times he was carried away by his own rhetoric, and his raillery probably provided him with a purgation of his own exasperation. For Throkmorton was a deeply frustrated reformer. In February 1586/87 his speech in the House of Commons, pertaining to foreign policy, had reflected on the monarchs of France, Spain, and Scotland, and had led not only to a rebuke by Lord Chancellor Hatton but also to the decision by Lord Burghley to imprison him in the Tower. Disappointed, Throkmorton fled to Hillingdon, and his parliamentary career came to a sudden end. He was also frustrated by the failure of the Puritan legislative program in the Parliaments of 1586/87 and 1588/89, by the shifting of power in the Privy Council, and the growing influence of Archbishop Whitgift. He was incensed by the treatment accorded his book, *The State of the Church of Englande,* which was confiscated and burned, and he was angered by the punishment meted out to his printer, Waldegrave, whose shop had been raided, whose press and type had been destroyed. He denounced the harassment of such Puritans as Walter Travers, Giles Wigginton, Percival Wiburn, Eusebius Pagit, Robert Cawdrey, and John Udall.

If we consider Throkmorton as a frustrated idealist with a strong sympathy for Puritan aspirations, as expressed in the growing Reformed churches, we can understand his desire to replace lord bishops, deans, and priests with pastors, elders, and deacons. If we remember that he was dismayed by the problems of human conduct, greed, pride, hypocrisy, simony, bribery, and nonresidency, we may extenuate his conviction that a congregational and presbyterial form of discipline would be an improvement upon the procedure of ecclesiastical courts, which dispensed justice frequently by monetary fines or verdicts of contumacy, without changing the minds and hearts of the offenders, who were required by law to attend church services. If we note his love of thoughtful sermons, his wide reading, his belief in the efficacy of dividing the Word aright, we may sympathize with his protests against the dumb unpreaching ministry. After thirty years, from 1558 to 1588, the Church of England was still struggling with the difficult problem of providing able clergymen in some 8,700 parishes. The Puritan surveys of the ministry in various shires, though one-sided and incomplete, do reveal the large number of clergy inadequately educated, unable to preach and often unable to read effectively the homilies and the Book of Common Prayer. Too many lists reveal incumbents of low ethical and religious standards, vicars who are described as common swearers, gamesters, barrators, mass-mongers, and non-preachers. Others, morally blameless, are characterized as hirelings, unlearned readers, and servingmen. Therefore, when able preachers were suspended or deprived for non-subscription to Whitgift's Three Articles, for not wearing the surplice, or for not following the prescribed liturgy, Throkmorton was indignant at the Elizabethan scribes and Pharisees, blind guides "straining out a gnat and swallowing a camel."

As a member of Parliament, Throkmorton was a believer in free speech in the House of Commons, even on sensitive religious questions, which were usually referred to the bishops in the House of Lords or to Convocation. He believed in the corollary of free speech in the pulpit, and likewise advocated a policy of uncensored Puritan books. Consequently, he denigrated the efforts of the clerical censors to curtail Puritan printing. The Star Chamber decree of 23 June 1586 put great powers into the hands of Archbishop Whitgift and Bishop Aylmer, and empowered the Stationers' Company to keep a close check on secret presses. This company effectively checked the career of the most eminent Puritan printer for fifteen years. As Throkmorton's friend, Walde-grave was the source of the passages in the Martinist books relating to the printer's plight. As a supporter of the common-law courts, Throkmorton was an opponent of the ecclesiastical and prerogative courts. His denunciation of the Court of High Commission, dominated by Archbishop Whitgift, Bishop Aylmer, and Bishop Cooper, with its oath ex officio, his criticism of the chancellor's court in the diocese of London, of the archidiaconal courts, and of the lingering persistence of a quasi canon law in the decisions of the church courts, revealed his Puritan bias.

In a broad context, the Marprelate literature was a culmination of sixteen years of opposition to the polity and practices of the Church of England from the outbreak of the Admonition Controversy in 1572 to the appearance of the *Epistle* in October 1588. In a limited sense the Martinist attack represented a one-man crusade for reform directed against the hierarchy. In a personal sense it was a satirical onslaught against Archbishop Whitgift, who was a choleric, strong-minded, able, and uncompromising martinet, but who was also unflinching, sincerely committed to the queen and the Church of England, and fearless in enforcing uniformity. His unswerving loyalty to the queen was rewarded by unquestioned support from his monarch. Royal paternalism, fortified by political acumen and uncommon common sense, kept the forces of reform under control.

The publication of the Martinist books constitutes a new chapter in the history of secret printing. Though Throkmorton worked alone with utmost secrecy, though he kept discreetly in the background, though he published his books pseudonymously, he was unable to cover his tracks. He needed a printer, whose identity was quickly discovered. He required a co-ordinator, John Penry, whose activities were speedily reported. And he needed distributors for his books, agents such as Humphrey Newman, Mrs. Waldegrave, John Bowman, and Henry Sharpe, whose participation could not be concealed.

In the fifteen years following the Martinist episode, the

queen, Privy Council, and archbishop achieved a Pyrrhic victory. By 1589 and 1590 the Martinists were silenced. In 1590–92 the Puritan classis movement was effectively curbed by Bancroft and the courts of High Commission and Star Chamber. On 6 April 1593, the Separatist leaders, John Greenwood and Henry Barrow, were hanged. In the same month a law was enacted, "An Acte to Retayne the Quenes Majesties Subjects in Their Due Obedyence," which provided for conformity and prescribed imprisonment and banishment for nonconformity. On 29 May John Penry's life terminated at the end of a noose for publishing in 1590 a "seditious" book in Scotland, *Reformation No Enemie*. Penry was not indicted for writing the Marprelate books, as Throkmorton was, but his participation in the project as a business manager was a factor in the minds of his judges. The death of Thomas Cartwright on 27 December 1603, the Hampton Court Conference of January 1603/04, the death of Archbishop Whitgift on 29 February 1603/04, and the promulgation of the "Constitutions and Canons Ecclesiastial 1604" by the Canterbury Province, marked the end of a chapter in the struggle between Puritan and Anglican.

In the field of literature Throkmorton contributed seven Marprelate items and five related books. As the author of the *Epistle, Hay Any Worke for Cooper, Martin Senior,* and *Master Some Laid Open in His Coulers*, he has earned a secure place in the history of satire. His three parliamentary speeches of 1586/87 and his *Defence* of 1594 still make for fascinating reading and provide source material for the historian of Parliament and Puritanism. As a zestful, droll, frolicking, frivolous, humorous, and satirical writer, his patter on the printed page is reminiscent of Richard Tarleton's palaver on the public stage. Throkmorton has modified the stereotype of a Puritan writer as necessarily serious, theological, and obscurantist. Although it is easy to catch Throkmorton in exaggeration and in glib, garrulous, and voluble distortion, it is more difficult to accuse him of outright prevarication. He had read widely, had pondered deeply, and had experienced the life of country and court.

Throkmorton's fulminations and strictures, his jesting and satirizing, produced the hostile stage productions of the spring and summer of 1589. Likewise, his writings provoked the spate of anti-Martinist books that followed in the next four or five years. He attracted the attention of Elizabeth and Lord Chancellor Hatton, of Parliament and Convocation, of Privy Council and Court of Star Chamber, of at least six judges, of Francis Bacon, Archbishop Whitgift, Bishop Cooper, Dean Sutcliffe, Richard Hooker, Thomas Nashe, John Lyly, Gabriel and Richard Harvey, and Anthony Munday. Equally important, he appealed to the rank and file reader. Although Throkmorton's reforms were delayed, he did contribute to the ongoing debates regarding the respective jurisdiction of magistrates and prelates, the place of secular and ecclesiastical courts, the justice or injustice of subscription and ex officio oaths, the right not to testify against oneself, the need of free speech in Parliament, pulpit, and press. Some of his ideals were realized in the 1640s, but it was not until 1689—one hundred years after the publication of his *Protestatyon*—that the Bill of Rights, the Toleration Act, and the supremacy of Parliament were achieved.

APPENDIXES

THE FIRST SIX appendixes describe items which Throkmorton wrote from 1572 to 1588. Since these items are anonymous, I have presented brief summaries of reasons for attributing these works to Throkmorton. Although all of these writings appeared before the publication of the first Marprelate book, the *Epistle*, and although the authorship of the Marprelate tracts does not depend on the evidence for Throkmorton's authorship of these six items, it is helpful to know that Throkmorton's anti-episcopal career began not in 1588 but in 1572, and that his early views correspond to those found in the Marprelate books.

Appendix A. "An Answer to Certen Peeces of a Sermon"

About 10 June 1572, Field and Wilcox's revolutionary and censorious *An Admonition to the Parliament* was published while Elizabeth's fourth Parliament was in session. This presbyterian manifesto had "an enormous effect," as Bishop Walter H. Frere noted. With Cartwright's lectures and sermons in 1570, it launched a twenty-year campaign against the Anglican polity, ceremonies, and Book of Common Prayer. Reaction was immediate and sharp. The authors were arrested about 23 June and on 27 June Bishop Cooper delivered an official reply. One of the bishop's listeners was Throkmorton, who had attended the University of Oxford when Cooper was the master of Magdalen College School and when Field and Wilcox were undergraduates. Throkmorton immediately wrote "An Answer to Certen Peeces of a Sermon Made at Paules Crosse on Sunday the xxviith of June in *Anno* 1572 by Doctor Cowper, Bishop of Lincoln."[1] Since Cooper had excused the low state of the English clergy by asserting that the frequent alteration of religion after 1534 had discouraged students from entering the ministry, Throkmorton asked why pastors were discouraged by episcopal license from preaching and why bishops excommunicated, banished, and imprisoned godly preachers of the Word. He berated the bishop for his defense of the English liturgy and suggested that the simpler forms of common prayer used in the Reformed churches in Geneva, France, and Scotland would be more apposite. He decried the unscriptural titles of dignity such as primate, metropolitan, suffragans, lord bishops, chancellors, and commissaries. Although the bishop considered external government and discipline as variable and subject to the pleasure of church and magistracy, Throkmorton asserted that polity was a divinely prescribed institution. He also accused Cooper of having "wrested and perverted sundrie places of Scripture"—a familiar complaint in Tudor polemical literature.

The author of "An Answer" has never been identified, but the writer probably was Throkmorton. As his earliest extant writing, this treatise is trebly important because it presents his views as of 1572, it reveals his connection with Field and Wilcox in the Admonition Controversy, and it clarifies his hostile and impertinent criticisms of Bishop Cooper as seen in all of the Marprelate writings. It also facilitates the attribution of authorship to him of four succeeding works in 1572–73.[2] One clear indication of Throkmorton's pen is the use of strong, stinging, and colorful words: "carnally, choler, craftie, depraving, espied, fleshlie, hierlings, hypocrites, juggling, maugre, mychers [thieves], myslyked, pratle, rhetoricians, ruffianlike, scowring, skullion, smacking, whorehunters, wresting." A second indication of Throkmorton's style of writing is the occurrence of at least twenty-five oft-repeated phrases, such as "with what face," "of your own coat," and "repugnant to Gods Worde." As in most of his books, Throkmorton's fondness for classical or biblical allusions is evident, since he uses seven Latin quotations and four Greek words. Fourthly, there are typical examples of his sarcasm, such as his description of pluralists as "galloping Sir Johns in the countrey" and his insulting characterization of Cooper ("as for your honour I let that passe, as smacking to[o] muche of Antichrists stenche"); (fol. 459).

Throkmorton's predilection for alliteration is illustrated by seventeen examples: "deterred from doing their duties, doughtie divines, followers and favourers, gay geare, lewde and loytering, loytering lubbers, mended the matter, mens mynds from medling in the ministerie, mumble mattens, patches and peeces, preache or professe, reforme and re-dresse, seasoned with such salte, shiftes and shewes, sight of the samme sunne, simplicitie and sinceritie, not unwilling onely, but unable too." Also, Throkmorton's predisposition toward certain topics is displayed by the following twenty-four subjects: banishment, bare readers, bishops and lord bishops, ceremonies, church government, conscience, depri-vation, free will, joining of civil and ecclesiastical offices, nonresidency, papists, Paul's Cross, Pelagianism and predestination, persecution, pluralism, preaching, prisons, promotions, Reformed churches, sermons, superstitions, un-learned clergy, will of God, and worldly preferment.

There are ten parallels which point toward Throkmorton's authorship of "An Answer." In each following example the folio number in the first line is taken from "An Answer." The reference (IV:37) indicates Throkmorton's *Hay Any Worke for Cooper*, page 37, and (7:70) indicates *Master Some Laid Open*, page 70. For other arabic and roman numerals, see the complete listing in chapter six. Page references to the *Exhortation* and *A Second Admonition* are taken from the edi-tions printed in Frere and Douglas, *Puritan Manifestoes.*

nam qui pergit, ea quae vult dicere, ea quae non vult audiet
  (fol. 461)
qui pergit quod vult dicere quae non vult audiet (IV:37)

spoileth and robbeth (fol. 461)
spoile and robberie (VII:18, 21)

what that good acceptable and perfect will of God is (fol. 462)
what that good, acceptable and perfect wil of God is (*Exhorta-tion*, 61)

runne out into blinde and odde corners (fol. 459)
runne into corners (I:52)

to let thes passe (fol. 462)
to let these passe (*Second Admonition*, 116)

the minister must be didaktikos [apt to teach] (fol. 460)
and are in some measure thithacticoi [didacticoi, the Greek
  nominative plural; "thithacticoi" is a printer's error] (7:24)

being so repugnant to Gods Worde (fol. 461)
these are not repugnant, saithe one, to the Woorde of God
  (*Second Admonition*, 92)

carnal . . . but of fleshlie reason and worldlie policie (fol. 459)
which is not fleshlye or carnally, or for any worldly respecte
  (*Exhortation*, 69)

if you vewe the place well (fol. 460)
if you vewe it attentively (7:70)
I have vewed it meetly wel (7:93)

consider what came upon Nadab and Abihu [sons of Aaron]
  for offering strange fire (fol. 459)
he that could not abide straunge fire in the olde law (*Second
  Admonition*, 91)
by any other than a sonne of Aaron, consumed by any strange
  fire (II:B3)

In addition to the seven reasons presented thus far, we
note that in "An Answer" there are also six small indications
which reveal Throkmorton's pen because of the occurrence
of similar points in his other writings. Throkmorton mentioned "one Hermannus" who compiled a book "full of cor-
ruptions" (fol. 460). The reference is to Hermannus of Wied
(1477–1552), archbishop of Cologne, 1515–47, who published an
ad interim book.[3] Under pressure from the emperor, Charles
V, Hermannus and others sought to reconcile Catholic and
Protestant views. Compromise settlements were arranged at
the Interim of Regensburg of 1541 and the Augsburg Interim
of 1548, but were unsatisfactory to both sides. Throkmorton
believed that the imperial efforts on the Continent were a
warning to England, which had been involved in an *ad interim*

establishment of religion during the years 1558–72. Therefore, the allusion to Hermannus seems to cohere with Throkmorton's early use of the very unusual phrases, "interimisticall state of our church," "interimisticall reformation," and "fie upon you, you interimistical traditioners," which he employed in "A Friendly Caveat to Bishop Sands." He denounced the bishop as "Master Doctor Drawbacke," as one who favored the Elizabethan interim settlement, "which is but a little step from Papistrie," and as one who opposed the establishment of a pure uncompromising religion.[4]

Another clue is Throkmorton's interest in the education of divinity students. His exaggerated claim that he "could finde meanes that both the universities and cathedrall churches" would produce a sufficiency of preachers in a decade (fol. 460) is similar to his promise in *Hay Any Worke* (page 35) to "helpe those good young students unto a means to live." A third indication of Throkmorton's mind is his familiar threat to publish his "An Answer" and also "further confutations" if Bishop Cooper refused to give serious attention to the criticisms leveled against him.[5] A fourth clue is Throkmorton's characterization of Cooper as a man "better seen [versed] in physick, or teaching a schole, than in the mysteries and secrets of holy Scripture"; this is reminiscent of his denunciation of the bishop as "a siely Schoolemaster, being also as unlearned, as a man of that trade and profession can be."[6] Fifthly, Throkmorton's sharp disagreement with Cooper's praise of the English liturgy as "the most agreeable to Gods Worde of any since the Apostles time" (fol. 460) is similar to his criticism of Cooper's claim that "there had not bin since the Apostles time, such a flourishing estate of a Church, as we have now in England" (I:33). A sixth observation is the writer's common practice of omitting "for" in a clause such as "finde me any forme of praier"; one also notes his use of proverbs, his utilization of patristic writers, his Scriptural allusions, especially to Paul, his choice diction, and his clarity revealed in a direct, blunt, and conversational style.

When I first encountered the manuscript of "An Answer,"

I sensed that Throkmorton was a possible author. This recognition factor, intuition, or sense of affinity is difficult to explain. It is a subjective judgment and must be used cautiously, but it serves as a guide in determining what anonymous items should be thoroughly studied. After many years of close analysis of Throkmorton's manner of writing, I have experienced by a kind of literary osmosis an absorption of his diction, style, irony, interests, reactions, and techniques. "An Answer" provides a sense of coherence with the works of Throkmorton but not with the writings of such potential authors as Field, Wilcox, Cartwright, Travers, Anthony Gilby, or Christopher Goodman.

---

1. Petyt MSS. 538(47), fols. 459–62, Inner Temple Library.

2. See Appendixes B, C, D, E.

3. *Einfaltigs Bedencken einer christlichen Reformation*. This book, also known as *Didagma* (1543), was published in English, *A Simple, and Religious Consultation* (London, 1547, 1548). It was used in the preparation of *The Order of the Communion* (1548) [*S.T.C.*, 16456].

4. See Appendix E. The pages in "A Friendly Caveat," *A Parte of a Register*, are 376, 379, 380. The *N.E.D.* cites the first occurrence of "Interimist" as 1560 and of "Interimisticall" as 1643. Throkmorton's use of it in 1573 may be the first occurrence of it as an adjective, perhaps one of his coined words. See the book, *Interim, hoc est, constitutio*, published in 1548 at Cologne. For other Latin and German editions, see the British Museum, *General Catalogue*, vol. 84, column 428. See also Philipp Melanchthon, *A Waying and Considering of the Interim*, translated by John Rogers (London: E. Whitchurche, 1548).

5. Both Throkmorton and Martin threaten or promise about sixteen times to answer their opponents. See the *Epistle*, pp. 40–43.

6. "An Answer," fol. 460; *Hay Any Worke*, p. 22; *Protestatyon*, p. 20.

APPENDIX B. *An Exhortation to the Byshops*

An Exhortation to the Byshops to Deale Brotherly with Theyr Brethren, dated 30 September 1572, was probably published in October, together with a second part, *An Exhortation to the Bishops and Their Clergie*. The first *Exhortation* justified the criticism presented in the *Admonition* and rebuked the bishops for their harsh dealing with Field and Wilcox, who had been thrust into prison with common felons. Although they had been confined as "close prisoners" in Newgate, yet the bishops allegedly had not practiced Christian charity by succoring them; although the prisoners had been kept in fetters, the bishops had not urged their liberty; even though the admonitors had spoken the truth, the bishops had resented any references to their own "lordships and livings." The writer urged the bishops to "deale more christianly for the Lordes sake with your brethren; let not lawes that were purposely made for the wicked, be made snares by you to catch the godly; lay aside this Lording, and shew your selves brethren in deede."[1]

The second *Exhortation* was a demand that the bishops reply fully and frankly to the *Admonition*. For the benefit of simple and unlearned men, the learned clergy should refute the *Admonition* by the Word of God; they should know that "there is a better way for Bishops, and Bishops of Christ, to confute a schisme by, than prisons and chaines." Therefore, in preparing their refutation, the higher clergy were urged not to "wring the Scripture to serve their owne turne, or other mennes phantasies. For if they do, it wil easely be spied." The bishops were also admonished: "Cogge [cheat] not therfore, nor foiste [insert sneakingly], neither bumbaste [stuff, inflate] it with rhetoricke, or mans authoritie to make a shew, but let the word of the eternall be judge betweene bothe, which is goulde and silver, and which is drosse and stubble, which is corne, and which is chaffe."[2]

Among the numerous indications of Throkmorton's pen, we observe the use of proverbs and Latin sentences and phrases;[3] criticism against the titles, lordships, and dignities of bishops; the references to persecution and prisons; the emphasis on conscience; the accusation of double-talk, or "Bishops English," as also discussed in *Martin Senior* (Civ-Di). There are eight common phrases or clauses, used by Martin and Throkmorton, such as "I have tolde you," "beare us in hande," "take this matter in hande," and "nowe to the matter." Although sparingly used by other writers, these phrases and clauses in their variety and frequency suggest

Throkmorton's pen. Less common expressions, which also occur in Marprelate's books, are: "spoile and robbe us," "greene heades," "flymme flamme," "flatly and plainly," "without controlment," "to serve their owne turne," and *"cum privilegio."*[4] Another indication is the occurrence of fourteen examples of alliteration, found throughout the works of Throkmorton and Martin: "bewitched and blineded," "bragged and boasted," "burthen your brethrens backes," "disclose the disorders," "disorderous discipline," "false fodder," "favoure and frendship," "fond and feeble," "frankly and freely," "licenciously and losely," "lordships and livings," "paine and punishment," "pastors and preachers," "redresse and Reformation." We also note the use of balanced sentences:

> as thoughe to honor the Almightie,
>> were to dishonor the Prince.
> what he hathe commaunded we may strive to maintain,
>> and what he hath forbidden, we may indevor to suppresse.[5]

There are eight suggestive parallels in the *Exhortations* and in the works of Throkmorton and Martin:

> inter vos autem non erit sic (*Exhortation*, 68)
> inter vos autem non sic (*Certaine Articles*, 141)[6]

> which are of the inferioure sort (*Exhortation*, 73)
> any of the inferior sorte ("Speech on the Bill and Book," Phillipps MS. 13891, MA 276, fol. 13)

> overthrowe of the whole state (*Exhortation*, 64)
> overthrowe of the state (VI:Civ v)

> take the scepter out of his hande (*Exhortation*, 69)
> wrest the scepter out of her hand (VI:Civ v)

> as fast as they can trotte (*Exhortation*, 59)
> as fast as a dog can trot (I:33)

> the prescripte rule of Gods holy Woorde (*Exhortation*, 63)
> which God hath prescribed in the Worde (II:D1)

> much like to galled horsses (*Exhortation*, 61)
> horse with a gald backe (6:Civ)

delt as close prisoners a long time, so that no frende, no not skarce their wives may come to them (*Exhortation*, 64)

two godly ministers in close prison, so that no frends can come to visit them: Do you not separate them and their wives? ("An Answer," fol. 461)

---

1. Frere and Douglas, *Puritan Manifestoes*, p. 67.

2. Ibid., p. 71.

3. Ibid., pp. 66, 68, 71–75.

4. Ibid., pp. 69, 73, 59, 58, 65, 65, 71.

5. Ibid., pp. 65, 60, 67, 63, 63, 70, 75, 63, 58, 67, 66, 62, 64, 58. Throkmorton's use of structural balance is apparent in his three parliamentary speeches.

6. These references are to the editions in Frere and Douglas.

APPENDIX C. *Certaine Articles*

After the publication of *An Admonition*, an anonymous Anglican reader collected thirty-seven extracts from this work and published them with the title, "A Viewe of the Churche, That the Authors of the Late Published *Admonition* Would Have Planted within This Realme of Englande, Containing Such Positions as They Hold against the State of the Said Churche, as It Is Nowe." To this manuscript book Throkmorton replied with "A Reproufe of This Viewe, Made as It Is Thought, by the Byshops, and a Confirmation of the Booke in Short Notes," which listed and refuted the thirty-seven extracts. Most of Throkmorton's rebuttals indicated that the extracts were misinterpreted, exaggerated, or falsified, but some of the refutations amplified, clarified, or justified the presbyterian positions found in the *Admonition*. It is possible that "A Reproufe" first appeared in September 1572 as a manuscript book, but about October "A Viewe" and "A Reproufe" were printed in black letter, with the title, *Certaine Articles*, and appended to *A Second Admonition to the Parliament*, which was also printed in black letter.[1]

The title page of *Certaine Letters* contains three clues to authorship: (1) the initials J.T.J.S., which probably indicate Job Throkmorton as author and John Strowd[2] as printer;

(2) eight lines of doggerel, not unlike that found in Martin's *Epitome* and *Martin Senior;*[3] and (3) a humorous imprint reminiscent of four Martinist imprints.[4] Several stylistic clues indicate Throkmorton's pen. The coined word "pervertisements" is substituted for "advertisements." The familiar masculine possessive "his" is used for "its," the phrase "and you can" appears for "if you can," and the preposition "a" occurs in "now a dayes." There are fifteen Latin phrases and quotations. Anti-prelatical and anti-Catholic attitudes are revealed in the phrase "stinking portuise," in the assertion that "popes are the children of perdition," and in the references to the High Commission, the Donation of Constantine, and "pope Jones [Popess Joan]."

Irony creeps in with "your pretie using of it," "Christe in deed erred in this," and "either folish Paule and wise you, or folish you, and wise the Apostles." Sarcasm is displayed in the query, "why not a Cardinall at Canterburye," and in the remark, "speake truthe if thou can, and shame the devill." Even more caustic was the assertion that "the Psalmes would [ought] not be handled in greasie alehouse chaunters mouthes." In criticizing the Anglican prayer to be delivered from thunder and lightning, the writer revealed himself as "gibing Job" with his officious taunt, "put in too, [to be delivered] from sparrow blasting."[5] Other small indications of Throkmorton's pen are his promise or threat to publish some items despite the opposition of the bishops' officers; his allusion to the printer John Day, to a pursuivant, and to episcopal persecution. There is a reference to Demetrius, who appears as an interlocutor and usurer in Throkmorton's *The State of the Church of Englande,* and there is an allusion to Humphrey Toy the bookbinder and sleuth, who may be related to Mrs. Toy.[6]

Throkmorton's familiar phrases and clauses appear, such as "yet marke I pray you," "I tell you," "this geare," and "cleane against the truthe." Also, Throkmorton's penchant toward deliberate alliteration is seen in "just judgement," "patched Portuise," and "reprehending and reproving." There are seven parallels:

quidlibet ex quolibet (*Certaine Articles,* 141)
quidlibet ex quolibet (12:A3)

I cry them mercy (*Certaine Articles,* 139)
I crye him mercy (I:11)

inter vos autem non sic (*Certaine Articles,* 141)
inter vos autem non erit sic (*Exhortation,* 68)

loitering lubbers (*Certaine Articles,* 146)
loytering lubbers ("An Answer," fols. 460, 461)

by patches and peeces (*Certaine Articles,* 141)
by patches and pieces (10:Bii)

the state of the church (*Certaine Articles,* 146)
The State of the Church of Englande (Throkmorton's book)

no ground nor warrant in Gods book (*Certaine Articles,* 139)
sure of his grounde and warrant (10:Aii v)

---

1. In *Certaine Articles,* p. 147, the reference to the Massacre of Saint Bartholomew's Day, 24 August 1572, provides a *terminus a quo;* Whitgift's *An Answere* of November gives a *terminus ad quem. Certaine Articles, S.T.C.,* 10850, is reprinted in Frere and Douglas.

2. For Strowd, see Peel, *The Seconde Parte of a Register,* 1:10, 108–20, and Collinson, *The Elizabethan Puritan Movement,* pp. 139–40.

3. *Epitome,* signature A2 v; *Martin Senior,* signature Diii and Diii v.

4. Title pages of the *Epistle, Epitome, Hay Any Worke,* and *Martin Junior.*

5. *Certaine Articles,* pp. 142, 141, 141, 140, 141, 144. The reference to "thunder and lightning" is from the Litany; see William Benham, *The Prayer-Book of Queen Elizabeth, 1559* (Edinburgh, 1911), p. 55.

6. In *Hay Any Worke,* p. 48, Throkmorton makes a cryptic comment: "Though in deed, I never said in my life, that there was ever any great familiaritie (though I know there was some acquaintaunce) betweene mistris Toye and John Whitgift."

APPENDIX D. *A Second Admonition to the Parliament*

Unlike *An Admonition to the Parliament,* which described what was amiss in the Church of England, *A Second Admonition to the Parliament* prescribed a program of reform. Thus, it was an attempt to implement the recommendations and to supplement the findings of the first *Admonition.* It was also a protest against the imprisonment of Field and Wilcox, a defense of their actions, and a refutation of the criticisms expressed by official spokesmen such as Edwin Sandys, bishop of London, and Thomas Cooper, bishop of Lincoln. Justifying his use of hot sentences and sharp words, the author roundly accused the bishops and members of Convocation of being time-servers and sycophants, men who were motivated more by expediency and tradition than by principle and truth. Among the recommended reforms, one notes that the writer advocated an adequate salary for the underpaid clergy. This could be accomplished, he asserted, by the removal of impropriated livings controlled by the crown, by colleges, courtiers, and other secular patrons. Small parishes should be united. Ministers should be selected by the eldership and the congregation, and the individual church should be directed by the pastor, teacher, assistants or elders, and deacons. The local consistory, the conference or classis, the provincial and national synods should replace the rule of archbishops, bishops, and archdeacons, together with their various courts. Excommunication should be the prerogative of the local church, not of the chancellors, deans, commissaries, and officials principal. Much preferred was the Apostles' Creed instead of the Athanasian Creed, and more beloved was the Geneva Bible of 1560 than the Bishops' Bible of 1568. Also, strongly recommended was the preaching of the Word instead of the reading of the liturgy of the Book of Common Prayer.

The authorship of the *Second Admonition* has been attributed, without evidence, to Cartwright, Anthony Gilby, and Christopher Goodman. There are clues, however, that the author, "a practical but hot-blooded man, who wields a facile pen," was Job Throkmorton.[1] It is highly probable that the writer who penned *Certaine Articles*, and who appended it to the *Second Admonition*, was the author of both treatises. Throkmorton's irrepressible animus against the bishops is prevalent in all his writings from 1572 to 1596, and his stinging phrases in *A Second Admonition* are similar to invectives found throughout his books. Some examples are: "sencelesse asses, blindest bussarde, fat canons, cormorant masters, dolts, theevish nonresidentes, spoilers, the popes underlings, loitering and idell bellyed epicures, gredy bellied wolves." His penchant toward deliberate alliteration is a special characteristic which sets him apart from other writers: "archbuilders, not the archbishops; cleane contrary to the course; deserveth no dispraise; drawne and driven; falleth forthe; fitte furniture; foster fathers; hardly handeled; learned letters; losse of living; mistresse money; neither in matter nor manner; persecute and prisone them; the place of Peter is plaine; preservation and prosperitie; raile upon, and revile; ready and a right way; receive it or rejecte it; rightly reformed; by roate, rather than by reason; so sharpe a sight to see; that sort who are so soft set, and fat fed; stiffe and sturdie; veriest varlets; this were a worldy wise way; we wot not what." Furthermore, there are many familiar phrases, common and ordinary but noteworthy because of their overuse: "it must needes passe, we wold be sory, put you in minde, I canne tell you, out of square, I should be lothe, I dare say, give over, if this be true."

Another characteristic of Throkmorton's works and the *Second Admonition* is the use of colorful, strong, and unusual words. Some examples are: "afterclaps, bawdie, brawned, caveats, currishly, flap, fisking, frie, galleth, hainous, minse, nobilitating, privities, pratling, quiresters, ribaude, seered, stomacke, surbatted, sustentation, totquots, trialities, ulcer, underprop." Throkmorton provides variety by the use of Latin words and phrases, and interjects an occasional proverb—"ill will (they say) never said well." His habit of using double negatives is seen in such expressions as "nor he may not have that," in "can never be no priestes after," and in "nor for any of God his matters neither." His use of the personal pronoun for the reflexive and the omission of "to" or "for" are exemplified in "and gette them officers, wrong offered us, if they wil keepe them to the truth, I reporte me to these examples." Irony is utilized: "the men that sette upon them, are no worsse men than bishops;" "that is a thing that I would gladly learne;" "the persones that are thoughte to have made them, are laide in no worsse prison than Newgate."[2]

Another feature appearing in the *Second Admonition* and Throkmorton's writings is his choice of favorite subjects, since he repeatedly deals with prisons, persecutions, and martyrs; with the Court of High Commission, excommunication, discipline, lord bishops, and Convocation; with the ex officio oath, praemunire, and role of civil magistrats; with polity and ceremonies. Other small touches include his emphasis on acting in accordance with a sensitive conscience, his oft reiterated promise or threat to write book against an opponent, and his accusations of bribery or usury. We also find references to "olde Doctor Turner," Théodore de Bèze, and Bishop John Hooper, who are mentioned in Martin's books,[3] and to John Day and Humphrey Toy, as "persecuting printers," who are alluded to in *Certaine Articles* (page 148).

There are enough parallels of language and of ideas to indicate Throkmorton's pen and mind. About forty of his ideas as set forth in Martin's writings cohere with his views in *A Second Admonition*.[4] In the following list of sixteen parallels, each first line is taken from this treatise:

> within the compasse of suche statutes (91)
> within the compasse of the statute (1:1)
>
> he is not so narowly loked unto (101)
> if he were narrowly loked into (7:111)
>
> lette the Worde of God have the free course (103)
> let the Gospell have a free course (I:28)
>
> the pope of Lambeth (111)
> the pope of Lambeth (I:17, 26)
>
> Her Majestie of her wonted rare clemencie (130)
> Her Majestie of her wounted clemency (2:8)
>
> that is a thing that I would gladly learne (90)
> I would gladlie knowe for my learning (10:Ciii v)
> I would faine know for my learning (12:A3)
>
> this dung shall be throwne openly in their faces (91)
> their dung be . . . throwne into their faces (*Exhortation*, 61)

with a single eye (86)
with a single eie (6:A3 v) with a sengle [*sic*] eye (3:38)

a boye of ten yeares olde (101)
a boye of twelve yeare olde (VII:28)

the prescripte of the Woorde of God (100)
the certaine prescript rule of the Worde (II:B4 v)

the blindest bussarde (101)
so buzzardly blynde (3:39)

face oute the matter (107) it will be faced out (99)
face it out (6:C4 v) (I:33) (II:F2 v)

to the greedy use of many cormorant masters (96)
to the spoyle of such cormorants (VII:18)

daunger of a premunire (93)
danger of a premunire (I:21)

we flie to the lawes of this realme (130)
it is Her Majesties authoritie we flye to (130)
I have made bold to flye unto your Lordship (8:1)
I like better to flye to that hav[en] (8:1)

ministers that strain curtesie to forbeare to lie (117)
he strayneth a little curtesie with the *Learned Discourse* (II:D3)

---

1. A. F. Scott Pearson rightly rejected Cartwright's authorship. Gilby's and Goodman's writings do not reveal similar phrases, diction, topics, or alliteration.

2. *A Second Admonition*, pp. 88, 90. Printed in Frere and Douglas, *Puritan Manifestoes*. The original edition is rare.

3. Ibid., pp. 104, 82, 112; *Epistle*, p. 43; *Epitome*, signatures D3 v and F3; *Hay Any Worke*, p. 21; *Martin Junior*, signature Civ v.

4. Ideas such as: dioceses including several shires are too large, strange fire, ostentation of learning, a free conference, commingling of civil and ecclesiastical jurisdiction, learning Dean Nowell's *Catechism* by rote, Noah's nakedness and Ham's act, education of divinity students, lenient treatment of papists.

APPENDIX E. "A Friendly Caveat to Bishop Sands"

One of the most impertinent letters which Throkmorton ever wrote was entitled: "A Friendly Caveat to Bishop Sands

Then Bishop of London, and to the Rest of His Brethren the Bishops: Written by a Godly, Learned, and Zealous Gentleman, about 1567" [1573].[1] Like his two *Exhortations* of 1572, this letter was written on behalf of Field and Wilcox. After they had been imprisoned for nine months, the Privy Council on 20 March 1572/73 recommended that Edwin Sandys seek "to bring them to conformitie, and thereupon to shew them more favour." About 30 March they were transferred to the custody of John Mullins, archdeacon of London. On 30 April the prisoners petitioned Bishop Sandys "to set them at libertie or at the least to be in their owne houses." On the same day the bishop informed Lord Burghley that several noblemen had written letters on behalf of the prisoners, and he complained that "the whole blame is layde on me for ther imprisonment." Consequently, he requested Burghley to relieve him of his unpleasant responsibility.[2] By June the prisoners had been confined for twelve months, but their sentence of a year actually began after their arraignment on 2 October 1572. Believing that the Privy Council desired their liberty, and misconceiving that Sandys was the one who delayed the prisoners' release, Throkmorton in June rebuked the bishop in his chiding and obtrusive letter for persecuting God's children. He stigmatized Sandys as "a dissembling hypocrite," as "shamelesse and wicked," and as "Master Doctor Drawbacke in the band, with the rest of your mates." Then he added: "without all hypocrisie or deceite I cannot chuse, but lay unto your charge all the want of reformation of the Churche, and oppression of your brethren, that hath been since you were first consecrated."[3]

Indications of Throkmorton's authorship are seen in his charge of persecution, ridicule of Bishop Cooper as a "maggot-a-pie," and criticism of papist-minded and promotion-seeking clergy. He emphasized his own sensitive conscience and principles, and threatened to write another work, a treatise for the queen, designed to disclose the bishops' "usurped titles and other abuses." He utilized nine Latin expressions, quoted five proverbs, appended one stanza of doggerel, and twice resorted to the double negative. Although he accused the bishops of harping "upon one string," he himself sounded the familiar notes of lord bishop, dignities, seared consciences, cruel oppression, withstanders of reformation, precepts of men, hypocrisy, and sycophantic complacency. Throughout his letter he used at least a dozen familiar phrases, and resorted to his deliberate alliteration: "doctrine and doinges," "doting divinitie," "hunting and hawking," "leape if you list," "like lambes of Libanus," "loftie looke," "points and partes," "reject and refuse," "requiring a reformation," "stumble not at the stinging stile," "sufficient sureties."

The derision and name-calling are pronounced. Bishops were called "proud Pythagorasses, timeservers, men pleasing mungerelles, popish wolves, idle overseers, slow preaching pastours, bussards, beasts, interimistical traditioners." Then came the crowning insult to the "bellie filling, but small flocke feeding divines:" "But now, for as much as like blinde bayardes yee hoppe, the longer the worse, I am right gladd, that divers good and godlie men, set too their hand to make an end of the rodde, which I hope, afore it bee long, will make your proude buttockes to smart."[4]

The following ten parallels indicate similarities in language and ideas appearing in Throkmorton's and Martin's writings. Fortunately, he repeats himself, and thus it is possible to perceive the author behind the distinctive style and diction. In each first line the page number refers to Throkmorton's letter to Bishop Sandys, as printed in *A Parte of a Register.*

a Spade must be called a Spade (371)
I must needs call a Spade a Spade (II:A2)

I care not, if I helpe you my selfe (379)
I care not if they be sett downe (I:13)
I care not an [if] I now leave masse Deanes Worship (I:19)

bieflesse, and fat brewes (380)
beefe and brewesse (I:32)

with a great traine of Ruffians after you, and your Gentlemen
Ushers afore you (378)

did his gentlman Usher go bareheaded before him? (II:F3)
to bee in the traine of an English Priest (VI:Bi)

as woulde overthrow the whole state of the Realme (372)
as for the overthrowe of the whole state (*Exhortation*, 64)
to seeke the overthrowe of the state (VI:Civ v)

your companions white coates doinges (372)
a fewe white coates stande for hundred poundes (*Certaine Articles*, 139)

that can neither rule, neither your selves, neither your wives,
nor your children, nor the rest of your familie (378)
reform your families and your children (I:53)

a rule and warraunt out of Gods Worde (374)
neither rule nor warrant in the whole Scripture of God (10: Diii v)

for never a barrel is the better herring (378)
never a barrel better hearring (7:68)

yea, I my selfe hearde one maggot-a-pie [Bishop Cooper]
of your profession, opening afore the Queene and the Counsell, boldlie and stoutly say, and an other at Paules Crosse,
that there is no church in Europe better reformed than this
is; and that all things were so well, as were possible to bee
in the Primitive church (373)
[Bishop Cooper] protested before God, and the congregation
where he stood, that there was not in the world at this day;
nay there had not bin since the Apostles time, such a flourishing estate of a Church, as we have now in England (I:33)[5]

---

1. Printed in 1593, *A Parte of a Register*, pp. 371–81. The title of the letter was supplied by the anonymous editor of *A Parte* (*S.T.C.*, 10400). Edwin Sandes or Sandys was consecrated bishop of Worcester in 1559, confirmed as bishop of London in 1570, and became archbishop of York in March 1576/77. He died 10 July 1588.
2. Sandys's three letters to Burghley are printed in Frere and Douglas, *Puritan Manifestoes*, pp. 152–55.
3. "A Friendly Caveat," *A Parte of a Register*, pp. 376, 373.
4. Ibid., p. 375. The marginal note reads: "B[ishops] blinde bussards."
5. There are two other similar passages in Cooper, "A Defence of the Ceremonies," a manuscript in the "Seconde Parte of a Register," vol. B, part 2, fols. 236–37, in Dr. Williams's Library. See Peel, *The Seconde Parte*

of a Register, 1:125. The second passage is in Cooper, *An Admonition to the People of England*, pp. 64–65 of the first edition of 252 pages.

APPENDIX F. *The State of the Church of Englande*

About March or April 1588, Waldegrave printed in London a book, *The State of the Church of Englande, Laide Open in a Conference betweene Diotrephes a Bishop, Tertullus a Papist, Demetrius an Usurer, Pandocheus an Inne-Keeper, and Paule a Preacher of the Worde of God.* On 16 April Waldegrave's shop "at the sign of the Crane in St. Paul's Churchyard" was raided and most of these books were confiscated. On 13 May by the full court of the Stationers' Company the books were ordered to be burned, and it was further ordered that Waldegrave's "presse, letters and printinge stuffe [be] defaced and made unserviceable."[1]

The State of the Church of Englande, sometimes referred to as *Diotrephes* or as a *Dialogue*, is really a new vehicle to convey the old and cherished ideas of Throkmorton.[2] It is a dialogue which occurs at an English inn. Diotrephes, an Anglican bishop, and Tertullus, a papist, both traveling from Scotland, encounter Demetrius, a usurer, and Paul, a Puritan preacher, both coming from London. In their conversations Paul, as the mouthpiece of Throkmorton, praises the Puritans and advocates frequent sermons; he denounces clerical simony and oppression; he decries the bishops as too worldly, too much concerned with their titles and dignities, and too eager to seek ecclesiastical promotions. Paul also accuses the prelates of misinforming and misleading the queen and of mistreating the Puritans, her loyal subjects, by silencing, deprivation, and imprisonment. He stresses Throkmorton's familiar complaint of the lack of a learned ministry. To counter this point, Diotrephes asks his Catholic friend "what shall wee doe to make the worlde beleeve we would have the ministery learned"? Tertullus replies that the clergy should learn by rote a part of Alexander Nowell's *Catechism* or Heinrich Bullinger's "Decades."[3] Since Throkmorton frequently complained against alleged favorable treatment accorded papists, it is not surprising that Tertullus pleads for lenient treatment of Catholics and for a relaxation of the laws against them. In case it was necessary to imprison them, the papist added, they ought to be given the "best chambers" and accorded the full liberties of the prison, but if the Puritans should be incarcerated, they should "have the most stincking place that can be found." Tertullus, having ingratiated himself with the Anglican, Bishop Diotrephes, and gradually becoming his initimate counselor, suggests that the Puritans should steadily and cautiously be reduced in power by keeping them out of royal chapels, chaplainships, collegiate fellowships and headships, and by denying them access to the pulpit at Paul's Cross.[4]

Although anonymous, *The State of the Church of Englande* has been assigned to John Udall by Arber, Dexter, Pierce, Peel, and McGinn. The British Museum *General Catalogue* lists it as an anonymous item and also as Udall's work, and the *Short-Title Catalogue* assigns it both to Udall and Penry. There is no convincing evidence for these attributions, however, and despite the conjectures of the last hundred years the book may be assigned with high probability to Throkmorton, who referred to it in his *Epistle* as "my frend and deare brother Diotrephes his *Dialogue*," and as "my friend Tertullus in the poore *Dialogue* that the bishops lately burned."[5] There is a possible hint here that Throkmorton is expressing his resentment because his own book was ordered to be burned.

The reasons for attributing *The State of the Church of Englande* to Throkmorton, despite the consensus in Udall's favor, deserve careful consideration. It should be noted that the book is not written in Udall's manner of writing.[6] When Udall was adjudged guilty of felony by the justices of Assize at Croydon for writing *A Demonstration of Discipline*, he was not accused of writing *The State of the Church of Englande*, although he had been interrogated by Judge Edmund Anderson about this book six months previously, on 13 January 1589/90. Again, it should be remembered that all the ascriptions of *The State of the Church of Englande* to Udall ultimately derive from the testimony of Nicholas Tomkins, a servant of Elizabeth Crane. Tomkins conjectured that John Davidson or more likely Udall was the author, since he had seen a catalog in Udall's possession which listed a dialogue of 1588.[7] On this one conjecture of Tomkins, the warning of Richard Hooker is apropos: "Though ten persons be brought to give testimonie in any cause, yet if the knowledge they have of the thing whereunto they come as witnesses appeare to have growen from some one amongst them, and to have spred it selfe from hand to hand, they all are in force but as one testimonie."[8] We may conclude that the evidence for Udall's authorship is weak.

Dean Sutcliffe was the best informed critic of Throkmorton and also the author of two books on Udall and Throkmorton. When Sutcliffe ascribed to the Haseley squire his "dialogues," he implied that the first dialogue of 1588, *The State of the Church of Englande*, and the second dialogue of 1589, *A Dialogue. Wherin Is Plainly Laide Open*, were both written by Throkmorton. When we compare these two works, we find that they correspond to each other in form, diction, style of writing, and recurrent ideas. Both were printed by Waldegrave. Throkmorton's favorite and colorful words are apparent: "bawds, break-necke, bridle, chollericke, cloyed, derogation, descried, eversion, hangbies, jugling, kicke, mislike, nay soft, peevish, rayling hypocrits, sawcie, tendring," and "sleevelesse answere." Seventeen of Throkmorton's common phrases appear, such as "we care not, I tell you, I pray you (twenty times), in your eare, serve our turnes, what say you, I warrant you," and the ironic "I thank you." Many of Throkmorton's familiar themes and topics recur: alterations, bribery, chaplains, college heads, conscience, discipline, episcopal dignities and privileges, innovations, lord bishops, nonresidency, persecution, pluralism, preferment, prisons, subscription, supplications, and usury. One finds allusions to Puritan books, such as Cartwright's *The Second Replie agaynst Maister Whitgiftes Second Answer* (1575), Laurence Chaderton's *A Fruitful Sermon upon . . . the 12 Chapter of the Epistle to the Romanes* (1584), William Fulke's *A Briefe and Plaine Declaration (A Learned Discourse)* (1584), Dudley Fenner's *Counter-Poyson, Modestly Written for the Time* (1584 or 1585), and Walter Travers' *A Defence of the Ecclesiastical Discipline* (1588), all of which are mentioned in the Marprelate books.

Throkmorton's style is evidenced by his use of proverbs, a Latin phrase, a pun, as well as by his resort to irony, sarcasm, and satire. It is further illustrated by his constant utilization of alliteration: "the Cananit[e]s (I should say) the Canonists; a consent and conformitie; clean contrarye; made manifest unto all men; it muste needes make him mute; I perceive he is one of these peevish puritanes; sectes and schismes; stand you in such great steed; stand stiffe; unreverently and uncharitably; unlearned and unsufficient; wax worse and worse."

There are thirty parallels in language and ideas which clearly indicate Throkmorton's pen. In the following list, the page number of the first line of each example is taken from Arber's edition of Udall, *The State of the Church of England*, no. 5 in The English Scholar's Library of Old and Modern Works (London, 1879). Page references to *A Second Admonition* and to the *Exhortation* are from the editions in Frere and Douglas, *Puritan Manifestoes*. Other references to Martin's and Throkmorton's works are the same as the roman and arabic numbers listed in chapter six.

I will make thee kiss the Clinke for this geare (22)
you will for all this lustines, kisse the Clinke or Gatehouse for this geare (6:C4)

the Clynke, Gate-house, White-lyon (22)
the Clinke, Gatehouse or White Lyon (6:D1 v)

the Clynke, Gate-house, White-lyon, and the Fleet, have bin your onely argumentes whereby you have proved your cause (22)
there is a better way for Bishops, and Bishops of Christ, to confute a schisme by, than prisons and chaines: those were and are Antichristes bishops argumentes (*Exhortation*, 71)

give over their bishoppricks (10)
give over your bishopdomes (V:Ciii v)

such chollericke fellowes as you (14)
my Lord of Winchester [Cooper] is very chollericke (I:2)
Thomas of Winchester [Cooper] is a cholerick member (IV:30)

laye open your former speches (8) lay open the sinne (14)
layd open the very quintessence (III:t.p.)
laying open of their bishopprickes (VII:18)
laide open the tyrannicall dealing of lord bishopps (6:t.p.)
laid open in his coulers (7:t.p.)

if it please your Lordship (5)
may it please your Lordship (8:1—letter to Lord Hatton)

greene heades (11)
green heads (II:B2)

I do therfore much marvail (12)
I doe much marvell (II:A2 v)

some of which bookes [by Cartwright] have beene extant this
  dozen yeres (10)
Cartwrights workes, nowe a dozen yeares extant and more
  (6:A3 v)

I dealt somwhat roundly (14)
I dealt plainlie and roundly (10:Bi)

your owne Ordinary to whom you are sworne, to give canon-
  ical obedience (15)
was there canonicall obedience sworne to Archbishopp Titus
  (II:F3)

we have received many a foyle (27)
you first have received the foyle (I:3)

if all wee were turned out (17)
if . . . Lords weare turned out to grasse (IV:6)
if I turne you not all out of your places (VI:Aiii)

with a single eie (18)
with a single eie (6:A3 v)
with a single eye (*Second Admonition*, 86)

stinke in the nostrels both of God and man (20)
smelling in the nostrels of Her Majestie and the State (IV:t.p.)

looke so narrowly into the cause (21)
if he were narrowly loked into (7:III)
he is not so narowly loked unto (*Second Admonition*, 101)

is tooth and naile (20)
with tooth and naile (II:E1 v)
with tooth and naile (VI:Aiii v)

which Christe himselfe hath prescribed in his Word (21)
which God hath prescribed in the Worde (II:D1)

fire and fagotte (27)
fire, and fagot (V:Aii v)

care . . . but for a byshoppricke (22)
assure him of a bishoppricke (6:D1)
to get a bishoppricke (6:C4 v)
suche as gape after bishoppricks (6:D2)

I will tell you one thing in your eare (28)
to tell you my opinion in your eare (I:44)

yet it easeth my stomacke to tell it (7)
after that his Grace had eased his stomacke in calling him
  "boy," "knave," "varlet" (I:30)

both in Court and countrie (23)
eyther from countrie or Court (II:A2 v)

neither in matter nor maner (24)
bothe in matter and manner (*Second Admonition*, 93)
neither in methode, matter, nor manner (10:Aiii)

lose his credit (24)
loose his credite (7:86)
loose my credit (7:86)

enemies to the Gospel (23)
enemies of the Gospell (I:25)

he setteth men together by the eares (31)
the puritane and the vicker will goe by the eares (6:D4 v)

at that dead lift (25)
at a dead lift (I:7 margin)

doe stand stiffe against us (11)
stood stiffe in their former opinions (II:B1 v)

1. W. W. Greg and E. Boswell, eds., *Records of the Court of the Stationers'
Company, 1576 to 1602, from Register B*, pp. 27–28.

337

2. Dexter considers *The State of the Church of Englande* as "the pioneer" of the Marprelate series and as "a little pilot balloon sent up to test the direction and force of the wind then blowing" (*Congregationalism*, pp. 139–42). It was reprinted in *A Parte of a Register* (1593).

3. *The State of the Church of England*, p. 29, and *A Second Admonition*, p. 110.

4. *The State of the Church of England*, pp. 24–30.

5. *Epistle*, pp. 6, 13.

6. It is written in Throkmorton's manner of writing. Of the twelve stylistic characteristics discussed in chapter seven, eight are found in *The State of the Church of Englande*.

7. For Tomkins, see Arber, *Introductory Sketch*, pp. 85, 87. On page 87, section 9, Arber has misread the manuscript. It should be: "But he knoweth that Udall was the author of the *Demonstration of Disciplyne* for that Udall hym selfe tolde hym so and that he saw in Kyngeston upon Thames either in Udalls owne house or Chelsonnes howse a catalog of such books as Udall had Mad[e] [dyd make—crossed out] and printed, and in that catalog he sawe that book of *Demonstration of Discipline* for one." Section 11 reads: "To the eleventh he sayethe that he beleaveth that Udall was the author of *Diotrephes* bicause he sawe that book allso in the sayde catalog and bicause he is a northerne man." This one conjecture by Tomkins is outweighed by other evidence which points to Throkmorton's authorship. Tomkins also named Davidson as a possible author. See Harley MSS. 6848, fols. 81, 89.

8. *Of the Lawes of Ecclesiasticall Politie* (1593), pp. 23–24.

Appendix G. Anonymous Relevant Works in the *Short-Title Catalogue:* Confirmations, Rejections, and Suggestions of Authorship

S.T.C.

534—Probably T. Nashe
681—By A. L.; see 15102
1344—By Bancroft. Also 1345
1351—By Penry
1352—By Bancroft
1521—By Throkmorton, not Barrow
2021—By de Bèze
4712—Not by Cartwright
4713—By Throkmorton, not Cartwright
5147—Printed at London by Robert Waldegrave
5815—By R. Cosin
5820—By R. Cosin
5821—By R. Cosin

5823—By R. Cosin
6006—Cranmer, Parker, Haddon, Cheke, Foxe?
6805—By Throkmorton
7584—Cf. 7739; 7585 reprints 7584, 7739, 10397
7739—Printed by Waldegrave
7754—Printed at Edinburgh by Robert Waldegrave
10392—By Throkmorton
10393—Not by Cartwright. Possibly by Henry Howard
10394—Probably by a Puritan lawyer
10395—By William Fulke
10396—By Throkmorton, not Udall. See 24505
10397—Reprinted, *A Parte of a Register*. See 10400
10400—Printed at Middelburg by Schilders
10770—By Fenner
10771—By Fenner
10772—Not by Fenner; probably by Throkmorton partly
10850—By Throkmorton, who defended the *Admonition*
12342—By Throkmorton; printed at La Rochelle in 1589 by Waldegrave
12914—By Richard Harvey
17452—Probably by Nashe
17453-17459—By Throkmorton
17460—By Throkmorton, not Penry. See 6805
17461—Anti-Martinist
17462—Anti-Martinist
17463—By Lyly or Nashe?
17464—By Lyly?
17465—By Lyly?
19292a—Not by Throkmorton
19450—Probably by Nashe
19456—Probably by Nashe
19457—Probably by Nashe
19603—By Penry
19611—By Penry
20201—Printed by Robert Waldegrave. Reprinted, *A Parte of a Register*
20881—By M. Sutcliffe
21769—Not by Throkmorton. Probably by Tyndale
23318—Stoughton
23628—Not T. Turswell; probably T. Tymme
24499—By John Udall
24505—By Throkmorton, not Udall

The above fifty-nine items are taken from the first edition of Pollard and Redgrave, *A Short-Title Catalogue*. In the second edition (1976), volume 2, I-Z, there is a new item, no. 19903a.5, by Piers, the Ploughman, *O Read Me*, supposedly written by "the Gransier of Martin Mare-prelitte." These proof sheets, which repeat or paraphrase some of the language of Martin Marprelate, probably were issued in London about 1589.

In Wing, *A Short-Title Catalogue, 1641–1700*, there are three relevant items:

B 343   Francis Bacon, *A Wise and Moderate Discourse* (1641, which is the first printed edition. It was reprinted in 1663, with the title: *True Peace, or a Moderate Discourse to Compose the Unsettled Conscience and Greatest Differences in Ecclesiastical Affaires*. Both of these editions are derived from a manuscript in the Bodleian Library, E. Mus 55, with help from Additional MS. 4263, item 10, and Harley MSS. 3795, item 21, both in the British Library. The original title was "An Advertisement Touching the Controversies of the Church of England," which appeared anonymously in 1589.

C 1987   *The Character of a Puritan*. A reprint of 1643. There is a second edition of 1640, entitled *A Dialogue. Wherin Is Plainly Layd Open the Tyrannicall Dealing of Lord Bishopps against Gods Children*. The first edition is in Pollard and Redgrave, *Short-Title Catalogue*, no. 6805. Throkmorton was the author.

R 741   *Reformation No Enemie*, 1641. This is a second edition of *Hay Any Worke for Cooper*, 1589, by Throkmorton, with a new title.

APPENDIX H

APPENDIX H. **Job Throkmorton's Petition to Lord Treasurer Burghley (Endorsement: "3 Aprill 1587")**

May it please your Honor. To challenge any favor from your L[ordship] by deserte I can not: yet to dispayre of your favor for all that I may not. The lesse deserte the more honor to yow. Neyther am I the first man, I know, by many a hundred to whom yow have stoode an honorable frynde [friend] without cause. My faulte I were to blame, yf I would excuse. I doe heere confesse it before your L[ordship] with sorowe of harte. Yet my prayer is that it be not overstrayned into so hurtefull a sense. I have reade indeede long agoe, but I never felt it by experience till now: That th' indignation of the Prince was death. A just judgement of God (I confesse) uppon me for my unpenitent lyfe. Yet was it the first tyme that ever I so faulted, and in nature (as I take it) no contempte but meere unadvysednesse. In weight no desloyaultye but rashenesse. The priviledge of the place [House of Commons] apte enough to bring a young heade into a distemperature. I would to Christ thease consyderaciones might be some leni-tyve to her Highnesse indignation towards me. For the which my humble sute is that your L[ordship] would vouch-safe me what favor yow may when yow see your tyme. I say no more. But the Lorde moove your harte to somme tender compassion of my estate. The same God blesse your gray heares [hairs] with comforte, that as yow have lyved in honor, so yow may dye in peace, with peace of conscience for ever.

Humbly at your L[ordships] commaundement
Job Throkm[or]ton

British Library
Lansdowne Manuscripts 53
    item 71, folio 148
[Reproduced by permission of the British Library Board]

342

May it please yo'r hono'r: To challenge any favo'r from yo'r L: by deserte I can not yet to dispayre of yo'r favo'r for all that I may not: The losse deserve the move. hono'r to yo, neyther am I the first man I knew by many a hundred, to whom y have stoode an honorable frynde w'thout cause. my faulte I were to blame, yf I would excuse. I doe heere cofesse it before yo'r L: w'th sorow of harte: yet my

too hurtful a prayer is that it be not over strayned in'to too hurtful a sense: I have read indeede long agoe, but I never felt it by experience till now. That th'indignation of the Prince was death: A Just Judgm't of god I cofesse uppon me for my unpenitent lyfe: yet was it the first tyme that ever I so faulted. & in naturl (as I take it) no cotempt but meere unadvysednesse. In weight no dysloyaltye but rashenesse, The priviledge of the place ayd enough to bring a yong heade into a distempature: I would to Christ those cosyderacions might be some senityve to her highnesse indignation toward me: for the w'th my humble suit is that yo'r L: would vouchsafe me what favo'r yo may when yo see yo'r tyme: I say no more. But the Lorde moove yo'r haste to some tender cosideracion of my estate: The same god blesse yo'r ayay hearts w'th comforte, that as yo have lyved in hono'r so yo may dye in peace w'th peace of coscience for ever

Humbly at yo'r L: Comaundem't

Joh Throkmorton

NOTES—Introduction

1. Martin Marprelate, Martin Senior, Martin Junior, Gravener, Grivel, Johnson, Juell, Robinson, Stone, Tomson, and Warner. He also addressed Augustine Maicocke as "May" and John Bowman as "Archer."

2. Henry VIII, c. 1, *The Statutes of the Realm*, 11 vols. in 12 (London, 1810–28), 3:492. The phrase, "Supreme Heede," occurs in the Act of 1533. See ibid., p. 427.

3. 1 Elizabeth, c. 1, sections vii, ix, ibid., 4, pt. 1:350–55.

4. For the Convocation of 1562/63, see Edward Cardwell, *Synodalia. A Collection of Articles of Religion, Canons, and Proceedings of Convocations in the Province of Canterbury, from the Year 1547 to the Year 1717*, 2 vols. (Oxford, 1842), 1:34–72; 2:495–527. See also Edmund Gibson, *Synodus Anglicana*, ed. Edward Cardwell (Oxford, 1854), pp. 145–63. See further William P. Haugaard, *Elizabeth and the English Reformation. The Struggle for a Stable Settlement of Religion* (Cambridge, 1968), and Carl S. Meyer, *Elizabeth I and the Religious Settlement of 1559* (St. Louis, [1960]).

5. The best work on Cartwright is by A. F. Scott Pearson, *Thomas Cartwright and Elizabethan Puritanism, 1535–1603* (Cambridge, 1925).

6. *An Admonition* was published about 10 June in black letter, without a title page and indication of printer, place, or date. In late June Field and Wilcox were imprisoned at Newgate, and on 11 September confessed they were the authors. A second edition appeared about July, with changes possibly made by Job Throkmorton, and a reprint of the new edition was published before 25 August. John Strowd, a deprived clergyman, was probably the printer. The anonymous *A Second Admonition to the Parliament* appeared about October-November, lacking a title page and imprint. Although Cartwright has been commonly thought to be the author (*S.T.C.*, 4713), Pearson positively rejected the ascription (*Thomas Cartwright*, p. 74). It has been conjectured that Christopher Goodman was the author, but this attribution may be rejected because of stylistic differences. The style of writing is very close to that of Job Throkmorton, as indicated in App. D. See W. H. Frere and C. E. Douglas, eds., *Puritan Manifestoes. A Study of the Origin of the Puritan Revolt. With a Reprint of the Admonition to the Parliament and Kindred Documents, 1572* [and of *A Second Admonition*] (London, 1907; reprinted 1954), pp. vii–xxx. See also Donald J. McGinn, *The Admonition Controversy* (New Brunswick, N.J., 1949).

7. Whitgift's *Answere* (London, 1572), was published in November and two new editions appeared in 1573. Cartwright's *A Replye* was published in April 1573 by John Strowd near London, and a second edition followed two months later. These two editions are misdated as 1574 in the *S.T.C.*, 4711, 4712. In February 1573/74 Whitgift's *Defense* was published; it was an-

swered in *The Second Replie of Thomas Cartwright: Agaynst Maister Doctor Whitgiftes Second Answer, touching the Churche Discipline* ([Heidelberg: Michael Schirat], 1575), and also in *The Rest of the Second Replie of Thomas Cartwright: Agaynst Master Whitgifts Second Answer, touching Church Discipline* ([Basel: Thomas Guarinus, 1577]). See A. F. Johnson, "Books Printed at Heidelberg for Thomas Cartwright," *The Library* 2 (March 1948): 284–86. *Epistle*, pp. 3, 17.

8. For the articles, subscription, and opposition thereto, see John Strype, *The Life and Acts of John Whitgift, D.D.*, 3 vols. (Oxford, 1822), 1:227–60; Patrick Collinson, *The Elizabethan Puritan Movement* (London, 1967), pp. 243–48.

9. Mary Ballantine Hume, "The History of the Oath *ex officio* in England" (Radcliffe College Ph.D. dissertation, 1923—H922); also her article, Mary Hume Maguire, "Attack of the Common Lawyers on the Oath *ex officio* as Administered in the Ecclesiastical Courts in England," *Essays in History and Political Theory in Honor of Charles Howard McIlwain* (Cambridge, Mass., 1936), pp. 199–229.

10. Bridges' *Defence* (London, 1587) has a long title of twenty-five lines. It was a reply not only to Fulke's book but also to Théodore de Bèze's *Judgement*, and to arguments of Calvin, Lambert Danaeus, Robertus Caenalis or Cenalis, and Jean Bodin.

11. (London: Robert Waldegrave, 1584). The article in the *D.N.B.* on Walter Travers wrongly assigns this book to him. W. W. Greg, *A Companion to Arber* (Oxford, 1967), pp. 35–36, says that Travers' *De disciplina ecclesiae sacra ex Dei verbo descripta* "is apparently not extant," but was "printed as *A Brief and Plain Declaration.*" The manuscript "De disciplina" is extant, and was printed by Francis Paget, *An Introduction to the Fifth Book of Hooker's Treatise of the Laws of Ecclesiastical Polity* (Oxford, 1899), pp. 238–51. *A Briefe and Plaine Declaration* is a different book written by William Fulke. The *Ecclesiasticae Disciplinae et Anglicanae . . . Explicatio* ([Heidelberg: Michael Schirat], 1574), was published; it was translated by Cartwright as *A Full and Plaine Declaration* ([Heidelberg: Michael Schirat], 1574). See A. F. Johnson, "Books Printed at Heidelberg for Thomas Cartwright," *The Library* 2 (March 1948): 284–86.

12. Translated by John Field ([London: Robert Waldegrave, ca. 1580]). John Lyon, eighth Lord Glammis, and Scotland's lord high chancellor, desired the judgment of de Bèze on episcopacy. Replying to his query, de Bèze sent his answer, about 1576, called "de triplici episcopatu." See Gordon Donaldson, *The Scottish Reformation* (Cambridge, 1960), p. 191. See further Collinson, *The Elizabethan Puritan Movement*, pp. 110, 477, n. 2. Frédéric Gardy and Alain Dufour, editors of *Bibliographie des oeuvres . . . de Théodore de Bèze* (Geneva, 1960), question the attribution (p. 161).

13. Fenner's book was published at Middelburg by Richard Schilders. Its full title is *A Defence of the Godlie Ministers, against the Slaunders of D. Bridges, Contayned in His Answere to the Preface before the Discourse of Ecclesiasticall Governement, with a Declaration of the Bishops Proceeding against Them.* Bridges, in his *Defence*, pp. 1–53, replied to the "Praeface," leaves 2–4, of *A Briefe and Plaine Declaration*, which is the same as the *Discourse*, or "A Learned

Discourse of Ecclesiasticall Government." Travers' *A Defence* was published by Richard Schilders at Middelburg. Fenner's and Travers' books preceded Throkmorton's attack on Dr. Bridges by a few months.

14. Throkmorton's "Speech on the Low Countries" is in the Pierpont Morgan Library, Phillipps MS. 13891, reclassified as MA 276, fols. 3–9. Burghley's letter to Douglas is in Margaret Warrender, *Illustrations of Scottish History. Sixteenth Century* (Edinburgh, 1889), pp. 31–33. For Penry, see *Th'Appellation of John Penri, unto the Highe Court of Parliament, from the Bad and Injurious Dealing of the Archbishop of Canterbury and Other His Colleagues of the High Commission* ([La Rochelle: Robert Waldegrave], 1589), pp. 3–7, 39–43. His letter to Field is summarized in Ellesmere MS. 2148, fol. 85. This manuscript, at the Henry E. Huntington Library, San Marino, California, is entitled "Mr. John Penrye[s] Proceeding upon Couler of a Pretended Reformation," and is an important compilation of extracts from Martinist depositions, hitherto unused. For Waldegrave, see Edward Arber, *A Transcript of the Registers of the Company of Stationers of London; 1554–1640 A.D.*, 5 vols. (London, 1875–94), 1:248, 372, 501, 507, 512, 517, 528; 2:102, 106, 282, 848; 3:237; 5:lii. See also W. W. Greg and E. Boswell, eds., *Records of the Court of the Stationers' Company, 1576 to 1602, from Register B* (London, 1930), pp. 27–28. For Udall, see *A New Discovery of Old Pontificall Practises for the Maintenance of the Prelates Authority and Hierarchy* (London, 1643), pp. 1–25 et passim. Matthew Sutcliffe's reply to Udall is in *A Remonstrance: or Plaine Detection of Some of the Faults and Hideous Sores of Such Sillie Syllogismes and Impertinent Allegations, as out of Sundrie Factious Pamphlets and Rhapsodies, Are Cobled up together in a Booke, Entituled, A Demonstration of Discipline* (London, 1590 [1591]). (*S.T.C.*, 20881).

15. The *Epistle* has a long title of twenty lines. It begins: *Oh Read Over D. John Bridges, for It Is a Worthy Worke: Or an Epitome of the Fyrste Booke, of That Right Worshipfull Volume, Written against the Puritanes, in the Defence of the Noble Cleargie, by as Worshipfull a Prieste, John Bridges, Presbyter, Priest or Elder, Doctor of Divillitie, and Deane of Sarum . . . The Epitome Is Not Yet Published, but It Shall Be When the Bishops Are at Convenient Leysure to View the Same. In the Meanetime, Let Them Be Content with This Learned Epistle.* Allegedly the book was "printed oversea, in Europe, within two furlongs of a Bounsing Priest," but actually was printed at East Molesey, Surrey, near the Thames and Hampton Court Palace, by Waldegrave in October 1588.

16. *Epistle,* p. 5.

17. For praemunire, see 25 Edward III, statute 4, "The Statute of Provisors or Benefices," *Statutes of the Realm*, 1:316–18; 16 Richard II, c. 5, ibid., 2:85–86; 25 Henry VIII, c. 20, section vi, "An Acte Restrayning the Payment of Annates," ibid., 3:462–64.

18. 13 Elizabeth, c. 12. "A priest or minister of Godes holy Word" . . . shall "declare his assent and subscribe to all the Artycles of Religion which onely concerne the Confession of the true Christian Faithe and the Doctine of the Sacramentes." Ibid., 4, pt. 1:546.

19. *Epistle,* pp. 26–27, 29–30, 34–36.

20. Ibid., pp. 2, 3, 10, 17. Dudley Fenner's book, *A Counter-poyson* (London: Robert Waldegrave, [1584]), was a reply to Cosin's *An Answer to the Two First and Principall Treatises of a Certeine Factious Libell* (London, 1584), which was a reply to *An Abstract of Certaine Acts of Parlement* ([London: Robert Waldegrave, 1583 or 1584]), in which Throkmorton may have had a hand.

21. The *Epitome* also has a long title of twenty-six lines, beginning: *Oh Read Over D. John Bridges, for It Is a Worthy Worke.* The first twelve lines are identical with those of the *Epistle*, since the two books were regarded as two parts of Martin's reply to Dean Bridges. Line eighteen finally supplies the title: *In This Epitome.* The book was printed by Robert Waldegrave at Fawsley, Northamptonshire, in November 1588.

22. Aylmer's *An Harborowe* was published anonymously. It is dated 26 April 1559 at "Strasborowe," but it was printed in London by John Day. It was a reply to [John Knox], *The First Blast of the Trumpet against the Monstruous Regiment of Women* ([Geneva: John Crespin], 1558).

23. The pages in the *Epitome* for Aylmer's views on Parliament and for the quotations are E2, D4, C2, D4 v; for the name-calling, D4 v and E3. The pages in *An Harborowe* do not correspond with Martin's pagination. The correct references to *An Harborowe* are H3, D4 v, G4, and O4 v, which by Martin are cited as 53, 24, 47, 103. Martin began counting from signature B1.

24. Cooper's *An Admonition*, which is signed "T.C." in the preface, was entered in the Stationers' Register on 10 January 1588/89. I have used the first edition of 252 pages. Two further editions of 245 and 244 pages quickly appeared. The *S.T.C.*, 5682, wrongly implies that the edition of 244 pages was the first. Other editions were issued by John Petheram (1847) and Edward Arber (1882, 1883). Dr. McGinn asserts that the second edition "undoubtedly appeared after the publication of *Hay Any Worke for Cooper,* that is, after 23 March 1588–89," but this is undoubtedly wrong. Penry used the second edition in late January or February—before 7 March—in his *Appellation.* The authorities wished to correct immediately the mistakes or concessions in the first edition. See Donald J. McGinn, "A Perplexing Date in the Marprelate Controversy," *Studies in Philology* 41 (April 1944): 176.

25. *Certaine Minerall, and Metaphisicall Schoolpoints, to Be Defended by the Reverende Bishops, and the Rest of My Cleargie Masters of the Convocation House, against Both the Universities, and Al the Reformed Churches in Christendome. Wherin Is Layd Open, the Very Quintessence of All Catercorner Divinitie. And with All, to the Preventing of the Cavels of These Wrangling Puritans, the Persons by Whom, and the Places Where These Misteries Are So Worthely Maintayned, and for the Most Part, Plainly Set Downe to the View of All Men, and That to the Ternall Prayse of the Most Reverend Fathers* ([Coventry: Robert Waldegrave, 1588/89]). "Minerall" means "hidden," "abstruse," "recondite," and also "profound" in an ironic sense. The broadside is usually referred to as the *Mineralls.* Formerly a unique copy existed at Lambeth Palace Library, but a second copy was discovered as an endsheet in the Bodley Library (shelf-mark: Vet. AI. b. 9.).

26. Deans Richard Cosin, Gabriel Goodman of Westminster Abbey, and George Boleyn of Lichfield, and bishops Middleton, Edmund Freke, and William Overton were each named in one.

27. For the troubles of Marmaduke Middleton, bishop of St. Davids, see R. E. Head, *Royal Supremacy and the Trials of Bishops, 1558–1725* (London, 1962), pp. 20, 23–28; F. O. White, *Lives of the Elizabethan Bishops of the Anglican Church* (London, 1898), pp. 253–59; *Acts of the Privy Council, A.D. 1587–1588* (London, 1897), pp. 339–40; ibid., *1589–90*, pp. 337, 379; ibid., *1591–2*, p. 430. John Roche Dasent edited thirty-two volumes for the years 1542–1604, which were published from 1890 to 1907.

28. Bridges, *Defence of the Government*, pp. 339–40. Note the ironic "I thank him," a Throkmorton touch.

29. The *Mineralls* was published in the last week of January 1588/89, and *Hay Any Worke* appeared during the last week of March 1589.

30. *Hay Any Worke for Cooper: Or a Briefe Pistle Directed by Waye of an Hublication to the Reverende Byshopps, Counselling Them, if They Will Needs Be Barrelled up, for Feare of Smelling in the Nostrels of Her Majestie and the State, That They Would Use the Advise of Reverend Martin, for the Providing of Their Cooper. Because the Reverend T.C. (by Which Misticall Letters, Is Understood, Eyther the Bounsing Parson of Eastmeane, or Tom Coakes His Chaplaine) [Hath Shewed Himselfe in His Late Admonition to the People of England] to Bee an Unskilfull and a Beceytfull Tubtrimmer. Wherein Worthy Martin Quits Himselfe Like a Man I Warrant You, in the Modest Defence of His Selfe and His Learned Pistles, and Makes the Coopers Hoopes to Flye Off, and the Bishops Tubs to Leake Out of All Crye* ([Coventry: Robert Waldegrave, 1589]). The twelve words in square brackets have been added, as suggested in "Falts escaped," p. 48.

31. See Cooper, *An Admonition*, pp. 40 and 135; see also *Hay Any Worke*, p. 38.

32. Cooper, *An Admonition*, pp. 82, 83, 77 v, 77; *Hay Any Worke*, pp. 26, 25, 26, 24.

33. Ibid., pp. 34, 39–43.

34. *Theses Martinianae: That Is, Certaine Demonstrative Conclusions, Sette Downe and Collected (as It Should Seeme) by That Famous and Renowned Clarke, the Reverend Martin Marprelate the Great: Serving as a Manifest and Sufficient Confutation of Al That Ever the Colledge of Catercaps with Their Whole Band of Clergie-Priestes, Have, or Can Bring for the Defence of Their Ambitious and Antichristian Prelacie* ([Wolston, Warwickshire: John Hodgskin and Valentine Symmes, 1589]).

35. See *The Whole Workes of W. Tyndall, John Frith, and Doctor Barnes, Three Worthy Martyrs, and Principall Teachers of This Churche of England, Collected and Compiled in One Tome Togither, Beyng Before Scattered, and Now in Print Here Exhibited to the Church. To the Prayse of God, and Profite of All Good Christian Readers.*, 1 vol. in 2 parts and 3 divisions. Ed. John Foxe (London, 1573, 1572). *S.T.C.*, 24436. See also a helpful monograph on all three martyrs by William A. Clebsch, *England's Earliest Protestants, 1520–1535* (New Haven, 1964).

36. "An Act to Refourme Certayne Dysorders touching Ministers of the Churche," *Statutes of the Realm*, vol. 4, pt. 1:546.

37. The first English edition of Foxe's book was published as a folio in 1563; further editions in two volumes appeared in 1570, 1576, and 1583, all published in London by John Day.

38. *Martin Junior*, signatures Civ v, Dii, Dii v, Diii v, and Dii v. *Mar-Martin* is not listed in the first edition of the *S.T.C.* (1926), but it appears in the second edition (1976), 17461. 5. Another edition, almost identical, is *Marre Mar-Martin*, which is *S.T.C.* 17462. But *Mar-Martine*, *S.T.C.* 17461, is a different work.

39. *The Just Censure and Reproofe of Martin Junior. Wherein the Rash and Undiscreete Headines of the Foolish Youth, Is Sharply Mette with, and the Boy Hath His Lesson Taught Him, I Warrant You, by His Reverend and Elder Brother, Martin Senior, Sonne and Heire unto the Renowmed Martin Mar-prelate the Great. Where Also, Least the Springall Shold Be Utterly Discouraged in His Good Meaning, You Shall Finde, That Hee Is Not Bereaved of His Due Commendations* ([Wolston, Warwickshire: John Hodgskin and Valentine Symmes, 1589]). Usually referred to as *Martin Senior*. Note the familiar Throkmorton phrase, "I warrant you," as in n. 30.

40. *Martin Senior*, signatures Aii v–Bi. Martin's mention of names revealed no new information, since pursuivants had sought Penry and Sharpe in Northampton six months earlier. Nicholas Tomkins' examination in February 1588/89, had confirmed the role of Waldegrave, and it had been "discovered [revealed] by manye, that Humphrey Newman a Cobbler in London is the principall utterer [vendor]." No mention was made of Hodgskin. See Edward Arber, *Introductory Sketch to the Martin Marprelate Controversy, 1588–1590* (London, 1879), p. 116. Arber's work was reprinted in 1880, 1895, and 1964.

41. *Martin Senior*, signatures Civ–Dii.

42. Martin denounced William Gravett, vicar, as "one of dumbe Johns [Aylmer's] bousing mates." Tobias Bland, chaplain to John, Baron St. John of Bletso, Bedfordshire, was the author of *A Baite for Momus, So Called upon Occasion of a Sermon at Bedford Injuriously Traduced by the Factious* (London, 1589). His book was a criticism of Anabaptists, Brownists, Puritans, and of Martinism by innuendo. See pp. 22, 23, 25–27, 29–30, 35–36. See also *Martin Senior*, signatures Cii–Ciii, Dii–Diii v, and *Hay Any Worke*, p. 33.

43. *The Protestatyon of Martin Marprelat. Wherin not wi[t]hstanding the Surprizing of the Printer, He Maketh It Known unto the World That He Feareth, neither Proud Priest, Antichristian Pope, Tiranous Prellate, nor Godless Catercap: but Defiethe All the Race of Them by These Presents and Offereth Conditionally, as Is Farthere Expressed Hearin by Open Disputation to Apear in the Defence of His Caus aginst Them and Theirs. Which Chaleng if They Dare not Maintaine aginst Him: Then Doth He Alsoe Publishe That He Never Meaneth by the Assi[s]taunce of God to Leave the Assayling of Them and Theire Generation untill They Be Uterly Extinguis[h]ed out of Our Church* ([Wolston, Warwickshire, 1589]). Signature A was printed by amateurs; the last three signatures were printed by Waldegrave. In signature A there are sixty-one printing mis-

takes; in B, two; in C, none; and in D, four. See John Dover Wilson, "A Date in the Marprelate Controversy," *The Library* 8 (October 1907): 353–57.

44. *Protestatyon*, pp. 17, 14–16, 18.

45. Ibid., pp. 21–22, 12, 19–20, 16, 13–14.

46. Ibid., pp. 25, 28–29.

47. Dr. Some wrote four books entitled *A Godly Treatise*. The one intended here is *A Godly Treatise, Containing and Deciding Certaine Questions, Mooved of Late in London and Other Places, touching the Ministerie, Sacraments, and Church. Whereunto One Proposition More Is Added. After the Ende of This Booke You Shall Find a Defence of Such Points as M. Penry Hath Dealt against: And a Confutation of Many Grosse Errours Broched in M. Penries Last Treatise* (London, 1588). Penry wrote a reply to this book, but his manuscript was seized in January 1588/89. Job Throkmorton refuted it unmercifully in his *Master Some Laid Open in His Coulers* ([La Rochelle: Robert Waldegrave, 1589]), which was published in September, just a month after the confiscation of his own manuscript, *More Worke for Cooper*. The reference to Dr. Some's "conscience at Gyrton" refers to a benefice at Girton, near Cambridge, which he held as a pluralist in addition to his position as master of Peterhouse as the successor of Dr. Andrew Perne.

48. John Frégeville wrote *The Reformed Politicke. That Is, an Apologie for the Generall Cause of Reformation, Written against the Sclaunders of the Pope and the League. With Most Profitable Advises for the Appeasing of Schisme, by Abolishing Superstition, and Preserving the State of the Clergie. Whereto Is Adjoyned a Discourse upon the Death of the Duke of Guise, Prosecuting the Argument of the Booke. Dedicated to the King by John Frégeuille of Gaut* (London, 1589). The phrase and argument for "Preserving the State of the Clergie," that is, the English clergy, irritated Martin, who insisted that "reformation importeth the overthrow of the state of the cleargie." See the *Protestatyon*, p. 31.

49. Leonard Wright, author of *A Summons for Sleepers* (London, 1589). As a controversialist and writer of books on religious subjects, he was a critic of Martin Marprelate.

50. *Protestatyon*, pp. 26, 30–31. The bishops alluded to are Whitgift (Canterbury), Aylmer (London), and William Overton (Lichfield and Coventry) on the first rank; Richard Howland (Peterborough), Richard Rogers (suffragan of Dover), and Cooper (Winchester) on the second rank; John Bullingham (Gloucester) or John Young (Rochester), William Wickham (Lincoln) or William Chaderton (Chester), and Marmaduke Middleton (St. David's) on the third rank. In *The Marprelate Tracts, 1588, 1589* (London, 1911), William Pierce lists Richard Fletcher and Richard Barnes on the second rank, but Fletcher did not become bishop of Bristol until December 1589, and Barnes (Durham) died in August 1587. For the third rank, William Blethin of Llandaff is a doubtful alternative, but William Hughes of St. Asaph, to whom Martin referred as "the Bishop of Sir Asse," is a possible alternative to William Wickham or William Chaderton.

51. Pasquill of England, *A Countercuffe Given to Martin Junior: by the Ven-*

turous, Hardie, and Renowned Pasquill of England, Cavaliero ([London: John Charlewood], 1589). On signature Aiv v is the date, 8 August 1589, which indicates that Pasquill had read *Martin Junior* a week or two after it had been printed by 22 July. Pasquill promised a reply.

52. *Protestatyon*, p. 23 [32]; *Mineralls*, no. 27.

53. The first four Marprelate items were printed in black letter or Gothic type by Waldegrave on the press in Penry's custody; *Martin Junior* and *Martin Senior* were printed with roman type on the same press by Hodgskin and his assistants; the partial printing with roman type of *More Worke* was done on Hodgskin's press at Manchester. The *Protestatyon* was printed on Penry's press which had been hidden at Wolston on 29 July 1589. Two fonts of type, larger than those in the previously mentioned books, were used.

54. See Julia Norton McCorkle, "A Note concerning 'Mistress Crane' and the Martin Marprelate Controversy," *The Library* 12 (December 1931): 276–83. See also P.R.O., Star Chamber, 5/A 30/22, for Attorney General John Popham's "Bill of Complainte" of 11 February 1589/90, and "The Aunswere of Elizabeth [Crane] Carleton to the 'Bill of Informacion,' " dated 17 May 1590. See also B.L., Harley MSS., 2143, fols. 48 v–49. Mrs. Crane was the wife of Anthony Crane, not of Nicholas Crane the Puritan minister. Sometime in 1589, being a widow, she married George Carleton of Overstone, Northamptonshire.

55. The article by Sidney Lee on Throkmorton in the *D.N.B.* is wrong in stating that "a printing press was secretly set up in his house," and that *Theses Martinianae*, the *Just Censure and Reproofe*, and the *Protestatyon* "were put into type under Throckmorton's roof."

56. Wigginton's examination is in Albert Peel, ed., *The Seconde Parte of a Register. Being a Calendar of Manuscripts under That Title Intended for Publication by the Puritans about 1593, and Now in Dr. Williams's Library, London*, 2 vols. (Cambridge, 1915), 2:253–58 and 238–53. The original "Seconde Parte of a Register" is in Dr. Williams's Library; see vol. B, pt. 2, fols. 26–39; vol. A, pt. 1, fols. 29–32, and pt. 2, fols. 36–44; vol. C, fols. 753–72, 843–50. See also my article, "A Corpus of Elizabethan Nonconformist Writings," in *Studies in Church History*, 16 vols., ed. C. W. Dugmore, Charles Duggan, G. J. Cuming, and Derek Baker (London, 1964–), 2 (1965): 292–309.

57. For Udall, see *A New Discovery of Old Pontificall Practises for the Maintenance of the Prelates Authority and Hierarchy*, pp. 1–7. This work is a collection of documents on Udall, by an anonymous editor. See *S.T.C.*, U14 (Wing). See also Arber, *Introductory Sketch*, pp. 87–95, 121–22, 169–72.

58. The best work on Field is by Patrick Collinson, "John Field and Elizabethan Puritanism," *Elizabethan Government and Society. Essays Presented to Sir John Neale*, ed. S. T. Bindoff, J. Hurstfield, C. H. Williams (London, 1961), pp. 27–62. See also Arber, *Introductory Sketch*, p. 94, and "Feilde," *D.N.B.*, Supplement, II.

59. For Fenner, see Peel, *Seconde Parte*, 1:230, 238, 240–41, 296. See also Ronald Bayne's article in the *D.N.B.*

60. Tomkins' examinations are in Harley MSS. 6848, fols. 81, 89. See also Arber, *Introductory Sketch,* pp. 84–87. For Pagit, see Pierce, *The Marprelate Tracts,* pp. 62, 63, 246. For Pagit and Cartwright, see *Hay Any Worke,* pp. 21, 36 and Thomas Fuller, *The Church History of Britain; from the Birth of Jesus Christ until the Year 1648,* ed. J. S. Brewer, 6 vols. (Oxford, 1845), 5:149–50; the first edition appeared in 1655 or 1655/56. See also Pearson, *Thomas Cartwright,* pp. 285–89.

61. See William Maskell, *A History of the Martin Marprelate Controversy in the Reign of Queen Elizabeth* (London, 1845), pp. 101–03. See also Maskell, "Martin Marprelate," *The Christian Remembrancer* (April, 1845): 338–406. Since Travers was second only to Cartwright as a Presbyterian leader, the suggestion that he was Marprelate is plausible. In 1574 he had published *Ecclesiasticae Disciplinae, et Anglicanae Ecclesiae ab illa aberrationis, plena e verbo Dei, et dilucida explicatio,* which Cartwright translated the same year as *A Full and Plaine Declaration of Ecclesiasticall Discipline owt off the Word off God, and off the Declininge off the Churche off England from the Same.* Both books were published at Heidelberg by Michael Schirat in 1574, not at La Rochelle and Geneva. The Latin work has a false imprint: Rupellae [La Rochelle]: Adamus de Monte, 1574. In the years 1586–89 Travers' manuscript book, "De disciplina ecclesiae sacra ex Dei verbo descripta," was submitted to various classes or presbyteries for revision, but the brethren could not agree, and the work was not published in Travers' lifetime. Found in Cartwright's study after his death, it finally appeared as *A Directory of Church-Government* (London, 1644 [1644/45], in twenty-four pages). Francis Paget published the Latin edition from a manuscript in Lambeth Palace Library (Codd. MSS. CXIII, no. 10, p. 180), in *An Introduction to the Fifth Book of Hooker's Treatise of the Laws of Ecclesiastical Polity,* app. 3, pp. 68–75, 238–51. Travers also published in 1588 a reply to Dean Bridges, to which Martin alludes: *A Defence of the Ecclesiastical Discipline Ordayned of God to Be Used in His Church.* See S. J. Knox, *Walter Travers: Paragon of Elizabethan Puritanism* (London, 1962), pp. 25–107 and 116–17. See also Richard Bauckham, "Hooker, Travers and the Church of Rome in the 1580s," *Journal of Ecclesiastical History* 29 (1978): 37–50. Dr. Bauckham corrects Thomas Fuller's statement: "Here the pulpit spake pure Canterbury in the morning, and Geneva in the afternoon, until Travers was silenced." See Thomas Fuller, *The History of the Worthies of England* (London, 1662), p. 264 in the section on "Devon-Shire."

62. A. L. Rowse, *The England of Elizabeth. The Structure of Society* (New York, 1951), p. 476, n. There is a new biography by Alan G. R. Smith, *Servant of the Cecils. The Life of Michael Hickes, 1543–1612* (Totowa, N.J., 1977). Dr. Smith finds no connection for Hickes and Marprelate. Dr. Rowse, who is certainly well read in Tudor history and literature, illustrates the complexity of the Marprelate problem. In 1951 he suggested Hickes as a possible Martin, but in 1962 he spoke of Job Throkmorton as "the celebrated Puritan and Martin Marprelate pamphleteer" (*Ralegh and the Throckmortons* [London, 1962], pp. 22, 25, 114, 190, 196). But in 1968, in his review of Donald J. McGinn's book, *John Penry and the Marprelate Controversy* (New Brunswick, N.J., 1966), he supported the thesis that Penry was Martin and that

Throkmorton "was also involved." He then stated: "The summing up of the *D.N.B.* on the subject provides the common-sense of the matter and is not superseded" (*English Historical Review* 83 [1968]:169). Unfortunately, Sir Sidney Lee's two articles on Penry and Throkmorton contain about thirty-five errors in addition to the major fallacy of identifying Martin with Penry. Sir Sidney's summary has been superseded by the work of William Pierce, John Dover Wilson, Georges A. Bonnard, Albert Peel, Glanmor Williams, David Williams, Sir John Neale, and Patrick Collinson.

63. For Tomson, see Pearson, *Thomas Cartwright*, pp. 279–80; for Cecil and the earl of Essex, see John Penry, *The Notebook of John Penry, 1593*, ed. Albert Peel, Camden Third Series, no. 67 (London, 1944), pp. 66, 70; see also Martin's *Just Censure*, signature Aiv and Pierce, *Marprelate Tracts*, p. 37.

64. "An Advertisement for Papp-hatchett, and Martin Mar-prelate," *The Works of Gabriel Harvey, D.C.L.,* ed. Alexander B. Grosart, 3 vols. (London, 1884, 1885), 2:131. See also R. Warwick Bond, *The Complete Works of John Lyly, Now for the First Time Collected and Edited from the Earliest Quartos, with Life, Bibliography, Essays, Notes, and Index,* 3 vols. (Oxford, 1902), 3:390–91, for Harvey's statement; page 400 for Lyly's accusation. Cf. Ronald B. McKerrow, *Works of Thomas Nashe,* 5 vols. (London, 1904–[1910]), 3:138. This edition was reprinted in 1958 with new material.

65. *Acts of the Privy Council*, A.D. *1588–9*, p. 131; ibid., A.D. *1590*, pp. 68–69 (Norwich, 1898; London, 1899).

66. Collinson, *Elizabethan Puritan Movement*, p. 395. Martin's reference to Tarleton's soul could not relate to Carleton, who was living in 1589. Tarleton died on 5 September 1588. See *Hay Any Worke*, p. 46.

67. For Dexter's views, see the "Argument by the Rev. H. M. Dexter, D.D., of New Bedford, Massachusetts, U.S., in Favour of the Authorship Being Assigned to Henry Barrow," in Arber, *Introductory Sketch,* pp. 187–92. See also his *Congregationalism of the Last Three Hundred Years as Seen in Its Literature, . . . with a Bibliographical Appendix* (New York, 1880), pp. ix, x, 129–202. For Dexter's life and work, see the *Proceedings of the Massachusetts Historical Society,* Second Series, 6 (1891): 176–84, and 7 (1892): 90–103. His remarkable bibliography of 7,250 items is still useful. Barrow would not have written anonymous or pseudonymous books.

68. *The Library*, Third Series 3 (April, July 1912): 275–76.

69. Ibid., pp. 243–44, 248–52.

70. Ibid., pp. 133–35.

71. John X. Evans, ed., *The Works of Sir Rogers Williams* (Oxford, 1972), p. 172.

72. For Pierce and McKerrow, see their separate replies, "Did Sir Roger Williams Write the Marprelate Tracts?" in *The Library* 3 (October 1912): 345–74. For Wilson's response, see "Did Sir Roger Williams Write the Marprelate Tracts? A Rejoinder," *The Library* 4 (January 1913): 92–104.

73. For criticism of Wilson, see Milton Crane, *Shakespeare's Prose* (Chicago, [1951]), pp. 203–08; S. Schoenbaum, *Shakespeare's Lives* (Oxford, 1970), pp.

704, 718–23; C. J. Sisson's review of Wilson's book, *The Essential Shakespeare, a Biographical Adventure* (Cambridge, 1932), in *The Modern Language Review* 26 (1932): 473–76. A. L. Rowse writes: "Of superfluous suggestions as to the authorship of the tracts the most absurd is that of Professor Dover Wilson suggesting Sir Roger Williams. No evidence for it, nor reason for it whatever; while the propagation of doubt where there is no need for it is as deplorable as the assertion itself" (*English Historical Review* 83 [1968]: 169–70). Wilson's essay is in *The Cambridge History of English Literature*, 3 (1930): 374–98.

74. *The History of the Early Puritans*, 2d ed. (London, 1853), p. 207.

75. William Pierce, *An Historical Introduction to the Marprelate Tracts. A Chapter in the Evolution of Religious and Civil Liberty in England* (London, 1908), chap. six and pp. 307–08; Champlin Burrage, *The Early English Dissenters in the Light of Recent Research (1550–1641)*, 2 vols. (Cambridge, 1912), 1:131; *The Notebook of John Penry, 1593*, ed. Albert Peel, p. xiii.

76. Virginia Miller Cornell has written a Ph.D. thesis, "Understanding Elizabethan Laughter. The Martin Marprelate Tracts," at Arizona State University (1974). This dissertation is helpful in the study of English prose style and in providing a discussion of Martin's words and phrases. On the authorship, however, Mrs. Cornell states that she has not been able "to present conclusive results because I lack the expertise and facilities to evaluate my raw data" (p. 212). She conjectures that there were three Martins. The first Martin was John Field, but "his material was rewritten by Udall." The second Martin was John Penry, whose hand may be detected especially in the serious passages. The third Martin "is possibly Job Throkmorton—but his presence may be far more pervasive than we now realize." It is possible that Throkmorton used some material from reports by Penry, Udall, and Wigginton in Field's corpus, but much of his material comes from his teeming mind and broad experience. The death of Field in March 1587/88 and the absence of Udall in Newcastle-upon-Tyne during all of 1589, make unlikely any participation by them in the Marprelate books, and make impossible any contribution to the last five works of Martin.

NOTES—Chapter I

1. See "Minutes of a Letter to the Archbishop of Canterbury from the Lord Chanceler [and] Lord Threasurer, 14 November, 1588," in Lansdowne MSS. 103, item 43, fol. 102; printed in Arber, *Introductory Sketch*, pp. 107–08. Arber has "serch" but the manuscript reading is "fetch." William Brooke (1527–96/97), eighth Lord Cobham, Lord Warden of the Cinque Ports, and Lord Chamberlain, became a privy councilor in 1585/86. Thomas Sackville (1536–1608), created Lord Buckhurst in 1567 and earl of Dorset in 1603/04, became a privy councilor about February 1585/86. Sir John Wolley (1540?–95/96), Latin secretary, dean of Carlisle, and diplomatist, was appointed to the Privy Council on 30 September 1586.

2. The depositions are in Harley MSS. 6849, fols. 157, 159. Thomas Baker's transcripts of them are in Harley MSS. 7042, fol. 34, but lack John Good's deposition. They are printed, not always correctly, in Arber, *Introductory Sketch*, pp. 81–104. Arber has "Stanghton," but "Staughton" seems the better manuscript reading.

3. Stephen Chatfield's deposition is in Harley MSS. 6849, fol. 130; Baker's transcript of it is in Harley MSS. 7042, fol. 31. See Arber, *Introductory Sketch*, p. 83. Arber dates this deposition as probably 1589, but November 1588 seems preferable, since Chatfield in November had volunteered to make a deposition. See ibid., p. 81.

4. Martin had written: "Is this your meaning (M. Doctor [Bridges])? You have spun a fayre thred. Can you tell your brother Marprelate, with all your learning, howe to decline what is Latine for a goose?" See the *Epitome*, signature C4 v; Pierce's edition, *Marprelate Tracts*, p. 140. In Pierce's edition all signatures, such as B3 v, or Cii, indicate the end of the page, but all arabic page numbers, such as 9 or 30, indicate the beginning of the page. The facsimile edition of *The Marprelate Tracts (1588–1589)*, published by the Scolar Press (Leeds, 1967), is useful. Martin's references to a goose point toward Throkmorton. Other sarcastic allusions to a goose are in the *Epistle*, pp. 18, 19, 47, and in *Martin Senior*, signature Diii, and in Throkmorton, *The Defence of Job Throkmorton* ([Middelburg], 1594), signature Dii v.

5. See the list of ecclesiastical commissioners in app. 2 of Roland G. Usher, *The Rise and Fall of the High Commission* (Oxford, 1968), pp. 345–61. This second edition has a new introduction and bibliography by Philip Tyler. Richard Young's name does not appear on the lists for 1584 or 1589, but it appears on two lists of special commissioners for 1593 and 1594, in Harley MSS. 6849, fol. 239. Usher's list is incomplete because he did not use the commission for 20 June 1589. Bancroft and Whitgift are the only ones listed for 1589 by Usher, but Cooper, Aubrey, Cosin, and Goodman also belong to the 1589 commission. See SP 12/228/ fol. 19, and especially Ellesmere MS. 1988, in the Huntington Library. See also the "Seconde Parte

of a Register," vol. B, pt. 1, fols. 427–34, and vol. C, fols. 524–30, both in Dr. Williams's Library. See further G. W. Prothero, *Select Statutes and Other Constitutional Documents Illustrative of the Reigns of Elizabeth and James I*, 4th ed. (Oxford, 1913), which contains "A Copie of the High Commission, 1584," pp. 472a–472k, and six other commissions, pp. 227–42.

6. *Epistle*, pp. 26–27; Pierce, *Marprelate Tracts*, pp. 57–59.

7. Perhaps Wigginton was thinking of such lawyers as Robert Beale, Nicholas Fuller, James Morice, and Peter Wentworth. For the ex officio oath, see James Morice, *A Briefe Treatise of Oathes* ([London?, 1600?]). A recent helpful book is by Leonard W. Levy, *Origins of the Fifth Amendment. The Right against Self-Incrimination* (New York: Oxford University Press, 1968). Wigginton's examination is printed in Peel, ed., *The Seconde Parte of a Register*, 2:253–58; see also 2:238–53 for supplementary material.

8. Barrow's examination at the Fleet is printed in Leland H. Carlson, ed., *The Writings of Henry Barrow, 1587–1590* (London, 1962), pp. 170–72.

9. Nicholas Tomkins' original examination is in Harley MSS. 6848, fol. 81. In his *Introductory Sketch*, pp. 84–86, Arber prints this examination from Baker's transcript in Harley MSS. 7042, fol. 13, but the transcript is both inaccurate and incomplete.

10. According to Sharpe, there were about 900–1,000 copies printed, of which Sharpe bound and stitched 700, but Newman said that 1,500 were printed. See Arber, *Introductory Sketch*, pp. 98–99, and Ellesmere MS. 2148, fol. 86.

11. *Martin Senior*, signatures Aiii v–Bi, and Pierce, *Marprelate Tracts*, pp. 355–60.

12. Arber, *Introductory Sketch*, pp. 114–15. The earl of Hertford was the brother of Elizabeth, Sir Richard's wife.

13. Although the printing ceased during these three months, Throkmorton was busy with his writing. His *Dialogue. Wherin Is Plainly Laide Open the Tyrannicall Dealing of Lord Bishopps against Gods Children* (*S.T.C.* 6805) was completed in this period. Throkmorton was also writing his *More Worke for Cooper* at this time, and it is probable that he was penning "Martins Interim." See Arber, *Introductory Sketch*, p. 180, and Matthew Sutcliffe, *An Answere unto a Certaine Calumnious Letter Published by M. Job Throkmorton, and Entituled, A Defence of J. Throkmorton against the Slaunders of M. Sutcliffe* (London, 1595). pp. 72 and 72 v.

14. The first Roman Catholic English version, the Douai-Rheims New Testament, translated mainly by Gregory Martin, was published in 1582. Thomas Cartwright was requested to answer this "heretical" translation, based on Jerome's Vulgate, and Secretary Francis Walsingham promised him £100 annually for the task. Cartwright began his labors, but Archbishop Whitgift commanded him to desist, and Waldegrave was unable to realize his wish. In 1588 and 1589 William Whitaker and William Fulke at Cambridge wrote against the Catholic version, and in 1602 Cartwright published his first reply, printed in 1602 by Waldegrave in Edinburgh.

His second reply was published posthumously by William Brewster and the Pilgrim Press at Leyden in 1618.

15. Ellesmere MS. 2148, fol. 86 v; Sutcliffe, *An Answere*, p. 71; B.L., Additional MSS. 48064, fol. 146 (formerly Yelverton MSS. 70); Pierce, *Historical Introduction*, pp. 333–39.

16. Whitgift's letter is in Lansdowne MSS. 61, item 3, fol. 5. See Arber, *Introductory Sketch*, pp. 112–13. Arber wrongly entitles this letter "Archbishop Whitgift's autobiographic report to Lord Burghley of the discovery of the Martinist Press by the Earl of Derby; dated 24th August 1589." Actually, it is Whitgift's reply to information provided by Burghley and other privy councilors.

17. *Acts of the Privy Council, A.D. 1589–90*, pp. 59, 62.

18. Hatton's "memorial" of 2 September 1589, possibly from the queen or expressing her desires, is in the *Calendar of State Papers, Domestic Series, Elizabeth, 1581–1590*, p. 614. The *Calendar* speaks of the "examination of Martin Marprelate," but the original record reads: "Item, the examynacon of Martin Marprelate toe be thoroughlye persevered in." See P.R.O., State Papers Domestic, Elizabeth, vol. 226, for 2 September 1589. In his *Historical Introduction* Pierce has "by his one [own] confession," but the manuscript reading is clearly "one"; Hodgskin contrasted one confession against another. Hodgskin was examined at least seven times: by the earl of Derby, the privy councilors, the special committee at the Bridewell, the Tower officials during his racking, his examiners on 25 and 27 November, and the lords commissioners in December 1589. See Ellesmere MS. 2148, fols. 86 v, 87, Harley MSS. 7042, fols. 1–11, Lansdowne MSS. 238, fols. 326–34; see also Arber, *Introductory Sketch*, pp. 101–04, 115–16, 119–36, and Pierce, *Historical Introduction*, pp. 333–39, 197.

19. Arber, *Introductory Sketch*, pp. 114–16, 125; T. B. Howell and T. J. Howell, *A Complete Collection of State Trials*, 34 vols. (London, 1811–28), 1:1,265, 1,269. The pagination in William Cobbett's edition of 1809–26 is the same.

20. The "Summary" is in Lansdowne MSS. 61, article 22, and is printed in Arber, *Stationers' Registers*, 2:816–17, with his own title: "Secret Report to Lord Burghley of the Authors of the Martin Marprelate Tracts," and in Arber, *Introductory Sketch*, pp. 114–17.

21. The conjectures in this "Summary" are not evidence and must be balanced by Symmes's testimony, Ellesmere MS. 2148, and Sutcliffe's *An Answere*, pp. 68–75. Failure to do so leads to erroneous conclusions, as seen in McGinn, *John Penry*, pp. 116, 117, 125, 128, 129, 130, 144, 231.

22. Ellesmere MS. 2148, fol. 86 v; Arber, *Introductory Sketch*, p. 135; Pierce, *Historical Introduction*, pp. 333–39.

23. The bond of Henry Sharpe, stationer, of All Saints, Northampton, is dated 14 October 1589. See MSS. Carte Antique et Miscellanee, IV, 161, in Lambeth Palace Library. As early as February 1588/89, the mayor of Northampton, Thomas Crasswell, had been ordered by the authorities to apprehend Sharpe. See Penry, *Appellation*, p. 46.

24. Sharpe's examination is printed in Arber, *Introductory Sketch*, pp. 94–104. This is based on Harley MSS. 7042, fols. 15–19 (old folios 19–27), which is a transcript. What may be the original manuscript is in Lansdowne MSS. 830, fols. 114–18. One Pigot, whose house at Coventry was searched by pursuivants, said Sharpe was responsible for this action, and accused him of having "done wickedly in taking his Oath before the Lord Chancelor"—and that "against Christian liberty."

25. Ellesmere MS. 2148, fols. 85, 86 v, 87; Arber, *Introductory Sketch*, p. 133.

26. The eight privy councilors were: Lord Cobham, Lord Buckhurst, Mr. Comptroller (Sir James Croft), Mr. Vice Chamberlain (Sir Thomas Heneage), Mr. Secretary (Sir Francis Walsingham), Sir John Perrot, Mr. John Wolley, and Mr. John Fortescue, but later the names of Walsingham and Perrot were omitted and that of Francis Gawdy, justice of the Queen's Bench, was added. See *Acts of the Privy Council, 1589–90*, pp. 225, 227; also *Acts of the Privy Council, 1590*, p. 292. The letter on p. 225 (1589) and the letter on p. 292 (1590) are almost identical. The letter of November 1589 established a commission to carefully examine Knightley, Wigston, and Hales. It is likely that the letter of 29 June 1590 establishes the same commission, with the addition of the name of Justice Gawdy, for the examination of Newman in July 1590. Two former commissioners are missing: Walsingham (died 6 April 1590) and Sir John Perrot.

27. Arber, *Introductory Sketch*, p. 129. For portraits of Knightley and his wife, see Oswald Barron, ed., *Northamptonshire Families* (London, 1906), pp. 184–86.

28. Arber, *Introductory Sketch*, pp. 123–26, 129–31.

29. Ibid., p. 132.

30. Ibid., p. 133.

31. Ellesmere MS. 2148, fols. 86 v, 87; Arber, *Introductory Sketch*, pp. 101, 127, 134–35; Pierce, *Historical Introduction*, pp. 333–35; Sutcliffe, *An Answere*, pp. 71, 71 v, 72.

32. Pierce, *Historical Introduction*, pp. 334–39; Arber, *Introductory Sketch*, pp. 135–36; Sutcliffe, *An Answere*, pp. 71, 71 v.

33. Arber, *Introductory Sketch*, pp. 81–83, 88–93. Tomkins' examination of 15 February 1588/89, is in Harley MSS. 6848, fol. 81; the transcript is Harley MSS. 7042, fol. 13; for his 29 November examination, the original is Harley MSS. 6848, fols. 89–90; the transcript is Harley MSS. 7042, fols. 21 v–22—old fol. 32. Arber, *Introductory Sketch*, pp. 84–87, prints not the originals but the incomplete transcripts. *Diotrephes*, sometimes carelessly referred to as *Dialogue*, is entitled: *The State of the Church of Englande*, and actually is a dialogue (*S.T.C.*, 24505).

34. Three of the commissioners were privy councilors: Lord Cobham, Lord Buckhurst, and John Fortescue; the other five were Bishop John Young, judges Edmund Anderson, William Aubrey, William Lewin, and Solicitor General Thomas Egerton. For the name of the mayor, I am indebted to B. W. Beckingsale of the Department of History, University of Newcastle-upon-Tyne.

35. Howell, *State Trials*, 2:1,271–77. See also [Udall], *A New Discovery of Old Pontificall Practises for the Maintenance of the Prelates Authority and Hierarchy. Evinced by Their Tyrannicall Persecution of That Reverend, Learned, Pious, and Worthy Minister of Jesus Christ, Mr. John Udall, in the Raigne of Queene Elizabeth.* This work was issued at London in 1643 by an anonymous compiler. It contains Udall's examination, pp. 1–7, his arraignment at Croydon, pp. 7–26, and his appearance before the court at Southwark, pp. 26–44. Arber prints only four pages of Udall's examination on 13 January before the commissioners, *Introductory Sketch*, pp. 169–172.

36. Harley MSS. 7042, fols. 1–11; printed by Arber, *Introductory Sketch*, pp. 119–36. Arber entitles this as "The Brief Held by Sir John Puckering, while attorney general, against the Martinists." Since this "Brief" may be dated about January 1589/90, prior to Knightley's trial before the Court of Star Chamber on 13 February, it is anachronistic to refer to Puckering as "Sir" and it is erroneous to refer to him as "Attorney General." Puckering was the queen's serjeant, became Keeper of the Great Seal in succession to Lord Chancellor Hatton in 1592, and was knighted the same year. John Popham was the attorney general from 1581 to 1592, and then was appointed lord chief justice of the Court of Queen's Bench (1592–1607). He had served as a privy councilor since 1571. Thomas Egerton was attorney general from 1592 to 1594.

37. Ellesmere MS. 2148, fol. 88; Sutcliffe, *An Answere*, pp. 72, 73; Arber, *Introductory Sketch*, p. 181.

38. Ellesmere MS. 2148, fols. 85–88; Sutcliffe, *An Answere*, pp. 70 v–73. Arber, *Introductory Sketch*, pp. 131, 176–82.

39. Ellesmere MS. 2148, fols. 85 v–88 v. Sutcliffe, *An Answere*, pp. 70 v, 72, 72 v, 73.

40. Ellesmere MS. 2148, fols. 88 v, 89. Arber, *Introductory Sketch*, p. 182.

41. Ibid., pp. 180–82, 184.

42. Ellesmere MS. 2148, fols. 88 v, 89.

NOTES—Chapter II

1. The letter of 14 November is in Lansdowne MSS. 103, fol. 102. Arber prints this letter and also the six depositions in his *Introductory Sketch*, pp. 81–83, 107–08. There is an order from the Court of High Commission, dated 16 December 1588 to officials in Kent, requesting a search for Martin's books. See Kent Archives Office, High Commission Act Book, PR C44/3, fols. 5–6.

2. Shortly after the first edition of 252 pages was published, it was speedily revised. Bishop Cooper had acknowledged that the pristine government of the apostolic and New Testament church was democratic, congregational, and non-episcopal or non-papal. He had written: "I grant it was so," and "I will not deny it." But the revision stated: "that is not yet proved." The words "do what he dare" are changed to "do what he can." Martin informed his readers: "Here you see that if this patch T.C. had not used two patches to cover his patcherie, the bishops woulde have accounted him to be as very a patch as Deane John [Bridges]" (*Hay Any Worke*, p. 38; Pierce, *Marprelate Tracts*, pp. 269–70). In Cooper's first edition, pages 40 and 135, there are two pasted slips or patches which cover the original wording.

3. *An Admonition*, signatures Aii and Aii v, 1st ed.

4. Ibid., p. 1.

5. Ibid., p. 2.

6. Ibid., pp. 35, 36.

7. Ibid., pp. 33, 34, 36, 37, 74, 75.

8. Arber, *Introductory Sketch*, pp. 95–97, 115, 125, 129.

9. The first edition of the *Exhortation*, with 66 pages, was published in London. There are copies at Oxford, Cambridge, Dr. Williams's Library in London, and at the Huntington Library. The second edition, consisting of 110 pages, includes the reprinting of the first edition, with only minor changes (pp. 1–40); it includes supplementary material (pp. 41–52), plus fifty-three reasons or syllogisms relating to Welsh ministers, especially non-preaching curates (pp. 52–65). Then follows a long address: "To the Lords of the [Privy] Counsel" (pp. 65–110). A unique copy is in The National Library of Wales, Aberystwyth, as part of the Sir John Williams Collection, W.A. 13. The third edition, published about August-September 1588, does not include the last section, pp. 65–110. It is printed from the same type as the second edition, except for page 65, which has been reset. Robert Waldegrave printed all three editions, in London and East Molesey. See John Williams, "Undescribed Edition of a Work of Penry," *Transactions of the Congregational Historical Society* 2 (October 1906): 430–31.

10. During his examination on 13 January 1589/90, Udall was asked by Lord Buckhurst if he knew that Penry was Martin Marprelate. Udall replied that he did not, nor did he suspect him, because Penry had written a letter, "wherein he did deny it, with such tearmes as declare him to be ignorant and cleere in it." This letter, written about November 1588, after the publication of the *Epistle*, is an important early denial. See [Udall], *A New Discovery of Old Pontificall Practises*, pp. 1–7; Arber, *Introductory Sketch*, p. 172.

11. Penry, *Appellation*, pp. 6, 7, 45, 46.

12. J. E. Neale, *Elizabeth I and Her Parliaments, 1584–1601* (London, 1957), p. 198.

13. Richard Bancroft, *A Sermon Preached at Paules Crosse the 9 of Februarie, Being the First Sunday in the Parleament, Anno 1588* [1588/89] (London, 1588 [1588/89]). In two later books, both published anonymously in 1593, Bancroft continued his attacks: *Daungerous Positions and Proceedings* (London, 1593), and *A Survay of the Pretended Holy Discipline* (London, 1593). See further W. D. J. Cargill Thompson, "A Reconsideration of Richard Bancroft's Paul's Cross Sermon of 9 February 1588/9," *Journal of Ecclesiastical History* 20 (1969): 253–66. See also *The Judgement of Dr. Reignolds* [John Rainolds] *concerning Episcopacy, whether It Be Gods Ordinance. Expressed in a Letter to Sir Francis Knowls concerning Doctor Bancrofts Sermon at Pauls Crosse, the Ninth of February 1588* [1588/89] (London, 1641). Also included in *Informations, or a Protestation, and a Treatise from Scotland* ([London], 1608), *S.T.C.* 14084. See Owen Chadwick, "Richard Bancroft's Submission," *Journal of Ecclesiastical History* 3 (1952): 58–73; Champlin Burrage, *The Early English Dissenters in the Light of Recent Research (1550–1641)*, 2:127–33; I.D. [John Davidson], *D. Bancrofts Rashnes in Rayling against the Church of Scotland* (Edinburgh: Robert Waldegrave, 1590); [John Penry], *A Briefe Discovery of the Untruthes and Slanders (against the True Governement of the Church of Christ) Contained in a Sermon, Preached the 8. [9] of Februarie 1588* [1588/89] *by D. Bancroft, and Since That Time, Set Forth in Print, with Additions by the Said Authour* ([Edinburgh: Robert Waldegrave, 1590]). Bancroft is not listed as a high commissioner in the Letters Patent of January 1583/84, but he was appointed about 1586–87, and he is listed in the commission dated 20 June 1589. See Ellesmere MS. 1988, fol. 2, and Additional MSS. 32092, fols. 123–25, in the British Library.

14. *A Second Admonition to the Parliament*, signature Hii. This *Admonition*, which was published about October-November 1572, has been wrongly attributed to Cartwright, but stylistic evidence points to Throkmorton as the author. The quotation is in *Puritan Manifestoes*, edited by W. H. Frere and C. E. Douglas, p. 129. See my App. D and Pearson, *Thomas Cartwright*, pp. 73–75.

15. [Udall], *A Demonstration of Discipline*, the last page of his preface (unnumbered). See also the reprint in *A Parte of a Register* ([Middelburg, 1593]), p. 5, and Arber's edition (1880, 1895), p. 7.

16. Martin's daring statement about "twenty fistes about your eares" is in the *Epistle*, p. 2; see Pierce, *Marprelate Tracts*, pp. 18, 216–17, 246. See

also *Hay Any Worke,* signature A3, and Cooper, *An Admonition,* p. 40. Martin's statement on "putting downe lord bishops" is in the *Epitome,* signature E2.

17. Bancroft, *A Sermon,* pp. 83–84.

18. The proclamation of 13 February 1588/89, is in the B.L., Grenville Collection, 6463, fol. 273. See Arber, *Introductory Sketch,* pp. 109–11, and Paul L. Hughes and James F. Larkin, *Tudor Royal Proclamations,* 3 vols. (New Haven, 1964, 1969); vol. 3: *The Later Tudors (1588–1603),* 3 (1969): 34–35. See also two recent works, Rudolph Heinze, *The Proclamations of the Tudor Kings* (Cambridge, 1976), and Frederic A. Youngs, Jr., *The Proclamations of the Tudor Queens* (Cambridge, 1976).

19. Penry, *Appellation,* pp. 46–47.

20. See the "Epistle to the Reader," *A Summons for Sleepers.* Martin ridiculed Wright in *Martin Junior,* signature Diii v, in *Martin Senior,* signature Cii v, and in the *Protestatyon,* p. 31, where he is called "wringlefaced Wrighte." He was also refuted in *More Worke for Cooper.*

21. *Mar-Martine* (London, 1589), signature A4 v. It is reprinted in *Transactions of the Congregational Historical Society* 5 (October 1912): 357–67. Martin Marprelate's ridicule of Mar-Martine is in *Martin Junior,* signature Dii, and *Martin Senior,* signature Dii v–Div.

22. *Marre Mar-Martin* (n.p., n.d.), signature A4. The *S.T.C.,* 17462, conjectures 1590, but a reference in *Plaine Percevall the Peace–Maker,* signature A2, proves that it was published before October 1589. It is reprinted in *Transactions of the Congregational Historical Society* 5 (October 1912): 367–69.

23. *Mar-Martin,* as another edition of *Marre Mar-Martin,* is not the same as *Mar-Martine.* All three were probably printed in 1589.

24. *A Whip for an Ape* (London, summer, 1589).

25. *Antimartinus, sive Monitio cuiusdam Londinensis ad Adolescentes utriusque Academiae, contra personatum quendam rabulam, qui se Anglice Martin Marprelat, hoc est, Martinum Mastigarchon, e Misarchon vocat* (London, 1589).

26. *Asinus Onustus. The Asse Overladen. To His Loving, and Deare Mistresse, Elizabeth the Blessed Queene of England* (London, 1642), pp. 7, 11–12, 17.

27. (London, 1589), p. 35. The sermon was preached on 6 May; it was entered in the Stationers' Register 7 June; the preface is dated 14 June 1589.

28. *A Countercuffe Given to Martin Junior; by the Venturous, Hardie, and Renowned Pasquill of England, Cavaliero. Not of Olde Martins Making, Which Newlie Knighted the Saints in Heaven, with Rise up Sir Peter and Sir Paule; but Lately Dubd for His Service at Home in the Defence of His Countrey, and for the Cleane Breaking of His Staffe uppon Martins Face,* signatures Aii, Aii v, Aiii. The imprint, inspired by Martin's examples, reads: "Printed, betweene the Skye and the Grounde, within a Myle of an Oake, and Not Many Fieldes of[f], from the Unpriviledged Presse of the Ass-ignes of Martin Junior."

29. Bacon's essay, discreetly not published in his lifetime, is in *The Works of Francis Bacon,* edited by James Spedding, Robert Leslie Ellis, and Douglas

Denon Heath, 14 vols. (London, 1857–72), 8:74–95. Vol. 8 (1862) is the same as vol. 1 (1861), *The Letters and the Life of Francis Bacon*. Bacon's *An Advertisement* was first printed separately in 1640 or 1641 during a period of strong anti-episcopal agitation. It was also included in *Resuscitatio*, a collection of Bacon's works edited by William Rawley (London, 1657), pp. 162–179.

30. *The Works of Francis Bacon*, 8:76–77, 85, for the quotations.

31. *Martins Months Minde, That Is, a Certaine Report, and True Description of the Death, and Funeralls, of Olde Martin Marreprelate, the Great Makebate of England, and Father of the Factious. Contayning the Cause of His Death, the Manner of His Buriall, and the Right Copies Both of His Will, and of Such Epitaphs, as by Sundrie His Dearest Friends, and Other of His Well Willers, Were Framed for Him* ([London], 1589).

32. See especially signatures F1 v–F3 v, G1, G3 v, H2 and H2 v. The phrase "month's mind" refers to a celebration of the mass one month after Martin's death.

33. ([London], 1589). Signature Diii v gives the date for "Pasquils Protestation" as 20 October. For the quotations and main assertions, see signatures Aiii, Bii, Bii v, Ci, Ciii v, Civ v, Diii.

34. *Pappe with an Hatchet. Alias, a Figge for My God Sonne. Or Cracke Me This Nut. Or a Countrie Cuffe, That Is, a Sound Boxe of the Eare, for the Idiot Martin to Hold His Peace, Seeing the Patch Will Take No Warning* ([London, ca. October 1589]), signatures A4–B2 v, D1, E2. See also *The Complete Works of John Lyly*, edited by R. Warwick Bond, 3:393–413, 573–89.

35. *Plaine Percevall the Peace-Maker of England. Sweetly Indevoring with His Blunt Persuasions to Botch up a Reconciliation between Mar-ton and Mar-tother* ([London, 1589]). It was probably published shortly before Richard Harvey's *A Theological Discourse of the Lamb of God*, which was entered on 23 October 1589 in the Stationers' Register, but not published until 1590. Nashe and McKerrow assign this book to Richard Harvey, but Edward George Harman asserted it is "quite impossible that this book [*Plaine Percevall*] can be by the author of the *Lamb of God*" (*Gabriel Harvey and Thomas Nashe* [London, 1923], pp. 57–58). But Nashe wrote: "Thy hot-spirited brother Richard [Harvey] (a notable ruffian with his pen), having first tooke upon him in his blundring Persival, to play the Jacke of both sides twixt Martin and us, and snarld privily at Pap-hatchet, Pasquill, and others . . . presently after dribbed forth another fooles bolt, a booke I shoulde say, which he christened *The Lambe of God*." See Nashe, *Strange Newes, of the Intercepting Certaine Letters, and a Convoy of Verses, as They Were Going Privilie to Victuall the Low Countries* (London, 1592 [1592/93]), signature C2 v. See also McKerrow, *The Works of Thomas Nashe*, 1:270.

36. *Plaine Percevall*, pp. 8, 14, 21–22. "Mocchat" and "moccabitur" are coined Latin words. The Latin verbs for "mock" are "ludo" and "ludoficor." "Tuft mock-adoo mak-a-dooes" were tasseled, tuft, gowned trouble-makers.

37. (London, 1593). Also printed in *The Works of Gabriel Harvey*, edited by Alexander B. Grosart, 2:124–221.

38. *Pierces Supererogation*, pp. 69, 137, 138, 129, 122.

39. *A Myrror for Martinists, and All Other Schismatiques, Which in These Danger-ous Daies Doe Breake the Godlie Unitie, and Disturbe the Christian Peace of the Church* (London, 1590). It was entered in the Stationers' Register on 22 December 1589 and very likely was published in January 1589/90 by T.T. These initials also suggest Thomas Twyne, but they probably pertain to Thomas Tymme or Thomas Timme. Compare his *A Preparation against the Prognosticated Dangers of This Yeare 1588* (London, 1588). Both books were printed by J. Wolfe. See *S.T.C.*, 23628 and 24420.

40. *A Friendly Admonition* (London, 1590), was entered in the Stationers' Register on 19 January 1589/90. It contains one of the earliest references to Throkmorton's *Master Some Laid Open in His Coulers* (p. 2, margin). For Wright's statements, see pp. 1–4. For Cartwright's letter to Harrison, see *Cartwrightiana*, edited by Albert Peel and Leland H. Carlson (London, 1951), pp. 48–58.

41. The title page continues: "Rimarum sum plenus" [I am full of cracks or chinks, that is, I cannot keep a secret]. "Therefore Beware (Gentle Reader) You Catch Not the Hicket with Laughing." There is a humorous imprint, mimicking Martin: "Imprinted at a Place, Not Farre from a Place, by the Assignes of Signior Some-body, and Are to Be Sold at His Shoppe in Trouble-knave Street, at the Signe of the Standish." See Donald J. McGinn, "Nashe's Share in the Marprelate Controversy," *PMLA* 59 (1944): 952–84. McGinn assigns this work to Nashe, but McKerrow, our leading authority on Nashe, is dubious of his authorship.

42. For name-calling and quotations, see signatures B3 v, C2, C3 v, D2 v, D3 v, E1 v–E3 v.

43. ([London], 1590). On signature E1 v the date 2 July 1590 is given. The imprint reads: "Printed Where I Was, and Where I Will Bee Readie by the Helpe of God and My Muse, to Send You the May-game of Martinisme for an Intermedium, betwene the First and Seconde Part of the Apologie." The probable author, Thomas Nashe, never published his promised "May-game" or the "Seconde Part of the Apologie."

44. *A Treatise Wherein Is Manifestlie Proved, That Reformation and Those That Sincerely Favor the Same, Are Unjustly Charged to Be Enemies, unto Hir Majestie, and the State. Written Both for the Clearing of Those That Stande in That Cause: and the Stopping of the Sclaunderous Mouthes of All the Enemies Thereof* ([Edin-burgh: Robert Waldegrave], 1590). Usually referred to as *Reformation No Enemie*, this treatise was written in the latter part of 1589 and published about January 1589/90. Penry's name is not on the title page but appears on signature A2. The preface is bitterly critical of the Privy Council and ecclesiastical authorities. The original book, from which passages were underlined and extracted to be used against Penry at his trial, 21–25 May 1593, is at the Huntington Library. See Ellesmere MS. 2148, fol. 88 v. ·

45. *The First Parte of Pasquils Apologie*, signatures A3 v, A4, B2 v, and C2. Martin's books were published *after* the Armada was repelled.

46. (London, 1590). In 1591 an English translation was published: *Of the Diverse Degrees of the Ministers of the Gospell*. Saravia also wrote *Defensio tractationis de diversis ministrorum evangelii gradibus* (London, 1594), against

Théodore de Bèze. See also W. D. J. Cargill Thompson, "Anthony Marten and the Elizabethan Debate on Episcopacy," *Essays in Modern English Church History. In Memory of Norman Sykes*, edited by Gareth V. Bennett and J. D. Walsh (London, 1966), pp. 44–75.

47. I have not included R.W., *Martine Mar-Sixtus* (London, 1591), which is a reply to Pope Sixtus V. The writer justified his use of the name "Martine": the first syllable meant to mar, and the second syllable, tine, indicated "the murdering end of a forke." He also charged that Martin the Great "laid siege against his native soyle," but that Martine Mar-Sixtus combatted "a forreine adversary." I have excluded John Davies, *Sir Martin Mar-People, His Coller of Esses* [Collar of SS—an ornamental badge or chain], since this book of six pages of stanzas bewails the state of affairs: "O wayward, wicked, wanton world, O gaping gulfe of griefe, O sinke of sinne, O sea of shame." The author may be glancing at Martin Marprelate when he writes: "such baudy bookes abounding now for sinfull delectation," or "such volumes vile such venome have, as soone corrupts the readers."

48. Bacon, "An Advertisement touching the Controversies of the Church of England," *Works of Francis Bacon*, 8:70–95 and 76.

49. *Mar-Martine*, signature A4 v.

50. *Martins Months Minde*, signature E4, E3 v.

51. *A Whip for an Ape* (London, 1589), signature A2.

52. *The Returne of the Renowned Cavaliero Pasquill of England* (London, 1589), signature Ciii v.

53. John Payne Collier, *The History of English Dramatic Poetry to the Time of Shakespeare; and Annals of the Stage to the Restoration*, 3 vols. (London, 1831), 1:271–77, and in the new edition (1879), 1:264–70; E. K. Chambers, *William Shakespeare, a Study of Facts and Problems*, 2 vols. (Oxford, 1930), 1:33–34; Chambers, *The Elizabethan Stage*, 4 vols. (Oxford, 1923), 1:294–95, 319, and chaps. 8 and 9; 2:18, 110, 395; 3:412, 444–45; 4:229–33. *Acts of the Privy Council, 1589–90*, pp. 214–16. The lord admiral was Charles Howard, of Armada fame, and later (1596) earl of Nottingham. Lord Strange was Ferdinando Stanley, who became the fifth earl of Derby in 1593.

NOTES—Chapter III

1. The trials of Sir Richard Knightley, Hales, Wigston and his wife in the Court of Star Chamber are available in Howell, *State Trials*, 1:1,263–72, and in William Cobbett, *A Complete Collection of State Trials*, 34 vols. (London, 1809–26), 1:1,263–72. T.B. and T. J. Howell added about 200 cases to the older edition of Francis Hargrave. The date given in the title of the case is 31 Eliz., Feb. 31, A.D. 1588, which should be 32 Elizabeth, 13 February A.D. 1589/90. I wish to thank Dr. W. H. C. Frend and the Fellows and librarian of Gonville and Caius College, Cambridge, for the use of the original manuscript, No. 197, Class A 1090, 8.

2. Knightley was wrong in stating that Penry's book was unobjectionable; the entire edition of 500 copies had been seized in March 1586/87 by officials of the Stationers' Company. It seems unlikely that Knightley was ignorant of the kind of book printed in Fawsley; in March 1589 he did send copies of Marprelate's *Epitome* or *Hay Any Worke* or both to his brother-in-law, Edward Seymour, earl of Hertford. See Arber, *Introductory Sketch*, p. 114, and Howell, *State Trials*, 1:1,266–67, 1,271.

3. Hales's aunt was Mary Fermor, the first wife of Knightley. For Hales, see Howell, *State Trials*, 1:1,267–68, and Arber, *Introductory Sketch*, p. 133. A new source for Hales is in the B.L., Additional MSS. 48039, fol. 63, formerly Yelverton MSS. 44.

4. The most recent proclamation was that of 13 February 1588/89 against the works of Marprelate and Udall. There was a proclamation of 30 June 1583 against the books of Robert Browne and Robert Harrison, and another of 12 October 1584 against books defacing true religion. See Paul L. Hughes and James F. Larkin, *Tudor Royal Proclamations*, vol. 2, *The Later Tudors (1533–1587)*, pp. 501–08; vol. 3, *The Later Tudors (1588–1603)*, p. 34. For the Star Chamber decree of 23 June 1586, see Lansdowne MSS. 905, no. 15, and P.R.O., State Papers Domestic, Elizabeth, vol. 190, no. 48. Printed in Arber, *Stationers' Registers*, 2: 807–12.

5. Howell, *State Trials*, 1:1,267; Arber, *Introductory Sketch*, p. 133.

6. Ibid., p. 123.

7. For the Bill of Complaint and "The Aunswere of Elizabethe [Crane] Carleton Widdow to the Bill of Informacion Exhibited againste Her by John Popham," see P.R.O., Star Chamber 5/A 30/22. See also Harley MSS. 2143, fols. 48 v, 49, which mentions her two fines and imprisonment. See further Julia Norton McCorkle, "A Note concerning 'Mistress Crane' and the Martin Marprelate Controversy," *The Library* 12 (December 1931): 276–83. Mrs. McCorkle refers to "an undated bill of information" by John Popham, but it is dated xi^mo Febr. A° xxxii. She also refers to Elizabeth Carleton's "appearance before the Commission on 1 October 1589." But

John Popham wrote that "the said Elizabeth Carleton was sythence the first daie of October nowe last paste called before certeine of your Majestyes most honorable Pryvye Councell and others to be examined." Since her servant, Nicholas Tomkins, was questioned about her activities on 29 November 1589, it is likely that Mrs. Crane was first examined in December or January 1589/90.

8. *Acts of the Privy Council, 1591*, p. 130.

9. B.L., Additional MSS. 48064, fol. 181 v (Yelverton MSS. 70).

10. Ellesmere MSS., vol. 52, no. 3318.

11. B.L., Additional MSS. 48064, fol. 146 (Yelverton MSS. 70). See *Statutes of the Realm*, 4, pt. 1:659. *Acts of the Privy Council, 1590*, p. 308. Pierce, *Historical Introduction*, pp. 333–35.

12. Ibid., pp. 334–35. *Statutes of the Realm*, 4, pt. 1:660.

13. *Acts of the Privy Council, 1591*, p. 130. In 1595 Sutcliffe wrote about the dropping of the manuscript of *More Worke for Cooper* into a low room where Hodgskin worked, and then added: "An unhappy droppe for poore Hodgskin, who, if Her Majestie had not bene gracious to him, had dropped off the gibet for it." See *An Answere*, p. 72.

14. For Symmes, see Arber, *Stationers' Registers*, 1:578, 581; 2:829, 833, 836, 840; 3:249, 661, 677, 678, 702, 703. William A. Jackson, *Records of the Court of the Stationers' Company, 1602 to 1640* (London, 1957), pp. 24, 152, 380–81.

15. Ibid., p. 381.

16. W. Craig Ferguson, *Valentine Simmes, Printer to Drayton, Shakespeare, Chapman, Greene, Dekker, Middleton, Daniel, Jonson, Marlowe, Marston, Heywood, and Other Elizabethans* (Charlottesville, Virginia, 1968), pp. 5–26, 104–09.

17. For Udall's court appearances, see Howell, *State Trials*, 1:1,271–316. See [Udall], *New Discovery*, passim, and John Strype, *Annals of the Reformation*, 4 vols. in 7 (Oxford, 1824), 4:28–41. For material incriminating Udall, see Arber, *Introductory Sketch*, pp. 81–83, 85, 87–95, 121–22, 169–72. *Acts of the Privy Council, 1590*, p. 224; ibid., *1591–2*, p. 474. *Calendar of State Papers Domestic, Elizabeth, 1591–4*, p. 35. Harley MSS. 360, items 45–47, fols. 75–77; 787, item 65, fol. 66b; 6849, fols. 120–42, 151–70, 235–36; 6995, item 48. Lansdowne MSS. 68, fols. 48–49; 69, items 40–45. SP 12/244/item 64/fol. 156, is Udall's letter to Lord Burghley, dated 3 March 1592. Since this is old style, the date is 1592/93, which establishes Udall's death as 1593, not 1592, as given in the *D.N.B.* See Robert Parker, *De Politeia Ecclesiastica Christi et Hierarchica Opposita, Libri Tres* ([Leyden], 1621), p. 328, for Udall's death. Matthew Sutcliffe refuted Udall's book in an anonymous work, *A Remonstrance: or Plaine Detection of Some of the Faults and Hideous Sores of Such Sillie Syllogismes and Impertinent Allegations, as Out of Sundrie Factious Pamphlets and Rhapsodies, Are Cobled up Together in a Booke, Entituled, A Demonstration of Discipline.*

18. See Ellesmere MS. 2147, fol. 83, for the examination of Penry on 24 May 1593 regarding his authorship of this book. Some of his strictures on the queen, taken from this volume, constituted evidence for adjudging him guilty of felony on 25 May, in violation of "An Acte against sedicious

Wordes and Rumors uttered againste the Queenes moste excellent Majestie," 23 Elizabeth, c. 2, section 4, *Statutes of the Realm*, 4, pt. 1, 659–61. The main counts were seditious words, slanders, and promoting insurrection. See *Reformation No Enemie*, signatures A2-AA2 v. See also Ellesmere MSS. 2147, fol. 83; 2149, fol. 91; 2152, fols. 104–07; 2153, fol. 111; Harley MSS. 6848, fol. 91; 6849, fols. 198–200; Lansdowne MSS. 75, no. 26, fols. 54, 55, no. 27, fols. 56–57. P.R.O., KB9/683/parchment 38; SP12/245/item 21/fol. 45.

19. [Edinburgh: Robert Waldegrave, 1590]. This book has no imprint and no author's name. The reason for the secrecy was that the English ambassador, Robert Bowes, checked closely on Penry's and Waldegrave's activities. Penry was banished in August, at the same time that this book was published. Both Kildale and Bancroft asserted correctly that Penry was the author. See Ellesmere MS. 2148, fols. 88 v, 89.

20. P.R.O., SP 52/46/no, 64, fols. 487–92. Burghley's marginal note reads: "Penry the seditious libeller." *Calendar of the State Papers Relating to Scotland and Mary, Queen of Scots, 1547–1603*, vol. 10, A.D. *1589–1593*, ed. W. K. Boyd and H. W. Meikle (Edinburgh, 1936), pp. 280–81, 292, 363–64, 368, 380, 383, 419–22, 435. The order for Penry's banishment is in *The Register of the Privy Council of Scotland*, vol. 4, *1585–1592*, ed. David Masson (Edinburgh, 1881), pp. 517–18. There is a stray letter of Bowes to Burghley, 4 May 1590, in Harley MSS. 4648, no. 23, fol. 28.

21. *Propositions and Principles of Divinitie, Propounded and Disputed in the Universitie of Geneva, by Certaine Students of Divinitie There, under M. Theod. Beza, and M. Anthonie Faius, Professors of Divinitie. Wherein Is Contained a Methodicall Summarie, or Epitome of the Common Places of Divinitie. Translated out of Latine into English, to the End That the Causes, Both of the Present Dangers of That Church, and Also of the Troubles of Those That Are Hardlie Dealt with Els-where, May Appeare in the English Tongue* (Edinburgh: Robert Waldegrave, 1591). Also, 1595.

22. See Richard Cosin, *Conspiracie, for Pretended Reformation: viz. Presbyteriall Discipline. A Treatise Discovering the Late Designments and Courses Held for Advancement Thereof, by William Hacket Yeoman, Edmund Coppinger, and Henry Arthington Gent. out of Others Depositions and Their Owne Letters, Writings and Confessions upon Examination* (London, 1592). This book, published anonymously, carries on the title page the date "Ultimo Septembris. 1591." See also Richard Bancroft, *Daungerous Positions and Proceedings*, pp. 141–76, and Francis Paget, *An Introduction to the Fifth Book of Hooker's Treatise of the Laws of Ecclesiastical Polity*, app., pp. 260–62. The best recent article is by John Booty, "Tumult in Cheapside: The Hacket Conspiracy," *Historical Magazine of the Protestant Episcopal Church* 42 (September, 1973): 293–317. For Penry's trip to London, see Ellesmere MS. 2148, fol. 89; for his translation of *Propositions and Principles*, see his examination of 5 April 1593 in Ellesmere MS. 2113, printed in Leland H. Carlson, ed., *The Writings of John Greenwood and Henry Barrow, 1591–1593* (London, 1970), pp. 356–57.

23. For Penry's examinations and imprisonment, see Harley MSS. 6849, fol. 204; Ellesmere MSS. 2113, fol. 25; 2148–2156, 2158, fols. 85–125 v. For his trial, see Champlin Burrage, *John Penry, the So-called Martyr of Congregationalism, as Revealed in the Original Record of His Trial and in Documents Related*

Thereto (Oxford, 1913). There is material on his last year of life in Carlson, *The Writings of John Greenwood and Henry Barrow, 1591–1593.* Other works are John Waddington, *John Penry, the Pilgrim Martyr, 1559–1593* (London, 1854); Pierce, *John Penry, His Life, Times, and Writings,* pp. 303–485; Peel's edition of the *Notebook;* McGinn, *John Penry and the Marprelate Controversy.* Waddington, Arber, and Sidney Lee, in his *D.N.B.* article, misdate Penry's birth as 1559, but 1563 is the correct date.

24. For Bowes's correspondence regarding Waldegrave, see *Calendar of the State Papers Relating to Scotland and Mary, Queen of Scots, 1547–1603,* vol. 10, *A.D., 1589–1593,* pp. 280–81, 292, 294, 361–64, 420–21, 430, 435, 702; vol. 11, *A.D. 1593–1595,* ed. Annie I. Cameron (Edinburgh, 1936), pp. 53, 114, 420, 430–31, 487, 502. For Waldegrave's seeking a pardon, see SP 52/46/item 22, fol. 347; SP 52/46/no. 64, fols. 487–92; SP 52/48/item 52/20 June 1592; SP 52/54/27 August, 3 December 1594; Cotton MSS., Titus, Bvi, fol. 154 (old fol. 148). For Waldegrave's printing, see Paul G. Morrison, *Index of Printers, Publishers and Booksellers in A. W. Pollard and G. R. Redgrave, A Short-Title Catalogue of Books Printed in England, Scotland, and Ireland and of English Books Printed Abroad, 1475–1640* (Charlottesville, Virginia, 1950), p. 74, and Harry G. Aldis, *A List of Books Printed in Scotland before 1700 Including Those Printed Furth of the Realm for Scottish Booksellers, with Brief Notes on the Printers and Stationers* (Edinburgh, 1904). The new edition of 1970 has additions. For Cartwright's book, see *S.T.C.,* 4716. The first four words are in Greek: Σὺν θεῷ ἐν χριστῷ.

NOTES—Chapter IV

1. Two helpful bibliographies are George W. Marshall, *The Genealogist's Guide* (Guildford, 1903), and John Beach Whitmore, *The Genealogical Guide*, 4 parts (London, 1947–53). For Fladbury and the early genealogy of the Throckmortons, see Treadway Nash, *Collections for the History of Worcestershire*, 2 vols. (London, 1799), 1:445–54. The pedigree from 1248 to 1779 does not include the children of Clement Throkmorton (died 1573) or of Job, but it is valuable for the families of Sir John (died 1446), Sir Thomas (died 1472), Sir Robert (died 1519), Sir George (died ca. 1553), and Sir Robert (died 1570 or 1580). See William Dugdale, *The Antiquities of Warwickshire*, ed. William Thomas, 2 vols. (London, 1730), 1:654–55, 749–56. This edition is superior to that of 1656. See Herbert M. Jenkins, *Dr. Thomas's Edition of Sir William Dugdale's "Antiquities of Warwickshire"* (Oxford, 1931). Dugdale Society Occasional Papers, no. 3.

2. William Camden, *The Visitation of the County of Warwick in the Year 1619*, ed. John Fetherston. Harleian Society, no. 12 (London, 1877), pp. 86–89, 111, 206–07. For Sir Nicholas and Sir Arthur and Elizabeth (Bess), see A. L. Rowse, *Ralegh and the Throckmortons*, chaps. 2, 3, 9, 10. For Sir Nicholas and the family, see a long poem of 229 stanzas, in Harley MSS. 6353, item 1, and Additional MSS. 5841, fols. 129–46, and John Gough Nichols, ed., *The Legend of Sir Nicholas Throckmorton* (London, 1874).

3. For Clement, see Camden, *Visitation*, pp. 88–89, 207; Charlotte Carmichael Stopes, *Shakespeare's Warwickshire Contemporaries* (Stratford-upon-Avon, 1907), chap. 9; *Acts of the Privy Council*, A.D. *1550–1552*, 3:325; ibid., A.D. *1558–1570*, 7:34. Clement was a "king's receiver" in 1541–42 and surveyor of the woods of the Duchy of Lancaster in 1551. For his appointment as a Merchant Adventurer or member in the Russia Company, see *Calendar of the Patent Rolls*, A.D. *1554–1555*, 2:55–59, and T. S. Willan, *The Muscovy Merchants of 1555* (Manchester, 1953), pp. 13, 125. For Hauckes, see John Foxe, *Acts and Monuments*, 4th ed., ed. Josiah Pratt, 8 vols. (London, 1877), 7:117–18.

4. For Katherine Neville's pedigree, see G. E. Cokayne, *The Complete Peerage*, ed. Vicary Gibbs et al., 13 vols. in 14 (London, 1910–40), 1:19–41; 9:502–05; 12, pt. 2:544–65. She was the niece of George, Lord Bergavenny, 1497–1534, and the sister of Edward Neville, Lord Bergavenny, who died 1588/89. Her father, Sir Edward, was beheaded in 1538 for his support of the Pole faction—Margaret, Reginald, and Henry. The latter was married to Jane, daughter of George Neville, Lord Bergavenny. See also Daniel Rowland, *An Historical and Genealogical Account of the Noble Family of Nevill, Particularly of the House of Abergavenny, and Also a History of the Old Barony of Abergavenny. With Some Account of the Illustrious Family of the Beauchamps* (London, 1830). See also Ellesmere MSS. 5984, 5985, in the Huntington Library.

5. In Camden, *Visitation*, pp. 88–89, 207; Clement, brother of Job, is omitted, but he appears in *Middle Temple Records*, ed. Charles H. Hopwood and Charles Trice Martin, 5 vols. (London, 1903–05), 1:251, and in the *Register of Admissions to the Honourable Society of the Middle Temple*, ed. Henry F. Macgeagh and H. A. C. Sturgess, 3 vols. (London, 1949), 1:45, 50.

6. For Tudor Oxford University, see Charles Edward Mallet, *A History of the University of Oxford*, 3 vols. (London, 1924–27); see especially chaps. 11–14, vol. 2; Mark H. Curtis, *Oxford and Cambridge in Transition, 1558–1642; an Essay on Changing Relations between the English Universities and English Society* (Oxford, 1959); *The Victoria History of the County of Oxford*, vol. 3: *The University of Oxford* (London, 1954). A recent work is *The University in Society*, ed. Lawrence Stone, 2 vols. (Princeton, 1974).

7. Martin Marprelate refers to Humphrey in the *Epitome*, signature F3 v; to Cole in the *Epistle*, p. 46; to Pagit in the *Epistle*, p. 28, *Hay Any Worke*, p. 21, and *Martin Senior*, signature Dii. Throkmorton's letter to Warcuppe on 13 January 1583/84 is in the P.R.O., SP 12/167/21.

8. Martin refers to Culpepper as "Dr. Culpable," warden of New College, in *Hay Any Worke*, p. 47; to Cooper in six of the seven Marprelate works; to Underhill in *Martin Junior*, signature Diii v, *Martin Senior*, signature Cii v, and the *Protestatyon*, p. 25; to Kennall in the *Epitome*, signature E4 v, and *Hay Any Worke*, p. 47. Throkmorton also refers to Colepepper or Culpepper and Bond in *A Dialogue. Wherin Is Plainly Laide Open*, signature D3 and D3 v.

9. The election of Bond to the presidency on 5 April 1589, after Ralph Smith had been elected, became a cause célèbre. Queen Elizabeth interfered, and Bond was the winner. Once again, in 1687, James II intervened in the affairs of Magdalen College, but he did not succeed, despite the precedent of 1589. See H. A. Wilson, *Magdalen College* (London, 1899), pp. 133–40, and William Dunn Macray, *A Register of the Members of St. Mary Magdalen College, Oxford, from the Foundation of the College*, 8 vols. (London, 1894–1915), 2:171–82. See also *The History of England from the Accession of James the Second by Lord Macaulay*, ed. C. H. Firth, 6 vols. (London, 1913–15), 2 (1914): 934–55.

10. Kennall is not noticed in the *D.N.B.* See Joseph Foster, *Alumni Oxonienses*, 2 (1891): 843. Foster's four volumes for 1500–1714 were published in 1891–92 at Oxford.

11. Martin refers to Dr. Day in *Hay Any Worke*, signature A3 v and p. 10; to Matthew in the *Epitome*, signature F3 v; to Rainolds or Reynolds, in the *Epistle*, p. 25. Martin does not refer to Campion or Gregory Martin except under the general name of papists and Rhemists, but Throkmorton refers to Campion in *Master Some Laid Open*, p. 87.

12. It is uncertain which college Throkmorton attended. Two of his sons and two of his grandsons matriculated in the university from The Queen's College; also, the *Victoria History of the County of Warwick*, 3 (1945): 106, states that Throkmorton was educated at Queen's, but no evidence is provided. Officials at Queen's have informed me that Throkmorton is not listed in their College Entrance Books, and A. B. Emden, whose *Biographical*

Register of the University of Oxford comes down to 1540 in his fourth volume, kindly has informed me Throkmorton is not listed for any Oxford college. He does appear, however, as a graduate in 1565/66; see C. W. Boase, *Register of the University of Oxford* (Oxford, 1885), 1:258, and Foster, *Alumni Oxonienses*, 4:1,483.

13. R. H. Hodgkin, *Six Centuries of an Oxford College. A History of The Queen's College, 1340–1940* (Oxford, 1949), p. 70.

14. Ibid.

15. This summary on The Queen's College is based on Hodgkin, *Six Centuries*, and especially on John Richard Macgrath, *The Queen's College*, 2 vols. (Oxford, 1921), 1: ch. 6 and pp. 185–205; 2:296.

16. For Throkmorton's use of legal language, see chap. seven. Inns of Chancery were preparatory schools, residence halls, and/or social and dining clubs for young law students. Attached to Middle Temple were New Inn and Strand Inn. See Hugh H. L. Bellot, *The Inner and Middle Temple, Legal, Literary, and Historic Associations* (London, 1902), p. 3.

17. For the period 1558–72, see Wallace MacCaffrey, *The Shaping of the Elizabethan Regime* (Princeton, 1968). For John Field, see Patrick Collinson, "John Field and Elizabethan Puritanism," *Elizabethan Government and Society. Essays Presented to Sir John Neale*, ed. S. T. Bindoff, J. Hurstfield, and C. H. Williams (London, 1961), pp. 127–62. On the Admonition Controversy, see Frere and Douglas, eds., *Puritan Manifestoes*, pp. vii–xxxi; *An Admonition* is printed therein, pp. 8–55. See also McGinn, *The Admonition Controversy*.

18. "An Answer" is in the Inner Temple, Petyt MSS. 538(47), fols. 459–62. It is printed in Styrpe, *Annals*, 2, pt. 1:286–304. Strype or his copyist has misread twenty-seven words and has omitted 1,402 words, especially sentences and sections where the manuscript reading is very difficult. The crabbed, careless, and blurred writing is so small that three and one-third folios approximate twenty-six typed pages, double spaced. For the authorship, see App. A, which presents reasons for attribution to Throkmorton.

19. These four works are printed in Frere and Douglas, eds., *Puritan Manifestoes*, pp. 57–148. For authorship, see Apps. B, C, D.

20. Printed in *A Parte of a Register*, pp. 371–81. The anonymous editor has misdated it as 1567, but the correct date is June 1573. Edwin Sandes or Sandys was bishop of Worcester, 1559–70, and did not become bishop of London until 13 July 1570. See App. E.

21. The letters of Sandys are in Frere and Douglas, eds., *Puritan Manifestoes*, pp. 152–55.

22. The letter is in the P.R.O., SP 12/167/21. See also J. W. Ryland, *Records of Rowington* (Oxford, 1922), 2:128–29. Warcuppe (ca. 1542–1605) matriculated from Peterhouse, Cambridge, in 1559; he was admitted to Christ Church, Oxford, in 1561, and received his B.A. in 1564. Since Throkmorton was at Oxford from 1562 to 1566, he may have known Warcuppe as an undergraduate. Wood describes him as "the most accomplished gentleman of the age he lived in," and as a linguist (*Athenae Oxonienses*, 1:754). He was an M.P. for Warwickshire in 1601.

23. There are no returns for the Parliament of 1571, but Frederick Leigh Colvile states that Clement Throkmorton was "M.P. for West Looe in 1571" (*The Worthies of Warwickshire Who Lived between 1500 and 1800* [Warwick, 1870, p. 752]).

23. Bancroft, *Survay*, p. 369. Bancroft was quoting a letter from Edmund Chapman to John Field.

25. *The Black Book of Warwick*, ed. Thomas Kemp (Warwick, [1898]), pp. 387, 389. The laws referred to, requiring citizens and burgesses to be residents "dwelling and free in the same Cities and Boroughs," were 1 Henry V, section 1, and 23 Henry VI, c. 13; see *Statutes of the Realm*, 2:170, 340.

26. *The Black Book of Warwick*, pp. 385–97; see also *The Book of John Fisher, Town Clerk and Deputy Recorder of Warwick (1580–1588)*, ed. Thomas Kemp (Warwick, [1900]), pp. xi–xv and passim. The *D.N.B.* is wrong in stating that Job had served in the Parliament of 1572–83 for East Retford, Notts. The incumbent was John Throckmorton.

27. Neale, *The Elizabethan House of Commons* (London, 1949), pp. 250–54.

28. Dr. Plumb's essay is in *Seventeenth-Century England*, ed. Paul S. Seaver (New York, 1976); see p. 144. See also Throkmorton's letter to the bailiff and principal burgesses of Warwick in Thomas Kemp, ed., *The Black Book of Warwick*, pp. 391–92. This letter may be dated about 25 September–5 October 1586. See further, Derek Hirst, *The Representative of the People? Voters and Voting in England under the Early Stuarts* (Cambridge: Cambridge University Press, 1975), pp. 210–12.

29. For the Parliament of 1586/87, see Neale, *Elizabeth I and Her Parliaments, 1584–1601*, pp. 103–91.

30. Phillipps MSS. 13891, reclassified as MA 276, fols. 5, 7, in the Pierpont Morgan Library.

31. Ibid., fols. 28, 46, 43, 43. For Burghley's letter, see Warrender, *Illustrations of Scottish History. Sixteenth Century*, pp. 31–33. Neale, *Elizabeth I and Her Parliaments, 1584–1601*, pp. 169–75: on pp. 164 and 174 Neale suggests that Throkmorton was sent to the Tower, but this is incorrect. For Hatton's criticism, see Harley MSS. 7188, fols. 89, 92.

32. Neale, *Elizabeth I and Her Parliaments, 1584–1601*, pp. 149 and 148–52; see "Dr. Bancroft's Discourse upon the Bill and Booke," P.R.O., SP 12/199/ items 1 and 2; Harley MSS. 7188, fols. 91 v–93 v; Peel, *The Seconde Parte of a Register*, 2:212–18. The "Book" had been printed by Waldegrave in 1584 and by Schilders in 1586 (*S.T.C.* 16567, 16568); for earlier models in Geneva and Scotland, see *S.T.C.* 16560, 16561, 16564, 16577.

33. Phillipps MSS. 13891, reclassified as MA 276, fol. 13.

34. Ibid., fols. 17, 18.

35. Ibid., fol. 23.

36. Sutcliffe, *An Answere*, p. 74. Job's sister, Katherine, married Thomas Harby, esquire, who was from Adstone, Northamptonshire, and Hillingdon, Middlesex.

37. Lansdowne MSS. 53, item 71, fols. 148–49.

38. Note the phrase "Laide Open." It also occurs in Throkmorton's *Master Some Laid Open* and his *A Dialogue. Wherin Is Plainly Laide Open.*

39. The books were seized on 16 April 1588. The Stationers' Company, at a full Court meeting on 13 May 1588, ordered "that ye said bookes shalbe burnte and the said presse letters and printinge stuffe defaced and made unserviceable accordinge to the said Decrees" [of the Star Chamber Court]. On 10 June two wardens and a pursuivant with five other men visited Kingston-upon-Thames and searched a poor woman's house in the hope of capturing Waldegrave. It is possible that at this time Waldegrave was already reprinting Throkmorton's *The State of the Church of Englande.* Martin gloated that the trip to Kingston-upon-Thames was a failure: "and many such journies may you make" (*Epistle,* p. 42). The 1593 edition appeared in *A Parte of a Register.* See Greg and Boswell, eds., *Records of the Court of the Stationers' Company, 1576 to 1602, from Register B,* pp. lviii, 27–28. See also Arber, *Stationers' Registers,* 1:528–29. For authorship, see infra, App. F.

40. The contents of the Marprelate books are summarized in the Introduction. They are briefly listed here in one paragraph to give a complete record of Throkmorton's writings in chronological order. For the evidence of authorship, see chapters six and eight.

41. Ellesmere MS. 2148, fol. 88.

42. Ibid. In his *An Answere,* p. 73, Sutcliffe mentions "Penries *Appellations,* and *Some in His Colours,*" but the Ellesmere MS. also includes *A Dialogue. Wherin Is Plainly Laide Open.*

43. John Dover Wilson, "A Date in the Marprelate Controvery," *The Library,* New or Second Series, 8 (October 1907):354–57.

44. Pierce, *Historical Introduction,* p. 339. Sutcliffe, *An Answere,* pp. 71 v–72.

45. For *Master Some,* see chapter five. The third consignment was Penry's *Appellation*—500 copies. We may conjecture 500 for *A Dialogue.* In addition, there were 500 copies of the *Protestatyon* brought from Wolston to Throkmorton's house.

46. Ellesmere MS. 2148, fol. 86 and 86 v. *A Dialogue* may have been printed in La Rochelle, but the place of printing is uncertain.

47. Sutcliffe, *An Answere,* pp. 56, 72, 72 v; Ellesmere MS. 2148, fols. 87 v, 88 v; on fol. 89 v, the writer speaks of treatises "taken in one of his [Penry's] chests which came lately owt of Scotland." This capture is most likely related to the search in April 1593 for Penry's books, as indicated in Arber, *Stationers' Registers,* 1:562. These sources indicate that Penry's treatises, including "Martins Interim," which had been sent to him in Scotland, were seized in the London area and not in Edinburgh. See chapter six.

48. Sutcliffe, *An Answere,* p. 72 v.

49. Ibid., pp. 2 v, 3, 4, 66 v, 67, 74 v, 75, 75 v, 76, 76 v, 77, 80, 80 v.

50. Throkmorton's petition was in the Manchester Papers, P.R.O., 30/15/124. See the "Report on the MSS. of His Grace the Duke of Manchester," *Eighth Report of the Royal Commission on Historical Manuscripts. Appendix.-(Part*

II) (London, 1881), p. 27, no. 124. No. 123 is the examination of the Marprelate printers on 10 December 1589. These papers are now in Lambeth Palace Library.

51. Coppinger wrote a letter to Throkmorton about May 1591, which is printed in Bancroft, *Daungerous Positions*, pp. 153–54, and in Cosin, *Conspiracie*, p. 26.

52. Throkmorton, *Defence*, signature Dii v.

53. This letter was first referred to by Cosin, *Conspiracie*, p. 17; it was printed in full by Bancroft in *Daungerous Positions*, pp. 154–55, and in Sutcliffe, *An Answere*, pp. 18 v–19. See also John Booty, "Tumult in Cheapside: The Hacket Conspiracy," *Historical Magazine of the Protestant Episcopal Church* 42 (1973): 293–317.

54. Rowse, *Ralegh and the Throckmortons*, pp. 158–64. Sir Walter and Elizabeth were married in October or November 1591; their son Damerei was born on 29 March 1592; on 7 August they were sent to the Tower by the queen. Cf. Pierre Lefranc, "La Date du Marriage de Sir Walter Ralegh: Un Document Inédit," *Etudes Anglaises* 9 (1956): 193–211.

55. Sutcliffe, *An Answere*, p. 73 v. The letter was sent to Penry in 1590 or 1591. The likelihood is that Sutcliffe obtained this letter after it had been found in Penry's chest in April 1593.

56. See pp. 9, 17, 22, 23, 26.

57. The *S.T.C.*, 1521, misdates this book as 1590 and wrongly attributes it to Barrow, but the author is clearly a Presbyterian and not a Separatist. F. J. Powicke and Bancroft suggested that Penry was the author, but Sutcliffe intimated that Throkmorton at least had a hand in part of the treatise. It exists in manuscript in Harley MSS. 7581, fols. 2–49. The printed book may be dated in 1592 from the references to it by Sutcliffe, *An Answere*, signature A4 v, and by Bancroft, *A Survay*, pp. 5–6, 429. Sutcliffe's reply to *A Petition*, entitled *An Answere to a Certaine Libel Supplicatorie, or Rather Diffamatory* (London, 1592), is dated 20 December 1592 (signature B1 v). Any reference to this book will be given with the date 1592; most of my references are to Sutcliffe's *An Answere* of 1595 without a date given.

58. *A Petition*, p. 3. Richard Hooker criticized this statement. See note 75.

59. Ibid., pp. 6, 13, 16, 25, 45, 46, 48, 49, 76, 80.

60. Ibid., pp. 6–7, 14, 17, 38, 76.

61. Ibid., p. 8. Both quotations have minor differences and are insignificant, but except for one sentence they begin and end at the same place. The passage is in Aylmer, *An Harborowe*, signature O4 and O4 v.

62. *A Petition*, pp. 45, 46, 76. Martin's phrases, "twentie fistes" and "an hundred thousande handes" are in the *Epistle*, p. 2, and in *Martin Senior*, signature Civ. The discussion on the "Bishops English" in *A Petition*, p. 45, is similar to the presentation in *Martin Senior*, signatures Civ-Di. His correction of Dr. Cosin is given on page 46.

63. For references to Tyndale, Barnes, and Hooper, see *Martin Junior*, signatures Bii v, Civ v, and the *Protestatyon*, p. 12. Martin alludes to statutes

in the reign of Henry VIII and especially of Elizabeth. See *Epitome*, signature E2 and *Martin Junior*, signatures Bii, Bii v, Civ; see also the *Epistle*, pp. 14, 38.

64. *Hay Any Worke*, p. 26 and A3 v.

65. In *A Petition*, p. 34, the writer refers to Piers Plowman, who "wrote against the state of Bishops and prophecied their fall in these wordes." Then he adds: "Geffrey Chaucer also in Henry the fourths time [Edward III and Richard II] wrote effectuallie against the state of the Bb. in this maner." What is worth noting is that in 1589 an unusual edition of Piers Ploughman was published, containing "proof sheets with MS. corrections." Previously unrecorded, it appears in the second edition of the *S.T.C.* (1976), 19903a.5. The title page paraphrases parts of the title page of Martin's *Epistle*, and on signature A2 we read: "To the puissant paltrypolitanes, bounsing Lord Bishops, Popish parsons, Fickars, and Currats, with all that Romish rable, Piers, Grandsier of Martin Marprelate, wisheth you better then I thinke you wishe your selves." The factotum used is one that Waldegrave also had used, and the type seems to be the same as used in the first four Marprelate items. It may have been issued by Throkmorton or it may have been published by someone using Martin's book as a model. Dr. William A. Ringler, Jr., kindly called my attention to this unusual work.

66. *An Answere* (1592), pp. 200–02.

67. The *S.T.C.* dates Hooker's work as conjecturally 1594, but 1593 is the correct date. See Raymond Aaron Houk, *Hooker's Ecclesiastical Polity, Book VIII* (New York, 1931), pp. 53–59, and C. J. Sisson, *The Judicious Marriage of Mr Hooker and the Birth of "The Laws of Ecclesiastical Polity"* (Cambridge, 1940), pp. 60–66. Hooker's pertinent letter of 13 March 1592/93 is paraphrased by Strype in *The Life and Acts of John Whitgift*, 2:147–49. For the latest edition of Hooker's writings, see the helpful preparatory book, *Studies in Richard Hooker. Essays Preliminary to an Edition of His Works*, ed. W. Speed Hill (Cleveland and London, 1972). The first two volumes have just been published (1977) by Harvard University Press: Books I-IV by Georges Edelen; Book V, W. Speed Hill.

68. Bancroft does not attribute *A Petition* to any author, but he does ascribe *A Dialogue* to Throkmorton (*Daungerous Positions*, pp. 45, 57, 58, 59). In *A Survay* there are thirty allusions to Field's correspondence, and thirty-one in *Daungerous Positions*.

69. See Peel, ed., *The Seconde Parte of a Register*, 1:12–14, and Collinson, *The Elizabethan Puritan Movement*, p. 440.

70. *Daungerous Positions*, p. 46.

71. See John Dover Wilson, "Richard Schilders and the English Puritans," *Transactions of the Bibliographical Society*, 11 (October 1909 to March 1911) (London, 1912): 98. See also p. 119, no. 27, which is a reproduction of Schilders' factotum, used in *A Parte of a Register*, opposite p. 546. William Herbert has implied that these books were seized in London and delivered to the archbishop of Canterbury, but this seems to be a reference to a book by Alexander Hume, *Christes Descention into Hell*, seized on 4 December 1594

"in a ship of Andrew Blakes that came forth of Scotland." See Joseph Ames, *Typographical Antiquities*, 3 vols., ed. William Herbert (London, 1785–90), 3:1,514 and footnote. See Peel, *The Seconde Parte of a Register*, 1:12, and Arber, *Stationers' Registers*, 1:567 and 2:40.

72. *An Answere* (1592), pp. 78, 202.

73. *Defence*, signatures Cii, Ciii, Eii; Sutcliffe, *An Answere* (1592), pp. 78–79.

74. *Defence*, signature Civ.

75. Richard Hooker, *Of the Lawes of Ecclesiasticall Politie* (London, [1592/93]), p. 44. See Throkmorton's *Defence*, signatures Ciii v-Civ v, and Sutcliffe's *An Answere* (1595), pp. 43, 51 v-54. Hooker had expressed his sentiments when he commented on *A Petition* without knowing that Throkmorton was the author. Hooker wrote: "When they which write in defence of your discipline and commend it unto the Highest not in the least cunning manner, are forced notwithstanding to acknowledge, that *with whom the truth is they know not*, they are not certaine; what certainty or knowledge can the multitude have thereof?" The eight italicized words are Throkmorton's (*A Petition*, p. 3); see Hooker, *Of the Lawes*, p. 14.

76. *Defence*, signature Eii.

77. Ibid., signature Ei and Ei v; Sutcliffe, *An Answere* (1595), p. 67.

78. *Defence*, signature Bii. Sutcliffe, *An Answere* (1595), p. 2; see pp. 18 v-19 for the complete letter. Sutcliffe's printing of the incomplete letter is in his *Answere* (1592), p. 201, with three "etc.'s"

79. *An Answere* (1595), pp. 76 v-77.

80. Ibid., pp. 28, 2 v, 76 v, 80 v, 3 v.

81. Ibid., pp. 49 v and 75.

82. Ibid., pp. 43, 14 v, 74.

83. Ibid., signature B1 v, pp. 7 v, 46, 56, 70 v-77 v, 83 v.

84. Printed by Richard Schilders in Middelburg. The factotum on signature A2 is reproduced by Wilson, "Richard Schilders and the English Puritans," *Transactions of the Bibliographical Society* 11 (October 1909 to March 1911): 118, no. 13. The ornament on the title page is reproduced by Wilson on p. 122, no. 49; it is similar but not identical. Throkmorton's *A Petition*, his *A Defence*, Cartwright's *A Brief Apologie*, and *A Parte of a Register* were all printed by Schilders. This indicates that after 1590 Waldegrave was not available for printing English books. Schilders also printed books for Travers and Fenner.

85. Sutcliffe, *An Answere* (1595), p. 48; *A Brief Apologie*, signature C2 v; in October 1590, Cartwright was examined in the consistory of St. Paul's by six commissioners. Among the thirty-one articles tendered to Cartwright were: "XXIII. *Item*, That he doth know, or credibly heard, who were the penners, printers, or some of the dispersers of the several libels, going under the name of *Martin Mar-Prelate*, of *The Demonstration of Discipline*, of *Diotrephes*, and such-like books, before it was known to authority; and yet, in favour of such and contempt of good laws, did not manifest the same to any who had authority to punish it. XXIV. *Item*, That being

377

asked his opinion of such books, he answered thus in effect, or something tending this way, viz. (meaning the bishops and others there touched) would not amend by grave books and advertisements, and therefore it was meet they should thus be dealt with, to their further reproach and shame" (Fuller, *The Church History of Britain*, 5 [1845]: 142, 146, 149–50). Fuller gives the date as 1 September 1590, but October seems more likely. Consult Pearson, *Thomas Cartwright*, pp. 318–20. Cartwright preached at Throkmorton's home at the baptizing of his child in 1586. See Fuller, *The Church History*, 5:146, article 13, and Bancroft, *Survay*, p. 377.

86. Sutcliffe correctly surmised that Throkmorton was the editor who was responsible for the preface of seven pages. Throkmorton was also the one who added two marginal notes. In the second note occurs the expression, "is put to the jumpe," which has a parallel in Throkmorton's *Defence*, "to put them to the jumpe" (Civ). Cartwright was in Guernsey from 1595 to 1601. Probably for this reason he entrusted Throkmorton with the task of seeing the book through the press. The preface is clearly in Throkmorton's style of writing.

87. Historical Manuscripts Commission, *Second Report of the Royal Commission on Historical Manuscripts* (London, 1871), app., p. 78.

88. The source of this account is in "Some Remarkable Passadges Concerning Mr. Throgmorten Which Hapned aboute Some Tenn Dayes before His Death, A.D. 1637," Additional MSS. 25037, fols. 84 v-97. It was printed by Samuel Clarke, *A Generall Martyrologie* (London, 1651), p. 409, in the second section, "The Lives of Sundry Modern Divines." See also the third edition, p. 172 (London, 1677). Although neither the manuscript nor Clarke's editions specified the first name, it was attributed to *Job* Throkmorton by Benjamin Brook, *The Lives of the Puritans*, 3 vols. (London, 1813), 2:361–62. Following Brook, Sir Sidney Lee repeated the error in his *D.N.B.* article.

89. Evelyn Fox, "The Diary of an Elizabethan Gentlewoman," [Lady Margaret Hoby], *Transactions of the Royal Historical Society*, Third Series, 2 (1908): 171. See also Dorothy M. Meads, *Diary of Lady Margaret Hoby, 1599–1605* (London, 1930), pp. 156–57. Also in 1600 Throkmorton as lord of Hatton was involved in a dispute with Robert Burgoyne regarding the ownership of Shortwood, a wood near Beausale Heath, in the parish of Hatton (*Victoria History of the County of Warwick*, 3:115).

90. For Dorothy Vernon, see Stebbing Shaw, *The History and Antiquities of Staffordshire*, 2 vols. (London, 1798, 1801), 1 (Hanbury): 85–88, 398–404; Camden, *Visitation*, pp. 89, 207, 395.

91. For Oxford colleges, matriculation, and degrees, I have utilized C. W. Boase, *Register of the University of Oxford*, vol. 1 (Oxford, 1885); Andrew Clark, *Register of the University of Oxford*, vol. 2, pts. 1–4 (Oxford, 1887–89); Joseph Foster, *Alumni Oxonienses*, 4 vols.; Anthony a Wood, *Athenae Oxonienses*, ed. Philip Bliss, 4 vols. (London, 1813–20); vol. 2, which includes *Fasti Oxonienses*, is helpful. For the admission of two brothers and two sons of Throkmorton to an Inn of Court, see *Register of Admissions to the Honourable Society of the Middle Temple*, 3 vols., compiled by Henry F. Macgeagh and H. A. C. Sturgess, 1:45, 50, 77, 95, 144; *Middle Temple Records*,

ed. Charles Henry Hopwood and Charles Trice Martin, 1:230, 251, 266, 409; 2:528.

92. Dugdale, *Antiquities of Warwickshire*, 2 (1730): 654. Clement was also a sheriff in the reign of James I; ibid., p. 1,152.

93. (Oxford: Joseph Barnes?, 1610). The sermon caused "tumultuous rumors" and "was by many more hainously taken than either heresie or treason." For other dedications by James Martin and John Rider, see *S.T.C.* 17509 and 21036a.

94. Job Throkmorton's second son was Job, who was born in 1594, matriculated from The Queen's College in 1609, admitted to Middle Temple in 1610. Katherine was the only daughter.

95. Fuller's editor, J. S. Brewer, mistakenly identifies the dedicatee as Job's son instead of the grandson. Camden's characterization is in his *Britain* (London, 1610 and 1637), p. 565. See Thomas Fuller, *The Church History of Britain; from the Birth of Jesus Christ until the Year M.DC.XLVIII*, ed. J. S. Brewer, 2:235 and note a. See page 89 in the first edition of 1655.

NOTES—Chapter V

1. *Master Some Laid Open in His Coulers: Wherein the Indifferent Reader May Easily See, Howe Wretchedly and Loosely He Hath Handeled the Cause against Master Penri. Done by an Oxford Man, to His Friend in Cambridge* ([La Rochelle: Robert Waldegrave, 1589]). Listed erroneously in the *S.T.C.*, 11498, 12342, under I.G. and John Greenwood. See signature A2 for the quotation, and note that Throkmorton anticipates "some offence to my friende," that is, Penry, who disliked Throkmorton's railing and invective.

2. Arber, *Introductory Sketch*, p. 68.

3. Frederick J. Powicke, *Henry Barrow Separatist (1550?–1593) and the Exiled Church of Amsterdam (1593–1622)* (London, 1900), pp. 84, 329, 352.

4. John Dover Wilson, "A Date in the Marprelate Controversy," *The Library* 8 (October 1907): 337–59.

5. Pierce, *Historical Introduction*, p. 235.

6. McKerrow, *Works of Thomas Nashe*, 4:55 and 5:374.

7. McGinn, "A Perplexing Date in the Marprelate Controversy," *Studies in Philology* 41 (1944): 169–80; *John Penry and the Marprelate Controversy*, pp. 158, 147–57, 165. Wilson made no such assumption.

8. *Appellation*, pp. 46–47. Note the contrast: "nowe fearing"—"sometimes." See McGinn, *John Penry and the Marprelate Controversy*, p. 153.

9. See P.R.O., Council Register, vol. 4, 1577–80, P. C. 2/12/fol. 531. *Acts of the Privy Council of England, A.D. 1578–1580*, 11:182. For Sharpe's difficulties in 1581, his interrogatories, and his replies on 13 April 1581, see SP 15/27A/ fols. 9, 12–23.

10. Ellesmere MS. 2148, fol. 86 and 86 v. The "litle jarre" probably refers to Penry's desire to have his *Appellation* printed immediately before Parliament adjourned and Waldegrave's refusal to remain at Coventry or Wolston.

11. Ellesmere MS. 2148, fol. 88. In the manuscript words "Fawsley" and "Haseley" seem almost identical, but in the third paragraph there are two references to "Haseley" which are easily decipherable and conclusive.

12. Ibid. The manuscript has "Gardiner" but Sutcliffe has "Garnet."

13. Further evidence for 1589 is found in an allusion to *Master Some* by Leonard Wright, *A Friendly Admonition*, p. 2, margin; this book was entered in the Stationers' Register on 19 January 1589/90. The anonymous author of *An Almond for a Parrat*, which may be dated about February or March 1589/90, also alludes to *Master Some*, signature E1 v or page 13 v. Therefore *Master Some* must be dated 1589.

14. Sutcliffe, *An Answere* (1595), p. 72; Sutcliffe, *An Answere* (1592), p. 202.

See also Arber, *Introductory Sketch*, p. 179.

15. *Master Some Laid Open*, pp. 10, 34, 14, and signature A2.

16. *A Defence of That Which Hath Bin Written*, pp. 5–6.

17. *Master Some Laid Open*, p. 72. Robert Some, *A Godly Treatise . . . Whereunto One Proposition More Is Added* (September 1588), p. 140.

18. Sutcliffe, *An Answere* (1595), pp. 67, 75.

19. Ibid., p. 72 v; Arber, *Introductory Sketch*, pp. 180–81. The phrase and title occur in *Master Some Laid Open*, p. 105, and in Sutcliffe, *An Answere* (1595), p. 72 v.

20. *Master Some Laid Open*, pp. 21–22. The Greekword "orthotomein" means to cut straight, to divide correctly; see 2 Tim. 2:15.

21. Arber, *Introductory Sketch*, pp. 85, 87, 125–27, 129–30.

22. *A Viewe*, p. 70; *Three Treatises concerning Wales*, ed. David Williams (Cardiff, 1960), p. 158; Penry, *Notebook*, p. 65.

23. These two lists comprise twenty items and three non-extant items; if we add the seven Marprelate works and the three non-extant writings, *More Worke for Cooper*, "Martins Interim," and *The Crops and Flowers of Bridges Garden*, we have a complete list of thirty items by Throkmorton.

24. Dexter, *Congregationalism*, p. 234, n. 76; Pierce, *Historical Introduction*, p. 234; Pierce, *John Penry*, p. 244; Wilson, "The Marprelate Controversy," *Cambridge History of English Literature* 3 (Cambridge, 1930): 390–91, or (New York, 1933): 443–44; McGinn, *John Penry and the Marprelate Controversy*, p. 127.

25. Sutcliffe, *An Answere* (1595), p. 73; Arber, *Introductory Sketch*, pp. 179, 181. On 18 December 1590 Robert Bowes, the English ambassador to Scotland, notified Burghley that James VI had "planted Wal[de]grave to be his printer upon caution given that he shall not hereafter offend her majestie or estate." See the letter of 20 June 1592 from James VI to Burghley regarding a pardon for Waldegrave. Both letters are in the *Calendar of the State Papers Relating to Scotland and Mary, Queen of Scots, 1547–1603*, ed. William K. Boyd and Henry Meikle, X, *A.D. 1589–1593*, 10:435, 702. It is possible that Sutcliffe's reference to Waldegrave's deposition may be derived from Waldegrave's "caution given," or his confession, or from Jenkin Jones's examination on 6 November 1590, or from Henry Kildale's examination on 3 October 1591. See Ellesmere MS. 2148, fol. 88 v and Arber, *Introductory Sketch*, p. 179.

26. Sutcliffe, *An Answere* (1592), p. 202; *An Answere* (1595), pp. 70 v–72 v. Since he mentions "dialogues" in the plural, he may intend also *The State of the Church of Englande*, which is referred to as a *Dialogue* or as *Diotrephes*.

27. *Introductory Sketch*, pp. 193–96.

28. *Henry Barrow Separatist*, pp. 84–85, 329, 352.

29. Wilson, "Martin Marprelate and Shakespeare's Fluellen," *The Library* 3 (April and July 1912): 249–51, 260–62; "The Marprelate Controversy," *Cambridge History of English Literature*, 3 (1930): 390–91.

30. *Historical Introduction,* pp. 210, 233–35; *John Penry,* pp. 201, 244–48.

31. Bonnard, *La controverse de Martin Marprelate, 1588–1590. Épisode de l'histoire littéraire du puritanisme sous Élizabeth* (Geneva, 1916), pp. 196–97.

32. Collinson, *The Elizabethan Puritan Movement,* p. 395.

33. Neale, *Elizabeth I and Her Parliaments, 1584–1601,* p. 220. In his seminars, private conversations, and letters, Neale ruled out Penry as a candidate for Martin's writings. My mentor at the University of Chicago, Marshall M. Knappen, a superb Tudor scholar, concluded: "The available evidence as to the identity of this recruit is more than a little confusing and contradictory, but in the main it points to Job Throckmorton, a wealthy country gentleman of the neighborhood, and one of the parliamentary champions of the Puritan bill of 1572." See his *Tudor Puritanism. A Chapter in the History of Idealism* (Chicago, 1939), p. 295.

34. John Penry, *The Aequity of an Humble Supplication,* ed. Alexander James Grieve (London, 1905), pp. iii-xv.

35. *Three Treatises concerning Wales,* ed. David Williams, pp. xxi-xxii. Clarke, *A General Martyrologie,* 3d ed. (London, 1677), p. 13 of "The Lives," 2d section. Cf. Richard Greenham, *The Workes* (London, 1612), pp. 788–94, 851–52.

36. Dexter, *Congregationalism,* p. 234, n. 76, p. 197; see also his "Argument," in Arber, *Introductory Sketch,* pp. 187–92. See further Leland H. Carlson, ed., *The Writings of John Greenwood, 1587–1590, Together with the Joint Writings of Henry Barrow and John Greenwood, 1587–1590,* pp. 93–94, and *The Writings of John Greenwood and Henry Barrow, 1591–1593,* pp. 1–89.

37. Dexter clearly ruled out Penry as Martin Marprelate. He stated "that there is not the requisite resemblance between Penry's books and the Martin Mar-Prelate tracts to make a common authorship probable." He also wrote: "The weight of evidence is against the theory that John Penry was their Author," and concluded that "there is nothing in the style and manner of Penry's acknowledged works to make it probable that he wrote the Martinist tracts." See his "Argument," in Arber, *Introductory Sketch,* pp. 189, 187, 188, and in *Congregationalism,* p. 234, n. 76.

38. Maskell, *A History of the Martin Marprelate Controversy,* pp. 10, 11, 16, 120.

39. McGinn, *John Penry and the Marprelate Controversy,* pp. 158–65.

40. Ibid., pp. 148, 158, 165; McGinn, "A Perplexing Date in the Marprelate Controversy," *Studies in Philology* 41 (1944): 180. McGinn dates the *Appellation* 7 March 1589/90, and says that Master Some was "probably published later in 1590." His argument that the *Appellation,* as well as *Master Some Laid Open,* was written *after* 17 November 1589, is based on Penry's statement, "nowe after 31. yeares of the gospell enjoyed" (*Appellation,* p. 34). But this means *within* the thirty-first regnal year, as is clearly indicated in Penry's statement, "in the 31. yeare of the raigne of Queene Elizabeth" (*Appellation,* p. 27), which McGinn does not mention.

41. McGinn, *John Penry and the Marprelate Controversy,* pp. 144–46.

42. Ellesmere MS. 2148, fol. 88.

43. McGinn weakens his argument when he writes: "Nevertheless, it must be admitted that the attacks on Bridges in *M. Some Laid open in his coulers* are written not as a Welsh jeremiad, as in Penry's *Exhortation,* but rather in the tarletonizing vein of Martin's *Epistle.*" This is tantamount to saying that *Master Some* is not written in Penry's style but in that of Martin and Throkmorton, whose styles are identical.

McGinn's generalization that "the commonly accepted evidence" connects *Master Some* "not only with the Martinist tracts but also with Penry's acknowledged writings" is a half-truth. There is much evidence linking *Master Some* with the Martinist tracts but none whatsoever with Penry's "acknowledged writings." McGinn's constant efforts to press guilt by association and linkage without evidence are disturbing. He refers to *Master Some,* which appears to be "the product of Penry writing in his Martinist style," but Penry has no Martinist style. When McGinn discusses Barrow's critique of *Master Some,* he writes: "Although Barrowe is willing to play along with the fiction of the pamphlet's being written by Penry's friend, he directs his remarks to Penry himself." There is no evidence that Barrow was "willing to play along with the fiction," and there is plenty of evidence that Barrow directs his remarks not to Penry but to Penry's friend. When McGinn writes: "Particularly significant to the student of the Marprelate Controversy is the subtle identification of Penry with Martin, as though Barrowe himself were aware of the secret," he is presenting unsupported conjecture. Barrow was blunt and forthright and did not make subtle identifications. When McGinn asserts: "Slyly Barrowe insinuates that 'if Mr Penry provide not better stuffe for his owne defence than his friend of Oxenford hath as yet brought,' he and his companions 'must become Brownists,'" McGinn himself is supplying the misleading word "Slyly." And when he speaks of "Penry's concession that since Elizabeth is persuaded in her conscience that she has received the true sacrament in the 'popish' church, she is baptized and needs no further outward sign of baptism," he should speak of the friend of Oxenford's concession, who was Throkmorton as the author of *Master Some.* Barrow referred at least fourteen times to Penry's "advocate," his "proctor," his "friend," the "scholler of Oxford," and "the clerk of Oxenford." To identify these references with Penry himself and to assign the authorship of *Master Some* to Penry is a violation of the canons of historical scholarship. McGinn's statements are in *John Penry and the Marprelate Controversy,* pp. 161, 164, 184. Barrow's references are in Leland H. Carlson, ed., *The Writings of Henry Barrow, 1587–1590,* pp. 425–52. Throkmorton's statements are in *Master Some Laid Open,* pp. 52, 58–60.

44. Turney, "A Critical Edition of the Puritan Pamphlet, *M. Some Laid Open in His Coulers,*" pp. 3, 47, 55–56.

45. McKerrow, *The Works of Thomas Nashe,* 5:35. Wilson, "The Marprelate Controversy," *Cambridge History of English Literature,* 3 (1930): 398, 390, 391. The later edition (1933) omits "most famous" and "humble." See also Wilson, "A Date in the Marprelate Controversy," *The Library* 3 (1907): 349.

NOTES—Chapter VI

1. See Part I, pp. ii-xl, li-lii. The thesis is at Rutgers University.

2. One clue is that Waldegrave's press and equipment "were destroied about Ester was a twelve moneth," which indicates a date after 30 March 1589. The second clue is the implication that Dr. Perne, master of Peterhouse, is still living. Martin's first reference to Perne's death occurs in July 1589. See *A Dialogue*, signatures B4 and D2 v, and *Martin Senior*, signature Cii.

3. Penry's *Appellation* has an initial ornament letter T on page 1, which is identical with that used by the French printer in La Rochelle, Jerome Haultin. See Louis Desgraves, *Les Haultin, 1571–1623* (Geneva, 1960), p. 62. Haultin, who was in England about 1574–85, was a Huguenot and probably a close friend of Waldegrave, whose italic type in the Marprelate books was cut by Haultin. See Talbot Baines Reed and A. F. Johnson, *A History of the Old English Letter Foundries* (London, [1952]), pp. 96, 161.

4. For the Hampstead story, see *A Dialogue*, signature C3 v. Thornby is John Thornborough (1551–1641), who became bishop of Limerick in 1593 or 1593/94, of Bristol in 1603, and of Worcester in 1617. See Robert Somerville, *The Savoy. Manor: Hospital: Chapel* (London, 1960), pp. 238–39. Dr. Culpepper was warden of New College, Oxford, 1573–99; Dr. Bond became president of Magdalen College and vice-chancellor of Oxford University. George Acworth, as the bishop's commissary and Visitor to New College, made serious charges against Culpepper. See Hastings Rashdall and Robert S. Rait, *New College* (London, 1901), p. 126. For Dr. Bond, see H. A. Wilson, *Magdalen College* (London, 1899), pp. 133–40.

5. Bancroft, *Daungerous Positions*, pp. 45, 57, 58, 59; Sutcliffe, *An Answere* (1595), p. 46; *A Dialogue*, signature C4; Sutcliffe, *An Answere* (1592), pp. 201–02. By "theses" Sutcliffe means *Martin Junior*; by "protestations," the *Protestatyon*; by "dialogues" he means *A Dialogue* and *The State of the Church of Englande*; by "arguments," probably the *Mineralls*; by "laying men out in their coulours," *Master Some Laid Open*. All six were written by Throkmorton, as Sutcliffe correctly asserted.

6. *A Dialogue*, signature C3.

7. Ibid., signatures C4 and D2.

8. Ibid., signatures C3 (Aylmer), B3 (Cooper), B2 v (Middleton), D2 v (Perne), C2 (Some), D2 v (Kennall), D3 v (Bond), D3 (Culpepper), C3 v (Marprelate), and also the *Protestatyon* (allusion to *More Worke*).

9. Bertande de Loque [François de Saillans], *A Treatie* [sic] *of the Churche*, trans. T. W. (London, 1581), p. 4 of "An Admonition to the Reader." This work was first published as *Traité de l'Église* (Geneva, 1577), and was translated by Thomas Wilcox, one of the authors of the *Admonition to the Parlia-*

384

ment. It was reissued in 1582. The words referred to by Martin are: "Thus may they [who oppose the titles of Metropolitans, Archbishops, and Bishops] make our Saviour Christ inferiour to his Father, concerning his divinitie, because the title *homousios* is no where literally expressed, although the same by sundrie places may be well and justly gathered."

10. Marmaduke Middleton was bishop of Waterford and Lismore in Ireland, 1579–82, and bishop of St. David's 1582–92, and then suspended. His death in 1593 may have made unnecessary deprivation from his see. In the P.R.O., see SP 12/228/fol. 15; 230/fol. 78; see also Star Chamber 5/A—Index Vol. 2, Attorney General vs. Marmaduke Middleton, Bundle; see G XV, no. 23. Printed material is available in Historical Manuscripts Commission, *Calendar of the Manuscripts of the Most Hon. the Marquis of Salisbury, K.G.* (London, 1892), pt. 4, 4:279–84; *Calendar of State Papers, Domestic, Elizabeth, 1581–1590.* pp. 119, 143, 335, 629, 648.

11. An example of Throkmorton's playing with words.

12. In bowling, a rub is an obstacle to the course of the bowl.

13. Since the date 1587 is old style, it should be 1587/88. The Lenten season began on Ash Wednesday, 21 February 1587/88. The older priory of Saint Mary Overy or Overie (over the ferry) became in 1540 the parish church of Saint Saviour of Southwark, and today is a part of the rebuilt Cathedral Church of Southwark. For Martin's playing with "Sir" and "Saint" see *Hay Any Worke*, pp. 1–2.

14. Cooper, *An Admonition*, 1st ed. of 252 pp., p. 62.

15. Aylmer, *An Harborowe*, signature O4 and O4 v. The quotation as given in II:D4 v is accurate, but the other three seem to derive from Throkmorton's memory.

16. Sir Edward Horsey, of Dorsetshire, was dubbed a Knight Bachelor at Hampton Court in December 1577. The *D.N.B.* article states that he was knighted at Westminster, but see William A. Shaw, *The Knights of England* (London, 1906), 2:78. Sir Edward was captain of the Isle of Wight; he was also a friend of the earls of Leicester and Warwick.

17. John Udall, *A Demonstration of Discipline*, signature B1 v; see p. 6 of Arber's edition of 1895.

18. Actually, Cooper's Dictionary was entitled *Bibliotheca Eliotae.* Martin is unfair to Bishop Cooper. Throkmorton's disdain for Cooper begins in the 1560s, and was first expressed in his "An Answer" (1572).

19. Cooper, *An Admonition*, p. 135, 1st ed. of 252 pp.

20. During Lent, 1587/88, Whitgift ordered that no Bible should be bound without the Apocrypha. Bishop Cooper defended the archbishop and said that "such giddie heads, as seeke to deface them [the Scriptures] are to be bridled." See Cooper, *Admonition*, p. 49.

21. Robert Some, *A Godly Treatise, Containing and Deciding Certaine Questions*, signature Giii. Dr. Some writes that Penry's view on baptism "is a most absurd heresie."

22. Cooper, *An Admonition*, p. 33. The bishop was referring to Throkmorton's *Epistle* and *Epitome* and to Udall's *Demonstration*.

23. Aylmer, *An Harborowe*, signature H1. Although Martin has "to defende their head, etc.," Aylmer wrote: "to defende their head, their head Christe, I saye, and his crosse."

24. See Carl S. Meyer, *Elizabeth I and the Religious Settlement of 1559*, chaps. 2, 3. See also J. E. Neale, "The Elizabethan Acts of Supremacy and Uniformity," *English Historical Review* 65 (July 1950). The most recent work is Winthrop S. Hudson, *The Cambridge Connection and the Elizabethan Settlement of 1559* (Durham: Duke University Press, 1980). There were lords spiritual in the Upper House during Elizabeth's first Parliament, 25 January–8 May 1559. On 28 April nine Catholic bishops voted against the Act of Uniformity. On 23 May fifteen bishops refused the oath required by the Act of Supremacy, but Anthony Kitchin, bishop of Llandaff, did take the oath.

25. The bishop is Archbishop Whitgift; the dean of Westminster is Gabriel Goodman; Cousins is Richard Cosin, dean of the Arches; Pearne is Andrew Perne, master of Peterhouse, Cambridge.

26. Whitgift's books were: *An Answere to a Certen Libel* (1572), and *The Defense of the Aunswer to the Admonition* (1574). The "foule heape" was Bridges' *A Defence*.

27. Waldegrave's press and type were seized on 16 April 1588; they were destroyed on 13 May by the Stationers' Company. Pursuivants raided his house in November, hoping to capture copies of the *Epistle*.

28. This is the first *Exhortation*, which should not be confused with the second *An Exhortation to the Bishops and Their Clergie*. These two *Exhortations* are available in Frere and Douglas, *Puritan Manifestoes*, pp. 57–78.

29. *Hay Any Worke*, signature B1 v, pp. 26, 30, 35, 37, 43, 43.

30. Throkmorton's summary is in the *Protestatyon*, pp. 24–32; see Sutcliffe, *An Answere* (1595), pp. 54 v, 71 v, 72. See also Arber, *Introductory Sketch*, pp. 117, 176–79.

31. Pierce, *Historical Introduction*, pp. 334, 338.

32. Sutcliffe, *An Answere* (1595), p. 71 v. On the same page Sutcliffe asserted that Throkmorton "wrote most of *More Worke for Cooper*, which is knowne to be M. Throkmortons." The Ellesmere MS. 2148, fol. 87, says that "a third part of [the] book is of Penries hand writinge." Penry may have been an amanuensis for Throkmorton, or he may have written a separate reply to Dr. Some's second or third *A Godly Treatise*.

33. Sutcliffe, *An Answere* (1595), pp. 71 v, 72. Arber, *Introductory Sketch*, p. 117.

34. Ibid. The first admission was made in *Hay Any Worke*, p. 35.

35. Sutcliffe, *An Answere* (1595), pp. 56, 72, 72 v, 77, 77 v. Arber, *Introductory Sketch*, p. 180.

36. Ellesmere MS. 2148, fol. 89 v.

37. Sutcliffe, *An Answere* (1595), pp. 77, 77 v, 56, margin.

38. Arber, *Introductory Sketch*, pp. 180–81; Sutcliffe, *An Answere* (1595), p. 72 v.

39. See the valuable article by John Dover Wilson, "Richard Schilders and the English Puritans," *Transactions of the Bibliographical Society* 11 (1909–11): 65–134. For Throkmorton's letter, see Sutcliffe, *An Answere* (1595), p. 72 v.

40. Ibid., pp. 72 v, 75.

NOTES—Chapter VIII

1. See chapter seven for stylistic peculiarities and parallels.

2. Two-thirds of this chapter pertains to the *Epistle* and *Martin Senior*. Since the *Epitome* and *Hay Any Worke* are by the same author, these two works are briefly discussed in two paragraphs.

3. "To the Lords of the [Privy] Counsel," *Exhortation*, 2d. ed., pp. 71–88, and also *A Viewe*, pp. 20–41.

4. The only stylistic characteristic not found in the *Epistle* is the use of "his" for "its," but in the *Epitome*, which is a continuation of the *Epistle* by the same author, there are two examples on signatures B1 and C1. Examples of colorful writing, existing on almost every page, are not listed.

5. See chapter seven, the section on "The Diction of Martin and Throkmorton."

6. See chapter seven for the numbering system.

7. Martin quotes and paraphrases proverbs: "al is fish that comes to the net," "I have two strings to my bow," "well fare him that sayd thought is free," "unles it be at a dead lift," "you cannot daunce so cunningly in a net but I can spie you out," "Dr. Perne shall be in there by the weekes."

8. Penry wrote: "what I have written, shalbe recorded and called in question in the church of God, (when I am gone the way of all flesh)." See his *Exhortation*, in Williams, *Three Treatises concerning Wales*, p. 97, and his *A Defence of That Which Hath Bin Written in the Questions of the Ignorant Ministerie, and the Communicating with Them* (East Molesey: Robert Walde-grave, 1588), pp. 5–6.

9. In Marprelate's writings there are references to five men (all at Oxford in the 1560s) who were later college heads at Oxford: Nicholas Bond, William Cole, Martin Culpepper, John Underhill, and Thomas Cooper. See the *Epistle*, p. 46; *Hay Any Worke*, p. 47; *Martin Junior*, signature D3 v; *Martin Senior*, signature C2 v; *Protestatyon*, p. 25. In *A Dialogue*, see signatures B3, D3 and D3 v. In *Master Some Laid Open* there are ten references to Oxford and four contrasting references to Cambridge. See the title page, signature A2, and pages 10, 14, 18, 33, 34, 38, 41, 46, 54, 86, 87, 97. Throkmorton refers to "your two Cambridge doctors," "your Universitie," "ye Cambridge men," and also speaks of "our Oxford doctors," and "we Oxford men." He writes: "If I shoulde name Oxforde men unto you, it may be you woulde thinke me partial." In the *Mineralls*, no. 7, and in *Hay Any Worke*, p. 47, there are references to Solihull, which lies about twelve miles northwest of Throkmorton's manor at Haseley. In the *Protestatyon*, p. 25, there is a reference to Dr. William Wood of Alsolne College [All Souls], Oxford.

10. In the *Epitome*, signature G1 v, Edmund Scambler, bishop of Norwich, and in *Hay Any Worke*, signature A3 v, Bishop William Chaderton of Chester, are attacked. The only prelates not mentioned by Marprelate are Thomas Godwin of Bath and Wells, John May of Carlisle, John Piers of Salisbury, John Meyrick of Sodor and Man, Hugh Bellot of Bangor, and William Blethin of Llandaff. In 1588 Ely, Oxford, and Durham were vacant, and York was also vacant for a few months after the death of Archbishop Edwin Sandys on 10 July 1588. In 1589 John Piers was translated to York.

11. Penry, *Notebook*, pp. 63–64. Likewise, in *A Briefe Discovery*, p. 42, Penry writes: "Let Martin in other points answere for himselfe."

12. In a percipient article, Raymond A. Anselment indicates that "the dramatic satire of Martin Marprelate is actually a unique adaptation of traditional rhetoric. The standard Elizabethan authorities on rhetoric—Aristotle, Cicero, Quintilian, and [Sir Thomas] Wilson—all justify Marprelate's decision to answer serious religious arguments facetiously, but the complex dramatic manner in which he assumes the classical posture of the eiron [dissembler] and forces his opponent John Bridges into the role of the alazon [boaster] reveals an original satiric genius. Consciously manipulating a variety of ironic postures, Martin extends his personae of the vociferous clown, country simpleton, and dissembling auditor into the posture of an antirhetorician." See his article, "Rhetoric and the Dramatic Satire of Martin Marprelate," *Studies in English Literature, 1500–1900* 10 (1970): 103–19, and 103 for the quotation. See also three helpful articles: Travis L. Summersgill, "The Influence of the Marprelate Controversy upon the Style of Thomas Nashe," *Studies in Philology* 48 (1951): 145–60; John S. Coolidge, "Martin Marprelate, Marvell, and *Decorum Personae* as a Satirical Theme," *PMLA* 74 (1959): 526–32; Donald J. McGinn, "Nashe's Share in the Marprelate Controversy," *PMLA* 59 (1944): 952–84.

13. *Epistle*, pp. 19, 38–39.

14. Arber, *Introductory Sketch*, p. 94.

15. [Udall], *A New Discovery*, p. 3; Arber, *Introductory Sketch*, p. 172.

16. The only criterion not found is the use of "his" for "its."

17. The word "alterius" seems to be a misreading by the printer, who read "ni" in the manuscript as "iu." Throkmorton probably never saw the proof, since he relied on the printers for checking the sheets.

18. *Martin Senior*, signature Bi v, Bii; *Epistle*, p. 26. See also the *Epitome*, signature A2 v. If the reader accepts the evidence in the first section for Throkmorton's authorship, then the parallel is valid.

19. *Martin Senior*, signatures Aii v-Bi v, Cii-Ciii.

20. Ibid., Dii and Dii v; Biii v-Civ.

21. Ibid., Civ-Di v.

22. Ibid., Bii v and Div v; *Epistle*, p. 3; for doggerel, see the *Epitome*, signature A2 v, and *Martin Senior*, signature Diii and Diii v. See also *Certaine Articles*, in Frere and Douglas, *Puritan Manifestoes*, pp. 135–36.

23. *Martin Senior*, signature Bii.

24. Sutcliffe, *An Answere* (1595), p. 71; Pierce, *Historical Introduction*, p. 339.

25. Sutcliffe, *An Answere* (1595), p. 71 v; Pierce, *Historical Introduction*, pp. 336–37.

26. Sutcliffe, *An Answere* (1595), pp. 71 and 71 v.

27. Pierce, *Historical Introduction*, p. 334.

28. Sharpe's date is 20 February, but his chronology is defective. John Hales testified that Penry's *A Viewe* was published before the proclamation of 13 February; since the *Mineralls* was printed before *A Viewe*, it must be dated earlier. The best authority is Newman, who said the *Mineralls* "came owt about a fortnight before Shroftide." Since Shrovetide in 1588/89 fell on 9–11 February, Newman's date is 26–28 January. See Ellesmere MS. 2148, fol. 86; Larkin and Hughes, *Tudor Royal Proclamations*, vol. 3, *The Later Tudors (1588–1603)*, 3:34–35; Howell, *State Trials*, 1:1,263–67.

29. Arber, *Introductory Sketch*, pp. 97–98.

30. Throkmorton's authorship of the *Epistle* has been established previously. Since the author of *Hay Any Worke* (p. 35) admitted that he wrote the *Epistle*, Throkmorton is responsible for these two parallels, as well as five others in *Hay Any Worke*, pp. 16, 17, 19, 21, 24. These parallels in turn help to establish Throkmorton's authorship of the *Mineralls*, since the parallel in the *Mineralls* (III:12) is almost verbatim.

31. *Mineralls*, nos. 2, 29; *Epistle*, p. 50; *Hay Any Worke*, signature A2 v. Anthony a Wood has identified Dr. Day as *Thomas* Day, canon of Christ Church and Fellow of All Souls, but this is an error, which his editor repeats in 1813. The culprit was Dr. *John* Day, of Magdalen College, and later chancellor of Wells Cathedral. Wood prints thirteen stanzas of "Mr [Thomas] Buckley's libell of divers persons of Oxford," which refers to the amours of Dr. Day and Mrs. Thomas (Amey) Cooper. See the *Summary Catalogue of Western Manuscripts in the Bodleian Library at Oxford*, 3 (1895): 338, no. 14703. See also Anthony a Wood, *Athenae Oxoniensis*, ed. Philip Bliss, 4 vols. (London, 1813–20), 1:608–13; *Hay Any Worke*, signature A3 (twice), pp. 10, 37; *Protestatyon*, p. 23. See also chapter ten, note 12.

32. Sutcliffe, *An Answere* (1595), pp. 71 and 71 v. For the law of 23 Elizabeth, c. 2, see *Statutes of the Realm*, 4: pt.1:659–60. See also Pierce, *Historical Introduction*, pp. 333–35.

33. *Martin Junior*, signature Ciii v. Martin ironically referred to the bishops who were "seeking for more costly houses than ever his father built for him." Throkmorton was alluding to the Haseley manor house which his father Clement rebuilt or restored.

34. Ibid., signatures Div, Ciii v, Civ v, Ci and Ci v, Civ.

35. After the capture of the printers and all the equipment on 14 August 1589, new supplies were needed. Penry's press remained hidden at Wolston; his role in obtaining paper, ink, an iron frame, and type from London is presented in Ellesmere MS. 2148, fol. 88.

36. Penry, *Notebook*, pp. 63–65, 71. Penry did not attach his name to his first book, *A Treatise Containing the Aequity of an Humble Supplication*, but

it was presented to the House of Commons with his petition, and the authorship was known. His book, *A Briefe Discovery,* did not carry his name, but it may have been removed because Waldegrave did not wish to offend Ambassador Bowes or James VI, who had taken umbrage after Penry's *Reformation No Enemie* was published. Penry admitted his authorship of *A Briefe Discovery,* which indicates that he acknowledged all nine of his works, but Throkmorton refused to acknowledge eighteen of his books, and he did not admit his responsibility for the preface of Cartwright's *A Brief Apologie.* The one exception was his *Defence of Job Throkmorton,* but even this book carried the transparent subterfuge that it was "taken out of a copye of his owne hande as it was written to an honourable personage."

37. Martin's denial of having a wife or children is in the *Protestatyon,* pp. 14–16, 23[32]. His statement seems designed to throw the pursuivants off the track. Martin theoretically had two sons, Martin Senior and Martin Junior, and Throkmorton had a wife, two sons, and a daughter. Penry was married on Wednesday, 5 June 1588.

38. *Protestatyon,* pp. 12, 16, 23, and *Martin Junior,* signature Bii v, Biii, no. 57.

39. *Epitome,* signature F2 v, and A2.

40. Ibid., B1 v, and *Epistle,* p. 41, margin.

41. For the parallels and examples of stylistic characteristics, see chapter seven.

42. *Hay Any Worke,* signature B1 v, pp. 26, 30, 35, 37, 43, 43. In each reference, Throkmorton told the readers what he intended to say in *More Worke.*

43. Not with Penry's book, *A Defence,* which was excessively polite. See Arber, *Introductory Sketch,* p. 117, which gives the first conjectures of the investigators on authorship. These conjectures of September 1589 are premature and inaccurate, since the investigators had not seen the testimony of the printers and had no suspicion as yet of Throkmorton's role. It was not until 10 December 1589 that Symmes revealed what he knew about Throkmorton.

44. *Hay Any Worke,* p. 35.

45. For the criteria and examples, see chapter seven. One of the parallels, previously mentioned, deserves special attention:

> Qui pergit quod vult dicere quae non vult audiet (IV:37, margin)

> Nam qui pergit, ea quae vult dicere, ea quae non vult, audiet ("An Answer to Certen Peeces of a Sermon . . . in Anno 1572 by Doctor Cowper, Bishop of Lincoln"). It is remarkable that Throkmorton used this quotation from Terence in his first writing in 1572 and also in 1589—both times against Bishop Cooper.

NOTES—Chapter IX

1. *An Exhortation to the Byshops to Deale Brotherly with Theyr Brethren*; *An Exhortation to the Bishops and Their Clergie*; *Certaine Articles*; *A Second Admonition to the Parliament*; *The State of the Church of Englande*. See *S.T.C.*, nos. 10392, 10850, 4713, 24505. The first four are reprinted in Frere and Douglas, *Puritan Manifestoes*. The fifth book was printed in *A Parte of a Register* in 1593 (*S.T.C.*, 10400); Edward Arber reissued it in 1879.

2. For the decree, see Arber, *Stationers' Registers*, 2:807–12, printed from State Papers, Domestic, vol. 190, article 48, in the P.R.O.

3. Burghley's letter is available in Warrender, *Illustrations of Scottish History. Sixteenth Century*, pp. 31–33.

4. William Camden, *Annales Rerum Anglicarum, et Hibernicarum, Regnante Elizabetha, ad Annum Salutis M.D.LXXXIX* (London, 1615), p. 498. He writes: "Iobus Throcmortonus vir doctus et facete dicax." See also Camden, *Annales. The True and Royall History of the Famous Empresse Elizabeth* (London, 1625), book 3, pp. 290–91.

5. Sutcliffe, *An Answere* (1595), pp. 76–78. On 25 February 1586/87 Hatton rebuked Throkmorton for his speech, "On the Low Countries," delivered in the House of Commons on 23 February. See Harley MSS. 7188, fols. 89–92.

6. Arber, *Introductory Sketch*, pp. 175, 178, 179, 180, 183, 184. Sutcliffe, *The Examination of M. Thomas Cartwrights Late Apologie* (London, 1596), p. 7 v.

7. *The Protestatyon*, p. 24. Since the evidence for Throkmorton's authorship of various books has been presented in chapters five–eight, Martin and Throkmorton are considered identical.

8. For Symmes and Thomlin, see Sutcliffe, *An Answere* (1595), pp. 71, 72, and Pierce, *Historical Introduction*, pp. 333–39. For Sharpe, see Arber, *Introductory Sketch*, pp. 94–104, 114–36, and Lansdowne MSS. 830, fols. 114–18. For Newman, see Sutcliffe, *An Answere* (1595), pp. 70–73, and Ellesmere MS. 2148, fols. 85–88.

9. Sutcliffe, *An Answere* (1595), pp. 68 v–70 v, 74–78 v, 80 v.

10. Ibid., pp. 71–72 v, and Pierce, *Historical Introduction*, p. 336.

11. Items 5 and 6 were both published in 1593 in *A Parte of a Register*. Sutcliffe published item 12 in *An Answere* (1595), pp. 18 v-19. Throkmorton's authorship of twenty-two unacknowledged items is premised on the arguments in chapters five–nine and in the appendixes.

12. *Hay Any Worke*, pp. 1, 6.

13. *Epistle*, p. 4. In the margin is the additional comment: "What malapert knaves are these that cannot be content to stand by and he[a]re, but they must teach a gentleman how to speake."

14. *Epitome*, signature B3 v-B4.

15. *Hay Any Worke for Cooper*, p. 34.

16. *Epitome*, signature C2. In replying to Dean Bridges, Martin wrote: "You may see then, how headie and perverse these our brethren are, that had rather sticke unto a poore fisherman and Tentmaker, Peter and Paule, in a matter of trueth, than imbrace the manifest falsehood of so plaine an untrueth, with a fat deane, and all the brave spiritual Lordes in the lande" (ibid., signature C3).

17. *Epistle*, p. 15; *Martin Senior*, signatures Bii v, Div; *Hay Any Worke*, pp. 2, 36.

18. *Master Some Laid Open*, p. 76.

19. "Speech on the Low Countries," Phillipps MSS. 13891, reclassified as MA 276, fol. 31.

20. *Epistle*, p. 49. *Master Some Laid Open*, p. 65.

21. "Speech on the Low Countries," Phillipps MSS. 13891, reclassified as MA 276, fol. 36; *Epistle*, p. 48. In *Master Some Laid Open*, p. 76, Throkmorton wrote: "Was not his head smitten with a *lethargie* that spied nowe a time to speake of a *liturgie.*"

22. "Speech on the Bill and Book," Phillipps MSS. 13891, reclassified as MA 276, fol. 16.

23. *Martin Senior*, signature Div. The quotation is from *Mar-Martine*, signature A3 (*S.T.C.* 17461), and may be dated April–June 1589, after the publication of *Hay Any Worke* in March and before the publication of *Martin Senior* in July. The original reads: "O England now full eften must thou Pater Noster say." Anthony Munday is possibly the author of *Mar-Martine*.

24. *Martin Senior*, signature Div. The reference to "Nicholas Priestes" derives from a line in *Mar-Martine*, signature A3, "that fend S. Nichols rights." There is another work in the Huntington Library, entitled *Mar-Martin*, with three pages of doggerel. It is a reprint of *Marre Mar-Martin: Or Marre-Martins Medling, in a Manner Misliked*, without a title page, and with a few minor changes. Note Throkmorton's familiar "we thanke him."

25. *Martin Junior*, signature Dii and Dii v.

26. *Martin Senior*, signature Dii v.

27. *Certaine Articles*, title page. Following the humorous imprint are the initials of J.T.J.S., which refer to Job Throkmorton and John Strowd. This book is listed in the *S.T.C.*, 10850, under the names of John Field and Thomas Wilcox, probably because it contains extracts from the *Admonition to the Parliament*, but it is a defense of the *Admonition* by Throkmorton, aided by the printer, Strowd. Field and Wilcox were in jail when *Certaine Articles* was published in the autumn of 1572. On the *verso* of the title page there is also a poem, "To the Prelacie," with seven stanzas, probably by Throkmorton.

28. *Master Some Laid Open*, pp. 30–31; *Epitome*, signature A2 v. Just before his "rime doggrell" Martin has written: "Eyther from countrie or Court,

M. Martin Marprelate will do you hurt." The use of doggerel and humorous imprints typify Throkmorton but not Penry.

29. Many of these names are from Throkmorton's *Master Some Laid Open*, pp. 33, 34, 69, 81, 82, 91, 106. See also his *A Dialogue*, signature C4 and C4 v. Other names are scattered throughout Martin's books: *Epistle*, pp. 1, 8, 17, 23, 31, 34; *Epitome*, signature A2; *Hay Any Worke*, p. 9. Since Penry does not indulge in name-calling, it seems highly probable that Throkmorton and Martin are identical. The unusual phrase, "Lockewoode of Sarum," is found in Throkmorton's *Master Some Laid Open*, p. 81, and in Martin's *Protestatyon*, p. 26.

30. These names are widely scattered. See examples in *Master Some Laid Open*, p. 73. See also the *Epistle*, pp. 17, 32, 35, 36, 40, and *Martin Junior*, signature Di v. In Throkmorton's three parliamentary speeches, see Phillipps MSS. 13891, fols. 9, 16, 17, 21, 43. Name-calling is also characteristic of Throkmorton's writings in 1572 and 1573.

31. *Epistle*, pp. 19, 38–40; *Epitome*, signature A2.

32. *Martin Junior*, signatures Ai v, Ciii v, Civ, Div.

33. *Martin Senior*, signatures Aii v-Bi; Dii and Dii v; Biii v-Ciii; *Protestatyon*, pp. 30–31.

34. Throkmorton's *Defence* is the only book listed under his name in the British Museum *General Catalogue* and in the *Short-Title Catalogue*. Both of these reference works err in ascribing *A Petition Directed* to Henry Barrow.

35. *Master Some Laid Open*, pp. 9, 11, 14, 16, 42, 44, 70, 73, 91.

36. Ibid., pp. 30–31.

37. Signature B1 and B1 v.

38. For references to Waldegrave, see the *Epistle*, pp. 6, 23–24, 25; *Epitome*, signature F4; *Hay Any Worke*, pp. 39–43; *Martin Senior*, signatures Aii v-Aiv, Bii; *A Dialogue*, signature B3 v-B4. Ellesmere MS. 2148, fol. 88.

39. See John Dover Wilson, "Richard Schilders and the English Puritans," *Transactions of the Bibliographical Society* 11(1909–11): 65–134, and the *Epitome*, signature A2.

40. *Epistle*, pp. 6–7. The *Harmony of the Confessions* was first printed in Latin at Geneva in 1581; the English edition was published at Cambridge in 1586. It is listed in the *S.T.C.*, 5155; in the British Museum *General Catalogue*, it is difficult to find, since it is catalogued under "Europe, Christian and Reformed Churches." See vol. 69, p. 664.

41. Throkmorton is referring here to his own *Dialogue*, correctly entitled as *The State of the Church of Englande*, listed in the *S.T.C.*, 24505.

42. For Thomas and Chard, see the *Epistle*, pp. 6, 10, 13; *Master Some Laid Open*, pp. 64, 86; *Hay Any Worke*, p. 37. See also Allan Stevenson, "Thomas Thomas Makes a Dictionary," *The Library* 13 (December 1958): 234–46. See further Geoffrey Keynes, "The Hand of Thomas Thomas," *Transactions of the Cambridge Bibliographical Society*, 4, pt. 4 (1967): 291–92; see also John Morris, "Restrictive Practices in the Elizabethan Book Trade: The Station-

ers' Company v. Thomas Thomas 1583–8," ibid., 276–90, and 4, pt. 5 (1968): 339–62.

43. The figure 1,401 refers to the numbered pages of Dr. Bridges' *Defence*. Since there is an unnumbered final page 1,402, and since there are 10 pages of prefatory material, the book is sometimes cited as having 1,402 or 1,412 pages. Martin described it as "a very portable booke, a horse may cary it if he be not too weake." The figure 812 refers to the numbered pages of Whitgift's *The Defense of the Aunswere to the Admonition* (1574). See the *Epitome*, signature B1, and *Martin Junior*, signature Aiii.

44. *Epistle*, pp. 12–15, 17, 21, 22, 26, 32; *Epitome*, signature A2 v; *Hay Any Worke*, pp. 37, 38, 43; *Martin Junior*, signature Cii; *Martin Senior*, signature Biv v; *Master Some Laid Open*, p. 73. See also *The Statutes of the Realm*, 2:85–86. Penry avoided the issue of treason (*Exhortation*, 2d ed., pp. 82–85).

45. *Epistle*, pp. 5, 10, 43, 49; *Mineralls*, conclusion; *Hay Any Worke*, signature A2 and p. 42; *Martin Junior*, signatures Biii v, thesis 71, Ciii and Ciii v; *A Dialogue*, signature C4. For Benison, see Pierce, *The Marprelate Tracts*, pp. 93–95.

46. *Master Some Laid Open*, p. 42. Richard Walton was the pursuivant who raided Penry's study on 29 January 1588/89. Anthony Munday was the one who brought Giles Wigginton before the Court of High Commission on 6 December 1588. For Munday, see *Martin Senior*, signature Aii v. See also John Dover Wilson, "Anthony Munday, Pamphleteer and Pursuivant," *Modern Language Review* 4 (1909): 484–90. For Walton, see Penry, *Appellation*, pp. 6, 45–46.

47. *Epitome*, signature E1 v. The same idea is expressed in *Master Some Laid Open*, p. 10: "Why, is this your manner of canvasing of controversies in Cambridge? Or is it your custome nowe a daies, to drawe the most of your arguments *a fustibus et fascibus, a vinculis et carceribus?*" [by means of clubs and rods, by fetters and jails]. Also, in the *Protestatyon*, p. 13, Martin accuses the lord bishops of using the weapons of "slanders, ribaldry, scurrillity, reviling, imprisonment, and torture . . . as beside whorish impudencie, halter, axe, bonds, scourging and racking." For pursuivants, see *Hay Any Worke*, p. 41; *Martin Senior*, signatures Aii v-Bi, Dii and Dii v.

48. *Hay Any Worke*, p. 41; *Protestatyon*, p. 20; *The Defence of Job Throkmorton*, signature Ciii v.

49. Ibid., signature Ciii.

50. *Master Some Laid Open*, p. 56.

51. *Martin Junior*, signature Aii v.

52. *Epistle*, pp. 11, 17, 18; *Epitome*, signatures C2, C4; *A Dialogue*, signatures C4 v, D1.

53. *Master Some Laid Open*, pp. 17, 42, 122–23. In 1555 Whitgift became a Fellow of Peterhouse; in 1563 he was named Lady Margaret professor of divinity; in April 1567 he was elected master of Pembroke College; in July 1567 he was elected master of Trinity College, and in the same year was made the Regius Professor of divinity; in 1570 he served as vice-chancellor; in

1571 he was elected dean of Lincoln Cathedral; in 1577 he became bishop of Worcester, and in 1583 was confirmed as archbishop of Canterbury. In February 1585/86, he became a member of the Privy Council.

54. The strongest condemnations of Whitgift are in *Martin Senior*. See also the *Epistle*, p. 32 and margin.

55. *Epistle*, pp. 4, 5, 6, 8, 48, 52, 53; *Epitome*, signatures B1 v, B2, B3 v, B4, C1 and C1 v, C3 and C3 v, F2 v; *Hay Any Worke*, pp. 1, 6, 7, 18, 21, 36; *Martin Junior*, signature Aii; *Martin Senior*, signatures Aii v, Bii v; *Protestatyon*, p. 7.

56. *Hay Any Worke*, p. 36; *Protestatyon*, pp. 7–8.

57. *Epistle*, pp. 48, 52; *Martin Senior*, signature Bii v; *Master Some Laid Open*, pp. 39, 52, 59, 79, 80, 95, 100, 102.

58. *Epistle*, p. 48; *Master Some Laid Open*, p. 55.

59. *Epitome*, signature E4 v. In form, this syllogism is in the first figure. Whereas the first mood or mode is "*Barbara*"—AAA (All M is P), this syllogism is in the second mode, "*Celarent*,"—EAE (no M is P). The vowels in the first syllable of each of the three names nicely correspond to EAE— cE lA rEnt.

60. Occasionally Penry quoted from the Book of Proverbs, but he does not quote proverbs. He did use the expression—"the apple of his eye"— from Deut. 32:10. Wit and humor are lacking.

61. *Epistle*, pp. 15, 45; *Epitome*, signature E1.

62. *Hay Any Worke*, p. 29.

63. Ibid., pp. 14, 20, 21, 24; *Martin Junior*, signatures Aii, Civ v; *Protestatyon*, p. 17. Martin anticipates Dean Swift, who wrote: "THUS, I find it by Experiment, Scolding moves you less than Merriment" (*The Poems of Jonathan Swift*, ed. Harold Swift, 3 vols. [Oxford, 1937; 2d ed., 1958], 2:636, lines 207–08).

64. Penry, *Appellation*, pp. 4–5, 40–41; *Epistle*, pp. 29–30, 26–27, 31, 34–36; *A Dialogue. Wherin Is Plainly Laide Open*, signature C3 v-C4.

65. *Epistle*, pp. 41–42, 43; *Hay Any Worke*, pp. 3–4; *Master Some Laid Open*, pp. 21–22; *Epistle*, pp. 46–48; *A Dialogue. Wherin Is Plainly Laide Open*, signature D3 v.

66. *Epistle*, p. 36–37.

67. Ibid., pp. 20–21.

68. Sutcliffe, *An Answere* (1592), pp. 200–02; *An Answere* (1595), pp. 70–73. Penry, *Notebook*, p. 65; Bancroft, *Daungerous Positions*, pp. 45, 57–59; Pierce, *Historical Introduction*, pp. 333–38.

69. Martin's interest in sermons and sermon-criticism may be seen in the *Epistle*, pp. 32–35, 38, 44, 47–50; *Epitome*, signatures D1 v, E2, F1 v, F2, F4; *Mineralls*, nos. 11, 13, 19; *Hay Any Worke*, pp. 44–46; *Martin Junior*, signature Cii; *Martin Senior*, signatures Aiii v, Aiv v, Ciii; *Protestatyon*, pp. 26, 27. Throkmorton's interest in sermons is revealed as early as 1572, in his "An Answer to Certen Peeces of a Sermon . . . by Doctor Cowper," in

1573, in "A Friendly Caveat to Bishop Sands," in 1589, in *A Dialogue*, signatures C1, C1 v, C3, D2, and in *Master Some Laid Open*, pp. 21, 22, 43–45, 117.

70. Penry wrote seven books; he was the translator of the eighth, *Propositions and Principles of Divinitie* (*S.T.C.* 2053); his ninth book was incomplete at his death, but it was published posthumously in 1609, *The Historie of Corah, Dathan and Abiram*. It was probably seen through the press by Francis Johnson, and printed in Amsterdam.

NOTES—Chapter X

1. Ellesmere MS. 2148, fol. 85; Penry, *Appellation*, pp. 4–5, 39–46.

2. *Epistle*, pp. 29–30. Martin speaks of Penry's "bolde attempt" in presenting a book and petition to Parliament. If Penry had written this account, he probably would have said, "this just appeal."

3. *A Viewe*, pp. 47, 48, 53, 54; *Appellation*, pp. 39–41; *Reformation No Enemie*, signatures C4 v, G3. There are also brief allusions to the archbishop in *A Briefe Discovery*, pp. 52–54, and in the manuscript Notebook, Ellesmere MS. 483, fols. 31, 48; see Peel, *Notebook of John Penry*, pp. 64, 71. Penry's nine allusions to Whitgift, which approximate one page of material, should be contrasted with 130 references by Martin, who hated the archbishop.

4. *Notebook of John Penry*, p. 64. By contrast, Throkmorton hopes for an early death for the archbishop (*A Dialogue*, signature D4).

5. *Hay Any Worke*, p. 44; *Martin Senior*, signature Aiii; *Epitome*, signature D2 v.

6. *Martin Senior*, signature Aiv v, Bi, Biii v.

7. *Martin Junior*, signature Diii; *Martin Senior*, signature Ci–Cii; *Epistle*, p. 2; *Hay Any Worke*, p. 36.

8. Cooper, *Admonition*, p. 75; see also signature Aii v, pp. 74–84, 134–35; in the 2d ed., consult signature Aii v, pp. 81–94, 140. Martin used the first edition, Penry the second. Hemingius, or Niels Hemmingsen (1513–1600), was a Danish clergyman and the king's professor at the University of Copenhagen (Hafnia). At least six of his books were translated into English.

9. *Appellation*, p. 29.

10. *Hay Any Worke*, p. 22. Martin's treatment here of "a siely Schoolemaster" is similar to Throkmorton's accusation against Cooper in "An Answer to Certen Peeces of a Sermon," Inner Temple, Petyt MSS. 538(47), fols. 459, 461.

11. *Epistle*, pp. 28, 46. Martin is unfair and unscholarly in his criticisms of Cooper's dictionary and his *Thesaurus*. In 1538 *The Dictionary of Syr Thomas Eliot, Knyght*, appeared. After the death of Sir Thomas in 1546, Thomas Cooper, "schoolmaster of Maudlens in Oxford," issued three expanded and enriched editions, in 1548, 1552, and 1559, with the title, *Bibliotheca Eliotae*.

The *Thesaurus Linguae Romanae et Britannicae*, based on the work of Robert Stephanus [Éstienne] and edited by Thomas Cooper, appeared in 1565. Later editions appeared in 1573, 1578, 1584, and 1587. These folios represent an enormous amount of labor, "opera et industria Thomae Cooperi." The 1584 edition has about 1,762 pages, including the *Bibliotheca Eliotae*.

For an excellent discussion of Cooper's role, see two articles by DeWitt T. Starnes, "Thomas Cooper and the *Bibliotheca Eliotae*," University of

Texas *Studies in English* 30 (1951): 40–60; "Thomas Cooper's *Thesaurus:* A Chapter in Renaissance Lexicography," ibid. 28 (1949): 15–48; DeWitt T. Starnes, *Renaissance Dictionaries. English-Latin and Latin-English* (Austin: University of Texas Press, 1954), chaps. 6–8. See also the biographies of Elyot by Stanford E. Lehmberg and Pearl Hogrefe; of Robert Éstienne, by Elizabeth Armstrong.

12. *Hay Any Worke*, p. 10. There is one other passage which is relevant. Martin writes: "The stile and the phrase [of Cooper's *Admonition*] is very like her [Mrs. Cooper's] husbands, that was sometimes woont to write unto Doctor Day of Welles. You see I can do it in deed" (ibid., signature A3). Dr. Day has been wrongly identified by Anthony a Wood as Thomas Day, who was born about 1495, became a Fellow of All Souls in 1518, received a B.C.L. degree in 1521, became a canon of Christ Church in 1546, and died in February 1567/68. Since he was not a doctor, was not associated with Magdalen College, and was not employed at Wells, he does not satisfy Martin's requirements. The correct identification is John Day, who was born in 1529, attended Magdalen College as a demy from 1544 to 1551, served as a Probationary Fellow, 1551–86, obtained his M.A. in 1555, and earned a D.C.L. degree in 1579. In 1587 he was appointed vicar-general or chancellor in the diocese of Bath and Wells, serving with Bishop Thomas Godwin, also a Magdalen Fellow (1544–49). See Wood, *Athenae Oxonienses*, 1 (1691): 119, 229, 232, 746; *Athenae*, 1 (1813): 610; 2 (1815): 213 of the *Fasti Oxonienses*, in the latter part of vol. 2, both edited by Philip Bliss (4 vols.; London, 1813–20). See also Joseph Foster, *Alumni Oxonienses*, 1 (Oxford, 1891): 387; John Harington, *A Briefe View of the State of the Church of England* (London, 1653), pp. 61–65; John Rouse Bloxam, *A Register of the Presidents, Fellows, Demies . . . of Saint Mary Magdalen College*, 8 vols. (Oxford, 1853–85), 2: lxxii; 3:108–24; 4:102, 113, 171; William Dunn Macray, *A Register of the Members of St. Mary Magdalen College, Oxford*, 8 vols. (London, 1894–1915), 2 (1897): 37, 128; 3 (1901): 87. John Day appeared before Dr. George Ackworth, the commissary for Robert Horne, bishop of Winchester, during the period 16–28 September 1566. Perhaps at this time he was required to furnish bond of £100 with a promise not to visit Mrs. Amey Cooper, wife of Thomas, later bishop of Lincoln, 1570/71, and of Winchester, 1584–94. See Macray, *A Register*, 2:36–37, and John Le Neve, *Fasti Ecclesiae Anglicanae* (London, 1716), p. 234. In the three-volume edition of T. Duffus Hardy, *Fasti Ecclesiae Anglicanae* (Oxford, 1854), see 1:266, and 2:521.

13. *Hay Any Worke*, p. 37.

14. *Epistle*, pp. 33–34. Cooper's reply is in his *Admonition*, pp. 64–73. Penry disagrees with Martin. See *A Viewe*, pp. 11, 15, 67.

15. *Hay Any Worke*, p. 5.

16. "An Answer to Certen Peeces of a Sermon," Inner Temple, Petyt MSS. 538(47).

17. "To the Lords of the [Privy] Counsel," *Exhortation*, 2d ed., pp. 71–88; *A Viewe*, pp. 20–41.

18. *Epistle*, pp. 10–17. *Exhortation*, 2d ed., pp. 84, 88. *Epitome*, signature B1.

19. *Master Some Laid Open*, pp. 10, 14, 20, 30–35, 38, 39, 42, 64, 65, 68, 69, 71,

72, 82, 86, 88, 91, 102, 103, 105, 106, 116, 121. Throkmorton also ridiculed Bridges in *A Dialogue*, signatures A1, C1, C4 v, D1, D2 v.

20. *Epistle*, p. 18.

21. *A Briefe Discovery*, pp. 30, 50.

22. *Hay Any Worke*, pp. 36–37; *Martin Junior*, signature Ci and Ci v. This statement provides a clue that Throkmorton had written anonymously against the bishops before 1588. Both Cartwright and Throkmorton wrote against the prelates in the 1570s.

23. Whitgift's *An Answere* has 246 numbered pages, plus 54 pages of prefatory material and appended items. This work was reissued in 1573, and a second edition, "newly augmented by the authore," also appeared in 1573. There is a new section, "Certayne Notes and Properties of Anabaptistes," pp. 19–31. The *Defense* of 1574 has 36 plus 812 pages. In *Martin Junior*, signature Aiii, the mysterious numbers occur, "their 812, their 1401," which refer to the number of pages in Whitgift's *Defense* and Bridges' *Defence*. Pierce, in *The Marprelate Tracts, 1588, 1589*, p. 306, misinterprets 812.

24. See Donald J. McGinn, *The Admonition Controversy*, which prints selections from Cartwright's and Whitgift's writings. See also *The Works of John Whitgift, D.D.*, ed. John Ayre for the Parker Society, 3 vols. (Cambridge, 1851–53).

25. *Epistle*, p. 17; see also pp. 3, 28, 38; *A Dialogue*, signature C4 v; *Master Some Laid Open*, p. 34.

26. Pearson, *Thomas Cartwright and Elizabethan Puritanism*, pp. 303–04, 365–70, 451; Bancroft, *Survay*, p. 377; Fuller, *The Church History of Britain*, ed. J. S. Brewer, 5:146, 149, 154; Throkmorton, *Defence*, signature Aiii. Cartwright's book was quickly answered by Dean Sutcliffe in *The Examination of M. Thomas Cartwrights Late Apologie* (1596). Sutcliffe ironically suggests to Cartwright: you should talk "with your friend Master Throkmorton, to whom, I doubt not, but you will discommend me, and therefore I desire not to be commended to him" (p. 5 *verso*). Of the preface by Throkmorton, Sutcliffe writes: "Yet of the two the preface is more fond, advancing M. Cartwright to the state of innocencie, and more odious, being fraught with divers rayling reproches. The authour seemeth to [be] Master Job Throkmorton, an olde friend of mine, who by commending of M. Cartwright, sought to be revenged on mee. And what he could not winne by commending him, that he seeketh by rayling and gnashing his teeth upon me. But mery malicious fellowes well doeth the Prophete describe in his 35 Psalme [verse 16]. And such dealing is not strange in that gentleman, to whom I wish no other paine, than that for his scorning and rayling, for which his owne friendes call him *gibing Job*, he doe not in the ende weepe full bitterly" (p. 7 *verso*).

27. *Epitome*, signature D3 v. Aylmer's book is anonymous, and carries the imprint, "Strasborowe, 1559," but more likely it was printed by John Day in London, while Elizabeth's first Parliament was meeting. The book is a reply to John Knox's *The First Blast of the Trumpet against the Monstruous Regiment of Women* (1558), and a denunciation of the Catholic bishops carried over from the reign of Mary Tudor. The phrase, "without rime, and with-

out reason," is used by Throkmorton in *Master Some Laid Open,* p. 85, and in his *Defence,* signature Dii v.

28. *Epitome,* signature D4 v; [Aylmer], *An Harborowe,* signature O4 and O4 v. The phrase "with your hundreths" should be "with hundreds."

29. Penry, *Notebook,* ed. Albert Peel, pp. 64, 71. Penry's criticisms of Martin in his private Notebook, never intended for publication and therefore more forthright, indicate two persons, and preclude the possibility that Penry was Martin. See McGinn, *John Penry,* pp. 49–50.

30. See Sidney Lee's article in the *D.N.B.,* "Andrew Perne." See also John Foxe, *The Acts and Monuments,* 4th ed., by Josiah Pratt, 6 (1877): 320–22, 327–32, 336, 405; 8 (1877): 258–63, 269, 272, 277, 280–81, 287.

31. *Martin Senior,* signature Cii. For other references to Dr. Perne, see *Epistle,* pp. 10, 13, 32, 51; *Epitome,* signatures C4 v, D1, E4 v, G1; *Hay Any Worke,* pp. 44, 47; *Protestatyon,* p. 26.

32. *A Defence of That Which Hath Bin Written in the Questions of the Ignorant Ministerie, and the Communicating with Them,* pp. 5–6, 9, 23, 30, 63.

33. *Mineralls,* nos. 16, 25; *Martin Junior,* signature Ciii; *Martin Senior,* signature Cii v; *Protestatyon,* pp. 28–29. A saunce bell, or Sanctus bell, was a handbell used to focus attention in the church services after the pealing of the larger turret bell. The Sanctus refers to the thrice-repeated Sanctus (Tersanctus), and is a part of the rite following the Preface and preceding the Canon.

34. *Master Some Laid Open,* signature A2, pp. 1, 43, 46, 49, 70.

35. Ibid, pp. 6, 7–8, 9–10, 106, 124. Also, Luke 22:26.

36. *Master Some Laid Open,* pp. 43, 56, 41–42.

37. Ibid., p. 44; *Protestatyon,* p. 29.

38. *A Viewe,* p. 44. 1 Tim. 3:1–7.

39. *Martin Senior,* signature Bii; *Epistle,* pp. 40–41; *Epitome,* signatures D4 v, G1 v. Martin's contemplated book, *Epistomastix,* more correctly should be *Episcopomastix* (a whip for the bishop), and suggests *Papistomastix* (a whip for the papists), as Laurence Humphrey, president of Magdalen College, was called, or William Prynne's *Histrio-Mastix* (1633), a scourge for the actor.

40. *Epistle,* pp. 4–6, 46–47, 50; *Mineralls,* no. 2; *Hay Any Worke,* p. 6; *Martin Senior,* signature Civ.

41. *Epistle,* pp. 4, 5, 11, 49–52; *Epitome,* signature E3 v; *Mineralls,* no. 6; *Hay Any Worke,* signature A3 v, p. 43.

42. Martin's characterization is manifestly unfair (*Epistle,* pp. 2–3; *Hay Any Worke,* p. 42). Richard Cosin entered Trinity College, Cambridge, before he was twelve years old, and was like Francis Bacon and Cotton Mather in his precocity. William Barlow's biography, *Vita et obitus ornatissimi celeberrimiq[ue] viri Richardi Cosin, legum doctoris, decani curiae de Arcubus, cancellarii seu vicarii generalis reverendissimi patris Ioannis Archiepiscopi Cantuariensis* (London, 1598), praises his learning and achievements. Cosin wrote not only *An Answer* to *An Abstract,* but also *Conspiracie for Pretended Reformation*

(1592), an exposé of the Hacket-Coppinger-Arthington fiasco of July 1591, and an attack on the Puritan reformers. His *An Apologie: of, and for Sundrie Proceedings by Jurisdiction Ecclesiasticall* (London, 1591), is a defense of the ex officio oath, which Throkmorton hated, against James Morice's "A Brief Treatise of Oaths," a manuscript in the British Library, Cottonian MSS., Cleopatra F i. 2. It was published posthumously, about 1600, probably at London and Middelburg. See *S.T.C.*, 18106–07. Cosin's *Ecclesiae Anglicanae Politeia in Tabulas Digesta* (London, 1604), was a posthumous work, and was republished *anno salutis* 1634 as a staunch defense of the Anglican polity in the turbulent period of William Laud, John Hampden, Henry Burton, John Bastwick, and William Prynne.

43. In *Master Some Laid Open*, p. 18, Throkmorton ridicules Dr. Some's "authenticall principles," and "deep misteries." Then he adds: "I thought certainly I had bene at one of M. Deane of Westminster his sermons, because he, good soule, seldome handeleth any controversies, but tels the people in good sound English, *'That vertue is good, and vice is evil.'* " See also *Mineralls*, no. 14; *Epistle*, p. 34.

44. *Mineralls*, thesis or no. 27; *Protestatyon*, p. 32. In *Master Some Laid Open*, p. 58, Throkmorton utilized the doctrine of the elect and of eternal security: "That whom God loveth he loveth for ever, and that it is unpossible for al the power of hell and darknes, to wipe Her Majestie out of the booke of life, wherein she is written."

45. *Epitome*, signature E4 v; *Hay Any Worke*, p. 47. The name is spelled Kenal, Kenold, Kenolde, Kennolde, Kennell, and Kennall. Martin's strictures against Dr. Kennall possibly may be explained by the fact that Kennall was appointed archdeacon of Oxford in 1561, shortly before Throkmorton became an undergraduate at the university (1562–66). Since there was no bishop of Oxford in 1557–67, 1568–89, and 1592–1604, the archdeacon must have been an important and busy official, who confronted such staunch nonconformists as Thomas Sampson, dean of Christ Church, and Dr. Laurence Humphrey, president of Magdalen College. As commissary or vice-chancellor of the university from 1564 to 1567, Dr. Kennall administered his office during Throkmorton's last two years at Oxford. Kennall's successor as commissary was Thomas Cooper, whom Throkmorton also disliked.

46. *Epistle*, pp. 34–35; *Epitome*, signature G1.

47. *Epistle*, p. 46; *Hay Any Worke*, pp. 37, 47; *Martin Junior*, signature Diii v; *Martin Senior*, signature Cii v; *Protestatyon*, p. 25. For Bond and Culpepper, see *A Dialogue. Wherin Is Plainly Laide Open*, signature D3 and D3 v. Culpepper is mentioned both by Martin and Throkmorton.

48. The picture of Dr. Copcot in the *D.N.B.* is that of a man of macerated flesh, worn out by hard study. Martin's description seems accurate and prophetic, since Copcot died the next year, 1590, approximately forty-two years old. Martin refers disrespectfully to him as Capcase, Copcoat, and Copquot, and Throkmorton reveals the same disrespect in his *Master Some Laid Open*, p. 86: "I appeale to the flowre of your own universitie [of Cambridge]. I do not mean D. Copquot, for we count him but of the

middle sort, as we set D. Bridges and D. Pearne in the seventeenth fourme behind him." There is a possible explanation of Martin's and Throkmorton's dislike of Dr. Copcot. After Dudley Fenner published his anonymous *A Counter-Poyson* in 1584, defending Puritan polity, Copcot replied to this book the same year in a sermon at Paul's Cross. Then in 1586 another anonymous book was published, *A Defence of the Reasons of the Counter Poyson, for Maintenaunce of the Eldership, against an Answere Made to Them by Dr. Copequot, in a Publike Sermon at Paules Crosse, upon Psalm 84, 1584* ([Middelburg: Richard Schilders], 1586). From the preface it is clear that Fenner did not write this *Defence*, erroneously attributed to him in the *S.T.C.*, no. 10772. It is possible that Throkmorton wrote *A Defence of the Reasons*, or a part of it, since it contains many indications of his style and ideas. When Martin taunts Copcot to "answere the confutation of your sermon at Pauls Crosse," he may be challenging Copcot to "confute if he can" Martin's own book. There is scattered information on Copcot in A. L., *Antimartinus*, pp. 53–54; John Lamb, *Masters' History of the College of Corpus Christi and the Blessed Virgin Mary in the University of Cambridge* (Cambridge, 1831), pp. 136–43; James Bass Mullinger, *The University of Cambridge from the Royal Injunctions of 1535 to the Accession of Charles the First* (Cambridge, 1884), pp. 321–23; and Thomas Fuller, *The History of the University of Cambridge*, ed. James Nichols (London, 1840), p. 208. Dr. Copcot's sermon was not published, except a small part in *A Defence of the Reasons*, signatures A3 and A4, but it is available in Lambeth MSS. 374, fols. 113 v-153, renumbered 1–39.

49. *Epistle*, pp. 10, 19, 22–23, 35–36. Lucius Tarquinius Superbus (the Proud), who died in 495 B.C., was the last Roman king.

50. Ibid., p. 34; *Protestatyon*, p. 25. The book probably was *A Short Christian Instruction for the Use of a Private Family* (London: Robert Waldegrave, [1588]). The copy at the Bodleian Library may be unique. See *S.T.C.*, no. 6173. Davidson was neither "an obscure person" nor "an unlearned Scot," as Strype and Whitgift suggest. See Robert M. Gillon, *John Davidson of Prestonpans. Reformer, Preacher, and Poet in the Generation after Knox* (London, [1936]). Davidson wrote *D. Bancrofts Rashnes in Rayling against the Church of Scotland* (1590), which supplemented Penry's *A Briefe Discovery of the Untruthes and Slanders Contained in A Sermon Preached the 8. [9] of Februarie 1588* [1588/89] *by D. Bancroft*, and which brought the future archbishop in trouble with James VI and Lord Burghley. See Owen Chadwick, "Richard Bancroft's Submission," *Journal of Ecclesiastical History* 3 (January-April 1952): 58–77. William Wood was a Fellow of All Souls College and a doctor of Civil Law.

51. *John Penry and the Marprelate Controversy*, pp. 71, 61, 61, 84, 71, 105, 55. "Penry's evasive remark may represent the equivocation characteristic of Puritan 'confessions,' " ibid,. p. 227.

52. "A Date in the Marprelate Controversy," *The Library* 8 (1907): 359.

53. McGinn, *John Penry*, pp. 200–01.

54. Ibid., p. x.

55. McGinn, "The Real Martin Marprelate," *PMLA* 58 (1943): 84–107.

56. *Journal of Modern History* 40 (1968): 420–21.

57. McGinn, *John Penry*, p. 118.

58. Since McGinn relies solely on Arber, his listing of suspects and witnesses is incomplete. He omits Edward Sharpe, Peter Graye, John Wright, and Lawrence Wood, who are presented in the Puckering Brief; he omits Grimston, Richard Holmes, Jenkin Jones, and Henry Kildale, who are included in the very important Ellesmere MS. 2148; he does not mention Augustine Maicocke and John Bowman, who are listed in Sutcliffe's summary. Furthermore, McGinn speaks of "the testimony" of Newman, Penry, Throkmorton, and Waldegrave in "the brief held by the Attorney General Sir John Puckering." There is no testimony by these important participants in the Puckering Brief, but there are reports *pertaining to* these persons. "Attorney General Sir John Puckering" was a queen's serjeant, but was never attorney general; in 1590 he was not "Sir," since he was not knighted until 1592. See McGinn, *John Penry*, pp. 93, 94, 118, and also his article, "The Real Martin Marprelate, *PMLA* 58 (1943): 95, where he writes: "Regarding the depositions of the Martinist supects, what impresses us most is that Penry directly or indirectly figures in every one." But if the reader will check the first six depositions in Arber (pp. 81–83), he will see that all six relate to John Udall, whom McGinn omits in his list of deponents.

59. McGinn, *John Penry*, p. 118.

60. For the "similarities," see ibid., pp. 121–32. See Glanmor Williams, review of McGinn's book, *Welsh History Review* 3 (1967): 312. I compiled a long list of tendentious statements, wrote a separate chapter refuting each, and then decided to omit the chapter because I wanted to give more space to Throkmorton. Six examples of tendentious statements relate to (1) the mysterious writer at Richmond; (2) Dr. Perne as Penry's legendary foe; (3) McKerrow's opinion on the identity of Martin; (4) Tomkins' opinions on the identity of Martin: (5) Sharpe's generalization on Penry's intimates; (6) Sharpe's note "of that he had confessed." For (1), see Arber, *Introductory Sketch*, pp. 81–83; McGinn, *John Penry*, pp. 8, 96, 97. For (2), see McGinn, *John Penry*, pp. 50, 49, 122, 122 on Perne. It should be noted that Perne is never mentioned in all nine of Penry's books. For (3), see ibid., p. 116, and McKerrow, *The Works of Thomas Nashe* 4 (1908): 55 and 5 ([1910]): 192. For (4), see McGinn, "The Real Martin Marprelate," *PMLA* 58 (1943): 96, and Arber, *Introductory Sketch*, p. 87, no. 9, and p. 84, no. 3. For (5) and (6), see McGinn, *John Penry*, pp. 104, 91; Sutcliffe, *An Answere* (1595), p. 73; and Arber, *Introductory Sketch*, p. 182.

61. McGinn, *John Penry*, p. 126.

62. Ibid., p. 128.

63. *Martin Junior*, signature Ciii *verso*.

64. Pierce, *An Historical Introduction to the Marprelate Tracts*, p. 336.

65. Sutcliffe, *An Answere* (1595), p. 71; Arber, *Introductory Sketch*, p. 177. Dr. McGinn's assumption of "foreknowledge" depends on the authorship of *Martin Junior*, which he mistakenly assigns to Penry. See my chapter eight

for reasons why *Martin Junior* and *Martin Senior*, which belong together, were written by Throkmorton.

66. See the list of Throkmorton's works in chapter seven. *Master Some Laid Open, A Dialogue,* and *More Worke for Cooper* were not written by Penry; *A Second Admonition to the Parliament* was written by Throkmorton, not by Cartwright; it is probable that Throkmorton, not Udall, wrote *The State of the Church of Englande (Diotrephes);* it is incorrect to assign *A Petition Directed to Her Most Excellent Maiestie* to Henry Barrow; Penry did not write *An Humble Motion with Submission* (*S.T.C.,* 7754), as we learn from the printer Henry Kildale. *A Defense of the Ecclesiastical Regiment* was not written by Whitgift. In S. Halkett and J. Laing, *Dictionary of Anonymous and Pseudonymous English Literature,* new and enlarged ed. (Edinburgh, 1926), 2: 34, this work is ascribed to Lord Henry Howard. *A Defence of the Reasons of the Counter Poyson* was not written by Fenner, as the preface makes clear. Throkmorton may have collaborated in this *Defence,* but I am uncertain. If we add to these nine books the seven Marprelate books, which I have assigned to Throkmorton, then there are sixteen books concerning which McGinn and I differ on attribution.

67. McGinn, *John Penry,* p. 117.

68. "The Real Martin Marprelate," *PMLA* 58 (1943): 106.

69. McGinn, *John Penry,* p. x.

70. "The Real Martin Marprelate," *PMLA* 58 (1943): 96–97.

71. McGinn refers to the deposition and examination of Hodgskin, but does not seem to realize that the "deposition" or "examination" is an account of Hodgskin's arraignment and trial before the court. See McGinn, *John Penry,* p. 224, n. 1, and Pierce, *An Historical Introduction to the Marprelate Tracts,* pp. 333–35.

72. McGinn does not heed the warning of the compiler of the Puckering Brief, nor does he refer to it: "It is to be noted, that the said Hodgkins in diverse of his examinations, went about to conceale his being at Master Throckmortons for delivering or freeing of him from suspicion of any such matter." See Arber, *Introductory Sketch,* p. 134.

73. McGinn, "The Real Martin Marprelate," *PMLA* 58 (1943): 98–107. In many years of research, I have not encountered such a garbling of evidence and such a barrage of accusatory statements. There are at least twenty pejorative accusations which are inaccurate. McGinn writes: "As perhaps the outstanding example of Sutcliffe's distortion of facts, he presents the testimony of Tomlyn and Symmes—as he himself assures us, though no such testimony remains on record." "Again appealing to Symmes' testimony no longer extant—if, indeed it ever did exist . . . ," with the implication that Sutcliffe has manufactured his evidence. Symmes testimony is extant. The original document is Manchester Papers, no. 123, recatalogued as Lambeth MSS. 2686. For McGinn this is the non-extant testimony, and he regards the defective summary in the Puckering Brief as the extant testimony. See McGinn, ibid., pp. 102–03; Arber, *Introductory Sketch,* p. 134. The original document is conveniently available in Pierce, *An Historical Introduction to the Marprelate Tracts,* pp. 335–39. Sutcliffe is the only person

who utilized all the relevant testimony, including the "lost documents," which McGinn derides, even though some have come to light.

74. McGinn, *John Penry*, pp. 113–15; "The Real Martin Marprelate," *PMLA* 58 (1943): 102–04.

75. Ibid., p. 104, and Pierce, *An Historical Introduction to the Marprelate Tracts*, pp. 336–37.

76. McGinn refers to "Newman's deposition in Arber," but there is no deposition by Newman in Arber. What we find in Arber, *Introductory Sketch*, p. 131, are statements by four persons *pertaining to* Newman as a disperser of Marprelate books. McGinn's statement is in "The Real Martin Marprelate," *PMLA* 58 (1943): 102. For Newman, see further Additional MSS. 48064, fol. 181 *verso*, and Ellesmere MSS. 3318.

77. McGinn, "The Real Martin Marprelate," *PMLA* 58 (1943): 86.

78. McGinn, *John Penry*, p. 217; Williams, *Three Treatises concerning Wales*, p. xxviii.

79. McGinn, *John Penry*, p. 20 for both quotations. Perhaps McGinn should consider such Puritans as John Robinson, Peter Wentworth, Sir John Eliot, and John Milton, and the books of Joseph Lecler and W. K. Jordan.

80. Martin's statement is in the *Protestatyon*, p. 12. Pierce's perplexity is expressed in his edition, *The Marprelate Tracts, 1588, 1589*, p. 402, n. 2. McGinn's comments are in *John Penry*, pp. 130–31.

81. Sir John Williams, "Undescribed Edition of a Work of Penry," *Transactions of the Congregational Historical Society* 2 (Oct. 1906): 430–31. Wilson, *The Library* 10 (July 1909): 225–40.

82. McGinn, *John Penry*, p. 131.

83. Ibid., pp. 89, 94, 117, 89.

84. McGinn, "A Perplexing Date in the Marprelate Controversy," *Studies in Philology* 41 (1944): 177–78. Wilson is correct in his dating. There is no deposition by Waldegrave in the state documents. It would be a real find if it could be located. What we have in the state documents is an item in the Puckering Brief, a collection of statements *pertaining to* Waldegrave. Sutcliffe's account is valuable, since it is our only source which informs us of Waldegrave's printing of books at La Rochelle. Wilson was correct in his selection of this source.

85. McGinn, *John Penry*, p. 90. This statement is an unkind, unnecessary, and unscholarly reproach on "most students of the Controversy." I take no delight in reporting these inaccurate statements, but I feel honor bound to substantiate the scholarly research of my predecessors who no longer can defend themselves.

86. The book reviews of McGinn's *John Penry and the Marprelate Controversy* provide a diversity of opinions, many of which are percipient and informed. See the following by British reviewers: B. W. Beckingsale, *Notes and Queries* 212 (September 1967): 352; Peter Brooks, *Bibliothèque d' Humanisme et Renaissance* 29 (1967): 285–86, and also *Anglican Theological Review* 49 (1967): 237; John Carey, *Renaissance Quarterly* 20 (1967): 375–77; Patrick Collinson,

Journal of Ecclesiastical History 18 (1967): 134; C. G. Harlow, *Review of English Studies* 20 (1969): 82–83; Derek Holmes, *Heythrop Journal* 8 (1967): 91–92; Christopher Hill, *New Statesman* 72 (1966): 556; A. L. Rowse, *English Historical Review* 83 (1968): 169–70; N. R. N. Tyacke, *History* 52 (1967): 199; David Williams, *Studia Neophilologica* 38 (1967): 370–72; Glanmor Williams, *Welsh History Review* 3 (1967): 311–12; and also ibid., 361–80, "John Penry: Marprelate and Patriot?" for an extended review published six months after his first review; Penry Williams, *The Library* 23 (1968): 72–73. There is also an article by David Williams, which is not a book review but perhaps an article review, published two years after McGinn's article, "The Real Martin Marprelate," *PMLA* 58 (March 1943): 84–107, in *The Welsh Review* 4 (March 1945): 50–54. In addition to these fourteen reviews, there are ten American reviews, of which two are anonymous. These are: Leland H. Carlson, *Church History* 36 (1967): 90–91; Rudolf Kirk, *Seventeenth Century News* 25 (1967): 16; Kenneth R. R. Gros Louis, *Modern Language Journal* 51 (1967): 426–27; John R. Roberts, *Journal of English and Germanic Philology* 66 (1967): 254–57; Paul S. Seaver, *Journal of Modern History* 40 (1968): 420–21; Edward O. Smith, Jr., *Journal of Presbyterian History* 45 (1967): 150–51; W. M. Southgate, *American Historical Review* 72 (1967): 579–80; Thomas B. Stroup, *Modern Philology* 65 (1968): 247–49. The two anonymous reviews are in *Choice* 3 (1966): 668, and *Christian Century* 83 (1966): 561.

87. My research on style influenced me against any theory of composite authorship. Penry was sensitive to the accusation that he was Martin Marprelate, and denied that he was Martin. Since he resided with Throkmorton from 2 March to 2 October 1589, one must conclude that there was much general discussion, and perhaps some disagreement, on the question of priority for printing Penry's or Throkmorton's books. The only likely indication of collaboration occurs in *Hay Any Worke for Cooper*, pp. 15–18, where there is material on church polity, common to both Penry and Throkmorton. Throkmorton may be writing his own material, or he may be paraphrasing Penry, or Penry may have submitted oral or written material. It is difficult to form any conclusion on authorship from a list of short three-line points or theses.

A SELECT BIBLIOGRAPHY

MANUSCRIPTS

BODLEIAN LIBRARY
Additional Manuscripts
c. 302, fol. 38
c. 303, fols. 200–07
Douce Manuscripts
309

BRITISH LIBRARY
Additional Manuscripts
1330, fols. 48, 49
5841, fols. 129–46
23241, 23242, 25037
32092, fols. 106–07, 123–33
32485, M I. 2
32490, EE(26)
48039, fols. 63–70
48064, fols. 9–24, 118–31, 144–
46, 181–85, 220–22, 253–56
Cotton Manuscripts
Julius, F vi, fol. 76 (old fol.
71)
Titus, B vi, fol. 154
Egerton Manuscripts
2598, fols. 242–43
2603, fol. 49
2645, fols. 156 et seq.
2713, fols. 144, 145
Harley Manuscripts
360, fols. 45–47
361, fols. 68–74
787, items 65, 66b
831, fols. 14–19
834, fols. 62–75
1100, fols. 32, 33

2143, fols. 48–49
6353, item 1
6848, fols. 30–36, 81, 85–94,
150, 154–79, 193
6849, fols. 120–49, 154–79,
198–210, 235–36, 239
6866, fols. 82–135
6995, 6996, 6997, 6998, 7028–
50
7042, fols. 6–34, 47–49, 54–55,
193–200, 204, 375
7188, fols. 89–93
7581, fols. 2–49
Landsdowne Manuscripts
53, item 71, fols. 148–49
58, items 17–21
61, item 3, fol. 5; item 22, fols.
68–69; item 27, fols. 78–80;
item 29, fol. 83
64, item 16, fols. 51–56
68, articles 5, 41–47, 50–60,
62, 84, 86
69, items 40–45
75, fol. 25; items 26, 27, 28,
fols. 54–59
80, no. 63, fol. 160
101, item 51, fols. 186–98
103, item 43, fol. 102; item 71
109, items 12, 13, fols. 34–36
111, item 4
120, fols. 21–28
238, fols. 326–34
808, fol. 63
830, fols. 114–18

982, fols. 118, 127, 139, 155–61, 177–79

Sloane Manuscripts
885, fols. 101–105

UNIVERSITY OF CAMBRIDGE

Emmanuel College
Sutcliffe Manuscripts
(Matthai Sutlivii Opera, 14 vols.)

Gonville and Caius College
197, fols. 206, 211–21
(Class A. 1090. 8)

University Library
M. m. i. 47, fols. 333–35
Thomas Baker Transcripts, xxiv-xlii. Volumes i-xxiii are the Harley Manuscripts in the British Library, 7028–50

DOCTOR WILLIAMS'S LIBRARY

Morrice Manuscripts
Seconde Parte of a Register. Volume B
Loose Papers. Volume A
Transcript. Volume C
A Chronological Account of Eminent Persons; Letters; etc., from 1534 to 1695
H. Volume I, 1534 to 1585
I. Volume II, 1585 to 1627: 373(14), 395(13), 397(2), 405(2), 419(2, 4), 441(8), 487(2, 5, 6)

HENRY E. HUNTINGTON LIBRARY

Ellesmere Manuscripts
483 (Penry's notebook)

1988 (High Commission, 20/6/1589)
2101–2117, 2121, 2145–2156, 2158, 3318, 5984, 5985

Hastings Manuscripts
5092

INNER TEMPLE LIBRARY

Petyt Manuscripts
538/47/fols. 459–62

KENT COUNTY ARCHIVES OFFICE

Court of High Commission, Act Book, 1584–1603
(C44/3, fols. 5–6)

LAMBETH PALACE LIBRARY

Lambeth Manuscripts
374, fols. 113–53
445, items 5, 6
650, no. 232; 2686
Carte Antique et Miscellanee IV, 161

PIERPONT MORGAN LIBRARY

Throkmorton Manuscripts
MA 276, fols. 3–9, 13–27, 28–51
(Phillipps Manuscript 13891)

PUBLIC RECORD OFFICE

King's Bench, Indictments, Ancient
KB9/683/Part I
Parchments 36, 37 (Penry)
King's Bench, Controlment Roll
KB29/230/Membranes 59 v, 68, 75 (Penry)
King's Bench, Coram Rege Roll

KB27/1325/Easter Term, 35 Elizabeth (Penry)

Manchester Papers
30/15/123 (Symmes)
30/15/124 (Throkmorton)
(See Lambeth Manuscripts, 2686)

Privy Council
2/12/fol. 531 (Sharpe)
2/16/fols. 249, 250, 253, 398 (Martinist Printers)
2/17/fol. 809 (Hodgskin)
2/17/fols. 796–97 (Privy Council letter, dated 3 July 1590; is almost identical with a letter of November 1589)
2/18/fols. 276, 277, 411, 414, 417, 435, 441

Prerogative Court of Canterbury
P.C.C. 38 Rutland. (John Field's Will)

Star Chamber
5/A 30/22 (J. Popham, Elizabeth Crane)
5/A 30/22 (Elizabeth Crane Carleton)

State Papers, Domestic, Elizabeth
SP 12/167/21 (Throkmorton)
SP 12/199/1, 2 (Bancroft)

SP 12/212/fol. 49
SP 12/219/21, 22
SP 12/226/4, 8 (Marprelate)
SP 12/227/2 September 1589 (Printers)
SP 12/227/37 (Hodgskin)
SP 12/228/fol. 15 (Middleton)
SP 12/228/fol. 19 (High Commission)
SP 12/229/48, fols. 113–14 (Symmes)
SP 12/230/fol. 78 (Middleton)
SP 12/235/no. 6 (Penry)
SP 12/244/fol. 62 (Penry)
SP 12/244/item 64, fol. 156 (Udall)
SP 12/245/item 21/fols. 45, 112 (Penry)
SP 12/245/item 30 (Penry)
SP 15/21/121 (Carleton)
SP 15/27A/fols. 9, 15 (Sharpe)
SP 15/31/14/fols. 58, 60 (Marprelate)

State Papers, Scotland, Elizabeth
SP 52/45/44
SP 52/46/nos. 22, 64, 73 (Penry)
SP 52/48/nos. 52, 53 (Waldegrave)

BOOKS

There are useful bibliographies in *The Cambridge Bibliography of English Literature* 1(1940):685–94; in volume 5, *Supplement: A.D. 600–1900* (1957):321–22; in *The New Cambridge Bibliography of English Literature* 1(1974):1,950–64; in *The Cambridge History of English Literature* 3(1930):537–45; in Henry M. Dexter, *Congregationalism* (1880), pp. 1–288, chronologically arranged—7,250 items; in T. G. Crippen, "Early

Nonconformist Bibliography," *Transactions of the Congregational Historical Society* 1(1901–1904):44–57, 99–112, 171–84, 252–65, 410–20; 2(1905–06):61–71, 219–29, 432–44. See also Conyers Read, *Bibliography of British History, Tudor Period, 1485–1603* (1933); 2d ed. (1959), and Mortimer Levine, *Tudor England, 1485–1603* (1968), which continues a bibliographical survey to September 1966. Dr. Williams's Library has published a *Guide to the Manuscripts*, compiled by Kenneth Twinn (1969), and also *Early Nonconformity, 1566–1800. A Catalogue of Books*, in 12 volumes (1968). The standard monographs on nonconformity and Tudor Puritanism by Patrick Collinson, Christopher Hill, Marshall M. Knappen, A. F. Scott Pearson, Albert Peel, and William Pierce are rich in footnotes and bibliographical suggestions. William Haller's books reveal wide reading in history and literature.

My original bibliography has been drastically pruned. Most of the books listed below have been retained because they are not in the usual bibliographies or because they have been published in the last three decades. Occasionally an older book is listed with additional bibliographical details.

Anselment, Raymond A. *'Betwixt Jest and Earnest': Marprelate, Milton, Marvell, Swift and the Decorum of Religious Ridicule*. Toronto, ca. 1979.

Aylmer, John. *An Harborowe for Faithfull and Trewe Subjectes*. [London], 1559. See "The Puritan Palinodia." "The Harborough for Faithful Subjects," in Samuel R. Maitland, *Essays on Subjects Connected with the Reformation in England*. London, 1899. First appeared in *The British Magazine* for 1846–47.

Burgess, Alan. *Warwickshire*. London, 1950.

Carlson, Leland H. and Paulson, Ronald. *English Satire. Papers Read at a Clark Library Seminar, January 15, 1972*. Los Angeles, 1972.

Coke, Edward. *A Booke of Entries*. London, 1614. Penry's trial.

Collier, Jeremy. *An Ecclesiastical History of Great Britain. Chiefly of England*. 2 vols. London, 1708, 1714. Later editions in 1840–41, 1845–46, and 1852, all in nine volumes.

Collinson, Patrick. *Archbishop Grindal, 1519–1583. The Struggle for a Reformed Church*. Berkeley, 1979.

Collinson, Patrick. *The Elizabethan Puritan Movement*. London, 1967.

Colvile, Frederick Leigh. *The Worthies of Warwickshire Who Lived between 1500 and 1800*. Warwick, [ca. 1870].

Colville, John. *Original Letters of Mr. John Colville, 1582–1603. To Which Is Added, His Palinode, 1600.* Ed. David Laing. Edinburgh: Bannatyne Club, 1858.

Couper, W. J. *Robert Waldegrave, King's Printer for Scotland.* Glasgow, 1916.

Cross, Claire, ed. *The Letters of Sir Francis Hastings, 1574–1609.* Somerset Record Society, 69. Frome, 1969.

Davies, Horton. *Worship and Theology in England from Cranmer to Hooker, 1534–1603.* Princeton, 1970.

Dawley, Powel Mills. *John Whitgift and the English Reformation.* New York, 1954.

Desgraves, Louis. *Les Haultin, 1571–1623.* Geneva, 1960.

Doubleday, H. Arthur; Page, William; Salzman, L. F.; and Pugh, R. B., eds. *The Victoria History of the Counties of England. Warwickshire.* 8 vols. London, 1904–69. Especially helpful for Throkmorton and Haseley.

Eccles, Mark. *Shakespeare in Warwickshire.* Madison, 1961.

Erdman, David V. and Fogel, Ephim G., eds. *Evidence for Authorship. Essays on Problems of Attribution, with an Annotated Bibliography of Selected Readings.* Ithaca, New York, 1966.

Ferguson, W. Craig. *Valentine Simmes. Printer to Drayton, Shakespeare, Chapman, Greene, Dekker, Middleton, Daniel, Jonson, Marlowe, Marston, Heywood, and Other Elizabethans.* Charlottesville, Virginia, 1968.

Gasquoine, Thomas. *John Penry and Other Heroes of the Faithfull and Suffering Church.* London, 1909.

Gillon, Robert Moffat. *John Davidson of Prestonpans. Reformer, Preacher and Poet in the Generation after Knox.* London, [1936].

Greg, W. W. and Boswell, E. *Records of the Court of the Stationers' Company 1576 to 1602, from Register B.* London, 1930.

Haller, William. *The Rise of Puritanism.* New York, 1938.

Hill, Christopher. *Economic Problems of the Church, from Archbishop Whitgift to the Long Parliament.* Oxford, 1956.

Hunt, John. *Religious Thought in England from the Reformation to the End of the Last Century.* 3 vols. London, 1870–73. 1:70–107. This author provides original comments on Marprelate nine years before Arber's *Introductory Sketch* was published.

Isaac, Frank. *English Printers' Types of the Sixteenth Century.* Oxford, 1936.

Kemp, Thomas, ed. *The Black Book of Warwick.* Warwick, [1898].

Knappen, Marshall M. *Tudor Puritanism. A Chapter in the History of Idealism.* Chicago, 1939. Bibliography, pp. 521–31.

Lecocq, Louis. *La Satire en Angleterre de 1588 à 1603.* Paris, 1969.

Marprelate, Martin. *The Marprelate Tracts [1588–1589].* Leeds, 1967. Scolar Press Facsimile.

[Nashe, Thomas]. *An Almond for a Parrat, or Cutbert Curry-Knaves Almes. Fit for the Knave Martin.* [London, 1590]. Reprinted in 1846.

Nashe, Thomas. *The Works of Thomas Nashe.* Ed. Ronald B. McKerrow. 5 vols. London, 1904–[10]. See especially "The Martin Marprelate Controversy," 5:34–65. The reprint, 1958, has new material in volume 5:1–84, "A Supplement," by F. P. Wilson.

Neale, J. E. *Elizabeth I and Her Parliaments, 1584–1601.* London, 1957. The first volume for 1559–81 appeared in 1953.

O'Day, Rosemary and Heal, Felicity, eds. *Continuity and Change. Personnel and Administration of the Church in England 1500–1642.* Leicester University Press, 1976.

A Parte of a Register. [Middelburg: Richard Schilders, 1593].

Paule, George. *The Life of the Most Reverend and Religious Prelate, John Whitgift, Lord Archbishop of Canterbury.* London, 1612. The edition of 1699 includes Richard Cosin's *Conspiracy for Pretended Reformation.*

Pearson, A. F. Scott. *Church and State. Political Aspects of Sixteenth Century Puritanism.* Cambridge, England, 1928.

Pearson, A. F. Scott. *Thomas Cartwright and Elizabethan Puritanism, 1535–1603.* Cambridge, England, 1925.

Peel, Albert. *The Christian Basis of Democracy.* London, 1943. Lectures 2 and 3 pertain to Penry.

Peel, Albert, ed. *The Seconde Parte of a Register. Being a Calendar of Manuscripts under That Title Intended for Publication by the Puritans about 1593, and Now in Dr. Williams's Library, London.* 2 vols. Cambridge, England, 1915. Five helpful indexes.

Peel, Albert and Carlson, Leland H., eds. *Cartwrightiana.* London, 1951.

Peirce, James. *A Vindication of the Dissenters.* London, 1717. Latin edition, 1710.

Porter, H. C. *Reformation and Reaction in Tudor Cambridge.* Cambridge, England, 1958.

Rowse, A. L. *Ralegh and the Throckmortons.* London, New York, 1962.

Schoenbaum, Samuel. *Internal Evidence and Elizabethan Dramatic Authorship. An Essay in Literary History and Method.* Evanston, 1966.

Simpson, Percy. *Studies in Elizabethan Drama.* Oxford, 1955. See chapter 7, "The Official Control of Tudor and Stuart Printing."

Smith, John James et al. *Index to the Baker Manuscripts.* Cambridge, England, 1848.

Stopes, Charlotte C. *Shakespeare's Warwickshire Contemporaries.* Stratford-upon-Avon, 1907. Chapters 9 and 10 for the Throkmortons.

Throkmorton, Job. *The Defence of Iob Throkmorton, against the Slaunders of Maister Sutcliffe, Taken out of a Copye of His Owne Hande as It Was Written to an Honorable Personage.* [Middelburg: Richard Schilders], 1594.

Udall, John. *A Demonstration of the Trueth of That Discipline Which Christe Hath Prescribed.* [East Molesey: Robert Waldegrave, 1588]. Included in *A Parte of a Register* (*S.T.C.*, 10400). Reprinted 1641, 1642, with title: *The True Form of Church Government.* Reissued by Edward Arber, 1880, 1895.

Usher, Roland G. *The Rise and Fall of the High Commission.* Oxford, 1968. A reprint of the 1913 edition, with a new introduction and a supplemental bibliography by Philip Tyler, pp. i-xxxviii.

Waddington, John. *Congregational History, 1567–1700, in Relation to Contemporaneous Events, and the Conflict for Freedom, Purity, and Independence.* London, 1874.

[Waddington, John]. *Historical Papers (First Series). Congregational Martyrs.* London, 1861. The edition of 1862 is a reprint, without the epilogue (pp. 195–96) in the first edition.

White, Francis O. *Lives of the Elizabethan Bishops of the Anglican Church.* London, 1898.

Williams, David, ed. *Three Treatises concerning Wales.* Cardiff, 1960.

Williams, Samuel. *John Penry, 1563–1593.* Cardiff, 1956.

Wilson, John Dover. *Martin Marprelate and Shakespeare's Fluellen. A New Theory of the Authorship of the Marprelate Tracts.* London, 1912. Reprinted from *The Library* 3(1912): 113–51, 241–76.

Youngs, Frederic A., Jr. *The Proclamations of the Tudor Queens*. Cambridge, England, 1976.

ARTICLES

This select list includes mainly recent articles and a few older articles omitted in standard bibliographies.

Anselment, Raymond A. "Rhetoric and the Dramatic Satire of Martin Marprelate." *Studies in English Literature 1500–1900* 10 (1970): 103–19.

Booty, John. "Tumult in Cheapside: The Hacket Conspiracy." *Historical Magazine of the Protestant Episcopal Church* 42 (1973): 293–317.

Bühler, Curt F. "Robert Waldegrave and the Pirates of Dunkirk." *The New Colophon*, 1, pt. 4 (1948): 377–82.

Cargill Thompson, W. D. J. "A Reconsideration of Richard Bancroft's Paul's Cross Sermon of 9 February 1588/9." *Journal of Ecclesiastical History* 20 (1969): 253–66.

Cargill Thompson, W. D. J. "Sir Francis Knollys' Campaign against the *Jure Divino* Theory of Episcopacy." C. Robert Cole and Michael E. Moody, eds., *The Dissenting Tradition. Essays for Leland H. Carlson* (Athens, Ohio: Ohio University Press, 1975), pp. 39–77.

Carlson, Leland H. "A Corpus of Elizabethan Nonconformist Writings." *Studies in Church History*, ed. G. J. Cuming, 2 (1965): 297–309.

Chadwick, Owen. "Richard Bancroft's Submission." *Journal of Ecclesiastical History* 3 (1952): 58–77.

Collinson, Patrick. "John Field and Elizabethan Puritanism." *Elizabethan Government and Society. Essays Presented to Sir John Neale*. Ed. S. T. Bindoff, J. Hurstfield, and C. H. Williams (London, 1961), pp. 127–62.

Collinson, Patrick. "Towards a Broader Understanding of the Early Dissenting Tradition." C. Robert Cole and Michael E. Moody, eds., *The Dissenting Tradition*, pp. 3–38.

Coolidge, John S. "Martin Marprelate, Marvell, and *Decorum Personae* as a Satirical Theme." *PMLA* 74 (1959): 526–32.

[Crippen, T. G.?]. "A Remarkable Puritan Maunscript" [Wigginton]. *Transactions of the Congregational Historical Society* 2 (1905–06): 147–50. See also 2 (1906): 379–86, and 3 (1907): 27–32.

Edgerton, William L. "The Calendar Year in Sixteenth-Century Printing." *The Journal of English and Germanic Philology* 59 (1960): 439–49.

Ferguson, F. S. "Relations between London and Edinburgh Printers and Stationers (–1640)." *The Library* 8 (1927): 145–98.

[Green, Joseph J.]. "Some Puritan Genealogies [Throkmorton]." *Transactions of the Congregational Historical Society* 4 (1909): 96–97.

Jackson, William A. "Robert Waldegrave and the Books He Printed or Published in 1603." *The Library* 13 (December 1958): 225–33.

Johnson, A. F. "Books Printed at Heidelberg for Thomas Cartwright." *The Library* 2 (March 1948): 284–86.

[Maskell, William]. "Martin Marprelate." *The Christian Remembrancer* (April 1845): 338–406.

McGinn, Donald J. "Nashe's Share in the Marprelate Controversy." *PMLA* 59 (1944): 952–84. See also *PMLA* 61 (1946): 431–53.

McKerrow, Ronald B. "Did Sir Roger Williams Write the Marprelate Tracts?" *The Library* 3 (October 1912): 364–74.

Morris, John. "Restrictive Practices in the Elizabethan Book Trade: The Stationers' Company *v.* Thomas Thomas, 1583–8." *Transactions of the Cambridge Bibliographical Society* 4, pt.4 (1967): 276–90.

New, John F. H. "The Whitgift-Cartwright Controversy." *Archiv für Reformationsgeschichte* 59 (1968): 203–12.

Pierce, William. "Did Sir Roger Williams Write the Marprelate Tracts?" *The Library* 3 (October 1912): 345–64.

Pierce, William. "The Marprelate Tracts." *Transactions of the Congregational Historical Society* 2 (1905): 81–88.

Summersgill, Travis L. "The Influence of the Marprelate Controversy upon the Style of Thomas Nashe." *Studies in Philology* 48 (1951): 145–60.

Williams, David. "The Enigma of John Penry." *Welsh Review* 4 (1945): 50–54.

Williams, Glanmor. "John Penry: Marprelate and Patriot?" *Welsh History Review* 3 (1967): 361–80.

Williams, John. "Undescribed Edition of a Work of Penry." *Transactions of the Congregational Historical Society* 2 (October 1906): 430–31.

Wilson, John Dover. "Anthony Munday, Pamphleteer and Pursuivant." *Modern Language Review* 4 (1909): 484–90.

Wilson, John Dover. "A Date in the Marprelate Controversy." *The Library* 8 (October 1907): 337–59; see also 10 (July 1909): 225–40; 3 (1912): 113–51, 241–276; 4 (January 1913): 92–104.

Wilson, John Dover. "The Marprelate Controversy." *The Cambridge History of English Literature* 3 (1909): 374–98.

Wilson, John Dover. "Richard Schilders and the English Puritans." *Transactions of the Bibliographical Society* 11 (1909–11): 65–134.

Zinberg, Cecile. "The Usable Dissenting Past: John Strype and Elizabethan Puritanism." C. Robert Cole and Michael E. Moody, eds., *The Dissenting Tradition*, pp. 123–139.

DISSERTATIONS

Bauckham, Richard. "The Career and Thought of Dr. William Fulke (1537–1589)." University of Cambridge, 1973.

Breward, Ian. "The Life and Theology of William Perkins, 1558–1602." University of Manchester, 1963.

Collinson, Patrick. "The Puritan Classical Movement in the Reign of Elizabeth I." University of London, 1957.

Cornell, Virginia Miller. "Understanding Elizabethan Laughter. The Marprelate Tracts." Arizona State University, 1974.

Donaldson, Gordon, "The Relations between the English and Scottish Presbyterian Movements to 1604." University of London, 1938.

Gabriel, Richard C. "Members of the House of Commons, 1586–7." University of London, 1954.

Greene, Walter Kirkland. "The Martin Marprelate Controversy." Harvard University, 1923.

Hume, Mary Ballantine. "The History of the Oath *ex officio* in England." Radcliffe College, 1923.

King, Joy Lee Belknap. "A Critical Edition of *A Dialogue Wherin Is Plainly Laide Open, the Tyrannicall Dealing of L. Bishopps against Gods Children.*" Rutgers—The State University, 1968.

Owen, H. Gareth. "The London Parish Clergy in the Reign of Elizabeth I." University of London, 1957.

Sheils, W. J. "The Puritans in Church and Politics in the Diocese of Peterborough, 1570–1610." University of London, 1975.

Turney, Charles. "A Critical Edition of the Puritan Pamphlet *M. Some Laid Open in His Coulers.*" Rutgers—The State University, 1965.

INDEX

Abbot, George, archbishop of Canterbury, 82

Abington, 68

An Abstract, of Certain Acts of Parliament, 293; *STC* 10394

Acosta, Joseph de, author, 83

Act of Supremacy (1559), 3

Act of Uniformity (1559), 3. *See also* Statutes

Acworth or Ackworth, Dr. George, commissary for Bishop Horne, 384, 399

Acts and Monuments (Foxe), 16, 284

Adams, widow, 22, 137

Adderbury, Oxfordshire, 47

Admonition Controversy, 238, 278–79, 282, 311, 315

An Admonition to the Parliament (Field and Wilcox), 4, 98, 101, 102, 278, 282, 314, 319, 320, 322, 324, 344

An Admonition to the People of England (Cooper), 12, 13, 54, 58, 61, 227, 248, 254, 256, 278, 295, 347, 360

"An Advertisement for Pap-hatchet" (Gabriel Harvey), 68

"An Advertisement touching the Controversies of the Church of England," a manuscript book of 1589, printed in 1640 or 1641 (F. Bacon), 64

Aequity (Penry). See *A Treatise Containing the Aequity*

An Agnus Dei (John Weever), 83

Airay, Henry, provost of Queen's, Oxford, 101

Alford, Lincolnshire, 36

All Souls College, Oxford, 388; Alsolne College, 201, 388

Allde, Edward, printer, 82

Allde, Elizabeth, wife of Edward, 82

Allde, Margaret, mother of Edward, 82

Allen, William, cardinal, 3, 256

Alliteration, 55, 65, 70, 117, 161, 180, 186–89, 234, 266, 316, 321, 323, 326, 330, 335, 365

An Almond for a Parrat (Nashe), 70, 118

Anabaptisme, 69

Anabaptist, 66, 70, 400

Anatomie of Abuses (Philip Stubbes), 70

Anderson, Anthony, 225

Anderson, Sir Edmund, chief justice, Court of Common Pleas, 44, 49, 79, 125, 333

Andrewes, Lancelot, master of Pembroke College, Cambridge, 79, 81, 85

Anecdotes, 142–43, 214, 219, 262–65, 283

Anglicanism, 13, 14, 54, 57, 97, 102, 106, 120, 314, 323

Anglicans, 3, 14, 17, 96, 108, 111, 156, 312, 333

Anne, queen of Scotland, wife of James VI and I, 90

Anselment, Raymond A., 389

"An Answer to Certen Peeces of a Sermon" (Throkmorton), 101, 206, 217, 242, 314–19, 321, 324, 372

An Answer to the Two First and Principall Treatises (Richard Cosin), 293

"An Answer unto a Letter of Master Harrisons by Master Cartwright," 69

An Answere to a Certaine Libel (Sutcliffe, 1592), 138

An Answere to a Certen Libel (Whitgift), 4, 282, 324

An Answere unto a Certaine Calumnious Letter (Sutcliffe, 1595), 125–28, 138, 152, 205, 304, 305

419

Antimartinus (by A.L.), 62
Apocrypha, 13, 168–69
Apologie (Cosin), 116
Appelbie, Christopher, 48
Appellation (Penry), 37, 51, 88, 111, 134, 135, 136, 137, 138, 143, 156, 159, 211, 273, 307
Appollinaris, 69
Arber, Edward, xv, 31, 151, 152, 296, 307, 333, 335, 338, 357
Aretius, Benedictus, Swiss writer, 216, 255
Aristotle, 100
Arius, 69
Arthington, Henry, 85, 87, 88, 114, 116, 120, 123, 241
Articles of Religion, 5, 9, 16, 238, 263, 310
Asaph, bishop of (William Hughes), 199, 212
Ascham, Roger, 67
"Asinus Onustus. The Asse Over-ladened," a manuscript book of 1589, printed 1642, 63
Assize, justices of, 52, 83–84, 115, 194, 240–41, 333
Atkinson, [Nicholas?], parishioner at Sedbergh, Yorkshire, 34, 263
Attributions of authorship, 69, 101–02, 152, 153, 154, 155, 156, 157, 160, 172, 179–81, 227–29, 315, 320–22, 322–24, 325–28, 328–32, 333–38, 338–40, 344, 361, 364, 375, 376, 378, 382, 383, 390, 391, 392, 394, 403, 404–05
Aubrey, William, 32, 33, 44
Augsburg, West Germany, 317
Auncient Historie of the Destruction of Troy (Raoul Le Fèvre), 83
Aylmer, John, bishop of London, 11, 20, 216, 225, 227, 234, 290, 291, 310; challenge to, 110, 250; criticism of, 9, 12, 18, 19, 160, 162, 164, 168, 251, 262; defendant, 13, 170, 257; defense of, 56; *An Harborowe*, 118, 167; High Commission, 119, 238, 273, 283, 311; Privy Council, 136; ridicule of, 165, 191, 192, 214, 215, 224, 245, 246, 248, 264–65, 267

Babington, Anthony, 103
Babington, Zachary, son-in-law of

William Overton, bishop of Coventry and Lichfield, 292
Bacon, Lady Ann, wife of Sir Nicholas and mother of Francis, 64, 122
Bacon, Francis, 64–65, 71, 313
Baginton Hall, Warwickshire, 128
Bainbridge, Robert, 238
A Baite for Momus (Tobias Bland), 63
Baker, Edward, prebendary of Peterborough Cathedral, 40, 57
Baker, Thomas, 355, 356, 358
Banbury, Oxfordshire, 22, 51
Bancroft, Richard, xxi, 361; books of, 121, 190, 361; criticism of, 18, 118, 166, 225, 256, 281; defense of, 53, 71; chaplain to Hatton, 59; member of High Commission, 59; licenser of press, 82; authorship of *A Dialogue*, 160, 265, 302; *A Parte of a Register*, 122–23; Penry, 218, 368; proclamation of 13 February 1588/89, 60; Puritan classis movement, 312; sermon of 9 February 1588/89, 20, 58, 59, 60, 61; on Throkmorton, 239
Bangor, Caernarvonshire, 291
Baptism, 13, 133, 169, 286
Barnardus. *See* Bernarde
Barnes, Joseph, printer, 7
Barnes, Richard, bishop of Durham, 350
Barnes, Robert, 16, 118, 233
Barrow, Henry, xi, xiv, 3, 25–26, 28, 35, 58, 62, 121, 134, 141, 152, 153, 155, 312, 383
Basel, 97
Basilikon Doron (James VI), 91
Bauckham, Richard, 352
Baxter, Richard, 152
Beale, Robert, 27, 102, 116, 238
Becke, Edmund, translator, 204
Beckingsale, B. W., xiv, 358, 406
Becon, Dr. John, 292
Bedford, 225
Bedill, William, registrar, 44
Bell, Dr. John, master of Jesus College, Cambridge, 217, 294
Bellarmine, Robert, cardinal (Roberto Bellarmino), 12, 168, 169, 197, 279

Bellot, Hugh, bishop of Bangor, Caernarvonshire, 291, 389

Benison, Barnaby, 56, 255, 257

Bergavenny, 97. The older dignity was styled Bergavenny, the later one, Abergavenny

Berkshire, 160

Bernarde or Barnard, Dr. Daniel, Oxford vice-chancellor, 139, 197, 267

Bèze, Théodore de (Beza), 6, 98, 121, 170, 205, 223, 252, 255, 327

Bickley, Thomas, bishop of Chichester, Sussex, 293

Bigamy, 162, 165, 228, 292

"Bill and Book," 24, 106, 107, 238, 255, 321, 373

Bilson, Dr. Thomas, warden of Winchester College, 120, 121

Bishop, George, printer, 62

Bishops' Bible (1568), 325

Bishops' English, 18, 118, 225, 320

Blackfriars, 17, 49, 255

Bland, Tobias (Tom Blan o Bedford, writer), 18, 63, 225

Blasphemy, 9, 166, 273

Blatcher, Marjorie (Mrs. S. T. Bindoff), xv

Blethin, William, bishop of Llandaff, Glamorgan, 291, 389

Bodleian Library, 98, 179, 347

Bodley, Sir Thomas, 98

Bond, Nicholas, president of Magdalen College, Oxford, 85, 98, 160, 162, 264, 267, 294, 371

Bonnard, Georges A., 151, 153, 296

Bonner, Edmund, bishop of London, 96

Book of Common Prayer, 2, 4, 132, 166, 224, 310, 314, 325

Book of Martyrs. See Acts and Monuments

Book reviews of McGinn's John Penry, 404, 406–07; also, 178, 298–99

Booke of the Forme of Common Prayers (Calvinist and Reformed), 106, 373

Boulogne, 96

Bousfield, Bartholomew, Oxford provost of Queen's, 101

Bowes, Robert, English ambassador in Edinburgh, 86, 87, 89, 90, 91, 111, 175, 368, 381

Bowman, John, 22, 52, 176, 241, 311

Boyle, Richard, his bookshop in Blackfriars, 17, 208

Brecknockshire, Wales, 217

Brecon, Wales, 140

Brewster, William, 357

Bribery, 9, 167, 192, 216, 280, 309, 327, 334

Bricot, Father Thomas, Oxford don, 216

Bridewell prison. See Prisons

Bridges, John, dean of Sarum, 177, 183, 188, 205, 216, 225, 228, 234, 244–45, 282, 290, 306, 308; Defence, 5, 83, 258; Mineralls, 13, 227; Sacro-sanctum Novum Testamentum, 83; Fenner, 23; Sir Sidney Lee, 152; Penner, 218, 279, 296; denunciation of, 10, 118, 204, 213, 215, 217, 250, 251, 256; criticism of, 12, 111, 167, 260; name-calling, 248, 252; ridicule of, 11–12, 18, 20, 112, 185, 190, 191, 203, 211, 219, 223, 224, 235, 246, 247, 249, 252–53; sermons, 12, 267; bishopric, 160, 258

Brief Apologie of Thomas Cartwright (introductory epistle by Throkmorton), 128, 179, 254, 283

Briefe and Plaine Declaration (Fulke), referred to as "A Learned Discourse," which is the running title, 328, 354

Briefe Discovery (Penry), 52, 86, 268, 281, 368

Bristow or Bristol, 252

Bristow, Richard, Catholic author, 256

Bromley, William, 131

Bromley-Davenport, W., M.P., 128

Brook, Benjamin, author of Lives of the Puritans, 296

Brooke, William, Lord Cobham, 5, 32, 53, 358

Brooks, Peter, 406

Browne, Robert, xiv, 3, 62, 152

Browniste, 20, 66, 70, 235, 287

Bruges, 83

Bucer, Martin, 71, 255, 284

Buckhurst, Lord. See Sackville

Buckley, Thomas, of Oxford, 390

Bullen, George (Boleyn), dean of Lichfield, 21, 294
Bullinger, Heinrich, 98
Bullingham, John, bishop of Gloucester, 20, 165, 166, 214, 264, 267, 292
Burghley, Lord, William Cecil, lord treasurer, 24, 31, 35, 39, 242; appeals to, 90; London plays, 73; "Summary of the Information," 40, 171; Bowes, 86, 87, 89, 381; Coppinger, 113–14; Penry, 218, 232, 284; Sandys, 102, 329; Job Throkmorton, 6, 106, 107–08, 113, 238–39, 309, 342; Sir Nicholas Throckmorton, 96; Whitgift, 38, 39, 53
Burgoyne, Robert, dispute with Job Throkmorton, 378
Burrage, Champlin, 28, 296
Byfield, Northamptonshire, 67

Calling, 113, 132–33
Calvin, John, 98, 121, 170, 204, 205, 223, 252, 255, 288
Cambridge, 62, 76, 138, 155, 187
Cambridge, University of, 97, 139, 254, 281, 284, 289, 295, 388
Camden, William, historian, 28, 239, 392
Camerarius, Joachimus, 255
Campion, Edmund, 3, 69, 99, 252, 371
Cannon, John, ed., Letters of Junius, xi
Canon law, 14–15, 195
Canons Ashby, Northamptonshire, 129
Canterbury, city of, 38, 294. See also Whitgift
Canterbury Cathedral, 54
Carey, Henry, Lord Hunsdon, 39, 48
Carey, John, 95, 406
Cargill Thompson, W.D.J., 361, 365
Carleton, George, second husband of Elizabeth Crane, 24, 25
Carleton, Mrs. George. See Crane, Elizabeth
Carlson, Leland H., 297, 407
Carmarthen, Carmarthenshire, 57
Cartwright, Thomas, 3, 4, 12, 34, 54, 69, 70, 87, 101, 121, 225, 290, 314, 319, 325, 328, 377; books, 19, 37, 76, 77,

91, 179, 242, 254, 334, 336, 344–45, 356–57; Puritan classis movement, 4, 116, 312; Throkmorton, 23, 113, 216, 217, 282–83, 378; Sutcliffe, 124, 128, 283; Whitgift, 160, 166, 260, 281–82
Catechism, or First Instruction (A. Nowell), 328, 332
Catherine de Médicis, queen of France, 105
Catholics, 10, 64, 75, 95, 96, 99, 102–03, 108, 142, 160, 279, 284, 293, 317–18, 323, 332–33, 356, 386
Cato, 197
Cawdrey, Robert, 119, 255, 309
Caxton, William, 83
Cecil, Robert, earl of Salisbury, 24
Cecil, William. See Burghley
Ceremonies, 2, 13
Certaine Articles (Throkmorton), 102, 243, 247, 321, 322–24, 325, 327, 393
Certaine Minerall, and Metaphisicall Schoolpoints (Throkmorton), 21, 60, 160, 179, 268, 347; authorship of, 151, 227, 228, 229, 242; date of, 51, 109, 279, 390; defendants, 12–13; parallels in A Dialogue, 164; printing of, 22, 42, 77; schoolpoints, 13, 119, 227, 286; thirty-seven theses, 12; Sutcliffe on authorship of, 151
Chaderton, Laurence, master of Emmanuel College, Cambridge, 111, 129, 255, 334
Chaderton, William, bishop of Chester, 20, 119, 292, 389
Chadwick, Owen, 361
Chard, Thomas, printer, 216, 254
Charke, William, cleric, 255
Charles V, emperor, 317
Charles IX, king of France, 105, 246
Charlewood, John, printer, 216, 254
Chatfield, Stephen, 23, 32, 48, 83, 84, 248
Chaucer, Geoffrey, 159
Cheapside, 87, 88
Chemnitius or Kemnitius, Martinus, Lutheran theologian, 255
Christ Church, Oxford, 97, 98, 372
Church Government. See Polity
Church History of Britain (T. Fuller), 130
Church of England, 1–3, 303, 310; crit-

icism of, 8–9, 14, 36, 101, 117, 310; defense of, 54–56, 58–59, 61, 69, 71–72, 116; doctrine of, 16; Bilson as advocate of, 121; Hooker as apologist for, 120; Sutcliffe as defender of, 118, 151, 304; Throkmorton's attack upon, 108, 115, 128, 174, 217, 311

Clarke, Robert, baron of the Court of Exchequer, 83, 84

Clarke, Samuel, 155

Cobham. *See* Brooke, W.

Cockfield, Suffolk, 255

Coggeshall, Essex, 96

Cole, Dr. William, president of Corpus Christi College, Oxford, 97–98, 217, 267, 294

Colepepper, Martin (Culpepper), warden of New College, Oxford, 98, 160, 200, 246, 267, 294

Colet, John, 32

Coligny, Gaspard de, French Huguenot admiral, 105

Collier, Jeremy, 28

Collinson, Patrick, author and Elizabethan scholar, xiv, 25, 151, 154, 297, 351, 406–07

Collyns, Markes, 32

Cologne, West Germany, 317

Commons, House of. *See* House of Commons

Compendious Discourse (Bilson), 121

Confession of Faith, STC 22023, 89

Confutation of the Rhemish Translation (Cartwright), 37. *See also* Douai-Rheims. *See further* Rhemish New Testament

Congregationalism, 25

Conscience, 19, 20, 78, 118, 233, 261–62, 287, 320, 327, 330, 334

Conspiracie, for Pretended Reformation (Cosin), 116, 121

Convocation, 2–4, 6, 8, 13, 107, 117, 238, 273–74, 294, 310, 325, 344

Cook, Cutbert, 32

Cooke, Sir Anthony, father-in-law to Lord Burghley and Sir Nicholas Bacon, 64

Cooper, Thomas, bishop of Winchester, 11, 20, 60, 167, 168, 169, 188, 233, 234, 285, 290, 291, 313, 325; *Admonition*, 12, 13, 54, 58, 227, 248, 278,

314, 347, 360; "An Answer" (by Throkmorton), 206, 314; dangers of Presbyterianism, 14, 15, 56–57; defense of bishops, 15, 54, 56, 275, 314; denunciation of, 19, 110, 111, 118, 160, 166, 200, 215, 228, 250, 251, 277, 281, 318, 335; *Hay Any Worke for Cooper*, 171; High Commission, 33, 238, 273, 311, 355; Marprelate, 54–56, 225, 273–74; *Mineralls*, 227; *More Worke for Cooper*, 171; polity, 71, 244, 277, 315; refutation of by Penry, 218; ridicule of, 162, 204, 245, 256, 259–60, 276, 279, 295, 329; sermons, 214, 277–78, 331; University of Oxford, 98, 216, 267, 276, 278

Cooper, Mrs. Thomas, 99, 228, 233, 267, 276, 277, 278, 390

Cooperism, 201

Cooperist, 20, 201, 235

Copcot, John, master of Corpus Christi, Cambridge, 10, 200, 217, 267, 295, 402–03

Cope, Sir Anthony, M.P., 24, 106, 238

Coppinger, Ambrose, servant of the earl of Warwick, Ambrose Dudley, 113

Coppinger, Edmund, brother of Ambrose, 85, 87, 113, 116, 120, 121, 123, 125, 126, 141, 172, 241, 242

Corley, Warwickshire, 217, 263

Cornell, Virginia Miller, 354

Corpus Christi College, Cambridge, 10, 217, 295

Corpus Christi College, Oxford, 97–98, 217, 255, 294

Corunna, Spain, 67

Cosin, Richard, dean of the Arches, 10, 33, 36, 111, 116, 118, 120, 121, 123, 126, 170, 188, 217, 227, 251, 273, 285, 293, 401–02

Cottington, James, 10, 217, 263, 294, 295

Cotton, John, cleric, 296

Coughton, Warwickshire, 95

Countercuffe (Pasquill), 21, 64, 68

Counter-Poyson (Fenner), 10, 293, 334

Courts: Admiralty, 15, 195; Arches, 15, 195; Chancellor's diocesan, 195, 311; church courts, 65, 195, 311; Common Pleas, 44, 79, 125; Ecclesiastical Commission, *see* High Commission; Exchequer, 83–84; King's Bench or Queen's Bench, 18, 78, 80, 81, 88, 196, 229, 298; Newgate Sessions, 88; Prerogative Court of Canterbury, 15, 44; Requests, 10, 195, 264; Star Chamber, *see* separate entry; various Assizes, 52, 83, 115, 194, 240, 333

Coventry, Warwickshire, residence of John Hales, 42, 43, 44, 45, 47, 67, 71, 76, 109, 130, 227, 302, 304

Crane, Anthony, first husband of Elizabeth Crane, 351

Crane, Elizabeth, first wife of Anthony Crane, then married George Carleton, 22, 23, 24, 25, 36, 40, 50, 78, 143, 334, 351, 366–67

Cranmer, Thomas, archbishop, 2, 16

Crasswell, Thomas, mayor of Northampton, 61, 135

Creede, Thomas, printer, 83

Crippen, T. G., Congregationalist, editor, 296

Cripplegate, 79

Croft, Sir James, comptroller, 358

Crops and Flowers of Bridges Garden (Throkmorton), 22, 51, 52, 112, 127, 128, 141–42, 148, 151, 175–77, 180, 205, 242, 254, 265, 266, 302

Cross Keys, 73

Croydon, 83, 333

Culpepper. *See* Colepepper

Cursus optimarum questionum (Thomas Bricot), 216

Curtain theater, 72

Daemonologie (James VI), 91

Dalton, James, prosecutor of Udall, 84, 117

Danaeus or Daneau, Lambert, 255

Daniel, Samuel, 83

Daungerous Positions (Bancroft), 121

Davenport, Humphrey, M.P., 116

Davidson, John, Scottish divine, 36, 255, 295, 334, 403

Davies, Sir John, 82

Day, John, paramour of Mrs. Cooper, 99, 228, 267, 277, 278, 390, 399

Day, John, printer, 323, 327, 400

Day, Thomas, canon, Christ Church, 390, 399

"De disciplina ecclesiae sacra ex Dei verbo descripta" (Travers), printed as *A Directory of Church-Government* in 1644 or 1645. It was "entered at Stationers' Hall on the 11th of February, 1644/5." Cartwright may have been the editor or reviser. *See* page 352

De diversis ministrorum Evangelii gradibus (Hadrian Saravia), 71

"Decades," by Heinrich Bullinger. First Latin edition 1549; extracts published in English, 1566; three volumes published in 1577 as *Fiftie Godlie and Learned Sermons,* 332

Defence of Job Throkmorton (Throkmorton), 123, 125–28, 152, 153, 156, 179, 214, 217, 241, 242, 251, 254, 255, 283, 312

Defence of That Which Hath Bin Written (Penry), 57, 133, 139, 144, 145, 227, 233, 285, 286, 289, 290

Defence of the Ecclesiastical Discipline (Travers), 6, 10, 256, 335

Defence of the Godlie Ministers (Fenner), 6, 10, 23

Defence of the Government (Bridges), 5, 8, 83, 249, 256, 258, 279, 308

Defence of the Reasons of the Counter-Poyson (not by Fenner; probably by Throkmorton), 122, 403

Defense of the Aunswere (Whitgift), 4, 282

Dekker, Thomas, 83

Demonstration . . . of Discipline (Udall), 8, 24, 35, 36, 40, 48, 49, 58, 84, 116, 122, 333, 338

Denmark, 275, 276

Depositions, 32, 50, 54, 137, 138, 151, 161, 173, 175, 176, 299, 355, 404, 405, 406

Derby, 4th earl of. *See* Stanley, Henry

Devereux, E. J., 204

Devereux, Robert, 2d earl of Essex, 308

Devonshire, 37

Dexter, Henry M., Congregationalist writer and editor, 25, 26, 141,

150, 151, 152, 153, 155, 158, 296, 333, 338, 352, 382. See *The State of the Church*

Dialogue concerning the Strife of Our Church (anonymous, 1584), xvii

Dialogue. Wherin Is Plainly Laide Open (Throkmorton), 242, 250, 253, 255, 266, 268, 302, 303; anti-episcopal, 217; Bancroft on authorship, 122, 160, 265; Sutcliffe on authorship, 151, 160, 334; parallels in, 162–71, 220, 229; printing of, 88, 159; publication of, 51, 110, 137, 160; style, 150, 161, 179, 184

"Diary of an Elizabethan Gentlewoman," by Margaret Hoby, 129, 378. *Diary*, ed. Dorothy M. Meads, 378

Diction, 198–202, 212, 223–24, 230–31, 233, 243–44, 246, 266, 315, 318, 320–21, 323, 325–26, 330, 334

Dieppe, 26

Diotrephes. See *The State of the Church*

Discipline, 4, 75, 116, 121, 124, 156, 168, 170, 327, 334. *See also* Polity

Dissenters. *See* Nonconformists

D. Bancrofts Rashnes in Rayling (Davidson), 403

Dod, John, 129

Doddeson, Robert, 32

Dorbel of Sarum, olde (Bridges), 202

Douai-Rheims. *See* Rhemish New Testament

Douglas, Archibald, Scottish ambassador in London, 6, 106, 238

Drayton, Michael, 83

Dryden, John, 95

Dudley, Ambrose, earl of Warwick, 113, 217, 238, 251, 263

Dudley, Anne (Russell), countess of Warwick, third wife of Ambrose Dudley, 114, 251

Dudley, John, duke of Northumberland, 96

Dudley, Robert, earl of Leicester, 100, 238, 308

Dugdale, William, 130

Duport, John, master of Jesus College, Cambridge, 294

Durham, 350

Dyke, William, preacher at St. Albans, 66

East Molesey, Surrey, 8, 22, 31, 36, 44, 48, 78, 109, 143, 302

Ecclesiasticae Disciplinae . . . Explicatio (Travers), translated by Cartwright, *A Full and Plaine Declaration*, 345, 352

Ecclesiastical polity. *See* Polity

Edinburgh, Scotland, 52, 86, 87, 89, 91, 111, 115, 151, 156, 159, 268, 281

Edward VI, 2, 43, 284

Egerton, Stephen, 70, 124, 255

Egerton, Thomas, solicitor general, 75, 268

Elders, 4, 11, 14, 121, 133, 168

Elderton, William, ballad writer, 67

Election in Warwick, 1586, 103–04

Eliot. *See* Elyot

Elizabeth, Queen, 2, 20, 31, 53, 71, 75, 79, 85, 96, 105, 114, 194, 195, 213, 226, 291, 313; appeals to, 17, 81, 84, 85, 91, 107–08, 342; conspiracy against, 28, 103; Cooper's sermon before the queen, 331; loyalty to, 76–77, 107, 125, 246, 308, 311; malice against, 80, 84, 87–88, 175, 234; opposes Puritans, 3, 59, 97, 312; supreme governor, 36; Throkmorton's speech offends, 105, 107; queen grants clemency to Throkmorton, 115

Elizabethan period, 96, 116, 157, 298, 310, 318

Elizabethan Puritan Movement (Collinson), 154

Ellesmere MS. 2148, "Mr. John Penrye[s] Proceeding upon Couler of a Pretended Reformation," 346, 367–68, 370, 386, 390 et passim

Elmar, "mar-elme." *See* Aylmer

Elton, G. R., 204

Ely, dean of. *See* Perne

Elyot, or Eliot, Sir Thomas, diplomatist, compiler of a dictionary (1538), 216, 276–77, 385, 398–99

Emmanuel College, Cambridge, 255

England, Church of. *See* Church of England

Epigrammes (Sir John Davies), 82

Epigrammes (Weever), 83

Epistle, 8–10, 42, 48, 112, 134, 162, 180, 226, 228, 242, 249, 268, 280, 314, 333; anti-clerical attacks, 217–18; Cooper attacks, 13; humor, 211, 215, 226, 247; parallels in *A Dialogue*, 164, 212; personal references, 217, 218, 220, 267; printing of, 21, 22, 24, 31, 36, 53; publication date, 51, 57, 109; Puritans defended in, 23; similarity to *Master Some*, 153; source for *A Dialogue*, 160; stylistic features of, 211, 213–15, 219–20, 236; suspected authors of, 26, 32–36, 49, 58, 127, 174; Throkmorton's authorship of, 210–20, 235, 266, 274, 302, 312; unusual diction of, 199, 212

Epitome, 10–12, 21, 112, 118, 153, 160, 180, 218, 226, 235–236, 242, 247, 249, 256, 323; allusions to Aylmer, 10, 12; to Bridges, 11–12, 280; to Sharpe, 61; to Tomkins, 36; to Wigginton, 33, 34; Fawsley, 22, 45; parallels in *A Dialogue*, 164; polity, 11; printing and distribution of, 51, 57, 61, 76; reaction to, 10–11; suspected authors, 23, 26, 44, 127, 174, 221, 235, 266, 280, 300, 302

Erasmus, Desiderius, 203–04, 256

Essayes (Montaigne), 83

Essex, 2d earl of. *See* Devereux, Robert

Eucharist, 133

Euphues (Lyly), 67, 68

Evans, [Hugh?], 56, 263

Evans, John X., editor of works of Sir Roger Williams, 27

Ex officio oath, 16, 19, 33, 35, 116, 233, 238, 273, 295, 311, 313, 327, 345, 356

Examination of T. Cartwrights Late Apologie (Sutcliffe), 128

Examinations of Martinist suspects, 32–36, 38–39, 40–49, 50–52, 175

Excommunication, 9, 16, 71, 195, 230, 325, 327

Exhortation to the Bishops and Their Clergie, II (Throkmorton), 101, 242, 316, 317, 319–22, 329, 335

Exhortation to the Byshops, I (Throkmorton), 10, 164, 171, 242, 316, 319–22, 324, 327, 329, 331

Exhortation unto the Governours (Penry), 57, 138, 178, 211, 259, 279, 285, 305, 306, 307, 360

Fagius, Paul, 284

Familists, Family of Love, 66

Father Admonitor, name for Bishop Cooper, author of *An Admonition*, 202

Fawsley, Northamptonshire, residence of Sir Richard Knightley, 22, 40, 43, 44, 45, 57, 58, 71, 109, 137, 143, 227, 302, 304

Felony, 79, 80, 81, 84, 113

Fen, Humphrey, preacher at Coventry, 67

Fenner, Dudley, 6, 10, 19, 23, 28, 255, 293, 306, 334

Fenner, Edward, judge of Queen's Bench, 84, 113, 122, 241, 302

Fermor, Mary, first wife of Sir Richard Knightley, 366

Field, John, 3, 124, 238, 319; *Admonition to the Parliament*, 54, 98, 101, 314, 315; Cooper denounces, 278; correspondence and documents, 121, 122; death of, 23–24; election efforts, 103; incarceration, 102, 325; Marprelate suspect, 28, 36; Penry's letter to, 7; *Second Admonition*, 102, 325; Collinson, 415; *DNB*, "Feilde," Supplement, II, 205–06

First Blast (Knox), 347, 400

First Parte of Pasquils Apologie (Pasquill), 70

Fisher, John, burgess, 104

Fladbury, Worcestershire, 95, 370

Fleetwood, William, recorder of the City of London, 39

Fletcher, Richard, bishop of Bristol, 350

Florence, Italy, 71

Fludd, William, puritan, 25

Fortescue, John, privy councilor, 39, 358

Foxe, John, martyrologist, 16, 255, 284, 349

Francis, Thomas, provost of Queen's, Oxford, 100

Freedom of speech, 106, 238

Frégeville, John or Jean de, 18, 20, 223, 225, 234

Freke, Edmund, bishop of Norwich and of Worcester, 292, 293

Frend, W. H. C., 366

Frere, Walter H., bishop of Truro, xv, 296, 314

Friendly Admonition (Leonard White), 69

"A Friendly Caveat to Bishop Sands" (Throkmorton), 102, 217, 242, 250, 318, 328–32

Frith, John, 16, 233

Fruitful Sermon (Laurence Chaderton), 334

Fulham, 264, 265

Fulke, William, master of Pembroke College, 5–6, 69, 111, 141, 183, 255, 334, 345

Fuller, Nicholas, puritan lawyer, 84

Fuller, Thomas, 130

G., I., pseudonym used by Job Throkmorton, 140, 243

Gambling, 118–19, 145, 192–93, 212, 222, 294

Gardiner of Northampton. *See* Garnet

Garnet of Northampton, 22, 137

Gasquoine, Thomas, writer on Penry, 297

Gawdy, Francis, judge of Queen's Bench, 81, 113, 229, 241, 302, 358

Genealogies, 95–97, 129–31, 370–71, and endsheets

Geneva, 97, 98, 106, 121, 185, 238, 281, 315

Geneva Bible, 204, 325

Gibson, James, 141

Gifford, George, 159

Gigge, Elizabeth, 13, 165, 228

Gilby, Anthony, 122, 159, 255, 319, 325, 328

Glibberie, a vicar in Halstead, Essex, 263–64

Gloucester, 252

Godley, Henry, Penry's father-in-law in Northampton, xix, 22, 58, 137

Godly Treatise Containing and Deciding (Robert Some, May 1588), 20, 35, 57, 133, 138, 156, 285, 350

Godly Treatise . . . Whereunto One

Proposition More Is Added (Robert Some, September 1588), 20, 57, 58, 133, 138, 143, 169, 220, 286

Godwin, Thomas, bishop of Bath and Wells, 99, 389

Good, John, 32

Goodman, Christopher, 319, 325, 328, 344

Goodman, Gabriel, dean of Westminster, 33, 166, 170, 217, 293–94, 402

Gosson, Stephen, 83

Gower, John, 159

Grammar and Accidence (William Lily and John Colet), 46, 81–82; STC 5542

Gravat or Gravett, William, 18, 192, 225

Gravelines, battle of (fought 29 July 1588), 26

Gravener, pseudonym of Throkmorton, 243

Greene, Robert, 83

Greenham, Richard, 155, 253, 255

Greenwich, 107

Greenwood, John, 3, 88, 141, 151, 152, 153, 155, 312

Greg, W. W., 345

Greye or Graye, Peter, 45

Grieve, Alexander J., 151, 154, 296, 306

Grimston, of Northampton, 22, 50, 109

Grindal, Edmund, archbishop, 5

Grivel, pseudonym of Throkmorton, 243

Gros Louis, Kenneth R.R., 407

Gualter, Rudolph, 98

Guernsey, Channel Islands, 378

Guinea, Africa, 85

Gyfford, Stephen, 42, 43, 44, 45

Gyrton or Girton, Cambridgeshire, 20, 287, 350

Hacket, William, 85, 87, 88, 114, 116, 120, 123, 125, 190, 241

Hales, John, 22, 42, 43, 44, 45, 50, 75, 76, 77, 366, 390

Hall, William, printer, 82

Haller, William, xv

Halstead, Essex, 263

Hampstead, 263

Harborowe (Aylmer), 11, 12, 118, 167, 283

Harding, Michael, 204

Harding, Thomas, Catholic writer, 256, 279

Harlow, C. G., 407

Harman, Edward George, 363

Harmony of the Confessions of the Faith, 254, 394; *STC* 5155

Harrison, Robert, 3, 69

Harrowden, Northamptonshire, 95

Harte, John, mayor of London, 73

Hartwell, Abraham, 33

Harvey, Gabriel, 24, 68–69, 82, 313

Harvey, Richard, 313

Harvye, Master, a usurer, 141, 204, 263, 294

Haseley, 101–02, 115, 128, 129, 216, 228, 237, 239, 267, 390; books delivered to, 137; books packed up at, 137, 232, 254, 267; Cartwright visits, 282; Hodgskin at, 46, 47, 51, 301; Newman at, 51, 137; Penry at, 85, 303; Clement Throkmorton purchases property of, 96, 390; Waldegrave at, 26, 89, 110, 111, 137, 151, 160, 254

Haslop, a pursuivant, 257

Hastings, Henry, 3d earl of Huntingdon, 8

Hatton, Christopher, 31, 41, 75, 313, 357; Bancroft chaplain to, 18, 59; estimate of Throkmorton, 239, 309; privy councilor, 5, 39; rebukes Throkmorton, 106; Sharpe and, 41, 42, 136; speech to Parliament, 58, 59; Throkmorton's petition to, 112–13, 115, 119, 239, 242, 268, 302, 336; Whitgift and, 31, 35, 53

Hauckes, Thomas, 96

Haultin, Jerome, 384

Haultin, Les, 88, 159

Hay, Alexander, lord clerk register, Scotland, 90

Hay Any Worke, 13–15, 55, 134, 153, 160, 171, 180, 203, 225, 227, 228, 247, 279; author of, 26, 127, 174, 221, 236, 242, 266, 300, 302, 312; binding of, 304; parallels in *A Dialogue*, 164; Penry's aid to, 51; personal allusions, 236, 268, 324; printing of, 21, 22, 24, 37, 42, 77, 88, 109, 137, 151, 159; title, 249

Hemingius, or Hemmingsen, Niels, Danish professor, 275, 398

Heneage, Thomas, 75, 77, 358

Henry III, king of France, 6, 105

Henry VIII, of England, 2, 12, 96, 196, 284

Henry of Lorraine, duke of Guise, 96

Henry Barrow Separatist (Powicke), 152

Herbert, William, 376–77

Heresy, 21, 34, 169

Hermannus of Wied, archbishop of Cologne, 317, 318

Heylyn, Peter, 28

Hickes, Michael, 24, 352

High Commission, 25, 36, 136, 233, 307, 312, 327, 355; Cawdrey's appearance before, 119; criticism of, 16, 19, 35, 238, 311; defense of, 235; functions of, 5, 9, 31–33, 53–54, 61, 82, 87, 113; members of: Aubrey, 355; Aylmer, 273, 283, 311; Bancroft, 59, 355; Cooper, 273, 311, 355; Cosin, 273, 355; Goodman, 355; Lewin, 273; Whitgift, 273, 311, 355; Wickham, 273; Middleton and, 13, 165, 195; Penry and, 7, 9, 58, 211, 214, 273–74; warrants of, 257

Hildersam, Arthur, cleric, 296

Hill, Christopher, xiv, 407

Hillingdon, Middlesex, near Uxbridge, 6, 107, 127, 309, 373

Hinton, Dr. William, archdeacon of Coventry, 130

Hirst, Derek, 373

History of the Martin Marprelate Controversy (Maskell), 155–56

Hoby, Sir Edward, brother of Sir Thomas, 129

Hoby, Margaret, wife of Sir Thomas, 129

Hoby, Sir Thomas Posthumous, 129

Hodgskin or Hodgkins, John, 41, 43, 47, 79, 112; employment of, 173, 229; replaces Waldegrave, 15, 21, 38; his printing press, 22, 38, 126; printed *Martin Junior*, 15, 40, 47, 48, 229, 250, 301–02; printed *Martin Senior*,

428

40, 48; at Wolston, 22, 38, 110; at Warrington, 22, 38; at Manchester, 22, 38; *More Worke* secretly delivered to, 48, 110, 173, 266; printing of, 172; seizure of, 232; possible second part of, 110, 171; capture of, 38, 232; racked in the Tower, 39; examinations of, 39, 45–46, 357; shields Throkmorton, 46, 299, 304; confession of, 50; Newman's testimony on, 51; Sharpe's testimony on, 40; Symmes's testimony on, 41, 47; arraignment and trial, 80–81, 227, 229, 265; received the queen's favor, 367; McGinn's reliance on, 303–04

Hodgson, Hugh, provost of Queen's, 100

Holmes, Derek, 407

Holmes, Richard, 22, 50, 109, 138, 241

Holyoke, Francis, 130

Hone, Dr. John, 10, 32, 215, 217, 248, 263, 295

Hooker, Richard, 120, 124, 313, 334, 376, 377

Hooper, John, bishop of Gloucester and Worcester, 2, 16, 118, 233, 327

Hopkins, Samuel, American Congregationalist, 296

Horace, Quintus Horatius Flaccus, *De Arte Poetica*, 196

Horne, Robert, bishop of Winchester, 399

Horsey, Sir Edward, 167, 385

Horton, Thomas, 32

Hounslow, 70, 225

House of Commons, 14, 57, 105, 106, 108, 115, 237, 309, 310, 342, 391, 392

Howard, Charles, lord high admiral, earl of Nottingham, 39

Howell, David, 36, 48

Howland, Richard, bishop of Peterborough, 20, 293

Hughes, William, bishop of St. Asaph, is a possible alternative to William Wickham or William Chaderton, 20, 291, 292

Human body, allusions to, 244, 249

Humble Motion (anonymous), 52, 89, 159

Humor, 18, 215, 237, 240, 261, 275, 291, 303, 312; in the *Epistle*, 10; in the *Epitome*, 235; comic imagination in *Master Some*, 132; humorous writing on Dr. Bridges, 252, 253, 280, 286; humorous writing on Dr. Some, 142, 286–90; mirth and humor in Martin's and Throkmorton's books, 106, 210–13, 244, 245, 247; humorous and playful expressions, 212; doggerel, 18, 61, 62, 226, 247, 323; name-calling, 248, 274, 330; punning, 246, 323; unexpected humorous endings, 226, 245; humor and syllogisms, 259–61; humorous anecdotes, 264–65; Lyly's humor, 67; lack of humor in Penry's writings, 178, 263, 285

Humphrey, Laurence, president of Magdalen College, Oxford, 97, 98, 267

Hunsdon, Lord. *See* Carey, Henry

Hunt, John, author of *Religious Thought*, 296

Hunting of Antichrist (Leonard Wright), 61

Huntingdon, earl of. *See* Hastings, Henry

Hutchinson, Anne, 23

Hypocrisy, 12, 126, 309

I.G. *See* G., I.

Inns of Court, 101, 372

Interim, interimist, and interimistical, 317–19

Introductory Sketch (Arber), reprints portions of Penry, *A Treatise Containing the Aequity*, 56–67; *Appellation*, 68–74; Bacon, *Advertisement*, 146–68; Udall, *New Discovery*, 169–72; Dexter, "Argument," 187–92

Invective, against bishops, 19, 54–56, 60, 215, 248, 278, 330; against clergy of Church of England, 174–75, 248; against the hierarchy, 9, 86, 215, 224, 248, 275; against Martinists, 69–70; against Dr. Bridges, 8–9, 11, 211, 248; against Sutcliffe, 123–24, 128; Sutcliffe, against Throkmorton, 126–27, 173–74, 175; Throkmorton, against Dr. Some, 134, 172, 173, 251–52; Dr. Some, against Penry,

133; invective in the *Epistle*, 214; invective, in *Martin Junior*, 230
Ipswich, Suffolk, 255
Irony, 161, 169, 213, 235, 245, 251–53, 273–74, 288, 289–90, 323, 326–27, 334, 335
Islington, 88

Jackson, Lawrence, servant of Knightley, 44, 45, 76, 143
Jackson, William A., bibliographer, 83
James VI and I, 6, 85, 86, 89, 90, 91, 105, 175, 239
Jan of Leyden, 55
Jeffs, R., of Upton, Northamptonshire, 42, 43, 44
Jerome, 121
Jesuits, 12, 27–28, 75, 76, 102, 103, 141
Jesus College, Cambridge, 217, 294
Jewell, John, bishop of Salisbury, 71
John Lord Saint John, baron of Bletsoe, 63
Johnson, Francis, Separatist, 88
Jones, Jeffry, Jerrerie, or Gefferie, "Sir," of Corley, Warwickshire, 73, 193, 214, 217, 263
Jones, Jenkin, xix, 52
Jonson, Benjamin, 83
Judgement (de Bèze), 6
Judgement of Dr. Reignolds (John Rainolds or Reynolds), 361. *See* Ussher, in Wing, *STC*, U 186
Junius, letters of, xi
Junius (Du Jon), Franciscus, 255
Just Censure. See Martin Senior

Kennall, John, archdeacon of Oxford, vice-chancellor of the University, 99, 139, 162, 165, 166, 200, 217, 261, 267, 294, 402
Kildale, Henry, 21, 37, 45, 52, 57, 61, 368, 405
Kilkhampton, Cornwall, 23
King, Sir James, of Hertfordshire, 294
King, Joy Lee Belknap, 158
King, P. I., xv
King's Bench or Queen's Bench. *See* Courts

Kingston-upon-Thames, 8, 23, 32, 42, 48, 215, 248, 263, 338
Kirk, Rudolf, 407
Kitchin, Anthony, bishop of Llandaff, 3
Knappen, Dr. Marshall M., Rhodes scholar, xv, 297
Knewstub, John, Puritan writer against the Family of Love, 255
Knightley, Sir Richard, 50, 238; estate at Fawsley, 22, 40, 43, 143; Waldegrave arrives at, 45; *Epitome* printed at Fawsley, 76; Newman at Fawsley, 45; brother-in-law to the earl of Hertford, 37; writes a letter to John Hales on Waldegrave's behalf, 45, 76; Sharpe's testimony on, 42; Knightley's conjectures on authorship of *Epitome*, 299; examination of, 44, 75–77; testimony of his employees, 44–45, 57
Knightley, Lady, Mrs. Richard. *See* Fermor, Mary, and Seymour, Elizabeth, 43, 366
Knightley, Valentine, son of Sir Richard, 42, 76
Knipperdollinck, Bernt, German Anabaptist from Münster, 55
Knollys, Sir Francis, 27, 116
Knox, John, 347, 400
Kydwell, Nicolas, 32
Kyldale. *See* Kildale

L., A., 62–63
La Rochelle, France, 88, 89, 109, 111, 134, 135, 137, 138, 151, 153, 154, 156, 159, 160
Lambert, John, 16
Lambeth Palace, 36, 119, 179, 259, 285, 286, 287, 298
Lambethetical, 201; Lambethisme, 192, 199; Lambethiste, 20, 201
Lancashire, 39
Langland, William, 159
Latimer, Hugh, bishop of Worcester, 2, 118
Lawson, Dame Margaret, 65, 72, 257, 277
Lawson, Thomas, husband of Dame Lawson, 277

Le Fèvre, Raoul, 83
Learned ministry, 106–07, 238, 310, 332
Lee, Edward Dunn, M.P. for Carmarthen, xvii, 57
Lee, Sir Sidney, 129, 151, 152, 284, 351, 353
Les Haultin. *See* Haultin
"Letter to Edmund Coppinger" (Throkmorton), 242
Levy, Leonard W., xv, 356
Lewin, Dr. William, xix, 44, 273
Leyden, The Netherlands, 55, 357
Lichfield, Staffordshire, 21
Lily, William, 82
Lincoln, bishop of. *See* Wickham, William
Lincoln Cathedral, 259, 277
Lincoln College, Oxford, 18, 99, 294
Lincoln's Inn, 17
Llandaff, bishop of. *See* Blethin, William
Lockwood of Sarum, Old, name given to Dean Bridges, 201, 202, 203, 235, 248, 394
London, 58, 76, 101, 110, 135, 217, 225, 237, 245, 295, 332; Jenkin Jones transports Penry's books to, 52; Marprelate books delivered to, 43; manuscript of the *Mineralls* sent from London to Penry, 227, 297; Newman visits, 173; Penry's chest seized in area of, 111, 175; printing supplies obtained in, 109; Mrs. Sharpe visits, 42; tumult in Cheapside, 87; Throkmorton's ancestor a mayor of, 95; Throkmorton in, 113, 143
London, bishop of. *See* Aylmer, John
Long Meg of Westminster, 16
Longley, Katherine M., 24
Loque, Bertrand de (François de Saillans), 164, 165, 255
Lord Bishops, 20, 60, 327, 330, 334; Cooper's defense of, 276; Penry's criticism of, 291; regarded as unscriptural by Martin, 9, 16, 194; accused of being tyrannical, 336, and in title of *A Dialogue. Wherin Is Plainly Laide Open the Tyrannicall Dealing of Lord Bishopps against*

Gods Children; ridicule of, 13, 19, 20, 192, 200, 226, 245, 249, 283, 350
Lyly, John, 24, 56, 67, 74, 75, 152, 261, 313
Lyon, John, 8th Lord Glammis, 345

McGinn, Donald J., 151, 155, 157, 333; criticism of Waddington, Pierce, Arber, Sutcliffe, Williams, Wilson, 305–07; depositions of Martinist suspects, 299, 404; errors in dating, 135–38, 156, 382; estimate of Penry's character, 297–98; external and internal evidence, 299; failure to utilize available source materials, 298–99; misattribution of *Master Some*, 143, 156, 383; "most important evidence for Penry's authorship," 300; "most convincing evidence for Penry's authorship," 300–03; similarities in *Master Some, A Dialogue*, and Martin's books, 150; reviews of his *John Penry*, 178, 298–99; 404, 406–07; sources improperly evaluated, 303–05; tendentious statements, 404
Machiavelli, Niccolò, 62, 66, 70
McKerrow, Ronald B., 27, 135, 157, 237, 296
Madox, John, 191, 214, 219, 264, 265, 283
Magdalen College, Oxford, 97, 98, 99, 162, 277, 295, 371
Magdalen College School, Oxford, 98, 99, 276, 314
M[agistri] Sutliuii de catholica, orthodoxa, et vera Christi ecclesia libri duo (Sutcliffe), 116
Maicocke, Augustine, 22, 52, 241
Maitland, Sir John, chancellor of Scotland, 89
Manchester Papers, 374–75. Given to the Public Record Office in 1880 by William Drogo (Montagu), duke of Manchester (1823–90). Numbers 123 and 124 now at Lambeth Palace Library
"Manuscript Reply to Dr. Some" (Penry), 133

Mar-Martin (person), 16, 20, 68, 222, 223, 225, 226, 247, 250, 393

Mar-Martin (book), 62, 393

Mar-Martine (person), 72

Mar-Martine (book), 61, 393

Marbury, Francis (Merbury), Puritan cleric, father of Anne Hutchinson, 23, 24, 36

Marian exiles, 2, 97, 98, 99

Marks or notes of a true church, 133

Marlowe, Christopher, 83

Marphoreus, Mar-foreus, or Marphoreus, 65, 68

Marre Mar-Martin, 62, 393

Marsden, J. B., 27

Marston, John, 82

Marten, Anthony, royal librarian, 71

Martin, Gregory, 99

Martin Junior (Theses Martinianae), 40, 45, 64, 67, 159, 171, 176, 221, 225, 241, 242, 274, 283, 304; printing of, 15, 21, 46, 47, 80, 81, 109, 301, 302, 303; "Martin Juniors Epilogue," 15, 16; theses, 16, 20–21, 26; authorship of, 26, 80, 127, 144, 151, 172, 173, 226, 227, 229, 230, 250, 265; satire in, 16–17, 286; stylistic features in, 230–31

Martin Junior, author, 16, 17, 18, 64, 67, 191, 222, 225, 226, 247, 257

Martin Marprelate the Great, 16, 19, 250

Martin Senior, 17–18, 21, 45, 46, 67, 211, 229, 250, 268, 286, 304, 312; manuscript copy delivered to Hodgskin, 47; printing of, 21, 40, 41, 109, 302; type used in, 159; authorship of, 80, 127, 152, 172, 173, 221, 226–27, 265, 304–05; Bishops' English, 18, 320; doggerel, 247, 323; Sharpe designated in, 40; Dr. Some ridiculed in, 286; stylistic features in, 221–26

Martin Senior, author, 17, 18, 222, 224, 225, 226, 245, 250

Martin the Great, 17

Martinism, 19, 191, 201; Martinist, 20, 201, 311, 312

"Martins Interim," 111–12, 127, 152, 174–75, 180, 242, 266, 302, 374

Martins Months Mind (by Mar-phoreus), 65, 68, 118

Martyr, Peter, 71

Martyrs, 2, 16, 97, 327, 348

Mary, queen of Scots, 96, 103, 104–05, 293

Mary Tudor, 2, 16, 96, 284

Maskell, William, Anglican writer on Puritan authors, 23, 151, 155–56

Mason, Sir John, 99, 100

"Mr. John Penrye[s] Proceeding upon Couler of a Pretended Reformation." *See* Ellesmere MS. 2148

Master Some Laid Open, 112, 132–35, 164, 172, 179, 211, 216, 236, 255, 302, 303, 312; views on authorship: Waldegrave, 138, 265; Sutcliffe, 127; Wilson, 27; I.G., 140–41, 243; Throkmorton's authorship of, 138–57, 233, 266; conjectures on Penry's authorship, 41, 143, 383; manuscript delivered to Waldegrave about 1 April, 146–50; printing of, 88, 159, 254; printed book delivered by Waldegrave to Throkmorton, 51, 110; date of, 134–38; denunciation of Dr. Some, 287–90; humor in, 142, 227, 252–53, 280; parallels in, 146–50, 176–77; references to Penry, 268

Matthew, Tobias, president of St. John's College, Oxford, 99

May, John, bishop of Carlisle, 389

Meddows or Meddowes, James, 22, 109, 176, 267

Melville, Andrew, rector of the University of St. Andrews, 90

Melville, Sir Robert, deputy chancellor of Scotland, 90

Merbury. *See* Marbury

Merchant Adventurers Company, 96

Merton College, Oxford, 98

Meyrick, John, bishop of Sodor and Man, 389

Middelburg, Zeeland, where a nonconformist church was served by Cartwright and Dudley Fenner, 6, 23, 112, 123, 176, 254

Middle Temple, 101, 129

Middleton, Marmaduke, bishop of St. David's, 13, 20, 160, 162, 165, 228, 292, 385

Midlands, 25, 216

Mildmay, Sir Walter, 129

Mineralls. See *Certaine Minerall, and Metaphisicall Schoolpoints*

Montaigne, Michel de, 83

More, John, 33, 255

More Worke for Cooper, 18, 55, 162, 223, 236, 240, 242, 277, 301; authorship of, 26, 41, 80, 152, 172–74, 220, 227, 229, 265–66; promised in *Hay Any Worke*, 174, 223, 236, 266, 277; manuscript secretly dropped, 48, 176, 241; manuscript seized at Manchester, 115, 172, 232; printing of, 21, 22, 38, 39, 45, 46, 109; summarized in the *Protestatyon*, 19–21, 110, 221, 232, 266, 286; supposed second part, 171

Morice, James, 27, 116, 238

Moses, 14

Münster, 55

Mullins, John, archdeacon of London, 102, 329

Munday, Anthony, 33, 225, 257, 313

Myrror for Martinists (by T.T., Thomas Tymme?), 69

Name-calling. *See* Invective

Nashe, Thomas, 27, 70, 82, 83, 95, 135, 152, 261, 283, 313

Nashes Lenten Stuffe, 82

National Library of Wales, 306

Naturall and Morall Historie (Joseph de Acosta), 83

Neale, Sir John, xiv, 104, 106, 151, 154, 296

Nestorius, 69

Neville, Sir Edward, 1st baron of Bergavenny, great-great-grandfather of Job, 97

Neville, Sir Edward, Job's grandfather, executed in 1538, 97

Neville, Sir George, 2d baron of Bergavenny, great-grandfather of Job, 97

Neville, Katherine (Throkmorton), Job's mother, 97, 140, 251, 370

Neville, Sir Ralph, 1st earl of Westmorland, great-great-grandfather of Katherine Neville (Throkmorton) and great-great-great-grandfather of Job, 97

New College, Oxford, 98, 99, 294

New Discovery (Udall), 346

New Inn, London, 101

Newbery, Ralph, 62

Newcastle-upon-Tyne, 8, 48

Newgate Sessions, 88

Newman, Humphrey or Humfrey, 17, 41, 43, 44, 50, 179, 225, 241, 267, 303; distributor of Marprelate books, 22, 40, 42, 45, 159, 311, 406; aids employment of Hodgskin, 38, 109, 173; assisted in delivering manuscript of *More Worke*, 48; unwilling to deliver manuscript of "Martins Interim" to printers, 111; arrest, 50–52, 78; sentenced to death, 78; pardoned, 79–80; promised profits of *Crops and Flowers of Bridges Garden*, 51, 112, 141–42, 175–77, 265; deposition of, 137, 138, 153, 156, 161, 229, 240, 304, 305

Newton Lane, Manchester, 22, 38

Nonconformists, 2, 5, 9, 25, 28, 64, 97, 98, 99, 112, 140, 155, 176, 238, 295, 297, 312

Nonresidency, 9, 71, 162, 230, 273, 309, 326, 334

Norris, Sir John, 26

Northampton, Grimston of, 22, 50, 109, 159; Richard Holmes, 50, 109; Thomas Crasswell, mayor of, 135–36; Penry's study raided at, 51, 58, 286; Sharpe of, 17, 40, 41, 42, 57, 136, 159; Mrs. Sharpe of, 42; rumors at, 57, 58

Northamptonshire, 22, 23, 24, 25, 36, 41, 43, 67, 143

Norton, near Daventry, Northamptonshire, 45

Norton, Thomas, 116

Norway, 90

Norwich, 34, 255

Notebook, by Penry, 154, 218, 265, 268, 274, 284, 298, 300

Nowell, Alexander, dean of St. Paul's, 78–79, 81, 85, 328, 332

Oaths, 3, 65, 78, 124–25, 127, 138, 151
Oatlands, Surrey, 39
Of the Diverse Degrees (Saravia), 116
Of the Lawes of Ecclesiasticall Politie (Hooker), 120, 338
Origen, 69
Orléans, 160
Orwin, Thomas, printer, 216, 254
Overstone, Northamptonshire, 24
Overton, William, bishop of Coventry and Lichfield, 20, 292
Oxford, 62, 76, 138, 139, 264
Oxford, archdeacon of (Kennall), 99, 294
Oxford, University of, 97–101, 139, 153, 162, 371; curriculum, 100; enrollment in 1564, 100; Oxford associations as clues to authorship, 216–17, 228, 266–67; Puritans at, 97–98; Throkmorton at, 237, 276, 278, 294, 314, 388

Paddington, London, 170
Pagit, Eusebius (Paget), 23, 24, 66, 70, 98, 225, 255, 309
Pappe with an Hatchet (Lyly), 24, 67, 68, 75
Parallel expressions, 28, 235, 390; "An Answer," 316–17; *Exhortation,* 321–22; *Second Admonition,* 327–28; "A Friendly Caveat," 330–31; *State of the Church,* 335–37; *Protestatyon,* 234–35; *A Dialogue,* 162–71, 220; unusual parallels, 203–06, 266; parallels with three or more words, 206–07; verbatim parallels, 207, 266; close parallels, 207–09, 266; *Master Some,* 146–50; *A Petition Directed,* 119; *Epistle,* 212–13; *Mineralls,* 228–29; *Martin Junior,* 230, 300; *Martin Senior,* 222–23
Parker, Matthew, archbishop, 3, 4
Parliaments, 14, 57, 60, 65, 105, 108, 117, 118, 140, 144, 170, 194, 310; Parliament of 1541/42 (Henry VIII): 96, 103; Parliament of 1545: 96, 103; Parliament of 1547: 96, 103; Parliament of 1553 (Edward VI): 96, 103; Parliament of 1553 (Mary): 96, 103; Parliament of 1559 (Elizabeth): 3, 96, 103; Parliament of 1562/63: 96, 103; Par-

liament of 1571: 96, 103; Parliament of 1572: 96, 103, 105, 314; Parliament of 1584–86: 5, 103, 104; Parliament of 1586/87: 5, 6, 24, 57, 103–08, 127, 129, 154, 211, 237, 238, 239, 240, 309, 312, 321, 322; Parliament of 1589: 59, 134, 309; 1623/24 (James I): 130; 1625 (Charles I): 130; 1625/26: 130
Parr, Queen Katherine, sixth wife of Henry VIII, 95, 96, 115
A Parte of a Register (Puritan documents), 122–23, 254, 330, 331, 338
Pasquill, 21, 64, 66, 71
Patrick, Richard, 189
Paul the Apostle, 12, 206, 245, 273, 318, 393
Paul, the spokesman for Throkmorton in *The State of the Church of Englande,* 332
Paule, Sir George, historian, 28
Paul's Churchyard, 7, 37, 332
Paul's Cross Sermons, 10, 59, 60, 101, 246, 314, 331, 333
Pearson, A. F. Scott, best biographer of Cartwright, 141, 158
Peel, Albert, author, editor, xi, xv, 28, 151, 154, 297, 333
Peirce, James, nonconformist cleric, 271, 296
Pembroke College, Cambridge, 5, 68, 69, 79, 141, 255, 259
Pencaitland, Scotland, 141
Penry, John, xi, 6, 19, 36, 37, 48, 49, 56, 67, 87, 88, 134, 152, 252, 256, 368–69; Penry's style, 178, 193, 196, 198, 210–20, 224, 228, 230, 233, 243, 244, 251, 253, 263; Penry as a Marprelate suspect, 25, 28, 34–35, 41, 43, 46, 49, 50, 58, 71, 151, 152, 154–55, 226, 227; Penry's books: *Aequity,* 57, 76; *Exhortation,* 57, 132, 178, 259; *Defence,* 57, 103; manuscript reply to Dr. Some, 58, 133; *A Viewe,* 77, 159; *Appellation,* 51, 111, 134, 135, 136, 137, 138; *Reformation No Enemie,* 52, 70, 71, 86, 268, 312, 367–68; *Briefe Discovery,* 52, 86, 268; *Propositions and Principles,* 87; Penry as business manager and co-ordinator, 8, 21, 79, 109, 232, 241, 311; before High Commission, 9; his printing press, 22,

38; raid on his study, 51, 58, 133–34; second raid, 51, 137; leaves Haseley for Scotland, 85; banishment from Scotland, 86, 87; secret return to, 87; in London and Scotland, 1591–92, 87–88; in London, 1592–93, 88; joins Separatists, 88; captured, 88; chest of papers seized, 111, 175; arraigned and hanged, 88, 268, 312; associations with: Field, 23; Hales, 45; Hodgskin, 46; Jackson, 44–45; Knightley, 44, 57; Newman, 51, 137, 176; Sharpe, 40, 43, 84; Dr. Some, 132–34, 138–40; Waldegrave, 37; Penry and Throkmorton, 17, 115–16, 124, 138, 141, 143–46, 172, 173, 232, 236, 267, 268, 271–97; McGinn and Penry, 155–57, 297–307; denunciation of Penry by Nashe, 70; by Pasquill, 71

Penry, Mrs. John (Helen or Eleanor), xviii, 87, 88, 111

Penry, Safety, third daughter, 88; other daughters are Deliverance, Comfort, and Sure Hope

Percevall, or Richard Harvey, 68

Perkins, William, leading Puritan theologian, 91

Perncanterburikenolde, humorous name of a syllogism, 200, 261, 285, 294

Perne, Andrew, 111, 170, 200, 215, 217, 219, 225, 234, 256, 261, 267, 274, 285, 290, 293; Penry and, 283–84; turncoat reputation of, 162, 165, 166, 192, 204, 214, 248, 284; Sir Sidney Lee's article in the *DNB* on Penry, 152; Sir Sidney's seven other relevant articles in the *DNB*, 152; death of, 20, 159, 192

Perpetual Governement of Christes Church (Bilson), 120

"A Perplexing Date" (McGinn), 135

Perrot, Sir John, lord deputy of Ireland, and one of the Star Chamber judges at the trial of Martinists, 75, 77, 358

Persecution, 15, 160, 162, 170, 192, 224, 230, 233, 285, 295, 319–20, 323, 325, 327, 334, 337, 395

Persons, Robert, 3

Peterborough Cathedral, 57, 293

Peterhouse, Cambridge, 35, 259, 283–84, 372

Petheram, John, editor, 180

Petition Directed to Her Most Excellent Majestie (Throkmorton), 117–20, 122, 242, 250, 254, 375, 377

Petitions, by Penry, 7, 22, 45, 57, 144; by Puritans, 17–18; by Throkmorton, 107–08, 117–20; by Udall, 85

Philip II, king of Spain, 2, 6, 105

Pierce, William, xi, xv, 135, 140, 150, 151, 153, 154, 158, 179–80, 296, 297, 305–07, 333

Pierces Supererogation (Gabriel Harvey), 68–69

Piers, John, bishop of Salisbury, 389

Piers Plowman, "Grandsier of Martin Marprelate," 376

Pigot, of Coventry, 43, 358

Pilgrim Press, 357

Pilkington, James, bishop of Durham, 122

Pius V (Impius Quintus), 197, 202

Plaine Percevall (Richard Harvey), 67, 363

Plato, 197, 198, 222

Plumb, J. H., 104, 373

Pluralism, 9, 13, 230, 294, 334

Pole, Reginald, cardinal, 2, 96, 99–100

Polity or church government, 13, 231, 233, 277, 295, 308; Anglican views on church government: Bacon's assertions, 65; Bridges' views on, 11; Cooper's ideas on, 14, 275–76; Elizabeth's convictions on, 59; Anthony Marten's defense of, 71–72; Popham's warnings on, 75–76; Anglican attacks on Presbyterian polity, 69, 116, 251; Martin advocates the Presbyterian polity, 11, 14; Throkmorton supports Puritan polity: in *An Admonition*, 314, 315; in the *Second Admonition*, 325, 327; in *Martin Junior*, 163; in *A Petition Directed*, 117, 251; Penry critical of Whitgift's views, 274; criticizes Dr. Bridges' views, 279; Udall opposes the polity of the Church of

435

England, 32; Throkmorton's platform of church government, 308, 309, 310, 311, 315

Popham, John, attorney general, 75, 76, 77, 78

Powell, Thomas, 82

Powicke, Frederick J., father of Sir Maurice, 134, 151, 152, 153, 296

Practize of Prelates, by Tyndale, 233, 234 (1530 edition has "Practyse")

Praemunire, 9, 195, 196, 215, 224, 293, 295, 327

Preaching, 13, 162, 163, 165, 169, 189

Precisian, 190

Predestination, 192

Preface to Thomas Cartwright, *A Brief Apologie* (by Throkmorton), 242

Prestonpans, Scotland, 255

Principis Scoti-Britannorum Natalia (Andrew Melville), 90

Presbyterian, 3, 4, 5, 8, 9, 16, 26, 54, 56, 57, 59, 65, 66, 85, 87, 116, 117, 120, 121, 308

Presbyterianism, 6, 14, 16, 56–57, 59–60, 65, 66, 69, 106, 120, 121, 314

Presbyters, 121

Prime or Pryme, Ales or Alice, 13, 165, 228

Prime, Dr. John, 13, 225

Printers, 34, 35, 38–40, 172, 215, 224, 253; Catholic printers, 10; Puritan printers, 10; Martinist printers, 10. *See also* Chard, Charlewood, Haultin, Hodgskin, Kildale, Orwin, Schilders, Symmes, Thackwell, Thomas, Thomlin, Waldegrave

Printing, 21, 22, 33, 36, 37, 42, 43, 44, 45, 47, 50, 52, 53, 57, 62, 76, 77, 78, 80–83, 88–91, 137, 153, 156, 159, 171, 220, 229, 253–55, 302–03, 309, 310, 311, 332

Prisons: Bridewell, 39, 88, 216, 257; Clink, 1, 162, 194, 216, 256, 257, 335; Compter or Counter, 88, 216, 257; Fleet, 25, 35, 78, 113, 231, 257, 282–83, 335; Gatehouse, 1, 7, 35, 49, 83, 162, 231, 256, 257, 335; King's Bench prison, 88; Marshalsea, Southwark, 80, 257; Newgate, 101, 102, 231, 238, 257, 320; Tower, 6, 39, 46, 80, 107, 231, 257, 309, 373; White Lion, Southwark, 84, 335; general references, 19, 32, 33, 77, 79, 215, 224, 233, 327, 332, 333, 334

Privy Council, 14, 17, 25, 31, 35, 40, 44, 73, 102, 107, 117, 125, 136, 264, 312; appoints examiners for printers, 110; Bancroft advises, 53; Carleton summoned to, 24; Cooper speaks to, 331; Penry's *Exhortation* addressed to, 57; Penry criticizes, 86; Clement Throkmorton employed by, 96; Udall petitions the, 85

Proclamacion, printed illegally in 1601 by Symmes, 82

Proclamations, 12, 31, 58, 60, 76, 77, 362, 366

Promotions, 9, 73, 160, 162, 170, 192, 216, 258–59, 280, 288, 290, 332, 337, 395–96

Propositions and Principles of Divinitie (translated by Penry), 87

Protestatyon, 18–21, 139, 228, 313, 391; printed at Wolston, 22, 50, 109–10; assistance from Waldegrave, 110; stylistic features in, 233–36; satire in, 233, 250; parody of Dr. Some, 286–87; authorship of: Sutcliffe's assertion of Throkmorton's authorship, 127, 151; Penry on Throkmorton's authorship, 232–33, 265; Lyly and, 67; Nashe quotes from, 70; Newman's deposition on, 137; Wright ridiculed in, 69; summarizes *More Worke*, 172, 221, 232, 266, 286. *See also* 26, 232–35, 266

Proverbs, 213, 224, 243, 261, 318, 320, 326, 329, 335, 388, 396

Providence, 192

Pryme. *See* Prime

Pseudonyms, of Throkmorton, 52, 141, 177, 179, 344; of Bowman and Maicocke, 52

Puckering Brief, 50, 359, 404, 405

Puckering, John, keeper of the Great Seal, knighted in 1592, 50, 75, 80, 84–85

Puritan Classis Movement, 87, 113, 116, 121, 238, 312, 325

Puritan Manifestoes (Frere and Douglas, eds.), 171, 206

Puritanism. *See also* Presbyterian and Presbyterianism, and Puritans, 24, 25, 69, 97, 107, 108, 218, 255, 293, 309, 310, 312

Puritans, allusions to, 192, 220, 231, 255, 281–82, 297; leading Puritans: *see* Cartwright, Chaderton, Mrs. Crane, Coppinger, Fenner, Field, Humphrey, Pagit, Penry, Sampson, Throkmorton, Travers, Udall, Waldegrave, Wigginton; Puritan documents in *A Parte of a Register*, 122; Puritan disapproval of Martin, 11, 21, 37, 308; attacks on the Puritans, 61, 66, 71, 108, 116, 309; Anglican Puritans, *see* Foxe, Fulke, Chaderton, Rainolds, Whitaker; Anglicans and Puritans, 17–18, 56–57, 59, 111, 116, 121, 156, 160, 165, 167, 224–25, 233–34; Puritan printers not favored by Anglicans, 10, 254; Paul, a Puritan interlocutor in *The State of the Church*, 332; Puritane, an interlocutor in *A Dialogue*, 159–60

Pursuivants, 25, 162, 170; Aylmer exhorts his, 225; Martin alludes to, 216, 224, 233, 257, 258, 260, 286, 323; Munday as a, 33; raid Penry's study, 22, 137, 286; raid on Waldegrave's house, 171; Throkmorton evades, 115; Whitgift's imaginary speech to, 17; Whitgift's pursuivant, 139

Queens' College, Cambridge, 35
Queen's College, Oxford, 99–101, 129, 371–72

Racking, 39, 46, 81, 233, 258, 260
Raillery, 54, 55, 219, 293–95; against bishops, 19, 54, 56, 60, 257, 258, 274, 278, 291–93, 296, 309, 325, 329, 330, 332, 334; against the State, 60, 268; against particular clerics: Aylmer, 19, 273, 283; Bridges, 211, 280; Cooper, 19, 273, 278, 279; Perne, 284, 285; Some, 20, 236; Sutcliffe, 124, 241, 258; Whitgift, 19, 273, 274–75, 282; against raillers, 55, 58, 60, 63, 64, 65, 66, 67, 70; against Throk-

morton, 55, 60, 66, 126, 127, 239, 240; against Penry, 70, 268

Rainolds, John (Reynolds), president of Corpus Christi College, Oxford, 99, 111, 255, 267

Rainolds, William, papist exile, brother of John, 99, 256, 267

Ralegh and the Throckmortons (A. L. Rowse), 96

Raleigh, Sir Walter (Ralegh), 85, 96, 115, 375

Ramist, 70

Reconciliation (Anthony Marten), 71

Redman, William, archdeacon of Canterbury, 294

Reformation No Enemie (Penry), short title of *A Treatise Wherein Is Manifestlie Proved*, 52, 71, 86, 89, 268, 312, 364

Regensburg, West Germany, 317

Relation of the State of Religion (Sir Edwin Sandys), 82

Remonstrance (Sutcliffe), 116

Replye to an Answere (Cartwright), 4, 282

Rest of the Second Replie (Cartwright), 20, 282

Returne of the Renowned Cavaliero Pasquill of England, 66

Rheims, or Douai-Rheims Version of the New Testament. *See* Rhemish

Rhemish New Testament (The New Testment of Jesus Christ) (1582), *STC* 2883, 37, 75–76, 76–77, 99, 356–57

Rich, Barnaby, 83

Richmond, Surrey, 32, 48, 160

Ridley, Nicholas, bishop of London, martyr, 2, 16, 96

Ringler, William A., Jr., xiv, 376

Roberts, John R., 407

Robinson, Henry, provost of Queen's, 101

Robinson, John, Separatist, 152

Rogers, [Christopher?], cleric, 67

Rogers, Richard, bishop suffragan of Dover, 20

Rogers, Walter, 32

Rokeby, Ralph, master of Requests, 39

Roman Catholic Church, 64
Rowse, A. L., 353–53, 354, 407
Rythmes against Martin Marre-Prelate,
STC 17465, 62

Sackville, Thomas, Lord Buckhurst,
5, 32, 49, 53, 358
Sacraments, 2, 16, 133, 140, 285, 289
Sacro-sanctum Novum Testamentum
(Bridges), 83
Sadel or Sadeel, Antoine (Antoine
La Roche Chandieu), 256
St. Andrew's Church, Norwich, 34
St. Andrews, University of, 90
St. Anne's, Blackfriars, Stephen Eg-
erton minister of, 70
St. Asaph, formerly Llanelwy, dio-
cese of, 291, 292. *See also* Hughes
St. Bartholomew's Church, Lon-
don, 142, 143
St. David's, Pembrokeshire, 161, 291.
See also Middleton
St. Giles's, Cripplegate, 79
St. John's College, Cambridge, 255
St. John's College, Oxford, 99
St. Mary Overy, Southwark, 385
St. Mary (Great St. Mary's), Cam-
bridge, 155
St. Nicholas Church, Newcastle-
upon-Tyne, 8
St. Paul's Cathedral, 79, 278
St. Paul's Churchyard. *See* Paul's
St. Paul's Cross. *See* Paul's Cross
St. Peter's Church, Cambridge, 284
St. Sepulcher, London, 18. *See also*
Gravat
St. Thomas a Watering, Southwark
(Penry hanged at), 88
Salisbury or Sarum, 217, 224, 226, 235,
260
Sampson, Thomas, dean of Christ
Church, Oxford, 97
Sanders, Nicholas, 279
Sands, Edwin. *See* Sandys
Sandys, Edwin, bishop of London,
102, 122, 242, 250, 267, 318, 325, 328–
31, 372; archbishop of York, 389
Saravia, Hadrian, 71, 121
Sarum, dean of. *See* Bridges
Satire, 19, 25, 56, 59, 64, 65, 66, 138,
158, 251, 267, 271, 296, 299, 312; in the

Epistle, 215, 219; in the *Epitome,* 235;
in *Martin Junior,* 247, 274–75; in
Master Some, 134, 142–43, 211, 251–52;
against Bridges, 10, 11–12, 20, 252–
53, 280; against Cooper, 9, 15, 245,
274; against Lyly, 68; against Martin, 67, 70, 72–73; against Perne,
20, 284, 285; against Some, 20, 286–
90; against Whitgift, 311; against
Throkmorton, 112, 126; Throkmor-
ton indicted for satirical libels, 112;
praised by Wilson for, 157
Savonarola, Girolamo, 66, 71
Savoy Palace, 160
Saxony, 276
Scambler, Edmund, bishop of Norwich, 291, 389
Schilders, Richard, Dutch printer,
112, 117, 123, 176, 254, 376, 377
Schoeck, R. J., ed., *Editing Sixteenth*
Century Texts, 204
Scolar Press, 179
Scot, Alan, provost of Queen's, Ox-
ford, 100
Scotland, 88, 106, 111, 121, 122, 136, 141,
156, 175, 177, 248, 268, 309, 315, 332.
See also Edinburgh
Scourge of Villanie; Three Books of Sa-
tyres, 82
Seaver, Dr. Paul S., Tudor-Stuart
historian, 298, 407'
Second Admonition (Throkmorton), 4,
59, 101, 102, 242, 316, 317, 322, 324–
28, 336, 337, 344
Seconde Parte of a Register, Puritan
corpus of manuscripts calendared
by Albert Peel, 356
Seconde Replie (Cartwright), 10, 282,
334
Sedbergh, Yorkshire, 9, 23, 32, 214,
263. *See also* Wigginton
Seekers of Reformation, 117, 119, 251
Selby, William, mayor of Newcas-
tle-upon-Tyne, 48
Separatism, 25, 88
Separatists, 3, 26, 35, 69, 152, 308
Sermon of Obedience (Hinton), 130
Sermon Preached at Paules Crosse the
9 of Februarie (Bancroft), 60, 61
Sermons, 9, 130, 158, 224, 263–64, 267,
310, 396–97; by Bancroft, 59–60, 61;

438

by Bullingham, 292; by Cooper, 101, 166, 267, 277–78; by Goodman, 293; by Dr. Some, 142–43, 267; Puritan sermons, 64, 282, 332

Settle, Thomas, 170, 255

Seymour, Edward, duke of Somerset, protector (1506?–52), 43, 284

Seymour, Edward, earl of Hertford, son of the duke of Somerset (1539?–1621), 37

Seymour, Elizabeth, second wife of Sir Richard Knightley, and daughter of the duke of Somerset, 43

Shakespeare, William, dramatist, sonnet dedicated to by John Weever, 83

Shakespeare, William, a tenant in one of Job Throkmorton's cottages, 83, 128

Sharpe, Edward, vicar at Fawsley, Northamptonshire, 40, 45, 57

Sharpe, Henry, Marprelate bookbinder: attempts to arrest him, 61, 136; arrest of, 40; bookbinding, 21, 159; his chronology defective, 51, 390; conjectures that Penry was Martin, 43; considers making a confession, 37, 41; seeks a pardon, 42; refuses to set type, 37; purchases and sells copies of the Epitome, 57, 61; testimony of, 23, 40–43, 220, 227, 240, 299; consequences of his examination, 44, 83, 84; McGinn's praise of, 302–04

Sharpe, Mrs. Henry, 42, 137

Shaw, Lancelot, provost of Queen's, Oxford, 100

Shoreditch, county of London, 72

Shorte Introduction of Grammar (William Lily and John Colet), 81–82. See also Grammar and Accidence

Sidney, Sir Philip, 68, 91

Simmes. See Symmes

Simony, 9, 162, 216, 280, 309, 332

"Sir Maries Church in Cambridge" (Great St. Mary's), 12

Skynner, William, recusant, 102–03

Smith, Edward O., 407

Snape, Edmund, of Northampton, 87, 116

Some, Robert, master of Peterhouse, 185, 264; his first A Godly Treatise Containing, 35, 57, 156, 285; Penry's replies to, 57, 220, 285–86; his second A Godly Treatise . . . Whereunto, 57, 286; Penry wrongly suspected of writing against Some in More Worke, 41; Penry's courtesy to, 139–40, 144, 146, 190, 233; Throkmorton's ridicule of, 13, 20, 139, 142, 145, 162, 169, 227, 233, 246, 251, 252, 258–59, 260, 267, 286–90

Somerset, duke of. See Seymour

Southgate, W. M., 407

Southwark, Surrey, 80, 84

Southwell, Robert, 83

Spanish Armada, 55, 71, 215

Speaker of the House of Commons, 1586–87, John Puckering, 106

Speech, "Againste the Scottishe Queene" (Throkmorton), 104, 145

Speech, "The Bill and Book" (Throkmorton), 106–07, 373, 393

Speech, "On the Low Countries" (Throkmorton), 105, 144, 180, 203, 393

Stafford Law (a rare phrase, and a significant parallel), 105, 203–04

Stage players and plays, 72, 73, 74, 75, 192

Stanghton. See Staughton

Stanhope, Edward, diocesan chancellor, 9, 197, 217, 295

Stanley, Ferdinando, Lord Strange, became 5th earl of Derby in 1593, 73, 365

Stanley, Henry, 4th earl of Derby, 38, 39, 109, 115, 172, 174

Stapleton, Thomas, Catholic author, 256

Star Chamber, 5, 8, 53, 75, 77, 87, 113, 121, 195, 238, 295, 310, 312, 374

Starnes, DeWitt T., 398–99

State of the Church of Englande, also referred to as A Dialogue and as Diotrephes (by Throkmorton, not Udall), 7, 8, 36, 48, 49, 108, 112, 122, 127, 242, 254, 309, 323, 324, 332–38, 374

Stationers' Company, 7, 81, 82, 214, 254, 310, 332, 374

Statutes, 2, 3, 9, 16, 78, 80–81, 88, 118, 194, 195, 196, 222, 312, 346, 373, 375–76; Act of Supremacy in 1534, 2; Act of Supremacy in 1559, 3, 386; Act of Uniformity in 1559, 386; Act to Refourme Certayne Dysorders, 9; Act of Praemunire, 9, 196, 222, 256, 346; Statute of 13 Elizabeth, c. 12, 9, 16, 195, 346, 349; Statute of 23 Elizabeth, c. 2, 78, 80–81, 88, 230, 390; Acte to Retayne the Quenes Majesties Subjects in 1593, 312; of the University of Oxford, 100; of the University of Cambridge, 283

Staughton or Stanghton, William, 32

Stephanus, Robert (Éstienne, Robert the Elder), 167–68, 216, 276, 277, 398

Stepney, 175

Story of the Pilgrim Fathers (Arber), 152

Strange, Lord. See Stanley, Ferdinando

Strange Newes (Nashe), 363

Strassburg, 12, 97

Stratford-on-Avon, 282

Stroup, Thomas, 407

Strowd, John, printer, 243, 322, 324, 344, 393

Strype, John, xv, 28, 53, 372

Stubbes, Philip, 70

Stubbs, John, 115

Stylistic features, 178, 181–98, 198–202, 210, 261, 266, 271, 309, 319, 388; in the Epistle, 211–16, 219–20; in Hay Any Worke, 236; in Martin Junior, 230–31; in Martin Senior, 221–26; in "An Answer," 315–16; in An Exhortation to the Byshops, 320–21; in Certaine Articles, 323; in the Second Admonition, 325–27; in "A Friendly Caveat," 329–30; in The State of the Church of Englande, 333–35; in More Worke, 172–73; in A Dialogue. Wherin, 161–62; in "Martins Interim," 174–75. See also Diction

"Summary of the Information," a report to Lord Burghley, 40, 41, 171, 174

Summons for Sleepers (Wright), 61

Sun Theoi en Christoi [With God in Christ]. The Answere to the Preface of the Rhemish Testament (Cartwright), STC 4716, 37

Supplication to the Parliament. See A Viewe (Penry)

Surrey, county of, 10; parish of, 32, 217, 247, 263, 294, 295

Survay (Bancroft), 121, 190

Sutcliffe, Matthew, 123, 138, 153–54, 172, 179, 193, 220, 241, 405; his competency, 302, 304, 307; only source for Waldegrave's deposition, 89, 138, 151; studied More Worke, 6, 110; on the Crops and Flowers, 112; paraphrase of Throkmorton's letter to Penry, 115–16; accuses Throkmorton of writing anonymous and pseudonymous letters, 141; refutes A Petition Directed, 120; accuses Throkmorton of writing Martinist libels, 123, 265, 299: Epistle, 127; Epitome, 127; Mineralls, 120, 151; Hay Any Worke, 127, 152; Martin Junior, 120, 127, 151, 160, 226–27; Martin Senior, 127, 152, 226–27; Protestatyon, 120, 127, 151, 160, 265; More Worke, 127, 152, 232, 266; A Dialogue. Wherin, 120, 127, 151, 160; Master Some, 120, 127, 138, 151, 160; "Martins Interim," 127, 152, 174–75, 266; Crops and Flowers, 127, 128, 152, 176–77, 266; State of the Church, 120, 127, 160; excoriates Throkmorton, 126–27, 239–40; Sutcliffe's An Answere (1592), 138; his An Answere (1595), 125, 127, 138, 305; Cartwright answers Sutcliffe in A Brief Apologie, 128; Sutcliffe replies to Cartwright and Throkmorton's preface, 400; Throkmorton refutes Sutcliffe, 118, 123–24, 128, 258

Swift, Jonathan, xiii, 157

Syllogisms, 10, 211, 216, 231, 233, 240, 244, 259–61, 279, 284–85, 306, 307

Symmes, Richard, father of Valentine, 47

Symmes, Valentine, 21, 50, 205, 242, 301; employed by Hodgskin, 38, 39; examination of, 41, 46–48, 81, 112,

173, 240, 266, 304, 405; on Throkmorton's authorship, 48, 52, 226, 229, 232, 304–05; Marprelate books printed by: *Martin Junior*, 15, 47, 173, 176; *Martin Senior*, 47, 173; *More Worke*, 115, 172; non-Marprelate books printed by, 115, 172
Syria, 85

T., T. (Thomas Timme or Tymme), 69, 364
Tamlin. *See* Thomlin
Tarleton, Richard, jester, 25, 72, 252, 312, 353
Tarquinius Superbus. *See* Stanhope
Taverner, Richard, biblical scholar and translator, 204
Temple Church, 6, 256
Terence, Doctor, University of Oxford, 216
Terence, Publius Terentius Afer, Roman author, 391
Thackwell, "knave," printer, 216, 254
Theater, at Shoreditch, 72
Theological Discourse of the Lamb of God (Richard Harvey), 363
Thesaurus (Stephanus, and revised by Cooper), 167, 168, 216, 276, 277, 398–99
Theses Martinianae. See *Martin Junior*
Thomas, Thomas, printer at the University of Cambridge, 216, 254, 394
Thomlin or Tomlyn, Arthur, printer, 21, 38, 39, 41, 47, 50, 81, 109, 173, 229, 240, 242, 304
Thornborough, John, 160, 259
Thornby. *See* Thornborough
Thrasonicall, from Thraso or Thrason, a boastful soldier in Terence's play, the *Eunuch*, 202
Three Treatises (David Williams, ed.), 146, 155, 178, 307
Throckmorton, Sir Arthur, diarist, cousin of Job, brother of Elizabeth, 96
Throckmorton, Elizabeth, daughter of Sir Nicholas, and cousin of Job, 96, 115, 375

Throckmorton, Francis, Catholic plotter, son of John, cousin of Job, 96
Throckmorton, Sir George, grandfather of Job, 95
Throckmorton, John, justice in Chester, uncle of Job. *See* endsheet
Throckmorton, Katherine, great-grandmother of Job, 95
Throckmorton, Katherine, grandmother of Job, 95
Throckmorton, Michael, 96
Throckmorton, Sir Nicholas, diplomat, father-in-law of Sir Walter Raleigh, and uncle of Job, 95, 96
Throckmorton, Sir Robert, great-grandfather of Job, 95
Throckmorton, Sir Robert, grandfather of Job, 95
Throckmorton, Sir Robert, uncle of Job, 95, 96
Throgmorton. *See* Throkmorton, Job
Throkmorton, Clement, son of Sir George and father of Job, 96, 97, 115, 370, 373, 390
Throkmorton, Clement, brother of Job, 371
Throkmorton, Sir Clement, son of Job, 101, 129, 378
Throkmorton, Clement, grandson of Job, 130, 131
Throkmorton, Dorothy Vernon, Job's wife, 129, 378
Throkmorton, Job, 1, 5, 8, 25, 28, 41, 50, 95–131, 307; education at Oxford, 97–101, 237; authorship of: "An Answer," 314–19; *Exhortation*, 319–22; *Certaine Articles*, 322–24; *Second Admonition*, 4, 324–28; "A Friendly Caveat," 329–32; *State of the Church*, 332–38; Marprelate books: *Epistle*, 210–20; *Epitome*, 235–36; *Mineralls*, 227–29; *Hay Any Worke*, 236; *Martin Junior*, 15, 48, 80, 229–31; *Martin Senior*, 48, 211–27; *Protestatyon*, 232–35; related works: *Master Some*, 132–57; *A Dialogue. Wherin*, 158–71; non-extant works: *More Worke*, promised by, 48, written by, 48, 171–73; "Martins In-

terim," 111–12, 174–75; *Crops and Flowers of Bridges Garden*, 175–77; *Defence of*, 123–25; summary arguments for Throkmorton's authorship, 265–68; his writings, 101–03, 108–12, 117–20, 242–43; stylistic peculiarities of, 178–98, 243–51; diction, 198–202; parallels in his works, 202–09; satire of, 251–53, 263–65; special interests and topics, 253–62; in the House of Commons, 103–07; parliamentary speeches, 6, 104–07, 144, 145, 154, 179, 180, 203, 237, 239–40, 321, 322, 393; indictment at Warwick, 112–13, 114–15, 117, 126, 156, 161, 194, 240–41, 268; submission of, 239–40; petitions of, 17–18, 107–08, 113, 118, 119, 239–40; other events in his career: collaborated with Penry, 51; letter to Penry, 115–16; collaborated with Newman, 79; employed Hodgskin, 38, 46; visited printers at Wolston, 47; received newly printed books at Haseley, 88, 89; used pseudonyms, 52; was a friend of Cartwright, 282–83; was contemptuous of Perne, 285; was scornful toward Dr. Some, 286–90; was critical of bishops and other clerics, 290–96; feud with Sutcliffe, 123–28; wife and children, 8, 129–30; McGinn's neglect of, 302–03
Throkmorton, Job, younger son of Job, 101, 378
Throkmorton, Josias, brother of Job, 101
Throkmorton, Katherine, daughter of Job, 379
Throkmorton, Katherine Neville, wife of Clement, Job's mother, 97, 140, 251, 370
Tilney, Edmund (Tylney), master of the Revels, 73, 74
Timme or Tymme, Thomas, 69, 364
Tirrell, Edward (Tyrrell), 35
Titles of dignity, 101, 315, 320, 330, 332, 334
Tomkins, Nicholas, 23, 36, 40, 48, 50, 78, 83, 84, 333, 334

Tomson, Laurence, biblical scholar, 24
Torture, 39, 41, 46, 81
Tower, 39, 46, 80, 107, 237
Toy, Humphrey, printer, 323, 327
Toye, "mistris," acquaintance of Whitgift, 323, 324
Traitors Lately Array[g]ned, 82
Transactions of the Congregational Historical Society, 152
Travers, Walter, Puritan leader, 6, 10, 19, 70, 225, 319; prominent Puritan, 3; Presbyterian ordination at Antwerp, 66; regarded as a Marprelate suspect, 23, 24; denounced in *An Almond for a Parrat*, 70; derided by Bancroft, 121, 276–77, 309; praised by Throkmorton, 111, 255; held preaching position at the Temple, 256; important writings of, *Ecclesiasticae Disciplinae . . . explicatio*, 352; "De disciplina . . . descripta," 352; *Defence of the Ecclesiastical Discipline*, 6, 10, 256, 335; bishops taunted for not refuting him, 19; Aylmer and, 225; W. W. Greg refers to, 345; *DNB* article on, 345; *A Directory of Church-Government*, 352
Treason, 14–15, 34, 60, 118, 123, 125, 215, 216, 224, 230, 256, 273, 280
Treatise Containing the Aequity (Penry), 7, 44, 57, 76, 144, 155, 178
Treatise of Ecclesiasticall Discipline (Sutcliffe), 116
Treatise Wherein Is Manifestlie Proved (Penry). See *Reformation No Enemie*
Tremellius, Immanuel, Bible translator, 255
Trinity College, Cambridge, 4, 33, 259
Trinity College, Dublin, 6
Trinity Hall, Cambridge, 24
True Lawe of Free Monarchies (James VI), 91
Turner, Dr. William, 159, 214, 263, 327
Turney, Charles, 151, 155, 157
Turrianus, Franciscus, Spanish Jesuit, 256, 279

442

Turswell, Thomas, 69
Tyacke, N. R. N., 407
Tygurium or Tigurium. *See* Zurich
Tyler, Philip, 355
Tymme. *See* Timme
Tyndale, William (Tindale, Tindall), 16, 118, 233
Tyranny, 158, 192, 209, 233, 262, 295
Tyrrell. *See* Tirrell

Udall, John, Puritan writer, 6, 28, 36, 50, 70, 115, 117, 220, 255, 333, 334; his *A Demonstration*, 8, 35, 48, 58, 116, 122, 333, 338, 367; *A New Discovery*, 351, 359, 361; Sutcliffe's *Remonstrance* a refutation of, 367; dismissed as curate at Kingston-upon-Thames, 8, 10; pastor at Newcastle-upon-Tyne, 8, 24; a suspected Martinist, 23, 32; examination of, 48, 361; trial before judges of Assize, 83, 84; Tomkins' conjecture on Udall's authorship of *The State of the Church*, 334, 335, 338; Throkmorton's defense of, 124, 258, 263, 294, 295, 309; death of in prison, 85, 367
Underhill, Dr. John, rector of Lincoln College, Oxford, and bishop of Oxford, 18, 20, 98–99, 225, 267, 294
University of Wales, 306
Upton, Northamptonshire, 42, 143
Usher, Roland G., 355
Uxbridge, Middlesex, 107

Vernon, Dorothy, wife of Job Throkmorton, daughter of Thomas Vernon and Ellenor Shirley, 129
Vestments, 4
Viewe (Penry), 22, 42, 45, 51, 77, 144, 159, 178, 279, 286, 390
"A Viewe of the Churche," by an anonymous Anglican writer, 322
Villerius, Petrus Loseler (Pierre Loyseleur de Villiers), 255
Vituperation. *See* Invective
Vocation. *See* Calling

Vocht, Henry de, ed., *The Earliest English Translations of Erasmus' Colloquia, 1536–1566*, 204
Voltaire, François Marie Arouet de, xiii

Waddington, John, xi, 151, 154, 179, 296, 305
Wakefield, Yorkshire, home of Arthington, 87
Waldegrave, Robert, 10, 15, 36, 50, 152, 182, 298; his printing shop raided, 7, 170, 309; books printed by, 8, 21, 42, 44, 52, 88, 90, 132, 134, 151, 210, 227, 268, 332, 334, 374; his type, 40–41, 159; Waldegrave and Knightley, 76; Waldegrave at La Rochelle, 88, 109, 153, 154, 159; at Haseley, 89, 110, 111, 137, 160; in Edinburgh: appointed royal printer, 89, 151, 381; and James VI, 89–91, 175; efforts to obtain a pardon for, 89–91, 369, 381; Waldegrave and Throkmorton: his deposition on Throkmorton's authorship of *Master Some*, 151, 265, 307; as important source of information to Throkmorton, 254, 311; Waldegrave's nonexistent deposition "in the state documents," 307, 406; Sutcliffe's extant source of Waldegrave's deposition, 307, 381, 406; McGinn's confusion on deposition, 307, 381, 406
Waldegrave, Mrs. Robert, 22, 51, 86, 311
Wales, 133, 139, 217, 285, 297, 298, 305, 306
Walsingham, Sir Francis, secretary of State, 24, 358
Walton, Richard, pursuivant, 58, 133–35, 257, 286
Walton-on-Thames, 39
Warcuppe, Ralph, 98, 102, 242, 372
Warrington, Lancashire, 22, 38
Warwick, 47, 52, 95, 103, 104, 112, 128, 156, 161, 217, 225, 237, 240, 263, 268, 301, 302
Warwickshire, 96, 104, 109, 128, 130, 217, 237, 275
Watson, a pursuivant, 257

Weale, John, 128
Weever, John, 83
Welch Bayte (Powell), 82
Wentworth, Peter, M.P., 115, 238, 356
West Smithfield, 37
Westfaling, Herbert, bishop of Hereford, 293
Westminster, 114, 217, 241
Westminster School, 239
Westmorland, 97
Whip for an Ape, 62, 72
Whitaker, William, master of St. John's College, Cambridge, 111, 168, 169, 255
"White Friars," John Hales's house in Coventry, 22
Whitgift, John, 4, 8, 20, 59, 60, 139, 184, 193, 216, 218, 225, 227, 234, 250, 258, 309, 313; master of Trinity College, Cambridge, 4, 33; bishop of Worcester, 4, 259; archbishop of Canterbury, 5; president of the Privy Council, 16, 274; books by: *An Answere to a Certen Libel*, 4, 282; *Defense of the Aunswere*, 4, 282; Whitgift's opponents: Cartwright and his literary duel with, 160, 260, 281–82; Newman and, 78–79; Penry and, 218–19, 273, 274, 291; printers and, 38–39, 82; Throkmorton's submission to, 194, 268, 302; Udall and, 85; Wigginton and, 23, 32, 33–35, 214; denunciation of, 16, 18, 111, 118, 170, 238, 251; ridicule of, 11, 18, 168, 182, 188, 199, 201–04, 215, 228, 244, 245; challenge to, 110, 261; vituperation against, 175, 189, 206, 223, 224, 248, 274–75, 285; use of irony and taunts against, 17, 168, 169, 170, 204; his articles of religion, 5, 16, 238, 263; his biography in the *DNB* by Sir Sidney Lee, 152; censorship of plays, 73–74; defended by Cooper, 56; by Pasquill, 71; search for Martinists, 31–35, 38–39, 53–54; supported by the queen, 5; death of, 2, 312
Whittingham, William, 111
Wiburn, Percival, 255, 309

Wickham, William, bishop of Lincoln, 11, 20, 56, 267, 273, 293
Wied, West Germany, 317
Wigginton, Giles, 9, 23, 24, 32–35, 36, 56, 58, 67, 70, 255, 263, 309
Wigston, Roger, 22, 38, 41, 43, 44, 45, 50, 75, 77, 78, 176
Wigston, Mrs. Roger, 22, 38, 43, 44, 45, 46, 47, 48, 50, 75, 77, 78, 226, 229, 301, 302
Wilcox, Thomas, 98, 101, 102, 278, 314, 315, 319, 325, 329
Williams, David, xi, xv, 151, 154, 155, 178, 297, 305, 307, 407
Williams, Glanmor, xv, 178, 297, 407
Williams, Sir John, 306
Williams, Penry, 407
Williams, Sir Roger, a Marprelate candidate, xi, 25–27, 354
Wilson, John Dover, xv, 26–27, 109, 132, 135, 150, 151, 153, 156, 210, 296, 297, 306, 307, 354, 381, 406
Wilson, Sir Thomas, secretary of State, rhetorician, 389
Winchester, bishop of. *See* Cooper
Winchester College, 120
With God in Christ [*Sun Theoi en Christoi*]. *The Answere to the Preface of the Rhemish Testament* (Cartwright), 91
Wold, or Old, Northamptonshire, 24
Wolfe, John, printer, 254
Wolley, John, Latin secretary, 32, 39, 53, 358
Wolston, 43, 109, 110, 137, 159; *Martin Junior* printed at, 15, 47; *Martin Senior* printed at, 22; manuscript of *More Worke* delivered to, 176; Penry's press left at, 38, 390; Henry Sharpe at, 42; printers at, 301; Mrs. Wigston provided for printers at, 45; Throkmorton visits Wolston, 47, 229; arraignment of Roger Wigston and wife of Wolston, 77–78
Wood, Anthony a, 372, 390
Wood, Dr. William, cleric, a licenser of books, 20, 199, 246, 295–96, 388

Woolton, John, bishop of Exeter, 293

Worcester, 4, 217, 259, 264

Word preached, 9, 11, 34, 133, 165, 273, 294, 296, 309, 310, 315, 325

Wright, John, servant of Sir Richard Knightley, 45

Wright, Leonard, 18, 20, 61, 69, 189, 225, 234

Wright, Robert, of Ipswich, 255. Probably the chaplain to Robert Rich, second Lord Rich (1537? –81)

Wycliffe, John, 159

Young, John, bishop of Rochester, 20, 44, 56, 214, 292

Young, Richard, judge, special commissioner, 33, 35, 39, 73

Zurich, 12, 96, 198